T0133940

Software Engineering Handbook

Software Engineering Handbook

Jessica Keyes

AUERBACH PUBLICATIONS

A CRC Press Company

Boca Raton   London   New York   Washington, D.C.

Library of Congress Cataloging-in-Publication Data

Keyes, Jessica, 1950-
    Software engineering handbook / by Jessica Keyes.
        p. cm.
    Includes bibliographical references and index.
    ISBN 0-8493-1479-8
    1. Software engineering—Handbooks, manuals, etc. I. Title.

    QA76.758 .K48 2002
    005.1—dc21   2002031306

Visit the Auerbach Publications Web site at www.auerbach-publications.com

© 2003 by CRC Press LLC
Auerbach is an imprint of CRC Press LLC

No claim to original U.S. Government works
International Standard Book Number 0-8493-1479-8
Library of Congress Card Number 2002031306
Printed in the United States of America 2 3 4 5 6 7 8 9 0
Printed on acid-free paper

Dedication

This book is most appreciatively dedicated to
my clients and friends, old and new,
and particularly my family.

Contents

Foreword

In *Soul of a New Machine*, Tracy Kidder details the riveting story of a project conducted at breakneck speed, under incredible pressure. Driven by pure adrenaline, the team members soon became obsessed with trying to achieve the impossible. For more than a year, they gave up their nights and weekends — in the end logging nearly 100 hours a week each! Somewhere buried in the midst of Kidder's prose, we find that, at the end of this project, the entire staff quit. Not just one or two of them, but every single one!

The information technology field is ripe with stories such as this one. Software development projects are usually complex and often mission critical. As a result, the pressure on staff to produce is great. Sometimes, as in the Kidder example, even with success comes failure.

Successful software development projects (i.e., get the product done on time **without** losing staff members) have something in common. Each of these projects, in some way, shape, or form, followed one or more principles of applied methodology, quality, and productivity. Some of these principles are clearly intuitive, but most are learned or culled from vast experience over a number of years and projects.

In today's globally competitive environment, information technology is a major partner with business units; because of this, the push is on for enhanced software productivity and quality. Intuition just will not cut the mustard any longer. An organization cannot wait until software developers learn their quality lessons over so many projects in as many years.

This book was written to push the information technology industry up that learning curve in one fell swoop. Collected here are 65 chapters, 191 illustrations, 19 appendices filled with **practical** (the keyword here is practical) techniques, policies, issues, checklists, and guidelines, and complete "working" examples on methodology, quality, productivity, and reliability. All of this information was culled from over 25 years of experience on the front lines and experience as a professor of computer science as well.

Acknowledgments

This book would not have been possible without the help and encouragement of many people. First of all, I would like to thank my husband and parents, without whose unwavering support this book would never have been finished. I also thank my editors at Auerbach, who had great faith in this project.

I would also like to thank the following students at Fairleigh Dickinson and the University of Phoenix: Carol Neshat, Jing Xia, Qing Xue, David Goldman, Mark Reese, Susmitha S. Kancherla, Scott D. Reese, Steve Mann, Jyh Ming Lin, Len Baker, Yu-Ju Wu, Kanoksri Sarinnapakorn, Rod Berglund, and Gina Cobb, as well as all of my students at Virginia Tech.

These students acted as my research assistants and worked diligently on providing research, outlines, and very rough drafts for some of the chapters in this book. These shining lights also developed many of the appendices found at the back of this book.

JESSICA KEYES

Preface

Much has been said and written about software engineering.

Unfortunately, much of it is written from an academic perspective that does not always address everyday concerns that the software developer and his or her manager must face. With decreasing software budgets and increasingly demanding users and senior management, technology directors want and need a complete guide to the subject of software engineering. This is that guide.

This handbook is composed of three parts. Section I contains 20 chapters on all facets of software engineering — from planning to object-oriented design. In Section II, we change gears from method to metrics. In this section of the handbook, we find all manner of productivity, quality, and reliability methods, such as a technique for converting prototypes to operational systems and a methodology for establishing a productivity-enabling software development environment.

In Section III — Appendices — using the principle that examples speak louder than words, I have provided you with a set of "fully loaded" IT documentation including sample business-use cases, a test plan, a project plan, and even a full systems requirement specification.

The content of the handbook is extensive and inclusive. In it you can find everything from estimation methods to the seven principles of quality leaders to guidelines for structured methodologies to productivity through shared information technology.

And all of this is in the language of the software developer.

Note: I have made every attempt to acknowledge the sources of information used, including copyrighted material. If, for any reason, a reference has been misquoted or a source used inappropriately, please bring it to my attention for rectification or correction in the next edition.

The Author

Jessica Keyes is president of New Art Technologies, Inc., a high-technology and management consultancy and development firm started in New York in 1989. She is also a founding partner of New York City-based Manhattan Technology Group.

Keyes has given seminars for such prestigious universities as Carnegie Mellon, Boston University, University of Illinois, James Madison University, and San Francisco State University. She is a frequent keynote speaker on the topics of competitive strategy, productivity, and quality. She is former advisor for DataPro, McGraw-Hill's computer research arm, as well as a member of the Sprint Business Council. Keyes is also a founding board of directors member of the New York Software Industry Association. She has recently completed a two-year term on the Mayor of New York City's Business Advisory Council. She is currently a professor of computer science at Fairleigh Dickinson University's graduate center as well as the University of Phoenix and Virginia Tech.

Prior to founding New Art, Keyes was managing director of research and development for the New York Stock Exchange and has been an officer with Swiss Bank Co. and Banker's Trust in New York City. She holds a Masters of business administration from New York University where she did her research in the area of artificial intelligence.

A noted columnist and correspondent with over 200 articles published, Keyes is the author of 16 books on technology and business issues.

Section I

THESE 20 CHAPTERS COVER the entire spectrum of software engineering activities. Topics covered include: information engineering, software reliability, cost estimation, productivity and quality metrics, requirements elicitation, engineering life cycle, object-oriented analysis and design, system modeling techniques, using UML, using DFDs, feasibility studies, project planning, the system requirements specification, the system design specification, JAD, RAD, reverse engineering, re-engineering, the data dictionary, the repository, the process specification, TQM, user interface design, the test plan, use cases, methodologies, the class dictionary, outsourcing, software maintenance, and documentation.

Chapter 1
Introduction to Software Engineering

You must start somewhere so I have chosen to start this book at the beginning — with a very brief introduction to software engineering. In this chapter we are going to touch lightly on topics that we will cover in more depth in later chapters. Reading this chapter will give you a sense of the interconnectivity of the myriad of software engineering activities that we talk about.

Computer systems come in all shapes and sizes. There are systems that process e-mail and systems that process payroll. There are also systems that monitor space missions and systems that monitor student grades. No matter how diverse the functionality of these systems, they have several things in common:

- *All systems have end users.* It is for these end users that the system has been created. They have a vested interest in seeing that the system is correctly and efficiently doing what it is supposed to be doing. You might say that these end users have a "stake" in seeing that the system is successful so sometimes they are referred to as "stakeholders." There are different types of stakeholders. A good systems analyst is careful to make sure that he does not leave out stakeholders erroneously. This is indeed what happened when the post office started developing the automated system that you now see in use today at all post offices. This system was developed "in a vacuum." What this means is that only higher level employees were involved in system development. The clerks who actually man the windows were left out of the process; when it came time for this system to be deployed, the lack of involvement of this critical set of stakeholders almost led to an employee mutiny.
- *All systems are composed of functions and data.* All of us like to get our payroll checks. To create a payroll check requires us to define several functions (sometimes called processes). For example, there might be functions for: 1) obtaining employee information; 2) calculating payroll taxes; 3) calculating other deductions; and 4) printing the check. Systems analysts are not payroll clerks; nor are they accountants. A

typical systems analyst does not have the information at his fingertips to create a payroll processing system without the involvement of stakeholders. He needs to utilize several analytical techniques — including interviewing and observation — to get the details on how to perform these processes. Functions are only one half of the equation, however. The other half is the data. Sometimes the data will already be available to the systems analyst — i.e., via a corporate database or file. Sometimes, however, the systems analyst will have to "create" a new database for the application. For this particular task, he will usually work with a database administrator or data administrator. This person has the expertise and authority to create or modify a database for use with the new or enhanced application.

- *All systems use hardware and software.* A systems analyst has many decisions to make. He must decide on which platform to run this system: 1) PC only; 2) mainframe only; 3) client/server (i.e., PC client and mainframe or workstation server), etc. He also must decide whether or not to use any third-party software (i.e., Excel, SAP, etc.); He may even need to decide on which programming language and type of database to use.
- *All systems are written using programming languages.* If the IT (information technology) department is filled with COBOL programmers, it might not be a wise decision to use Java. If Java is mandatory, then the systems analyst needs to plan for this by training existing staff or outsourcing the development effort to a consulting firm. This information is contained within the "requirements document," which, in this handbook we will call the system requirements specification, or SRS.
- *All systems should be designed using a methodology and proper documentory techniques.* There are many developmental methodologies. The two main generic categories are structured and object-oriented. The tools and techniques surrounding these methodologies are part and parcel of "software engineering." A properly developed system is carefully analyzed and then designed. The first step of this process is the plan; the next step is the SRS, and the third step is the design document. Finally implementation, testing, and then deployment take place. These are some of the main steps in the software development life Cycle or SDLC.

THE SOFTWARE DEVELOPER

I started out in this field as a programmer. In those days (several eons ago) there were real boundaries between the different types of jobs one could do. If you were a programmer you did not do analysis work and vice versa. In fact, most analysts back then knew very little about programming.

That has all changed but, typically, you still start out as a programmer but then the sky's the limit. A programmer is a person who knows one or more programming languages (e.g., Java, C++, etc.). His job is to read a programming specification, which is usually written by the systems analyst, and then translate that specification into program code.

In most companies the programmer works within project teams that are managed by a project leader who, in turn, is managed by a project manager. Each project team has one or more programmers and probably one or more systems analysts. The programmer works on the code and seldom, if ever, works with the end users. The systems analysts, on the other hand, work directly with the end users to develop requirements and specifications for the system to be designed.

A programmer can lack all the social graces because few "outsiders" deal with him, but the systems analyst is on the front lines. He needs to be articulate, friendly, and a good listener. The systems analyst must also have the capability to pay a great deal of attention to detail and be creative in coming up with techniques for uncovering hidden information. For example, when developing the FOCUS system, I needed to uncover hundreds of mathematical formulas that could be used to analyze the financial forms. I also had to design dozens of screens that could be utilized efficiently by the end users. Instead of designing the screens (this was pre-Internet days), I turned the end users loose with a word processing programmer and asked them to list the information they wanted to see and where they wanted to see it. This is called JAD, or joint application development.

When I first starting working for the New York Stock Exchange, I was responsible for building a computer system that processed a series of financial forms (like your tax forms) that were required to be filled out by the various member firms (e.g., Merrill Lynch) of the Exchange. These forms contained hundreds of financial items.

My job as an analyst was to work with the people in the regulatory department who understood how to process these forms — these were the end users. Our job was a hard one; the financial forms were complex. The end users were accountant types with vast experience in interpreting these forms. The reason for looking at these forms at all was to determine whether the firm (i.e., Merrill Lynch) was financially healthy — a very important job.

As the systems analyst on the job I had to meet regularly with these end users to try to "pick their brains." We met several times a week to work on the project. There was lots of yelling and screaming and tons of pizza. In the end, however, we developed a document that was quite detailed in describing everything that the system — called FOCUS — was supposed to do. Once this document was complete it was turned over to the programmers whose job it was to turn the document into a complete working system.

7

As you can see from my description, I have left a few job titles out of the picture because each organization is structured a bit differently. For the most part, when one develops a system at least two departments are involved. One is the end-user department (e.g., marketing, operations). The end users have a "need" for a system to be developed or modified. They turn to the computer department, sometimes called IS (information systems), MIS (management information systems), or IT (information technology) to help them turn this need into a working system.

The end-user department is composed of experts who do a particular task. Maybe they are accountants or maybe they are in marketing — they still are experts in what they do. They are managed, just like IS people, by managers. We can refer to these managers as business managers just like we refer to a computer manager as an IS manager. Although most systems analysts work directly with those that report to the business manager, the business manager still plays a critical role. We need to turn to him if we need some information from the entire department or we need to have something done that only the business manager can direct.

THE SDLC: SYSTEMS DEVELOPMENT LIFE CYCLE

The development of computer systems has many moving parts. Each of these parts has a name — i.e., analysis, design, etc. We call the entirety of these steps a systems development life cycle.

Why do we call this a life cycle? A system has a life of its own. It starts out as an idea and progresses until this idea germinates and then is born. Eventually, when the system ages and is obsolete, it is discarded or "dies." So "life cycle" is really an apt term.

The idea phase of the SDLC is the point at which the end user, systems analyst, and various managers meet for the first time. This is where the scope and objectives of the system are fleshed out in a very high-level document.

Next, a team composed of one or more systems analysts and end users tries to determine whether the system is feasible. Systems can be NOT feasible for many reasons: too expensive, technology not yet available, not enough experience to create the system; these are just some of the reasons why a system will not be undertaken.

Once the system is determined to be feasible, systems analysis is initiated. This is the point when the analysts put on their detective hats and try to ferret out all the rules and regulations of the system. What are the inputs? What are the outputs? What kind of online screens will there be? What kind of reports will be needed? Will paper forms be required? Will any hook-ups to external files or companies be required? How shall this information be processed? As you can see, much work needs to be done at this point and many questions need to be answered. In the end, all of the answers to these questions will be fully documented in a requirements document.

Once all the unknowns are known and are fully documented, the systems analyst can put flesh on the skeleton by creating high-level and then detailed designs. This is usually called a specification and can be hundreds of pages long. This document contains flowcharts, file and database definitions, and detailed instructions for the writing of each program.

All along the way, the accuracy of all of these documents is checked and verified by having the end users and analysts meet with each other. In fact, most approaches to system development utilize the creation of a project team consisting of end users and IS staff. This team meets regularly to work on the project and verify its progress.

Once a complete working specification is delivered to the programmers, implementation can get underway. For the FOCUS system, we turned the specification over to a team of about 20 programmers. The systems analyst, project leader, and project manager were all responsible for making sure that the implementation effort went smoothly. Programmers coded code and then tested that code. When this first level (unit testing) of testing was done, there were several other phases of testing including systems testing, parallel testing, and integration testing. Many companies have QA (quality assurance) departments that use automated tools to test the veracity of systems to be implemented.

Once the system has been fully tested, it is turned over to production (changeover). Usually, just prior to this, the end-user departments (not just the team working on the project) are trained and manuals distributed. The entire team is usually on call during the first few weeks of the system after changeover because errors often crop up and it can take several weeks for the system to stabilize.

After the system is stabilized, it is evaluated for correctness. At this point a list of things to correct as well as a "wish list" of things that were not included in the first phase of the system is created and prioritized. The team, which consisted of technical and end-user staff, usually stays put and works on the future versions of the system.

THE FEASIBILITY STUDY: THE FIRST STEP (See Chapter 2)

It never pays to jump into developing a system. Usually, it is a good idea to conduct a feasibility study first. The easiest part of the feasibility study is determining whether the system is technically feasible. Sometimes, however, it might not be feasible because the company does not have the technical expertise to do the job. A good systems analyst will go one step further and see if it is feasible to outsource (i.e., let someone else do it) the project to people who can do the job. Sometimes, the technology is just not robust enough. For example, many years ago I wanted to deliver voice recognition devices to the floor of the New York Stock Exchange. The technology at that time was just too primitive so the entire project was deemed not feasible.

Discovering that the project is feasible from a technical perspective but would require vast organizational changes (e.g., creation of new end-user departments) adds a layer of complexity to the problem. This, then, would make the project organizationally not feasible.

Finally, the project just might cost too much money. To figure this out will require you to perform a cost/benefit analysis (take out those spreadsheets). To do this, you must figure out an estimated cost for everything you wish to do, including cost of hardware, cost of software, cost of new personnel, cost of training, etc. Then you need to calculate the financial savings for creating the new system: reduce staff by one third; save 5 hours a day. Sometimes the benefits are intangible; for example, allowing us to compete with our major competitor.

Once it has been determined that the project is feasible, a project plan is created that plots out the course for the entire systems development effort — i.e., budget, resources, schedule, etc. The next step, then, is to start the actual analytical part of systems development. For that we need to collect some information. (See Chapter 2 for more information on feasibility studies.)

INFORMATION-GATHERING CHANNELS

One of the first things you will do when starting a new project is to gather information. Your job is to understand everything about the department and proposed system you are automating. If you are merely modifying an existing system, you are halfway there. In this case you will review all of the system documentation and the system itself, as well as interview the end users to ferret out the changed requirements.

How can you make sense out of a department and its processes when you do not know anything about it? One of the things you do is to act like a detective and gather up every piece of documentation you can find. When I built the FOCUS system, I scrounged around and managed to find policy manuals and memos that got me part of the way toward understanding what these people did for a living. Other sources of information include: reports used for decision making; performance reports; records; data capture forms; Web sites; competitors' Web sites; archive data. Passive review is seldom enough, however. The next step is to be a bit more active and direct.

The first thing you can do is to interview end users. For our FOCUS project, I had already created a project team consisting of tech people and end users; however, I decided that it would be worthwhile to interview a representative sampling of people working in different jobs that "touched" the process to be automated.

You cannot interview someone without preparation. This consists first of understanding all that you can about the job and person being interviewed and then preparing a set of questions for this person. However, sometimes an interview is insufficient to meet your needs. Your subject may not be able to articulate what he or she does. The next step, then, is to observe the person at his job.

I've done much work in the artificial intelligence arena where observation is a large part of the systems analysis process. One of the case histories people in the field often talk about is one concerning building a tax expert system.

At one end of a large table sat a junior accountant. A large number of tax books were piled in front of the junior accountant At the other end sat some of the most senior tax accountants at the firm. Nothing was piled in front of them. In the center of the table sat the systems analyst armed with a video recorder. This person was armed with a script that contained a problem and a set of questions. The task at hand was for the junior accountant to work through the problem guided by the experts. The experts had nothing to refer to but what was in their memories. Thus they were able to assist the junior accountant to solve the problem while the video camera recorded the entire process.

Observation can only be done selectively — a few people at the most. Another technique, which will let you survey a broad number of people at one time, is the questionnaire. Building a questionnaire requires some skill. There are generally two types of questions:

Open-ended:
1. What are the most frequent problems you have in buying books from a book store?
2. Of the problems listed above, what is the single most troublesome?

Closed:
1. The tool is used as part of the program development cycle to improve quality   1   2   3   4   5
(circle appropriate response, where 5 is the highest score)

A good questionnaire will probably be a combination of both types of questions (hybrid). It is also important to make sure that you format your questionnaire for easy readability (lots of white space and even spacing), put all the important questions first (in case the respondents do not finish the survey), and vary the type of question so that participants do not simply circle 5s or 1s all the way down the page.

See Chapter 4 for more details on information-gathering channels.

DIAGRAMMING OR MODELING THE SYSTEM (See Appendices G and I)

You can use a wide variety of techniques to describe your problem and its solution diagrammatically as well as a wide variety of tools that can assist you in drawing these diagrams. One of the diagrammatic techniques is flowcharting and the tool of choice is Microsoft Visio, as shown in Exhibit 1-1.

One of the most practical of tools is the DFD, or data flow diagram, as shown in Exhibit 1-2. DFDs are quite logical, clear, and helpful when building systems — even Web-based systems. All inputs, outputs, and processes are recorded in a hierarchical fashion. The first DFD (referred to as DFD 0) is often the system from a high-level perspective. Child DFDs get much more detailed. Exhibit 1-2 is a snippet of a real online test system — a rather complicated system that lets people take tests online. This particular DFD shows the data flow through the log-in process. The rectangular boxes (i.e., D5) are the data stores. Notice that D5 is an online cookie; D1, on the other hand, is a real database. It is a relational database and this is one particular table. The databases and their tables are defined in a data dictionary. The square box is the entity (i.e., test taker) and can be a person, place, or thing; the other boxes are process boxes. Process 1.1 is the process for Get Name. There will be a child DFD labeled 1.1 Get Name. 1.1 Get Name will also appear in a process dictionary that will contain a detailed specification for how to program this procedure.

Other modeling tools include:

- *Entity relationship diagram.* An ERD is a database model that describes the attributes of entities and the relationships among them. An entity is a file (table). Today, ER models are often created graphically, and software converts the graphical representations of the tables into the SQL code required to create the data structures in the database as shown in Exhibit 1-3.
- *State transition diagram.* An STD describes how a system behaves as a result of external events. In Exhibit 1-4 we see the effects of a person reporting a pothole.
- *Data dictionary.* The data dictionary is a very organized listing of all data elements that pertain to the system. This listing contains some very specific information as shown in Exhibit 1-5. It should be noted that there are many variations in the formats of data dictionaries.
- *Process specification.* The PSPEC describes the "what, when, where, and how" of the program in technical terms. It describes just how the process works and serves to connect the DFD to the data dictionary. It uses pseudocode (sometimes called structured English or Program

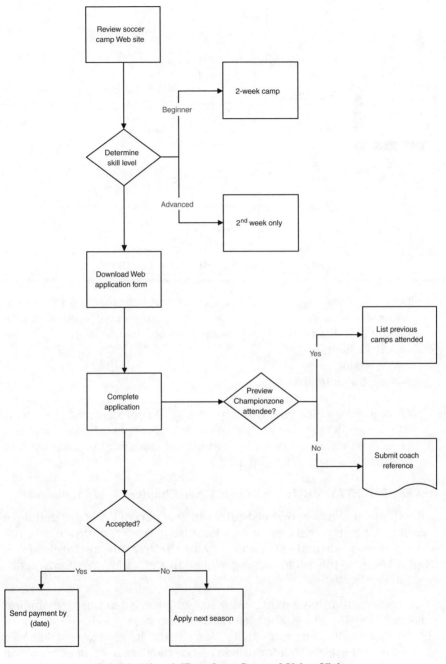

Exhibit 1-1. A Flowchart Created Using Visio

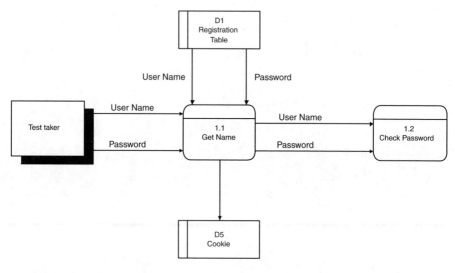

Exhibit 1-2.   The Data Flow Diagram (DFD)

Definition Language — PDL) to explain the requirements for programming the process to the programmer. An example is shown in Exhibit 1-6. Other ways of representing process logic are:
— A decision table
— A decision tree
— A mathematical formula
— Any combination of the above
- *Class diagrams.* Analysts working on an OO (object-oriented system) will utilize OO tools and diagrammatic techniques. One of these is a class diagram drawn using UML or unified modeling language. A class diagram is shown in Exhibit 1-7.

DEVELOPMENTAL METHODOLOGIES (See Chapters 7, 9, 11, and 13)

The Software Engineering Institute, which is part of Carnegie Mellon, in Pittsburgh, Pennsylvania, is famous for a framework that describes software process maturity. A summary of the five phases appears in Exhibit 1-8. Read this while keeping in mind that most organizations, sadly, are at stage 2 or 3.

Companies that have achieved a stage 2 process maturity or higher make use of methodologies to ensure that the company achieves a repeatable level of quality and productivity. Many methodologies are available for use. Some of these are vendor driven — i.e., they are used in conjunction with a software tool set. In general, methodologies can be categorized as

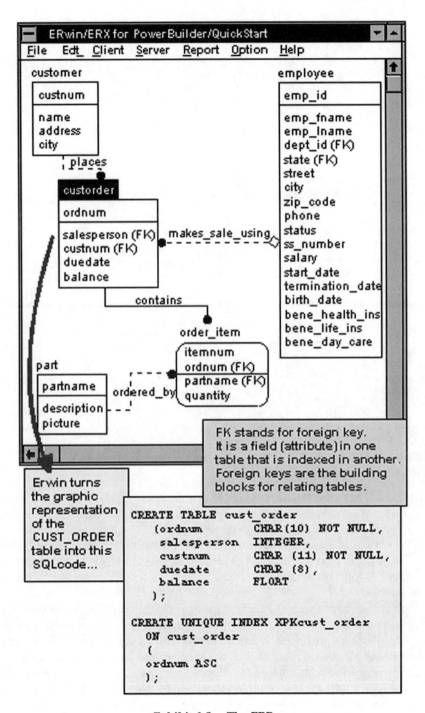

Exhibit 1-3. The ERD

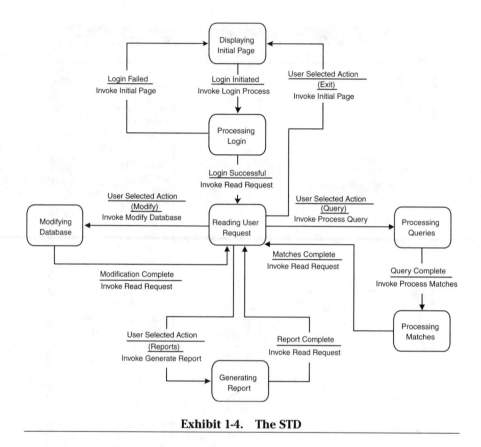

Exhibit 1-4. The STD

follows. It should be noted that a methodology can be used in conjunction with another methodology:

- *System development life cycle (SDLC)*. This is a phased, structured approach to systems development. The phases include requirements feasibility, analysis, system design, coding, testing, implementation, and testing. Please note that there are variations of these stated phases. Usually, each phase is performed sequentially, although some potential for overlap exists. This is the methodology used most often in industry.
- *Iterative (prototyping)*. Most of this approach is used to replace several of the phases in the SDLC, in which the "time to market" can be months (sometimes years). During this time, requirements may change; therefore the final deliverable might be quite outmoded. To prevent this from happening, it is a good idea to try to compress the development cycle to shorten this time to market and provide interim results to the end user. The iterative model consists of three steps:

Name:	Membership Database [D2]
Aliases:	None
Where Used/ How Used	Used by the Database Management System to process requests and return results to the Inquiry and Administration Subsystems
Content Description:	Attributes associated with each asset including: • Membership Number = 10 Numeric Digits • Member Since Date = Date • Last Name = 16 Alphanumeric Characters • First Name = 16 Alphanumeric Characters • Address = 64 Alphanumeric Characters • Phone Number = 11 Numeric Digits (1, area code, phone number) • Assets on Loan = Array containing 10 strings each containing 64 Alphanumeric Characters • Assets Overdue = Array containing 10 strings each containing 64 Alphanumeric Characters • Late Fees Due = 10 Numeric Digits • Maximum Allowed Loans = 2 Numeric Digits
Name:	Member Data [D3]
Aliases:	None
Where Used/ How Used	A file used to validate username and passwords for members, librarians, and administrator when attempting to access the system. The username and password entered is compared with the username and password in this file. Access is granted only if a match is found.
Content Description:	Attributes associated with each asset including: • Member Username = 16 Alphanumeric Digits • Member Password = 16 Alphanumeric Digits

Exhibit 1-5.   The Data Dictionary

1) listen to the customer; 2) build or revise a mock-up; 3) enable customer to test drive the mock-up and then return to step 1.

• *Rapid application development (RAD).* This is a form of the iterative model. The key word here is "rapid." Development teams try to get a first pass of the system out to the end user within 60 to 90 days. To accomplish this, the normal seven-step SDLC is compressed into the following steps: business modeling; data modeling; process modeling; application generation and testing and turnover. Note the term "application generation." RAD makes use of application generators, formerly called CASE (computer assisted software engineering) tools.

• *Incremental model.* The four main phases of software development are analysis, design, coding, and testing. If we break a business problem into chunks, or increments, then we can use an overlapping, phased approach to software development. For example, we can start the analysis of increment one in January, increment two in June, and

Exhibit 1-6. Pseudocode Example.

Process #1
Name Logon

Number: 1
Name: Logon

Description: Registered test takers will logon to their account
with their username and password through this process. Once they
register, they will be able to take the test.

Input data: User name from the test taker, password from the test
taker, user name from the registration tale, password from the
registration table

Output data: User name to the cookie

Type of process: Validation

Process logic:

Get user name and password from the user
If correct then
      Allow the user to take the test

else
      Produce an error
endif

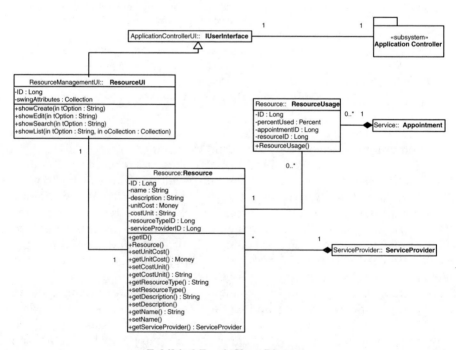

Exhibit 1-7. A Class Diagram

Exhibit 1-8.   Summary of the Five Phases of the Software Process Maturity Framework

Stage 1: Initial is characterized by processes:

- That are ad hoc
- That have little formalization
- That have tools informally applied

Key actions to get to the next step:

- Initiate rigorous project management; management oversight; quality assurance

Stage 2: Repeatable is characterized by processes:

- That have achieved a staple process with a repeatable level of statistical control

Key actions to get to next step:

- Establish a process group
- Establish an SW-development process architecture
- Introduce software engineering methods and tech

Stage 3: Defined is characterized by processes:

- That have achieved foundation for major and continuing progress

Key actions to get to next step:

- Establish a basic set of process managements to identify quality and cost parameters
- Establish a process database
- Gather and maintain process data
- Assess relative quality of each product and inform management

Stage 4: Managed is characterized by processes:

- That show substantial quality improvements coupled with comprehensive process measurement

Key actions to get to next step:

- Support automatic gathering of process data
- Use data to analyze and modify the process

Stage 5: Optimized is characterized by processes:

- That demonstrate major quality and quantity improvements

Key actions to get to next step:

- Continue improvement and optimization of the process

increment three in September. Just when increment three starts up, we are at the testing stage of increment one, and coding stage of increment two.

- *Joint application development (JAD)*. JAD is more of a technique than a complete methodology. It can be utilized as part of any of the other methodologies discussed here. The technique consists of one or more end users who are then "folded" into the software development team. Instead of an adversarial software-developer–end-user dynamic, the effect is to have the continued, uninterrupted attention of the persons who will ultimately use the system.
- *Reverse engineering*. This technique is used, first, to understand a system from its code and, second, to generate documentation based on the code and then make desired changes to the system. Competitive software companies often try to reverse engineer their competitors' software.
- *Re-engineering*. Business goals change over time. Software must change to be consistent with these goals. Re-engineering utilizes many of the techniques already discussed in this chapter. Instead of building a system from scratch, the goal of re-engineering is to retrofit an existing system to new business functionality.
- *Object-oriented*. Object-oriented analysis (OOA), object-oriented design (OOD), and object-oriented programming (OOP) are very different from what we have already discussed. In fact, you will need to learn a new vocabulary as well as new diagramming techniques.

SYSTEM DESIGN

Most of the models we have discussed fall under the structured rubric (except for the OO model). The requirements document, or SRS (systems requirement specification), is written for a broad audience (see Appendix G) and reflects this structured technique. Usually it is provided not only to IT staff but also to end users. In this way, the end users are able to review what they have asked for as well as the general architecture of the system. Once approved, the system now must be designed. The system specification, here called the SDS (systems design specification), contains a very finite level of detail — enough so that programmers will be able to code the entire system (See Appendices J and L for sample SDS and OOSDS, respectively). This means that the SDS must contain:

- Information on all processes
- Information on all data
- Information about the architecture

You must start somewhere. That "somewhere" is usually the very highest level of a design. There are three logical ways to do this:

- *Abstraction.* This permits you to concentrate at some level of generalization without regard to irrelevant low-level details. This is your high-level or logical design.
- *Stepwise refinement.* This is a successive decomposition or refinement of the specifications. In other words, you move from the high level to the detailed, from the logical to the physical.
- *Modularity.* This means that you know a good design when you see a compartmentalization of data and function.

Look again at the DFD in Exhibit 1-2; it was not the first in the series. The very first DFD would have been DFD 0, which is equivalent to the high level of detail that it is recommended you start from. Here you can see the logical components of the system. Underneath the 0 level we start to get more detailed and more physical. At these lower (or child) levels we start specifying files and processes.

The design document that you create will rarely look the same from one organization to another. Each has its own template and its own standard diagramming tool (i.e., Visio versus SmartDraw) and its own diagramming format (i.e., flowcharts versus UML (uniform modeling language) versus DFDs).

When the requirements document is high level, the specification is much more detailed; it is, after all, a programming specification. For the most part, the specification document for the testing system discussed included: 1) a general description of the system; 2) its users; 3) its constraints (i.e., must run on a PC); 4) the DFDs or other format; 5) the data dictionary; 6) the process dictionary; 7) a chart showing the tasks that need to be done (Gantt). The purpose of this specification (usually called a "spec" by those in the field) is to give the programmers a manual from which they can code. If it is a good spec the programmers should not need to come back to you time after time to get additional information. Chapters 12 through 14 have more information on this subject.

Design Strategies

Part of the process of designing a system is to make a bunch of decisions. For example, in creating an online testing system, I had to answer the following questions:

1. What platform should the testing software run on? PC? Internet? Both?
2. If it was going to run on the Internet, should it be compatible with all browsers or just one specific one?
3. What kind of programming language should be used? Should the client use VBScript? JavaScript? Should all process be on the backend? If so, which language should be used — Perl or Java?

4. What kinds of servers do I need? Do I run Microsoft NT, or UNIX, or Linux? Do I need an e-commerce server? How about a RealMedia server?

5. What kind of network am I going to use? VPN (virtual private network)? Internet? Intranet? LAN?

I had to answer hundreds of other questions before we were able to proceed. Answering these questions required much research. For example, if you were going to design a medical claims processing system, you would probably decide in favor of using an optical scanning system to process the thousands of medical claims that came in every day. There are many vendors of optical scanning equipment. Part of your job would be to make a list of the vendors, meet with them, and then perhaps beta one or two of the competitive products.

Essentially, the job of a systems analyst is to be an explorer — go out and wander the world and find the best combination of technologies to create the most cost-effective system. To do this may require a combination of strategies:

1. Program the whole thing in house.
2. Find out if there is a software package you can buy and use.
3. Let someone else program it (outsource).
4. Put together a combination of any of these items in any order.

OBJECT-ORIENTED METHODOLOGIES (See Chapter 13)

Object-oriented systems development follows the same pattern as structured systems development. First, you must analyze your system (object-oriented analysis or OOA). Next, you design the system using object-oriented design or OOD. Finally, you code the system using object-oriented (OOP) programming techniques and languages (i.e., C++, Java).

OO techniques may have some similarity to traditional techniques but the concept of OO is radically different from what most development people are used to. This methodology revolves around the concept of an object, which is a representation of any information that must be understood by the software. Objects can be:

- External entities: printer, user, sensor
- Things: reports, displays
- Occurrences or events: alarm, interrupt
- Roles: manager, engineer, salesperson
- Organizational unit: team, division
- Places: manufacturing floor
- Structures: employee record

The easiest way to think of an object is just to say it is any person, place, or thing. One of the important features of OO is the reusability of its objects. A well-coded object is often thought of as a "black box." What this means is that the programmer should be able to glue together several objects to create a working system. He should not need to know too much about any of these objects. Does anyone remember playing with Lego blocks as a child? It was easy to create incredible things such as bridges and building because each of the blocks was easily connected to all other blocks. It is the same with objects (see encapsulation below).

First some OO definitions:

- *Class:* in object technology, a user-defined data type that defines a collection of objects that share the same characteristics. An object, or class member, is one instance of the class. Concrete classes are designed to be instantiated. Abstract classes are designed to pass on characteristics through inheritance.
- *Object:* a self-contained module of data and its associated processing. Objects are the software building blocks of object technology.
- *Polymorphism:* meaning many shapes. In object technology, the ability of a generalized request (message) to produce different results based on the object that it is sent to.
- *Inheritance:* in object technology, the ability of one class of objects to inherit properties from a higher class.
- *Encapsulation:* in object technology, making the data and processing (methods) within the object private, which allows the internal implementation of the object to be modified without requiring any change to the application that uses it. This is also known as information hiding.

Take a look at Exhibit 1-9. Here we have a class, called automobile, that has several common attributes. One is that this thing has a motor. Another attribute is the fact that an automobile (usually) has four wheels. In an OO system you can create derived classes from the parent class. Notice the nice, shiny red sportscar. This is the derived class called "sports car." It also has a motor and four wheels that it **inherits** from the parent class. However, in this derived class we have some additional attributes: fast rpm and sleek design. The sports car is the **child** of the **parent** class named automobile. So we can say, "Every convertible is an automobile but not every automobile is a convertible."

To develop an OO application one must define classes. If you know anything about OO programming languages such as C++, all variables within a program are defined as some "type" of data. For example, in C and C++, a number is defined as a type called "integer." When we define a class in a programming language, it is defined as a type of class as shown below:

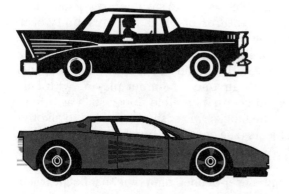

The class called automobile
- Motor
- Four wheels

PARENT

Inheritance ▼ Derived class

The class called sports car
- Inherits motor
- Inherits four wheels
- Fast RPM
- Sleek design

CHILD (extra features)

Exhibit 1-9. The Class Automobile.

```
//Program to demonstrate a very simple example of a class
called DayOfYear.

#include <iostream.h>

//This is where we define our class. We'll call it
DayOfYear//It is a public class. This means that there are
no//restrictions on use. There are also private classes.

//The class DayOfYear consists of two pieces of data: month
and//day and one function named output ()

class DayOfYear

{

public:

        void output();

        int month;

        int day;

};
```

Designing OO systems requires the use of different modeling and definitional techniques that take into account the idea of classes and objects. Unified modeling language (UML) is an emerging standard for modeling OO software. Exhibit 1-7 shows a sample class diagrammed using UML and Appendix L contains a complete SDS for an OO system. Contained within this SDS are numerous diagrams (models): 1) class diagrams, 2) object models, 3) package diagrams that show how the classes are grouped together, and 4) collaboration diagrams, which show how the classes "collaborate" or work with each other. (See Chapter 13 for more on object-oriented methodologies.)

TESTING (See Chapter 16)

When you tie many programs together you have a system. It is not uncommon for a system to have thousands of lines of code, all of which must be tested. The very first level of testing is at the programmer's desk. Here he works with whatever tools he is using to make sure that everything works.

Many applications are built using a Microsoft product called Visual Basic. Exhibit 1-10 shows what the debugger looks like. For those of you who do not know the derivation of the term, debug means to take the "bugs" out of a program. A bug is an error, but the term actually stems from an incident with one of the first computers in the early 1950s. A real bug crawled into the computer, which stopped working. Ever since, we use the term debugging to describe the process of ridding a program of its problems

The debugger will run only if your code "compiles and links" first. When you compile a program it goes through a syntax checker that checks for obvious errors (i.e., referencing a variable that does not exist).

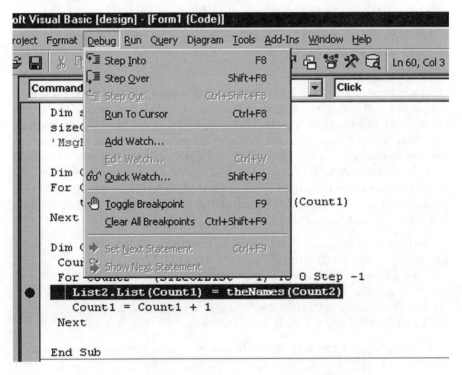

Exhibit 1-10. Visual Basic's Debugger.

When a group of programmers work together, their project manager might think it a good idea that a "walkthrough" be held. This is when the team gets together and examines the code as a group to find flaws and discuss better ways to do things. Usually this is not done. One reason is that programmers do not like to do this; another reason is that it is very time consuming.

You can consider the testing the programmer does at his own desk unit testing — meaning testing a unit of work (a program). When several programs must interact together, another type of test that you might want to perform is integrating testing. This test determines if the separate parts of the system work well together. For example, program 1 creates a file that contains a student file and program 2 processes that student file. If program 1 makes a mistake and creates the student file incorrectly, then program 2 will not work.

A system test tests the complete system — soup to nuts. All of the inputs are checked, all of the outputs are checked, and everything in between is checked. If there is an existing system, a parallel test is done. "Parallel" is a good term for this because you must run both systems in tandem and then check the results for similarities and differences.

Finally, acceptance testing is done. This means that you run a test and the end user agrees or disagrees with the test and approves or disapproves it.

In any case, testing is a lot of work that involves many people, including end users and, usually, a quality assurance (QA) department. QA people spend all of their time writing testing scripts (i.e., a list of things to test for) and then running those scripts. If they find an error they send a report to the programmer, who then fixes it. QA usually uses testing tools to assist with these massive jobs. These tools assist with the creation of scripts and then automatically run them. This is especially helpful when conducting stress testing — testing to see how well the system works when many people are using it at the same time.

Testing is usually not performed in a vacuum. An analyst or manager prepares a test plan that details exactly what must be tested and by whom (see Appendix A). The test plan contains the testing schedule as well as the intricate details of what must be tested. These detailed plans are called "test cases" and form the basis for the test scripts used by the programmer or QA staff member, usually in conjunction with a testing tool.

A sample test case that could appear in a test plan appears in Exhibit 1-11. This would be turned into a script for use by the testers. For more details of testing, see Chapter 16.

Exhibit 1-11. Sample Test Case.

1.1.1. Accounting: Payment

    1.1.1.1. Description

        The purpose of this test is to determine if a representative of the service care provider can enter a payment receipt within the accounting subsystem.

    1.1.1.2. Required Stubs/Drivers

        The accounting subsystem will be invoked with particular attention to the payment class.

    1.1.1.3. Test Steps

        1. The service care provider must successfully log into the system.

        2. The service care provider must invoke the accounting user interface to enter the payment receipt.

        3. The service care provider must enter a payment receipt and press the button to commit the transaction.

    1.1.1.4. Expected Results

        Test Success

        1. A subsequent query indicates the customer's balance reflecting the recent payment.

        2. A successful message is displayed.

        Test Failure

        1. The customer's balance does not reflect the payment receipt.

        2. The customer's balance reflects an incorrect amount that is a result of faulty logic within the program.

STANDARDS AND METRICS

When you build a house you must adhere to certain standards; otherwise, the homeowner's lamp will not fit into the electrical outlet. The size of the outlet is consistent with a standard used throughout the building industry. Those who travel know that they must bring an adaptor because a hair dryer brought from the United States into Italy will not fit into Italian outlets. This is because many standards in America are different from the standards in other countries.

Standards are an important fact of life; without them we would be living in chaos. This is especially true in the IT industry. The American National Standards Institute, which is located in New York (www.ansi.org), was founded in 1918 to coordinate the development of U.S. voluntary national standards in the private and public sectors. It is the U.S. member body to

ISO and IEC. Information technology standards pertain to programming languages, EDI, telecommunications and physical properties of diskettes, cartridges, and magnetic tapes. The IEEE (Institute of Electrical and Electronics Engineers — www.ieee.org) is another membership organization that develops standards.

For example, IEEE 1284 is an IEEE standard for an enhanced parallel port that is compatible with the Centronics port commonly used on PCs. Instead of just data, it can send addresses, allowing individual components in a multifunction device (printer, scanner, fax, etc.) to be addressed independently. IEEE 1284 also defines the required cable type that increases distance to 32 feet.

Your company might well adhere to ISO 9000 and 9001. As I mentioned, ANSI is the U.S. member body to ISO. The International Organization for Standardization is a Geneva-based organization that sets international standards. ISO 9000 is a family of standards and guidelines for quality in the manufacturing and service industries from the International Standards Association; it defines the criteria for what should be measured. ISO 9001 covers design and development, ISO 9002 covers production, installation and service, and ISO 9003 covers final testing and inspection.

If you live by the rule of standards you need to have a way to measure whether or not those standards are adhered to. In our field, we use metrics (measurements). The most prevalent metric used is lines of code, which is the number of lines of code a programmer can program in an hour. There are many more metrics. The second half of this handbook provides details on a variety of metrics that are in use (or should be in use) today. Appendix P is a software metrics capability evaluation guide that will be useful prior to starting on a measurement program.

A controlled development and maintenance program is essential for bringing down the cost associated with software development life cycle. The control mechanism can be implemented by setting up specific goals and then selecting the right set of metrics for measurements against those goals. Goals must be tangible and balanced or they will be too remote to be considered achievable. Intermediate targets are needed for monitoring the progress of the project and making sure that it is on the right track. Project data collection and analysis should also be part of the control mechanism.

A four-step procedure (Linkman and Walker, 1991) is outlined for establishing targets and means for assessment. The procedure is not focused on any particular set of metrics; rather, it believes that metrics should be selected on the basis of goals. This procedure is suitable for setting up goals for the entire project's deliverables or for any partial product created in the software life cycle. (More information on standards and metrics can be found in Section II.)

PROCEDURE

1. *Define measurable goals.* The project goals establishment process is similar to the development process for project deliverables. Software projects usually start with abstract problem concepts and the final project deliverables are obtained by continuously partitioning and refining the problem into tangible and manageable pieces. Final quantified goals can be transformed from initial intangible goals by following the same divide-and-conquer method for software deliverables. Three sources of information are helpful to establishing the targets:
   — Historical data under the assumptions that data is available, development environment is stable, and projects are similar in terms of type, size, and complexity
   — Synthetic data such as modeling results if models used are calibrated to the specific development environment
   — Expert opinions
2. *Maintain balanced goals.* The measurable goals are usually established on the basis of cost, schedule, effort, and quality. It is feasible to achieve a single goal, but it is always a challenge to deliver a project with the minimum staff and resource, on time, and within budget. It needs to be kept in mind that trade-off is always involved and all issues should be addressed to reach a set of balanced goals.
3. *Set up intermediate goals.* A project should never be measured only at its end point. Checkpoints should be set up to provide confidence that the project is running on course. The common practice involves setting up quantifiable targets for each phase, measuring the actual values against the targets, and establishing a plan to make corrections for any deviations. Cost, schedule, effort, and quality should be broken down into phase or activity for setting up intermediate targets. Measurements for cost and effort can be divided into machine and human resources according to software life-cycle phase so that expenditures can be monitored to ensure the project is running within budget. Schedule should always be defined in terms of milestones or check points to ensure intermediate products can be evaluated and final product will be delivered on time. Quality of intermediate products should always be measured to guarantee the final deliverable will meet its target goal.
4. *Establish means of assessment.* Two aspects are involved in this activity:
   — *Data collection.* Based on the project characteristics such as size, complexity, level of control, etc., a decision should be made in terms of whether a manual data collection process or an automated data collection process should be used. If a nonautomated way

is applied, then the availability of the collection medium at the right time should be emphasized.

— *Data analysis.* The following two types of analyses should be considered:

- *Project analysis,* a type of analysis consisting of checkpoint analysis and continuous analysis (trend analysis), is concerned with verifying that intermediate targets are met to ensure that the project is on the right track.

- *Component analysis* is a type of analysis that concentrates on the finer level of details of the end product and is concerned with identifying those components in the product that may require special attention and action. The complete process includes deciding on the set of measures to be analyzed, identifying the components detected as anomalous using measured data, finding out the root cause of the anomalies, and taking actions to make correction.

INSTALLATION

When you have a very small system you can just put it online (direct). If your system is larger then there are several ways to approach installing (implementing) the system. If you are going to replace an existing system, then you can install the new system in a parallel mode. This means that you run both systems at the same time for a period of time. Each day the end users check the outputs and, when they feel comfortable, turn the old system off.

Many companies run multiple servers with the same system running on each server. One good way to install a system is to install it on a single server first, see how it runs, and then install it on another server. This is called a phased approach.

DOCUMENTATION

One day all of the programmers who wrote the original system will leave. If documentation is not adequate then the new programmers will not understand how to work on the system. I recently worked on a project (Internet gambling for a foreign country) where the programmer did not have any documentation at all. The system was written in C++ and ASP and there were hundreds of programs. It was almost impossible to figure out which program ran first. So, you really do need system documentation.

It is also critical to have some documentation for the end users. You have seen the manuals that come with software that runs on your PC. Look at the manual that comes with Visio; you are the end user for this software. So, if you write a system, you will need to write a manual for your end users.

Finally, you will need to train your end users to use the system. When I worked for the New York Stock Exchange, we brought in a tool that permitted our end users to use a fourth generation language (4GL) to do their own queries against the system's database. We needed to train these end users to use the 4GL productively. Instead of writing and teaching a course ourselves, we hired an expert who did it for us (outsource). (See Chapter 19 for more on documentation.)

MAINTENANCE

Many, many years ago I worked with a project leader who wanted to play with a new toy. At the time databases were just coming into vogue, so the project leader decided to create a database for a new system. The problem was that this particular system did not need this particular database. The system was written but, as a result of the horrid choice of databases, it never ran well. In fact, it "bombed" out all the time.

After a year of problems, management decided that the system needed to be fixed, and fix it we did. This is called corrective maintenance — modifying an existing system so that it works correctly. Maintenance is done for lots of reasons.

One reason we are all familiar with is because of security and viruses. Systems people frequently make modifications to software because of problems such as this. The casino gaming programmers mentioned previously had to suspend programming new features into the system to take care of the "Code Red" worm. This is an example of preventative maintenance. Most often the reason for maintenance is simply to improve the system. If the casino end users decide to add a new game to the system or a new data field is added to a database or a new report is required — these are examples of maintenance for improvement purposes.

Some organizations have two types of programmers; one type usually works on new software and the other is stuck with maintenance. This is not often done anymore because maintenance programmers are usually an unhappy lot and, therefore, their turnover rate is quite high.

All systems need to be managed. You cannot make changes to a system willy-nilly. The way you control what happens to a system is to continue holding meetings with your end users and developing a prioritized list of changes and additions that need to be made. Occasionally, a change might come in from a person who is not on the end-user committee. To handle these requests, system personnel usually make use of a standard change request form. This form contains information such as desired change, reason for change, screen shots of the existing screen that needs to be changed, if applicable, and more, depending on the organization. Usually these changes must be authorized by the end user's management before it is sent to the computer department.

Once the change request comes to the computer department, if it is simple and there is some spare time, the modification is scheduled immediately. Usually, however, it is added to a prioritized list of things to do. When it reaches the top of the list, the same SDLC steps used during development are used during maintenance. In other words, you need to determine whether the modification is feasible, determine its cost, develop a specification, etc. (Chapter 18 provides additonal discussion on maintenance.)

TRAINING

After the system is installed the end users will require some training. The various ways to achieve this include in-house training to CAI (computer assisted instruction).

Once the end-users are trained they will need some support on a day-to-day basis. First, as already discussed, they will need a manual so they can look up answers to questions. Some systems do not use paper manuals; instead, everything is embedded in a Help file. If the manuals are insufficient then the company might want to do what most companies are doing and fund and staff a Help Desk. Sometimes people in end-user departments rely on a person within their department who has become quite expert at using the system. This person is usually referred to as the resident expert.

CONCLUSION

In this introductory chapter we have covered a broad array of systems development issues and methodologies. We started our grand tour by discussing the SDLC (systems development life cycle) that identifies the different steps IT team members take when developing a computer system using the traditional structured approach. These steps include, but are not limited to, feasibility study, analysis, design, testing, and implementation.

It is very important that an IT team use a methodology to build a system. Although systems can certainly be built without such a methodology, the resulting systems are usually quite flawed and inefficient, and cost too much money to build and maintain. One would not build a house without blueprints; therefore, it makes sense that one should not build a computer system without a blueprint for building it (the requirement document and design specification).

We have seen some of these "building tools" in action in the form of DFDs (data flow diagrams) and PSPECs (process specifications). There are many other diagrammatic techniques such as State transition diagrams, E–R diagrams (entity–relationship), and control flow diagrams. These tools are used by the analyst to lay out exactly what the system is going to do, how the system will interact with its data, how the databases will be laid out, and how the system will interface with other systems.

Of course, none of this is possible without first figuring out what the end user wants and needs for his or her system. The process of determining these requirements is usually called requirements elicitation and it is the information uncovered in this process that the analyst uses to model the system.

Once the system is deemed feasible and its requirements determined, it is now time to physically design the system. This is when the analyst or designer gets into the "bits and bytes" of the system: exactly what functions will be programmed, the logic of these functions, what data will be used, what network architecture should be used, etc. In this step, an extremely detailed design specification is created — so detailed that the programmers have all the information they need to write their programs.

The system is then tested (unit testing by the programmer, acceptance testing by the end users, system testing by the team, etc.). After the system has been thoroughly tested, it is time to implement the system; this is often called "putting it into production" by those in the field. Just prior to this, the IT team documents the system and trains the end users.

Finally, the system is in production and it is time to support it (help desk, training, etc.) and make changes (maintenance) as required.

References

1. Linkman, S.G. and Walker, J.G. (1991). Controlling programs through measurement, *Inf. Software Technol.*, 33, 93–102.

Chapter 2
The Feasibility Study and Cost/Benefit Analysis

A feasibility study is a detailed assessment of the need, value, and practicality of a proposed enterprise, such as systems development (Burch, 2000). Simply stated, it is used to prove that a project is either practical or impractical. The ultimate deliverable is a report that discusses the feasibility of a technical solution and provides evidence for the steering committee to decide whether it is worth going on with any of the suggestions.

At the beginning of every project, it is often difficult to determine if the project will be successful, if its cost will be reasonable with respect to the requirements of building certain software, or if it will be profitable in the long run.

In general, a feasibility study should include the following information:

- Brief description of proposed system and characteristics
- Brief description of the business need for the proposed system
- A cost/benefit analysis
- Estimates, schedules, and reports

Considerable research into the business and technical viability of the proposed system is necessary in order to develop the feasibility study.

FEASIBILITY STUDY COMPONENTS

There are actually three categories of feasibility.

Financial Feasibility

A systems development project should be economically feasible and provide good value to the organization. The benefits should outweigh the costs of completing the project. The financial feasibility also includes the time, budget, and staff resources used during all the stages of the project through completion.

A feasibility study will determine if the proposed budget is enough to fund the project to completion. When finances are discussed, time must also be a consideration. Saving time and user convenience has always been a major concern when companies develop products. Companies want to make sure that services rendered will be timely. No end user wants to wait for a long time to receive service or use a product, however good it is, if another product is immediately available.

Key risk issues include: 1) the length of the project's payback (the shorter the payback, the lower the risk), 2) the length of the project's development time (the shorter the development time, the less likely objectives, users, and development personnel will change and, consequently, the lower the risk), and 3) the smaller the differences people make in cost, benefit, and life cycle estimates, the greater the confidence that the expected return will be achieved.

Technical Feasibility

A computer system should be practical to develop and easy to maintain. It is important that the necessary expertise is available to analyze, design, code, install, operate, and maintain the system. Technical feasibility addresses the possibility and desirability of a computer solution in the problem area. Assessments can be made based on many factors — for example, knowledge of current and emerging technical solutions, availability of technical personnel on staff, working knowledge of technical staff, capacity of the proposed system to meet requirements, and capacity of the proposed system to meet performance requirements.

Developing new technology will need to take into account the current technology. Will today's technology be able to sustain what we plan to develop? How realistic is the project? Do we have the knowledge and tools needed to accomplish the job? Emerging technology is getting more and more advanced with each passing day; somehow we need to know if our objectives can be realized. It is not enough to note if the product in development is technologically feasible, we also must make sure that it is at par with or more advanced than technology in use today.

Key risk issues:

- Project staff skills and clarity of project design requirements — technical risk is reduced where similar problems have been solved or where the design requirements are understandable to all project participants.
- Proven and accepted equipment and software — tried and tested hardware and software components carry lower risk. Projects that are novel or break new ground carry higher risk.

- Project complexity — a project that requires a high degree of technical skills and experience will be a higher-risk undertaking than one that is not as sophisticated and can be handled by less specialized people.

Organizational or Operational Feasibility

A systems development project should meet the needs and expectations of the organization. It is important that the system be accepted by the user and be operational. The following requirements should be taken into consideration in determining if the system is operationally feasible: staff resistance or receptiveness to change, management support for a new system, nature or level of user involvement, direct and indirect impact of new system on current work practices, anticipated performance and outcome of the new system compared to the old system, and viability of development and implementation schedule. The following issues should also be addressed:

- Does the organization for which the information system is to be supplied have a history of acceptance of information technology or has past introduction led to conflict?
- Will personnel within the organization be able to cope with operating the new technology?
- Is the organizational structure compatible with the proposed information system?

Key risk issues:

- User acceptance — the more strongly the users support the project, the less risk of failure.
- Changes to organizational policies and structure — the more a project influences changes to relationships within an organization or modifies existing policies, the greater the risk.
- Changes to method of operation, practices, and procedures — the more a project necessitates major changes or modifications to standard operating procedures in an organization, the greater the likelihood of risk.

Depending upon the scope of the software to be developed, organization feasibility might require the following analyses, particularly if the software being developed is a product that will be introduced to the marketplace:

- *Competitive analysis* refers to the study of the current trends and different brand names available in today's market to enforce competitive advantage in product development.
- *New product development analysis* is a key factor in feasibility studies; it studies the need for and uniqueness of a product, justifying further study, development, and subsequent launching.

- *Performance tracking analysis* evaluates how well a product will perform technically and financially in relation to its features and requirements.

Competitive Analysis. How does your product or service measure up to the competition? What is your market share? Is there room for growth? Web sites can be visited, marketing literature reviewed, and financial reports analyzed. Surveys can be developed to figure out the competition and how the product will be needed.

Surveys are an important source of information on market needs and user expectations. In competitive analysis, the market is evaluated as well as the market standing value of existing products. Quantitative research is also useful in anticipating market changes and foreseeing how the competition will react.

New Product Development. The first goal in launching a new product is to identify a need. What will the software offer that is not offered right now in existing products? Are businesses, schools, or personal consumers interested in such a product? A feasibility study will allow an organization to find the right niche for products. The feasibility study also helps evaluate the market for growth, cost, and longevity of the product. This gives the company a chance to tweak a product before it is manufactured and subsequently launched.

Performance Tracking. There are many factors to consider when evaluating the market share of a product. Profits and sales certainly reflect customer acceptance, but true results can be known only when you evaluate brand awareness as well as consumer attitudes and satisfaction. Equally important to a healthy business are the people who make it happen. What is the morale within your company? Are your employees performing at their best? It is important to evaluate a company's internal and external behavior vis-à-vis the prospective end users of the product. If it is internal, will employees see the need to implement totally new software and thus relearn operations or will it hinder them from cooperating for fear that technology might replace them?

COST/BENEFIT ANALYSIS

One of the major deliverables of the feasibility study is the cost/benefit analysis. In this document the organizational, financial, and technical aspects of creating the software are put into a dollars and cents format. Appendix D (sample cost/benefit analysis worksheets) provides a good framework for this analysis.

The purpose of this analysis is to determine whether the costs exceed the benefits of the new or modified system. Costs associated with a computer project can be categorized as follows:

- Systems analysis and design
- Purchase of hardware
- Software costs
- Training costs
- Installation costs
- Conversion and changeover costs
- Redundancy costs
- Operating costs, including people costs

Many specific costs are subcategorized within these categories; for example: analyst calculations of total cost of project, alternatives to purchasing hardware, staff needed to train users, maintenance costs for hardware and software, costs of power and paper, and costs associated with personnel to operate the new system. A more detailed list includes:

- *Equipment* — disk drives, computers, telecommunications, tape drives, printers, facsimiles, voice and data networks, terminals, modems, data encryption devices, physical firewalls (leased or purchased)
- *Software* — application programs, operating systems, diagnostic programs, utility programs, commercial off-the-shelf (COTS) software such as word processors and graphics programs, database management software, communications software, server software (leased or purchased)
- *Commercial services* — teleprocessing, cell phones, voice mail, online processing, Internet access, packet switching, data entry, legal services
- *Support services* — systems analysis and design, programming, training, planning, project management, facilities management, network support
- *Supplies* — CDs, tapes, paper, pens, pencils, CD-ROMs, etc.
- *Personnel* — salary and benefits for all staff involved, usually calculated at a rate of 30 percent of the base salary

It is important that the benefits outweigh the costs. Some of the benefits cannot necessarily be measured, but nevertheless should be taken into consideration. Some of those benefits are intangible such as savings in labor costs, benefits due to faster processing, better decision making, better customer service, and error reduction. It may be difficult to determine benefits and costs in advance.

Cost information can be obtained from:

- *Experiences from the past.* Old documents and information will be useful in getting some ideas about the cost of software, hardware, and each service. Invoices for expenses for resources purchased for prior projects are particularly useful.
- *Costs from the market.* It is also important to get the price from the current market for your software system.
- *Publishing.* Business and trade publications and the Internet are another source of price information as well as product functionality.
- *Personal experience.* End users and system staff might have relevant information on costs and product feature sets.

SCHEDULING THE FEASIBILITY STUDY

Creating a schedule for the feasibility study is very important in that it puts into perspective the amount of time required, people involved, potential consumers, and competition that will provide the relevant information. Tasks include selecting a team, assigning appropriate tasks to each team member, and estimating the amount of time required to finish each task. Some of the scheduling tools that can be utilized are diagrams showing relevant work scheduling in relation to the tasks required to finish the feasibility study. Some of these use a table as shown below, a Gantt chart (Exhibit 2-1), or a PERT diagram (Exhibit 2-2), which is represented by a network of nodes and arrows that are evaluated to determine the project's critical activities. Precedence of activities is important in determining the length of the project when using a PERT diagram.

Exhibit 2-1. **Figuring the time schedule in relation to the related activity may also be accomplished using a two-dimensional Gantt chart.**

Feasibility Study Tasks	Detailed Activity	Weeks Required
Data gathering	Conduct interviews	3
	Administer questionnaires	4
	Read company reports	4
	Introduce prototype	5
	Observe reactions to prototype	3
Data flow and decision analysis	Analyze data flow	8
Proposal preparation	Perform cost/benefit analysis	3
	Prepare proposal	2
	Present proposal	2

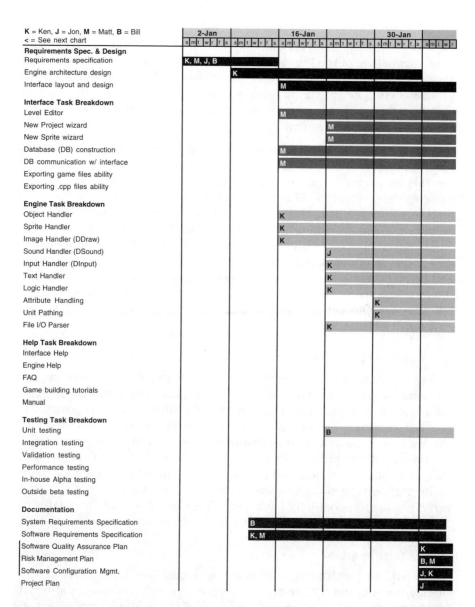

K = Ken, J = Jon, M = Matt, B = Bill <= See next chart	2-Jan	16-Jan	30-Jan
Requirements Spec. & Design			
Requirements specification	K, M, J, B		
Engine architecture design	K		
Interface layout and design		M	
Interface Task Breakdown			
Level Editor		M	
New Project wizard		M	
New Sprite wizard		M	
Database (DB) construction		M	
DB communication w/ interface		M	
Exporting game files ability			
Exporting .cpp files ability			
Engine Task Breakdown			
Object Handler		K	
Sprite Handler		K	
Image Handler (DDraw)		K	
Sound Handler (DSound)		J	
Input Handler (DInput)		K	
Text Handler		K	
Logic Handler		K	
Attribute Handling			K
Unit Pathing			K
File I/O Parser		K	
Help Task Breakdown			
Interface Help			
Engine Help			
FAQ			
Game building tutorials			
Manual			
Testing Task Breakdown			
Unit testing		B	
Integration testing			
Validation testing			
Performance testing			
In-house Alpha testing			
Outside beta testing			
Documentation			
System Requirements Specification	B		
Software Requirements Specification	K, M		
Software Quality Assurance Plan			K
Risk Management Plan			B, M
Software Configuration Mgmt.			J, K
Project Plan			J

Exhibit 2-2. A PERT (Program Evaluation and Review Techniques) Diagram

THE FEASIBILITY STUDY PROCESS

A feasibility study should follow a certain process. It should analyze the proposed project and produce a written description, define and document possible types of systems, and develop a statement of the probable types of systems. The feasibility study should analyze the costs of similar systems, produce a rough estimate of the system size, costs, and schedules, and define the benefits of the system. It should produce an estimate of the next stage of the life cycle. Analysis of the current system is necessary in order to establish feasibility of a future technical system. This will provide evidence for the functions that the new system will perform. Finally, a report should be written containing suggestions, findings, and necessary resources (Sauter, 2000).

A feasibility report will be written and submitted to management containing all relevant information, including financial expenses and expected benefits as shown in Exhibit 2-3. Based on this report, management will make its determination about the future of the project. Much of the information will come from the analyst and the systems investigation. The report should include information on the feasibility of the project, the principal work areas for the project, any needs for specialist staff that may be required at later dates, possible improvements or potential savings, costs and benefits, as well as recommendation. Charts and diagrams relative to the project, such as Gantt and Pert charts, should be included in the feasibility report. Obviously, the project cannot proceed until the feasibility report has been accepted.

Determining Feasibility

A proposal may be regarded as feasible if it satisfies the three criteria discussed at length earlier: financial, technical, and operational. Scheduling and legal issues must also be considered (Burch, 2000). It is possible to proceed with the project even if one or more of these criteria fail to be met. For example, management may find that it is not possible to proceed with the project at one point in time but that the project can commence at a later date. Another option would be for management to make amendments to the proposed agenda and agree to proceed upon those conditions. Conversely, a project that may have been determined feasible may later be determined infeasible due to changes in circumstances.

Other Considerations

When dealing with many kinds of projects, costs and benefits are usually the main concerns. Other concerns, however, should be considered. Project timeframes should also be addressed in the feasibility study; realistic estimates should be made detailing staff resources and time required to complete the different phases of the project.

In dealing with the project, it is also important to consider all legal or regulatory issues that may occur throughout the feasibility or any stage of the project. It may be wise to conduct a preliminary investigation of any obligations and regulatory or legal issues prior to commencement of the initial project stages.

Exhibit 2-3. Expected Benefits Compared to Expenses

Interest Rate	10.00%
NPV	$1,450,582.94
IRR	103%
Payback	2.0 years (payback manually calculated)
Assumptions	

Expenses

		Year 1	Year 2	Year 3	Year 4	Year 5
IT Related						
Initial hardware plus additional yearly capacity	Hardware	$304,000	$50,000	$50,000	$50,000	$50,000
Solution software and licensing costs for upgrades	Software	$111,000				
Project-related design and implementation costs	People	$90,000				
Training, policies, and procedures	Training/Materials	$250,000				
Costs associated with potential unknown factors	Variance	$75,000				
User Related						
Human resources for the project	Hardware					
	Software					
	People	$300,000				
Training for developers on application rollback	Training/Materials					
	Lost Opportunity	$10,000				
	TOTAL	**$1,140,000**	**$50,000**	**$50,000**	**$50,000**	**$50,000**

(continued)

43

Exhibit 2-3. (continued)   Expected Benefits Compared to Expenses

Benefits						
IT Related						
Gains achieved from buying fewer servers	Hardware	$83,300	$83,300	$83,300	$83,300	$83,300
	Software	$0				
1 man less spent managing storage	People	$50,000	$50,000	$50,000	$50,000	$50,000
Gains from more efficient use of storage	Productivity Gains	$75,000	$100,000	$125,000	$150,000	$175,000
User Related						
Improved development efficiency, based on company growth	Hardware	$0				
	Software	$0				
	People	$150,000	$175,000	$200,000	$225,000	$250,000
Improved profit margins on projects, based on company growth	Productivity Gains	$200,000	$225,000	$250,000	$275,000	$300,000
	TOTAL	$558,300	$633,300	$708,300	$783,300	$858,300
	TOTAL PMT	($581,700)	$583,300	$658,300	$733,300	$808,300

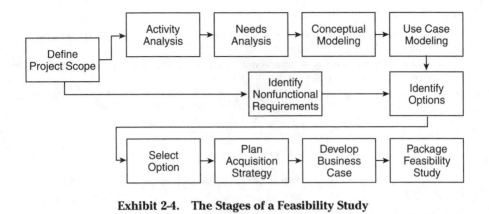

Exhibit 2-4. The Stages of a Feasibility Study

Stages of Feasibility Study

Robinson (2002) has neatly summarized the stages of a feasibility study (Exhibit 2-4):

1. Define project scope
2. Perform activity analysis
3. Perform needs analysis
4. Conduct conceptual modeling
5. Use case modeling
6. Identify nonfunctional requirements
7. Identify options
8. Select options
9. Plan acquisition strategy
10. Develop business case
11. Conduct package feasibility study

CONCLUSION

The primary goal of the feasibility study is to evaluate the risks, benefits, and potential of a proposed project. We also know that the study should aid in producing a solid plan for the research stage and stages to follow so that the project will be given careful consideration and be properly funded. According to Burch (2000), a feasibility study will help you make informed and transparent decisions at crucial points during the developmental process to determine whether it is operationally, economically, and technically realistic to proceed with a particular course of action. It should provide a means of minimizing risks, clarifying issues and expectations, and improving the decision making process and the stages to follow.

References and Further Reading

Allen, G.W. (1998). The position of the feasibility study in project management, (Online) Available: http://www.dis.port.ac.uk/~allangw/papers/feas-stu.htm.

Anonymous. (1996). Feasibility study and initial assessment, (Online) Available: http://cygnus.uwa.edu.au/~belle/ScafEng/feasibil.htm.

Burch, J. G. (2000). Designing and implementing record keeping systems, (Online). Available: http://www.records.nsw.gov.au/publicsector/DIRKS/exposure_draft/feasibility_analysis.htm.

Curtis, G., Hoffer, J., George, J., and Valacich, J. (2000). *Introduction to Business Systems Analysis,* Pearson Custom Publishing, Boston, 17, 19, 23, 25–229.

Kendall, K.E. and Kendall, J.E. (1999). *Systems Analysis and Design*, 4th ed., Prentice Hall, New York, 54–68.

Putnam, L. and Myers, W. (1997). How solved is the cost estimation problem? *IEEE Software*, 14(6), 105–107.

Pressman, R.S. (2001). *Software Engineering: a Practitioner's Approach*, 5th ed., McGraw Hill, New York, 117–118.

Robinson, P. (2002). Lyonsdale systems. Feasibility study, (Online) Available: http://members.iinet.net.au/~lonsdale/bm/bm21.htm.

Sauter, V. (2000). The feasibility study, (Online) Available: http://www.umsl.edu/~sauter/analysis/deliverables.htm.

Chapter 3
Writing the Project Plan

In the beginning there was just code and nothing but code. The art of software engineering was just a blip on the horizon and project planning did not even have a name. In the early days of software development, one person could carry out the whole process of requirement collection, analysis, designing, development, testing, and maintenance by himself. Of course, he did not recognize these processes as independent steps with the names I have used.

As computers became ubiquitous software engineering, the "policies and procedures" of developing computer systems became an important — and organized — discipline. Project planning became an indispensable part of software engineering.

The project plan is the roadmap that details all of the components of a software engineering effort. It is a work product generated by the planning tasks in a software engineering process that contains detailed information about budgets, schedules, and processes. It necessarily addresses a broad audience, including management, staff, and customers. For this purpose it should be comprehensive but concise.

WHY WRITE A PROJECT PLAN?

Projects often go awry. A China Airlines Airbus took off from Taipei International Airport on April 26, 1994, and continued flying according to its flight plan. While approaching Nagoya Airport for landing, the aircraft crashed. On board were 271 persons: 256 passengers (including 2 infants) and 15 crew members, of whom 264 persons (249 passengers including 2 infants and 15 crew members) were killed and 7 seriously injured. The aircraft ignited and was destroyed.

While the aircraft was making an approach under manual control by the flight officer, he inadvertently activated the GO lever, which caused the FD (flight director) to GO AROUND mode and caused a thrust increase. This made the aircraft deviate above its normal glide path, which, in turn led to the chain of events that ultimately caused the airplane to stall and then crash.

Computers are increasingly being introduced into safety-critical systems and, as a consequence, have been involved in more than a few accidents. Some of the most widely cited software-related accidents in safety-critical systems have involved a computerized radiation therapy machine called the Therac-25. Between June, 1985, and January, 1987, six known accidents involved massive overdoses by the Therac-25 — with resultant deaths and serious injuries. They have been described as the worst series of radiation accidents in the 35-year history of medical accelerators.

Software disasters like these could have been avoided had the software been designed and tested properly. Productivity and quality oriented software design cannot be accomplished without adequate project planning.

A realistic project plan must be developed at the beginning of a project. It must be monitored during the project and modified, if necessary. Ultimately, a project plan is a vehicle and focal point that enables the project manager to carry out all sorts of project management activities. It provides a roadmap for a successful software project.

WHO WRITES THE PROJECT PLAN?

The project manager or team leader normally writes the project plan, although experienced consultants are often called in for this aspect of the project. In truth, there are as many ways to write a project plan as there are companies that write them. If the project is large, the proposed system might be divided into subsystems — each with its own team. Each team leader may need to write his own part of the project plan. The project manager then compiles each subplan into a plan for the whole project.

Another alternative is to divide the project plan into discrete tasks and parcel out the effort to team members. Appendix F contains a sample project plan. As you can see from its table of contents, it is easily divisible.

WHAT GOES INTO THE PROJECT PLAN?

Pressman (2001) has defined the prototypical project plan. A student implementation of this guideline can be found in Appendix F; the reader is directed there for a concrete example of how a project plan is orchestrated.

The first section introduces the system and describes its purpose. The project scope and objectives need to be defined here. This subsection contains a formal statement of scope, description of major functions, concerns on performance issues, and a list of management and technical constraints.

The second section discusses project estimates and resources. Historical data used for estimates needs to be specified, as do estimation techniques. As a result of the estimation process, the estimates of effort, cost, and duration need to be reported here. Resources are required to be discussed in terms of people and minimal hardware and software requirements.

The third section discusses risk management strategy. A risk table needs to be created at first, followed by more detailed discussions on risks to be managed. Based on that, a risk mitigation, monitoring, and management (contingency) plan needs to be created for each risk that has been addressed.

The fourth section is an actual project schedule in terms of deliverables and milestones. A project work breakdown structure, or WBS, needs to be created, followed by a task network and a timeline chart (Gantt chart). In addition, a resource table describes the demand for and availability of resources by time windows. In a WBS the total task is broken down into series of smaller tasks. The smaller tasks are chosen based on size and scope to fit in the management structure of the project. Therefore, efficient planning and execution are possible.

The fifth section discusses staff organization. Usually a project is carried out by a group of people and therefore a team structure needs to be defined and a management reporting relationship specified.

The sixth section lays out a picture on tracking and control mechanisms. It can be divided into two subsections: quality assurance and control and change management and control.

At the end of the project plan, all supporting materials that do not fit into the body of the document can be attached in the appendices section.

Most project managers have a difficult time writing a project plan because it is often required at project inception, which, unfortunately, is when information is most scarce. The project manager must choose a process model most appropriate for the project, and then define a preliminary plan based on the set of common process framework activities. The possible models include linear sequential model, prototyping model, RAD model (Mantei, 1991), incremental model (McDermid and Rook, 1993), spiral model, etc. — many of which are described in other chapters of this handbook. Afterward, process decomposition (partitioning) is carried out, generating a complete plan reflecting the work tasks required to populate the framework activities.

THE PROJECT PLAN UNWRAPPED

Software Scope

Determination of software scope needs to be ascertained first. One establishes software scope by answering questions about context, information objectives, function, performance, and reliability. The context usually includes hardware, existing software, users, and work procedures. Normally a system specification developed by a system analyst supplies the information necessary to bound the scope.

Techniques like question and answer sessions and FAST (facilitated application specification techniques) can be used to gather requirements and establish project scope (Zahniser, 1990).

The following is a minimum that needs to be ascertained:

- *Major functions* are the customers' requirements as to what the software should be able to do.
- *Performance issues* are about speed, response time, and other performance-related requirements. They can have serious impacts on the requirement of effort and therefore should be clarified here.
- *Management and technical constraints* should be listed as foundation for the next section's estimation.

Project Estimates

Estimation is the one activity that lays a foundation for all other project planning activities. However, a project manager should not be overly manic in estimation. If an iterative process model is adopted, it is possible to revisit and revise the estimates when customer requirements change.

Historical Data Used for Estimates. Historical data is key to a good estimation. The availability of reliable historical software metrics from previous projects assists the project planner in translating the product size estimation into effort, time and cost estimations. Baseline productivity metrics (e.g., LOC (lines of code) or FP (function points)) should be stored by project domain for use in future estimation efforts.

Estimation Techniques. If similar projects have already been completed, estimates can easily be based on that available data. Otherwise, a decomposition technique or an empirical model can be used. There are also software tools that automate the process using the two preceding approaches. At least two estimation methods should be used, with the final estimation a triangulation of the two. Even so, common sense and experience should be the ultimate judge.

In the example provided in Appendix F two estimation methodologies are used:

- Process based where the system is decomposed into discrete tasks such as analysis of the user interface and design of the user interface with an estimated amount of time allocated to each. For the online resource scheduling system the process-based estimate was 7.5 person months.

- LOC, or line of code, estimation is much harder to estimate manually. A tool such as COCOMO (an abbreviation of cost construction model) makes the effort much easier. A wealth of information as well as a free version of the COCOMO automated tool can be found on the CSE center for software engineering web site (http://sunset.usc.edu/research/COCOMOII/index.html).

COCOMO II is a model that allows one to estimate the cost, effort, and schedule when planning a software developmental activity. It is based on the original COCOMO model devised by Dr. Barry Boehm in 1981. The COCOMO II model is actually derived from the following original mathematical formula that is described in the second half of this book:

$$m = c_1 * KLOC^a * PROD[f_i]$$

COCOMO II permits the estimator to estimate a project cost in terms of LOC or function points (FP). FP calculation is quite complex; a chapter explaining function points can be found in this section.

Exhibit 3-1 shows the COCOMO II tool set in action. Although a bit cumbersome — the nonfree COCOMO tools are much more user friendly — the free version is quite functional. In this real-world example, I used COCOMO to estimate the cost of building an Internet gaming system using the LOC option (see module size). If you look down at the bottom of the screen shot, you will notice three estimates: optimistic, most likely and pessimistic. The COCOMO tool set has many features. I would recommend that you download this tool and try it out.

Thus, the planner first needs to estimate the size of the product to be built, and then translate the size estimate into human effort, calendar time, and dollars.

Decomposition Techniques

According to Putnam and Myers (1992), several approaches can be used to handle the project sizing problem: "fuzzy-logic" sizing, which uses approximate reasoning technique as in the art of "guestimating," function point sizing, standard component sizing (i.e., modules, screens, reports, etc.), and change sizing, which is used in estimating the size of an effort to modify an existing system.

Problem-based estimation techniques include FP- and LOC-based estimation, which we just discussed. Both require the project planner to decompose the software into problem functions that can be estimated individually. Then the project planner estimates LOC or FP (or other estimation variable) for each function and applies the baseline productivity

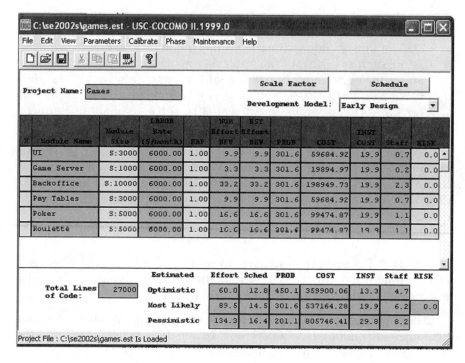

Exhibit 3-1. Using COCOMO for Estimation

metrics to derive the cost of or effort for the function. Finally, these function estimates are combined to produce the overall estimate for the whole project. Alternatively, a process-based estimation is commonly used. Here the process is partitioned into a relatively small set of activities (i.e., the large project is decomposed or segmented into more manageable tasks) or tasks and the effort required to accomplish each is estimated.

Empirical Model

A variety of empirical models are available to calculate the effort required based on the size estimation in FP or LOC. Other than COCOMO (Boehm, 1981), the most widely used model is the software equation (Putnam and Myers, 1992).

Putnam's cost estimation model is a macro-estimation model. The model recognizes the relationship between cost and the amount of time available for the development effort. The Putnam model supports the mythical man-month idea first put forth by Frederick Brooks that states that people and time are not always interchangeable. The software equation is explained in the second half of this book.

The results of these estimation techniques are estimates of effort, cost, and duration. They, in turn, are used in other sections of the project plan.

Risk Management Strategy

A proactive risk strategy should always be adopted. It is better to plan for possible risk than to need to react to it in a crisis. Software risks include project risks, technical risks, and business risks; they can also be categorized as known, predictable, or unpredictable risks. First, risks need to be identified. One method is to create a risk item checklist. The sample project plan in Appendix F lists the following risks:

- Customer will change or modify requirements
- Lack of sophistication of end users
- Users will not attend training
- Delivery deadline will be tightened
- End users resist system
- Server may not be able to handle larger number of users simultaneously
- Technology will not meet expectations
- Larger number of users than planned
- Lack of training of end users
- Inexperienced project team
- System (security and firewall) will be hacked

Then risks need to be projected in two dimensions: likelihood and consequences. This section can be a separate RMMM (risk, mitigation, monitoring, and management) plan and used as part of the overall project plan.

Risk Table. A risk table is a simple tool for risk projection. First, based on the risk item checklist, list all risks in the first column of the table. Then in the following columns fill in each risk's category, probability of occurrence, and assessed impact. Afterward, sort the table by probability and then by impact, study it, and define a cut-off line.

Discussion of Risks to Be Managed. All risks above the cut-off line must be managed and discussed. Factors influencing their probability and impact should be specified.

RMMM Plan for Each Risk. A risk mitigation plan is a tool that can help in avoiding risks. Causes of the risks must be identified and mitigated. Risk monitoring activities take place as the project proceeds and should be planned early. Risk management — i.e., the contingency plan — is a list of activities that are put into action in the event a risk is realized. A plan should be created well before that.

Schedules

Before drafting a schedule several things need to be done. The project manager needs to first decide the type of the project from four choices: concept development, new application development, application enhancement, and re-engineering projects. Then the project manager needs to compute a task set selector value (Pressman, 2001) by: 1) grading the project for a set of adaptation criteria including its size, requirements, and constraints, 2) assigning weighting factors to each criterion, 3) multiplying the grade by weighting factors and by the entry point multiplier for the type of the project, and 4) computing the average of all results in the previous step. Based on this average value, the project manager can choose the degree of rigor required for the project from four options: casual, structured, strict, and quick reaction. Afterward, the task set can be decided and distributed on the project time line based on the process model choice: linear sequential, iterative, or evolutionary.

A sample from the schedule created for use in Appendix F appears in Exhibit 3-2.

Project tasks, also known as project work breakdown structure (WBS) are now defined as shown in Exhibit 3-3.

Alternatively, a textual WBS can be created as shown in Exhibit 3-4.

Task Network. Interdependencies among tasks are defined using a task network as shown in Exhibit 3-5. A task network is also known as an activity network because it shows all of the activities for the project — and each activity's dependencies. In Exhibit 3-5, task 1.1 must be completed prior to initiation of task 1.2, and so on. A variety of automated tools implementing program evaluation and review technique (PERT) and critical path method (CPM) (Moder et al., 1983) can be used for project scheduling.

DuPont developed the CPM for use in chemical plants. The objective is to determine the trade-off between project duration and the total project cost, which is accomplished by identifying the critical path through activity network. The critical path can help management to change the duration of the project. In CPM, an activity time is assumed to be known or predictable.

Project evaluation and review technique was developed by the Navy when the Polaris missile was designed. When accurate time estimates are not available, PERT is an ideal tool for Project Planning since it uses probability theory.

Exhibit 3-2. Project Work Breakdown Structure

Activities	Deliverable	From Date	To Date	Milestone
Meetings	Weekly meetings	02/04/02	05/07/02	05/07/02

ID	ⓘ	Task Name	February				March			
			2/3	2/10	2/17	2/24	3/3	3/10	3/17	3/24
1	▦	Meetings								
2		**Requirements**								
3		**Assess functional requirements**								
4	▦	Number of versions				Jason				
5	▦	Hardware analysis				Jason				
6	▦	Language specification				Jason				
7		Select database				Kristina				
8	▦	Define functions				Kristina,Susan				
9	▦	Demonstrating system				Susan				
10		**Evaluation of testing needs**								
11	▦	Define activities								
12	▦	Define responsible person								
13		Define schedule								
14	▦	Assess non-functional requirements								
15	▦	Final requirements specification					Jason,Susan,Kristina			

Exhibit 3-3. Our Student Project Plan Uses Microsoft Project to Create a WBS.

Eventually CPM and PERT merged into a single technique. Events are shown as nodes and activities are shown as arrows that connect events. Arrows represent the effort required for achieving the next event; direction specifies the order in which events must occur. There are two types of times for each event. One is the "earliest time," the earliest possible time at which the event can be achieved. The other is the "latest time," which is the latest time the event can occur without delaying subsequent events and completion of the project. For an event, the slack time can be obtained or calculated by the difference between the latest and the earliest times.

Timeline Chart (Gantt Chart). Usually the timeline chart is generated using automated tools after inputting the task network or task outline and each task's effort, duration, start date, and resource assignment. This chart is visual and usually the most used part of a project plan. However, it is also possible to create a viable Gantt chart using Microsoft Excel as shown in Exhibit 3-6.

Resource Table. This is another output generated by the automated tool, with a focus on the workload for and utilization of the project resources, particularly human resources. Once a proper project schedule is developed, its tasks and milestones should be tracked and controlled as the project proceeds.

Exhibit 3-4.   Textual WBS

Phase I: Proposal

TASK	START	FINISH
Create budget	Thu 6/20/02	Fri 6/21/02
Define project team	Thu 6/20/02	Fri 6/21/02
Define material resources	Mon 6/24/02	Wed 6/26/02
Identify management team	Thu 6/27/02	Thu 6/27/02

Phase II: Planning

Determine performance goals	Thu 6/20/02	Thu 6/20/02
Conduct stakeholder interviews	Thu 6/20/02	Thu 6/20/02
Analyze current architecture	Thu 6/20/02	Fri 6/21/02
Produce operational metrics	Mon 6/24/02	Wed 6/26/02
Problem analysis	Thu 6/27/02	Fri 6/28/02
Problem resolution	Mon 7/1/02	Fri 7/12/02
Determine future needs	Mon 7/15/02	Tue 7/16/02

Phase III: Design

Produce topology maps	Wed 7/17/02	Tue 7/23/02
Determine capacity allocations	Wed 7/24/02	Thu 7/25/02
Determine backup requirements	Fri 7/26/02	Mon 7/29/02
Determine specific hardware req.	Tue 7/30/02	Tue 7/30/02
Determine specific software req.	Wed 7/31/02	Wed 7/31/02

Phase IV: Implementation

Install new SAN hardware	Wed 7/31/02	Tue 8/20/02
Install necessary supporting software	Thu 8/22/02	Thu 8/22/02
Verify SAN to topology maps	Fri 8/23/02	Fri 8/23/02
Perform system testing	Wed 8/21/02	Tue 8/27/02
Migrate hardware to SAN	Wed 8/28/02	Tue 9/3/02
Testing and verification	Wed 9/4/02	Tue 9/10/02
Collect operational metrics	Wed 9/11/02	Thu 9/12/02
Compare to existing system	Fri 9/13/02	Fri 9/13/02

Phase V: Support

Prepare training materials	Wed 7/31/02	Tue 8/13/02
Perform testing against materials	Wed 8/14/02	Wed 8/14/02
Training	Wed 8/14/02	Tue 8/20/02
Establish support needs	Mon 9/16/02	Tue 9/17/02
Implement tracking methodology	Wed 9/18/02	Thu 9/19/02
Determine additional follow-up needs	Wed 9/25/02	Wed 9/25/02

Project Resources

Estimation of resources required is an important component of software planning. For each resource the planner needs to specify with these characteristics: description, statement of availability, and time window.

- *People:* the planner needs to specify the organizational position and specialty of human resources required by the project. Only after estimating the development effort can we define the number of people required.
- *Hardware and software:* hardware and software form the foundation of the software engineering environment (Naur and Randall, 1969). The project planner must determine its time window and verify its availability. Reusable software components should also be specified, alternatives evaluated, and acquisition made early.
- *Special resources:* any other resources not covered in the previous two sections should be listed here.
- *Staff organization:* people are the critical factor in a software development effort. In a typical software project, the players fall into five categories: senior managers, project (technical) managers, practitioners, customers, and end users. A good team leader should be able to motivate other players, organize the process, and innovate or encourage people to be creative.
- *Team structure (if applicable):* a project manager should decide on the organizational structure for the team. According to Mantei (1981), these three generic team organizations exist: democratic decentralized (DD), controlled decentralized (CD), and controlled centralized (CC). The factors that influence the team structure decision include: difficulty of the problem, size of the resultant programs, team lifetime, problem modularity, criticality of the solution, rigidity of timeline, and communications required. Generally speaking, a DD structure is best for difficult problems and a CC or CD structure is best for very large projects.
- *Management reporting:* coordination and communication issues, including management reporting relationships, should be addressed here.

Tracking and Control Mechanisms

This may be the last section, but not the least important. Errors and changes are inevitable, and we need to plan ahead to stay prepared for when they actually happen.

- *Quality assurance and control:* software quality assurance activities (SQA) happen at each step of the software process and are carried out by software engineers and an SQA group. Software engineers assure quality by applying rigorous technical methods and measures, and conducting formal technical reviews and well-planned testing. SQA group assists software engineers through a set of activities that address quality assurance planning, oversight, record keeping, analysis, and reporting. We need to plan these activities in this subsection.

- *Change management and control:* the later the changes happen in a project, the higher the cost. Change control combines human procedures and automated tools to provide a mechanism for the control of changes that, if uncontrolled, can rapidly lead a large project to chaos. The change control process begins with a change request, leads to a decision to make or reject the request, and culminates with a controlled update of the software configuration item to be changed. This part of the activities should be planned here.

Appendices

Any supporting materials to the preceding sections should be attached in this section.

IS IT WORTH IT?

Like any other software engineering task, project planning and writing a detailed project plan take time and costs money. Therefore a natural question arises: is it worth it? The answer is yes. If you want a system that is cost effective, does not go over budget, and actually works, a project plan is mandatory.

More than a few people in this field use the "roadmap" metaphor to describe the role of a project plan; however, it is also a "compass." Its estimation and scheduling part may be like a rough roadmap (never precise enough at the beginning of a project), but its risk management, organization plan, tracking, and control part are definitely a compass. It guides the project team in handling unpredictable risks or undesired events.

A good project plan benefits not only the project, but also the domain as whole by its measures and metrics, which can be historical data for later projects.

References

Boehm, B. (1981). *Software Engineering Economics*, Prentice-Hall, New York.

Kerr, J. and Hunter, R. (1994). *Inside RAD*, McGraw-Hill, New York.

Mantei, M. (1981). The effect of programming team structures on programming tasks, CACM, 24, 106–113.

McDermid, J. and Rook, P., Eds. (1993). Software development process models, in *Software Engineer's Reference Book*, CRC Press, Boca Raton, FL, 28–66.

Moder, J.J., Phillips, C.R., and Davis, E.W. (1983). *Project Management with CPM, PERT and Precedence Diagramming*, 3rd ed., Van Nostrand Reinhold, New York.

Naur, P. and Randall, B., Eds. (1969). *Software Engineering: a Report on a Conference Sponsored by the NATO Science Committee*, NATO.

Pressman, R. (2001). *Software Engineering, a Practitioner's Approach*, 5th ed., McGraw Hill, New York.

Putnam, L. and Myers, W. (1992). *Measures for Excellence*, Yourdon Press, New York.

Chapter 4
Requirements Elicitation

Without proper information it is difficult, if not impossible, to define or start a systems development project. Information gathered in this process is called requirements elicitation; it will enable the project manager or analyst to create a blueprint of current systems and allow definition of objectives, description of processes, and deployment of objectives for the new system. In addition, if the systems analyst is careful, he can lay the foundation of efficient and effective communications with stakeholders that will lead to a higher likelihood of a successful project.

STAKEHOLDER ANALYSIS

Stakeholders are the people needed to ensure the success of the project, for example, daily users and their managers, as well as technical support people. It is important to find all the stakeholder groups and determine their interests and needs. The first step, then, in requirements elicitation is stakeholder analysis in which you try to find answers to the following questions:

- Who are the stakeholders?
- What goals do they see for the system?
- Why would they like to contribute?
- What risks and costs do they see?
- What kind of solutions and suppliers do they see?

Stakeholders could be:

- The sponsor who pays for the development of the product
- People who will be using the product on a daily basis
- Managers of departments looking to increase work force efficiency
- The company's customers (clients of the system), without whose support there will be no business advantages
- Business partners: suppliers, carriers, and banks that also need to interact with the system
- IT people and hotline staff in case the product is to be developed within the company
- IT people at the client's site

Stakeholders should be carefully interviewed (Curtis et al., 2000) to:

- Define financial constraints
- Define the current and proposed information systems
- Define current and proposed development process
- Define current and proposed hardware assets and availability
- Define current and proposed software assets and availability
- Define current and future goals and objectives of the stakeholders

Information gathered from the financial constraints will allow examination of realistic designs and eliminate unnecessary expenditures of resources on unrealistic approaches. One must also know the current information systems in place and hardware assets as well as the current software assets available within the company. It is also critical that the development team fully understand the current development methodologies and tool sets that the company utilizes. The goals and objectives of the information gathering process are to be able to accumulate enough information to define all of these items as well as the goals of the stakeholders.

ELICITATION TECHNIQUES

Various methods can be used to obtain the information necessary to prepare a project plan. These methods include interviewing, questionnaires, observation, participation, documentation, research, business intelligence (BI), competitive intelligence (CI), reverse engineering, and benchmarking.

Interviewing

The most common method of gathering information is by interviewing people. Interviewing can serve two purposes at the same time. The first is a fact-finding mission to discover what each person's goals and objectives are with respect to the project; the second is to begin a communications process that enables one to set realistic expectations for the project.

A wide variety of stakeholders can and should be interviewed. Stakeholders are those with an interest in seeing this project successfully completed — i.e., they have a "stake" in the project. As discussed earlier, stakeholders include employees, management, clients, and partners.

Employees. It is amazing to me that some analysts develop systems without ever interviewing those whose jobs will be affected the most. This occurred most notably at the U.S. Post Office when the clerical staff was automated in the 1980s. So little information was shared about what the new system was going to do that the clerks got the misimpression that they were soon to be replaced.

The number and type of employees that will need to be interviewed will depend on the type of system being developed. Systems generally fall into two categories: tactical and strategic. Tactical systems are usually transactional-based systems such as check processing, student registration, and medical billing where data volumes are high and staff members accessing those systems are clerical. Strategic systems support the decision making process and are utilized by middle and senior managers. It is possible for a system to be a hybrid of both these system types. An example of this would be a transactional back end that collects data for analysis by managers at the front end.

Interviews can have some major obstacles to overcome. The interviewee may resist giving information out of fear, may relate his perception of how things should be done rather than how they are really done, or may have difficulty in expressing himself. On the other hand, the analyst's own mindset may also act as a filter. The interviewer sometimes needs to set aside his own technical orientation and make a strong effort to put himself in the position that the interviewee is in. This requires that the analyst develop a certain amount of empathy.

An interview outline should contain the following information:

- Name of interviewee
- Name of interviewer
- Date and time
- Objectives of interview — i.e., what areas you are going to explore and what data you are going to collect
- General observations
- Unresolved issues and topics not covered
- Agenda — i.e., introduction, questions, summary of major points, closing

Recommended guidelines for handling the employee interview process include:

- Determine the system type (tactical, strategic, hybrid).
- Make a list of departments affected by the new system.
- For each department, request or develop an organization chart that shows the departmental breakdown along with the name, extension, and list of responsibilities of each employee.
- Meet with the department head to request recommendations and then formulate a plan that details which employees are the best interview prospects. The "best" employees to interview are those: 1) who are very experienced (i.e., senior) in performing their job functions; 2) who may have come from a competing company and, thus, have a unique perspective; 3) who have had a variety of positions within the department or company.

- Plan to meet with employees from all units of the department. In other words, if you are automating the marketing function and interviewing the marketing department, you will want to meet with employees from the marketing communications unit, marketing research unit, public relations group, etc. In some cases, you may find that interviewing several employees at a time is more effective than dealing with a single employee because interviewing a group of employees permits them to bounce ideas off each other.
- If a departmental unit contains many employees, it is not optimum to interview every one. It would be wrong to assume that the more people in a department, the higher the number of interviewees should be. Instead, sampling should be used. Sampling is used to: 1) contain costs; 2) improve effectiveness; 3) speed up the data-gathering process; 4) reduce bias. Systems analysts often use a random sample; however, calculating a sample size based on population size and your desired confidence interval is more accurate. Rather than provide a formula and instructions on how to calculate sample size here, I direct the reader to the sample size calculator located at http://www.survey-system.com/sscalc.htm.
- Carefully plan your interview sessions. Prepare your interview questions in advance. Be familiar with any technical vocabulary your interview subjects might use.
- No meeting should last longer than an hour. A half hour is optimum. There is a point of diminishing returns with the interview process. Your interviewees are busy and usually easily distracted. Keep in mind that some of your interviewees may be doing this against their will.

Customers. If the new or modified system will be affecting customers in any way, one should interview several customers to obtain their impressions of the current process and what features would be desirable. This information can be very enlightening. Often customers just live with the frustrations and never mention them to anyone at the company. Customers often have experiences with other vendors or suppliers and can offer insight into the processes that other companies use or that they have experienced.

Guidelines for interviewing customers include:

- Work with the sales and marketing departments to select knowledgeable and cooperative customers.
- Prepare an adequate sample size as discussed in the prior section.
- Carefully plan your interview sessions. Prepare your interview questions in advance.

Companies and Consultants. Another source of potentially valuable information is other companies in the industry and consultants who specialize in the areas that will change with the new processes. Consultants can be easily located and paid for their expert advice, but it is wise to tread slowly when working with other companies who are current or potential competitors.

Guidelines for interviewing other companies include:

- Work with senior management and marketing to create a list of potential companies to interview. This list should contain the names of trading partners, vendors (companies that your company buys from), and competitors.
- Attend industry trade shows to meet and mingle with competitor employees and listen to speeches made by competitive companies.
- Attend trade association meetings; sit on policy and standards committees.

Suppliers. Suppliers of the products you are considering are also an important source of ideas for the problem you are facing. These suppliers know a great deal about how their product has been used and how problems have been overcome in different systems. They can also give you a long list of features they provide.

Types of Questions. When interviewing anyone it is important to be aware of how to ask questions properly. Open-ended questions are best for gaining the most information because they do not limit individuals to predefined answers. Other benefits of using open-ended questions are that it: puts the interviewee at ease, provides more detail, induces spontaneity, and is far more interesting for the interviewee. Open-ended questions require more than a yes or no answer (Yate, 1993). An example of an open-ended question is "What types of problems do you see on a daily basis with the current process?" These questions allow individuals to elaborate on the topics and potentially uncover the hidden problems at hand that might not be discoverable with a question that requires a yes or no answer.

Often one starts a systems development effort with the intention of solving a problem that turns out to be a symptom of a larger problem. If the examination of problems leads to the underlying issues, the resolution of those issues will be more valuable to the company in the end. Many symptoms are a result of the same problem, and a simple change can fix many issues at once. One disadvantage of open-ended questions is that they create lengthier interviews. Another is that it is easy for the interview to get off track and it takes an interviewer with skill to maintain the interview in an efficient manner (Yates, 1993).

Closed-ended questions are, by far, the most common questions in interviewing. They are questions that have yes and no answers and are utilized to elicit definitive responses.

Past-performance questions can be useful to determine past experiences with similar problems (Yates, 1993). Often interviewees are reluctant to discuss problems so questions about past-performance can allow the person to discuss an issue with similar problems. An example of how a past-performance question is used is, "In your past job how did you deal with these processes?"

Reflexive questions are appropriate for closing a conversation or moving forward to a new topic (Yates, 1993). Reflexive questions are created with a statement of confirmation and adding a phrase such as: Don't you? Couldn't you? Wouldn't you?

Mirror questions are a subtle form of probing and are useful in obtaining additional detail on a subject. After the interviewee makes a statement, pause and repeat the statement with an additional or leading question: "So, when this problem occurs, you simply move on to more pressing issues?"

Often answers do not give the interviewer enough detail so one follows the question with additional questions to prod the interviewee to divulge more details on the subject. For example:

- Can you give some more details on that?
- What did you learn from that experience?

Another, more subtle, prodding technique can be used by merely sitting back and saying nothing. The silence will feel uncomfortable causing the interviewee to expand on his or her last statement.

Questionnaires and Surveys

If large numbers of people need to be interviewed, one might start with a questionnaire and then follow up with certain individuals that present unusual ideas or issues in the questionnaires. Survey development and implementation is composed of the following tasks, according to Creative Research Systems, makers of a software solution for survey creation (surveysolutions.com):

- Establish the goals of the project — what you want to learn.
- Determine your sample — whom you will interview.
- Choose interviewing methodology — how you will interview.
- Create your questionnaire — what you will ask.
- Pretest the questionnaire, if practical — test the questions.
- Conduct interviews and enter data — ask the questions.
- Analyze the data — produce the reports.

Similar to interviews, questionnaires may contain closed-end or open-ended questions or a combination of the two.

Appendix H contains a survey that was created for a Y2K software product. This survey demonstrates the use of a hybrid questionnaire. Although most of the questions are quite specific, and thus closed-ended, there are at least two open-ended questions. Questions 6 and 8 under the heading of "management aspects" permit the respondent to reply to an essay type of question.

Survey creation is quite an art form. Guidelines for creation of a survey include:

- Provide an introduction to the survey. Explain why it is important to respond to it. Thank participants for their time and effort.
- Put all important questions first because it is rare that all questions will be responded to. Those filling out the survey often become tired of or bored with the process.
- Use plenty of "white space." Use an appropriate font (i.e., Arial) and font size (i.e., at least 12), and do skip lines.
- Use nominal scales if you wish to classify things (i.e., What make is your computer? 1 = Dell, 2 = Gateway, 3 = IBM).
- Use ordinal scales to imply rank (i.e., How helpful was this class? 3 = not helpful at all, 2 = moderately helpful, 1 = very helpful).
- Use interval scales when you want to perform some mathematical calculations on the results; i.e.:

  How helpful was this class?
  Not useful at all   Very useful
    1   2   3   4   5

Tallying the responses will provide a "score" that assists in making a decision that requires the use of quantifiable information. When using interval scales, keep in mind that not all questions will carry the same weight. Hence, it is a good idea to use a weighted average formula during calculation. To do this, assign a "weight" or level of importance to each question. For example, the preceding question might be assigned a weight of 5 on a scale of 1 to 5, meaning that this is a very important question. On the other hand, a question such as "Was the training center comfortable" might carry a weight of only 3. The weighted average is calculate by multiplying the weight by the score (w * s) to get the final score. Thus the formula is

$$S_{new} = w * s.$$

Several problems might result from a poorly constructed questionnaire. Leniency is caused by respondents who grade nonsubjectively — in other

Exhibit 4-1. Different Approaches to Surveys

Speed	E-mail and Web page surveys are the fastest methods, followed by telephone interviewing. Mail surveys are the slowest.
Cost	Personal interviews are the most expensive, followed by telephone and then mail. E-mail and Web page surveys are the least expensive for large samples.
Internet Usage	Web page and e-mail surveys offer significant advantages, but you may not be able to generalize their results to the population as a whole.
Literacy Levels	Illiterate and less-educated people rarely respond to mail surveys.
Sensitive Questions	People are more likely to answer sensitive questions when interviewed directly by a computer in one form or another.
Video, Sound, Graphics	A need to get reactions to video, music, or a picture limits your options. You can play a video on a Web page, in a computer-direct interview, or in person. You can play music when using these methods or over a telephone. You can show pictures in the first methods and in a mail survey.

words, too easily. Central tendency occurs when respondents rate everything as average. The halo effect occurs when the respondent carries his good or bad impression from one question to the next.

Several methods can be used to deploy a survey successfully. The easiest and most accurate is to gather all respondents in a conference room and hand out the survey. For the most part, this is not realistic, so other approaches would be more appropriate. E-mail and traditional mail are two methodologies that work well, although you often must supply an incentive (i.e., prize) to get respondents to fill out those surveys on a timely basis. Web-based surveys (Internet and Intranet) are becoming increasingly popular because they enable the inclusion of demos, audio, and video. For example, a Web-based survey on what type of user interface is preferable could have hyperlinks to demos or screen shots of the choices.

Creative Research Systems summarizes the different approaches to surveys in the table shown in Exhibit 4-1.

Observation

Observation is an important tool that can provide a wealth of information. There are two forms of observation: silent and directed. In silent observation, the analyst merely sits on the sidelines with pen and pad and observes what is happening. If it is suitable, a tape recorder or video recorder can record what is observed. However, this is not recommended if the net result will be several hours of random footage.

Silent observation is best used to capture the spontaneous nature of a particular process or procedure. For example:

- When customers will be interacting with staff
- During group meetings
- On the manufacturing floor
- In the field

Directed observation provides the analyst with a chance to microcontrol a process or procedure so that it is broken down into its observable parts. At one accounting firm a tax system was being developed. The analysts requested that several senior tax accountants be coupled with a junior staff member. The group was given a problem as well as all of the manuals and materials needed. The junior accountant sat at one end of the table with the pile of manuals and forms while the senior tax accountants sat at the other end. A tough tax problem was posed. The senior tax accountants were directed to think through the process and then direct the junior member to follow through on their directions to solve this problem. The catch was that the senior members could not walk over to the junior person or touch any of the reference guides. This whole exercise had to be verbal and use just their memories and expertise. The entire process was videotaped. The net result was that the analyst had a complete record of how to perform one of the critical functions of the new system.

Participation

The flip side of observation is participation. Actually becoming a member of the staff and thereby learning exactly what it is that the staff does, so that it might be automated, is an invaluable experience.

Documentation

It is logical to assume that a wide variety of documentation will be available to the analyst. This includes, but is not limited to, the following:

- Documentation from existing systems, including requirements and design specifications, program documentation, user manuals, and help files. (This also includes whatever "wish" lists have been developed for the existing system.)
- Archival information
- Policies and procedures manuals
- Reports
- Memos
- Standards
- E-mail

- Minutes from meetings
- Government and other regulatory guidelines and regulations
- Industry or association manuals, guidelines, and standards (e.g., accountants are guided not only by in-house "rules and regulations" but also by industry and other rules and regulations)

Competitive Intelligence

Competitive intelligence (CI) is business intelligence that is limited to competitors and how that information affects strategy, tactics, and operations (Brock, 2000b). 4Sight partners (2000) define competitive intelligence as "a systematic and ethical program for gathering, analyzing, and managing external information that can affect your company's plans, decisions, and operations." 4Sight goes on to state that utilization of the Internet as the method of gathering information on individuals and companies has become widespread and automatic. CI enables management to make informed decisions about everything from marketing, R & D, and investing tactics to long-term business strategies (SCIP, 2002).

CI data can be gathered from the following sources:

- Internet discussion groups (listservs) and news groups (Usenet). Simple searches on the Internet can obtain expert discussions on issues in listservs and Usenet (Graef, 2002). Often a quick form of CI is to search these Internet postings for discussions of similar issues. The level of detail contained in these discussions is beneficial for things to do and also things that will not work (Graef, 2002). This is one of the quickest and most cost-effective methods of obtaining information about a project (Graef, 2002).
- Former employees of your competitors often are invaluable in providing information about your competitors' operations, products, and plans.
- Your competitors' Web sites usually contain marketing information about products and services offered as well as press releases, white papers, and even product demos. Product demos enable the analyst and business manager to effectively "reverse engineer" the competitive product (i.e., see how it ticks).
- If your competitor is a public company then its investor relations Web page will contain a wealth of financial information such as annual reports. An alternative source of financial filings can be found at www.sec.gov. A company's 10Q (quarterly) and 10K (annual) reports contain information on products, services, products, budgets, etc.

Normally, it is the role of the business or marketing manger to perform competitive intelligence. However, when this is obviously not being done, a proactive systems analyst will take the lead.

Brainstorming

In a brainstorming session you gather together a group of people, create a stimulating and focused atmosphere, and let people come up with ideas without risk of being ridiculed. Even seemingly stupid ideas may turn out to be "golden."

Focus groups

Focus groups are derived from marketing. These are structured sessions where a group of stakeholders are presented with a solution to a problem and then are closely questioned on their views about that solution.

Prototyping

A prototype is a simplified version of part of the final system. Developers experiment with the prototype to get an idea of how it would work in real life and what its problems and plus points are.

A CHECKLIST FOR REQUIREMENTS MANAGEMENT

The requirements management checklist shown in Exhibit 4-2 is used by the U.S. Department of the Navy.

CONCLUSION

Information gathering is a very intensive process with many aspects. The more information one has about a project from the start, the better prepared one will be to complete the project. Successful project management demands that enough information be known at the beginning of a project to anticipate potential problems in the systems development life cycle (Keogh, 2000). The role of a systems analyst in information gathering is to gain knowledge and interpret it to the benefit of the project plan. Anthony Smith said that turning information into knowledge is the creative skill of our age (ASH, 2002).

Exhibit 4-2. Requirements Management Checklist U.S. Department of the Navy

Commitment Planning:
1. Were all stakeholders identified?
2. Was the acceptance criteria defined?
3. Were nontechnical requirements identified and documented?
4. Has the project plan been developed or updated?
5. Has the project's risk been assessed?
6. Has the requirements management policy been reviewed?
7. Have the metric collection points and schedule for requirements management been identified?
8. Has the project plan been reviewed?
9. Did senior management review the project plan?
10. Was commitment to the project plan obtained?

Elicitation:
1. Was information concerning the problem's domain, open issues, and resolution identified?
2. Were the candidate technical requirements captured?
3. Were nontechnical requirements captured?

Analysis:
1. Were the requirements decomposed?
2. Were the quality attributes for each requirement determined?
3. Was traceability of the requirements established?
4. Was a reconciliation of the requirements performed?
5. Was the rationale for any decisions captured?
6. Were modifications to the requirements reflected in the project plan?

Formalization:
1. Were the informal requirements and supporting information documented?
2. Were formalized work products developed?
3. Were formalized work products placed under configuration management?

Verification:
1. Were the formalized requirements inspected for the quality attributes?
2. Were inconsistencies among the requirements identified and corrected?

(continued)

Exhibit 4-2. (continued)   Requirements Management Checklist U.S. Department of the Navy

3. Were redundant requirements identified and corrected?
4. Were deficiency reports generated and placed under configuration management?
5. Was the project plan updated to reflect changes made as a result of deficiency report resolution?
6. Are the formalized requirements traceable?
7. Have the stakeholders examined the formalized engineering artifacts and verified that they represent customer and end-user requirements?
8. Were the formalized engineering artifacts placed under CM?

Commitment Acceptance:
1. Were requirements metrics presented to the customer?
2. Was the project status presented to the customer?
3. Did the stakeholders approve the baselined requirements?
4. Did the customer provide approval to proceed?
5. Were periodic or event-driven reviews of the requirements held with project management?
6. Did QA audit the activities and products of requirements management?

References

4Sight Partners. (2000). Battleground: information gathering versus user privacy, (Online.) Available: http://www.4sightpartners.com/insights/watch082300.htm.

ASH (Action on Smoking and Health). (2002). Olympic questions, (Online) Available: http://www.teachers.ash.org.au/researchskills/questions.htm.

Bock, W. (2000a). Frequently asked questions about business intelligence, (Online.) Available: http://www.bockinfo.com/docs/bifaq.htm.

Bock, W. (2000b). Peter Drucker on information and information systems, (Online.) Available: http://www.bockinfo.com/docs/drucker.htm.

Creative Research Systems. Survey Design. http://www.surveysystem.com/sdesign.htm.

Curtis, G., Hoffer, J., George, J., and Valacich, J. (2000). *Introduction to Business Systems Analysis,* Pearson Custom Publishing, Boston.

Graef, J. (2002) Using the Internet for competitive intelligence, (Online) Available: http://www.cio.com/CIO/arch_0695_cicolumn.html.

Keogh, J. (2000). *Project Planning and Implementation,* Pearson Custom Publishing, Boston.

SCIP. (2002) What is CI? (Online) Available: http://www.scip.org/ci/index.asp.

Yate, M. (1997). *Hiring the Best,* 4th ed., Adams Media, Avon, MA.

Chapter 5
Designing User-Oriented Systems

Developers of system software need to involve users in the design process from the start. Until now, developers have kept the secrets of their trade to themselves. At the same time, they have failed to take an interest in the work of the business for which they are producing a tool. Users frequently share in the development process only through beta tests of products long after they have been designed. Users can frequently be a constant source of data on work habits, loads, and performance requirements. Developers can keep up with user needs the same way they are required to keep up with changes in technology. Maintaining a good relationship between the development and user communities ensures a healthy development process.

SECRETS OF THE TRADE

During the last few decades while automation of the business world has proceeded at an ever-accelerating pace, the practitioners of the black art of systems development have jealously guarded the secrets of their trade. Members of today's computer cult, who talk among themselves in tongues of Java, C++, and all things Internet, have forgotten the sounds of the human language — so much so that it is often necessary to hire a translator to explain the systems developer's work to the confused customer, the actual user of the cult's handiwork.

This translator would not be needed if companies would design their systems with the user in mind. That means involving end users at the start of the systems development process. To accomplish this, the technical staff must take some time away from studying the nuts and bolts of new tools to learn the tricks of the users' trades.

It also means that the end users need to be encouraged to get involved in the entire systems development effort, from the specification stage to actual application testing. Their involvement will help ensure that the finished system meets their needs and, in turn, the information needs of the corporation.

Today, under traditional systems analysis methods, the user is frequently left out of the loop. During the standard requirements definition phase, representatives from the user department are interviewed. Then a work flow analysis may be performed to determine the relationships between functions within that department. Finally, several months after the requirements definition, some customer testing is conducted — testing that unfortunately constitutes the sum total of user involvement. So it is not surprising that a plethora of changes must be made after the user finally reviews the test results.

TAILORING THE SYSTEM TO END USERS' NEEDS

The systems staff can avoid this last-minute retrofit by building a system tailored to specific end-user needs. To do that tailoring, the IT team should apply the same quick-study principle used in keeping up with new technology to learning end-user job functions. In fact, systems designers should know these functions at least as well as a six-month employee who is doing that work.

The necessary knowledge, however, is not always easy to come by because, all too often, systems gurus balk at attending user meetings. A big price tag may be attached to such behavior, as the New York Stock Exchange (NYSE) found out during my tenure there. During the mid-1980s, a series of user meetings was held to determine the rules and regulations of an important regulatory system that the Exchange wanted to develop. The NYSE's IT group found these critical meetings boring and, as a consequence, the finished system ended up incomplete; much money had to be spent adding enhancement features.

A thorough immersion in the customer's culture also negates the "we" versus "them" attitude that exists between many end users and the supporting IT staff. Top managers in the IT division at a major New York-based Swiss Bank learned this lesson the hard way. The bank's foreign exchange trading group was adamant about needing a foreign exchange trading system. The head of the Swiss Bank's IT department disagreed, so the trading group brought in an outside consultant who spoke their language and carefully listened to what they had to say.

As a result, the consultant was able to develop a usable, mostly error-free system that the users proudly showed off to other departments at the bank. At the next IT status meeting, users demanded to know why the IT staff could not or would not deliver systems as fast and as good as the one built by the foreign exchange group. Needless to say, the management of Swiss Bank's IT group was soon replaced.

DRUMMING UP ENTHUSIASM

Once you have a user-friendly IT staff, then you need to drum up enthusiasm and interest among the user community so that it will want to be involved every painful step of the way. "Community" is the operative word here because as many users as is feasible should be involved in the systems development process. In today's systems world, however, the norm is to have only one user who serves as the liaison for the entire group and assists the IT team as it develops specifications and tests the application.

Can one person adequately represent an entire user group? The answer is almost always no if you want a system worth its development dollars. Although involving many users can cause giant headaches, if the process is properly handled, the resulting system will be superior.

That was the experience I had at the NYSE when faced with the challenging chore of devising a system for over 150 professional users spread through five separate departments.

Despite the fact that each of the five departments did the exact same job, the diversity of opinion among the people in these units was nearly overwhelming. It took the great organizational skills of a talented analyst to pull all the heterogeneous information together into one cohesive specification. What resulted was far more complex, but a much more accurate and usable system that covered all the bases.

To cover all those bases, the NYSE IT team formed a working committee of users made up of one very verbal representative from each of the five departments. For roughly three months prior to the start of the specification stage, this working group would sometimes meet as often as two or three times a week.

The meetings were spent discussing actual use cases upon which the system would be based. In this way, the users were able to come up with all of the criteria that would ultimately be used in developing the system. It was during this conceptual phase of system definition that NYSE's IS staff and the departmental end users were able to reach a meeting of the minds in terms of desired inputs and outputs.

Determining the users' real information needs is indeed the stickiest wicket of the entire specification process. If all you do is translate the paper avalanche to the tube, then the ultimate system will not be much better than the former manual one. In fact, many of these paperwork clone systems actually decrease productivity.

The key to pinpointing the users' actual information needs is not to present more data, but to present less, but more meaningful or relevant, data. To date, IT has applied the pitch-hit-and-run theory to most systems development. Little, if any, consideration has been given to the differing information requirements of the various decision-making levels within an organization. As a result, you end up with fancy applications that spit out a kludge of irrelevant information.

METHODOLOGIES

To avoid that systems scenario and to present the optimum mix of detail and composite data to users, the developer can follow several time-tested methods. All of the methods recognize a relationship between the type of user and the level of detail needed to do the job or make a decision.

The three types of users — technical, tactical, and strategic — correspond to the three levels of workers in today's typical corporation. The technical users are generally the paper pushers in the corporate hierarchy. These employees —check processors and complaint takers, for example — are the people who need to see all the data. They input and review a wealth of data, normally in rote fashion.

At the opposite end of the spectrum are the senior managers, who use information gathered at the lower rungs for strategic purposes. A whole range of executive information and decision support systems is now available to help this corporate vanguard. These wares feature flashy colors on touch screens notable for the scarcity of data displayed. The data is likely to show sales projections, profitability numbers, and comparisons with the competition.

In the middle, between the strategic users and the technical users, are the tactical users. These are the middle managers, the poor unfortunates buried under the paper avalanche. It is these professionals who therefore need the most careful balance of data.

As always, users' needs dictate the data representation discipline used. Human resources or utility users, for example, are good candidates for descriptive models in the form of organization charts or floor plans. Modeling is also a good mode for operations management students who want to apply game theory to problems that lack supporting information. On the other hand, a normative representation of data is an apt choice for budget personnel, who need the best answer to a given problem.

Deciding on the type of information and how to present it to a particular group of users is the job of IT personnel. Sometimes they get carried away with their mission. At the NYSE, for example, the systems staff realized they had gone too far when a display for a large customer exceeded 91 screens of information. Going back to the drawing board, they came up with a plan to make the 91-screen monster more manageable. What they did was use graphics to tame the tangle of numbers displayed, coupled with embedded expert systems that enabled users to navigate quickly and more effectively through the data. In this filtering process, the systems developer sifts through the data, displaying only what is relevant at any point in time.

One way to do the filtering is by using the monitoring method, which serves up data to the user on an exception basis. This can take the form of variance reporting, in which the system produces only exceptions based on a programmatic review of the data. After reviewing credit card payments, a system can, for instance, display only those accounts where the payment is overdue or below the minimum. The monitoring method can also be used in programmed decision-making applications, in which case the system makes all of the technical decisions and many of the tactical ones as well.

American Express made the decision to go with a monitoring method that simplified its complex credit authorization chores. An expert system, aptly named Authorizer Assistant, helped Amex reduce the percentage of bad credit authorizations. It also reduced the number of screens needed to review customer data from a high of 12 to a manageable 2.

The advent of fourth generation languages (4GLs), which enabled end users to access corporate databases with an easy-to-use query syntax, has made interrogative methods of systems design more popular today. Implicit in this approach is the understanding that on many occasions users in complex decision-making environments cannot identify the information they need to perform ad hoc analyses. In these cases, all of the data elements must be resident in an accessible database. There must also be a tool that allows users to easily develop queries and variations on these queries against the data.

The ease-of-use factor provided by a 4GL came in very handy when Bankers Trust in New York (now Deutsche Bank) opted to leave the retail business. The data processing effort required to achieve this feat was enormous. With the help of Focus, the 4GL product from Information Builders in New York (www.ibi.com), the bank was able to ensure a smooth transfer of accounts from Bankers to many other far-flung financial institutions. Some accounts were spun off to a bank in Chicago and some to Albany, New York, while a few high rollers were retained as privileged Bankers Trust customers.

Once users are certain about the correct way to handle the data, the IT squad can then translate this information into the specification that spells out how the system should run. In many IT shops, how a system should run is a function of what is available in-house. This means that user requirements are forcibly fit into an existing tool set and — just like a bad shoe fit — a bad system fit causes users great pain.

Some of that pain was felt at the Securities Industry Automation Corp. (SIAC), which originally cramped its users by limiting itself to just one database product. SIAC began using Total from Cincom Systems Inc., Cincinnati, back in 1977, when few database tools were on the market. There was absolutely nothing wrong with Total; what was wrong was the implicit order to use it for all systems. Use it SIAC did — for everything!

Total is now gone from SIAC (Cincom has since retired the Total database and folded its functionality into the Supra product), replaced by a better stocked tool chest that includes a wide variety of database and 4GL tool sets. SIAC learned that a greater selection of software arms the designer with the options needed to tailor a system to specific user demands.

Good tailoring is particularly crucial when it comes to designing the external component of a system that the users see. Although users are not exposed to internal intricacies like utilities and overnight updating, they routinely work with external features such as on-line updates and reports, and PC uploading and downloading.

DISTRIBUTING DATA TO ITS RIGHTFUL OWNER — THE END USER

Most IT shops today design superbly efficient systems — for batch and transaction-based systems. Unfortunately, these systems are then jury-rigged for the part of the system visible to the user. Such technology tinkering often leaves the user out on a limb.

That is exactly where some end users at the NYSE found themselves when a billing system using a hierarchical production database was defined to a 4GL. The database, which was composed of numerous segments of data keyed by a brokerage firm number, ran very fast during overnight update processing due to its efficient design, specifically labored over for this purpose.

Meanwhile, some NYSE users were anticipating a new system with the extra added attraction of ad hoc inquiry. By a happy coincidence — or so it was originally thought —a 4GL had just been brought into the Exchange for end-user computing. The hierarchically defined database was dutifully defined to RAMIS; the users were trained and then let loose. RAMIS came up empty.

The problem was that bane of logic, the JOIN. Although the internal database was segmented into a logical structure for efficiencies, the data on every brokerage house was dispersed throughout, making it difficult for the users to get to it without understanding a bit more than they wanted to know about information processing.

There are as many ways of designing systems as there are people to use them. Most systems are designed out of prejudice: John Doe, the database administrator at the Widget Corp., is expert at Microsoft Access; therefore, all systems at the company are designed using Microsoft Access. Most corporate systems are designed around some sort of heavy-duty database. There are several types of database architectures: hierarchical, as in IBM IMS; networked, as in Computer Associates' IDMS, which has lately morphed into a combination networked and relational database; relational, as in Microsoft's SQL Server; and object oriented, as in Objectivity's Objectivity/DB. The proper choice depends upon many factors, not the least of which should be ease of access by the user.

Serious decisions must also be made regarding the system platform. In a world of mainframes, PCs, minicomputers, advanced workstations, Internet, and Intranets, the endless possibilities boggle the systems developer's mind. Solutions run the gamut from pure mainframe to a cluster of connected micros and minis to web-based distributed. In vogue today is an any-to-any environment where a user with a smart workstation has easy access to various mainframes, minis, or PCs across an Intranet.

THE SYSTEMS CHOICE

Choosing hardware and software is truly the fun part of systems design. Visits to vendors and trips to trade shows where you can play with test equipment transport you into an IT Disneyland. But while you are out there high-teching it up, at some point you had better come down to earth and get the user involved. If not, your dream machine will turn into an expensive nightmare. So, no matter what platform or program you pick, the user variables in making your selection must be examined at every technological turn. Among those user considerations are cost, ease of use, access to corporate data, graphics requirements compatibility with current environment, and particular preferences.

Ease of use was the major criterion that caused some equipment the NYSE was considering to be scuttled. Bar code readers for use in the field were the equipment under investigation. The technical group at the Exchange, who thought they had found the perfect solution, promptly ordered sample equipment and found that it worked like a charm. However, in order for it to work properly, the credit-card size readers had to be held at a certain angle. It was a good thing the users were consulted because it turned out that they were not able to hold the devices at that precise angle.

The lesson here is that just because you find it easy to use does not mean the user will necessarily agree with you. Also, keep in mind that just because it is state of the art and your technical staff adores it does not mean the user will concur. It all adds up to input: the user needs to have a say in the selection process.

This lesson is particularly pertinent when it comes to developing the specification for online screens and reports — the most visible part of any system. What frequently happens is that the IS people gather information and create a specification. After six to twelve months, they are ready to demo the system they developed to the users. With so much time intervening, the users have invariably changed their minds about or forgotten what they want.

At Bankers Trust, when it was developing an equipment leasing system, that time was not allowed to elapse without user feedback. Instead, the bank decided to rapid-prototype (RAD) the system for users. During the specification stage, a series of screens were put up on the system within a matter of days. Users were given an ID into the system so they could play with the prototype. They got the feel for the system and were able to voice their opinions and objections immediately.

An even more daring user approach was taken by the NYSE. Certain Exchange users were given an online editor and told to develop the screens utilizing a JAD (joint application development) methodology. IT staffers held their breath for many days, fearing the outcome of this experiment. They need not have feared; users know what they want to see and how they want to see it. Therefore, forget about textbook cases of good screen design and give your users a paintbrush.

Far more control is necessary in the system testing phase, however. Users are notorious for their lax standards when they are involved in testing. Therefore, the IT group must carefully oversee a test plan that covers all facets of the system, using as many test cases and as many users as possible.

In one company the systems squad exercised both caution and control in testing a very large financial system that was distributed across a group of seven users. The users were asked to compare test results with raw data and to annotate screen printouts or reports as appropriate. Because the users were given very specific tasks and very specific instructions (not the usual "take a look at the system and let me know if you see anything wrong"), the system was 99 percent debugged before it went into production.

Once the system has been tested, it is time to go live. Ideally, the users have been involved every step of the way in the design process, and pains have been taken to keep all those who will ultimately use the system informed of its progress.

Several years ago, the Securities & Exchange Commission stirred up user interest by running a contest to name their system and giving out awards to the winner — a move that would qualify as good user PR. Another tried-and-true PR ploy is to stage glitzy system demos complete with refreshments. After show time, it is important to keep the name of the system in front of the potential users. NYSE developers who designed a system named Force did just that by distributing pens inscribed with the slogan "May the FORCE be with you."

CONCLUSION

The points I have mentioned are all quite obvious, but they are often overlooked by harried IT staffs. This results in installed systems that are deemed successful by technicians but are dubbed flops by users. Thus, to design a system for all-around success, "May the USER be with you."

Chapter 6
The Outsourcing Decision

Outsourcing is a three-phased process:

> Phase 1. Analysis and evaluation
> Phase 2. Needs assessment and vendor selection
> Phase 3. Implementation and management

PHASE 1: ANALYSIS AND EVALUATION

In order to understand the services that need to be outsourced, organizational goals need to be identified — particularly the core competencies. Once the goals and core competencies are identified, information related to these activities is gathered to compare the cost of performing the functions in-house with the cost of outsourcing them. This enables the company to answer nonfinancial questions such as "How critical are these functions and activities?" or "What depends on these activities?" or "Will this activity become a 'mission critical' activity?" This will help organizations reach decisions about whether or not to outsource. Long-term cost and investment implications, work morale, and support should also be considered (see Appendix D for sample cost-benefit analysis worksheets).

PHASE 2: NEEDS ASSESSMENT AND VENDOR SELECTION

The objective of this phase is to develop a detailed understanding of the needs of the organization and the capabilities of possible solution providers.

In this phase a "request for a proposal" (RFP) is developed and delivered to applicable vendors. RFPs need to be structured in a manner to facilitate assessment and comparison of the various vendors. They should contain the complete requirements, problem that needs to be resolved, desires, etc. A clearly structured and documented RFP also helps vendors understand and evaluate what a company is looking for and assists them in assessing whether they can provide the required service.

When evaluating the vendor proposals, the organization should look not only at the technological capability of the vendor but also at factors such as the vendor's financial stability, track record, and customer support reputation. Contacting vendor's existing and previous clients would give the organization a good idea about the vendor's abilities.

Once a vendor is selected, the organization needs to make sure that a fair and reasonable contract, beneficial to the organization, is negotiated. It is imperative to define service levels and the consequences of not meeting them clearly. Both parties should make sure that they understand the performance measurement criteria (see Appendix Q for a software metrics capabilities guide).

PHASE 3: IMPLEMENTATION

The final phase in the outsourcing decision process is the implementation. During this phase a clear definition of the task needs to be identified, so establishing a time frame would be very helpful. Mechanisms need to be established to monitor and evaluate performance during the vendor's developmental process. This is important even after implementation to make sure that the outsourced tasks are being delivered by the vendor as agreed upon. Ability to identify, communicate, and resolve issues promptly and fairly will help the company achieve mutual benefits and make a relationship successful.

Depending on the size of the outsourcing contract, the manager responsible for the program's delivery and integration may be responsible for all of the process, or only some. These are the horizontal and vertical factors of outsourcing management. A manager of the horizontal process is often involved in the decision to outsource, and is then responsible for defining the work, selecting and engaging the vendor, and managing the delivery and completion of the program. This manager normally handles all day-to-day negotiations. With larger programs, particularly those on a global scale, a decision is often made at senior levels to outsource. A negotiation team is appointed to work through the complex agreements, usually under strict confidentiality, until the agreement is finalized and announced. It is then the role of the manager of the vertical component to implement and manage the ongoing program. Part of this role is the interpretation of the agreement and identification of areas not covered by the agreement.

AN OUTSOURCING EXAMPLE

In this chapter we will break down the outsourcing decision-making process using an e-business system as an example. Since the Internet opened for business just a short ten years ago and despite the boom–bust cyclical nature of the market, few companies have not jumped into the foray by building a corporate Internet presence. The Internet is the one thing most companies have in common.

Visit Gateway.com and wander over to their accessory store (http://www.gtwaccessories.com). Here you can buy everything from digital cameras to software to printers. Sounds like quite an operation does it not? The store might have the Gateway logo on it, but you will not find it on any Gateway corporate computer. Where you will find it is at Vcommerce.com — a company that is in the business of putting other companies in the e-commerce business. According to Gateway, by outsourcing the entire function, it is able to sell products and grow revenues while focusing its attention on its core competencies.

In other words, Gateway, no slouch in the computer expertise department, has decided that even they do not have the expertise or desire to run a sophisticated e-commerce site. Instead, they decided to give the problem to someone else — someone with the expertise. What, then, does this say about the rest of us?

Outsourcing Issues

It is important to understand the ramifications of systems development in the world of high-risk interconnected computers. In order to make an ROI-enhancing decision, the CIO must gather much information from a diversity of areas:

- *Legal issues.* It is amazing how many Web sites are without benefit of legal counsel. This stems from the days when the Web had the reputation of the "Wild, Wild West." Today, the CIO must be concerned about issues such as copyright infringement of images and text, the use of online warranties, licensing, contracts, and spamming.
- *Regulatory issues.* Right now purchases on the Web are not taxed but expect that this reprieve will not last forever. Other taxation issues to consider include the effect of telecommuting Web developers on the jurisdictional exposure of the corporation. Of course, we all know by now that online gambling is prohibited, but what about lotteries and contests — even if you offer them as a promotional gimmick? Then consider First Amendment issues, pornography issues — et cetera, et cetera, et cetera.
- *Security.* Once you open your doors you will probably be letting in more than customers. Hackers, crackers, and other malevolent creatures of the night seem to spend all of their waking hours figuring out new ways to wreak havoc on unsuspecting organizations. Top this off with a veritable plague of new viruses, concerns about fire, sloppy data entry, and attacks by internal employees and security becomes a full-time job. Things you need to understand are uses of firewalls, encryption, and authentication — ultracomplex technologies not for the technologically faint of heart. Even the most sophisticated of preventive measures will not ward off all attacks. Think back to the massive

denial of service attacks on sites such as Yahoo and eTrade in February, 2000, and the various klez viruses that plagued us in 2002.

- *Staffing issues.* Do you have the staff to implement an e-business initiative successfully? E-business is hard work; it is $24 \times 7 \times 52$. Also keep in mind that new bells and whistles are invented almost daily. You will need to invest a substantial sum to keep your staff trained so that they can take advantage of these new technologies.
- *System usability.* Long gone are the days when you could throw up a Web site and expect kudos. With a plethora of tool sets such as Macromedia Flash, Web conferencing, instant chat, etc., the stakes for a usable Web site have gotten a lot higher — and much more expensive. Given the size of many Web sites, ergonomics and navigability issues must be explored. Would GM ever release a new kind of car without some sort of driver-acceptance testing?
- *System functionality.* It was so much easier just five years ago to throw up a Web site and have it considered novel. Today all things novel probably have already been done so you will not be able to lure new web visitors to your site with the promise of the "newest and the greatest." Instead you must focus on your site's functionality. For example, a small golf Web site named swapgolf.com offers a wide variety of functions: a golf shopping mall, ability to swap golf tee times, a bulletin board, and even golf puzzles. Notice all the functionality is related to the golf theme. CNBC.com, on the other hand, is a large site with many more financial resources than swapgolf so it is no wonder that this site is loaded with functionality. Note too that CNBC.com offers theme-related functionality. Because CNBC is a financial news service, Web site functionality includes financial-related services such as MoneyTalk, Quote Box, and Markets. Also keep in mind that a Web site is a high maintenance project that needs to be fed constantly.
- *System reliability.* Perhaps the most irritating problem Web surfers encounter is sites that have bad links, databases that decline to work, and general overall system development sloppiness. It is almost as if many sites were thrown online without any testing whatsoever. Netslaves is a most intriguing Web site that takes delight in shooting down what they consider to be myths and outright lies about all things Internet. Self-professed Netslave media assassin Steve Gilliard has this to say about the Net myth that "things move fast online and we have to stay ahead." He explains, "It takes time to develop a reliable business. The faster you move, the more likely you are to screw up. It takes time, years, to get things right, develop trust in key employees and stabilize. Moving fast in many cases is an excuse for incompetence."
- *System integration.* Web-based systems should never operate in a vacuum. Instead, they should be fully integrated into your current corporate systems. For example, your marketing and sales systems need information about who is visiting your site, what they are looking at,

and what they are buying. Only a solid integrative infrastructure will accomplish this. Real synergy occurs when internal and external systems are effectively linked together, creating more efficient ways to market, sell, and process and deliver orders. This translates to integrating a whole spate of disparate systems, including inventory, ordering, and invoicing, along with supply-chain data from business partners — in other words, the organization's ERP (enterprise resource planning) resource.

- *Meaningful metrics.* It really does not pay to spend $5 million to build an e-commerce system if you will never know how it affects the bottom line. Will it increase sales by 10 percent or boost customer retention by 15 percent? Before you ever do the technology planning for an e-business, you should decide just what it is you are hoping to accomplish (i.e., your business strategy plan) and then develop meaningful metrics to measure your progress.
- *Costs.* Even if you plan carefully, there will always be those hidden and unexpected costs for hardware, software, communications, and even new staff.

What Does It Cost?

Back in 1995, Tom Vassos, an instructor at the University of Toronto, was part of an IBM team that created IBM's Web site. It had 10,000 documents spread across 30 Web servers around the world. Their requirements included everything from translation into multiple languages, downloadable documents, demonstration tools, contents of entire IBM magazines and publications, graphics images, audio clips, and fulfillment mechanisms for other deliverables such as CD Roms.

The site cost several million dollars initially, with an IBM commitment to spending several more to maintain and expand the site.

Some experts estimate that a large site should cost $6 million over two years, a medium site $2 million, and $500,000 for a small site over two years. These numbers include many costs for site and product promotion and content upkeep.

The Gartner Group surveyed 100 leading companies operating e-commerce sites and found that the average firm had spent three-quarters of a million dollars on the technology (i.e., hardware/software/peopleware) alone. Add to that the cost of marketing that site and you may need a budget as high as amazon.com, which now spends upward of $40 million per quarter to market itself.

Using an ISP (Internet Service Provider)

With the rise of Web-hosting companies, today the organization has a wide variety of less expensive alternatives. For example, a small business using a typical ISP such as VeriSign would pay about $376 per month for monthly service, file storage and data transfer fees, and a shopping cart. An even smaller business can get away with a bare-bones site for about $10 per month at Schogini.com. In neither of these cases does Web design figure into the equation. That is a separate cost.

Web site design costs vary considerably among web design firms. One company I have worked with charged $2,000 for a 10-page site and $10,000 for a 25-page site. A high-end site for a mid-sized business I worked with set the company back around $50,000. This got them about 50 pages and assorted add-ons such as user tracking, image maps, frames, Shockwave or Quicktime animation, audio, database, shopping cart, SSL (secure transaction server), creative illustrations, CGI, and database programming. Hosting charges were separate. For a mid-sized business low end costs about $100 to $160 a month, mid level $160 to $350 a month and high end about $350 a month. Add $1,500 a month for a T-1 communications line.

A good place to start doing comparative research is www.thelist.com, which provides a list of virtually all of the ISPs in the world and the services and price structures they offer. As mentioned, you will find wide variation in prices.

Rolling Your Own

The other choice, one that only very large companies seem to take today, is to roll your own. Rough estimates for a start-up configuration for a small to mid-sized company are as follows:

- *Computer.* Keep in mind that the IBM site described previously had 30 Web servers. Just one of them can cost you between $5,000 and $25,000, which includes only the hardware. This is a one-time cost although maintenance upgrades will need to be figured into the equation.
- *OS/server software.* This can cost anywhere from $0 if you run a free version of Linux to over $10,000. Usually either UNIX or Windows/NT/2000 is used, with Linux quickly gaining ground. You may also need to buy multiple Web servers. First there is the Web server that runs the actual Web site. Add an additional Web server if you are running an e-commerce server. Add a third server if you need to run something like RealAudio. Again, this is a one-time cost requiring maintenance upgrades.
- *Modems.* Modem pricing varies, depending upon how many you need and their capabilities. Modems, in case you did not know, are used for those people who might need to dial into your system. This is a one-time cost.

- *Connectivity hardware.* Hardware or software devices such as routers and couplers will run you anywhere from $1000 to $5000+. This is a one-time cost.
- *Communications.* You cannot simply hook up your PC to a slow modem and expect to be able to use that as your Web site. Connecting your PC to the Net will require you to lease a high-speed telephone line. A T-1 will cost you about $1500 a month. A T-3, which has a higher speed, will cost you even more.

Labor Costs

As is true for most labor costs, the price of labor is all across the board. Staff salaries for technology experts are rather high, with an average cost of about $60,000 a year for someone with several years of experience.

Hiring consultants will bring a variety of proposals to your doorstep. Web page authors charge anywhere from $30 to $150 an hour with the higher-end price going to those that can build you a database or write you a custom script using Perl or Java.

The Gartner Group has estimated that, through 2004, IT contractors and other outside resources will be used to complete 50 percent of the e-business work in large enterprises.

Costs Depend on What You Put on the Site

Whether you outsource or not, figuring out what your Web site will cost is a lengthy, complicated process. The first thing to do is to make a list (see Exhibit 6-1) of exactly what you expect to put on this site, how often you will update it, and the site's expected functionality.

Once this list is made, you can send out RFPs (requests for proposal) to various Web-hosting companies to determine their cost structure to develop your site. Your IT department should be given a chance to bid as well.

SHOULD YOU OUTSOURCE?

Moving to an e-business model requires an enormous commitment. Ask yourself whether you are up to it. Also ask yourself whether your company is up to it.

There are many good reasons to outsource as Gateway discovered when it decided to outsource many of its own e-business functions. Deciding whether or not to outsource is a very individual decision based on many corporate factors:

Exhibit 6-1. Figuring Out What Your Web Will Cost

Feature	IT Dept Price	Competitor 1 Price	Competitor 2 Price
Number of pages of text?			
a. Provide names and location of this text.			
Number of images?			
a. Provide name and location of each image file.			
b. Do any of these images need to be altered?			
Number of animations required?			
a. Provide name and location of each.			
b. If new ones must be designed, provide design information.			
Number of documents you wish to store on the Web?			
a. PDF files (name and location of each)			
b. Doc files (name and location of each)			
c. Powerpoint files (name and location of each)			
d. Wav or other audio files (name and location of each)			
e. Avi or other video file (name and location of each)			
f. Other files — list			
Will you be using RealAudio or video?			
a. Are media files already available or do they need to be created or digitized?			
Will you require SSL connectivity? This is secure server capability so that people can do things like enter private information online.			
a. Do you require encryption?			
b. Do you require digital certificates?			
c. What level of security do you need?			

(continued)

Exhibit 6-1. (continued)   Figuring Out What Your Web Will Cost

Feature	IT Dept Price	Competitor 1 Price	Competitor 2 Price
How many e-mail accounts do you need?			
a. Will you need e-mail routing?			
b. Will you need autoresponders?			
Will you need a shopping cart service for online purchases?			
a. Do you already have product information for those products you wish to sell, including images and text information? Provide file name and location for each.			
Will you need a chat room?			
Will you need a bulletin board?			
Will you need a guestbook?			
Will you need feedback forms?			
Will you need activity reports? What periodicity?			
Will you need banner creation?			
To which other sites do you wish to link?			
Do you need database lookup?			
Do you need a visitor registration program?			
Will you outsource or do it internally? If done internally, add costs for:			
a. Hardware			
b. Servers			
c. Modems			
d. Connectivity			
e. T1			
Will your company require Internet fax?			
Will the company require virtual private networks (VPNs)? (These are private networks between one or more locations, i.e., partners.)			

Here are some reasons why outsourcing might be a good idea for your company.

- *Price.* Rolling your own is often much more expensive than outsourcing to a reputable service provider.
- *Expertise.* Few companies have the level of expertise in-house that building a sophisticated Web site requires.
- *Obsolescence.* Hardware and software turn obsolete within six months and upgrades are often expensive. Outsourcing makes this someone else's problem. For the outsourcer to stay in business, it must stay at the most current release and use the most sophisticated equipment. It does this so you do not need to.
- *Security.* As mentioned earlier, encryption, virus protection, and all of the other security paraphernalia such as site backup and disaster recovery are quite expensive to perform on your own.
- *Complete solution.* If you select a reputable hosting company with lots of experience you benefit from this experience and its expertise. It can provide you with everything from hosting to design to maintenance, all in one place.
- *Scalability.* It is likely that your site will grow in complexity and functionality. A Web-hosting company will be able to scale up without service interruptions.
- Of course, there are disadvantages to outsourcing as well:
- *Hidden charges.* If you exceed your quotas (i.e., data transfer, disk space) you will be charged an additional premium.
- *Their rules and not yours.* The Web hosting company makes the rules and not you. You will need to modify your own corporate policy to accommodate the outsourcer.
- *Timeliness.* Say the Web hosting company runs an advertising blitz to get new customers — and it works. Your request for modifications might need to wait a while.
- *Mergers and acquisitions.* The Net world moves fast and is on an acquisition binge. What happens if the company you are using is acquired?

QUESTIONS TO ASK POTENTIAL OUTSOURCING COMPANIES

A company cannot choose a hosting company out of a hat. Ask the following questions:

- What capabilities do you offer and at what prices? Can you provide us with everything on our list of requirements?
- What is your level of expertise? Demonstrate by showing a portfolio of Web sites developed at different levels of sophistication.
- How long have you been in business?
- What are your sales?
- Provide three references.

- How quickly do you respond to telephone and e-mail customer service questions?
- What measures do you have in place to secure our data on your servers?
- Are you 24 × 7?
- What type of disaster recovery services do you provide?
- How often do you upgrade your hardware and software?
- If some of your staff are using dial-up lines to access your outsourced servers, can they get online without busy signals? Can staff members use local phone numbers to dial into the network?
- What are the speed and capacity of the hosting company's link to the Internet? (This is called throughput.)
- Will the hosting company accept large file transfers?
- Will the hosting company permit e-mail broadcasting?

OUTSOURCING MODELS

Outsourcing does not need to be an all or nothing proposition; several models are available:

- *In-house.* If you are a large company with a significant existing technology infrastructure with commensurate expertise, this approach might be the most cost-beneficial to you. Of course, you will not know whether this is the right approach unless you cost out the other alternatives.
- *Full outsource.* Turn over the entire spectrum of development to an outsourcing company or combination of outsourcing companies and consulting firms.
- *Partial outsource.* Possible alternatives are hosting your own servers but hiring a consultancy to program them; outsourcing your server hosting but programming it in-house, and hosting your servers but purchasing third-party software packages to run on those servers.

CONCLUSION

Whether to outsource or not is a difficult decision and involves the analysis of many variables. Ultimately the success — and bottom line — of the organization rests on making the right decision.

Chapter 7
Methodology Selection

It is surprising how few IT organizations utilize a formal methodology. Although the vast majority employ a wide variety of automated tool sets to assist their programmers in developing and testing complex code, the "process" of systems development is still largely chaotic in most organizations.

A systems methodology guides the activities of developing and evolving systems starting from the initial feasibility study and culminating only when the system is finally retired. Use of a methodology assures the organization that its process of developing and maintaining systems is sustainable and repeatable.

Life would be simple if there were only one methodology. Unfortunately, or fortunately depending upon your perspective, you can choose from hundreds of methodologies (http://www.wwweb.org/smo/bmc/). Some are industry standard and some are proprietary to a particular consulting organization. Given this vast choice, it is important that you are able to determine whether a systems methodology will meet the specific needs of your organization. The way to do this is by evaluating the methodology. This is the focus of this chapter.

A BRIEF SUMMARY OF COMMON GENERIC METHODOLOGIES

There is a wide variety of methodologies. Organizations will select the ones most appropriate for their mode of development. It is not unusual for an organization to utilize more than one methodology. Typically, a structured and an object-oriented approach can peacefully co-exist within one company.

- *System development life cycle (SDLC).* This is a phased, structured approach to systems development. The phases include requirements feasibility, analysis, system design, coding, testing, implementation, and testing. Please note that there are variations of these stated phases. Usually, each phase is performed sequentially, although some potential for overlap exists. This is the methodology that is used most often in industry.

- *Iterative (prototyping).* This approach is used to replace several of the phases in the SDLC. In the SDLC approach the "time to market," so to speak, can be months (sometimes years). During this time, requirements may change and the final deliverable, therefore, might be quite outmoded. To prevent this from happening it is a good idea to try to compress the development cycle to shorten the time to market and provide interim results to the end user. The iterative model consists of three steps: 1) listen to customer; 2) build and revise a mock-up; 3) have customer test drive the mock-up and then return to step 1.
- *Rapid application development (RAD).* This is a form of the iterative model. The key word here is "rapid." Development teams try to get a first pass of the system out to the end user within 60 to 90 days. To accomplish this, the normal seven-step SDLC is compressed into the following steps: business modeling; data modeling; process modeling; application generation, and testing and turnover. Note the term "application generation"; RAD makes use of application generators, formerly called CASE (computer-assisted software engineering) tools.
- *Incremental model.* The four main phases of software development are analysis, design, coding, and testing. If we break a business problem into chunks — or increments — then we can use an overlapping, phased approach to software development as shown below:

    Increment 1

            Analysis   Design   Code   Test
            → Delivery of first increment

    Increment 2

            Analysis   Design   Code   Test
            → Delivery of second increment, etc.

- *Joint application development (JAD).* JAD is more of a technique than a complete methodology and can be utilized as part of any of the other methodologies discussed here. The technique consists of "folding" one or more end users into the software development team. Instead of an adversarial software developer–end-user dynamic, the effect is to have the continued, uninterrupted attention of the persons who will ultimately use the system.
- *Reverse engineering.* This technique is used, first, to understand a system from its code, second, to generate documentation base on the code, and, third, make desired changes to the system. Competitive software companies often try to reverse engineer their competitors' software.
- *Re-engineering.* Business goals change over time. Software must change to be consistent with these goals. Re-engineering utilizes many of the techniques already discussed here. Instead of building a system from scratch, the goal of re-engineering is to retrofit an existing system to new business functionality.

- *Object-oriented (OO).* OO primarily consists of object-oriented analysis (OOA), object-oriented design (OOD), and object oriented programming (OOP). These methodologies are radically different from traditional, more structured methodologies.

RATING YOUR METHODOLOGY

1. Does the methodology identify the steps necessary to produce each deliverable of a systems development effort?

Methodologies are necessarily very "step" oriented. One cannot and should not proceed to step two without adequately completing step one. A person using a particular methodology should be provided with a clear delineation of all steps as well as what initiates and terminates each of these steps. A good methodology will define answers to the following questions:

- What must be done?
- How long will it take?
- Why is the step done?
- How should it be done?
- What is produced?
- Who will do it?
- When should it be done?
- Which tools are to be used?

Rate this attribute:

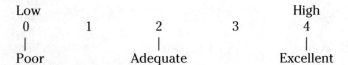

2. Does the methodology simplify the systems development process?

Some methodologies are so complicated that they are impossible to use. If it is not clear to the user of the methodology how to use that particular methodology, the systems development effort will fail.

Rate this attribute:

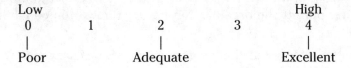

3. Does the methodology encourage and provide the means to implement a standard and repeatable approach to systems development?

The Software Engineering Institute (http://www.sei.cmu.edu/sei-home.html) in Pittsburgh is the creator of the well-known capability maturity model (CMM). The framework consists of several levels of maturity that an IT department goes through on its way to becoming completely optimized and productive:

- *Initial.* This level is ad hoc and chaotic.
- *Repeatable.* Basic project management processes are established to track cost, schedule, and functionality.
- *Defined.* Management and engineering activities are documented, standardized, and integrated into the organization.
- *Quantitatively managed.* This level uses detailed measures.
- *Optimizing.* Continuous process improvement is enabled by quantitative feedback and from testing innovative ideas and technologies.

An often quoted statistic is that 80 percent of us are sitting on top of level one. Use of a methodology implies that the organization is at level three — defined. A methodology enables the organization to implement a standardized procedure for the development of systems so that the process of developing these systems is standardized and can be repeated easily by one or more project teams.

Rate this attribute:

Low				High
0	1	2	3	4
Poor		Adequate		Excellent

4. Can the methodology be customized to meet the specific requirements of the organization or is it unyielding and uncustomizable?

Every organization is unique in terms of its policies and procedures, industry, and standards it applies to its practices. It makes sense, therefore, that any methodology selected needs to be flexible so that it can accommodate the way the organization works today — as well as the way the organization will work tomorrow. The very best methodologies are those that permit the organization full customization capabilities in terms of:

- Can the names of methodology components be changed to those the organization is more familiar with?
- Can the descriptions of methodology components be changed?
- Can new components be added and related to existing components?
- Can component definitions (designs) be altered, extended, or deleted?

- Can new paths be defined to describe unique uses of the methodology?
- Can the underlying methods and deliverables be changed?

Rate this attribute:

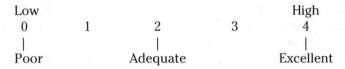

5. Is the methodology "state of the art?"

Each month brings new innovations to the IT industry. The Internet has been with us for less than a decade. Flat file systems have morphed into relational database systems that have morphed into object-oriented databases.

Because the tools and techniques of developing systems are continually improving, it makes sense that the methodology chosen needs to have the capability of interacting with these newer tools and techniques — in case the methodology becomes as obsolete as the tools it thinks you are using. Tools that your methodology should support include:

- Computer-assisted systems engineering (CASE), as well as visual development tools such as Visual Basic, Visual C++, etc.
- Data dictionaries, repositories, and data warehouses
- Java and XML
- Relational databases and object-oriented databases
- Client-server
- Cooperative and collaborative processing
- Internet and Intranet
- Accelerated and user-centered development such as JAD (joint application development) and RAD (rapid application development)
- Integration (across business area, system data, and function sharing)

Rate this attribute:

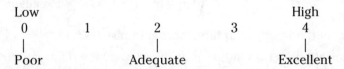

6. Is the methodology complete?

Most formal systems development activities are based around several steps collectively known as the SDLC or systems development life cycle. The SDLC consists of:

- *Planning.* In this step we uncover the mission and goals of the project and ascertain the resources required to implement the system.

101

- *Feasibility.* This step determines whether or not the project is economically or technically feasible.
- *Analysis.* In this step the business and technical requirements of proposed systems are uncovered, modeled, and documented.
- *Design.* During this phase system high-level as well as low-level architectures are crafted that are traceable back to the business requirements uncovered in the analysis phase.
- *Implementation.* In this phase programs are coded and tested.
- *Production.* Once the programs have been written and tested, this phase will oversee the introduction of the system into the business.
- *Maintenance.* No system is ever complete. During the maintenance phase, modifications are made to the system to fix errors and to enhance the system per new requirements.

Some methodologies pertain only to the latter phases of the SDLC. A preferred methodology will encompass the entire range of SDLC activities.

Rate this attribute:

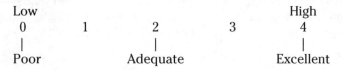

7. Can the methodology be broken down into components?

Although the methodology should cover all phases of the SDLC, the preferred methodology will be object oriented in nature. For example, it should be possible to extract the piece of the methodology relevant to the feasibility study easily.

Rate this attribute:

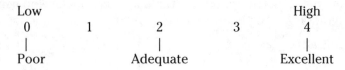

8. Is the methodology adaptable across industries?

Organizations across industry boundaries exhibit different attributes. A preferred methodology is adaptable to all industries, across all boundaries.

Rate this attribute:

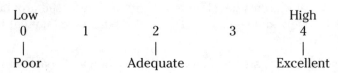

9. Does the methodology produce documentation?

A formal process necessitates the creation of deliverables at certain pre-designated milestones. For example, upon completion of the analysis phase it is typical that a requirements specification be created. The particular methodology will specify the format and timeliness of the document.

Rate this attribute:

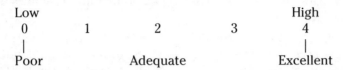

10. Does the methodology have discrete methods for each step in each phase of the SDLC?

A formal methodology breaks down the systems development process into phases (e.g., SDLC). Each phase, in turn, has its own unique steps. A good methodology will supply methods that will instruct the developer in applying that segment of the methodology to the particular step in question. For example, a unique step of the analysis phase is to interview end users. A good methodology will provide instructions on:

- Who performs this task
- How to perform this task
- What tools to use to perform this task
- What deliverable, if any, is required

Rate this attribute:

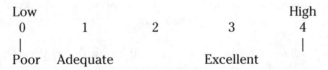

11. Does the methodology provide techniques that describe how to conduct its methods?

For a methodology to be usable it must detail the techniques of performing the tasks outlined within it. For example, for the task "interview end users" techniques should include:

- How to select the end users
- What sampling techniques to use
- How to devise questionnaires and surveys
- How to use a tape or video recorder effectively

Rate this attribute:

```
Low                                    High
 0         1         2         3         4
 |                                       |
Poor    Adequate            Excellent
```

12. Will the methodology incorporate standards and practices of the organization?

All organizations are different. Each publishes its own set of policies and procedures (i.e., naming conventions, tool usage guidelines, etc.), which may or may not be consistent within the industry. A good methodology enables the organization to maintain its unique set of standards and practices.

Rate this attribute:

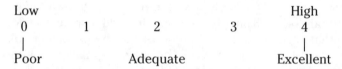

```
Low                                    High
 0         1         2         3         4
 |                                       |
Poor              Adequate         Excellent
```

13. Does the methodology identify roles played by various members of the project team?

A wide variety of people constitutes a typically project team.

- *Project manager* — manages one or more projects.
- *Project leader* — manages a specific project.
- *Systems analyst* — handles the analytical aspects of the system.
- *Designer* — designs the systems (might be the same person as the analyst).
- *Network administrator* — is responsible for implementing the network aspects of the system.
- *Database administrator* — designs the database and file systems.
- *Web designer* — handles the front end of any Internet or Intranet systems.

An effective methodology links required skills with each method in order to identify appropriate roles.

Rate this attribute:

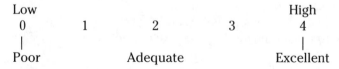

```
Low                                    High
 0         1         2         3         4
 |                                       |
Poor              Adequate         Excellent
```

14. Does the methodology identify support tools appropriate for execution of each method?

A wide variety of tools on the market will automate many of the tasks delineated in the methodology (i.e., survey generation, program code generation, model building).

It should be noted that many methodologies were developed by software vendors for the express purpose of supporting a particular tool set. In other words, the methodology was developed as a marketing vehicle for the tool set.

Rate this attribute:

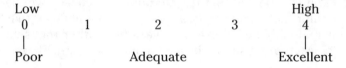

15. Is the methodology verifiable?

A formal methodology must have a visible model. This model must be able to be verified for correctness and completeness and modified as needs dictate. Only methodologies that are coupled with automated tool sets are capable of this.

Rate this attribute:

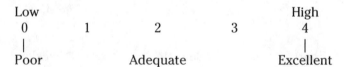

16. Can the methodology be searched?

Methodology is the road map to the development of a system. As discussed, the methodology contains information on how to approach each phase in the SDLC along with techniques and tools for executing the methods specified for that particular phase. From the perspective of the systems developer, the methodology is a knowledge base that instructs him or her on the "how-tos" as well as the "why tos" and "when tos" of systems development. It makes sense, therefore, that the system developer be permitted to search through this methodology knowledge base to retrieve specific information.

Because it is a knowledge base, the information contained there should be navigable from multiple perspectives. The systems developer should be able to forward chain through the knowledge base from top to bottom, as well as backward chain upward from the lowest level to the highest level of abstraction.

The methodology knowledge base should exhibit all of the features of an end-user-oriented, windows- or browser-based system, including search, print, save, edit, view, and help.

Rate this attribute:

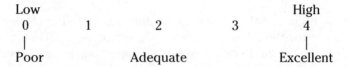

17. Does the methodology maintain standard industry interfaces?

Although it is expected that the methodology chosen will be coupled with one or more automated tools, a very strong possibility is that the organization will already be using a wide variety of other tool sets that the methodological tool set should be able to interface with. These interfaces include:

- Project management software
- CASE and application development tool sets
- Report writers
- Desktop publishing and word processing software
- Spreadsheets and databases

Rate this attribute:

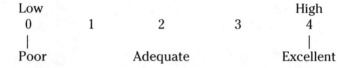

18. Is adequate training available for the methodology?

Whether the training is vendor oriented, in-house oriented or consultant/training company oriented, it is imperative that staff be fully trained on use of the methodology, as well as any tool sets, prior to use.

Rate this attribute:

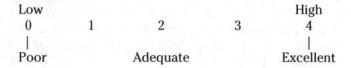

19. Has the vendor demonstrated that the methodology/tool suite is used at an organization similar to your organization?

Seeing the methodology and tool set, if applicable, in use at a comparable organization is reassuring and demonstrates the full range of the methodology's capabilities. Additionally, it demonstrates the capabilities of the vendor in terms of training, implementation, and support.

Rate this attribute:

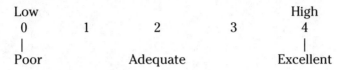

Low				High
0	1	2	3	4
|				|
Poor		Adequate		Excellent

DETERMINING YOUR METHODOLOGY'S RATING

Our questionnaire contained 19 questions or attributes. With a top score of 4 points for each question or attribute, the highest rating a methodology can receive is 76 points. An adequate rating, a point score of at least 2 per question, would be 36 points. Obviously, the higher the score is, the better the methodology.

References and Further Reading

Holcman, S. (1993). A systems methodology: a rating and evaluation guide, in *Software Engineering Productivity Handbook,* Keyes, J., Ed., McGraw-Hill, New York.

Chapter 8
Selecting and Integrating a Repository for Effective Resource Management

> The corporation of the future will be run with a vast mesh of interacting computers and data-based systems. It will be impossible to manage and build the procedures to take advantage of this technology without some form of information engineering, appropriately automated. The encyclopedia, which is the heart of information engineering, will be a vital corporate resource.
>
> — **James Martin (1989)**

EFFECTIVE INFORMATION RESOURCE MANAGEMENT

There are many roads to productivity. The one least traveled, but perhaps most profitable, is the one where software tools are integrated in a manner producing accessible and timely information.

The three keywords here are information, tools, and integration. Information is really the most important asset a company owns. With proper utilization, information becomes a potent competitive force. In today's very global — and very competitive — economy, information may, in fact, be the deciding factor in determining the color of the organization's bottom-line.

Understanding that information is a resource to be valued, organizations have made a heavy investment in information technology. This investment, to the tune of billions of dollars, included development of new systems as well as purchase of a variety of software tools.

Software tools are decidedly two-flavored. On the one hand are the end user-oriented tools, which include report writers and 4GLs; on the other hand are tools that specifically target the development function. These tools run the gamut from compilers to data administration tools to visual development tools. Common among all of these tools has been the decided lack of interconnectivity, or integration.

Lack of integration is a subtle defect with a powerfully negative impact on the productivity and competitiveness of an organization. It translates to an inability to manage information in a consistent and nonredundant fashion. Because software tools have seams, information cannot flow easily from one tool to anther, forcing organizations to move the information manually between tools — or worse, to create redundant and conflicting information stores.

Recognizing the ramifications of these problems, the industry has begun to move in the direction of development frameworks. The goal of these frameworks is to provide a boundaryless environment to spur the free flow of information through the use of standards and guidelines for development of software tools.

Metadata repositories, the focus of this chapter, have historically focused on application development and data warehousing. Recently this mission has been extended to support component middleware frameworks and business objects. In the near future, knowledge management and enterprise information portal environments will be supported as well.

A metadata repository, which I will call a repository workbench, has three functions. It is a repository, it provides tools, and it forms the "connecting glue" of the development framework — in other words, integration.

A short and standard definition of a repository is "an organized reference to the data content of something. That something could be a system, a database, or a collection of all the files, program databases, and manual records maintained by a large organization." Although the definition of tools should be self-evident, in this context it is not.

Tools in a repository workbench environment encompass a broad spectrum of functionality that goes beyond what is commonly available. The last component of the repository workbench equation is integration; this component meshes the repository and the repository-based tools into an organization's environment. The net sum of the repository equation is the ability to better leverage the skill set of a wide range of the organization's staff — from data administrators to programmers to analysts and end users. This leveraging of skill sets leads to a dramatic increase in productivity.

The remainder of this chapter assists the reader in three areas: evaluating the benefits of a repository workbench solution, planning for its implementation, and measuring it.

HOW TO USE THIS CHAPTER

In the first section — Evaluating the Repository Workbench — a quantitative approach is taken to assist the reader in understanding the features of a repository workbench and comparing these features across competitive products. Twenty-three distinct criteria are divided into three categories: repository, integration, and tools; each criterion is presented in the form of a set of features. To quantify the assessment, each should be rated in terms of its importance to the organization. A rating, or weight, of 1 to 3 should be used (1 = not important to the organization, 2 = required by the organization, 3 = of high importance to the organization).

Each of the features describing the criteria should next be rated according to how well the vendor fulfills the requirement. A scale of 1 through 5 should be used: (1 = fails, 2 = weak, 3 = adequate, 4 = good, 5 = excellent).

After you finish rating all 23 criteria, your scores can be transferred to the charts at the end of this chapter. These charts allow you to add up repository scores and to make overall evaluations and comparisons.

In the second section — Preparing for the Repository Workbench — a series of checklists is provided to assist the reader in deciding whether or not a repository workbench solution is desirable and in developing a plan for repository workbench implementation.

In the third section — Repository Metrics — a series of measurements is provided to assist the reader in determining how well the repository is utilized.

Evaluating the Repository workbench

Selecting a repository workbench is not a simple process. Repository workbench software is quite complex and the selection process mirrors this complexity. Because a repository workbench offers a composite of functionality, the evaluation team needs to review three discrete levels of functionality: the repository component, the workbench component, and the integrative component. What follows is a set of categories that will assist in this process; each represents a different level of functionality that a product of this type should have.

The repository is the heart of the repository workbench. It is much more than a data dictionary or a data warehouse. It stores information about objects — whether those objects are file definitions or process rules. The sections below itemize the major attributes of a repository. An effective and robust repository should meet the objects presented in this section:

1. Initial Data Capture:

For the most part, objects required to be entered into the repository already reside in catalogs, files, databases, and CASE encyclopedias, or as part of a program (i.e., working storage as well as the procedure division). Scanning enables an organization to populate the repository quickly through the importation of objects from a pre-existing source. Among the facilities that a robust repository product provides are:

Weighting: 1 2 3	Rating
Scan program source — file sections	1 2 3 4 5
Scan program source — working storage sections	1 2 3 4 5
Scan program source — procedure divisions	1 2 3 4 5
Scan copybooks	1 2 3 4 5
Scan multiple copybooks	1 2 3 4 5
Scan database catalogs	1 2 3 4 5
Scan CASE encyclopedias	1 2 3 4 5
Scan databases	1 2 3 4 5
Provide the ability to repopulate the repository as many times as necessary through versioning	1 2 3 4 5
Provide collision resolution	1 2 3 4 5
Multilevel impact analysis	1 2 3 4 5
Scan data dictionaries	1 2 3 4 5
Scan class dictionaries	1 2 3 4 5

2. **Tracking:** A repository should have the ability to keep detailed information about objects. The repository defines an object as more than the traditional data definition; an object may be a field, file, procedure, or system. Because the repository maintains detailed information about objects, the organization has an excellent opportunity to track the status of many of the formal processes that form the underpinnings of IT. A robust repository should be able to:

Weighting: 1 2 3	Rating
Keep track of jobs	1 2 3 4 5
Keep track of programs/objects	1 2 3 4 5
Document data content of files and databases	1 2 3 4 5
Document data processed by programs, jobs, systems	1 2 3 4 5
Document reports and screens	1 2 3 4 5
Document schedules	1 2 3 4 5
Document backup and retention	1 2 3 4 5
Document maintenance responsibilities	1 2 3 4 5

3. Source and Use: All organizations are different in the policies, methods, and procedures of their IT processes. The repository workbench must integrate itself as well as act as an integrator of these policies, methods, and procedures. The repository workbench must be flexible enough to:

Weighting: 1 2 3   **Rating**

Support data model	1 2 3 4 5
Support object model	1 2 3 4 5
Support information center usage	1 2 3 4 5
Support application generator	1 2 3 4 5
Support life cycle methodology	1 2 3 4 5
Support distributed processing	1 2 3 4 5
Document communications network	1 2 3 4 5
Maintain hardware inventory	1 2 3 4 5
Support data security planning	1 2 3 4 5
Support forms control	1 2 3 4 5
Support change and problem control	1 2 3 4 5
Support procedures and standards for repository update and maintenance	1 2 3 4 5

4. User Access: Studies on productivity have shown that the user interface has the greatest impact on the usability of the system. For the function of data administration, a flexible user interface is mandatory if the organization is to leverage the resources of skilled professionals. The repository workbench product should offer the following features:

Weighting: 1 2 3   **Rating**

Mainframe-based:	
Easy to use	1 2 3 4 5
Contextual help facility	1 2 3 4 5
SAA/CUA compliant	1 2 3 4 5
Customizable	1 2 3 4 5
Pull-down menus	1 2 3 4 5
Pop-up windows	1 2 3 4 5
Fast-path commands	1 2 3 4 5
Client/Server based:	
GUI	1 2 3 4 5
Graphical representation of E-R model	1 2 3 4 5
Point and click	1 2 3 4 5
Multiple platforms	1 2 3 4 5
CPI-C	1 2 3 4 5
XML	1 2 3 4 5
Online	1 2 3 4 5
Batch	1 2 3 4 5
Internet/Intranet	1 2 3 4 5

5. Dialog: A robust repository dialog should provide a simple, intuitive means for maintaining and querying information assets, as well as accessing tools. Features should include:

Weighting: 1 2 3	Rating
Contextual menus	1 2 3 4 5
Menus rebuilt automatically as tools are added	1 2 3 4 5
Self-maintaining	1 2 3 4 5
E-R rule-based data entry screens	1 2 3 4 5
Project-based menus	1 2 3 4 5
Context-sensitive feedback	1 2 3 4 5
Reusable panels	1 2 3 4 5
Scrollable panels	1 2 3 4 5
Spreadsheet-like displays	1 2 3 4 5
Customize forms	1 2 3 4 5
End-user SQL queries	1 2 3 4 5
Project-defined SQL queries	1 2 3 4 5
Multilevel impact analysis	1 2 3 4 5
Attribute anchoring	1 2 3 4 5
Meaningful labels for DB names	1 2 3 4 5
Multiple text types	1 2 3 4 5

6. Extensibility: A robust repository workbench is not rigid; it should support growth. This growth should not be limited merely to data definitions. In an object-based environment a repository workbench should have the flexibility to add new sources of information as well as new tools, reports, and procedures. Each of these is defined as an object. Extensibility features should include:

Weighting: 1 2 3	Rating
Dialog assistance	1 2 3 4 5
Automatic rebinding	1 2 3 4 5
Automatic creation of repository table spaces	1 2 3 4 5
(Re)creation of repository indices	1 2 3 4 5
Reorg	1 2 3 4 5
Error handling and correction	1 2 3 4 5
(Re)granting of table privileges	1 2 3 4 5
Integration with repository tools	1 2 3 4 5
Ability to add on in-house tools	1 2 3 4 5
Ability to add on third party tools	1 2 3 4 5
Ease in defining migration rules	1 2 3 4 5
Ease in defining security	1 2 3 4 5
Ease in defining validation rules	1 2 3 4 5
Ease in defining integrity rules	1 2 3 4 5
Ease in defining derivation rules	1 2 3 4 5
Ease in defining domain constraints	1 2 3 4 5

7. Project Control: A repository workbench must provide facilities to automate the enforcement of corporate and project standards and procedures, and to control distribution of repository resources. Capabilities should include:

Weighting: 1 2 3	**Rating**
Project-oriented security requirements	1 2 3 4 5
Clone function for rapid project definition	1 2 3 4 5
Access/update/migrate privileges	1 2 3 4 5
Ability to subset E-R types	1 2 3 4 5
Life cycle phase authorization	1 2 3 4 5
Project parameterization	1 2 3 4 5

8. Versioning: The repository workbench must provide a comprehensive set of facilities for supporting, monitoring, and auditing the evolution of repository definitions. This feature makes it possible to plan and implement the maintenance procedures that become necessary as systems mature and require modifications. A robust repository workbench provides the following capabilities:

Weighting: 1 2 3	**Rating**
Use of variation name attribute	1 2 3 4 5
Unlimited number of variations	1 2 3 4 5
Support of revision number attribute	1 2 3 4 5
Ability to perform set-level operations	
Set-rename	1 2 3 4 5
Set-delete	1 2 3 4 5
Set-copy	1 2 3 4 5
ANSI IRDS support	1 2 3 4 5
Alias support	1 2 3 4 5

9. Life Cycle Phase Management: Supporting an organization's methodologies is an essential role of a repository. A robust repository workbench provides an organization-extensible means for defining the various stages of object evolution. These stages are referred to as life cycle phases. Transition rules define the movement of an object from one phase to another. Relationships between entities based upon their respective life cycle phases should be verified to ensure proper migration results. Managing life cycle phases and object migration is a vital function within a repository if it is to control and participate in an organization's development and maintenance methodology. Features should include:

Weighting: 1 2 3	**Rating**
Customizable controls	1 2 3 4 5
Ability to add or remove life cycle definitions	1 2 3 4 5

(continued)

Weighting: 1 2 3 *(continued)*   **Rating**

Transition rules	1 2 3 4 5
Migration paths	1 2 3 4 5
Relationship-state rules	1 2 3 4 5
Project-controlled life cycle phases	1 2 3 4 5
Versioning within life cycle phase	1 2 3 4 5

Integration. Developmental frameworks like AD/Cycle are philosophies. For the most part, software engineering tools such as CASE maintain key positions within this framework but do little to integrate effectively with other tools in other quadrants of the framework — or even other tools within the same quadrant. The objectives in this section, if met by the tool being evaluated, will assure the organization that the repository will be seamlessly integrated with repository tools as well as in-house-developed and third-party tools.

10. Architecture: A repository workbench is a unique hybrid of repository, tools, and an integrative vehicle. In order to support this threefold functionality, the underlying architecture of a repository workbench product must provide openness and an extensible framework. The organization must be able to easily integrate into and expand upon the framework. The architectural features of a robust architectural framework include:

Weighting: 1 2 3   **Rating**

Object-based approach	1 2 3 4 5
Extensible	1 2 3 4 5
Easily configurable	1 2 3 4 5
Easily modifiable	1 2 3 4 5
Easy integration	1 2 3 4 5
Underlying meta–meta model	1 2 3 4 5
Vendor-supplied meta model	1 2 3 4 5
Security, backup, and recovery	1 2 3 4 5
Referential integrity	1 2 3 4 5

11. Standards: The basis of any open framework is the standards that it rests on. For this framework to be fully integrative with an organization's environment, the framework must conform to and support the standards and guidelines that the industry has embraced. Additionally, the repository workbench must provide the organization with the ability to support the standards that it has developed as part of its policies and procedures. This might includes where applicable:

Weighting: 1 2 3   **Rating**

XML	1 2 3 4 5
Web services	1 2 3 4 5

(continued)

Weighting: 1 2 3 *(continued)*	**Rating**
ANSI SQL	1 2 3 4 5
UML	1 2 3 4 5
Java community process	1 2 3 4 5
Internet engineering task force	1 2 3 4 5
OAG (open applications group)	1 2 3 4 5
OMG (object management group)	1 2 3 4 5
Business objects	1 2 3 4 5
Organizational naming conventions	1 2 3 4 5
Organizational keywords and abbreviations	1 2 3 4 5
Organizational custom rules	1 2 3 4 5
Other	1 2 3 4 5

12. Gateways: The basis of a repository product is information; however, information is not confined to a single source. A repository product must provide the organization with a series of gateways that allow the organization to export and import information among these information sources (e.g., application development tools, various databases, and files). Because the organization is expected to have multiple requirements for gateways, the most robust repository workbenches will generically define a gateway bridge that provides a commonalty of approach across diverse products. Features should include:

Weighting: 1 2 3	**Rating**
Generic bridge architecture	1 2 3 4 5
Bi-directional bridge	1 2 3 4 5
Upload/download facilities	1 2 3 4 5
Check in/check out	1 2 3 4 5
Collision resolution	1 2 3 4 5
Impact analysis	1 2 3 4 5
Import/export capabilities	1 2 3 4 5
Bulk population ability	1 2 3 4 5
Repopulate through versioning	1 2 3 4 5
Default rules	1 2 3 4 5
Variable name mapping	1 2 3 4 5
Catalog import	1 2 3 4 5
Source import from multiple catalogs	1 2 3 4 5
Flat file import	1 2 3 4 5
Obsolete file import	1 2 3 4 5
IMS bridge:	
Store and manage IMS objects	1 2 3 4 5
Generate copybooks, PSBs, DBDs	1 2 3 4 5
Impact analysis across objects	1 2 3 4 5
IMS SQL reporting writing	1 2 3 4 5

13. CASE Bridge: CASE (application development) tools require a very specific gateway that allows CASE objects to be integrated into the repository with the goal of permitting CASE users to have a more efficient way of controlling, securing, reporting, and distributing specifications captured in their workstations. A robust repository can be thought of as a clearinghouse between workstations and CASE products. The repository workbench should provide management tools that enable the organization to share data resources. This includes:

Weighting: 1 2 3	**Rating**
Shared model between different tools	1 2 3 4 5
Support change control	1 2 3 4 5
Report on design and analysis	1 2 3 4 5
Upload CASE product Encyclopedia	
Reporting	1 2 3 4 5
Rehearsal	1 2 3 4 5
Extend the definition of CASE objects	1 2 3 4 5
Reusability	1 2 3 4 5

14. Services: A product is only as good as the service provided by the product vendor. Toward this end, the following features should be evaluated:

Weighting: 1 2 3	**Rating**
Continuous support	1 2 3 4 5
Toll-free hotline	1 2 3 4 5
Timely assistance	1 2 3 4 5
Trial period provided	1 2 3 4 5
Customer references provided	1 2 3 4 5
Support during trial	1 2 3 4 5
Quality of staff	1 2 3 4 5
Maintenance program	1 2 3 4 5
Product improvement schedule	1 2 3 4 5
Responsiveness	1 2 3 4 5
Track record	1 2 3 4 5
Tailored training program	1 2 3 4 5
Online documentation	1 2 3 4 5
Manuals	1 2 3 4 5
Newsletter	1 2 3 4 5
User groups	1 2 3 4 5

15. Workbench Integration: The repository workbench creates a productive environment where repository information is integrated with an extensible tool set. This approach offers you the flexibility to incorporate your existing tools as well as those you may consider in the future. Tool integration capabilities include:

Weighting: 1 2 3	Rating
Ability to integrate user-defined tools	1 2 3 4 5
Ability to integrate third-party packages	1 2 3 4 5
All tools accessible through online dialog	1 2 3 4 5
Extensible end-user interface	1 2 3 4 5
Well-documented API	1 2 3 4 5
Easy incorporation into menuing system	1 2 3 4 5
User security	1 2 3 4 5
Customizable help dialogs and messages	1 2 3 4 5

Tools.   A robust repository workbench needs to supply a series of tools that take advantage of the repository and its integrative prowess. The features described in this section are those of a robust environment.

16. Tool Integration: The ability to integrate tools to the workbench is only one side of the coin. The other side is to have the facilities to develop in-house tools. A tool development environment should possess the following capabilities:

Weighting: 1 2 3	Rating
Vendor-supplied shell programs	1 2 3 4 5
Vendor-supplied subroutine libraries	1 2 3 4 5
Comprehensive assistance	1 2 3 4 5
Encapsulation	1 2 3 4 5
Tools developed in-house invoked through dialog	1 2 3 4 5
Vendor-supplied tools reusable	1 2 3 4 5

17. Groupware: Productivity is greatly enhanced when a facility is provided for project teams and users to communicate with each other. This is often referred to as groupware. Within a repository environment, this can be accomplished through the use of electronic mail. Features available should include:

Weighting: 1 2 3	Rating
Electronic mail available	1 2 3 4 5
Messaging to project members	1 2 3 4 5
Messaging to users	1 2 3 4 5
Batch output messaging	1 2 3 4 5
Edit output and resend	1 2 3 4 5
Reusable method	1 2 3 4 5

18. Reporting: Various levels of the organization require access to the repository for reporting. On one level, the end users require access to find out the types of information available within the organization. On another level, data administration staff has a real need to control the transition of information within the repository. Both levels of user access need to be supported. Reporting features include:

Weighting: 1 2 3	**Rating**
QMF reporting interface	1 2 3 4 5
FOCUS reporting interface	1 2 3 4 5
Canned reports should include:	
Repository detail	1 2 3 4 5
Catalog detail	1 2 3 4 5
Repository/catalog comparison	1 2 3 4 5
Table column cross reference	1 2 3 4 5
Table structure/element cross reference	1 2 3 4 5
Logical/physical element reference	1 2 3 4 5
Logical entity cross reference	1 2 3 4 5
Structure circular references	1 2 3 4 5
Catalog statistical and action summary	1 2 3 4 5
Repository/catalog comparison	1 2 3 4 5
Repository content detail	1 2 3 4 5
Catalog content detail	1 2 3 4 5

19. Impact Analysis: In nonrepository systems, a large percentage of nonproductive time is spent in determining the impact of change. Analysts and programmers must manually review documentation and program source listings to evaluate the extent of change necessary as well as the length of time required to make those changes. This can be a lengthy process. A repository-based system automates this process through the function of impact analysis. Automatic impact analysis deconstructs the repository to determine the level of change required. The impact analysis function should include the following capabilities:

Weighting: 1 2 3	**Rating**
Multiple level	1 2 3 4 5
Nested impact analysis	1 2 3 4 5
Interactive as well as batch	1 2 3 4 5
Immediate maintenance capabilities	1 2 3 4 5
"Uses" and "where-used" displayed concurrently	1 2 3 4 5

20. Scripting: Database administrative procedures are extraordinarily complex. The complexity of many of these tasks implies that the staff member involved must have the highest degree of skill and exercise the utmost level of care. Organizations that wish to leverage the skill set of the average user, increase the speed at which a task may be completed, or deploy vast functionality across differing layers of the organization require the means to decrease the complexity level of the activity and thereby reduce the risk of error. A repository-based scripting facility provides this functionality. Capabilities should include:

Weighting: 1 2 3	**Rating**
Recursive script development	1 2 3 4 5
Ability to invoke any vendor-supplied tool	1 2 3 4 5
Ability to invoke any vendor-supplied report	1 2 3 4 5
Ability to invoke any vendor-supplied script	1 2 3 4 5
Ability to invoke any in-house tool	1 2 3 4 5
Ability to invoke any in-house report	1 2 3 4 5
Ability to invoke any in-house script	1 2 3 4 5
Batch mode	1 2 3 4 5
Commit points and breakpoints	1 2 3 4 5
Script status feedback	1 2 3 4 5
Parameterized	1 2 3 4 5
Vendor-supplied base start-up scripts	1 2 3 4 5
Cut and paste facility	1 2 3 4 5
Invoked by electronic mail	1 2 3 4 5

21. Forms: Forms provide the ability to establish external layout definitions that present a modified view of the objects within the repository without altering the object itself. Although the definitions of objects in the repository are not altered, the user view can be modified to afford the greatest expediency in utilization of the repository without needing to write code. Features should include:

Weighting: 1 2 3	**Rating**
Project-level modification	1 2 3 4 5
Order of presentation	1 2 3 4 5
Alteration of the prompt label	1 2 3 4 5
Alteration of the annotation	1 2 3 4 5
Modification of display rules	1 2 3 4 5
Modification of item length	1 2 3 4 5
Customization of the default values	1 2 3 4 5
Object-orientation of form	1 2 3 4 5
Maintainable via a method	1 2 3 4 5
Accessible through dialog menus	1 2 3 4 5
Accessible via scripting	1 2 3 4 5

22. Generation: The repository acts as the central clearinghouse for corporate information resource management, so it must have the ability to act in concert with definitions used by application development and end-user tools. To enhance productivity, consistency, and security, the repository workbench must have the ability to generate syntax. This includes the ability to:

Weighting: 1 2 3   **Rating**

Use DDL, DML syntax including:

Create	1 2 3 4 5
Drop	1 2 3 4 5
Grant	1 2 3 4 5
Revoke	1 2 3 4 5
Bind	1 2 3 4 5
Rebind	1 2 3 4 5
Free	1 2 3 4 5
Generate and execute mode	1 2 3 4 5
Generate and save mode	1 2 3 4 5
Copybook generation	1 2 3 4 5
DBD, PSB for IMS	1 2 3 4 5
DCLGEN3	1 2 3 4 5

23. Managing Relational Tables: A repository workbench needs to be more than just a repository. Facilities to manage the underlying database should be fully integrated into the tool set. These tools should provide the ability to:

Weighting: 1 2 3   **Rating**

Unload/reload databases	1 2 3 4 5
Create and drop objects	1 2 3 4 5
Referential integrity support	1 2 3 4 5
Grant and revoke commands	1 2 3 4 5
Bind, rebind, and free commands	1 2 3 4 5
Reorg, runstats and copy commands	1 2 3 4 5

Preparing for the Repository Workbench

Preparing for any software implementation requires careful planning and control. In the case of a repository workbench, where information, systems, and integration factors must be considered, even more care is urged for a successful implementation. A series of checklists is provided for this purpose.

Preplanning Action Items:

1. Standardize the names, definitions, and physical descriptions of data elements used in all programs.
2. Document which data is kept in which files or databases or schemas.
3. Document which reports and screens are produced by which programs jobs and systems.
4. Document which programs, jobs, and systems access and update which data elements in which files or databases or schemas.

5. Document which modules and subprograms are included in which programs.
6. Document processing schedules, file back-up and retention, and responsibilities for program and jobstream maintenance.

Questions to ask for sizing of data collection effort:

1. How many systems are there?
2. What is the quality of system documentation?
3. If documentation is inadequate, can the required data be obtained from the original developers or from users?
4. How many programs are in each system?
5. How good are the run books and program documentation?
6. Have these been kept up to date as changes have been made?
7. Are job control statements kept in a single file or library?
8. Are program source statements kept in a single file or library?
9. Is some type of source library maintenance system in use?
10. Is library content really kept up to date?
11. How many FILEs, DATABASEs, and SCHEMAs are in each system?
12. How many different record types are there?
13. How many different relational tables are there?
14. Are standard record descriptions used?
15. Are they kept in a central library?
16. Are data element names standardized?
17. Are the names meaningful?
18. Are good definitions available?
19. Is there documentation of coding structures?
20. How well are reports, display screens, and input transactions documented?
21. Can the data content be obtained from user manuals?
22. If the information above is not readily available, how will it be obtained? Who will compile it?
23. Who will do the actual work of preparing repository input?
24. How will it be done?
25. Can part of the data be obtained by scanning source programs or copy libraries?
26. Who will review edit lists and resolve naming discrepancies and other problems?

Questions to ask concerning technical and operational issues:

1. Will the repository always be running? System initialization must be amended to include this.
2. Will reports be produced automatically on some predetermined schedule? Will they be triggered by specific events, such as the implementation of a new system? Will they be on a run-on-request

basis? Who will initiate the jobs to produce the reports? How will they be distributed? How will special requests be handled?

3. How will repository problems be reported and resolved?
4. Will computer operations think of the repository as a production system?
5. Will procedures for the turnover of new systems or system changes incorporate steps that will ensure that the repository has been correctly updated?

Questions to ask about security:

1. Who should be allowed to access what? Can project teams alter data that they think of as their own?
2. Will passwords be controlled and changed from time to time? Will they be changed when employees resign or are discharged?
3. Does repository software provide a mechanism to prevent access to the repository via means other than the repository software?

Questions to ask concerning redundant and inconsistent data:

1. Can you identify all occurrences of the same information?
2. Can you determine which elements are calculated or derived and how?
3. Will you know the original sources of all elements?
4. Will you know the uses of the elements?
5. Can the repository implementation help to determine whether there are procedures or programs to ensure consistency?
6. Will the repository implementation provide for validation rules and criteria?
7. Does it provide for data consistency and integrity rules?
8. What about procedures to ensure that such rules are entered in the repository?

Questions to ask about complexity and interdependence:

1. Does the repository help us determine who actually uses the reports or screens?
2. Does it help identify screens and reports that contain the same information?
3. Does it help the user identify the tasks and procedures that require use of the information contained in the reports and screens?
4. Will it help improve documentation?
5. Will it decrease complexity by providing reusability?

Repository Metrics

These criteria measure how well a repository or data dictionary collects, maintains, and retrieves information about data. The objectives of these measures are to offer users cost-effective means of retrieving relevant information and reducing information overload. Five criteria are proposed to evaluate data dictionaries and repositories: relevance, consistency, common use among information systems, degree of automation, and degree of security.

DBA Objective Metrics. The following criteria measure how well each commercial repository/repository product fulfills DBA objectives.

Relevance. This criterion measures the effectiveness of retrieving correct information in response to a request. It is measured by two factors: recall and precision.

$$\text{Recall} = \frac{\text{Number of matching data elements retrieved by a product}}{\text{Maximum number of matches possible}}$$

$$\text{Precision} = \frac{\text{Number of matching data elements retrieved by a product}}{\text{Number of data elements retrieved by a product}}$$

Consistency. This criterion measures the performance of the product in removing redundancies and storing the minimum number of elements from which all other elements can be derived. The result will be what James Martin (1990) refers to as a canonical data repository — a minimal and nonredundant representation of data elements in an enterprise.

$$\text{Consistency} = 1 - \frac{\text{Number of elements in the final repository}}{\text{Number of elements in the original data dictionaries}}$$

Common use among different IS: This criterion measures whether the product can be consistently applied to standardize IS in different departments and operations within an IS organization. Current trends toward integrating networks and information systems to build integrated repository-network management environments make it important that repositories handle multiple environments. Deciding which repository to use as the central repository may depend on its flexibility in handling a variety of software and hardware. The common use criterion measures this flexibility:

$$\text{Common Use} = \frac{\text{Number of elements standardized using particular product}}{\text{Number of elements standardized in the organization}}$$

Degree of automation. An active repository uses substantially less manpower than a passive one. In response to an inquiry, an active repository can locate the elements and find out who has access to them; it then directs the database management system to obtain those data elements. On the other hand, passive data dictionaries have no tie-ins to the operating system and require the user to write programs to gain access to the elements. This criterion measures the extent to which a product makes it easy for a DBA to standardize and store elements.

$$\text{Degree of automation} = 1 - \frac{\text{Time spent in training and using product}}{\text{Total time available}}$$

Degree of security: Overall security depends on managing the access controls to various data elements. Access control limits must be defined for each user and violations acted upon.

$$\text{Degree of security} = 1 - \frac{\text{Number of security failures}}{\text{Number of attempts to breach security}}$$

Repository Workbench Metrics. The following metrics measure additional attributes of the repository workbench.

- *Redundancy:* One of the objectives of a repository solution is to act as the single source for all information flows. To measure how successful the repository implementation is requires knowledge concerning the number of objects stored in the repository versus the number of objects stored, simultaneously, in different sources.

$$\text{Redundancy} = \frac{\text{\# redundant objects}}{\text{Total \# objects}}$$

- *Intuitive access:* One of the most important, but underrated, features of a repository workbench is its user interface. The more intuitive the dialog is, the more the repository workbench will be used. Frequency of use translates into higher productivity; a low rating implies need for tuning or training.

$$\text{Intuitiveness} = 1 - \frac{\text{\# users requiring manual}}{\text{Total number of users}}$$

- *Level of impact analysis.* This metric measures how well the impact analysis function is utilized.

$$\text{Level of impact analysis} = \frac{\text{\# levels being accessed}}{\text{Total \# levels in E-R model}}$$

- *Integration.* This metric determines the progress of the tool integration effort. Because a repository workbench enables complete tool integration, the level of integration implies progress — or lack of it.

$$\text{Integration} = \frac{\text{\# tools integrated}}{\text{Total \# tools in use}}$$

SCORING THE REPOSITORY WORKBENCH

The chart in Exhibit 8.1 provides a means to conduct a quantitative evaluation of several repository products. To use this chart, simply transfer the scores from each of the rating scales under the 23 criteria. To transfer the score, multiply the rating (1 through 5) by the weighting (1 through 3).

Exhibit 8-1. Evaluation of Products

	Product A	**Product B**
1. Initial data capture		
2. Tracking		
3. Source and use		
4. User access		
5. Dialog		
6. Extensibility		
7. Project control		
8. Versioning		
9. Life cycle		
10. Architecture		
11. Standards		
12. Gateways		
13. CASE bridges		
14. Services		
15. Workbench integration		
16. Tool development		
17. Groupware		
18. Reporting		
19. Impact analysis		
20. Scripting		
21. Forms		
22. Generation		
23. Table management		

References

Martin, J. (1989). *Information Engineering, Book I: Introduction,* Prentice Hall, Englewood Cliffs, NJ.

Martin, J. (1990). *Information Engineering, Book II: Planning and Analysis,* Prentice Hall, Englewood Cliffs, NJ.

Chapter 9
Structured Methodology Review

A variety of methodologies is available to the systems analyst. Many are proprietary methodologies utilized in conjunction with a software application development tool set (CASE — computer assisted software engineering).

The original and still frequently used systems development construct dictates that systems are developed through a series of distinct stages. It is necessary for each stage to be completed before going to the next. This is a linear progression of system development, hence the name "waterfall" method. Waterfall design methods are a one-way flow from the requirements process toward the working system (Coffee, 2001).

Once a stage of the project is complete, it is sent to the next stage with a "deliverable," which is evidence or documentation that the stage has been completed and the project is ready for the next process. There are eight generally accepted stages of a systems development life cycle technique (see Exhibit 9-1):

- *Determination of scope and objectives* — overall scope of the project is agreed upon.
- *Systems investigation and feasibility study* — a report on the feasibility of a technical solution to the problem is prepared.
- *Systems analysis* —a logical model of the existing system is built.
- *System design* — the analyst develops two or three alternative designs.
- *Detailed design* — detailed physical specifications are made so that the system can be built.
- *Implementation* — the system is physically created.
- *Changeover* — the old system is replaced by the new system.
- *Evaluation and maintenance* —hardware and software are maintained.

A real benefit of this approach is the division of a lengthy project into stages, which makes it more manageable. This is realized throughout the project in terms of better project control and communication, and during the working life of the system in terms of its meeting user requirements and

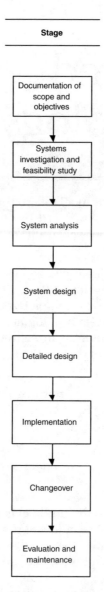

Stage

Documentation of scope and objectives

Systems investigation and feasibility study

System analysis

System design

Detailed design

Implementation

Changeover

Evaluation and maintenance

Exhibit 9-1. The Traditional SDLC

the ease with which it can be modified to take into account changes in these requirements (Curtis, 2000).

However, many in the field feel that the traditional waterfall method is outdated. The problem is that the waterfall models a one-way flow from requirements. You must be able to paddle upstream and take a different path if the one you first choose turns out to be too long — to practice white-water kayaking, rather than just going over the waterfall and hoping you will like where you land (Coffee, 2001). Today's business is fast paced and systems need to be developed as quickly as possible to meet organizational needs, with early delivery of the easy portions of an application for on-the-job testing and comments (Coffee, 1994).

Fast-changing requirements and shorter lead times might require the use of different methodologies.

RAPID APPLICATIONS DEVELOPMENT (RAD)

It is no longer adequate to take two or three years to build a system. More than ever, businesses are in a race against time (Glen, 1993). Directly opposed to the traditional and lengthy life cycle approach is rapid applications development, or RAD for short. RAD is a loosely used term (like many other design terms) that describes any approach to a fast-designed system.

RAD has been described as a set of tactics and techniques to minimize development time — a radical departure from the traditional waterfall method (Glen, 1993). Essentially, RAD uses time boxing to control development time for each phase of the project. If a deadline is in danger of being missed, lower-priority requirements are moved back to a later time box or the next phase of an incremental delivery (Tudhope, 2000). RAD requires management to accept consensus management and joint application design (JAD). Specialists with advanced technology (SWAT teams) work closely with the users to define and refine applications.

SWAT (also referred to by Glen as "slaves without any time") is an effective tactic in many RAD projects in that small, multidisciplined IT teams work with users directly. This fosters team building. SWAT members are not confined to separate floors or buildings. This approach is different than assembling many systems specialists with inch-wide and mile-deep knowledge in specific areas to build applications in IT ghettos (Glen, 1993).

RAD has four phases, as shown in Exhibit 9-2 (Curtis et al., 2000):

1. *Requirements planning* — joint requirements planning (JRP), establishes high-level objectives
2. *Applications development* — JAD follows JRP, involves users in workshops
3. *Systems construction* — design specifications, used to develop detailed and generate code
4. *Cutover* — users trained and the system tested

According to Tudhope (2000), the majority of developers who are aware of RAD tend to select elements of the methodology rather than following it strictly. Others use generally similar techniques without identifying them as RAD.

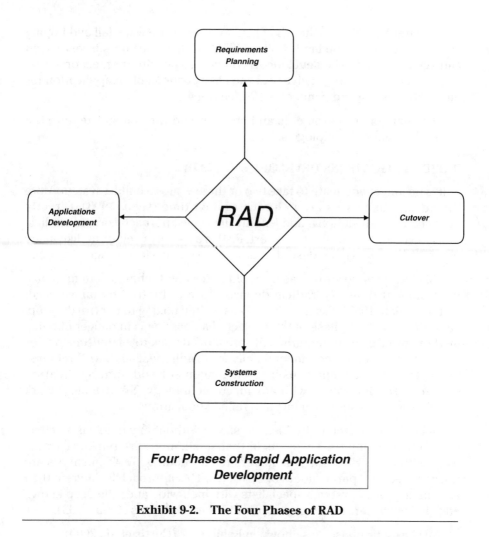

Four Phases of Rapid Application Development

Exhibit 9-2. The Four Phases of RAD

Proponents of the RAD design methodology say that business needs can change substantially during long development times, and meeting current needs when the system comes into operation is a better aim than meeting a "long-frozen" specification (Tadhope, 2000). However, others say you should never let developers write a line of code until the specifications are approved by all parties. Prudent managers might therefore follow the "waterfall" model, in which requirements are completed and flow downstream to design (Coffee, 1994).

A variation of the RAD technique dictates that design technique is to be deliberate in the systems foundation, but one should design some parts ahead of time. The foundation is the data model, which should be designed in partnership with the business side of the organization. A logical data or

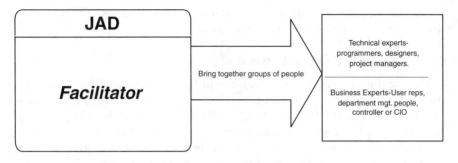

Exhibit 9-3. The JAD Process

object design process allows definition of how business is currently conducted and plans for future changes. RAD is used for screens, reports, business rules, and communications, but only after the database or object model is in place. Involving users in the process that takes the longest makes development time less of an issue; end users see the prototype in days or hours once the foundation is laid (Boyer, 1995). Boyer recommends that we build the walls of the application and roof as quickly as possible, but to make sure the foundation is in place first.

JOINT APPLICATION DESIGN (JAD)

In joint application design, analysts work with groups during the development of the system; they integrate groups of technical and business experts (Exhibit 9-3). These groups may include programmers, designers, and project managers, as well as user reps, department management people, and the controller or CIO. These JAD sessions are usually run by a trained facilitator.

The JAD process has four stages: framework presentation, project scoping, preliminary definitions development, and detailed requirements development (Dodson, 1994).

In the framework presentation stage the facilitator sets the tone for the project, explaining the JAD approach. Usually this stage involves a core team of business experts and will last between one half to a full day. Project scoping involves the same group of people identifying project priorities across department lines. This should take a total of 6 to 12 hours. The preliminary definitions stage produces the context diagram; the entire core team participates in this phase. The context diagram shows the system's place in the flow of the organization's information, which should take about one day. The detailed requirements stage should take five to ten days in session; however, the detailed requirements can take weeks to develop.

Attending all of these sessions is the "scribe" responsible for documenting all the information gathered during each meeting and providing it to the team as needed. This relieves other participants from taking notes, which diverts their attention from the matters at hand.

GROUP SUPPORT SYSTEMS (GSS)

One of the problems with meetings in the JAD approach is that only a limited number of people can participate effectively before the meeting becomes inefficient (Dennis et al., 1999). Nevertheless, it is important to receive input from all the experts because no one expert usually has the expertise to document business processes completely. Another problem with JAD sessions is that only one person can speak at a time. This creates a problem in that experts blocked from contributing their ideas while another is speaking may forget or suppress them because they seem less relevant later. Also, many times a group session is dominated by just a few people. This could lead to a model that favors the dominating participants.

In recent years computer technology called group support systems has been designed to provide same-time, same-place interactions in which participants use computers to interact and exchange ideas (Dennis et al., 1999). This is designed to reduce group interaction problems and may help to improve meetings by using parallel communication, anonymity, and group memory.

GSS also reduces meeting time and allows group members to share their ideas simultaneously through the use of the collaborative software. Participants can also remove themselves from the discussion to pause and think without worrying about remembering what the other members have said.

Of course electronic meetings also have their negative effects. It is said that this type of communication is often "less rich" than verbal communication and that resolving differences with electronic meetings is more difficult. The effectiveness of GSS greatly depends on the size of the group. GSS was found to produce greater gains with larger groups; however, verbal meetings are more effective where differences of opinion need to be resolved (Dennis et al., 1999).

CASE TOOLS

The broadest definition of a CASE tool is any software tool that provides automated assistance for software development, maintenance, or project management activities (McMurtrey et al., 2000). CASE tools are not end-user oriented; they are used by professionals for carrying out part of the design and helping to speed the development process.

They have been trumpeted as the "silver bullet" of applications development but have not necessarily lived up to that name because they are not a "fix-all" solution to systems design. However, they are a feasible option for practitioners of systems development.

Case tools assist in (Curtis et al., 2000):

- *Corporate planning of info systems* — used to track relationships between various components.
- *Creating specification requirements* — information system is analyzed into its data requirements.
- *Creating design specifications* —tools are used to specify a design for the system.
- *Code-generation tools* — accept output of the design specification and produce code for direct execution.
- *Information repository* — stores information on entities, processes, data structures, business rules, source code, and project management.
- *Development methodology* — provides automated diagramming facilities for data-flow diagrams.

The many benefits of CASE include increased productivity, restructuring of poorly written code, decrease of application development time, and aid in project management. However, with benefits there are usually drawbacks, and CASE is no exception. Some of the drawbacks are a reliance on structured methodologies, a lengthy learning curve, possible user resistance, limited functions, and a required working knowledge of the underlying methodology.

A VARIETY OF STRUCTURED METHODOLOGIES

As mentioned, a wide variety of systems development methodologies can be chosen from, some accompanied by CASE tools and some without them. Most are based on the methodologies discussed previously. A list of references to some of the most common structured methodologies follows:

1. Yourdon, E.E. and Constantine L.L. (1977). *Structured Design: Fundamentals of a Discipline of Computer Program and System Design*, Yourdon Press
2. DeMarco, T. (1979). *Structured Analysis and Systems Specification*, Prentice Hall, Englewood Cliffs, NJ.
3. Gane, G. and Sarson, T. (1979). *Structured Systems Analysis*, Prentice Hall, Englewood Cliffs, NJ.
4. Jackson, M. (1975). *Principles of Program Design*, Academic Press, New York.
5. Jackson, M. (1983). System Development, Prentice Hall, Englewood Cliffs, NJ.
6. Martin, J. (1988). *Information Engineering: Book 1 Introduction, Book 2 Planning and Analysis, Book 3 Design and Construction,* Prentice Hall, Englewood Cliffs, NJ.

James Martin worked with Clive Finkelstein in designing information engineering. Interestingly, two models were actually derived from this exercise. Martin's model is IT-driven while Finkelstein's model is enterprise, or business, driven. I find Finkelstein's the more useful of the two and have included a brief summary here.

Finkelstein Information Engineering

Clive Finkelstein's (1989) version of information engineering starts with a business strategic planning exercise to identify important information systems required by the business. Then it develops chosen priority systems through successively detailed analysis and design, through to implementation.

Strategic planning consists of the following stages:

- Stage 1. Identifying the current plan. Use any existing strategic or tactical statements that may exist or a management questionnaire to gather information about business strategy
- Stage 2. Evaluation of current status consists of eight steps:
  1. Analyze mission and purpose to identify major data subjects that are represented in a high level mission model
  2. Identify potential goals (critical success factors)
  3. Define goals
  4. Identify issues
  5. Define strategies to deal with each issue
  6. Identify current functions (e.g., personnel, finance, etc.)
  7. Allocate strategies to functions
  8. Define functional responsibility (a detailed functional specification for each functional manager)
- Stage 3. Setting strategic direction consists of three steps: (1, 2) internal, and external appraisal: analysis of business, and business environment (3) strategic evaluation: create the strategic agenda; devise proactive strategic options and select; define strategic statement: formal documentation of strategic decisions, rational, assumptions, conclusions and alternatives.

Once we complete the strategic plan we can proceed to the development of more detailed data models and process models. These are built up in three successive levels:

- *Strategic modeling:* a high-level schematic data model, of interest to senior managers. Steps involve:
  1. Identifying data subjects
  2. Identifying data entities from mission
  3. Identifying preliminary functions
  4. Identifying data entities from strategies
  5. Identifying potential functions
  6. Identifying strategic attributes

7. Defining purpose descriptions
- *Tactical modeling:* the strategic model is refined into areas of more detail to describe data of more interest to middle managers. Typically approximately 20 of these tactical areas exist for any one strategic model.
- *Operational modeling:* any one tactical area may have typically three operational systems that need to be developed. Operational modeling develops the data and process models for a particular operational area to a level of detail to enable implementation.
- The final phase of the Finkelstein methodology is implementation. Implementation is technology dependent and is carried out using suitable DBMS, CASE, and other development tools. The major techniques used are:
- *Business data modeling:* a "business oriented" version of data modeling
- *Process modeling:* modeling of processes acting on "data," especially generic, reusable processes such as: Verify, Add, Read, Display, Change, Delete.
- *Dynamic performance monitoring:* the use of a generic approach to performance monitoring (a common requirement for most systems).

EXTREME PROGRAMMING

Extreme programming (XP) is a new programming methodology that is getting fairly heavy notice these days. Kent Beck (1999) is one of its main proponents and seems to have coined the term, so it seems reasonable to treat his book as the defining standard of the field. XP is the application of a group of practices to software development projects:

- *The planning game:* collaboration of business and programming professionals to estimate the time for short tasks (called "stories" in XP)
- *Small releases:* a ship cycle measured in weeks rather than years
- *Metaphor:* "a single overarching metaphor" to guide development substitutes for a formal architectural specification
- *Simple design:* no provision in the code for future changes or flexibility
- *Testing:* every piece of code exercised by unit tests when written, and the full suite of tests when integrated
- *Refactoring:* any piece of code subject to rewriting to make it simpler
- *Pair programming:* all production code jointly written by two developers
- *Collective ownership:* the right of any developer to change any piece of code on the project
- *Continuous integration:* code integrated to the main line every few hours
- *40-hour week:* no overtime
- *On-site customer:* a business person dedicated to the project
- *Coding standards:* one standard per project

XP amounts to abandoning the traditional "waterfall model" of development entirely in favor of what has often been called "cowboy coding." Beck argues that it is no longer vastly more expensive to fix problems in production than in planning; as a result, it is not necessary to plan. Instead, let your programmers program, trust them to solve problems as they come up, and plan and ship frequently so that you get feedback from the customer on a regular basis.

CONCLUSION

In this handbook's chapter on OO methodologies you will find a completely different take on the topic of methodologies. OO is a newer, fast method for creating software. In spite of OO's increasing popularity, it is not expected that the more traditional methodologies discussed in this chapter will fade into oblivion any time soon.

References

Beck, K. (1999). *Extreme Programming Explained*, Addison-Wesley, Reading, MA.

Boyer, P. (1995). Is RAD all wet? *Datamation*, 41(16), 84.

Coffee, P. (2001). Coding over the waterfalls, *eWeek*, 18(13), 39.

Coffee, P. (1994). The development dilemma: figuring out how to use contradictory techniques is the only safe bet in programming your C/S apps, *PC Week*, 11(36), 32.

Dennis, A.R., Hayes, G.S., and Daniels, Jr., R.M. (1999). Business process modeling with group support systems, *J. Manage. Inf. Syst.*, 15(4), 115.

Dodson, W.R. (1994). Secrets of a high performing teams: joint application design (JAD), *Data Based Advisor*, 12(12), 46.

Finkelstein, C. (1989). *An Introduction to Information Engineering*, Addison-Wesley, Reading, MA.

Glen, R. (1993). RAD requires radical thinking, *I.T. Mag.*, 25(11), 36.

McMurtrey, M.E., Teng, J.T.C., Grover,V., and Kher, H.V. (2000). Current utilization of CASE technology: lessons from the field, *Industrial Manage. Data Syst.*, 100(1/2), 22.

Tudhope, D. (2000). Prototyping Praxis, constructing computer systems and building belief, *Hum.—Comput. Interaction*, 15(4), 353.

Chapter 10
Extreme Programming Concepts

Extreme programming is a software methodology developed by Kent Beck to help software developers to design and build a system more efficiently and successfully. Extreme programming is a disciplined and well-planned approach to software development. What makes this programming so popular is that it is one of the first lightweight methodologies. A lightweight methodology has only a few rules and practices or ones that are easy to follow. Extreme programming does not require any additional paperwork and programmers do not need to go through tons of methods. It stresses customer satisfaction and can be used when the customer is not certain of his requirements or when new technology is to be introduced.

THE RULES OF EXTREME PROGRAMMING

Extreme programming applies four rules in developing the software project:

- *Communication*. The programmer must communicate with the customer and elicit his requirements, thus the emphasis on customer satisfaction. The programmer also needs to communicate with fellow workers, thus the emphasis on team work.
- *Simplicity*. The design is maintained as simply as possible.
- *Feedback*. The software is tested from its early stages, feedback is obtained, and changes are made. This is a cyclical process.
- *Courage*. The programmer can make changes even at the last stages and implement new technologies as and when they are introduced.

Extreme programming is a process of project development, as shown in Exhibit 10-1. Customer requirements are obtained in the form of user stories; the programmer selects the user stories to be implemented first with help from the customers. A plan is released that indicates how many user stories can be implemented in a single iteration, thus starting iterative development. The user stories are broken down into programming tasks

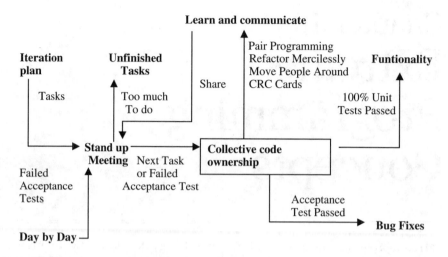

Exhibit 10-1. The Extreme Programming Process of Software Development

and assigned to programmers. The time required to complete these tasks is estimated first; these initial estimates are referred to as uncertain estimates. By using feedback, the programmer can adjust the estimates and make them more certain.

Once these programming tasks have been implemented, they are sent for acceptance testing. If these tasks produce an error or indicate a bug, they are sent back to be recoded in the next iteration. Once the programming tasks are approved by the customer, a small release of the tasks is made to check functionality.

The components of extreme programming include:

- *User stories.* User stories are written by the customer and describe the requirements of a system. The customer need not specify his requirements using any particular format or technical language; he merely writes these in his own words. Aside from describing what the system must be, the user stories are used to calculate the time estimates for release planning. At the time of the implementation of the user stories the developer obtains detailed information from the customer. The time estimate is usually in the form of ideal development time — defined as how long it would take to implement the story in code if there were no distractions, no other assignments, and the programmer knew exactly what to do. Typically, each story will get one to three weeks. The user stories are also used to produce test scenarios for acceptance testing by the customer as well as to verify that the user stories have been implemented correctly.

- *Release planning.* Release planning produces the release plan followed during development of the system; it is also called the "planning game." During release planning a meeting is set up with the customers and the development team. During this meeting a set of rules is set up by the customers and developers to which all agree. A schedule is then prepared. A development team is selected to calculate each user story in terms of ideal programming weeks, which is how long it would take to implement that story if absolutely nothing else needed to be done.

Release planning is guided by four values:

- *Scope* — how much needs to be done?
- *Resources* — how many people are available?
- *Time* — when will the project or release be done?
- *Quality* — how good and how well tested will the software be?

Candidate systems for XP are those that are reusable, testable, and have good business values.

Iteration

At the beginning of every iteration, an iteration planning meeting is held at which the user stories to be implemented during that iteration are chosen; the customer selects the user stories. The selected stories are broken down into discrete programming tasks during the planning session. The programming tasks are specified in the programmer's language.

The number of selected user stories or programming tasks increases or decreases the project velocity. Each programming task is estimated based on ideal programming days, which are the number of days it would take to program a task if no distractions or interruptions occurred.

After these programming tasks have been developed, they are tested. If bugs are found, the offending programming tasks are added back into the release plan to be handled by the next iteration.

During each iteration (see Exhibit 10-2), the plan is checked to detect duplicate programming tasks. If such tasks are found, they are removed or consolidated. If a single iteration has too much to do, several user stories are dropped; if the iteration has too little to do, a few are added.

Development

During the development phase, stand-up meetings are held every morning to discuss the problems faced during the development effort, to devise a solution to these problems, and, perhaps most importantly, to promote focus. No individual programmer owns his or her code. Instead, the code is

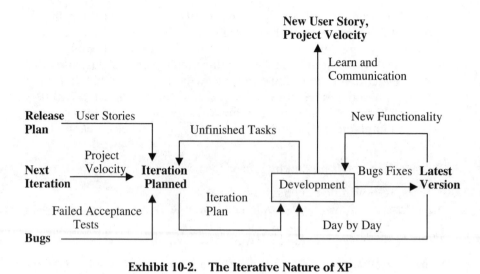

Exhibit 10-2. The Iterative Nature of XP

collectively owned and collaboratively worked upon. The focus of development is on small, manageable releases that can be thoroughly tested.

CRC Cards

CRC stands for class, responsibilities, and collaboration. CRC cards (Exhibit 10-3) contain information about the class, responsibilities and collaboration for designing the system as a team. CRC cards allow all the members of the project team to contribute to the project which will provide a number of good ideas which can then be incorporated in the design.

CLS025	
Class Name:	**ResourceUsage**
Class Type:	
Class Characteristics:	
Responsibilities:	**Collaborations:**
Receive Usage Information	Order
Store Usage Information	Resource
Provide Usage Information	Service Schedule
Authors:	Jane Doe

Exhibit 10-3.   CRC Card

Each CRC card is used to represent an object. The class name of the object can be written at the top of the CRC card; the responsibilities of the class are written on the left side of the card and the collaborating classes are written to the right of each responsibility. A CRC session consists of a person simulating the system by speaking about the relationships between the objects and the process. In this way, weaknesses and problems can be easily discerned and the various design alternatives can be explored quickly by simulating the proposed design.

System Metaphor

Classes, objects, and methods coded by the programmer can be reused. Instead of writing the code for a class, object, or method that already exists, it is important to name the objects in a standardized manner that enables other programmers to seek and reuse these objects. Thus, a common system or common system description is used by all programmers.

Collective Code Ownership

Collective code ownership is a contribution of the programmers to the project in the form of ideas to any segment of the project. Any programmer can add or change code, fix bugs, or refactor — i.e., reuse the code. The entire team is responsible for the system's architecture. Although it is hard to believe that a whole team can have authority over the entire project, it is actually possible. Each developer creates unit tests for his or her code as the code is developed. Code is released into a source code repository after being thoroughly tested.

Unit Test

Unit tests are written by the programmer before he starts coding. Writing the unit tests first gives the programmer a better understanding of the requirements specified by the customer. In addition, writing unit tests prior to coding helps programmers write the code more easily and faster.

Acceptance Test

Within the XP methodology, "functional" tests have been renamed "acceptance" tests to indicate that the system is accepted by the customer. The customer specifies the test scenarios during specification of the user stories; each story will have one or more acceptance tests. The acceptance tests are the expectation of the customer for the system. These acceptance tests are black box system tests, which enable the programmer to derive sets of input conditions that will fully exercise all functional requirements for a program. The user reviews the results of the acceptance tests and determines the priorities of the test failures. The team schedules time to fix the failed test for every iteration.

Project Velocity

The project velocity is used to measure how much work is being completed on the project; it is obtained by adding up the estimates of user stories completed during the iteration. Project velocity can also be obtained by adding up the estimates for tasks during the iteration. If the project velocity shows significant variations, a release planning meeting is conducted and a new plan is released. Project velocity is a measure of accuracy. How accurately are we able to produce results on time? How well are we able to make estimates?

Small Releases

The development team releases small iterative versions of the system to the customer. It is essential to get customer feedback on time instead of waiting until the last moment, which results in making changes at the last minute as well.

Simple Design

The design is kept as simple as possible. A complex design is hard to understand when changes are to be made in the future.

Coding Standard

Programmers follow a specific set of standard rules in writing code. This helps in communication among teams and enables a programmer to understand the code written by any other programmer easily.

Refactoring

Refactoring is the art of removing any duplicate code — i.e., the reuse of code that is already present. This helps in keeping the system design simple. Refactoring also saves a lot of time and increases the quality of the system.

Pair Programming

Pair programming specifies that a pair of programmers work collaboratively on a task. This helps assess the code as it is written. Pair programming increases software quality and takes the same time to deliver the system as a single programmer working on a single machine.

Continuous Integration

Coding is done by dividing big projects into small, manageable programming tasks. After coding, the discrete programming tasks are joined together; however, each of these tasks is tested individually for bugs. During integration of the programming tasks, it is quite possible that new bugs will arise. Therefore, after every integration, the integrated code is retested for bugs.

Changes may be made on the request of the customer. All the changes made to the code are integrated at least daily. The tests are then run before and after the changes. The code is not released if any bugs are found.

40-Hour Week

Each programmer works for only 40 hours per week. This helps the productivity of the project in the long term. No programmer is overloaded with work and no overtime is allowed. Overtime usually exhausts the programmer and chances are he or she will make mistakes.

On-Site Customer

A single customer or a group of customers is available at all times for the programmers. This helps in resolving the ambiguities that developers encounter during development of the project, in setting priorities, and in providing live scenarios.

CONCLUSION

Extreme programming can be stated as a fast and highly organized process for development of a software system. XP emphasizes communication, which is essential in order to encourage new ideas. Because pair programming is stressed in this method, the fear of losing any programmer in the middle of the project is substantially decreased. Theoretically, XP reduces competition among programmers by insisting that they all work as a single team.

Extreme programming can be used where the requirements change rapidly and the customer is not sure of those requirements. Feedback is integral to this process; thus, the end product will be developed according to customer requirements.

References

Beck, K. (1999). *Extreme Programming Explained*, Addison-Wesley, Reading, MA.

http://www.extremeprogramming.org. Extreme programming: a gentle introduction.

Chapter 11
Development Before the Fact Technology

I met Margaret Hamilton a little over a decade ago. At the time I was writing articles on software engineering for *Software Magazine*. I interviewed Hamilton for one of these articles. This is when I became intrigued by her radically different developmental technology called Development Before the Fact (DBTF).

Hamilton had run the software engineering division of the Charles Stark Draper Labs at MIT where the onboard flight software was being created under her direction for the Apollo and Skylab missions. As you can well imagine, software had to be developed to send people up into space and then to bring them safely home. It was critical, therefore, to develop software without any flaws. In her study of software developed for these missions, Hamilton tracked a variety of causes of software error — most notably interface errors. From her findings she developed the technology that is the topic of this chapter.

DBTF (and its associated 001 tool set) is quite unique. System models are visually created and then virtually bug-free code is automatically generated by the tool set, which generates the documentation as well. Astonishingly, the 001 tool set actually generated itself.

WHAT IS WRONG WITH SYSTEMS

Today's traditional system engineering and software development environments support their users in "fixing wrong things" rather than in "doing them the right way in the first place." Things happen too late, if at all. Systems are of diminished quality and an unthinkable amount of dollars is wasted. This becomes apparent when analyzing the major problems of system engineering and software development.

In defining requirements, developers rely on many different types of mismatched methods to capture aspects of even a single definition. In fact, the universal modeling language (UML) resurrects and supports this very practice. Among other things, data flow is defined using one method, state transitions another, dynamics another, data types another, and structures using still another method. Once these aspects of requirements are defined, there is no way to integrate them. Designers are forced to think and design this way because of limitations of technologies available to them.

This leads to further problems. Integration of object to object, module to module, phase to phase, type of application to type of application, or systems to software become even more of a challenge than solving the problem at hand. This is compounded by a mismatch of products used for design and development. Integration of all forms is left to the devices of a myriad of developers well into the development process. The resulting system is hard to understand, objects cannot be traced, and there is little correspondence to the real world.

With these traditional methods, systems are actually encouraged by informal (or semiformal) languages to be defined as ambiguous and incorrect. Interfaces are incompatible and errors propagate throughout development. Once again the developers inherit the problem. The system and its development are out of control.

Requirements are defined to concentrate on the application needs of the user, but they do not consider that the user changes his mind or that his environment changes. Developers are forced to use a technology without an open architecture. The result is "locked in" designs, such as being locked into a specific database schema or GUI; the user is forced to make resource allocation a part of the application. Porting becomes a new development for each new architecture, operating system, database, GUI environment, language, or language configuration; critical functionality is avoided for fear of the unknown and maintenance is both risky and the most expensive part of the life cycle. When a system is targeted for a distributed environment, it is often defined and developed for a single processor environment and then redeveloped for a distributed environment — another unnecessary development.

Insufficient information about a system's run-time performance, including that concerning the decisions to be made between algorithms or architectures, is incorporated into a system definition. This results in design decisions that depend on analysis of outputs from exercising a multitude of ad hoc implementations and associated testing scenarios. A system is defined without considering how to separate it from its target environment. It is not known if a design is a good one until its implementation has failed or succeeded.

The focus for reuse is late into development during the coding phase. Requirements definitions lack properties to help find, create, and inherently make use of commonality. Modelers are forced to use informal and manual methods to find ways to divide a system into components natural for reuse. Why reuse something in today's changing market if it is not able to be integrated, not portable or adaptable, and error prone? The result is little incentive for reuse, and redundancy is a way of life. Again, errors propagate accordingly.

Automation is an inherently reusable process. If a solution does not exist for reuse, it does not exist for automation. Systems are defined with insufficient intelligence for automated tools to use them as input. Too often, automated tools concentrate on supporting the manual process instead of doing the real work.

Definitions supported by "make work" automation are given to developers to turn into code manually. A process that could have been mechanized once for reuse is performed manually over and over again. When automation attempts to do the real work, it is often incomplete across application domains or even within a domain, resulting in incomplete code such as skeleton or shell code. Manual processes are needed to complete unfinished automations. An automation for one part of a system (e.g., the GUI) needs to be integrated manually with an automation for another part of the system (e.g., communications algorithms) or with the results of a manual process. The code generated is often inefficient or hardwired to a particular architecture, language, or even a particular version of a language. Most of the development process is needlessly manual. Again, all these manual processes are creating new errors each time.

A promising solution to these problems is DBTF. Whereas the traditional approach is after the fact, or curative, the DBTF approach is preventative.

DEVELOPMENT BEFORE THE FACT

With DBTF, each system is defined with properties that control its own design and development. With this paradigm, a life cycle inherently produces reusable systems, realized in terms of automation. Unlike before, an emphasis is placed on defining things the right way the first time. Problems are prevented before they happen. Each system definition not only models its application but also models its own life cycle.

From the very beginning, a system inherently integrates all of its own objects (and all aspects of and about these objects) and the combinations of functionality using these objects. It maximizes its own reliability and flexibility to change and the unpredictable; capitalizes on its own parallelism; supports its own run-time performance analysis and the ability to understand the integrity of its own design; and maximizes the potential for its own reuse, automation, and evolution. The system is developed with built-in quality and built-in productivity.

A curative means to obtain quality is to continue testing the system until the errors are eliminated; a preventative (i.e., DBTF) means is to not allow errors to creep in, in the first place. Whereas a curative means to accelerate a particular design and development process is to add resources such as people or processors, a preventative approach would find a more efficient way to perform this process, such as capitalizing more on reuse or eliminating parts of it altogether, yet still reaching the desired results. Effective reuse is a preventative concept. Reusing something with no errors, to obtain a desired functionality, avoids the errors of a newly developed system; time and money will not be wasted in developing that new system. For successful reuse, a system must be worth reusing and must be reused for each user requiring functionality equivalent to it. This means starting from the beginning of a life cycle, not at the end, which is typically the case with traditional methods. Then a system is reused for each new phase of development. No matter what kind, every ten reuses save ten unnecessary developments.

THE TECHNOLOGY

The DBTF technology embodies and is based on a formal theory; it has a formal systems language, a generic process, and an automation, all based on the formal theory. Once understood, the characteristics of good design can be reused by incorporating them into a language for defining any system. The language is the key to DBTF. It has the capability to define any aspect of any system (and any aspect about that system) and integrate it with any other aspect. These aspects are directly related to the real world.

This same language can be used to define and integrate system requirements, specifications, design, and detailed design for functional, resource, and resource allocation architectures throughout all levels and layers of "seamless" definition, including hardware, software, and peopleware. It could be used to define missile or banking systems as well as real-time, Internet, or database environments.

With this language, every object is a system-oriented object (SOO) developed in terms of other SOOs. An SOO integrates all aspects of a system including that which is function, object, and timing oriented. Every system is an object; every object is a system. Instead of object-oriented systems, DBTF has system-oriented objects and can be used to define systems with diverse degrees of fidelity and completeness. Such a language can always be considered a design language because design is relative: one person's design phase is another person's implementation phase.

This implementation-independent language has mechanisms to define mechanisms for defining systems. Although the core language is generic, the user "language," a by-product of a development, can be application specific because the language is semantics dependent but syntax independent. Unlike formal languages that are not friendly and friendly languages that are not formal, this language is formal **and** friendly.

The first step in building a DBTF system is to define a model (without concern for resource allocation details such as how many processes are needed) with the language. This process could be in any phase of development, including problem analysis, operational scenarios, and design. The model is automatically analyzed to ensure it was defined properly. This includes static analysis for preventative properties and dynamic analysis for user-intent properties.

A complete and fully production-ready and fully integrated software implementation (and documentation) for any kind or size of application, consistent with the model, is then automatically generated by the generic generator for a selected target environment in the language of choice (e.g., C, Java, or XML) and the architecture of choice. If the selected environment has already been configured, it is selected directly; if not, the generator is configured for a new language and new architecture before it is selected.

The resulting system can then be executed. If the desired system is software, the system can now be tested for further user-intent errors. It becomes operational after testing. *Before the fact testing* is inherently part of every DBTF development step. Errors are prevented simply by construction with the language and because of that which is inherent or automated; for example, since the generator automatically generates all the code, no manual coding errors will be made. Target changes are made to the definition, not to the code. Target architecture changes are made to the configuration of the generator environment, not to the code. If the real system is hardware or peopleware, the generated software system can serve as a form of simulation upon which the real system can be based.

DBTF is a system-oriented object approach based upon a unique concept of control. The foundations are based on a set of axioms and on the assumption of the existence of a universal set of objects. Each axiom defines a relation of immediate domination; the union of the relations defined by the axioms is control. Among other things, the axioms establish the relationships of an object for invocation, input and output, input and output access rights, error detection and recovery, and ordering during its developmental and operational states.

This approach is used throughout a life cycle, starting with requirements and continuing with systems engineering, specification, analysis, design, implementation, testing, and maintenance. Its users include managers, system engineers, software engineers, and test engineers, as well as end users.

In addition to experience with real-world systems, 001 takes its roots in many other areas, including systems theory, formal methods, formal linguistics, and object technologies. It would be natural to make assumptions about what is possible and impossible based on its superficial resemblance to other techniques such as traditional object technologies. It helps, however, to suspend any and all preconceived notions when first introduced to it because it is a world unto itself — a completely new way to think about systems and software.

The DBTF approach had its beginnings in 1968 with the Apollo space missions when research was performed for developing software for man-rated missions. This led to the finding that interface errors accounted for approximately 75 percent of all errors found in the flight software during final testing. These include data flow, and priority and timing errors at the highest and lowest levels of a system to the finest grain detail. Each error was placed into a category according to the means taken to prevent it by the very way a system was defined. A theory was derived for defining a system such that this entire class of interface errors would be eliminated.

INTEGRATED MODELING ENVIRONMENT

The first technology derived from this theory concentrated on defining and building reliable systems in terms of functional maps. Since that time this technology has been further developed to design and build systems with DBTF properties in terms of an integration of functional and type maps, where a map is a control hierarchy and a network of interacting objects. The philosophy behind this approach is inherently recursive and reusable where reliable systems are defined in terms of reliable systems. Only reliable systems are used as building blocks and as mechanisms to integrate these building blocks to form a new system. The new system becomes a reusable for building other systems.

Every model is defined in terms of function maps (FMaps) to represent the dynamic world of action by capturing functional and time (including priorities) behavior and type maps (TMaps) to represent the static world of objects by capturing space behavior (Exhibit 11-1). FMaps and TMaps guide the designer in thinking through concepts at all levels of system design. With these maps, everything you need to know (no more, no less) is available. All model viewpoints can be obtained from FMaps and TMaps, including data flow, control flow, state transitions, data and object structure, and dynamics. FMaps are inherently integrated with TMaps.

On an FMap, a function at each node is defined in terms of and controls its children functions. For example, the function "build the table" could be decomposed into and control its children functions "make parts and assemble." On a TMap, a type at each node is defined in terms of and controls its children types. For example, "type, table," could be decomposed into and control its children types, "legs and top."

Every type on a TMap owns a set of inherited primitive operations. Each function on an FMap has one or more objects as its input and one or more

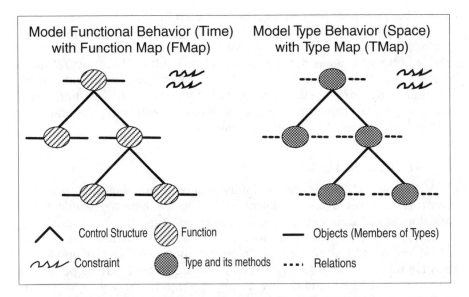

Exhibit 11-1.   FMaps Are Inherently Integrated with TMaps.

objects as its output. Each object resides in an object map (OMap), an instance of a TMap, and is a member of a type from a TMap. FMaps are inherently integrated with TMaps by using these objects and their primitive operations. FMaps are used to define, integrate, and control the transformations of objects from one state to another state (e.g., a table with a broken leg to a table with a fixed leg). Uses of primitive operations on types defined in the TMap reside at the bottom nodes of an FMap. Primitive types reside at the bottom nodes of a TMap.

When a system has all of its object values plugged in for a particular performance pass, it exists in the form of an execution map (EMap), an instance of an FMap.

Typically, a team of designers will begin to design a system at any level (hardware, software, peopleware, or some combination) by sketching a TMap of their application. This is where they decide on the types of objects (and the relationships between these objects) that they will have in their system. Often a road map (RMap), which organizes all system objects including FMaps and TMaps, will be sketched in parallel with the TMap. An RMap can also be automatically generated from a set of FMaps and TMaps upon demand.

Once a TMap has been agreed upon, the FMaps begin almost to fall into place for the designers because of the natural partitioning of functionality (or groups of functionality) provided to the designers by the TMap system.

The TMap provides the structural criteria from which to evaluate the functional partitioning of the system (e.g., the shape of the structural partitioning of the FMaps is balanced against the structural organization of the shape of the objects as defined by the TMap). With FMaps and TMaps, a system (and its viewpoints) is divided into functionally natural components and groups of functional components that naturally work together; a system is defined from the very beginning to inherently integrate and make understandable its own real world definition.

PRIMITIVE STRUCTURES

All FMaps and TMaps are ultimately defined in terms of three primitive control structures: a parent controls its children to have a dependent relationship, an independent relationship, or a decision-making relationship. A formal set of rules is associated with each primitive structure. If these rules are followed, interface errors are "removed" before the fact by preventing them in the first place. As a result, all interface errors (75 to 90 percent of all errors normally found during testing in a traditional development) are eliminated at the definition phase. Using the primitive structures supports a system to be defined from the very beginning to inherently maximize its own elimination of errors.

Use of the primitive structures is shown in the definition of the FMap for system, MakeATable (Exhibit 11-2). The top node function has FLATwood and ROUNDwood as its inputs and produces Table as its output. MakeATable, as a parent, is decomposed with a Join into its children functions, MakeParts and Assemble. MakeParts takes in as input FLATwood and ROUNDwood from its parent and produces Top and Legs as its output. Top and Legs are given to Assemble as input. Assemble is controlled by its parent to depend on MakeParts for its input. Assemble produces Table as output and sends it to its parent.

. As a parent, MakeParts is decomposed into children, MakeLegs and MakeTop, who are controlled to be independent of each other with the Include primitive control structure. MakeLegs takes in part of its parent's input and MakeTop takes in the other part. MakeLegs provides part of its output (Legs) to its parent and MakeTop provides the rest. MakeTop controls its children, FinishSoftWood and FinishHardWood, with an Or. Here, both children take in the same input and provide the same output because only one of them will be performed for a given performance pass. FinishSoftWood will be performed if the decision function "is:Soft,Wood" returns True; otherwise, FinishHardWood will be performed. Notice that input (e.g., FLATwood) is traceable down the system from parent to children and output (e.g., Table) is traceable up the system from children to parent. All objects in a DBTF system are traceable. MakeATable's TMap, Table, uses

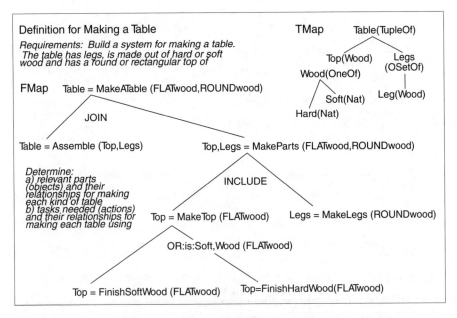

Exhibit 11-2. **The Three Primitive Structures Are Ultimately Used to Decompose a Map. The FMap Part of the System, MakeATable, Is Modeled Using JOIN, INCLUDE, and OR for Controlling Dependent, Independent, and Decision-Making Functions, Respectively.**

nonprimitive structures called type structures, a concept discussed in a later section.

Each type on a TMap can be decomposed in terms of primitive structures into children types where the defined relationships between types are explicit. In Exhibit 11-3, Table as a parent has been decomposed into its children, Top and Legs, where the relations between Top and Legs are on-1 and on-2, respectively, the relation between Table and legs is r-1, and the relation between Table and Top is r-0. Notice that making a Table Top depends on Legs to rest on (Exhibit 11-3a). On the other hand, an independency relationship exists between the front legs and the back legs of the Table (Exhibit 11-3b). The Table may have FrontLegs or BackLegs, or Front-Legs and BackLegs at once. In Exhibit 11-3c, which illustrates a decision structure with objects, unlike with the dependent and independent structures, the pattern of the OMap is always different from the pattern of the TMap because only one object is chosen to represent its parent for a given instance.

It can be shown that a system defined with these structures results in properties that support real-time distributed environments. Each system is event-interrupt driven; each object is traceable and reconfigurable, and

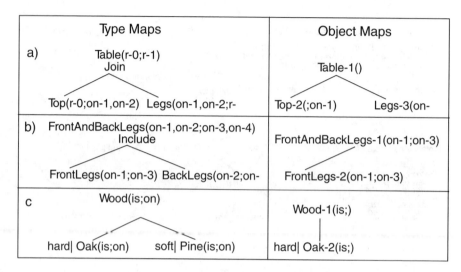

Exhibit 11-3. **A TMap (and Its Corresponding OMaps) Can Be Decomposed into Its Explicit Relationships in Terms of the Three Primitive Control Structures.**

has a unique priority. Independencies and dependencies can readily be detected and used to determine where parallel and distributed processing is most beneficial. With these properties, a system is defined from the very beginning to inherently maximize its own flexibility to change and the unpredictable and to capitalize on its own parallelism.

DEFINED STRUCTURES

Any system can be defined completely using only the primitive structures, but less primitive structures can be derived from the primitive ones and accelerate the process of defining and understanding a system. Non-primitive structures can be defined for FMaps and TMaps and can be created for asynchronous, synchronous, and interrupt scenarios used in real-time, distributed systems. Similarly, retrieval and query structures can be defined for client-server database management systems.

CoInclude is an example of a system pattern that happens often (Exhibit 11-4a). Its FMap was defined with primitive structures. Within the CoInclude pattern, everything stays the same for each use except for the children function nodes A and B. The CoInclude pattern can be defined as a nonprimitive structure in terms of more primitive structures with the use of the concept of defined structures. This concept is an example of available reusable patterns for FMaps and TMaps.

Included with each structure definition is the definition of the syntax for its use (Exhibit 11-4b). Its use (Exhibit 11-4c) provides a "hidden reuse" of

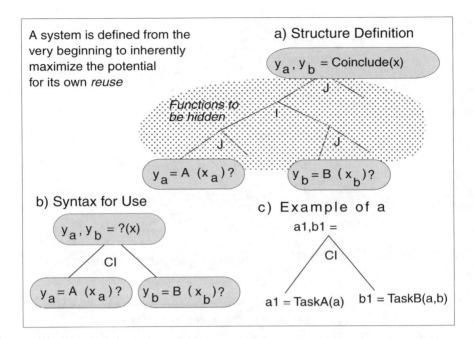

A system is defined from the very beginning to inherently maximize the potential for its own *reuse*

a) Structure Definition

$y_a, y_b = \text{Coinclude}(x)$

Functions to be hidden

$y_a = A (x_a)?$

$y_b = B (x_b)?$

b) Syntax for Use

$y_a, y_b = ?(x)$

CI

$y_a = A (x_a)?$

$y_b = B (x_b)?$

c) Example of a

$a1, b1 =$

CI

$a1 = \text{TaskA}(a)$

$b1 = \text{TaskB}(a,b)$

Exhibit 11-4. **Defined Structures Are Used to Define Nonprimitive Structure Reusables in Terms of More Primitive Structures. CO-INCLUDE is an Example of a System Pattern That Has Been Turned into a Defined Structure.**

the entire system as defined, but explicitly shows only the elements subject to change (that is, functions A and B). The CoInclude structure is used in a similar way to the Include structure except that, with the CoInclude, the user has more flexibility with respect to repeated use, ordering, and selection of objects. Each defined structure has rules associated with it for its use just as with the primitive control structures. Rules for the nonprimitives are inherited ultimately from the rules of the primitives.

Async, (Exhibit 11-5), is a real-time, distributed, communicating structure with asynchronous and synchronous behavior. The Async system was defined with the primitive Or, Include, and Join structures and the CoInclude user-defined structure. It cannot be further decomposed because each of its lowest level functions is a primitive function on a previously defined type (see Identify2:Any and Clone1:Any under End, each of which is a primitive operation on type Any), recursive (see Async under DoMore), or a variable function for a defined structure (see A and B under process). If a leaf node function does not fall into any of these categories, it can be further decomposed or it can refer to an existing operation in a library or an external operation from an outside environment.

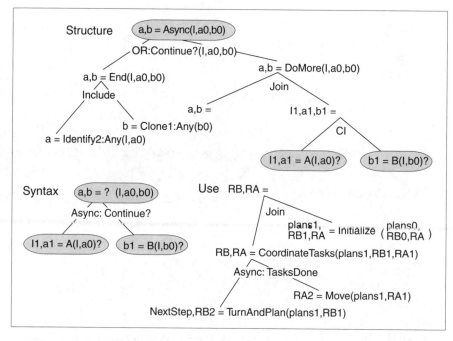

Exhibit 11-5.   Async is a Defined Structure That Can Be Used to Define Distributed Systems with Synchronous and Asynchronous Behavior.

CoordinateTasks uses Async as a reusable where TurnAndPlan and Move are dependent, communicating, concurrent, synchronous, and asynchronous functions. The two robots in this system work together to perform a task such as building a table. Here, one phase of the planning robot, RB, is coordinated with the next phase of the slave robot, RA.

Reusability can be used with a TMap model by using user-defined type structures, which are defined structures that provide the mechanism to define a TMap without their particular relations explicitly defined. TMap Table (Exhibit 11-2) uses a set of default user-defined type structures. Table as a parent type controls its children types, Top and Legs, in terms of a TupleOf type structure, Legs controls its child, Leg, in terms of OSetOf, and Wood controls Hard and Soft with a OneOf. A TupleOf is a collection of a fixed number of possibly different types of objects, OSetOf is a collection of a variable number of the same types of objects (in a linear order), and OneOf is a classification of possibly different types of objects from which one object is selected to represent the class. These type structures, along with TreeOf, can be used for designing any kind of TMap. TreeOf is a collection of the same types of objects ordered using a tree indexing system. With the use of mechanisms such as defined structures, a system is defined from the very beginning to inherently maximize the potential for its own reuse.

FMAPS, TMAPS, AND THEIR INTEGRATION

Exhibit 11-6 shows a complete system definition for a manufacturing company defined in terms of an integrated set of FMaps and TMaps. This company could be set up to build tables — with the help of robots to perform tasks — using structures such as those defined above. Because this system is completely defined, it is ready to be developed automatically to complete, integrated, and fully production ready to run code. This system's FMap, Is_FullTime_Employee, has been decomposed until it reaches primitive operations on types in TMap, MfgCompany. (See, for example, Emps=Moveto:Employees (MfgC) where MfgC is of type MfgCompany and Emps is of type Employees.) MfgCompany has been decomposed until its leaf nodes are primitive types or defined as types that are decomposed in another TMap.

System, Is_FullTime_Employee, uses objects defined by TMap, Mfg-Company, to check to see if an employee is full or part time. First a move is made from the MfgCompany type object, MfgC, to an Employees type object, Emps. The defined structure, LocateUsing:Name, finds an Employee based on a name. Once found, a move is made from Emp (an Employee) to PS (a Payscale). The primitive operation YN=is:FullTime(PS)

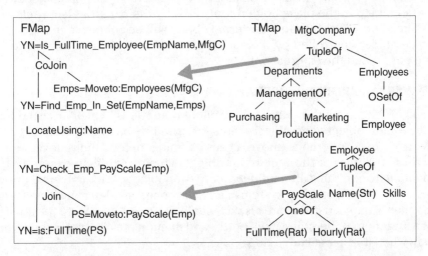

Exhibit 11-6.   A Complete System Definition Is an Integration of FMaps and TMaps, Where the FMaps Have Been Decomposed Until Reaching Primitive Functions on the Types in the TMaps and the TMaps Have Been Decomposed Until Reaching the Primitive Types. Specific Abstract Types Inherit Methods from User-Defined Type Structures and Are Applied as Leaf Function in FMaps.

is then used to determine from PS if Emp is full time. When PS is FullTime, YN will be True.

Each type structure assumes its own set of possible relations for its parent and children types. In this example, TMap, MfgCompany is decomposed into Departments and Employees in terms of TupleOf. Departments is decomposed in terms of ManagementOf (a user-defined type structure) into Purchasing, Production, and Marketing. Employees is decomposed in terms of OSetOf. One of the children of Employee, PayScale, is decomposed in terms of the type structure, OneOf.

Abstract types decomposed with the same type structure on a TMap inherit (or reuse) the same primitive operations and therefore the same behavior. So, for example, MfgCompany and Employee inherit the same primitive operations from type structure, TupleOf. An example of this can be seen in the FMap where both types, MfgCompany and Employee, use the primitive operation, MoveTo, which was inherited from TupleOf.

Here each use of the MoveTo is an instantiation of the Child=MoveTo: Child(Parent) operation of the TupleOf type structure. For example, Emps=MoveTo:Employees(MfgC) allows one to navigate to an employee's object contained in a MfgCompany object. A type may be nonprimitive (e.g., Departments), primitive (e.g., FullTime as a rational number), or a definition that is defined in another type subtree (e.g., Employees). When a leaf node type has the name of another type subtree, the child object will be contained in the place holder controlled by the parent object (defined as Skills) or a reference to an external object will be contained in the child place holder controlled by the parent object (forming a relation between the parent and the external object).

UNIVERSAL PRIMITIVE OPERATIONS

The TMap provides universal primitive operations, which are used for controlling objects and object states inherited by all types. They create, destroy, copy, reference, move, access a value, detect and recover from errors, and access the type of an object. They provide an easy way to manipulate and think about different types of objects. With universal primitive operations, building systems can be accomplished in a more uniform manner. TMap and OMap are also available as types to facilitate the ability of a system to understand itself better and manipulate all objects the same way when it is beneficial to do so.

TMap properties ensure the proper use of objects in an FMap. A TMap has a corresponding set of control properties for controlling spatial relationships between objects. One cannot, for example, put a leg on a table where a leg already exists; conversely, one cannot remove a leg from the table where there is no leg. A reference to the state of an object cannot be modified if there are other references to that state in the future; reject values exist in all types, allowing the FMap user to recover from failures if they are encountered.

The same types of definition mechanisms are used to define RotateRotateArm, a hardware system (Exhibit 11-7), as were used to define the preceding software system. Note that this system also includes the use of primitives for numeric calculation. In this system, the rotation of the robot arm is calculated to move from one position to another in a manufacturing cell to transfer a part. The universal operation (an example of another form of reusable with polymorphism), Replace, is used twice in this example. Each use of a universal operation has function qualifiers that select a unique TMap parent–child combination to be used during the application of the function.

Exhibit 11-8 has a definition that takes further advantage of the expressive power of a TMap with the option of using explicitly defined relations. In this example, a stack of bearings is described. A bearing in the stack may be under (with relation on-0) or on (with relation on-1) another bearing object in the stack as defined by the DSetOf structured type. A bearing object is decomposed into a Cap, a RetainerWith Balls, and a Base. Object relationships at this level show that the Cap is above the RetainerWithBalls, which is, in turn, above the Base. Further detail reveals that a Retainer has (with the has-n relation) some number of RetainerHoleWithBall objects. The set of RetainerHoleWithBall objects are independent of each other, defined by the ISetOf structured type. This structure allows for physically independent relations on the objects in the set. Here, different portions of the Cap surface are independently related (with the on-Balls relation) to each individual Ball object (with the on-Ball relation).

As experience is gained with different types of applications, new reusables emerge for general or specific use. For example, a set of reusables has been derived to form a higher level set of mechanisms for defining maps of interruptable, asynchronous, communicating, distributed controllers. This is essentially a second-order control system (with rules that parallel the primary control system of the primitive structures) defined with the formal logic of user-defined structures that can be represented using a graphical syntax (Exhibit 11-9).

In such a system, each distributed region is cooperatively working with other distributed regions and each parent controller may interrupt the children under its control. In this example, the robot controller may apply an arm controller or a sensor controller. If the arm controller is activated, the two grippers may concurrently use an Include to hold two ends of some object. If the sensor controller is activated, a sensor unit uses a Join to sense some image, followed by an image unit matcher. These reusables can also be used to manage other types of processes such as those used to manage a software development environment or a corporation.

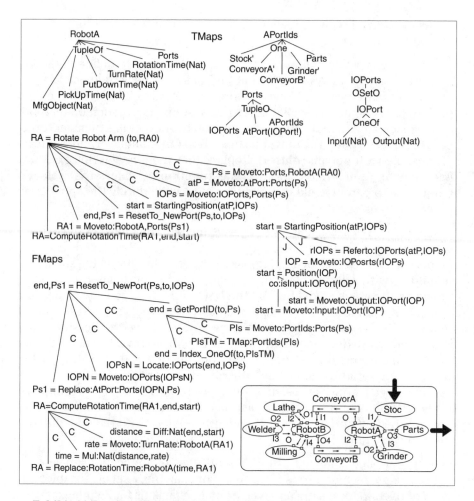

Exhibit 11-7. Any Kind of System Can Be Defined with this Language, Including Software, Hardware, and Peopleware. Rotate Robot Arm is an example of a Hardware System Defined in FMaps and TMaps.

The extent to which reuse is provided is a most powerful feature of DBTF. *Everything* developed is a candidate — reusable (and inherently integratable) within the same system, other systems, and these systems as they evolve. Commonality is ensured simply by using the language. The designer models the objects and their relationships and the functions and their relationships; the language inherently integrates these aspects as well as takes care of making those things that should be objects become objects. In fact, FMaps are defined in terms of TMaps and use TMaps as reusables, while TMaps are defined in terms of FMaps and use FMaps as reusables.

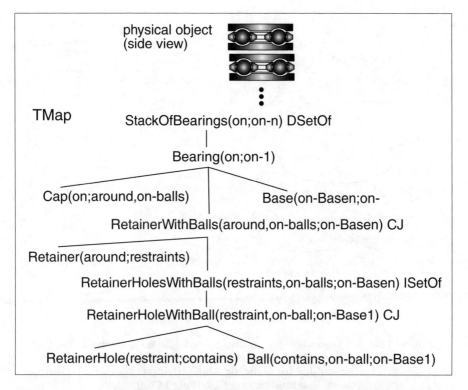

physical object
(side view)

TMap

StackOfBearings(on;on-n) DSetOf

Bearing(on;on-1)

Cap(on;around,on-balls)

Base(on-Basen;on-

RetainerWithBalls(around,on-balls;on-Basen) CJ

Retainer(around;restraints)

RetainerHolesWithBalls(restraints,on-balls;on-Basen) ISetOf

RetainerHoleWithBall(restraint,on-ball;on-Base1) CJ

RetainerHole(restraint;contains) Ball(contains,on-ball;on-Base1)

Exhibit 11-8. Explicitly Defined Relations Can Be Used to Take Further Advantage of the Expressive Power of a TMap. Here, a TMap Is Used for Defining a Bearing Manufacturing Process.

PERFORMANCE CONSIDERATIONS

When designing a system environment, it is important to understand the performance constraints of the functional architecture and to have the ability to change configurations rapidly. A system is flexible to changing resource requirements if the functional architecture definition is separated from its resource definitions. To support such flexibility with the necessary built-in controls, with DBTF the same language is used to define functional, resource, and allocation architectures. The meta-language properties of the language can be used to define global and local constraints for FMaps and TMaps. Constraints can be defined in terms of FMaps and TMaps. If we place a constraint on the definition of a function (e.g., Where F takes between two and five seconds), then this constraint influences all functions that use this definition. Such a constraint is global with respect to the uses of F.

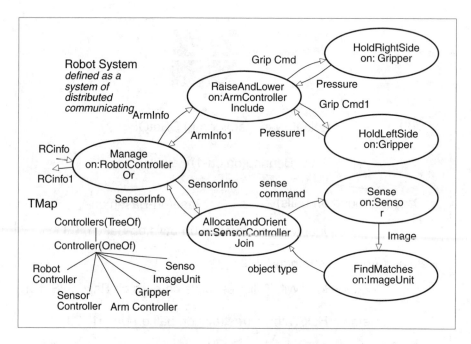

Exhibit 11-9.   A Second-Order Control System Has Been Derived That Parallels the Primary Control System to Form a Powerful Set of Reusables for Defining Maps of Interruptable, Asynchronous, Communicating, Distributed Controllers.

A global constraint of a definition may be further constrained by a local constraint placed in the context of the definition using that definition; e.g., when function G uses F, where F takes six seconds (not two to five seconds). The validity of constraints and their interaction with other constraints can be analyzed by static or dynamic means. The property of being able to trace an object throughout a definition supports this type of analysis and provides the ability to collect information on an object as it transitions from function to function. As a result, one can determine the direct and the indirect effects of functional interactions of constraints.

INHERENT INTEGRATION WITH SYSTEM-ORIENTED OBJECTS

A DBTF system is by nature an inherent integration of function (including timing) and object orientation from the beginning, i.e., it is a system-oriented object. The definition space is a set of real-world objects, defined in terms of FMaps and TMaps.

Objects, instantiations of TMaps, are realized in terms of OMaps. An execution, which is an instantiation of an FMap, is realized in terms of an

EMap. Definitions are independent of a particular implementation — e.g., building block definitions with a focus on objects are independent of particular object-oriented implementations. Properties of classical object-oriented systems such as inheritance, encapsulation, polymorphism, and persistence are supported with the use of generalized functions on OMaps and TMaps.

The DBTF approach derives from the combination of steps taken to solve the problems of the traditional "after the fact" approach. Collective experience strongly confirms that quality and productivity increase with the increased use of DBTF properties. A major factor is the inherent reuse in these systems, culminating in ultimate reuse, which is either inherent or automation itself.

From FMaps and TMaps, any kind of system can be automatically developed, resulting in complete, integrated, and production-ready target system code and documentation. This is accomplished by the 001 Tool Suite, an automation of the technology. The tool suite also has a means to observe the behavior of a system as it is evolved and executed in terms of OMaps and EMaps.

If asked if there were a way to develop any kind of software with:

- Seamless integration, including systems to software
- Correctness by built-in language properties
- No interface errors
- Defect rates reduced by a factor of ten
- Guarantee of function integrity after implementation
- Complete traceability and evolvability (changing applications, architectures, and technologies)
- Full life cycle automation
- No manual coding
- Maximized reuse including that which is automated or inherent
- Minimum time and minimum effort
- A tool suite

— all defined and automatically generated by itself, most people would say this is impossible, at least in the foreseeable future.

This is not impossible; in fact, it is possible today with the 001 systems design and software development environment (Exhibit 11-10 contains a summary that compares the traditional "after the fact" environment with a DBTF environment). Why can it do what it does? It is not magic. Simply put, it is because this environment automates and is based on the Development Before The Fact paradigm.

**Exhibit 11-10. Summary Comparing Traditional "After the Fact"
Environment with a DBTF Environment.**

Traditional (After the Fact)	DBTF (Before the Fact)
Integration ad hoc, if at all ~Mismatched methods, objects, phases, products, architectures, applications, and environment ~System not integrated with software ~Function oriented <u>or</u> object oriented ~GUI not integrated with application ~Simulation not integrated with software code	*Integration* ~Seamless life cycle: methods, objects, phases, products, architectures, applications, and environment ~System integrated with software ~System oriented objects: integration of function, timing, and object oriented ~GUI integrated with application ~Simulation integrated with software code
Behavior uncertain until after delivery	*Correctness by built-in language*
Interface errors abound and infiltrate the system (over 75% of all errors) ~Most of those found are found after implementation ~Some found manually ~Some found by dynamic runs analysis ~Some never found	*No interface errors* ~All found before implementation ~All found by automatic and static analysis ~Always found
Ambiguous requirements, specifications, designs introduce chaos, confusion and complexity ~Informal or semi-formal language ~Different phases, languages and tools ~Different language for other systems than for software	*Unambiguous requirements, specifications, designs remove chaos, confusion, and complexity* ~Formal, but friendly language ~All phases, same language and tools ~Same language for software, hardware and any other system
No guarantee of function integrity after implementation	*Guarantee of function integrity after implementation*
Inflexible: Systems not traceable or evolvable ~Locked in bugs, requirements products, architectures, etc. ~Painful transition from legacy ~Maintenance performed at code level	*Flexible: Systems traceable and evolvable* ~Open architecture ~Smooth transition from legacy ~Maintenance performed at specification level
Reuse not inherent ~Reuse is ad hoc ~Customization and reuse are mutually exclusive	*Inherent Reuse* ~Every object a candidate for reuse ~Customization increases the reuse pool
Automation supports manual process instead of doing real work ~Mostly manual: documentation, programming, test generation, traceability, integration ~Limited, incomplete, fragmented, disparate, and inefficient	*Automation does real work* ~Automatic programming, documentation, test generation, traceability, integration ~100% code automatically generated for any kind of software
Product x not defined and developed with itself	*001 defined with and generated by itself* ~#1 in all evaluations
Dollars wasted, error prone systems ~High risk ~Not cost effective ~Difficult to meet schedules ~Less of what you need and more of what you don t need	*Ultra-reliable systems with unprecedented productivity in their development* ~Low risk ~10 to 1, 20 to 1, 50 to 1 dollars sa ved/dollars made ~Minimum time to complete ~No more, no less of what you need

Note:

001, 001 Tool Suite, DBTF, Development Before the Fact, FunctionMap, FMap, TypeMap, TMap, ObjectMap, OMap, RoadMap, RMap, ExecutionMap, EMap, RAT, System Oriented Object, SOO, 001AXES, are all trademarks of Hamilton Technologies, Inc.

Selected Bibliography

Hamilton, M. (1986). Zero-defect software: the elusive goal, *IEEE Spectrum*, 23, 48–531986.

Hamilton, M. and Hackler, R. (1990). 001: a rapid development approach for rapid prototyping based on a system that supports its own life cycle, *IEEE Proc. 1st Int. Workshop Rapid Sys. Prototyping*, Research Triangle Park, NC, June 4, 1990.

Hamilton, M. and Hackler, W.R. (in press). System Oriented Objects: Development Before the Fact

Hamilton, M. and Hackler, W.R. (2000). Towards cost effective and timely end-to-end testing, HTI, prepared for Army Research Laboratory, Contract No. DAKF11-99-P-1236.

Hamilton, M. (1994). Inside Development Before the Fact, Electron. Design, 31.

Hamilton, M. (1994). Development Before the Fact in action, *Electron. Design*, (ESSoftware Engineering Tools Experiment-Final Report, Vol. 1, Experiment Summary, Table 1, p. 9, Department of Defense, Strategic Defense Initiative, Washington, D.C.)

Hornstein, R. and Hamilton, M. (in preparation). Realizing the potential for COTS utilization: creating and assembling reusable components right the first time, NASA, Washington, D.C., Hamilton Technologies, Inc., Cambridge, MA.

Krut, Jr., B. (1993). Integrating 001 tool support in the feature-oriented domain analysis methodology (CMU/SEI-93-TR-11, ESC-TR-93-188), Pittsburgh, Software Engineering Institute, Carnegie Mellon University.

Ouyang, M. and Golay, M.W. (1994). An integrated formal approach for developing high quality software of safety-critical systems, Massachusetts Institute of Technology, Cambridge, MA, Report No. MIT-ANP-TR-035.

001 Tool Suite. Hamilton Technologies, Inc. Version 3.3.1 (1986-2002) [www. htius.com]

Chapter 12
The Design Specification

The process of information systems development must pass through a number of distinct phases in order to be successful. This process is commonly known as the systems development life cycle (SDLC) and the design specification is an essential and integral component of it. Design specifications are blueprints showing what to build and how to build it.

THE PROCESS

By the time the systems designer comes to the design phase of the system life cycle, he or she has a pretty clear understanding of what the new system should do and why. This information is recorded in several documents:

- The feasibility study discusses the pros, cons, and costs of building the system (see Appendix C).
- The project plan provides preliminary information about the project, its mission and goals, its schedule, and its cost estimate (see Appendix F).
- The system requirements specification (SRS) contains detailed information about the requirements of the system (see Appendix G).

In spite of this detailed documentation, there may still be some uncertainty regarding future capabilities of the new system due to the different and changing perspectives of the end users and other stakeholders. Different people will see different possibilities for the new system, which is why a push to propose alternative solutions may take place. The designer must then consider the different views, covering all structured requirements, and transform them into several competing design strategies. Only one design will eventually be pursued.

THE DETAILS OF DESIGN

A variety of models were used in the analysis phase to help create a high-level process model. These tools, which include data flow diagrams (Exhibit 12-1), entity relationship diagrams (Exhibit 12-2), and state transition

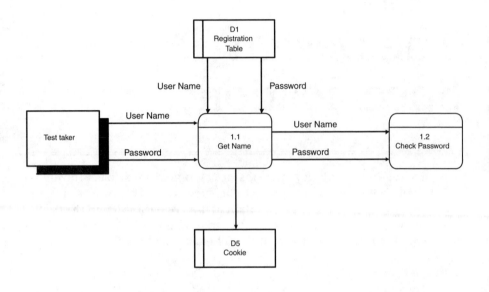

Exhibit 12-1.   The Data Flow Diagram

diagrams (Exhibit 12-3), are invaluable in producing program specifications as the move is made from logical models toward the physical design of the system.

Newcomers to the field often insist that analysis tools and deliverables be different from the design phase tools and deliverables. More commonly, many of the modeling tools and techniques used in the analysis phase are also used during the design stage. In addition, there is definitely an overlap between information contained within the SRS and information contained within the SDS. For example, when developing structured systems, analysts frequently use the DFD to describe the flow of information throughout the system for the analysis phase — the logical DFD. A more detailed set of DFDs is then created for the design phase — the physical DFD. The same can be said for ERDs, STDs, data dictionaries, and even process specifications.

The DFD provides a good example of how a document created originally during the analysis phase can be expanded during the design phase. In the analysis phase a DFD is developed that shows a conceptual — or context — view of the system as shown in Exhibit 12-4. The Level 0 diagram serves as a "table of contents" for subsequent DFDs. Note that it shows a generic "0" process with attendant data flows.

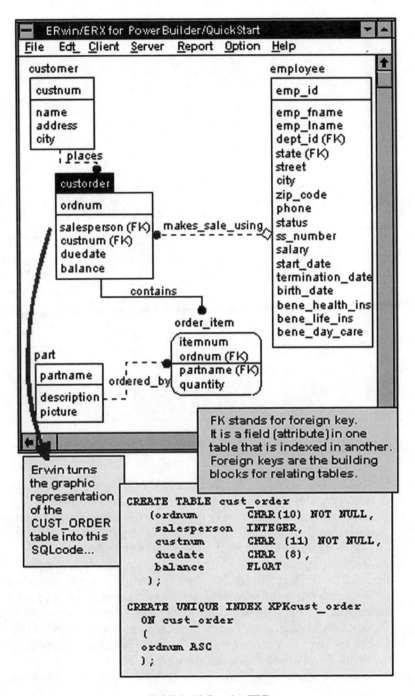

Exhibit 12-2. An ERD

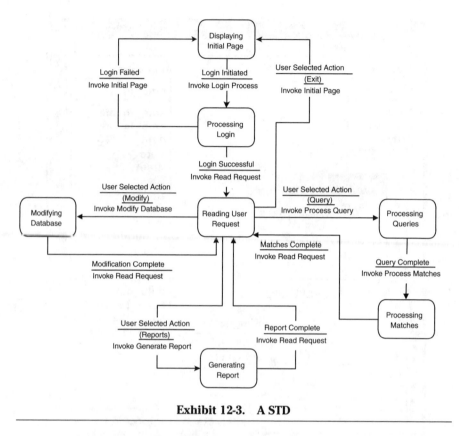

Exhibit 12-3. A STD

When drawing a DFD, a top–down approach is the most effective. Steps include (Kendall, 2002):

1. Develop a list of typical business activities and use it to determine external entities, data flows, processes, and data stores.
2. Draw a context diagram that depicts external entities and data flows to and from the system. The context diagram should be abstract — i.e., do not show any detailed processes or data flows.
3. Now draw diagram 0, which can be likened to a table of contents. Diagram 0 is the next level of detail when using a top–down approach. As we move down the hierarchy, we move from abstract and less detailed to more detailed and more concrete.
4. Create a child diagram for each process depicted in diagram 0.
5. Check for any errors and make sure the labels assigned to processes and data flows are logical and meaningful.
6. Now develop a physical data flow diagram from the logical data flow diagram.
7. Partition the physical data flow by separating the parts of the diagram to facilitate programming and implementation.

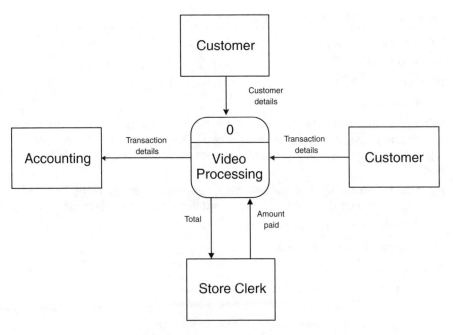

Exhibit 12-4.   The Context DFD

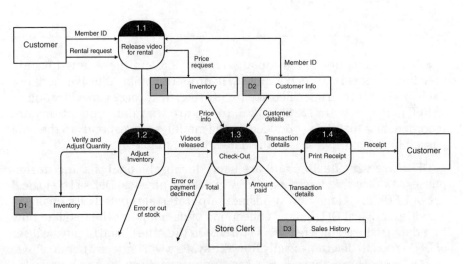

Exhibit 12-5.   DFDs Grow Successfully More Detailed

In the design phase the designer analyzes the DFD and determines how the data processes can be segregated into groups, each associated with a type of process, as shown in Exhibit 12-5. Note that now far more detail is specified.

Exhibit 12-6. The Process Specification

Process #1

Name: (LOGON)

Number: 1

Name: Logon

Description: registered test takers will log on to their accounts with their user names and passwords through this process. They do not need to register again. Once they log on, they enter their test subject and then they can take the test.

Input data: user name from the test taker, password from the test taker, user name from the registration table, password from the registration table

Output data: user name to the cookie

Type of process: manual check

Process logic:

```
Get user name and password from the user
if correct then
    Allow the user to take the test
else
    produce an error
endif
```

Key functions of each group are determined and these functions are then broken down (i.e., decomposed) in order to obtain cohesive modules. Each module is then specified separately (i.e., the process specification or PSPEC), as shown in Exhibit 12-6, to ensure that data collections are recorded, and that data produced by the modules corresponds to the data passed between processes in the data flow diagrams.

DFDs are very flexible and are used during the analysis and design phases. As discussed, you may draw logical or physical DFDs. The logical set of DFDs diagrams how a business operates and details its business activities. Logical DFDs show collections of data but not the detail of how that data is stored or where it is stored. On the other hand, a physical set of DFDs tries to diagram exactly how the system will or does operate. Physical DFDs show programs, databases, and other information necessary for the implementation of a particular system.

Designers must obtain a deep appreciation of the system and its functions because the production of a modular structural chart is not a mechanical task (Curtis et al., 2000).

LOGICAL AND PHYSICAL DESIGN

Design consists of two discrete steps: logical design and physical design. To understand the components of each it is necessary to discuss logical and physical analysis.

Logical and physical analysis

The physical analysis phase requires the systems analyst to determine the specifics of the existing processes that the system will automate, whether these processes are currently part of a technology system or are completely manual. Physical analysis involves the process of determining, in specific detail, exactly who does what and when he or she does it in the process or problem being solved (Curtis et al., 2000). This analysis shows what is really going on in the system, and helps the systems analyst put some structure around the new system's requirements.

Physical analysis occurs after the initial round of interviews with stakeholders and end users. At this point in the process, the systems analyst is likely to have an unwieldy batch of interview notes, details of observations, questionnaire responses, and sundry documents (Curtis et al., 2000). This information provides the basis for building a methodical description of the existing manual system. Building this description is the foundation of physical analysis. This work is considered *physical* analysis because the ultimate result of this work is a very nuts-and-bolts description of the actual (manual) steps and processes comprising the system, with little to no logical abstraction.

A primary vehicle for accomplishing the physical analysis phase is the manual system flowchart. This chart is very much like the process flowcharts that many people are familiar with, with some minor changes. The chart is structured in such a way that it is apparent which department, organization, or person owns each task, as shown in Exhibit 12-7.

As you can see, this is a very detailed and physically oriented diagram, showing the passage of documents and data through very specific checkpoints. This provides the data presentation required in order to gain the required level of understanding of the system as it exists, but you could not develop a system from this picture; a logical diagram is required for that.

The logical analysis phase is focused on abstracting the details uncovered during physical analysis out to a level of logical representation, which will allow them to be manipulated. Logical analysis produces the ultimate result of the systems analysis process: the decomposition of the functions of the system into their logical constituents and the production of a logical model of the processes and data flows (Curtis et al., 2000).

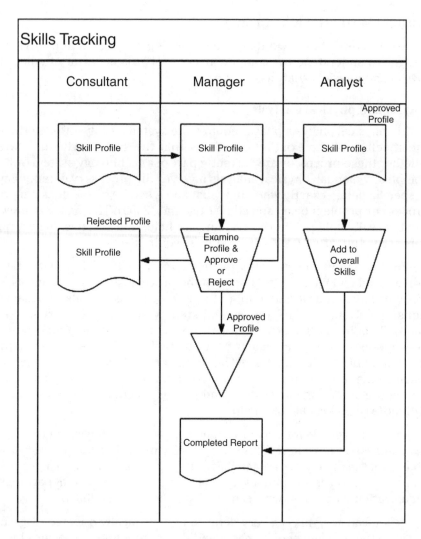

Exhibit 12-7. Task Analysis Flowchart

As the systems analyst and end user work through the flowcharts produced from the physical analysis and the preliminary logical model based upon it, the goal should be to jointly produce a detailed written description of all activities within the end user's purview that fall within the scope of the system (Bloor and Butler, 1989). The systems analyst and the end user must agree that this list is complete and precise. The entries in the list should be mutually exclusive and the list must be comprehensively exhaustive. Combined with the manual system flowcharts and logical diagrams, this list will serve as basic system requirements. Ultimately a detailed system requirements specification will be created (see Appendix G). With these documents in hand, the design phase can begin.

The analysis phase was broken down into two components: physical analysis and logical analysis. The design phase is also broken down into two components, although in the design phase logical design precedes physical design.

Logical Design

The logical analysis and logical design phases are very similar and over-lapping. Martin Butler and Robin Bloor stress that, in the logical phase, we create a model of the application area that matches the events occurring within the intended system. As these events are identified, each must be examined to determine specific criteria for it (Bloor and Butler, 1989):

- What initiates the event?
- What is changed by the event?
- What subsequent events are triggered by the event?
- What error conditions can arise?

These descriptions are crucial inputs for the physical design phase because they will allow us to derive the required objects and methods. It is this process that is likely the most important aspect of systems design; all of the blueprints for future code are based upon this logical model.

The tools of the logical paradigm are somewhat different from those of physical analysis discussed previously. Physical analysis tools, such as manual system flowcharts, are very concerned with the specific steps and decision points inherent in moving through the system. The logical analy-sis and design tools are more focused on definition of individual compo-nents of the system and the ways these components interact. The tools of choice for the logical phase of the systems development process are the data-flow diagram (DFD) and the entity-relationship diagram when using the traditional, structured paradigm.

At this stage of the process, with the logical design of the system com-plete, all that remains to complete the design is to define the physical design of the software.

Physical Design

The physical design is the blueprint for actual development of the soft-ware and deployment of the system. The physical phase is concerned with matching the logical model to the hardware and software at our disposal. Thus, we are transforming a logical model into a workable model that can be implemented (Bloor and Butler, 1989). Unlike the logical phases that immediately precede this work, the physical design phase is focused on specific implementation of the system. The logical design was built on the requirements defined during the physical and logical analysis phases. This fact allows the designer to build a physical design that implements the logical design without worrying about meeting the functional requirements of the end users; if the logical design is implemented, these requirements will be fulfilled.

The physical design phase is also where some specific implementation decisions must be made. Many, if not most, automated systems today use third-party software for pieces of the solution. Database software, Java application server software, and object messaging software are some examples of the kinds of third-party components that are often required. The logical design need not be concerned with the specific vendor choice, only with a requirement for one, because the logical design is intended to be abstracted away from the specific details of the implementation. The physical design, however, must answer these questions (Curtis et al., 2000). This fact illustrates the true distinction between the logical and physical design phases: the logical design is focused on what the system will do and the physical design is focused on how the system will do it.

THE SYSTEMS SPECIFICATION

The detailed design that has been achieved at this point in the process results in a systems specification. No agreed-on standard format for this specification exists and some insist that writing a design spec is more of an art form than a scientific process. Most IT professionals have sought a "cookie-cutter" explanation of how to write a good design spec, but one simply does not exist. Curtis et al. (2000) give a good basic outline of what a design specification should include:

- An executive summary in order to provide a quick summary of the major points in the specification
- A description of the proposed system and its objectives (may also include flow block diagrams and data flow diagrams may be used)
- A description of all programs to include module specifications and structure charts, together with test data
- A description of all input to include specimen source documents, screen layouts, menu structures, and control procedures
- A description of all output to include specimen output reports and contents of listings.
- A description of all data storage to include specification of file and database structure
- A detailed specification of controls operating over procedures within the system
- A specification of all hardware requirements and performance characteristics to be satisfied

- A specification of clerical procedures and responsibilities surrounding the system
- A detailed schedule for the implementation of the system
- Cost estimates and constraints

Appleton (1997) states that the design specification should meet the following criteria:

- It should adequately serve as training material for new project members so that they are able to understand what is said in design meetings.
- It should serve as "objective evidence" that the designers are following through on their commitment to implement the functionality described in the requirements spec.
- It needs to be as detailed as possible, while at the same time not imposing too much of a burden on the designers.

A SYSTEM SPEC WALKTHROUGH

Appendix J is a complete SDS for a working student-created system:

- Section 1 provides an overview of the system, its mission and goals, and any other supporting documentation deemed necessary by the support team. Much of this can be copied from the SRS (Appendix G), project plan (Appendix F), and feasibility study (Appendix C).
- Section 2 provides a list of design considerations that includes: assumptions, dependencies, frequency of use, database requirements, memory, and hardware and software constraints, as well as a description of the system environment — i.e., user interfaces, software interfaces, and communications interfaces. Section 2 also discusses policies and procedures, design methodology, and system risks.
- Section 3 specifies the architecture of the system. (Appendix I)
- Section 4 provides a high-level design spec of the system. A detailed set of DFDs can be found in this section.
- Section 5, the low-level design, provides a complete set of PSPECs as well as a data dictionary (Appendix K).
- Section 6 is reserved for a list of business-use cases as well as a series of screen shots showing the design of the user interface. (Appendix E).

CONCLUSION

Davis (2002) makes an important point when he states that without a complete, unambiguous design specification document, one could be setting oneself up for "costly" rewrites. Therefore it is important to recognize that the systems specification is used as (Curtis et al., 2000):

- The exit criterion from the stage of detailed design prior to the stage of implementation

- A source documentation from which programs are written and hardware "tenders" are brought about
- A historical reference of the system for future users and developers
- A comparative document during the assessment phase once the system is being used

An analyst who refers to the basic outline of design specification that considers everything from goals and objectives, to subsystems description, to potential project issues, should be able to develop a spec document that is understood by developers and at least somewhat by customers. These specifications should also help in avoiding errors and expensive rewrites.

A functional design specification is like a pyramid. The top reflects a broad overview that describes the wide spectrum of the system and its components. At each level below the overview, one has an overview of each of the primary components and as much detail as one's developers require (Davis, 2002).

References

Bloor, R. and Butler, M. (1989a). Object orientation…let's get physical, *DEC User*, December, 42.

Curtis, G., Hoffer, J.A., George, J.F., and Valacich, J. (2000). *Introduction to Business Systems Analysis*, Pearson Custom Publishing, Boston.

Davis, J. (2002). Design specifications: how much detail is enough? Available: http://builder.com.com/article.jhtml?id = r00120020206jed03.htm&src = search:.

Harrington, J.L. (1998). *Relational Database Design Clearly Explained*, Morgan Kaufmann, San Diego.

Kendall, K.E. and Kendall, J.E. (2002). *Systems Analysis and Design*, Prentice Hall, New York.

Chapter 13
Object-Oriented Design

Current code is a liability, not an asset. The challenge is to develop new code that is truly an asset. This challenge was issued by Vaughan Merlyn, one of the luminaries of our industry. It is one that bottom-line-conscious software engineering managers are now taking seriously. To meet this challenge, developers will need to do more than just tweak some code and liven up user interfaces. They will need to dramatically alter the way in which they code.

WHAT IS OO?

Object orientation (OO), which views the abstractions manipulated by computer software as counterparts to real-world objects, has promised developers a brave new world. Object-oriented development emerged as the dominant software development methodology of the 1990s. Not surprisingly, many organizations are jumping on the OO bandwagon.

The concept of an object is the fundamental building block on which the object-oriented paradigm rests. Four pivotal concepts are behind object orientation: encapsulation, message passing, dynamic binding, and inheritance. To the extent that a tool or language incorporates these concepts, it becomes qualified as an object-oriented tool kit.

We can explain these concepts using a simple letter as an analogy. Suppose a user wrote an e-mail letter to a colleague in another department. The letter is an object that has many properties in common with other letters: it contains information and has associated procedures that allow the user to manipulate it (read, write, and send). These properties, when grouped together, constitute the concept of the letter object. This process of combining data and functions all in one object is encapsulation.

Now suppose the e-mail system only allows users to write letters in English, but the company just hired an employee who speaks only Japanese. The company now needs the facility to create and manipulate Japanese letters. This is done by putting letter objects in discrete categories, referred to as classes.

A class is a collection of objects that share the same functionality and characteristics (procedures and data). In this example, two classes are created: an English letter class and a Japanese letter class. Both classes have many functions and characteristics in common. By identifying those things held in common we can create a super or parent class. Thus, the English letter and the Japanese letter become subclasses with each pinpointing how it differs from its parent and siblings.

The English and Japanese letter subclasses inherit the functionality of "reading, writing, and sending" from the parent object. However, the Japanese subclass is different in that it has the extra characteristic of translating text into the Japanese language, and the English subclass is different in that it translates into English. This is the meat behind the OO concept of inheritance.

The letter object permits the user to request certain tasks or services, such as "read a letter," "write a letter," or "send a letter." This is commonly called "sending a message to an object" — or to use OO parlance, message passing.

Sending a message is not quite the same as issuing a function call, a process familiar to most developers. Different objects can respond to the same message in different ways. For example, as just discussed, the "read" message is handled one way by the English object and another way by the Japanese object. In fact, the OO term "polymorphism" is used to describe the ability to send general-purpose messages to objects that will then handle them appropriately. The objects handle the specific details.

In sending these messages, the user never needs to specify the type of object with which he or she is dealing. OO systems utilize what is known as dynamic binding to determine the object type at run time when the code is executed.

The benefits of OO can be summed up as: quality, productivity, predictability, and control of complexity.

OO FROM THE BOTTOM UP

If we build object-oriented systems, we need tools that support the building of these applications. Developers building today's applications are essentially using the traditional, structured process methodologies developed by experts like Ed Yourdon, Tom DeMarco, and Chris Gane and Trish Sarson, as well as the data modeling methodology pioneered by Peter Chen.

Currently, information engineering techniques pivot around data and its relationships as documented in data-flow diagrams (Exhibit 13-1) and entity-relationship diagrams (Exhibit 13-2). Structured analysis is not based on objects, however.

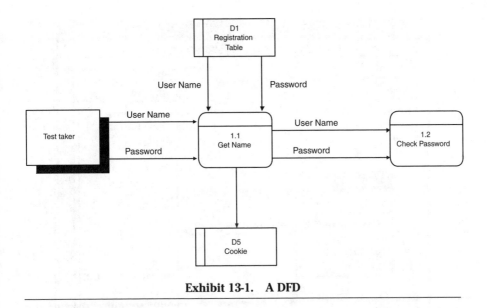

Exhibit 13-1. A DFD

Interestingly, not everything using objects is object oriented. Professor Paul Wegner of Brown University has defined three levels of object orientation for this purpose. The first level is object based. Object-based languages, tools, and methodologies support the concept of the object and use of messages to communicate between objects. The second level is what is known as class based, which supports the concepts of objects, messaging, and classes. The third level is object oriented, which supports the definition that this chapter has already supplied.

There are three levels of object orientation utilized in systems development. Object-oriented analysis (OOA) coincides with traditional analysis but utilizes OO techniques. Object-oriented design (OOD) is the design phase of the OO methodology and OOP (object-oriented programming) is the programming phase. The reader is urged to review the definitions at the end of this chapter for a better feel for the vocabulary of this methodology.

OO seems to have penetrated the organization in a bottom–up manner. Though the benefits of OO have been touted for at least a decade, it was only when OO languages became widely available that these methods began to be widely adopted. A big part of this can be attributed to the introduction of the Internet and Java programming language, which is OO. The introduction of "visual" program development environments for C++ (Exhibit 13-3) and Visual Basic.Net was also a contributing factor.

Classes are actually the building block of OO systems. Classes are built to be reusable and are often thought of as "black boxes." The programmer

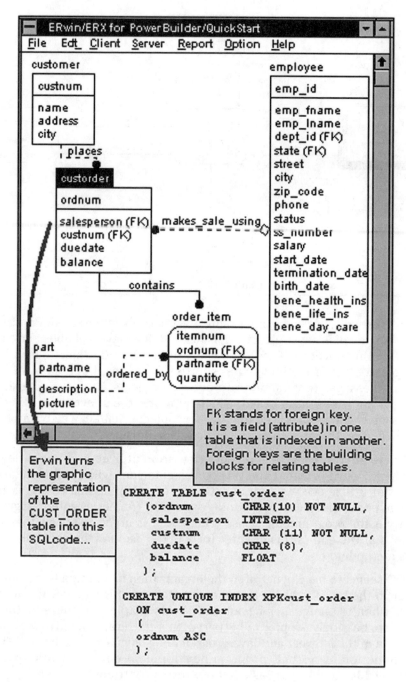

Exhibit 13-2. An ERD

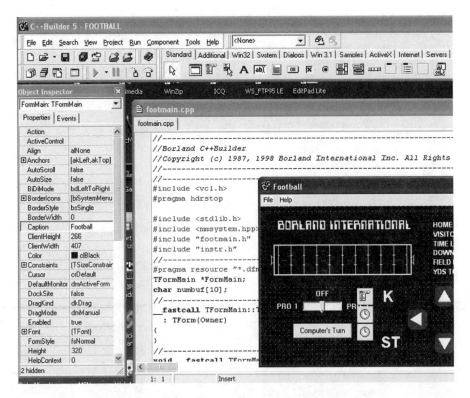

Exhibit 13-3.   The Borland Visual C++ Environment

should have only the details he or she needs to get the class to work. Classes can be stored in a class library. If enough classes are available to the programmer, the task of programming becomes less burdensome and the code is of a much higher quality because classes and objects available in a class library have been thoroughly tested.

The best way to explain the inner workings of classes is to show you a very simple program. In the C++ program displayed in Exhibit 13-4, we create a class named DayOfYear. Class DayOfYear encapsulates data (the integers month and day) and function (the function called output). If you read through the program (//denotes comments), you will immediately see the flexibility and power of classes and objects. As you can see, classes are the heart of an OO system. It makes sense, then, that OOA and OOD revolve around identification and specification of classes.

OOAD METHODOLOGIES

Object-oriented analysis and design (OOAD) benefits from a variety of competing but similar methodologies. The major OO methodologies are described by Gora (1996):

Exhibit 13-4.   Creating Class DayOfYear

```
//Program to demonstrate a very simple example of a class.
#include <iostream.h>
//This is where we define our class. We will call it DayOfYear
//It is a public class. This means that there are no
//restrictions on use. There are also private classes.

//The class DayOfYear consists of two pieces of data: month
and//day and one function named output ()
class DayOfYear
{
public:
    void output();
    int month;
    int day;
};//Notice the semicolon
//All classes are defined before main.
int main()
{
// We define variables of type char, integer and float (and
// others). A class is a kind of type. Below we are defining two
// classes of type DayOfYear. One is called today and the other
// is called birthday. Both instances of the class DayOfYear have
// a variable named month, another called day and a function
// called output()
    DayOfYear today, birthday;
    int temp;//to keep out window open
    cout << "Enter today's date:\n";
    cout << "Enter month as a number: ";
// Since both objects (today and birthday) use the variable month
// we have to have some way of distinguishing one from the other.
// We'll use the object as the distinguishing factor. The period
// in this case is called the dot operator. today.month is
// different from birthday.month

    cin >> today.month;
    cout << "Enter the day of the month: ";
    cin >> today.day;
    cout << "Enter your birthday:\n";
    cout << "Enter month as a number: ";
    cin >> birthday.month;
    cout << "Enter the day of the month: ";
    cin >> birthday.day;
```

(continued)

Exhibit 13-4. (continued)   Creating Class DayOfYear

```
// Now we will call the function called output for the two
// objects: once for today and once for birthday.
// Notice — because we see nothing between the parentheses — that
// no arguments are passed to the output function
    cout << "Today's date is ";
    today.output();
    cout << "Your birthday is ";
    birthday.output();
// The && means AND
    if (today.month = = birthday.month
      && today.day = = birthday.day)
      cout << "Happy Birthday!\n";
    else
      cout << "Happy Unbirthday!\n";
    cin >> temp;
    return 0;
}
// Here is the function output that was defined in the class
// DayOfYear. Notice the interesting way of starting this
// function. The :: is called a scope resolution operator
void DayOfYear::output()
{
    cout << "month = " << month
      << ," day = " << day << endl;
}
```

Booch

Grady Booch's approach to OOAD (*Object-Oriented Design with Applications*, Benjamin/Cummings, 1994) is one of the most popular and is supported by a variety of reasonably priced tools ranging from Visio to Rational Rose.

Coad and Yourdon

Coad and Yourdon published two of the first books on OOAD (*Object-Oriented Analysis* and *Object-Oriented Design*, Prentice-Hall, New York, 1990 and 1991, respectively). Their methodology focuses on analysis of business problems. Analysis proceeds in five stages, called SOSAS:

- *Subjects:* these are similar to the levels or layers in data-flow diagrams.
- *Objects:* object classes are specified in this stage.
- *Structures:* there are two types: classification structures and composition structures. Classification structures correspond to the inheritance relationship between classes. Composition structures define the

other types of relationships between classes. Methodologies deal with these structures.

- *Attributes:* these are handled similarly to attributes in relational analysis.
- *Services:* what other methodologies call methods or operations is identified.

In design, these activities are refined into four components:

- *Problem domain component:* classes that deal with the problem domain; for example, customer classes and order classes
- *Human interaction component:* user-interface classes such as window classes
- *Task management component:* system-management classes such as error classes and security classes
- *Data management component:* database access method classes and the like

Jacobson: Objectory and OOSE

Jacobson's full OOAD methodology, Objectory, is proprietary. His object-oriented software engineering (OOSE) is a simplified version of Objectory (*Object-Oriented Systems Engineering*, Addison-Wesley, Reading, MA, 1992).

The major distinguishing feature in Jacobson is the use case. A use-case definition consists of a diagram and a description of the interaction between the actor and a system. An actor may be an end user or some other object in the system.

According to Jacobson, a use case is any description of a single way to use a system or application, or any class of top-level usage scenarios, that captures how actors use their black-box applications. A use case is any behaviorally related sequence of transactions that a single actor performs in a dialog with a system in order to provide some measurable value to the actor.

Use cases are used to document user requirements in terms of user dialogs with a system. They appear first in the requirements model and are then used to generate a domain object model with objects drawn from the entities of the business, as mentioned in the use cases. This is then converted into an analysis model by classifying the domain objects into three types: interface objects, entity objects, and control objects.

LBMS SEOO

Systems engineering OO (SEOO) is a proprietary methodology and tool kit from the U.K.-based company LBMS. The four major components of the SEOO methodology are:

- Work-breakdown structures and techniques
- An object modeling methodology
- GUI design techniques
- Relational database linkages to provide ER modeling and 4GL-specific features

Rumbaugh OMT

James Rumbaugh's methodology is described in his book *Object-Oriented Modeling and Design* (Prentice-Hall, New York, 1991). Rumbaugh starts by assuming that a requirements specification exists. Analysis consists of building three separate models:

- The object model (OM): definition of classes, together with attributes and methods; the notation is similar to that of ER modeling with methods (operations) added
- The dynamic model (DM): state transition diagrams (STDs) for each class, as well as global event-flow diagrams
- The functional model (FM): diagrams very similar to data-flow diagrams

Shlaer and Mellor

Shlaer and Mellor's work is one of the earliest examples of OO methodology. (See Shlaer and Mellor's books, *Object-Oriented Systems Analysis: Modeling the World in Data* and *Object Lifecycles: Modeling the World in States*, Prentice-Hall, New York, 1988 and 1992, respectively.)

The Shlaer and Mellor methodology starts with an information model that describes objects, attributes, and relationships. Next, a state model documents the states of objects and the transitions between them. Finally, a data-flow diagram shows the process model.

OOAD SIMPLIFIED

Organizations that have purchased an OO software tool generally adhere to the OOAD methodology that the tool encompasses (i.e., Objectory, LBMS, etc.). Other organizations, however, are free to mix and match the "best of breed" components of a wide variety of OOAD methodologies. This section explains one such simplified approach.

1. Create the system boundary diagram. The first step in the analysis and design is the creation of a system boundary diagram. This diagrams the domain model and its relationship with external systems or users, as shown in Exhibit 13-5. The model structure diagram depicts the relationship of the domain objects.

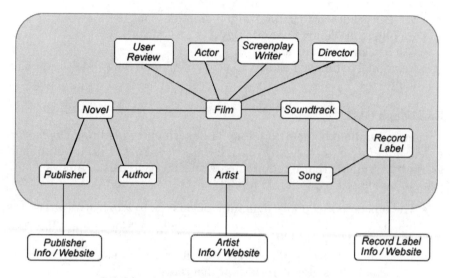

Exhibit 13-5. The System Boundary Diagram

2. Develop an actor list of external systems and users (Exhibit 13-6). The actor list shows each actor and his or her role in the domain model. Gather information about these actors.

3. Create use cases and scenarios. Use cases are a user-centered analysis technique to capture requirements from a user's point of view; they describe the possible sequences of interactions among the systems with one or more actors. Use cases illustrate high-level abstract functions without writing code. Scenarios capture the exceptions, nonstandard responses, and problems from the normal use case flow. Exhibit 13-7 shows a sample use case diagram and Appendix E shows a set of use case diagrams with associated scenarios.

4. Generate CRC cards, which are note cards that contain the domain model's classes, their responsibilities, and collaborators (Exhibit 13-8). The nouns used in the uses cases become the potential classes in the CRC cards. The verbs are the class's responsibilities; the collaborators help the classes do their jobs.

5. Draw a collaboration graph depicting the collaborations (i.e., relationships between objects) uncovered during the CRC process (Exhibit 13-9) and event traces to represent how events cause flow from one object to another (Exhibit 13-10).

6. Create a system class diagram from the information derived in the preceding exercises. Exhibit 13-11 shows a class diagram depicted in terms of a system's subsystems. In the case of an OO system we use the term package, which is a collection of classes. Subsequent diagrams will depict each class as shown in this highest level class diagram (Exhibit 13-12).

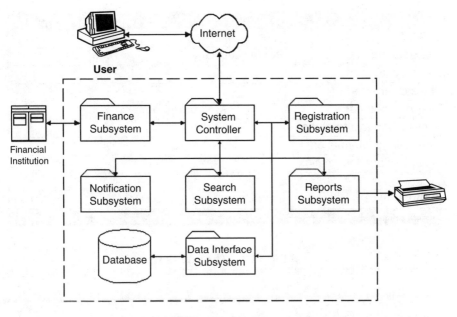

Exhibit 13-6. External and Internal Actors

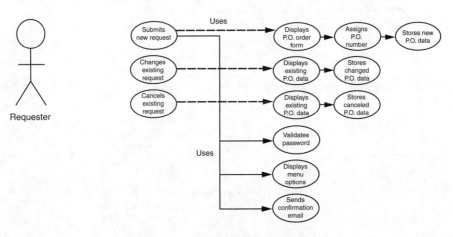

Exhibit 13-7. A Sample Use Case Diagram

7. A data dictionary (Exhibit 13-13) and set of process specifications (Exhibit 13-14) can then be created for all data and processes identified along with all screen designs.

Using this OO methodology is an iterative process; all of the steps described and illustrated above are constantly changing and evolving.

CLS025	
Class Name:	ResourceUsage
Class Type:	
Class Characteristics:	
Responsibilities:	Collaborations:
Receive Usage Information	Order
Store Usage Information	Resource
Provide Usage Information	Service Schedule
Authors:	Jane Doe

Exhibit 13-8. The CRC Card

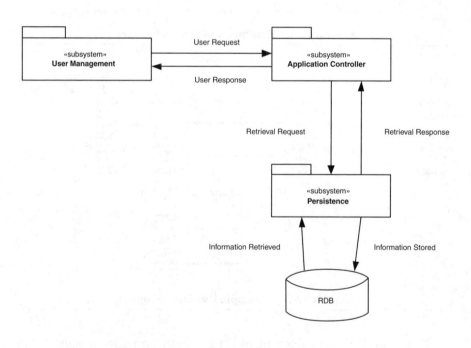

Exhibit 13-9.   The Collaboration Graph

Event Trace Diagram

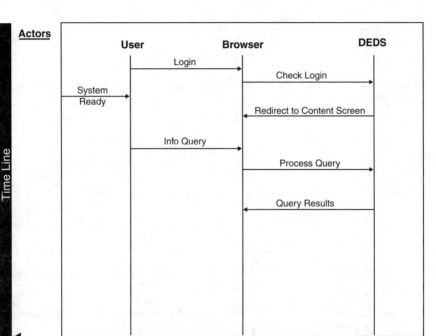

Exhibit 13-10. An Event Trace

Definitions:

- *Class* — a template comprising a definition of behavior and supporting information; each instance created from the class has its own copy of the information and utilizes a single copy of the methods that implement the class' behavior.
- *Class hierarchy* — a tree-structured aggregation of class definitions in which vertical link establishes a superclass-subclass relationship between a pair of classes; the subclass is a specialization of the superclass.
- *Information hiding* — a technique by which the structure and precise usage of information (data) are concealed. The information is private to its own objects and accessible to all other objects only via message sends to the owner; this is the basis of encapsulation.
- *Instance* — a particular occurrence of an object defined by a class. All instances of a class share the behavior implemented and inherited by the class; each instance has its own private set of the instance variables implemented and inherited by the class.

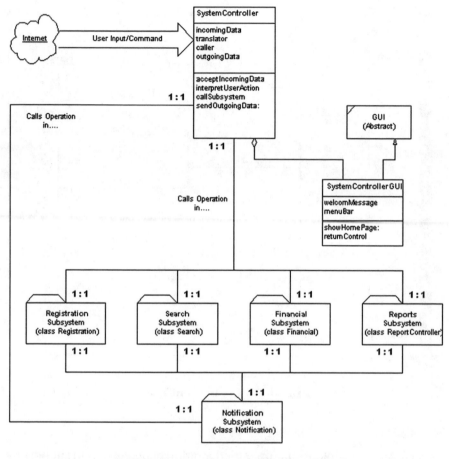

Exhibit 13-11. A System Class Diagram

- *Instantiation* — the act of creating an instance of a class.
- *Method* — a procedure whose code implements the behavior invoked by a message.
- *Object* — an entity capable of exhibiting a defined set of behaviors and interacting with other objects.
- *Object-oriented technology* — a collection of languages, tools, environments, and methodologies aimed at supporting development of software application centered around interrelated, interacting objects.
- *Reuse and reusability* — an approach to software engineering that emphasizes reusing software assets, including designs and code; and building software assets likely to be reusable in future applications.

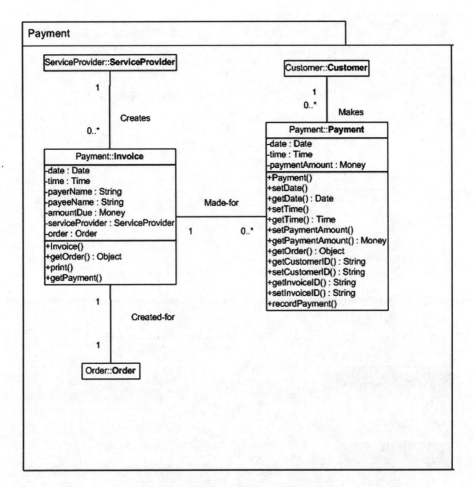

Exhibit 13-12.   A Class Diagram

TBL_USER	THIS TABLE CONTAINS INFORMATION ABOUT USERS			
COLUMN NAME	TYPE	LEN	DESCRIPTION	REQ
OUID_USER_ID	NUMBER	8	USER ID	Y
LOGON_ID	VARCHAR2	8	USER LOGIN ID	Y
PASSWORD	VARCHAR2	22	USER PASSWORD – HASHED	Y
FORGOT_PASSWORD_ QUESTION	VARCHAR2	50	FORGOT PASSWORD QUESTION	N
FORGOT_PASSWORD_ ANSWER	VARCHAR2	20	FORGOT PASSWORD ANSWER	N
FIRST_NAME	VARCHAR2	20	FIRST NAME	Y
LAST_NAME	VARCHAR2	20	LAST NAME	Y
TITLE	VARCHAR2	3	TITLE – MR, MS, MRS	Y
ADDR1	VARCHAR2	30	FIRST ADDRESS LINE	Y
ADDR2	VARCHAR2	30	SECOND ADDRESS LINE	N
CITY	VARCHAR2	20	CITY	Y
STATE	VARCHAR2	2	STATE	Y
ZIP	NUMBER	5	ZIP CODE	Y
ZIP_4	NUMBER	4	4 DIGIT ZIP QUALIFIER	N
HOME_PHONE	VARCHAR2	10	HOME PHONE NUMBER	Y
WORK_PHONE	VARCHAR2	10	WORK PHONE NUMBER	Y
OTHER_PHONE	VARCHAR2	10	OTHER PHONE NUMBER	N
E_MAIL	VARCHAR2	30	E-MAIL ADDRESS	N
GENERAL_NOTES	VARCHAR2	1000	MISCELLANEOUS NOTES	N
SYSID_ROLE_ID	CHAR	1	USER ROLE – 1:ADMINISTRATOR, 2:MANAGER, 3:EMPLOYEE, 4:CUSTOMER	Y
ACTIVE	CHAR	1	ACTIVE OR NOT	Y
USER_CREATED	NUMBER	8	USER WHO CREATED THE RECORD	Y
DATE_CREATED	DATE		DATE RECORD CREATED	Y
USER_MODIFIED	NUMBER	8	USER WHO MODIFED THE RECORD	N
DATE_MODIFIED	DATE		DATE RECORD MODIFIED	N
TBL_ROLE	THIS TABLE CONTAINS INFORMATION ABOUT A USER'S ROLE (ADMIN, MANAGER, EMPLOYEE, CUSTOMER, ETC.)			
COLUMN NAME	TYPE	LEN	DESCRIPTION	REQ
SYSID_ROLE_ID	NUMBER	4	ROLE ID	Y
ROLE_NAME	VARCHAR2	30	NAME OF THE ROLE	Y
ROLE_DESC	VARCHAR2	30	DESCRIPTION OF THE ROLE	N
TBL_AUTH_RULE	THIS TABLE CONTAINS INFO ABOUT WHAT FUNCTIONALITY IS (ADD_INVENTORY_ITEM, SCHEDULE_SERVICE, ETC.)			
COLUMN NAME	TYPE	LEN	DESCRIPTION	REQ
SYSID_AUTH_RULE	NUMBER	4	AUTH RULE ID	Y

Exhibit 13-13.   A Data Dictionary Entry

Exhibit 13-14.   A Process Specification

```
PACKAGE DatabaseManager IS

PROC addAppObject(appObject:IN, statusBoolean:OUT);

PROC modifyAppObject(appObject:IN, statusBoolean:OUT);

PROC deleteAppObject(appObject:IN, statusBoolean:OUT);

PROC queryAppObject(appObject:IN, resultObject:OUT);

PROC loadDatabase(databaseFileName:IN, statusBoolean:OUT);

PROC saveDatabase(databaseFileName:IN, statusBoolean:OUT);

PROC convertAppToSQL(app(bject:IN, sqlObject:OUT);

PROC convertSQLToApp(sqlObject:IN, appObject:OUT);

PROC issueDBCommand(sqlCommand:IN, statusBoolean:OUT);

PROC getDatabaseResult(resultObject:OUT);

////////////////////////////////////////////////////////////
//

//addAppObject — Adds an application object to the database

//returns BOOLEAN

//TRUE — success

//FALSE — error

////////////////////////////////////////////////////////////
//

PROC addAppObject(appObject:IN, statusBoolean:OUT)

TYPE returnCode IS INTEGER;

TYPE sqlCommand IS STRING;

sqlCommand = converTAppToSQL(appObject)

If sqlCommand ! = "" convert sqlCommand to ADD returned
sqlCommand;

returnCode = issueDBCommand(sqlCommand);

else
```

References

Gora, M. (1996). Object-oriented analysis and design, DBMS Online. http://www.dbms-mag.com/9606d15.html.

Chapter 14
User Interface Design

Like many aspects of software engineering, in order to be effective, user interface design needs to be analyzed, planned, and implemented in a detailed and organized manner. With the demand for enhanced functionality and implementation of increasingly complex systems, the pressure to produce user interfaces that satisfy all user requirements becomes a great challenge. Without guiding principles and a fundamental plan of attack, developers are doomed to failure. Fortunately, as computer systems have grown more complex, facilities for creating user interfaces quickly and more efficiently have also come on stream. However, tools alone do not make for a good user interface design.

User interfaces have matured rapidly over the last decade. The increasing speed and power of the PC and the growth of the Internet have fueled the development of larger and more complex applications requiring easier and more intuitive user interfaces. As application developers deliver more sophisticated and robust applications, users expect and demand better and more intuitive user interfaces to accompany those applications. Competition among application developers is fierce and a product's user interface plays a key role in adoption and acceptance by its user community.

USER INTERFACE (UI) DESIGN PRINCIPLES

No discussion of user interface design would be complete without reference to the underlying principles that guide good user interface design. Volumes have been written on the subject. The following are pointers to a few of the lists of user interface design principles from various sources:

- *Design Basics*, from the Internet, http://www-3.ibm.com/ibm/easy/eou_ext.nsf/Publish/6 (IBM).
- *Practical Real World Design, First Principles*, from the Internet, http://www.asktog.com/basics/firstPrinciples.html (Tognazzini,).
- *Principles of Good GUI Design*, from the Internet, http://axp16.ii.e.,org.mx/Monitor/v01n03/ar_ihc2.htm (Hobart,).

The perspectives are somewhat different, but all espouse the same basic principles, reiterated here for emphasis:

- *Put the user in control.* The user is obviously the most important player in this game and should be able to customize the interface to suit his or her preferences or needs. Whenever possible, account for the user's skill level; categories such as novice, occasional user, and frequent user make a good starting point. One example of this is a Macintosh word processing product. A set of five options enables the user to set the desired level of experience ranging from "novice" to "power user." Choosing a level results in filtering menus for only those options required by a user of the selected experience. A user gaining more experience at a specific level can move to the next level when ready.

- *Be direct.* The user should be allowed to work with the information presented by the application directly. When a user performs an action, the result of the action should be immediately apparent.
- *Use appropriate metaphors.* Whenever possible use metaphors that are familiar to the user. Metaphors help to make the user more comfortable when using the software and provides for a more intuitive interface. For example, a checkbook is a suitable metaphor for an application that manages a user's bank account.
- *Make the interface consistent.* Consistency in design makes it easier for the user to apply skills learned on one task to another task. Users should not need to spend time trying to remember differences in behavior among objects. Many Windows applications, for example, have the same basic pattern for menus; File and Edit are always the first two menus on the left and Help is typically the last menu on the right, as indicated in Exhibit 14-1.

Regular users of Windows applications expect these menus in this order; therefore, it does not make sense to break this paradigm.

- *Provide shortcuts.* For novice users, shortcuts may not be all that important, but as the user gains experience with the interface, inevitably he will look for faster and more efficient ways of getting the job done.

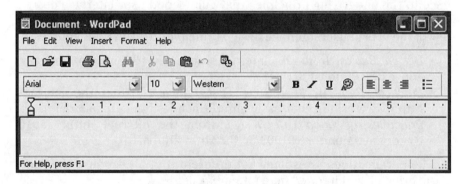

Exhibit 14-1.   Menu Order Consistency

Shortcuts play a key role here and are greatly appreciated by power users. I know one technical writer who works in Microsoft Word with the toolbar and menu bar hidden, doing all formatting work with only shortcuts. Quite amazing!

- *Be forgiving.* The user should be allowed to change his mind and reverse a previously performed action. If circumstances make it impossible to reverse the result of an action, provide an indication to the user up front, indicating that the action about to take place cannot be reversed. It is also important to make error recovery as easy as possible.
- *Provide feedback.* It is important that the user know what task is being performed. We all know how frustrating it can be when a program freezes the system while it is performing a task with no visual indication that the task is being performed or completed. Visual queues should be used to provide user interaction and feedback appropriate to the task performed.
- *Make the interface aesthetically pleasing.* An important aspect of the user interface is its visual appearance. Visual elements on the screen compete for the user's attention. It is not a simple task to get the right balance so that the user's attention is focused on the right elements at the right time. Often it is necessary to acquire the services of a graphics designer to get the right result. A professionally designed, aesthetically pleasing application is more likely to gain acceptance among users than one that lacks this characteristic.
- *Be as simple as possible.* This may sound simple, but from the developer's perspective simplifying the user interface typically involves quite a bit of work. In a complex application or product, try to develop a user interface that exposes only information necessary for the user to get the task done.
- *Provide help.* A help system is vital. Many different types of help systems are available. Embedded help is totally integrated within the application; it provides help instructions for every screen that is part of the user interface. Online help, typically accessible by choosing an item from the help menu, is a set of topics about the product; a table of contents, index, and search mechanism are typically provided so that the user can browse or search for a topic of interest. Context-sensitive help provides information about the current context; for example, when a specific dialog is displayed, the user can press F1 to get information about that dialog. Tooltip help displays hints; for example, when the cursor hovers over a toolbar button, help text is displayed as shown in Exhibit 14-2.

Two industry standards that provide excellent information on user interface design principles are The Windows Interface Guidelines for Software Design and Macintosh Human Interface Guidelines. Two websites that

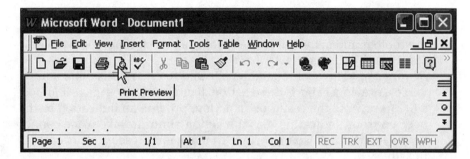

Exhibit 14-2.   Tooltip Help

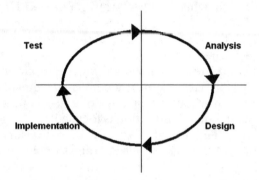

Exhibit 14-3.   Phases of User Interface Design

provide some excellent examples of good and bad user interface design are the Interface Hall of Fame, http://www.iarchitect.com/mfame.htm and the Interface Hall of Shame, http://www.iarchitect.com/mshame.htm. See the reference list at the end of this chapter for more details about these sources.

THE UI DESIGN PROCESS

Principles are good, but how and when do we apply them? One of the most popular user interface design methodologies is one that mimics the overall software development process. This process consists of four phases; each phase is repeated during each iteration of the cycle. A summary of the design process is shown graphically in Exhibit 14-3 and each of its phases is described briefly below:

- *Analysis.* This phase involves collection of information about the user and the tasks that he or she will want to perform using the application. An excellent, highly rated book on this subject is *User and Task Analysis for Interface Design* (Hackos and Redish, 1998). This book clearly separates analysis from design and provides guidelines and techniques for eliciting task information from prospective users.

- *Design.* Once the analysis has been completed and all tasks have been identified, the process of identifying the required objects and the actions to be performed can begin. User scenarios play a key role in this phase. From the scenario narrative, the designer can extract the objects (typically nouns) and the actions (typically verbs) to build a list of required elements. One book that addresses many of the issues that the developer faces during the design phase is *User Interface Design for Programmers* (Spolsky, 2000).
- *Implementation.* In the implementation phase, a prototype is produced. This is typically achieved using one of the many fourth-generation languages or programming development environments (Visual Basic, Visual C++, Visual J++, Java, etc.) that allow the rapid development of user interfaces using predefined libraries of components such as Windows, Menus, Buttons, Drop-Down list controls, Tree controls, etc.
- *Test.* When the prototype is complete, the developer can take the software to the customer for user interface evaluation. Users can test drive the software and make suggestions for improvements, which become part of the analysis phase. Then the cycle can begin again to refine the process further. Pamela Savage compares three different evaluation techniques: 1) expert reviews, 2) user reviews, and 3) interactive usability testing, with the conclusion that all three play a role in the evaluation process.

One aspect of good user interface design not immediately apparent from the four phases of the design cycle described here is that the design involves input from many different disciplines in addition to software development. These disciplines include visual designers, writers, human factors experts, and, of course, the user. A well-balanced team of people providing input from different perspectives is critical to the success of the user interface.

DESIGNING EFFECTIVE INPUT AND OUTPUT

Some systems analysts believe that designing input and output is the most important task in designing a system because it is the part the end user actually sees. Even though some people might disagree with this point of view, poorly designed input and output may cause an otherwise well-designed and solidly implemented system to fail. When systems analysts design input and output, there are three aspects of concern: (1) the input and output data (data flow) between software components, (2) the design of input and output between the software and other nonhuman producers and consumers of information, (3) the interaction between the user and the computer.

Designing Input

A key factor for developing the design input is the customer's requirements. This includes, but is not limited to: end-user expectations, patterns of end-user usage, security, and performance. The customer should not be the only consideration, however. All factors relevant to the design of the system should be considered, including management requirements, interface requirements, and other related processing requirements.

A variety of media and methods is used to capture and input data so that it can be used properly, including: (1) paper forms combined with data-entry screens, (2) electronic forms, and (3) direct entry devices.

Even though the usage of computers is very common, it would be surprising to find a system that did not have at least one input or output paper form. Paper forms carry data physically. In every business or organization there are manual transactions that might require the use of manual forms, such as order forms, sales transactions, and surveys. The data captured on these forms, therefore, must be entered into the system for processing. Guidelines for designing a paper form include:

- *Select proper paper.* Papers of different colors, grades, and weight might be used to print a form. When we select a paper for our form, we need to consider some factors, for example: how long the company will keep it, how to fill in the form (handwritten or printed), how it will be handled (gently, roughly), and if the paper is easy and convenient to use.
- *The size of paper should be appropriate.* The most popular size is 8.5 by 11 inches. If you require a smaller form, try to use half of this standard size: 8.5 by 5.5. For card forms, the standards start with 8 by 10 inches. It is best not to use nonstandard sizes because those sizes often have problems in handling and filing and usually increase the cost of devices and papers.
- *Forms should be easy to fill out.* To make forms easy to fill out, the following techniques are used: (1) Put simple instructions or examples on the form to assist users. (2) Form flow should be designed to follow a logical sequence (left to right, top to bottom) (See Exhibit 14-4). (3) Group-related data should be in the same section. (4) Each section and field should have a caption that tells the user what to put there. (5) Use proper space to make the form clearer. (6) Using lines and boxes can also help. (7) Have alternative selections capability (i.e., use of a check box).
- *Design to meet the purpose of a form.* A systems analyst should design different forms to better reflect different process requirements even if several forms are similar to each other.
- *Make the form attractive.* An attractive form can encourage the user to complete it. A form should be designed to look neat and the input

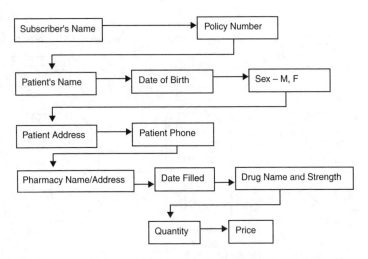

Exhibit 14-4. The Logical Flow of a Prescription Drug Claim Form

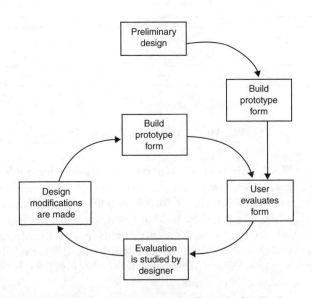

Exhibit 14-5. The Design of a Form Is Cyclical.

fields should be logically ordered. Aesthetic forms or usage of different fonts within the same form can help make it attractive.

- *Design evaluation.* After a form prototype has been created, we must give it to the user and check to see if it meets the user's requirements. The user can provide some suggestions and the designer can make modifications according to the suggestions. The evaluation cycle (see Exhibit 14-5) repeats until users are satisfied with the form.

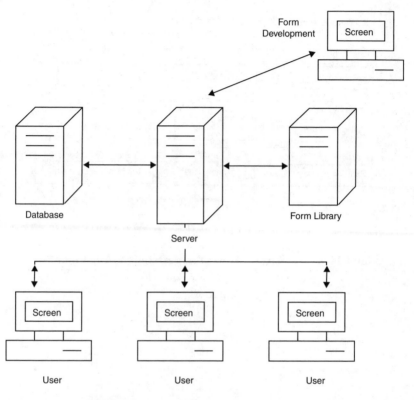

Exhibit 14-6. An Electronic Forms System

Designing Electronic Forms. When we talk about electronic forms systems (see Exhibit 14-6), we turn our attention from paper to screens. Designers must design electronic forms to reflect the organization of the data source. When it is used by people (customer, clerk, etc.), it must be designed with all the captions, data entry fields, and instructions arranged in a logical manner that can help users completing the forms. The designing guideline for the paper form can also apply to screen form because both have the same components.

Electronic forms have many advantages over paper that make use of this automated capability much more efficient: (1) the ability to process calculations; (2) the ability to retrieve data and populate the electronic form to reduce the number of fields that the user must fill in; (3) ability to validate each field automatically; (4) the ability to coordinate processes between tasks; (5) the ability to provide immediate help.

In most situations, electronic forms can replace all paper forms and substantially reduce the cost of a system. Factors that affect the cost include: (1) printers might run out of paper, causing the system to pause; (2) electronic forms can prevent many data entry errors and the end user from using the wrong form; (3) electronic forms can be easily modified to meet new business requirements; (4) electronic form databases efficiently manage the many forms in use in an organization.

Direct Entry Devices. When using electronic forms, the keyboard is the most common input device. However, there are some instances where data is not input by a user or a keyboard is not practical. Other data entry devices include:

- Scanner or optical character reader (OCR)
- Point-of-sale (POS) device
- Automatic teller machines (ATMs)
- Mouse
- Voice recognition

Designing Output

Output can be produced in a variety of ways: printing, screen, audio, microform, CD ROM, or electronic output. Each technology has different speed and cost, and affects the end user differently. When we choose an output technology, the following should be considered: (1) the purpose of the output; (2) the person who needs the information; (3) the reason the output is needed; (4) the way the output will be used; (5) what specific information will be included; (6) how the output will be viewed, i.e., printed on paper, stored on secondary storage such as tape, CD, tape, etc., or viewed on the screen; (7) how often the output is to be updated; (8) any security issues.

USABILITY TESTING

A user interface design can benefit greatly from usability testing. Although this testing involves quite a lot of up-front investment, the results are worth the investment, especially for commercial applications that have potentially a wide audience. Usability testing involves observing users as they use the application to perform their required tasks. The tests are generally administered by human factors specialists and are usually performed in a special work area where the specialists are separated from the users by a one-way mirror that enables the specialists to observer users as the tasks are performed. Users typically describe what they want to do and how they are going about it using the software. The specialists study these patterns and use the data to improve the user interface. This technique is a very effective means of detecting misunderstood or misinterpreted areas of the user interface. These areas can be redesigned and the tests can be performed again to check for improvement.

SUMMARY

Providing a good user interface is a critical skill for application developers today. Good user interface design does not happen automatically despite the myriad of tools available to help developers create them.

A good portion of this chapter has been devoted to stressing the design principles; this is not an accident. The developer must learn and apply basic principles and follow the tried and true process that leads to quality user interface designs. The formula already exists; it merely needs to be applied. The developer must always keep the users' interests in mind, especially in cases of conflict between satisfying a user requirement and taking an easier implementation route. The user interface should strive to delight and help the user get the job done faster and more efficiently. Developers must gain as much experience as possible when working with and being exposed to good user interface designs.

The user interface is a key component when it comes to the acceptance of an application or product. It can mean the difference between adoption and obscurity.

References

Hackos, J. and Redish, J. (1998) *User and Task Analysis for Interface Design*, John Wiley & Sons, New York.

Hobart, J. Principles of good GUI design, from the Internet, http://axp16.ii.e.,org.mx/Monitor/v01n03/ar_ihc2.htm.

IBM. Design basics, from the Internet, http://www-3.ibm.com/ibm/easy/eou_ext.nsf/Publish/6.

Isys Information Architects. *Interface hall of fame*, from the Internet http://www.iarchitect.com/mfame.htm.

Isys Information Architects. *Interface hall of shame*, from the Internet http://www.iarchitect.com/mshame.htm.

Macintosh Human Interface Guidelines. (1993) Addison-Wesley, Reading, MA.

Savage, Pamela. AT&T Bell Laboratories, *User interface evaluation in an iterative design process*: a comparison of three techniques, from the internet, http://www.acm.org/sigchi/chi96/proceedings/shortpap/Savage/sp_txt.html.

Spolsky, J. (2000) *User interface design for programmers*, from the Internet, http://www.joelonsoftware.com/uibook/chapters/fog0000000065.html.

The Windows Interface Guidelines for Software Design. (1995) Microsoft Press, Redmond, WA.

Tognazzini, B. *Practical real world design, first principles*, from the Internet, http://www.asktog.com/basics/firstPrinciples.html.

Two additional general sources of information that are worth a mention even though they are not explicitly referenced in this chapter are:

Sumit, GUI design links, from the Internet, http://www.sum-it.nl/enguilin.html.

Wilson, C. User interface design bibliography, from the Internet, http://world.std.com/~uieweb/biblio.htm.

Other Sources:

Blum, B.I. (1992) *Software Engineering: a Holistic View,* Oxford University Press, Inc., New York.

Burch, J.G. (1992) *System Analysis, Design, and Implementation,* Boyd & Fraser Publishing Company, Boston.

Kendall, K.E. and Kendall, J.E. (2001) *System Analysis and Design,* 5th ed., Prentice Hall, Inc., Upper Saddle River, NJ.

Pressman, R.S. (2001) *Software Engineering: a Practitioner's Approach*, 5th ed., McGraw-Hill Companies, Inc., New York.

Shaw, M. and Garlan, D. (1996) *Software Architecture: Perspectives on an Emerging Discipline*, Prentice Hall, Inc., Upper Saddle River, NJ.

www.sxu.edu/~rogers/bu433/index.html: System design: input, output, user interface.

www.webster.edu/~crawfodj/2810/pdf/2810ch07.pdf, User interface, input, and output design.

Chapter 15
Software Re-Engineering

Organizations spend much money building software applications customized according to their business rules. In other words, software is the realization of business rules. When business rules change, software must also change. Software change is very important because organizations are now completely dependent upon their software and have invested millions of dollars in these systems. Therefore, organizations must invest in system change to maintain the value of these systems. Software re-engineering is a strategy for software change. It rebuilds existing legacy systems that have become expensive to maintain or architecturally obsolete.

WHAT IS SOFTWARE RE-ENGINEERING?

Software re-engineering is (usually) concerned with reimplementing legacy systems to make them more maintainable. Re-engineering may involve redocumenting the system, organizing and restructuring the system, translating the system to a more modern programming language, or modifying and updating the structure and values of the system's data. The functionality of the software is not changed and, normally, the system architecture also remains the same. Re-engineering improves the system structure, creates new system documentation, and makes it easier to understand.

WHY WE NEED SOFTWARE RE-ENGINEERING

Computer software is the product that software engineers design and build. Once software is put into use, new requirements emerge and existing requirements change as the business rules change. Parts of software may need to be modified to correct errors or improve its performance.

As time goes on, software gets old and frequently breaks down. As the software is modified, it becomes more and more complicated and difficult to maintain. The level of difficulty of maintainability is directly proportionate to the cost of maintaining the system.

We are consequently faced with a dilemma. If we continue to use the system and make changes as required, our costs will inevitably increase. If we

211

decide to replace the system with a new system, costs will be incurred and the new system might not be as good as the old system.

Software engineering techniques extend the lifetime of legacy systems and reduce the costs of keeping these systems in use. We can create a product with added functionality, better performance and reliability, and improved maintainability by means of rebuilding the legacy system. Re-engineering may involve some structural modifications but does not usually involve major architectural change.

SOFTWARE RE-ENGINEERING STRATEGIES

A major problem for organizations is implementing and managing change to their legacy systems so that these systems continue to support the organization's business operations. There are a number of different strategies for software change:

- Software maintenance
- Architectural transformation — e.g., migration to servers or to Intranets
- Software re-engineering

Software maintenance is the general process of changing a system after it has been delivered; this strategy does not normally involve major architectural changes to the system. The following are three types of software maintenance:

1. Maintenance to repair software faults:
   - Coding errors are very cheap to correct.
   - Design errors are more expensive because this may involve rewriting several program components.
   - Requirement errors are most expensive to repair due to the extensive system redesign that may be necessary.
2. Maintenance to adapt the software to a different operating environment
3. Maintenance to add to or modify the system's functionality
   - External and internal factors, such as changing markets, changing laws, management changes, and structural reorganization, mean that businesses undergo continual change. These changes generate new or modified software requirements, so all useful software systems inevitably change as the business changes.

Approximately 20 percent of all maintenance efforts are spent fixing mistakes. The remaining 80 percent is spent adapting existing systems to changes in their external environment, making enhancements requested by users, and re-engineering an application for future use (Pressman, 2001).

After software has been corrected, adapted, and enhanced many times, it usually becomes unstable. The more maintainence on the software, the more frequently unexpected and serious side effects may occur. Although the system still works, its maintenance costs increase and its value decreases.

THE PROCESS OF RE-ENGINEERING

The main activities in a typical re-engineering process are:

1. Source Code Translation

The simplest form of software re-engineering is program translation where source code in one programming language is automatically translated to source code in another language (i.e., COBOL to Java). The structure and organization of the program are unchanged but have higher quality than the original program. One reason for this is that the target language may be an updated version of the original language or may be a translation to a completely different language. Source-level translation may be necessary for the following reasons:

- Hardware platform update: the organization may wish to change its standard hardware platform, but compilers for the original language may not be available on the new hardware.
- Organizational policy changes: an organization may want to standardize on a particular language to minimize its support software costs. Maintaining many versions of old compilers can be very expensive.
- Lack of software support: the suppliers of the language compiler may have gone out of business or may discontinue support for their product.
- Developers want to make the system easier to understand, test, and maintain: Some legacy systems have solid program architecture; however, individual modules were coded in a way that makes them difficult to understand, test, and maintain. In this situation, the code can be restructured (Pressman, 2001).

2. Reverse Engineering

Reverse engineering is the process of analyzing software with the objective of recovering its design and specification. The software source code is usually available as input to the reverse engineering process. Reverse engineering is different from re-engineering. Its purpose is to derive the design or specification of a system from its source code, while the objective of re-engineering is to produce a new, more maintainable system. Of course, reverse engineering to develop a better understanding of a system is often part of the re-engineering process.

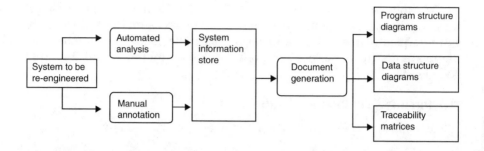

Exhibit 15-1. The Reverse Engineering Process

Reverse engineering can be used during software re-engineering to recover the original program design to help developers understand a program before reorganizing its structure. However, re-engineering need not always follow reverse engineering:

- The design and specification of an existing system may be reverse engineered so that they can serve as input to the requirements specification for that program's replacement.
- Alternatively, the design and specification may be reverse engineered so that they are available to help program maintenance. With this additional information, it may not be necessary to re-engineer the system source code.

The reverse engineering process is illustrated in Exhibit 15-1. The process starts with an analysis phase, during which the system is analyzed using automated tools to discover its structure. In itself, this is not enough to recreate the system design. Engineers then work with the system source code and its structural model, adding information that they have collected by understanding the system. This information is maintained as a directed graph linked to the program source code.

Information store browsers are used to compare the graph structure and the code and to annotate the graph with extra information. Documents of various types, such as program and data structure diagrams and traceability matrices, can be generated from the directed graph. Traceability matrices show where entities in the system are defined and referenced.

Tools for program understanding may be used to support the reverse engineering process. These usually present different system views and allow easy navigation through the source code. For example, they allow users to select a data definition, and then move through the code to where that data item is used. Examples of such program browsers are discussed by Cleveland (1989), Oman and Cook (1990), and Ning et al. (1994).

After the system design documentation has been generated, further information may be added to the information store to help recreate the system specification. This usually involves further manual annotation of the system structure. The specification cannot be deduced automatically from the system model.

3. Program Structure Improvement

The need to optimize memory use and the lack of understanding of software engineering by many programmers have meant that many legacy systems are not well structured. Their control structure is tangled with many unconditional branches and unintuitive control logic. This structure may also have been degraded by regular maintenance. Changes to the program may have made some code unreachable, but this can only be discovered after extensive analysis. Maintenance programmers often dare not remove code in case it may be accessed indirectly.

Typically, programs develop complex logic structure as they are modified during maintenance. New conditions and associated actions are added without changing the existing control structure. In the short term, this is a quicker and less risky solution because it reduces the chances of introducing faults into the system. In the long term, however, it leads to incomprehensible code. Complex code structures can also arise when programmers try to avoid duplicating code. Along with unstructured control, complex conditions can also be simplified as part of the program restructuring process. For instance,

Complex condition:

If not (a > b and (c < d or not (e > f)))...

Simplified condition:

If a < = b and (c > = d or e > f)...

This is how a conditional statement including "not" logic may be made more understandable.

If the program is data driven, with components tightly coupled through shared data structures, restructuring the code may not lead to a significant improvement in understandability. Program modularization may also be necessary. If the program is written in a nonstandard language dialect, standard restructuring tools may not work properly and significant manual intervention may be required.

In some cases, it may not be cost-effective to restructure all of the programs in a system. Some may be of better quality than others and some may not be subject to frequent change. Arthur (1988) suggests that data should be collected to help identify those programs that could benefit most from restructuring: The metrics, such as failure rate, percentage of source code changed per year, component complexity, and the degree to which programs or components meet current standards, can be used to identify the candidates for restructuring.

4. Program Modularization

Program modularization is the process of reorganizing a program so that related program parts are collected together and considered as a single module. Once this has been done, it becomes easier to remove redundancies in these related components, to optimize their interactions, and to simplify their interface with the rest of the program. A number of types of module may be created during the program modularization process.

- *Data abstractions.* In order to save memory space, many legacy systems depend on use of shared tables and common data areas. The information stored in these areas is globally accessible and may be used by different parts of the system in different ways. It is expensive making changes to these global data areas due to the costs of analyzing change impacts across all uses of the data. To reduce the costs of changes to these shared data areas, the program modularization process may focus on the identification of data abstractions. Data abstractions or abstract data types collect data and associated processing and are resilient to change.
- *Hardware modules.* These are related to data abstractions and gather all of the functions used to control a particular hardware device.
- *Functional modules.* For instance, all of the functions concerned with input and input validation may be incorporated in a single module. This type of modularization should be considered where it is impractical to recover program data abstractions.
- *Process support modules.* All of the functions and specific data items required to support a particular business process are grouped here.

5. Data Re-Engineering

Until now, most of our discussion on software evolution has focused on the problems of program modification. However, in many cases, associated problems of storage, organization, and format of the data processed by legacy programs may need to evolve to reflect changes to the software. The process of analyzing and reorganizing the data structures and, sometimes, the data values in a system to make it more understandable is called data re-engineering.

In principle, data re-engineering should not be necessary if the functionality of a system is unchanged. In practice, however, there are a number of reasons why you may need to modify the data as well as the programs in a legacy system:

- *Data degradation.* Over time, the quality of data tends to decline. Change to the data incurs errors, redundant values may have been created, and changes to the external environment may not be reflected in the data. This is unavoidable because the lifetime of data is often very long.
- *Inherent limits built into the program.* Programs are now often required to process much more data than was originally envisioned by their developers. Data re-engineering may be required to remove these limitations.
- *Architectural evolution.* If a centralized system is migrated to a distributed architecture, it is essential that the core of that architecture be a data management system that can be accessed from remote clients. This may require a large data re-engineering effort to move data from a mainframe to a server-based database management system. The move to a distributed program architecture may also be initiated when an organization decides to move from file-based data management to a database management system.

Because data architecture has a strong influence on program architecture and the algorithms that populate it, changes to the data will invariably result in architectural or code-level changes. Rickets (1993) mentions some of the problems with data that can arise in legacy systems made up of several cooperating programs:

- *Data naming problems.* Name may be cryptic and difficult to understand. Different names may be given to the same logical entity in different programs in the system. The same name may be used in different programs to mean different things.
- *Field length problems.* When field lengths in records are explicitly assigned in the program, the same item may be assigned different lengths in different programs or the field length may be too short to represent current data.
- *Record organization problems.* Records representing the same entity may be organized differently in different programs.
- *Hard-coded literals.* Absolute values, such as tax rates, are included directly in the program rather than referenced using some symbolic name.
- *Lack of a data dictionary.*
- *Inconsistent data definitions.* Data values may also be stored in an inconsistent way. After the data definitions have been re-engineered, the data values must also be converted to conform to the new structure.

Exhibit 15-2 illustrates the process of data re-engineering, assuming that data values converted. The change summary tables hold details of all the changes to be made. They are therefore used at all stages of the data re-engineering process.

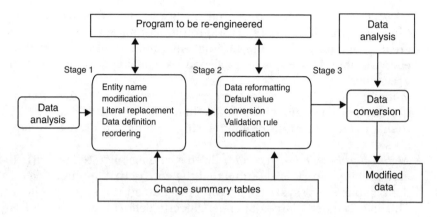

Exhibit 15-2. The Data Re-Engineering Process

In Stage 1 of this process, the data definitions in the program are modified to improve understandability; the data is not affected by these modifications. It is possible to automate this process to some extent using pattern matching systems such as Awk (Aho et al., 1988) to find and replace definitions or to develop XML descriptions of the data (St Laurent and Cerami, 1999) and use these to drive data conversion tools. However, some manual work is almost always necessary to complete the process. The data re-engineering process may stop at this stage if the goal is simply to improve the understandability of the data structure definitions in a program. If, however, there are data value problems as discussed earlier, Stage 2 of the process may then be entered.

If an organization decides to continue to Stage 2 of the process, it is then committed to Stage 3, data conversion, which is usually a very expensive process. Programs must be written that embed knowledge of the old and the new organization. These process the old data and output the converted information.

FORWARD ENGINEERING

The major distinction between re-engineering and new software development is the starting point for the development. For system re-engineering, the old system acts as a specification for the new system. Chikofsky and Cross (1990) call conventional development forward engineering (Exhibit 15-3) to distinguish it from software re-engineering (Exhibit 15-4). Forward engineering starts with a system specification and involves the design and implementation of a new system; re-engineering starts with an existing system and transformation of the old system.

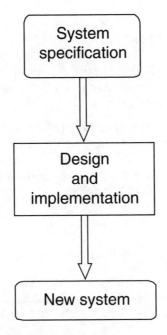

Exhibit 15-3. Forward Engineering

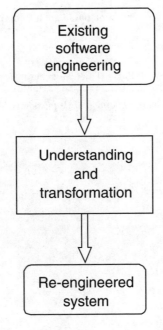

Exhibit 15-4. Software Re-Engineering

CONCLUSION

Developing a custom-built system requires a lot of money and time. Hence, organizations need to maintain their old systems in order to reduce the cost and increase the lifetime of the old system. For these purposes, re-engineering becomes a useful way to convert old, obsolete systems to more efficient, streamlined systems.

Software re-engineering encompasses a series of activities that include source code translation, reverse engineering, program structure improvement, program modularization, and data re-engineering. The intent of these activities is to create versions of existing programs that exhibit higher quality and better maintainability.

References

Aho, A.V., Kernighan, B.W., et al. (1988). *The Awk Programming Language*, Prentice-Hall, Englewood Cliffs, NJ, Chapters 8, 28.

CAS88. (1988). CASE tools for reverse engineering, *CASE Outlook*, CASE Consulting Group, 2, 1–15.

Chikofsky, E.J. and Cross, J.H. (1990). Reverse engineering and design recovery: a taxonomy, *IEEE Software*, 7, 13–17.

Cleveland, L. (1989). A program understanding support environment, *IBM Sys.J.*, 28, 324–344.

Ning, J.Q., Engberts, A., et al. (1994). Automated support for legacy code understanding, *IEEE Software*, 37, 50–57.

Oman, P.W. and Cook, C.R. (1990). The book paradigm for improved maintenance, *IEEE Software*, 7, 39–45.

Pressman, R.S. (2001). *Software Engineering: a Practitioner's Approach*, 5th ed., McGraw-Hill, Boston, 799–824.

Rickets, J.A. DelMonaco, J.C., et al. (1993). Data reengineering for application systems, in *Software Reengineering* Arnold, R.S., Ed., IEEE Press, Los Alamitos, CA, 288–293.

St Laurent, S. and Cerami, E. (1999). *Building XML Applications*, McGraw-Hill, New York, Chapter 9.

Chapter 16
Software Testing

Testing is a critical component of software development. Its goal is to uncover and correct errors found in software. Because software is complex, it is reasonable to presume that software testing is a labor- and resource-intensive process. Automated software testing helps to improve testers' productivity and reduce resources that may be required. By its very nature, automated software testing increases test coverage levels, speeds up test turnaround time, and cuts costs of testing. Unfortunately, due to a variety of reasons, not all test automation projects will achieve these returns on investment. In this chapter, a practical approach to automated software testing is discussed.

WHAT IS SOFTWARE TESTING?

A critical component in the process of software development is software testing. The classic software life cycle model suggests a systematic, sequential approach to software development that progresses through software requirements analysis, design, code generation, and testing. That is, once source code has been generated, program testing begins with the goal of finding differences between the expected behavior specified by system models and the observed behavior of the system.

The process of creating error-free software applications requires technical sophistication in the analysis, design, and implementation of that software and proper test planning, as well as robust automated testing tools. When planning and executing tests, software testers must consider the software and the function it performs, the inputs and how they can be combined, and the environment in which the software will eventually operate.

During early stages of the testing process, the programmer usually performs all tests. This stage of testing is referred to as *unit testing*. Here the programmer usually works with the debugger that accompanies his or her compiler. For example Visual Basic, as shown in Exhibit 16-1, enables the programmer to "step through" a program's (or object's) logic, one line of code at a time, viewing the value of any and all variables as the program proceeds.

A particular program is usually made up of many modules. An OO system is composed of many objects. Programmers usually architect their programs in a top–down modular fashion. *Integration testing* proves that

221

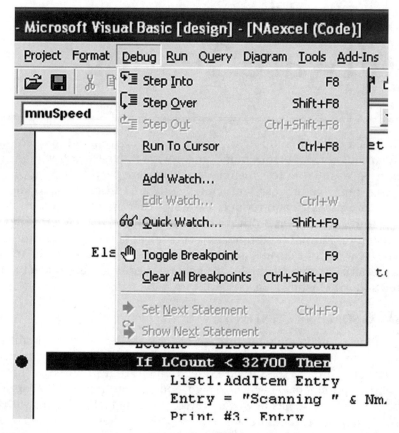

Exhibit 16-1. Visual Basic Providing Unit Testing Capabilities to Programmers

the module interfaces are working properly. For example, in Exhibit 16-2, a programmer conducting integration testing would ensure that Module2 (process module) correctly interfaces with its subordinate, Module2.1 (calculate process).

If module2.1 had not yet been written, it would have been referred to as a stub. Integration testing could still be performed if the programmer inserted two or three lines of code in the stub, which would act to prove that it is well integrated to module2.

On occasion, a programmer will code all the subordinate modules first and leave the higher-order modules for last. This is known as bottom–up programming. In this case module2 would be empty except for a few lines of code to prove that it is integrating correctly with module2.1, etc. In this case, module 2 would be referred to as a driver.

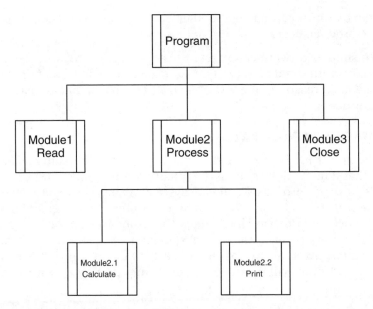

Exhibit 16-2.   Integration Testing Proving Module Interfaces Are Working Properly

Where integration testing is performed on the discrete programs or objects with a master program, *system testing* refers to testing the interfaces between programs within a system. Because a system can be composed of hundreds of programs, this is a vast undertaking.

It is quite possible that the system being developed is a replacement for an existing system. In this case, *parallel testing* is performed. The goal here is to compare outputs generated by each of the systems (old versus new) and determine why there are differences, if any.

Parallel testing requires end users to be part of the testing team. If the end user determines that the system is working correctly, we can see that the customer has "accepted" the system. This, then, is a form of *customer acceptance* testing.

As the testing progresses, testing specialists may become involved (see Appendix P for a sample QA handover document). Within the vernacular of IT, staff dedicated to performing testing are referred to as quality assurance engineers and reside within the quality assurance department. QA testers must have a good understanding of the program being tested as well as the programming language that the program was coded in. In addition, the QA engineer must be methodical and be able to grasp complex logic. Generally speaking, technical people with these attributes are hard to come by and even harder to keep because most of them aspire to become programmers.

Even simple software can present testers with obstacles. Couple this complexity with the difficulty in attracting and keeping QA staff and you have the main reason that many organizations now automate parts of the testing process.

SOFTWARE TESTING STRATEGY

Software testing is one critical element of software quality assurance (SQA) that aims at determining the quality of the system and its related models. In such a process, a software system will be executed to determine whether it matches its specification and executes in its intended environment. To be more precise, the testing process focuses on the logical internals of the software, ensuring that all statements have been tested, and on the functional externals by conducting tests to uncover errors and ensure that defined input will produce actual results that agree with required results.

To ensure that the testing process is complete and thorough it is necessary to create a test plan (Appendix O). A thorough test plan consists of the following:

1. Revision history
2. System introduction
    2.1. Goals and objectives
    2.2. Statement of scope
    2.3. Major constraints
3. Test plan
    3.1. System description
    3.2. Testing strategy
    3.3. Testing resources
    3.4. Testing metrics
    3.5. Testing artifacts
    3.6. Testing schedule
4. Test procedures
    4.1. Class testing
    4.2. Integration testing
5. Appendix 1: class testing test cases
    5.1. Application controller subsystem
    5.2. User management subsystem
    5.3. Resource management subsystem
    5.4. Order subsystem
    5.5. Accounting subsystem
    5.6. Customer relationship management subsystem
    5.7. Persistence subsystem

6. Appendix 2: integration testing test cases
   6.1. Customer registration
   6.2. Reallocate resources
   6.3. Search for service provider and initiate order
   6.4. Place order
   6.5. Pay for service
7. Appendix: project schedule

A sample test plan, created by my students for an OO dog grooming system, can be found in Appendix O. Although all components of this test plan are important, you will note that the plan is really focused around three things:

1. The test cases
2. Metrics that will determine whether there has been testing success or failure
3. The schedule

TEST AUTOMATION

The usual practice in software development is that the software is written as quickly as possible and, once the application is done, it is tested and debugged. However, this is a costly and ineffective way because the software testing process is difficult, time consuming, and resource intensive. With manual test strategies, this can be even more complicated and cumbersome. A better alternative is to perform unit testing independent of the rest of the code. During unit testing, developers compare the object design model with each object and subsystem. Errors detected at the unit level are much easier to fix; we only need to debug the code in that small unit. Unit testing is widely recognized as one of the most effective ways to ensure application quality; however, it is a laborious and tedious task. The workload for unit testing is tremendous, so to perform unit testing manually is practically impossible and hence the need for automatic unit testing. Another good reason to automate unit testing is that, when performing manual unit testing, we run the risk of making mistakes (Aivazis, 2000).

Besides saving time and preventing human errors, automatic unit testing helps facilitate integration testing. After unit testing has removed errors in each subsystem, combinations of subsystems are integrated into larger subsystems and tested. When tests do not reveal new errors, additional subsystems are added to the group, and another iteration of integration testing is performed. The re-execution of a subset of tests that have already been conducted is regression testing. It ensures that no errors are introduced as a result of adding new modules or modification in the software (Kolawa, 2001).

As integration testing proceeds, the number of regression tests can grow very large. Therefore, it is inefficient and impractical to re-execute every test manually once a change has occurred. The use of automated capture and playback tools may prove useful in this case. They enable the software engineer to capture test cases and results for subsequent playback and comparison.

Test automation can improve testers' productivity; they can apply one of several types of testing tools and techniques at various points of code integration. Some examples of automatic testing tools in the market include:

- C++Test for automatic C/C++ unit testing by ParaSoft
- Cantata++ for dynamic testing of C++ by IPL
- WinRunner for unit and system tests by Mercury Interactive

WinRunner is probably one of the more popular tools in use today because it automates much of the painful process of testing. Used in conjunction with a series of test cases (see Appendix O, Section 5), a big chunk of the manual processes that constitute the bulk of testing can be automated. The WinRunner product actually records a particular business process by recording the keystrokes a user makes (e.g., emulates user actions of placing an order). The QA person can then directly edit the test script that WinRunner generates and add checkpoints and other validation criteria.

When done correctly with appropriate testing tools and strategies, automating software testing provides worthwhile benefits such as repeatability and significant time saving. This is true especially when the system moves into system test. Higher quality is also a result because less time is spent in tracking down test environmental variables and in rewriting poorly written test cases (Raynor, 1999).

Principles for Test Automation

Test automation can be applied at unit testing, one or more layers of integration testing, and system testing (which is another form of integration). Tests should be executed soon after the code is written, before too much code integration has occurred, so that bugs will not be carried forward. When strategizing for test automation, consider automating these tests as early as possible, as well as later in the testing cycle (Zallar, 2002).

Pettichord (2001) describes several principles that testers should adhere to in order to succeed with test automation. These principles include:

- Taking testing seriously
- Being careful who you choose to perform these tests
- Choosing what parts of the testing process to automate
- Being able to build maintainable and reliable test scripts
- Using error recovery

Testers need to realize that test automation is a software development activity and so needs to adhere to standard software development practices. That is, test automation systems need to be tested and subjected to frequent review and improvement to make sure that they are indeed addressing the testing needs of the organization.

Because automating test scripts is part of the testing effort, good judgment is required in selecting appropriate tests to automate. Not everything can or should be automated. For example, overly complex tests are not worth automating; manual testing is still necessary in this case.

Zambelich (2002) provides a guideline to make automated testing cost effective. He says that automated testing is expensive and does not replace the need for manual testing or enable you to "down-size" your testing department. Automated testing is an addition to your testing process. Some pundits claim that it can take between three to ten times as long (or longer) to develop, verify, and document an automated test case than to create and execute a manual test case. Zambelich indicates that this is especially true if you elect to use the "record/playback" feature (contained in most test tools) as your primary automated testing methodology. In fact, Zambelich says that record/playback is the *least* cost-effective method of automating test cases. Automated testing can be made to be cost-effective, according to Zambelich, if some common sense is applied to the process:

- Choose a test tool that best fits the testing requirements of your organization or company. An automated testing handbook is available from the Software Testing Institute (http://www.softwaretestinginstitute.com).
- Understand that it does not make sense to automate everything. Overly complex tests are often more trouble to automate than they are worth. Concentrate on automating the majority of your tests, which are probably fairly straightforward. Leave the overly complex tests for manual testing.
- Only automate tests that will be repeated; one-time tests are not worth automating.

PRACTICAL APPROACH TO AUTOMATED SOFTWARE TESTING

Isenberg (1994) explains requirements for success in automated software testing. In order to succeed, the following four interrelated components must work together and support one another.

- *Automated testing system* — it must be flexible and easy to update.
- *Testing infrastructure* — this includes a good bug tracking system, standard test case format, baseline test data, and comprehensive test plans.
- *Software testing life cycle* — it defines a set of phases outlining what test activities to perform and when to conduct them. These phases are planning, analysis, design, construction, testing (initial test cycles, bug fixes, and retesting), final testing and implementation, and post-implementation.
- *Corporate support* — automation cannot succeed without the corporation's commitment to adopting and supporting repeatable processes.

Automated testing systems should have the ability to adjust and respond to unexpected changes to the software under test, which means that the testing systems will stay useful over time. Some of the practical features of automated software testing systems suggested by Isenberg are:

- Run all day and night in unattended mode
- Continue running even if a test case fails
- Write out meaningful logs
- Keep test environment up to date
- Track tests that pass, as well as tests that fail

USING AUTOMATED TESTING TOOLS

When automated testing tools are introduced, test engineers may need to face some difficulties. Project management should be used to plan the implementation of testing tools. Without proper management and selection of the right tool for the job, automated test implementation will fail (Hendrickson, 1998). Dustin (1999) has accumulated a list of "automated testing lessons learned" from his experiences with real projects and test engineer feedback. Some are presented here:

- The various tools used throughout the development life cycle do not integrate easily if they are from different vendors.
- Automated testing tools can speed up the testing effort; however, it should be introduced early in the testing life cycle in order to gain benefits.
- Duplicate information that is kept in multiple repositories is difficult to maintain. As a matter of fact, in many instances the implementation of more tools can result in less productivity.
- The automated testing tool drives the testing effort. Often when a new tool is used for the first time, more time is spent on installation, training, initial test case development, and automating test scripts than on actual testing.
- It is not necessary for everyone on the testing staff to spend his or her time automating scripts.

- Sometimes elaborate test scripts are developed through overuse of the testing tool's programming language, which duplicates the development effort. That is, too much time is spent on automating scripts without much additional value gained. Therefore, it is important to conduct an automation analysis and to determine the best approach to automation by estimating the highest return.
- Automated test script creation is cumbersome. It does not happen automatically.
- Tool training needs to be initiated early in the project so that test engineers have the knowledge to use the tool.
- Testers often resist new tools. When introducing a new tool to the testing program, mentors and advocates of the tool are very important.
- There are expectations of early payback. When a new tool is introduced to a project, project members anticipate that the tool will narrow the testing scope right away. In reality, it is the opposite — i.e., initially the tool will increase the testing scope.

CONCLUSION

Test engineers can enjoy productivity increases as a testing task becomes automated and a thorough test plan is implemented. Creating a good and comprehensive automated test system requires an additional investment of time and consideration, but it is cost effective in the long run. More tests can be executed while the amount of tedious work on construction and validation of test cases is reduced.

Automated software testing is by no means a complete substitute for manual testing. In other words, manual testing cannot be totally eliminated; it should always precede automated testing. In this way, the time and effort saved by using of automated testing can now be focused on more important testing areas.

References

Aivazis, M., (2000). Automatic unit testing, *Computer*, 33, back cover.

Dustin, E. (1999) Lessons in test automation, *STQE Mag.*, and from the World Wide Web: http://www.stickyminds.com/pop_print.asp?ObjectId = 1802&ObjectType = ARTCO, October, 41.

Hendrickson, E. (1998). The difference between test automation failure and success, Quality Tree Software, retrieved from http://www.qualitytree.com/feature/dbtasaf.pdf.

Isenberg, H.M. (1994) The practical organization of automated software testing, Multi-Level Verification Conference 95, December 1994, retrieved from http://www.automated-testing.com/PATfinal.htm.

Kolawa, A., (2001). Regression testing at the unit level? *Computer*, 34, back cover.

Pettichord, B. (2001). Success with test automation, retrieved from http://www.io.com/~wazmo/succpap.htm.

Raynor, D.A. (1999). Automated software testing, retrieved from http://www.trainersdirect.com/resources/articles/ProjectManagement/AutomatedSoftwareTestingRaynor.html.

Zallar, K. (2002). Automated software testing — a perspective, retrieved from http://www.testingstuff.com/autotest.html.

Zambelich, K. (2002). Totally data-driven automated testing, retrieved from http://www.sqa-test.com/w_paper1.html.

Chapter 17
The Process
of EDP Auditing

For as long as there have been computer departments there have been EDP (electronic data processing) auditors. These were and are the people who make sure a system does what it is supposed to do. In this chapter we discuss a methodology for EDP auditing using a Web-based system as an example.

In the "Wild West" days of the Internet, companies were "plopping" systems online faster than you could say "dot-com crash and burn." Now that those heady days appear to be over, smart organizations are beginning to think of their Web-based systems in the same terms as they do their more conventional systems.

In their quest toward increasing market share while lowering costs, these organizations are finally delving into the intricacies of the Web-based system to scrutinize such things as response time/availability, accessibility, ergonomics, logistics, customer service, and security and privacy.

This chapter provides the IT manager with a series of checklists that can be used to audit the Web-based system and easily modified to audit conventional systems. Audits should be done regularly, with the results used to fine-tune the system. Ultimately, think of these checklists as a set of issues that can be considered "food for thought."

ORGANIZING YOUR AUDIT

It is recommended that you hire an external consulting firm to perform this critical effort; however, your EDP audit department, with adequate training, would be a sufficient alternative. The reason why I much prefer an external auditor is that "neutral third parties" are usually more objective because they are not stakeholders and are not friendly with stakeholders. There is nothing like an unbiased opinion.

At a minimum, the auditor should obtain the following documentation:

- *A diagram of the application system.* A Web-based system is not unlike any other computer system. It has processes (e.g., process credit card) and entities (e.g., airline ticket) and shows the flow of data between the entities via the processes. Exhibit 17-1 shows an excerpt from a typical data-flow diagram.
- *A network diagram.* Most modern computer systems are developed using one of several traditional network architectures (i.e., two-tier, three-tier, etc.). Add EDI or Internet connectivity and you have quite a sophisticated environment. The auditor will need a roadmap to this environment to be able to determine any connectivity issues. Exhibit 17-2 demonstrates what a simple network diagram should look like.
- *Staff hierarchy diagram.* A complete list, preferably a diagram that shows direct reports, along with phone numbers and e-mail addresses is required. A good starting point is shown in Exhibit 17-3.

One would think that a modern organization would have these three items readily available. Think again. In my own experience, few of the organizations that I audit possess all three of these required items. Few possess even two.

If these are not available to the auditor, my recommendation is to start the audit effort with a series of brainstorming sessions in which at least the two diagrams are created. Even if diagrams are available, one or more brainstorming sessions are still advisable. This provides the auditors a "walk through" where system and network architects can be questioned directly and invariably speeds up the audit process.

Once the preliminary step has been completed (i.e., understanding the system), the auditor can proceed through his or her paces in a logical and methodical manner. The following sections, presented as a series of checklists, represent areas of the audit that can be performed in any order.

The checklist is actually a series of questions or areas to be studied. The responses to these questions form the data collected for input to the final audit report. This report will contain problems found and issues overlooked, as well as recommendations for improvement. For example, the auditor might find that the company has done inadequate security testing. The recommendation here might be to bring in a "white hat" to perform penetration as well as intrusion testing. Alternatively, the audit might uncover a deficiency in fulfillment processes the company follows to ship products to the customer. Again, the audit report will make recommendations for improvement.

We will begin at the beginning.

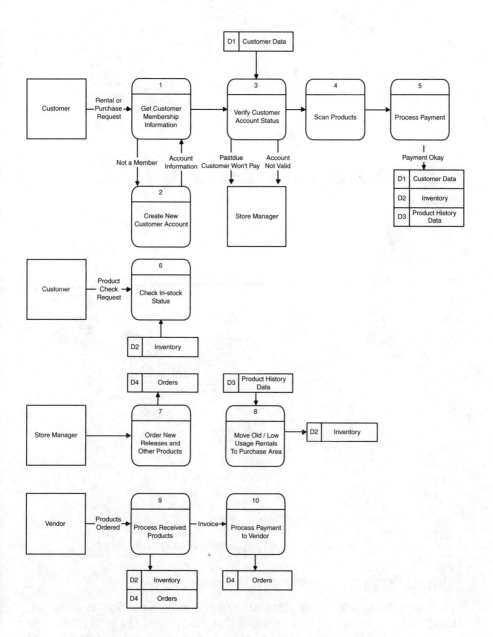

Exhibit 17-1.   A Data Flow Diagram for a Video Rental System

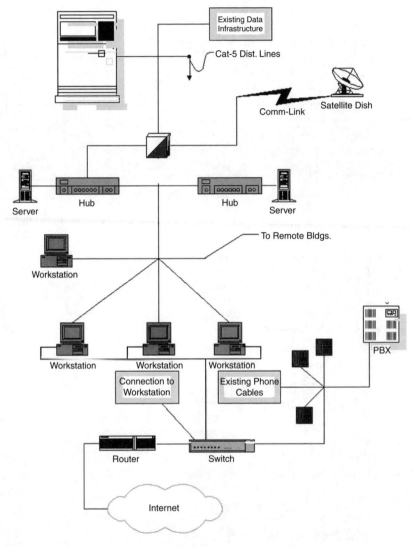

Exhibit 17-2. A Simple Network Diagram

SYSTEMIC AUDIT

It is surprising that many companies spend millions of dollars on advertising budgets to draw more "eyeballs" to their sites but never factor in whether or not the projected additional load can be supported by the current system configuration. A systemic audit looks at such things as response time, network architecture, and linkages.

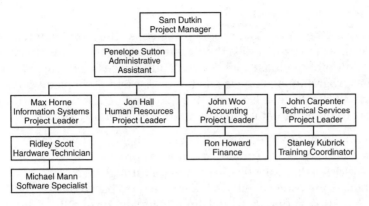

Exhibit 17-3. An Initial Staff Hierarchy Diagram

Response Time

Measurables in this section include actual response time versus projected response time. In spite of advances in supplying high-bandwidth connections to consumers, the vast majority of PCs are connected to the Web with little more than a 56-Kb modem and good intentions. This means that sites that are highly graphical or use add-ons such as Macromedia Flash will appear slow to download.

Given the wide variety of modem types, auditors should test the response time of the site using different scenarios such as:

- Using a DSL or cable modem connection
- Using a 56-Kb connection
- Using a 28-Kb connection
- At random times during the day, particularly 9 a.m (start of work day) and 4 p.m. (kids home from school)

Web sites such as netmechanic.com, a subscription service, can assist in this endeavor by checking for slow response time directly from their Web sites.

Broken Links

One of the top five irritants that Web surfers report is clicking on a link and getting a "nonexistent page" error message. This often results from system maintenance where Web programmers move the actual page but neglect to modify the link to that page. Unfortunately, this is a frequent occurrence. One of a number of tools, including netmechanic.com, can assist in tracking down these broken links.

Database Audit

Originally the Web was a simple place consisting mostly of text; nary a database was in sight. Today, the Web is filled to the brim with databases. The addition of databases makes the audit process even more complex. Because programming code is used to query, and perhaps even calculate, against that database, it is imperative that random checks be performed in an effort to pinpoint database query and calculation errors.

Essentially, auditing database access is similar to traditional IT (information technology) QA (quality assurance) process. One or more scripts must be written that will take that database through its paces. For example, if a database program calculates insurance rates based on a zip code, then that calculation should be duplicated manually or in a different parallel automated fashion to ensure that the result is correct. The same can be said for information that visitors to the site enter via a form. Is the information entered the same as that sent to the database?

Network Audit

The network, including node servers, should be tested to see if it is effectively configured to provide optimum response. It is not uncommon to find the Web development group separated from the traditional IT development group. This means that one frequently finds network configurations designed inappropriately for the task at hand. For example, a site attracting tens of thousands of hits a day would do well to run a multitude of Web servers rather than just one.

Most organizations use one or more ISPs (Internet service providers) to host their sites. The auditor should carefully gauge the level of service provided by these ISPs as well.

SECURITY AND QUALITY

No one topic is discussed more in the press than Internet security. From "love bug" viruses to wily hackers breaking into Western Union, security is an important component of the audit.

It is worthwhile to keep in mind that the auditor is not a security auditor, nor should he be. His role is to conduct a top level assessment of the security of the Internet- or Intranet-based system and, if warranted, recommend the services of a security firm well versed in penetration and intrusion testing. The entire issue of security is wrapped up within the more comprehensive issue of quality. This section will address both issues.

Review the Security Plan

All organizations must possess a security plan **in writing**. If they do not have this then they are severely deficient. The plan, at a minimum, should address:

- *Authentication.* Is the person who he says he is.
- *Authorization.* What users have what privileges; in other words, "who can do what?"
- *Information integrity.* Can the end user maliciously modify the information?
- *Detection.* Once a problem is identified, how is it handled?

Passwords

Passwords are the first shield of protection against malicious attacks upon your eBusiness. Questions to ask in this section include:

- Is anonymous login permitted? Under what conditions?
- Is a password scanner periodically used to determine if passwords can be hacked? Examples of this sort of utility include L0phtcrack.com for NT and www.users.dircon.co.uk/~crypto for UNIX.
- How often are passwords changed?
- How often are administrative accounts used to log on to systems? Passwords are hard to remember. This means that, in order to gain entrance to systems quickly, administrative and programming systems people often create easy-to-remember passwords such as "admin." These are the first passwords that hackers try to gain entrance into a system.

Staff Background

Administrative network staff must have a security background as well as a technical background. Those wishing to train their staffs would do well to look into the security skills certification program provided by www.sans.org.

Connectivity

Today's organization may have many external connections (i.e., partners, EDI, etc.), each of which the auditor should examine:

- The data passed between organizations: is what the company sent received correctly?
- The security of the connection: how is the data transmitted? Is it required to be secure? Is encryption used?
- If encryption is indeed used, it must be determined whether an appropriate algorithm is deployed.

The Product Base

All organizations invest in and then use a great deal of third-party software. As publicized by the press, much of this software — particularly browsers and e-mail packages, but word processing packages as well — contain security holes that, left unpatched, put the organization at risk. Therefore, for each software package used (for Net purposes):

- Check for publicized security holes.
- Check for availability of software patches. Always upgrade to the latest version of software and apply the latest patches.
- Check to see if patches have been successfully applied.
- Check security software for security holes. Security software, such as a firewall, can contain security holes just like any other type of software. Check for updates.

In-House Development

The vast majority of Web-based software is written by in-house programming staff. When writing for the Web it is important to ensure that your own staff does not leave gaping holes through which malicious outsiders can gain entrance. There are a variety of programming "loopholes" that open the door wide to hackers:

- In programming parlance, a "GET" sends data from the browser (client) to the server. For example, look at the query string below:

  ```
  http://www.site.com/process_card.asp?cardnumber = 123456789
  ```

  All HTTP (hypertext transport protocol) requests get logged as straight text into the server log as shown below:

  ```
  2000-09-15 00:12:30 — W3SVC1 GET/process_card.asp
  cardnumber = 123456789 200 0 623 360 570
  80 HTTP/1.1 Mozilla/4.0+(compatible;+5.01;+Windows+NT)
  ```

  Not only is the credit card number clearly visible in the log, but it might also be stored in the browser's history file, thus exposing this sensitive information to someone else using the same machine later. Security organizations recommend utilization of the POST method rather than the GET method for this reason.
- Are the programmers using "hidden" fields to pass sensitive information? An example of this is relying on hidden form fields used with shopping carts. The hidden fields are sometimes used to send the item price when the customer submits the form. It is rather easy for a malicious user to save the Web page to his own PC, change the hidden field to reflect any price he wants, and then submit it.
- One way to combat the problem discussed in the previous item is to use a hash methodology. A hash is a function that processes a

variable-length input and produces a fixed-length output. Because it is difficult to reverse the process, the sensitive data transmitted in this matter is secured. The auditor is required to assess the utilization of this methodology given any problems he might find in assessing the previous item.

- Is sensitive data stored in ASP or JSP pages? Microsoft's Internet information server (IIS) contains a number of security flaws that, under certain circumstances, allows the source of an ASP or JSP page to be displayed rather than executed. In other words, the source code is visible to anyone browsing that particular Web site. If sensitive data, such as passwords, is stored in the code then they will be displayed as well. The rule here is not to hardcode any security credentials into the page.
- Are application-specific accounts with rights identified early in the development cycle? There are two types of security. One is referred to as "declarative" and takes place when access control is set from outside the application program. "Programmatic" security occurs when the program checks the rights of the person accessing the system. When developing code for the Web, it is imperative that the rights issue be addressed early in the development cycle. Questions to ask include:
  — How many groups will be accessing the data?
  — Will each group have the same rights?
  — Will you need to distinguish between different users within a group?
  — Will some pages permit anonymous access while others enforce authentication?
- How are you dealing with cross-site scripting? When sites accept user-provided data (e.g., registration information, bulletin boards), which is then used to build dynamic pages (i.e., pages created on the spur of the moment), the potential for security problems is increased 100-fold. No longer is the Web content created entirely by the Web designers; some of it now comes from other users. The risk comes from the existence of a number of ways in which text can be entered to simulate code. This code can then be executed as any other code written by the Web designers — except that it was written by a malicious user instead. Javascript and html can be manipulated to contain malicious code, which can perform a number of activities such as redirecting users to other sites, modifying cookies, etc. More information on this topic can be obtained from CERT's Website at http://www.cert.org/advisories/CA-2000–02.html and http://www.cert.org/tech_tips/malicious_code_mitigation.html.
- Have you checked Wizard-generated or sample code? Often programmers "reuse" sample code they find on the Web or make use of generated code from Web development tools. Often the sample or generated code contains hardcoded credentials to access databases,

directories, etc. The auditor will want to make sure that this is not the case in the code being audited.

- Are code reviews performed? Nothing is worse than the lone programmer. Many of the problems discussed in the previous sections can be negated if the code that all programmers write is subject to a peer review. Code reviews, a mainstay of traditional quality-oriented programming methodology, are rarely done in today's fast-paced Internet environment. This is one of the reasons why so many security break-ins occur.

- It is necessary to conduct a Web server review. In order to run programs on the Web, many organizations use the CGI (common gateway interface) to enable programs (i.e., scripts) to run on their servers. CGI is not only a gateway for your programming code (i.e., via data collections forms) but also a gateway for hackers to gain access to your systems. Vulnerable CGI programs present an attractive target to intruders because they are easy to locate and usually operate with the privileges and power of the Web server software. The replacement of Janet Reno's picture with that of Hitler on the Department of Justice Web site is an example of this sort of CGI hole. The following questions must be asked of developers using CGI:

  — Are CGI interpreters located in bin directories? This should not be the case because you are providing the hacker with all the capabilities he needs to insert malicious code and then run it directly from your server.

  — Is CGI support configured when not needed?

  — Are you using remote procedure calls (RPC)? These calls allow programs on one computer to execute programs on a second computer. Much evidence indicates that the majority of distributed denial of service attacks launched during 1999 and early 2000 were executed by systems that had RPC vulnerabilities. It is recommended, wherever possible, to turn off or remove these services on machines directly accessible from the Internet. If this is not possible, then at least ensure that the latest patches to the software are installed; these mitigate some of the known security holes.

  — Is IIS used? This is the software used on most Web sites deployed on Windows NT and Windows 2000 servers. Programming flaws in IIS remote data services (RDS) are used by hackers to run remote commands with administrator privileges. Microsoft's Web site discusses methodologies to use to combat these flaws.

Testing

Pre-PC testing was a slow and meticulous process. Today's faster pace means that inadequate testing is performed by most organizations. In addition, many organizations forego security testing entirely. In this section of the audit, we determine whether adequate security is performed.

- Has penetration testing been done? This testing is used to assess the type and extent of security-related vulnerabilities in systems and networks, test network security perimeters, and empirically verify the resistance of applications to misuse and exploitation. It is possible that system administrators are sophisticated enough to be able to utilize the tool sets available to scan the systems for vulnerabilities; however, a whole host of "white hat" hacker security consulting firms have sprung up over the past several years and these people are recommended.
- Has intrusion testing been done? Many software tools are available on the market today that "monitor" systems and report on possible intrusions. These are referred to as intrusion detection systems (IDS). In this section of the audit, we determine whether an IDS is used and, if so, how effectively.
- Is there a QA (quality assurance) function? Although QA departments have been a traditional part of the IT function for decades, many newer pure-play Internet companies seem to ignore this function. In this section, the auditor will determine if the QA function is present; if it is, then it will be reviewed.

Reporting

Logging of all logins, attempted intrusions, etc. must be maintained for a reasonable period of time. In this section, the auditor will determine if these logs are maintained and, if so, for how long.

Backup

In the event of failure it is usual that the last backup be used to restore the system. In this section, the auditor will determine the frequency of backups and whether this schedule is reasonable.

ERGONOMICS

At this stage the auditor becomes involved in more abstract issues. In the last section on security, we could be very specific about what a system requires. In the section on ergonomics we need to be more subjective.

To achieve this end will require the auditor to meet with the system developers and with the end users. At times, these end users will be current or potential customers of the system; therefore, it might be necessary to develop surveys and perform focus groups. The goal here is nothing less than determining a "thumbs up" or "thumbs down" on the Web-based system vis-à-vis other Web-based systems.

Navigability

Navigation means determination of whether or not the site makes sense in terms of browsing it.

- How easy is it to find something on this site? If looking for a specific product, how many pages does one need to surf through to find it?
- Is there a search engine? If so, review for correctness and completeness. Many sites do not have search engines (in this instance we are talking about a search engine to search the site only, rather than the Internet). If the Web site exhibits depth (i.e., many pages), it becomes rather difficult to navigate around it. If a search engine is available, the auditor must check to see if what is being searched for can be correctly found.
- Is there a site map? If so, review for correctness and completeness. While not required and not often found, site maps are one of the most useful of site navigation tools. If available, the auditor will determine correctness of this tool.
- Are back and forward (or other) buttons provided? What tools are provided to the end user for moving backward and forward within the site? Are the browser's back and forward buttons the only navigation tools — or did the Web designers provide fully functional toolbars? If so, do these toolbars work on all pages? We have found that, of those firms audited, 10 percent of the pages pointed to by the toolbars cannot be found.
- Are frames used? If so, do toolbars and other navigation tools still work?

Usability

In the end it comes down to one question really: "How usable is the Web site?" In this section we ask:

- How easy is it to use this site? Although the auditor might have an opinion that might well be valid, here we resort to surveys and focus groups to determine the answer.
- How useful is this site?

Content

In this section we assess the value of the information contained within the site compared to competitive sites.

- Is content updated regularly?
- Is content relevant?
- Do visitors consider content worthwhile? The auditor will use survey techniques to determine the answer to this question.

- How does content compare with competitors'? The auditor will use survey techniques to determine the answer to this question.

Search Engine

The use of search engines as a way to find a site has declined in popularity, but it is still an important marketing vehicle on the Web. In this section the auditor will determine where the site places when performing a search using the top ten search engines.

CUSTOMER SERVICE

The Web is a doorway to the company's business; however, it is just one part of the business. Tangential services must be audited as well. Customer service is one of the biggest problem areas for Net firms. There have been many well-publicized instances of shoddy customer service. It is in the company's best interests, therefore, to assess customer service within the firm vis-a-vis its Web presence.

Accessibility

How easy is it for your customers to reach you?

- Review e-mail response. How long does it take you to respond to a customer e-mail?
- Review telephone response. How long does a customer wait on hold before a person answers his or her query?

E-Commerce

If your site doubles as an e-commerce site (i.e., you sell goods or services from your site), you need to assess the quality of this customer experience.

- Check shopping experience. Using a "mystery shopper" approach, the auditor will endeavor to make routine purchases using the Web site. Determine:
  — Is the shopping cart correct (i.e., are the goods you purchased in the shopping cart)?
  — Does the e-commerce software calculate taxes properly?
  — Does the e-commerce software calculate shipping charges properly?
- Check the fulfillment experience:
  — Is a confirmation e-mail sent to the purchaser?
  — Is the return policy carefully explained?
  — How quickly does the company refund money on returns?

Privacy

At a minimum, the auditor must review the company's privacy policy statement. He or she should then review the data flow to determine if the privacy policy is adhered to.

LEGALITY

The digital age makes it easy to perform illegal and potentially litigious acts. From a corporate perspective, this can be anything from a Web designer illegally copying a copyrighted piece of art to employees downloading pornography.

Copyright

Check the content ownership of text on your site. It is quite easy to copy text from one site to another. Ensure that your copy is completely original or that you have the correct permissions to reprint the data. In the same way, check image ownership.

Employee Web Usage

In a number of court cases employees have claimed harassment when other employees within the organization downloaded and e-mailed pornography. The company is responsible for the actions of its employees; therefore, it is highly recommended that the company:

- Create a policy memo detailing what can and cannot be done on the Internet (include e-mail). Make sure all employees sign and return this memo. Use tools such as those on surfcontrol.com to monitor employee Net usage.
- Determine whether any e-mail monitoring software is used and determine its effectiveness.

CONCLUSION

Auditing IT systems is an important activity. It is surprising, then, that so few companies take the time and effort to perform this necessary activity. EDP auditing not only pinpoints potentially troublesome technical areas but it can also serve as reinforcement for stakeholder support by identifying human factor issues as well.

Chapter 18
The Management of Software Maintenance

Maintenance is often called the enigma of software. Enormous amounts of dollars are spent on it but little management attention is given to it. Software maintenance presents a real conundrum — hardware deteriorates because of lack of maintenance, whereas software often deteriorates because of the presence of maintenance.

Maintenance is also the most expensive component of the software life cycle, as shown in Exhibit 18-1. IT departments spend from 75 to 80 percent of their budget (Guimaraes, 1983) and time on the maintenance process of system development. In addition, the cost of fixing an error rises dramatically as the software progresses through the life cycle. This amply demonstrates that maintenance costs more than any other phase and also that maintenance costs (per fixing the error) are enormous.

Once a new system is implemented, the real work begins for most IT departments. As users utilize the system, errors are discovered, and changes are requested. As systems have become more widely used within critical departments of the organization, the maintenance process has taken on a more important role. The management of systems maintenance has become perhaps the most critical phase of systems development.

THE MAINTENANCE PROCESS

As the new system is implemented and users begin to work with it, errors occur or changes are needed. Just as in the development of a new system, maintenance requires that steps be taken carefully in making changes or fixing errors. In the event of an error, this can be even more critical. Each step of the maintenance process is similar to steps in the systems development life cycle (Curtis et al., 2000) as seen in Exhibit 18-2. This is a logical extension of the development process because changes made to the system can affect the whole system and need to be controlled carefully.

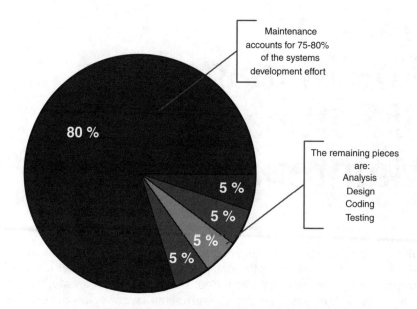

Exhibit 18-1.   The High Cost of Maintenance

SDLC					
Project Identification and Selection	Project Initiation and Planning	Analysis	Logical Design	Physical Design	Implementation
Obtain Maintenance Requests	Requests into Changes		Design Changes		Implementing Changes
Maintenance Process					

Exhibit 18-2.   The Maintenance Life Cycle Compared to the Development Life Cycle

The first step in the process is to obtain a maintenance request from a user. Many organizations use a system service request form (see Appendices A and B) that spells out the problem or need. Once the request has been received, the requests can be transformed into changes that can then be used to make design changes. After the changes are designed and tested, the changes can be implemented.

Exhibit 18-3 is an overview of system maintenance. Both the customer and maintainer are interacting with his or her own documentation, i.e., user manual and maintainer manual. The customer poses questions, problems,

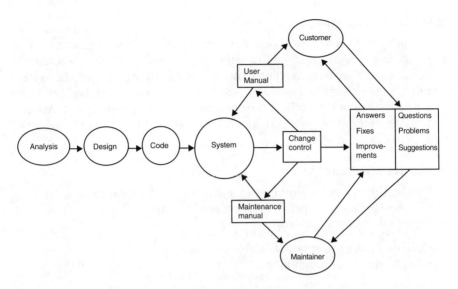

Exhibit 18-3. An Overview of System Maintenance

and suggestions to the maintainer who, in turn, gives the answers, which are filtered through a change control process and back into the system.

TYPES OF MAINTENANCE

Categorizing the types of maintenance required is helpful in organizing and prioritizing the requests of users. Software maintenance is more than fixing mistakes. Maintenance activities can be broken down into four sub-activities.

- Corrective maintenance
- Adaptive maintenance
- Perfective maintenance or enhancement
- Preventive maintenance or reengineering

Corrective Maintenance

Corrective maintenance involves fixing bugs or errors in the system as they are discovered. This maintenance is the type most users are familiar with because these problems are the most irritating to users. These usually receive top priority because they can paralyze the organization if not identified and fixed. Corrective maintenance consumes approximately 17 percent of the maintainer's time (Lientz and Swanson, 1978). Major skills required for corrective maintenance are:

- Good diagnostic skills
- Good testing skills
- Good documentation skills

Adaptive Maintenance

Adaptive software maintenance is performed to make a computer program usable in a changed environment. For example, if the computer on which the software runs is going to use a new operating system, the system requires some adaptive tweaking. Adaptive maintenance is typically part of a new release of the code or part of a larger development effort. Approximately 18 percent of software maintenance is adaptive (Lientz and Swanson, 1978).

Perfective Maintenance

This is the act of improving the software's functionality as a result of end-user requests to improve product effectiveness. This includes

- Adding additional functionality
- Making the product run faster
- Improving maintainability

This is the biggest maintenance time consumer. Approximately 60 percent of software maintenance is spent on perfective maintenance (Lientz and Swanson, 1978).

Preventive Maintenance

This refers to performing "premaintenance" in order to prevent system problems; it is different from corrective maintenance, which is performed to correct an existing problem. This is like maintaining a car in which you change the oil and air filter, not in response to some problem but to prevent a problem from occurring in the first place.

MAINTENANCE COSTS

As computers and their systems become more widely used, the need for maintenance grows. As these same systems age, maintenance becomes more critical and time consuming. Since the early 1980s, it is estimated that maintenance costs have skyrocketed from 40 percent of the IT budget to 75 to 80 percent (Exhibit 18-1). The reason for these increases stems from once newly designed systems aging. This shift from development to maintenance is a natural occurrence as organizations avoid the high cost of new systems and struggle to maintain their current systems.

Many factors affect the cost in time and money expended on system maintenance. One of the most costly is design defects. The more defects in a system, the more time is spent identifying and fixing them. If a system has been designed and tested properly, most defects should have been eliminated, but in the case of poor design or limited testing, defects can cause system downtimes that cost the organization in lost efficiency and perhaps sales.

The number of users can also affect the cost of system maintenance. The more users, the more time will be spent on changes to the system. More importantly, the more platforms the system is installed on, the higher the cost of maintenance. If a single system needs a change, then the time it takes to change the system is limited, but if that system resides on platforms across the country, e.g., in many branch offices of corporations, then the cost is increased significantly.

The quality of the documentation can also affect the overall cost of maintenance. Poor documentation can result in many lost hours searching for an answer that should have been explained in the documentation (Lientz and Swanson, 1981). The documentation is a type of road map to the system; when the map is well defined, finding your way through the system and understanding it become much easier.

The quality of the people and their skill level can also cost an IT department many wasted hours. An inexperienced or overloaded programmer can increase the cost of maintenance in two ways. First he or she can waste hours learning on the job at the IT department's expense. Second, a programmer overwhelmed with projects, may skip steps in the maintenance process and, in turn, make mistakes that cost time and money to fix.

The tools available to maintenance personnel can save many hours of work. Using automation tools such as CASE tools, debuggers, and others can help the programmer pinpoint problems faster or make changes more easily.

The structure of the software can also contribute to maintenance costs (Gibson, 1989). If software is built in a rational and easy-to-follow manner, making changes will be much easier and thus much faster, saving time and resources. Software maintenance costs can be reduced significantly if the software architecture is well defined and clearly documented, and creates an environment that promotes design consistency through the use of guidelines and design patterns (Hulse et al., 1989).

A MODEL FOR MAINTENANCE

Harrison and Cook have developed a new model of software maintenance based upon an objective decision rule, which determines whether a given software module can be effectively modified or if it should be rewritten. Their take is that completely rewriting a module can be expensive. However, it can be even more expensive if the module's structure has been severely degraded over successive maintenance activities. A module that is likely to experience significant maintenance activity is called "change prone." Their paper suggests that early identification of change-prone modules through the use of change measures across release cycles can be an effective technique in efficiently allocating maintenance resources.

In maintenance requests for nonchange-prone modules, the process flow is as follows:

Analyze code and identify change	→
Implement change and update documentation	→
Apply metric analysis	→
Compare with baseline	→
Check to see if it exceeds the threshold	→
If yes, then declare module to be "change prone;"	
otherwise, declare module to be non-change prone.	

The process for maintenance requests for a change-prone module is as follows:

Identify the highest level artifact affected by the request	→
Regenerate artifact	→
Identify artifacts that can be reused	→
Iterate through "development"	→
Declare module to be non-change prone.	

MANAGING MAINTENANCE PERSONNEL

As systems age and demand increases for maintenance personnel, there has been a loud debate over just who should be doing the maintaining. Should it be the original developers? Or should it be a separate maintenance department? Many have argued that the people who developed the system should maintain it because they will best understand the system and be better able to change it (Swanson, 1990). This logic is correct but difficult to fulfill because developers want to keep building new systems and consider maintenance a less desirable function. IT professionals view maintenance as fixing someone else's mistakes. One solution to this problem that has been tried recently involves rotating the IT personnel from development to maintenance and back to allow everyone to share in the desirable as well as undesirable functions of the department.

MEASURING EFFECTIVENESS

An important part of managing maintenance is to understand and measure the effectiveness of the maintenance process. As a system is implemented, service requests may be quite high as bugs are worked out and needs for change are discovered. If the maintenance process is operating properly an immediate decrease in failures should be seen (Exhibit 18-4). Good management of maintenance should include recording failures over time and analyzing these for effectiveness. If a decrease is not noticed, the problem should be identified and resolved.

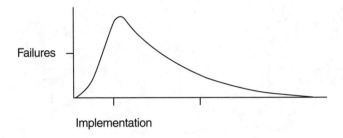

Failures

Implementation

Exhibit 18-4.   Normal Distribution of Failures Following Implementation

Another measure of success of the maintenance process is the time between failures. The longer the time between failures, the more time can be spent on improving the system and not just fixing the existing system (Lientz, 1983). Failures will happen, but more costly is the time fixing even the simplest failure.

Recording the type of failure is important to understanding how the failure happened and can assist in avoiding failures in the future. As this information is recorded and maintained as a permanent record of the system, solutions can be developed that fix the root cause for a variety of failures.

CONTROLLING MAINTENANCE REQUESTS

As problems arise or the need for change is discovered, the flow of these requests must be handled in a methodical way. Because all requests are not equal and they arrive at the project manager's desk at various times, a system has been developed by most IT departments. This system provides a logical path for the approval of requests and prioritizes and organizes those approved. The project manager has the job of categorizing the requests and passing them on to the "priority board" that decides if the request is within the business model and what, if any, priority to give the change. As decisions are made by the board, they are passed back to the project manager for action. The project manager then reports the decision to the user and acts on the change based on the priority given.

The type and severity of change help decide what priority it is given. If the change is important enough, it may be placed at the top of the queue for immediate action. If several changes occur in a single module a batch change may be requested. A batch change involves making changes to a whole module at once to avoid working on the same module several times. This also allows users to view the changes as a single update that may change the use of a module through screen changes or functionality.

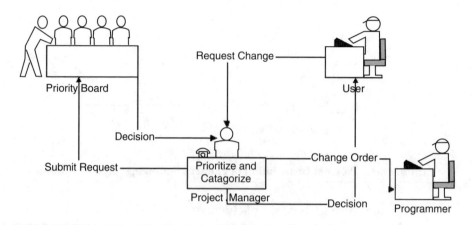

Exhibit 18-5. Change Request Flow

The queue of changes is a valuable tool in controlling work that needs to be done. Items high in the queue receive the immediate attention they deserve; those of lesser importance may never be acted on due to a change in needs or a new system that solves the problem.

CONCLUSION

Managing system maintenance requires that steps be taken similar to the development of new systems. System maintenance is in many ways an extension of the system development life cycle and involves similar steps to ensure that the system is properly maintained. As a new system is implemented, system maintenance is required to fix the inevitable errors and track them for future use. As a system ages and changes are requested, system maintenance has the job of categorizing, prioritizing, and implementing changes to the system. As these changes are made, the system librarian has the very important job of controlling the integrity of the system. The proper management of system maintenance is vital to the continued success of the system. A well managed systems maintenance department can save time and money by providing an error-free system that meets the needs of the users it serves.

References

Curtis, G., Hoffer, J., George, J., and Valacich, S. (2000). *Introduction to Business Systems Analysis*, Pearson Custom Publishing, Boston.

Gibson, V. and Senn, J. (1989). *System Structure and Software Maintenance Performance*, ACM Press, New York.

Guimaraes, T. (1983). *Managing Application Program Maintenance Expenditures*, ACM Press, New York.

Harrison, W. and Cook, C. Insights on improving the maintenance process through software measurement. http://www.cs.pdx.edu/~warren/Papers/CSM.htm.

Hulse, C., Edgerton, S., Ubnoske, M., and Vazquez, L. (1999). *Reducing Maintenance Costs through the Application of Modern Software Architecture Principles*, ACM Press, New York.

Lientz, B. (1983). *Issues in Software Maintenance*, ACM Press, New York.

Lientz, B.P. and Swanson, E.B. (1978). Characteristics of application software maintenance, *Commn. ACM*, 21, 466–481.

Lientz, B.P. and Swanson, B. (1981). *Problems in Application Software Maintenance*, ACM Press, New York.

Swanson, E. (1990). *Departmentalization in Software Development and Maintenance*, ACM Press, New York.

Chapter 19
The Science of Documentation

The one thing that software developers hate to do is to document their programs and their systems. Therefore, it is understandable that software documentation is the one of the most neglected areas in information technology. However, documentation is one of the most important components of systems development. Without adequate documentation, the system can be neither utilized efficiently nor maintained properly.

WHAT EXACTLY IS DOCUMENTATION?

According to Ambler (2002), a document is any artifact external to source code whose purpose is to convey information in a persistent manner; documentation includes documents and comments in source code. A model is an abstraction that describes one or more aspects of a problem or a potential solution.

All professionals in the field agree that documentation promotes software quality. There are numerous, well-documented reasons for this. David Tufflye, a consultant who specializes in producing high-quality documentation to a predefined standard, says that consistent, accurate project documentation is known to be a major factor contributing to information systems quality. He goes on to say that document production, version control, and filing are often not performed, contributing to a higher number of software defects that impact the real and perceived quality of the software, as well as leading to time and expense spent on rework and higher maintenance costs (Tufflye, 2002).

Marcello Alfredo Visconti proposes a software system documentation process maturity model that is consistent with — and runs in conjunction with — the Software Engineering Institute's (SEI) software process and capability maturity model. He argues that one of the major goals of software engineering is to produce the best possible working software along with the best possible supporting documentation.

Decades' worth of empirical data shows that software documentation processes and products are key components of software quality. These

Exhibit 19-1.   Visconti's Four-Level Documentation Maturity Model

	Level 1 Ad hoc	Level 2 Inconsistent	Level 3 Defined	Level 4 Controlled
Keywords	Chaos; variability	Standards check-off list; inconsistency	Product assessment; process definition	Process assessment; measurement control; feedback; improvement
Succinct Description	Documentation not a high priority	Documentation recognized as important and must be done.	Documentation recognized as important and must be done well.	Documentation recognized as important and must be done well consistently
Key Practices	Ad-hoc process; documentation not important	Inconsistent application of standards	Documentation quality assessment; documentation usefulness; assurance process definition	Process quality assessment and measures
Key Indicators	Documentation missing or out of date	Standards established and use of check-off list	SQA-like practices	Data analysis and improvement mechanisms
Key Challenges	Establish documentation standards	Exercise quality control over content; assess documentation usefulness; specify process	Establish process measurement; incorporate control over process	Automate data collection and analysis; continually striving for optimization

Source: Cook, C.R. and Visconti, M. (2000). Software system documentation process maturity model. http://www.cs.orst.edu/~cook/doc/Model.htm.

studies show that poor-quality, out-of-date, or missing documentation is a major cause of errors in future software development and maintenance (Visconti, 1993). For example, the majority of defects discovered during integration testing are design and requirements defects, e.g., defects in documentation that were introduced before any code was written

Visconti's four-level documentation maturity model provides the basis for an assessment of an organization's current documentation process and identifies key practices and challenges to improve the process. The four-level enhanced model appears in Exhibit 19-1.

Key practices as defined by Cook and Visconti (2000) are:

1. Creation of basic software documents
   — Consistent creation of basic software development documents
   — Consistent creation of basic software quality documents
2. Management recognition of importance of documentation
   — Documentation generally recognized as important
3. Existence of documentation policy or standards
   — Written statement or policy about importance of documentation
   — Written statement or policy indicating what documents must be created for each development phase
   — Written statement or policy describing the contents of documents that must be created for each development phase
4. Monitor implementation of policy or standards
   — Use of a mechanism, such as a check-off list, to verify that required documentation is done
   — Monitor adherence to documentation policy or standards
5. Existence of a defined process for creation of documents
   — Written statement to prescribe process for creation of documents
   — Mechanism to monitor adherence to prescribed process
   — Adequate time to carry out the prescribed process
   — Training material or classes about the prescribed process
6. Methods to assure quality of documentation
   — Mechanism to monitor quality of documentation
   — Mechanism to update documentation
   — Documentation is traceable to previous documents
7. Assessments of usability of documentation
   — Person or group perception of usability of documents created
   — Mechanism to obtain user feedback about usability of created documentation
8. Definition of software documentation quality and usability measures
   — Definition of measures of documentation quality
   — Definition of measures of documentation usability
9. Collection and analysis of documentation quality measures
   — Collection of measures about quality of documentation
   — Analysis of documentation quality measures
   — Recording of documentation error data
   — Tracking of documentation errors and problem reports to solutions
   — Analysis of documentation error data and root causes
   — Generation of recommendations based on analysis of quality measurements and error data
10. Collection and analysis of documentation usability measures
    — Collection of measures about usability of documentation
    — Analysis of documentation usability measurement

— Generation of recommendations based on analysis of usability measurements
— Generation of documentation usage profile
11. Process improvement feedback loop
   — Mechanism to feedback improvements to documentation process
   — Mechanism to incorporate feedback on quality of documentation
   — Mechanism to incorporate feedback on usability of documentation

An assessment procedure was developed to determine where an organization's documentation process stands relative to the model. This enables mapping from an organization's past performance to a documentation maturity level and ultimately generates a documentation process profile. The profile indicates key practices for that level and identifies areas of improvement and challenges to move to the next higher level.

Application of the model has a definite financial benefit. The software documentation maturity model and assessment procedure have been used to assess a number of software organizations and projects; a cost/benefit analysis of achieving documentation maturity levels has been performed using COCOMO that yielded an estimated return on investment of about 6:1 when moving from the least mature level to the next. According to Visconti, these results support the main claim of this research: software organizations that are at a higher documentation process maturity level also produce higher-quality software, resulting in reduced software testing and maintenance effort (Visconti, 1993).

METHODS AND STANDARDS

The many approaches to producing documentation are practically unique to each organization. Although the majority of software documentation is produced manually — i.e., done with word processing programs or with tools such as Microsoft Visio, some systems are designed to ease the process and will produce "automatic" documentation. Some of the automatic documentation capabilities are a subset of systems of a wider range of capabilities; this is the case with many computer-assisted software engineering (CASE) tools. These products are designed to support development efforts throughout the software development life cycle (SDLC), with documentation just one small part.

An example of one such tool is Hamilton Technologies 001 which is discussed at length in this handbook. 001 is a CASE tool (now usually called application development tool in lieu of the term CASE) that surrounds itself with an intriguing methodology called "development before the fact" (DBTF). The premise behind 001 and DBTF is that developing systems in a quality manner begets quality and error-reduced systems. One of the intriguing features of the 001 tool set is that it not only generates programming source code from maps (i.e., models) of a business problem, but also generates the documentation for the system.

On one end of the documentation spectrum, many companies utilize no tools other than a word processor and a drawing tool to extract documentation from their reluctant programmers. On the other end, forward-thinking companies make significant investments in their software development departments by outfitting them with tool suites such as 001. The vast majority of organizations lie somewhere between these two extremes.

The world of client/server has afforded the developer with new opportunities and decisions to make in terms of which tool set to use. When Microsoft Office was first introduced, it was utilized mostly for word processing. Today, Microsoft Access, the database component of the MS Office product set, has become a significant player in corporations with a requirement for a robust but less complex database than that of the powerhouse computers that run their back offices (i.e., Sybase, Oracle, Microsoft SQL Server).

Microsoft Access enables the automated production of several kinds of documents related to the datasets implemented with the program. The documents describe schemas, queries, and entity relationship diagrams (ERDs) as shown in Exhibit 19-2.

Some products are dedicated to producing documentation. One such product is Doc-o-Matic by toolsfactory.com. It is designed to work with the Borland Delphi software development environment. The product works with Delphi's internal structures, which may consist of: Author, Bugs, Conditions, Examples, Exceptions, History, Ignore, Internal, Notes, Parameters, Remarks, Return Value, See Also, Todo, and Version (Leahey, 2002). Doc-o-Matic has been compared to a gigantic parsing routine. As software systems grow in size and sophistication, it becomes harder for humans to understand them and anticipate their behavior, says Charles Robert Wallace in his dissertation, "Formal Specification of Software Using Abstract State Machines." This method essentially enables walk-through before code is written. Wallace argues that normal specification techniques aim to foster understanding and increase reliability by providing a mathematical foundation to software documentation (Wallace, 2000). His technique calls for layering information onto a model through a series of refinements.

GENERATING DOCUMENTATION THE RIGHT WAY

At present, many organizations are practicing a "hit or miss " form of software documentation. These are usually the companies that follow no or few policies and procedures and loosely follow standards. Good software development is standards based; thus, documentations must also be

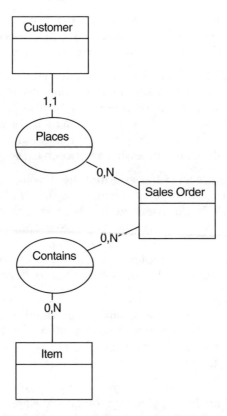

Exhibit 19-2.   An Access Entity Relationship Diagram (ERD)

standards based. At minimum, software documentation should consist of the following:

- *All documentation produced prior to the start of code development.* Most projects go through a systems development life cycle, which often starts with a feasibility study, goes on to create a project plan, and then enters into the requirements analysis and system design phases. Each of these phases produces one or more deliverables, schedules, and artifacts (examples of these can be found in the appendices to this handbook). In sum, the beginnings of your system documentation effort should include the feasibility study, project plan, requirements specification, and design specification, where available.
- *Program flowcharts.* Programmers usually, although not always, initiate their programming assignment by drawing one or more flowcharts that diagram the nuts and bolts of the actual program. Systems analysts can utilize diagrammatic tools such as data flow diagrams (DFD) or UML-based (unified modeling language) class diagrams

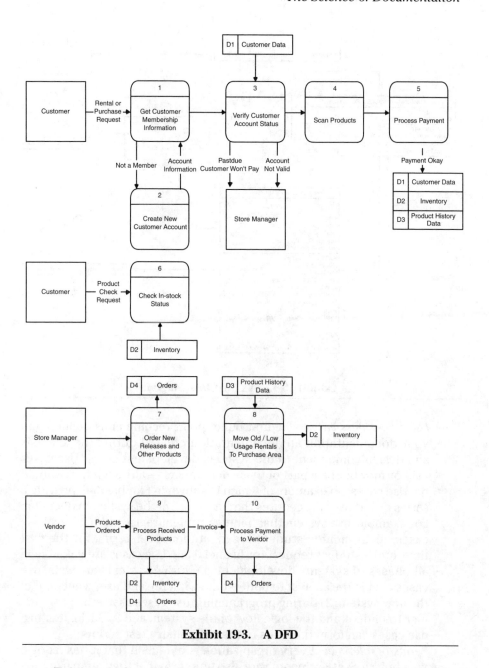

Exhibit 19-3.   A DFD

(Exhibits 19-3 and 19-4) to depict the entire system from a physical design level; however, the programmer is often required to utilize flowcharts (Exhibit 19-5) to depict the flow of a particular component of the DFD or UML class diagram.

261

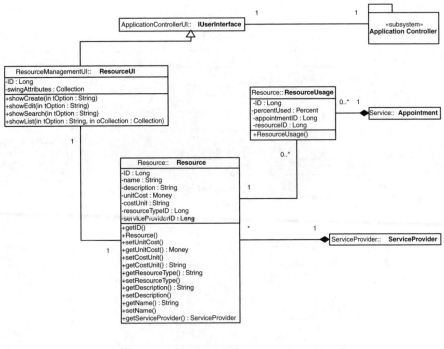

Exhibit 19-4. A UML Class Diagram

- *Use or business cases.* The first bullet point recommends including in your documentation all documentation created during the analysis and design component of the systems development effort. Use cases may or may not be a part of these documents — although they should be. Use cases, an example of which is shown in Exhibit 19-6, provide a series of end-user procedures that make use of the system in question. For example, in a system that handles student registration, typical use cases might include student log in, student registering for the first time, and a student request for financial aid. Use cases are valuable in all phases of systems development: 1) during systems analysis, use cases enable the analyst to understand what the end user wants out of the new system; 2) during programming, use cases assist the programmer to understand the logic flow of the system; and 3) during testing, use cases can form the basis of the preliminary test scripts.
- *Terms of reference.* Every organization is unique in that it has its own vocabulary. Systems people are also unique in that they often use a lingo incomprehensible to most end users. A "dictionary" of terms used is beneficial in clearing up any misunderstandings.

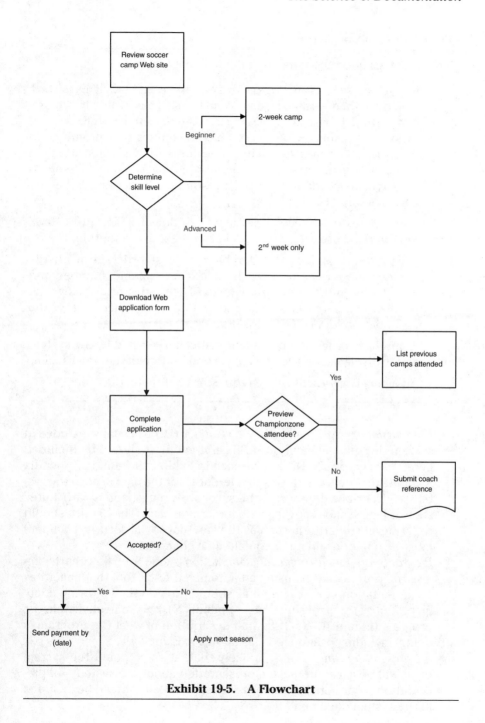

Exhibit 19-5. A Flowchart

Exhibit 19-6.   A Sample Use Case

Requestor logs into the system to submit a new request:

1. Requestor keys in his log-on ID and six- to eight-digit password, which are then verified against valid IDs and passwords in the procurement database. If the ID or password does not match, an error message is displayed on the screen. The requestor is prompted to re-key the ID or password. The requestor is allowed three attempts to log in. If unsuccessful, the password is flagged and a message is displayed to call data security for resolution. If successful, the procurement menu is displayed.

2. The requestor selects the menu option ENTER PURCHASE REQUEST by pressing the radio button next to that option.

3. The system displays the purchase request order form on the screen. The requestor keys the department name, number, and cost center in the appropriate fields. The requestor also keys the product numbers, selections, and quantities and then presses the radio button for SUBMIT ORDER.

4. A purchase order number is automatically assigned by the system and is displayed on the screen as confirmation of the order taken.

5. An e-mail is also sent to the requestor confirming the order.

- *Data dictionary.* Although a data dictionary (DD) is usually included in system design specification (SDS), if it is not, it should be included here. An excerpt of a DD can be seen in Exhibit 19-7 and in Appendix K. A data dictionary is "terms of reference" for the data used in the system. It describes database, tables, records, fields, and all attributes such as length and type (i.e., alphabetic, numeric). The DD also should describe all edit criteria such as the fact that social security numbers must be numeric and must contain nine characters.
- *Program/component/object documentation.* Aside from flowcharts, unless the programmer is using an automated CASE tool that generates documentation, the programmer should provide the following documentation: 1) control sheet (see Appendix N); 2) comments within the program (Exhibit 19-8); 3) textual description of what the program is doing, including pseudocode, as shown in Exhibit 19-8.
- *All presentation material.* It is likely that, at some point, the system team will be asked to make a presentation about the system. All presentation paraphernalia such as slides, notes, etc. should be included in the system documentation.

Exhibit 19-7. Data Dictionary

Name:	Membership Database
Aliases:	None
Where Used/How Used	Used by the database management system to process requests and return results to the inquiry and administration subsystems
Content Description:	Attributes associated with each asset including: • Membership number = 10 numeric digits • Member since date = date • Last name = 16 alphanumeric characters • First name = 16 alphanumeric characters • Address = 64 alphanumeric characters • Phone number = 11 numeric digits (1, area code, phone number) • Assets on loan = array containing 10 strings, each containing 64 alphanumeric characters • Assets overdue = array containing 10 strings each containing 64 alphanumeric characters • Late fees due = 10 numeric digits • Maximum allowed loans = 2 numeric digits

Name:	Member Data
Aliases:	None
Where Used/How Used	A file used to validate username and passwords for members, librarians, and administrator when attempting to access the system. The username and password entered are compared with the username and password in this file. Access is granted only if a match is found.
Content Description:	Attributes associated with each asset including: • Member username = 16 alphanumeric digits • Member password = 16 alphanumeric digits

Exhibit 19-8. Sample Program Comments

```
//Get cost of equipment

rsEquipment = Select * from Equipment Utilized Where Pothole ID =

NewPotholeID

Loop through rsEquipment and keep running total of cost by
equipment *

rsRepairCrew("Repair Time")

Total Cost = Total Employee Cost + Total Equipment Cost +
Material Cost

Update Employee Set Total Cost Where Pothole ID = NewPotholeID
```

- *Test cases (Appendix O) and test plan.* Although use cases form the basis of the initial set of test cases, they are a small subset of test cases. An entire chapter has been dedicated to software testing, so we will not prolog the discussion here. Suffice it to say that any and all test cases used in conjunction with the system — along with the results of those test cases — should be included in the system documentation.
- *Metrics.* It is sad to say that most organizations do not measure the effectiveness of their programmers. Those that do should add this information to the system documentation. This includes a listing of all metrics (formula) used and the results of those measurements. (This handbook contains many chapters on metrics.) At a minimum, the weekly status reports and management reports generated from toolsets such as Microsoft Project should be included in the system documentation.
- *Operations instructions.* Once the system is implemented, aside from the end users that the system was developed for, some computer support operations personnel may be required to support this system in some way. Precise instructions for these support personnel are mandatory and must be included in the documentation for the system.
- *End-user help files.* Most systems are built using a client/server metaphor that is quite interactive. Most systems, therefore, provide end users with online help. A copy of each help file should be saved as documentation. Most corporate systems are Windows-based; hence, a Windows-style format in creating help files (Exhibit 19-9) has become the de facto standard. Microsoft Help Workshop is often used to assist in developing these .hlp files, which are compiled from RTF (rich text format) files.

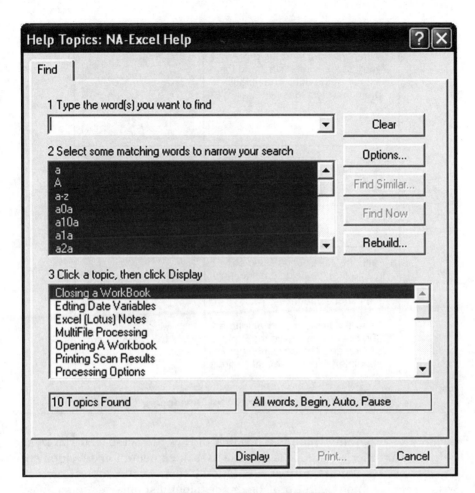

Exhibit 19-9. A Typical Help File

- *User documentation.* Aside from the built-in help file, a user manual should be included in what is provided to the end user. Increasingly, this user manual is supplied right on the CD rather than on paper. There are two different types of end-user manuals. One is more of an encyclopedia that explains the terms and workings of the system when the end user has a specific question. The second type is more of a tutorial.

User tutorials are easy to develop; it is important to approach the task step by step, going through all the motions of using the software exactly as a user would. Simply record every button you push and key you press. As seen in Exhibit 19-10, a table format works well documenting the use of the

Steps	Screen
1. When you first start the program, you'll see a screen similar to the screen at the right. The default protocol selected is telnet.	
2. Pick the down arrow on the drop-down box, and select the ssh1 option.	
3. With the ssh1 option selected, notice that the fields change, now different from those available on the telnet screen. Enter the appropriate Hostname and Username. Leave the Port, Cipher, and Authentication options populated with the default settings.	

Exhibit 19-10. Table Format for Developing Tutorials

SecureCRT program, which is a product of New Mexico-based Van Dyke Software. Another advantage is that the user documentation development process serves double duty as a functional test. As the analyst or tech writer is developing the tutorial, he or she might just uncover some bugs.

MAINTAINING DOCUMENTATION

In his discussion of system documentation for the article "Tools and Evidence," Scott Ambler (2002) suggests that modeling and documentation are effective, when employed with sense and restraint, and enhance system functionality. He makes a case that there is a need for restraint and that models should be discarded once they have fulfilled their purpose. As a project progresses, models are superseded by other artifacts such as other models, source code, or test cases that represent the information more effectively. Ambler takes a fresh approach — it is important to know what to keep, but it is also important to know what to throw away.

Documentation is particularly critical for maintenance work. Code can be mysterious to maintenance programmers who must maintain the system for years after the original system was written and the original programmers have moved on to other jobs (Graham et al., 2000).

Documentation is becoming more important. Ravi Shankar Kalakota (1996) wrote about organizing practices in his 1996 dissertation, "Organizing for Electronic Commerce." Organizing is crucial, he says, and the problem of organizing has three distinct dimensions:

- Organizing large amounts of data and digital documents
- Organizing business processes and workflows
- Organizing computing and processing

Kalakota offers resolution for each of these challenges, but for our purposes, I will limit discussion to the specific issues.

Distributed documents must be organized such that users and programs are able to locate, track, and use online documents. The growth of networking brings with it a corresponding increase in the number of documents to be organized. Current document organization techniques are derived from techniques used in file systems and are not sufficient for organizing the large number of heterogeneous documents that are becoming available for various purposes.

Second, Kalakota believes that new computing forms must be developed to process, filter, and customize online documents. He asserts that the traditional notion of client/server computing is not sufficient to deal with the complexity and needs of electronic commerce. Third, workflows need to be structured to take advantage of online documents. Workflows often dictate organization structure but are difficult to study because they are essentially complex patterns of interaction between agents (Kalakota, 1996). We can easily characterize the variable properties of sequential actions, but not real-time patterns for tasks occurring in parallel.

CONCLUSION

Documentation is an often neglected but very necessary component of the software development life cycle (SDLC). Numerous approaches and methods are available to software development teams to assist with the task. Most important are a commitment to documenting software, setting standards for the organization, and making them stick, that is, adhering to the standards.

References

Ambler, S.W. (2002). Tools and evidence. Software development. Online. Available: http://www.sdmagazine.com/documents/s = 7134/sdm0205i/0205i.htm.

Applied Information Science International. (1996). Entity relationship diagram. [Online]. Available: http://www.aisintl.com/case/olais/pb96/er_model.htm.

Cook, C.R. and Visconti, M. (2000). Software system documentation process maturity model. http://www.cs.orst.edu/~cook/doc/Model.htm.

Graham, C., Hoffer, J.A., George, J.F., and Valacich, J.S. (2000). *Introduction to Business Systems Analysis*. Pearson Custom Publishing, Boston.

Kalakota, R.S. (1996). Organizing for electronic commerce. DAI-A. 57/02. (From University of Phoenix Online Collection. [ProQuest Digital Dissertations]. Publication number: AAT 9617262. Available: http://www.apollolibrary.com:2118/dissertations/fullcit/9617262.)

Leahey, R. (2002). Doc-O-Matic 1.0: generates docs in WinHelp, RTF, HTML or HTML Help. Delphi Informant. Online. Available: http://www.delphizine.com/productreviews/2001/07/di200107rl_p/di200107rl_p.asp.

Tufflye, D. (2002). How to write, version and file software development documentation. Online. Available: http://tuffley.hispeed.com/tcs20006.htm.

Visconti, M.A. (1993). Software system documentation process maturity model. DAI-B. 55/03. (From University of Phoenix Online Collection. [ProQuest Digital Dissertations]. Publication number: AAT 9422184. Available: http://www.apollolibrary.com:2118/dissertations/fullcit/9422184.)

Wallace, C.R. (2000). Formal specification of software using abstract state machines. DAI-B. 61/02. (From University of Phoenix Online Collection. [ProQuest Digital Dissertations]. IBSN: 0–599–63514–2. Available: http://www.apollolibrary.com:2118/dissertations/fullcit/9959880.)

Chapter 20
Survey on IT Productivity and Quality

Who among us does not remember the soulful tale of Alice? In her journey through Wonderland she comes upon the Queen of Hearts who, at one point in the fantasy, makes sport of the game of chess with live chess pieces, including our very own Alice. The Queen makes Alice run fast, but Alice finds that she is merely running in place...running so very fast just to catch up.

Have productivity and quality risen? Or, like Alice, are more and more firms merely running in place — too tired from continual day to day operational battles or too shell-shocked from retrenching to support the new paradigms of client/server architectures, object orientation, and Intranets to pay heed to TQM (total quality management)?

Many years ago, sometime in the 1920s, some social scientists were studying the productivity of workers at a Western Electric plant in Hawthorne, Illinois. They discovered that when they turned up the lighting, productivity went up. They also found that when they turned down the lighting, productivity went up again. What these social scientists found was that when the Hawthorne workers realized that people were paying attention to them, they started to do better work. This became known as the "Hawthorne effect."

Even though the jury is still out on the effects of quality programs on the process of information technology, there is no doubt that the industry is extremely interested in its potential. According to some industry statistics, less than 5 percent of IT organizations are doing this sort of thing. Even though TQM is strongly rooted in many industries as a whole, for example, the 60 to 70 percent of those in manufacturing who have some sort of quality program in place, IT tends to be a black hole.

However, interest in the concept is increasing. One should start off the process by understanding a single principle — that change is painful and lengthy. In fact, to effectuate any kind of change you need something like a ten-year plan. Ten years is a long time, however, and management's patience is short. So how can you motivate change over that time period?

PLANNING FOR QUALITY

The secret is to make management extremely dissatisfied with the status quo; to do that, you need to look at the cost of the status quo. One way of accomplishing this is to examine the cost of poor quality.

By answering questions such as "what are we spending on detecting defects?" and "what are we spending on repairing defects?" the IT organization can begin to accumulate the statistics it needs to make the push for change. The data need not be hard to track; in most cases it is already available through project management systems that track walkthroughs, reviews, defect rates, etc. About 40 to 50 percent of the IT budget is spent on fixing defects due to poor quality. With statistics like this, it should be rather easy to motivate massive change.

Techniques to introduce TQM programs to the "black hole" of IT vary from company to company, but some commonalities are shown below:

- Conduct a customer satisfaction survey.
- Get management sponsorship to fix what the surveys found wrong.
- Top management needs to make a visible and personal commitment to any quality program.
- Customers as well as suppliers need to be involved.
- Define the processes.
- Come up with ways to improve the process.
- Determine metrics to measure the improvement of the process.

In the 1990s Coopers & Lybrand, now PriceWaterhouseCoopers after a merger, had a substantial TQM federal practice. This group focused on taking appropriate elements of TQM and applying them to software delivery organizations. The end result was the development of a specific methodology for doing that. This methodology provided a framework for managing continuous improvement for software delivery.

This group had first-hand experience of the endemic behaviors in most of us attracted to this business that are contrary to the quality tenets of TQM. One of these is the "code or die" syndrome. The greater the deadline pressures, the more we focus on "I got to code right now." This is a quality problem because it speaks to the fact that we are generally product oriented and when the pressure is on we fundamentally have no faith in the process. However, TQM says if you want to improve the quality of the product, you focus on improving the process. So this is a behavior that gets us into trouble every time. In order to combat behaviors that seem to sabotage the drive toward quality, Coopers & Lybrand modified their four-phase TQM methodology to suit the tenets of software engineering.

The centerpiece of the **assessment phase** of the Coopers & Lybrand methodology is development of metrics by which the quality baseline is assessed and by which improvements over time can be measured. There is no specific list of metrics; the choice of metrics depends upon the client because quality is different things for different people. What you think are key quality issues should drive what you are trying to measure. In order to determine the appropriate metrics for any particular client, Coopers consultants utilized a method first developed by NASA and then put into the public domain. Called goal–question–metric (GQM), it is a disciplined technique used to refine from key quality issues their individual components and, ultimately, the metrics that might be derived from them.

The second phase of the Coopers methodology, **planning**, is based on what we see today, our vision, or where we want to take ourselves. Here we look at the highest priority quality issues and think about what we want to do to build ourselves in that direction. The "plan" developed is actually a short list of things to do over the next six months. This is actually a list of "low-hanging fruit" — the list must contain the greatest near-term opportunities to increase quality.

The third phase, **process improvement**, is actually a phase of experimentation. It is here that the low-hanging fruit can be picked, and if determined not to have any nutritive value to the process, tossed quickly aside. Finally, in the fourth phase of the Coopers TQM methodology, **integration**, the best things from these experiments are built into the organization.

THE PROCESS OF MEASUREMENT

Organizations that apply measure productivity and quality do so for the same reasons. Software is becoming more complex and user demands and expectations are increasing. The need to develop better software, faster, translates to a need to quantify the project's progress and the system's attributes.

A variety of productivity and quality metrics are available; choosing the most appropriate one can be as tricky as picking winning lottery numbers:

- Lines of code
- Pages of documentation
- Number and size of texts
- Function count
- Variable count
- Number of modules
- Depth of nesting

- Count of changes required
- Count of discovered defects
- Count of changed lines of code
- Time to design, code, test
- Defect discovery rate by phase of development
- Cost to develop
- Number of external interfaces
- Number of tools used and why
- Reusability percentage
- Variance of schedule
- Staff years of experience with team
- Staff years of experience with language
- Staff years of experience with software tools
- MIPs per person
- Support to development personnel ratio
- Nonproject to project time ratio

Measuring does have its detractors. Many "artists" still refuse to be measured. Ironically, measuring often produces the unusual effect of increasing productivity only in the areas that are measured.

In most situations, the term "metric" is used in conjunction with the programming process only. However, programming is the smallest part of the systems development life cycle. For an effective measurement program, each component of the cycle must include its own measures — or a measure must be used that encompasses the entire spectrum of development.

The software development process is one of the most complex processes a human can perform; it includes numerous formidable tasks. Although variations abound in the number of executable steps in a life cycle, most IT organizations perform the same functionality.

Metrics must consider several esoteric items, such as user involvement, which is positively correlated with productivity increases. Human factors must also be taken into account, such as the square footage allocated per programmer. Capers Jones , a prominent researcher in this field, has shown that a full 78 square feet of floor space increases programmer productivity more than any application development tool. Design, programming, and quality factors must also be weighed.

Quality measurements are frequently overlooked in the race to implement on or before deadline. However, no matter what the time pressure, certain measures undertaken seriously can enhance the quality of output of any software investment. The following matrix has proven useful when filled out by end users:

Circle the number applicable to each measure.

	Add together for total score.	1 = low to 5 = high
1.	How easy is it to use?	1 2 3 4 5
2.	How secure is it?	1 2 3 4 5
3.	What is the level of confidence in it?	1 2 3 4 5
4.	How well does it conform to requirements?	1 2 3 4 5
5.	How easy is it to upgrade?	1 2 3 4 5
6.	How easy is it to change?	1 2 3 4 5
7.	How portable is it?	1 2 3 4 5
8.	How easy is it to locate a problem?	1 2 3 4 5
9.	Is the response time fast enough?	1 2 3 4 5
10.	How easy is it to train staff?	1 2 3 4 5
11.	How easy is it to test?	1 2 3 4 5
12.	Is there efficient use of computing resources?	1 2 3 4 5
13.	Is it easy to couple this system to another?	1 2 3 4 5
14.	Does the system minimize storage requirements?	1 2 3 4 5
15.	Is the system self-descriptive?	1 2 3 4 5
16.	Does the system exhibit modularity?	1 2 3 4 5
17.	Is there a program for on-going quality awareness?	1 2 3 4 5
18.	Is supplier quality checked?	1 2 3 4 5
19.	Is there a quality department?	1 2 3 4 5
20.	Is this the right system to be developed?	1 2 3 4 5

Measurement of quality is often thought of as a manufacturing process. Computer companies that manufacture hardware and software usually apply metrics to the manufacture of both. Digital Equipment, acquired by Compaq, which itself was acquired by HP in 2002, was famous for its software quality controls. DEC ran upward of 22,000 quality checks on the VAX Cobol compiler (Compaq recently retired the VAX computer in favor of its Alpha server (http://www.compaq.com/alphaserver/vax/).

With 22,000 tests, it was impossible to test the compiler thoroughly, so DEC wrote VaxScan, which looked at many micro-oriented measures such as rate of change and how much the program was tested. It also measured the introduction of new errors.

THE ORIGINAL METRIC

Those who measure most often use a simple source-lines-of-code (SLOC) metric. With this metric, however, there is room for variation. In their 1986 book, *Software Engineering Metrics and Models*, published by the

Benjamin/Cummings Publishing Company, Conte, Dunsmore, and Shen proposed this definition of SLOC:

> A line of code is any line of program text that is not a comment or blank line, regardless of the number of statements or fragments of statements on that line. This specifically includes all lines containing program headers, declarations and executable and nonexecutable statements.

The SLOC metric is often further redefined into distinguishing the number of noncomment source lines of code (NCSLOC) from the lines of code containing comment statements (CSLOC).

Along with SLOC measurements, the weekly time sheet provides other gross statistics often used for productivity measurement. The total number of labor hours expended, divided by the total number of NCSLOC, provides an overall statistic that can be used to compare productivity from project to project.

One problem with the SLOC measurement is that it does not take into account the complexity of the code being developed or maintained. Lines of code and man-months hide some very important things. For example, the SLOC measurement for a name and address file update program might be 600 lines of code per day. On the other hand, the output for software that tracks satellites might be in the range of 40 to 50 lines of code per day. To look at this output on a purely gross statistical level, one would conclude that the name and address project was more productive and efficient than the satellite project. This conclusion would be wrong.

Starting from this base, two researchers at the Massachusetts Institute of Technology's Center for Information Systems Research in Cambridge, Massachusetts, examined this complexity issue. Chris F. Kemerer and Geoffrey K. Gill studied the software development projects undertaken by an aerospace defense contracting firm from 1984 to 1989.

The Kemerer and Gill team began their research by reviewing the original measure for complexity as developed by Thomas McCabe, now president of McCabe & Associates, a Columbia, Maryland, consulting group, in his article, "A Complexity Measure." McCabe proposed that a valid measurement of complexity would be the number of possible paths in a software module. In 1978, W.J. Hansen in his article, "Measurement of Program Complexity by the Pair," interpreted McCabe's mathematical formula into four simple rules that would produce a numerical measure of complexity (i.e., the higher the number, the more complex):

- Add 1 for every IF, case, or other alternate execution construct.
- Add 1 for every iterative DO, DOWHILE, or other repetitive construct.
- Add 2 less than the number of logical alternatives in a case.
- Add 1 for each AND or OR in an IF statement.

Exhibit 20-1. Hewlett Packard TQC Metrics

Metric	Goal
Break-even time	Measures return on investment; time until development costs are offset by profits
Time to market	Measures responsiveness and competitiveness; time from project go-ahead until release to market
Progress rate	Measures accuracy of schedule; ratio of planned to actual development time
Post-release defect density	Measures effectiveness of test processes; total number of defects reported during the first 12 months after product release
Turnover rate	Measures morale; percentage of staff leaving
Training	Measures investment in career development; number of hours per year

The results of the Kemerer and Gill study showed that increased software complexity leads to reduced productivity. They recommended using more experienced staff and reducing complexity of the individual software module. To reduce complexity, they suggest establishing a complexity measure that could be in use as the code is written and then adhering to this preset standard.

THE HP WAY

Quality and productivity have been an explicit part of Cupertino, California-based, Hewlett Packard's (HP) corporate objectives. To help develop and utilize company-wide metrics, HP created the software metrics council. Today, dozens of productivity and quality managers within HP perform a variety of functions, from training to communicating the best software engineering practices to establishing productivity and quality metrics.

HP has adopted a methodology called total quality control (TQC). A fundamental principle of TQC is that all company activities can be scrutinized in terms of the processes involved; metrics can be assigned to each process to evaluate effectiveness. HP has developed numerous measurements, as shown in Exhibit 20-1.

The TQC approach places software quality and productivity assessment high on the list of software development tasks. When projects are first defined, along with understanding and evaluating the process to be automated, the team defines the metrics to be used to measure the process.

When HP decided to revolve the future of the company around Risc-based architecture in the 1990s, software reliability was deemed critical.

The development of the systems software was the largest development effort in HP's history, and the first that required multiple divisions to produce software that would be combined into a single software system.

Charles A. Krueger , a professor at the University of Wisconsin in Madison, has pointed out the productivity paradox of budget versus getting to market: is it more important to stay within the targeted confines of money allocated, or to get the product out on time? He quotes a McKinsey & Co. study indicating that going over budget by 50 percent and getting a product out on time reduces profits by only 4 percent. Staying on budget and getting to market five months late reduces profits to a third. Krueger insists that productivity is really a measure of how successfully you achieve your results.

Hewlett-Packard came to the same conclusion as Krueger, so the company insisted on reliable software and delivery on time. HP established the systems software certification program to ensure measurable, consistent, high-quality software through defining metrics, setting goals, collecting and analyzing data, and certifying products for release. This program developed four metrics for the Risc project:

- *Breadth* — measures the testing coverage of user-accessible and internal functionality of the product.
- *Depth* — measures the proportion of instructions or blocks of instructions executed during testing.
- *Reliability* — measures the stability and robustness of a product and its ability to recover gracefully from error conditions.
- *Defect density* — measures the quantity and severity of reported defects and a product's readiness.

HP's results were impressive. Defects were caught and corrected early, when costs to find and fix are lower. Less time was spent in the costly system test and integration phases, and on maintenance. This resulted in lower overall support costs and higher productivity. It also increased quality for HP's customers.

HP's success demonstrates what a corporate-wide commitment to productivity and quality measures can achieve. The commitment to these gains was so strong that HP invested in full-time productivity and quality managers, which is indeed unique.

THE FUNCTION POINT ADVANTAGE

In 1983, A.J. Albrecht, with IBM at that time, first proposed the function-point concept in a paper called "Software Function, Source Lines of Code and Development Effort Prediction: a Software Science Validation." This metric is a combination of metrics that assesses the functionality of the development process (see Appendix S for a more detailed description).

The function-point metric assesses the functionality of the software development process by first counting the number of external inputs (transaction types), external outputs (report types), logical internal files (nonphysical), external interface files (files accessed by the application but not maintained or updated by it), and external inquiries.

Using a set of standards for assessing complexity, these components are then classified as relatively low, average, or high. Once the total number of function counts is computed according to a statistical formula, the second step assesses the impact of 14 general system characteristics:

- Data communications
- Distributed functions
- Performance
- Heavily used configuration
- Transaction rate
- Online data entry
- End-user efficiency
- Online update
- Complex processing
- Reusability
- Installation ease
- Operational ease
- Multiple sites
- Facilitates change

These values are then summed to compute what is known as the value adjustment factor (VAF). The VAF is then multiplied with the total function count to create the number of function points.

The one aspect of function-point measurement programs that makes them so valuable is the presence of large databases of information that companies can use for comparison. SPR (www.spr.com), for example, maintains a database of over 9000 completed projects. It is used to compare an organization to industry norms — i.e., a benchmark.

Aside from these external comparative databases, many in-house databases have been painstakingly accumulated. As Kemerer states in his thesis, "from a control perspective, organizations using a variant method would have difficulty in comparing their function-point productivity rates to those of other organizations that switched methods; the new data might be sufficiently inconsistent as to render trend analysis meaningless."

Most people are using the function point metric because it offers the only metric that comes close to matching the economic definition of productivity — costs or services produced per unit of labor and expense. In the 1990s, using Capers Jones' SPR research base of 400 studied companies, the national average was calculated to be five function points per person-month; IT groups averaged eight function points per person-month. These numbers can dramatically increase with tool usage to the degree that it is possible to achieve 65 function points per person-month with a full application tool environment and reusable code. This metric will decrease when the development environment is new, but will regain momentum when familiarity with the tool set increases.

American Management Systems was an early believer in the function-point concept. With over 2200 systems professionals supporting 28 product lines, AMS needed a methodology that worked. The company had been measuring productivity for years, but found that its traditional metrics of lines of code and work-months was hiding some very important information: not all work-months are created equal. The problem was that there are experienced people and not so experienced people, expensive people and not so expensive people. If the company could find a way of optimizing this mix, then AMS would find increased productivity. To this end, AMS needed a measure that would foster economic productivity. Function points filled the bill.

Function points were created in an era prior to the Internet and prior to the introduction of object-oriented systems. As technologies and methodologies must grow to meet new business requirements, so too must our metrics.

Dr. Chris Kemerer, now at the University of Pittsburgh, but then a professor at MIT's prestigious Sloan School of Management, wrote a paper entitled, "Towards a Metrics Suite for Object-Oriented Design." This paper, authored with Dr. Shyam Chidamber, was presented at the October, 1991, ACM OOPSLA conference (object-oriented programming, systems, languages, and applications). Kemerer asserts his position as perhaps the first person to talk about measurement for object-oriented systems and proposes a series of six metrics that serve to measure the depth and breath of object-oriented design:

- *Metric 1: WMC (weighted methods per class).* This relates to the definition of complexity of an object. The number and complexity of methods involved are indicators of how how much time and effort is required to develop and maintain the object.
- *Metric 2: DIT (depth of inheritance tree).* DIT is a measure of how many ancestor classes can potentially affect a class. It is useful to have a measure of how deep a particular class is in the hierarchy so that the class can be designed with reuse of inherited methods.
- *Metric 3: NOC (number of children).* NOC is a measure of how many subclasses will inherit the methods of a parent class. NOC gives an idea of the potential influence a class has on the design. If a class has a large number of children, it may require more testing of the methods in that class.

- *Metric 4: CBO (coupling between objects).* This is a count of the number of noninheritance-related couples with other classes. Excessive coupling between objects outside the inheritance hierarchy is detrimental to modular design and prevents reuse. This measure is useful to determine how complex the testing of various parts of the design is likely to be.
- *Metric 5: RFC (response for a class).* The response set is a set of methods available to the object. Because it specifically includes methods called from outside the object, it is also a measure of communication between objects. If a large number of methods can be invoked, the testing and debugging of the object become more complicated.
- *Metric 6: LCOM (lack of cohesion in methods).* LCOM uses the notion of degree of similarity of methods. Fewer disjoint sets imply greater similarity of methods. Cohesiveness of methods within a class is desirable because it promotes encapsulation of objects.

It is easy to pinpoint how Kemerer's metrics differ from conventional measurements. Object-oriented metrics are specifically oriented to object-oriented methodologies, which are quite different from conventional methodologies. The notion is to try to go after those things that are different about the object-oriented approach.

The easiest one to explain to most people is the notion of inheritance. Our metric is to measure depth of inheritance. In this way we can determine to what degree people are using inheritance. The goal here is to address the optimal mix between complexity and usability. When a programmer uses no inheritance, then he is not taking advantage of reusability and therefore negates productivity gains of the object-oriented technique. When the programmer "goes really deep," this may also be bad because it will be hard to test. Indeed it may be too much for one person to keep in mind.

THE QUALITY EQUATION

Quality and productivity are tightly linked; the approaches used to address these issues — metrics, methodology, and tools — must be interconnected. Simply throwing technology or methodology at the problem is not enough. Information technology (IT) departments must also use "peopleware" solutions (Exhibit 20-2.).

Ed Yourdon (www.yourdon.com), an esteemed software guru, says that one way to improve development is to hire better developers. This solution is the closest thing to a silver bullet.

Rather than spend lots of money trying to bring in a new methodology, why not simply bring in better people? We know that there is a 25 to 1 differential between the best and the worst people and a 4 to 1 differential

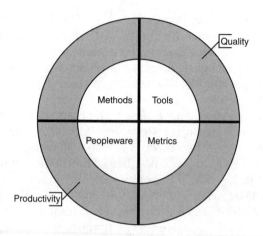

Exhibit 20-2. Layers to Quality and Productivity

between the best and the worst teams, so maybe the best way to improve productivity and quality is to improve hiring practices.

If you take a random group of 100 people and put them in a room with a complex programming exercise, one of them will finish 25 times faster than the others, Yourdon says. Another "peopleware" improvement to productivity is to help managers improve their skills, as well as to foster a teamwork approach among developers. Yourdon and many others believe that "peopleware" solutions boost productivity and quality more than any tools or techniques.

CONCLUSION

TQM is actually a process by which one manages continuous improvement. You need to learn the lessons in as close to real time as possible and implement lessons learned across the organization. For quality programs to be successful, you need to get scared enough to act.

References

A.J. Albrecht , A.J. (1983). Software function, source lines of code and development effort prediction: a software science validation, *IEEE Trans. Software Eng.*, 10, 1.

Conte, Dunsmore, and Shen, (1986). *Software Engineering Metrics and Models*, Benjamin/Cummings Publishing Company, San Francisco.

Hansen, W.J. (1978). Measurement of program complexity by the pair, (Cyclomatic Number, Operator Count) [ACM SIGPLAN Notices).

Kemerer, C. and Chidamber, S. (1991). Towards a metrics suite for object-oriented design, ACM OOPSLA Conference (object-oriented programming, systems, languages and applications).

Keyes, J. (1993). A Survey on IT productivity/quality, in *Software Engineering Productivity Handbook*, Keyes, J., Ed., McGraw-Hill, New York.

McCabe, T. (1976). A complexity measure, *IEEE Trans. Software Eng.*, SE-2, 4, 308.

Section II

This section is a compendium of techniques, guidelines, and philosophies that will assist the developer in understanding, and then putting into place a quality and productivity program. The 45 chapters contained in this section offer the reader a wealth of information and advice in a multitude of areas, including management of resources, methods, quality, and metrics.

Each chapter is composed of the following:

Abstract: discussing the goals and principles behind the technique
Procedures/Issues/Polices: a step-by-step implementation section
References: where the reader can obtain a detailed version of the technique synopsized in the chapter
Selected Bibliography: for further reading

Chapter 21
Putnam's Software Equation and SLIM

ABSTRACT

Putnam developed a constraint model called SLIM that would be useful for projects exceeding 70,000 lines of code. This model assumes that effort for software projects is distributed similarly to a collection of Rayleigh curves.

The Norden-Rayleigh curve (Exhibit 21-1) represents manpower as a function of time. Norden observed that the Rayleigh distribution provides a good approximation of the manpower curve for various hardware development processes. Development effort is assumed to represent only 40 percent of the total life cycle cost. Requirements specification is not included in the model. Estimation using SLIM is not expected to take place until design and coding.

Putnam suggests that staffing rises smoothly during the project and then drops sharply during acceptance testing. The SLIM model is expressed as two equations describing the relation between the development effort and the schedule. The first equation, called the *software equation*, states that development effort is proportional to the cube of the size and inversely proportional to the fourth power of the development time. The second equation, the *manpower-buildup* equation, states that the effort is proportional to the cube of the development time.

PROCEDURES/ISSUES/POLICIES

The software equation is calculated as follows:

$$S_s = CK^{1/3} t_d^{4/3}$$

where:

- S_s = the estimated size of the software system
- K = the total lifecycle effort in programmer years
- C = the technology constant
- T_d = the development time in years

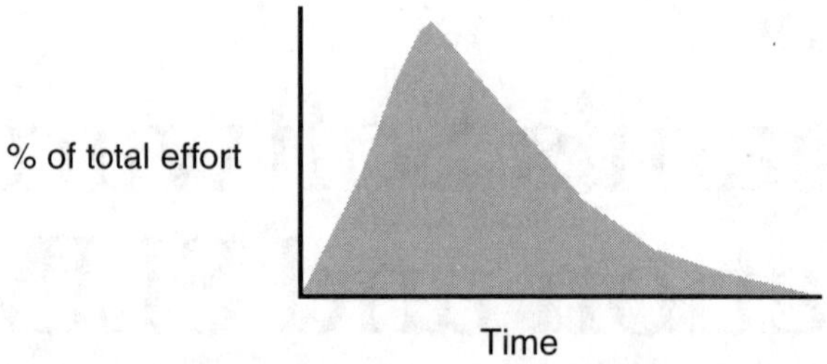

% of total effort

Time

Exhibit 21-1.   The Rayleigh Curve

Example:

$$S_s = 100 \text{ K and } y_{max} = 40 \text{ people}$$

- Using the programmerpower as a constraint, the shortest development time can be estimated.
- The maximum programmerpower occurs at the delivery time (i.e., $t = t_d$).
- This implies that $y_{max} = (K/t_d)e^{-1/2}$.
- This gives $K/t_d = 65.95$.
- Assuming that the technology constant is approximately 1000, we can substitute into the software equation.
- By solving for K and substituting, we get $t_d = 1.722$ years.
- By substituting the value for t_d, we get K = 113.57 programmer years.
- The development cost is 40 percent of K or 45.26 programmer years.
- The daily productivity of the programmers can be calculated. Assuming 250 workdays per year, the programmer productivity per day is equal to S/(.4K * 250) lines or 8.837 lines per day.

To allow effort estimation, Putnam introduced the manpower-buildup equation:

$$D = E/t^3$$

where D is a constant called manpower acceleration, E is the total project effort in years, and t is the elapsed time to delivery in years.

The manpower acceleration is 12.3 for new software with many interfaces and interactions with other systems, 15 for standalone systems, and 27 for reimplementations of existing systems.

Using the software and manpower-buildup equations, we can solve for effort:

$$E = (S/C)^{9/7} (D^{4/7})$$

References

Fenton, N.E. and Pfleeger, S.L. (1997). *Software Metrics: a Rigorous and Practical Approach,* International Thomson Computer Press. Stamford, CN.

Johnson, K. *Software Cost Estimation: Metrics and Models*, University of Calgary, Canada.

http://sern.ucalgary.ca/courses/seng/621/W98/johnsonk/cost.htm#The%20Software %20Equation.

Putnam, L.H. (1978). A general empirical solution to the macro software sizing and estimating problem, IEEE Transactions on Software Engineering, SE-4:4.

Dr. Shmuel Rotenstreich, Software cost estimation, http://www.seas.gwu.edu/~ shmuel/ cs272/14/index.htm. September 1999. George Washington University, Washington, D.C.

Chapter 22
The COCOMO II Model

ABSTRACT

COCOMO is very useful when used for custom, build-to-specification software projects; however, COCOMO II is useful for a much wider collection of techniques and technologies. COCOMO II provides up-to-date support for business software, object-oriented software, software created via spiral or evolutionary development models, and software developed using commercial off-the-shelf application composition utilities. COCOMO II provides models for early prototyping efforts and the more detailed early design and post-architecture models for subsequent portions of the life cycle.

APPLICATION COMPOSITION MODEL

The application composition model is used in prototyping to resolve potential high-risk issues such as user interfaces, software–system interaction, performance, or technology maturity. Object points are used for sizing rather than the traditional LOC metric.

An initial size measure is determined by counting the number of screens, reports, and third-generation components that will be used in the application. Fenton and Pfleeger (1997) classify objects as simple, medium, or difficult using the guidelines shown in Exhibits 22-1 and 22-2.

The number in each cell is then weighted according to Exhibit 22-3. The weights represent the relative effort required to implement an instance of that complexity level (Fenton and Pfleeger, 1997). The weighted instances are summed to provide a single object point number. Reuse is then taken into account. Assuming that r percent of the objects will be reused from previous projects, the number of new object points (NOP) is calculated to be:

$$NOP = (\text{object points}) \times (100 - r)/100$$

Exhibit 22-1. Object Point Complexity Levels for Screens

Number of Views Contained	Number and Source of Data Tables		
	Total <4	Total <8	Total 8+
<3	Simple	Simple	Medium
3–7	Simple	Medium	Difficult
8+	Medium	Difficult	Difficult

Exhibit 22-2. Object Point Complexity Levels for Reports

Number of Views Contained	Number and Source of Data Tables		
	Total <4	Total <8	Total 8+
<3	Simple	Simple	Medium
3–7	Simple	Medium	Difficult
8+	Medium	Difficult	Difficult

Exhibit 22-3. Complexity Weights for Object Points

Object Type	Simple	Medium	Difficult
Screen	1	2	3
Report	2	5	8
3GL component	—	—	10

Exhibit 22-4. Average Productivity Rates Based on Developer's Experience and the ICASE Maturity/Capability

Developer's experience and capability	Very Low	Low	Nominal	High	Very High
ICASE maturity and capability	Very Low	Low	Nominal	High	Very High
PROD	4	7	13	25	50

A productivity rate (PROD) is determined using Exhibit 22-4. Effort can then be estimated using the following equation:

$$E = NOP/PROD$$

THE EARLY DESIGN MODEL

The early design model is used to evaluate alternative software or system architectures and concepts of operation. An unadjusted function point

Exhibit 22-5.   Programming Language Levels and Ranges of Source Code Statements per Function Point

Language	Level	Min	Mode	Max
Machine language	0.10	—	640	—
Assembly	1.00	237	320	416
C	2.50	60	128	170
RPGII	5.50	40	58	85
C++	6.00	40	55	140
Visual C++	9.50	—	34	—
PowerBuilder	20.00	—	16	—
Excel	57.00	—	5.5	—

Exhibit 22-6.   Early Design Cost Drivers

Cost Driver	Description	Counterpart Combined Post-Architecture Cost Driver
RCPX	Product reliability and complexity	RELY, DATA, CPLX, DOCU
RUSE	Required reuse	RUSE
PDIF	Platform difficulty	TIME, STOR, PVOL
PERS	Personnel capability	ACAP, PCAP, PCON
PREX	Personnel experience	AEXP, PEXP, LTEX
FCIL	Facilities	TOOL, SITE
SCED	Schedule	SCED

count (UFC) is used for sizing. This value is converted to LOC using tables such as those published by Capers Jones (1996), excerpted in Exhibit 22-5.

The early design model equation is:

$$E = aKLOC \times EAF$$

where a is a constant, provisionally set to 2.45.

The effort adjustment factor (EAF) is calculated as in the original COCOMO model using the seven Boehm cost drivers shown in Exhibit 22-6.

THE POST-ARCHITECTURE MODEL

The post-architecture model is used during the actual development and maintenance of a product. Function points or LOC can be used for sizing, with modifiers for reuse and software breakage. Boehm advocates the set of guidelines proposed by the Software Engineering Institute in counting lines of code. The post-architecture model includes a set of 17 cost drivers and a set of 5 factors determining the project's scaling component. The five

Exhibit 22-7.   COCOMO II Scale Factors

W(i)	Very Low	Low	Nominal	High	Very High	Extra High
Precedentedness	4.05	3.24	2.42	1.62	0.81	0.00
Development/ Flexibility	6.07	4.86	3.64	2.43	1.21	0.00
Architecture/ Risk Resolution	4.22	3.38	2.53	1.69	0.84	0.00
Team Cohesion	4.94	3.95	2.97	1.98	0.99	0.00
Process Maturity	4.54	3.64	2.73	1.82	0.91	0.00

factors (Exhibit 22-6) replace the development modes (organic, semi-detached, embedded) of the original COCOMO model.

The post-architecture model equation is:

$$E = aKLOC^b \times EAF$$

where a is set to 2.55 and b is calculated as:

$$b = 1.01 + 0.01 \times SUM(Wi)$$

where W is the set of five scale factors shown in Exhibit 22-7.

The EAF is calculated using the 17 cost drivers shown in Exhibit 22-8.

References and Further Readings

Boehm, B. (1981). *Software Engineering Economics*, Prentice-Hall, Englewood Cliffs, NJ.

Boehm, B. (1975). The high cost of software, in *Practical Strategies for Developing Large Software Systems*, Horowitz, E., Ed., Addison-Wesley, Reading, MA, 4–14.

Boehm, B.W., Abts, C., Clark, B., and Devnani-Chulani, S. (1997). COCOMO II Model Definition Manual, The University of Southern California. http://sunset.usc.edu/research/COCOMOII/index.html.

Fenton, N.E. and Pfleeger, S.L. (1997). *Software Metrics: a Rigorous and Practical Approach*, International Thomson Computer Press,.

Johnson, K. Software Cost Estimation: Metrics and Models, University of Calgary. http://sern.ucalgary.ca/courses/seng/621/W98/johnsonk/cost.htm#The%20Software%20Equation.

Jones, C. (1996). *Applied Software Measurement*, McGraw-Hill, New York.

Exhibit 22-8. Post-Architecture Cost Drivers

Cost Driver	Description	Very Low	Low	Nominal	High	Very High	Extra High
						Rating	
Product							
RELY	Required software reliability	0.75	0.88	1.00	1.15	1.39	—
DATA	Database size	—	0.93	1.00	1.09	1.19	—
CPLX	Product complexity	0.70	0.88	1.00	1.15	1.30	1.66
RUSE	Required reusability	—	0.91	1.00	1.14	1.29	1.49
DOCU	Documentation	—	0.95	1.00	1.06	1.13	—
Platform							
TIME	Execution time constraint	—	—	1.00	1.11	1.31	1.67
STOR	Main storage constraint	—	—	1.00	1.06	1.21	1.57
PVOL	Platform volatility	—	0.87	1.00	1.15	1.30	—
Personnel							
ACAP	Analyst capability	1.50	1.22	1.00	0.83	0.67	—
PCAP	Programmer capability	1.37	1.16	1.00	0.87	0.74	—
PCON	Personnel continuity	1.24	1.10	1.00	0.92	0.84	—
AEXP	Applications experience	1.22	1.10	1.00	0.89	0.81	—
PEXP	Platform experience	1.25	1.12	1.00	0.88	0.81	—
LTEX	Language and tool experience	1.22	1.10	1.00	0.91	0.84	—
Project							
TOOL	Software tools	1.24	1.12	1.00	0.86	0.72	—
SITE	Multisite development	1.25	1.10	1.00	0.92	0.84	0.78
SCED	Development schedule	1.29	1.10	1.00	1.00	1.00	—

Chapter 23
Putnam's Cost Estimation Model

ABSTRACT

Putnam's (1978) cost estimation model is a macroestimation model that computes the relationship between cost and the amount of time available for the development effort. The model supports the "mythical man-month" idea first put forth by Frederick Brooks, who asserted that people and time are not always interchangeable.

PROCEDURES/ISSUES/POLICIES

The Putnam formula is as shown in Exhibit 23-1.

$$y = K\frac{t}{t_d^2} e^{-t^2/2t_d^2}$$

Exhibit 23-1.   The Putnam Formula

where

    y = instantaneous programmer power
    y = total life cycle cost in programmer years
    y = time from beginning of project
  td = delivery time
    e = 2.71828.

Reference

Putnam, L.H. (1978). A general empirical solution to the macro software sizing and estimating problem, IEEE Transactions on Software Engineering, SE-4:4.

Chapter 24
Malcolm Baldrige Quality Award

ABSTRACT

The Malcolm Baldrige Quality Award is an annual award to recognize U.S. companies that excel in quality achievement and quality management. The award promotes awareness of quality as an increasingly important element in competitiveness, understanding of the requirements for quality excellence, and sharing of information on successful quality strategies and on benefits derived from implementation of these strategies.

Although only one part of the examination is related to technology, all the Baldrige award tenets of quality apply to the IT process. In this chapter, a synopsis of the requirements is highlighted.

PROCEDURES/ISSUES/POLICIES
1. The award is built upon a number of key concepts:
   * Quality is defined by the customer.
   * The senior leadership of business needs to create clear quality values and build the values into the way the company operates.
   * Quality excellence derives from well-designed and well-executed systems and processes.
   * Continuous improvement must be part of the management of all systems and processes.
   * Companies need to develop goals, as well as strategic and operational plans, to achieve quality leadership.
   * Shortening the response time of all operations and processes of the company needs to be part of the quality improvement effort.
   * Operations and decisions of the company need to be based upon facts and data.
   * All employees must be suitably trained and developed, and involved in quality activities.
   * Design quality and defect and error prevention should be major elements of the quality system.
   * Companies need to communicate quality requirements to suppliers and work to elevate suppliers' quality performance.

2. Examination categories/items	Maximum points
1.0. Leadership	100
1.1 Senior executive leadership	40
1.2 Quality values	15
1.3 Management for quality	25
1.4 Public responsibility	20
2.0. Information and analysis	70
2.1 Scope and management of quality data and information	20
2.2 Competitive comparisons and benchmarks	30
2.3 Analysis of quality data and information	20
3.0. Strategic quality planning	60
3.1 Strategic quality planning process	35
3.2 Quality goals and plans	25
4.0. Human resource utilization	150
4.1 Human resource management	20
4.2 Employee involvement	40
4.3 Quality education and training	40
4.4 Employee recognition and performance measurement	25
4.5 Employee well-being and morale	25
5.0. Quality assurance of product and services	140
5.1 Design and introduction of quality products and services	35
5.2 Process quality control	20
5.3 Continuous improvement of processes	20
5.4 Quality assessment	15
5.5 Documentation	10
5.6 Business process and support service quality	20
5.7 Supplier quality	20
6.0. Quality results	180
6.1 Product and service quality results	90
6.2 Business process, operational and support service quality results	50
6.3 Supplier quality results	40
7.0. Customer satisfaction	300
7.1 Determining customer requirements and expectations	30
7.2 Customer relationship management	50
7.3 Customer service standards	20
7.4 Commitment to customers	15
7.5 Complaint resolution for quality improvement	25
7.6 Determining customer satisfaction	20
7.7 Customer satisfaction results	70
7.8 Customer satisfaction comparison	70

Reference

United States Department of Commerce, National Institute of Standards and Technology, Gaithersburg, MD.

Chapter 25
Zachman's Framework

ABSTRACT

In his seminal work, Zachman (1987) makes the observation that, just as a builder needs a detailed set of plans for a building, a systems developer needs a detailed set of plans for a complex system. He continues this observation by saying that different types of plans are prepared by different parties for different purposes and represent very different views of the same building. Zachman created an architectural framework that is basically a "set of representations" of differing orientations and focuses. This chapter gives a brief overview of Zachman's framework.

PROCEDURES/ISSUES/POLICIES

1. The framework is a two-dimensional classification of the various components of an information systems architecture. One dimension consists of scope description, business model, information system model, technology model and detailed description. The second dimension consists of data description, process description, and network description.
2. Zachman's framework (see Exhibit 25-1)
3. At the scope description level:
   - *Data description:* a list of entities relevant to the business or project
   - *Process description:* a list of business processes
   - *Network description:* a list of locations at which the business operates or at which the processes of interest are performed
4. At the business model level:
   - *Data description:* an entity-relationship diagram
   - *Process description:* possibly a functional flow diagram
   - *Network description:* some form of logistic definition of the enterprise

Exhibit 25-1. Zachman's Framework

	Data Description	Process Description	Network Description
Scope Description			
Business Model			
Information Systems Model			
Technology Model			
Detailed Description			

5. At the information system model level:
   - *Data description:* a detailed logical data model with all the necessary data element definitions
   - *Process description:* possibly a detailed data flow diagram with supporting documentation
   - *Network Description:* plan for system distribution
6. At the technology model level:
   - *Data description:* detailed definition of the external schemas
   - *Process description:* detailed structure chart with complete module specifications
   - *Network description:* system architecture of processors, nodes, and communication lines
7. At the detailed description level:
   - *Data description:* describing actual files, records, fields, etc. as understood by the data management software
   - *Process description:* consisting of the programs
   - *Network description:* in the form used by the communications software

Reference

Zachman, J.A. (1987). A framework for information systems architecture, *IBM Syst. J.*, 26(3).

Chapter 26
Linkman's Method for Controlling Programs through Measurement

ABSTRACT

A controlled development and maintenance program is essential for bringing down the cost associated with software development life cycle. The control mechanism can be implemented first by setting up specific goals and then selecting the right set of metrics for measurements against those goals. Goals must be tangible and balanced or they will be too remote to be considered achievable. Intermediate targets are needed for monitoring the progress of the project and making sure it is on the right track. Project data collection and analysis should also be part of the control mechanism.

A four-step procedure is outlined for establishing targets and means for assessment (Linkman and Walker, 1991). The procedure is not focused on any particular set of metrics; rather, metrics should be selected on the basis of goals. This procedure is suitable for setting up goals for the entire project deliverables or for any partial product created in the software life cycle.

PROCEDURE

1. Define measurable goals: the project goals establishment process is similar to the development process for project deliverables. Software projects usually start with abstract problem concepts; the final project deliverables are obtained by continuously partitioning and refining the problem into tangible and manageable pieces. Final quantified goals can be transformed from initial intangible goals by following the same divide-and-conquer method for software deliverables. Three sources of information are helpful to establishing the targets:

- Historical data is useful under the assumptions that data is available, development environment is stable, and projects are similar in terms of type, size, and complexity.
- Synthetic data such as modeling results is useful if models used are calibrated to specific development environment.
- Expert opinions can be helpful.

2. Maintain balanced goals: the measurable goals are usually established on the basis of four factors: cost, schedule, effort, and quality. It is feasible to achieve just a single goal, but it is always a challenge to deliver a project with the minimum staff and resources, on time, and within budget. It needs to be kept in mind that trade-off is always involved and all issues should be addressed to reach a set of balanced goals.

3. Set up intermediate goals: a project should never be measured only at its end point. Checkpoints should be set up to provide confidence that the project is running on course. The common practice involves setting up quantifiable targets for each phase, measuring the actual values against the targets, and establishing a plan to make corrections for any deviations. All four aforementioned factors should be broken down into phase or activity for setting up intermediate targets. Measurements for cost and effort can be divided into machine and human resources according to software life cycle phase so that expenditures can be monitored to ensure the project is running within budget. The schedule should always be defined in terms of milestones or checkpoints to ensure that intermediate products can be evaluated and the final product will be delivered on time. Quality of intermediate products should always be measured to guarantee the final deliverable will meet its target goal.

4. Establish means of assessment: two aspects are involved in this activity:
   - *Data collection:* based on project characteristics such as size, complexity, level of control, etc., a decision should be made in terms of whether a manual or an automated data collection process should be used. If a nonautomated process is applied, then the availability of the collection medium at the right time should be emphasized.
   - *Data analysis:* the following two types of analyses should be considered:
     — *Project analysis* — this type of analysis, consisting of checkpoint analysis and continuous analysis (trend analysis), is concerned with verifying that intermediate targets are met to ensure that the project is on the right track.
     — *Component analysis* — this type of analysis concentrates on the finer level of details of the end product and is concerned with identifying those components in the product that may

require special attention and action. The complete process includes deciding on the set of measures to be analyzed, identifying the components detected as anomalous using measured data, finding out the root cause of the anomalies, and taking actions to make corrections.

Reference

Linkman, S.G. and Walker, J.G. (1991). Controlling programs through measurement, *Inf. Software Technol.*, 33, 93–102.

Selected Bibliography

Kitchenham, B.A., Packard, L.M., and Linkman, S.G. (1990). An evaluation of some design metrics, *Software Eng. J.*, 5, 50–58.

Linkman, S.G. (1990). Quantitative monitoring of software development by time-based and intercheckpoint monitoring, *Software Eng. J.*, 5, 43–49.

Walker, J.G. and Kitchenham, B.A. (1989). Quality requirements specification and evaluation, in *Measurement for Software Control and Assurance*, Kitchenham, B.A. and Littlewood, B., Eds., Elsevier Applied Science, New York.

Chapter 27

Kellner's Nontechnological Issues in Software Engineering

ABSTRACT

Although much of the emphasis in current literature is on the technical issues of software engineering, a number of substantive nontechnological problems pose dangers to the effective practice of software engineering. A lack of software engineering productivity can be caused by managerial, organizational, economic, political, legal, behavioral, psychological, and social factors.

To achieve an acceptable level of software engineering productivity, as much emphasis must be placed on "people" issues as on technological issues. As Boehm puts it, "Personnel attributes and human relations activities provide by far the largest source of opportunity for improving software productivity" (Boehm, 1981).

PROCEDURES/ISSUES/POLICIES

1. Recognize that the process of software engineering is "sufficiently confused and incoherent that nontechnological factors impede the effective application of technology" (Humphrey, 1989).
2. Many nontechnological issues are intertwined with software engineering. Although any of these is a potential impediment, the Kellner panel focused on three:
   - The software engineering profession, for the most part, has not developed a block of capable and competent managers.
   - In spite of a concerted effort toward making software development an engineering discipline, it is still very much of an individual creative activity, rather than a team effort.
   - Little has been done to reduce performance differences among individuals or across teams.

3. Poor management produces:
   - Unrealistic project plans due to poor planning, scheduling, and estimation skills
   - Unmotivated staff due to inability of management to manage a creative staff
   - Lack of teamwork due to inability to build and manage effective teams
   - Poor project execution due to inadequate organization, delegation, and monitoring
   - Technical problems due to lack of management understanding of disciplines such as quality assurance and configuration management
   - Inadequately trained staff due to a short-sighted rather than a long-term perspective
4. Possible solutions to poor management problems:
   - Definition of dual career paths for technical and managerial staff
   - Training in managerial skills and techniques
   - Active mentoring and supervision by senior managers
   - Increased delegation of responsibility and matching authority
5. Reasons for lack of teamwork:
   - Desire for autonomy
   - A culture that reinforces individual efforts more than team efforts
   - Concentration of key application knowledge by a few individuals
   - Desire for privacy
   - The "not invented here" syndrome translated to the "not invented by me" syndrome
   - Large productivity differences from one individual to another
   - Political considerations between powerful individuals and managers
6. Possible solutions to teamwork problems:
   - Objective assessment of team contributions with appropriate rewards
   - Development of an organizational culture that condones and rewards group efforts
   - Active efforts to disperse crucial application knowledge across project staff
   - Improvements in communication and coordination across organizational layers
   - Adoption of "egoless" programming techniques
7. Large performance differences between individuals negate productivity increases. Boehm estimates that productivity ranges of 3:1 to 5:1 are typical, with some studies documenting differences as high as 26:1 among experienced programmers (Boehm, 1981). This variability is often due to:
   - Misguided staffing practices

- Poor team development
- Inattention to the critical role of motivation
- Poor management

8. Techniques to increase effective level of productivity:
   - Enhanced training
   - Investment in productivity tools (tools, methods)
   - Standard practices
   - Professional development opportunities
   - Recognition
   - Effective staffing
   - Top talent
   - Job matching
   - Career progression
   - Team balance
   - Improved management

References

Boehm, B.W. (1981). *Software Engineering Economics*, Prentice-Hall, Inc., New York.

Humphrey, W.S. (1989). *Managing the Software Process*, Addison-Wesley, Reading, MA.

Selected Bibliography

Brooks, F.P. (1987). No silver bullet, *Computer*, 20, 10–19.

Curtis, B., Krasner, H., and Iscoe, N. (1988). A field study of the software design process for large systems, *Commn. ACM*, 31, 1268–1287.

Humphrey, W.S., Kitson, D.H., and Kasse, T.C. (1989). The State of Software Engineering Practice: a Preliminary Report. Tech Rept. CMU/SEI-89-TR-1, Software Engineering Institute, Carnegie Mellon University, Pittsburgh.

Kellner, M.I. Software Engineering Institute, with panelists Bill Curtis, Software Engineering Institute, Tom DeMarco, The Atlantic Systems Guild, Kouichi Kisida, Software Research Associates, Inc., Maurice Schlumberger, Cap Gemeini Innovation, Colin Tully, Independent Consultant for IEEE, 1991, 144–146.

Chapter 28

Martin and Carey's Survey of Success in Converting Prototypes to Operational Systems

ABSTRACT

The use of prototyping has increased within the ranks of MIS groups during the last few years; however, a difference of opinion exists as to how a prototype should be implemented as well as about the steps taken to make the prototype operational. One school of thought stresses that the prototype is never meant to become an operational system. Therefore, the languages used as well as the platform selected should be experimental. On the other side of the argument are those stressing that the prototypical system should be as close to the operational system as possible. This disagreement has left MIS organizations without clear guidelines for the use of prototypes in their companies.

Martin and Carey (1991) conducted an extensive survey of a sector of MIS shops within the manufacturing industry and found that "prototype models were usually not thrown away, prototypes were usually programmed in the same language as the operational system, prototyping in third generational languages was common, and prototyping models were documented as they were developed." These findings, although contrary to much of the literature on prototyping, are important in that they open a fresh perspective on an important topic.

According to Martin and Carey, "prototyping is the process of quickly building a model of the final software system which is used primarily as a communication tool to assess and meet the information needs of the user."

Their survey found that the use of prototyping was born out of some major difficulties in the traditional software development approach, including:

- End users do not often possess a clear and concise understanding of what they need and what they want.
- The methodologies and tools currently employed by MIS, data-flow diagrams and the like cannot demonstrate the workings of an actual system to the liking, or understanding, of a naive end user.
- As the development team grows, so does the complexity of the task of communication between group members.
- Systems developed along traditional lines are often difficult to learn and use.
- As the technology becomes more complex, so do the systems created. As a result, systems are often developed over longer time periods.
- Traditional approaches have been plagued by late delivery and costly overruns.
- It comes as no surprise to MIS staff that a rather large application development backlog exists. According to Martin and Carey, "the users who requested them are frustrated, disillusioned, and ready to revolt."

Observed in the abstract, two schools of thought exist concerning prototypes; each has adopted a distinct type of prototype. The iterative type (labeled Type I by Martin and Carey) implements the final version of the prototype after a series of modifications. The Martin and Carey Type II prototype, the throwaway, is often built in a fourth generation language and is, indeed, only a model of the final system. At prototype's end, this model is "thrown away" and the system is ultimately implemented in a third generation language.

PROCEDURES/ISSUES/POLICIES

1. In general, the use of prototyping appears more appropriate for small decision support systems than for large transaction processing systems. Decision support systems may beneficially use Type I iterative systems. However, it has also been found that a transaction processing system might benefit from a Type II throwaway prototype.
2. In planning a prototype, the development team should take note of possible differences between the prototype and operational environments, including:
    - Language
    - Range of transactions
    - Documentation requirements
    - Computer architecture
    - Access control
    - Procedures

3. The programming language for the ultimate operational system should be self-documenting. There are inherent differences between third generation languages of the operational environment and fourth generation languages of the prototype environment. These include:
   - 4GLs are not as self-documenting as 3GLs.
   - 4GLs more than likely have features not available in 3GLs, such as rapid database inquiry.
   - 4GLs often use recursive paths not compatible with the structured, top–down operational language requirements.
4. Of a system's inputs, 4.20 percent usually represent 80 percent of the transaction volume. Therefore, it is this 20 percent that should be the domain of prototyping, according to Martin and Carey, because "a prototype is designed to show users what typically will happen, rather than all that can happen."
5. Turning a prototype into an operational system requires the development team to account for 100 percent of the system's transactions, rather than the 20 percent accountable in the prototype.
6. Prototypes are often run on a microcomputer because:
   - The PC is portable for demonstrations.
   - It will not be disrupted by operational problems.
   - It will not disrupt operations systems.
7. Systems are composed of more than just software. Systems also include hardware, people, and data. The procedures used to tie all of these together in the prototype are far less complex than procedures required in an operational system.
8. Conversion from an iterative prototype to a full operational system is complex and time consuming. Steps required include:
   - Language conversion
   - Expansion to full transaction range
   - Extensive documentation
   - Change from microenvironment to operational platform
   - Establishment of access control
   - Development of procedures
9. The pain of prototype to operational system conversion can be eased somewhat by careful development of the prototype. Approaches that accomplish this goal include:
   - The prototype should be programmed in the same language as the ultimate operational system.
   - The prototype should be documented as it evolves.
   - The prototype should be developed on the ultimate platform. If the system is intended for use on a mainframe, then prototype it on a mainframe

10. The Martin and Carey survey documented the prototyping characteristics discussed above as the techniques used in a segment of commercial industry. The specific survey results follow:
    - Prototype models were not usually thrown away.
    - Throwaway prototypes were not actually thrown away; they were often used for other purposes, such as training.
    - Prototypes were usually programmed in the same language as the operational system.
    - Prototyping in 3GLs was not uncommon. According to Martin and Carey, "the power of reusable code for a 3GL such as COBOL should not be underestimated."
    - Prototyping models were documented as they were developed.
    - The primary goal of the prototype process was user communications and involvement, not system development efficiency.

Reference

Martin, M.P. and Carey, J.M. (1991). Converting prototypes to operational systems: evidence from preliminary industrial survey, *Inf. Software Technol.*, 33, 351–356.

Selected Bibliography

Carey, J.M. and McLeod Jr., R. (1987). Use of system development methodology and tools, *J. Syst. Manage.*, 39, 30–35.

Carey, J.M. (1989). Prototyping:alternative systems development methodology, *Inf. Software Technol.*, September, 31(8).

Kingler, D.E. (1986). Rapid prototyping revisited, *Datamation*, 32, 131–132.

Martin, M.P. (1988). The transition between the prototype and the operational environment, Proc. Western Region of Deciison Sciences Institute (April 1988).

Martin, M.P. (1987). Designing systems for change, *J. Syst. Manage.*, 39, 14–18.

Chapter 29
Putnam's Trends in Measurement, Estimation, and Control

ABSTRACT

Although most MIS managers have read about the different techniques of measurement, estimation, and control, they are still confused about how to apply them to their own situations. In addition, a plethora of information about this topic has served only to confuse these practitioners, rather than enlighten them.

Putnam estimates that, in the development of complex systems, from 50 to 70 percent of these projects come in late, over budget, or in error. Most academicians as well as notables in the field, Putnam included, conclude that one of the major problems is that MIS departments have not developed the facilities to gauge where they are or where they should be. The old stand-by, lines of code (LOC), is, according to Putnam, "the worse metric." Twelve years of Putnam's research has shown that "both the numerator (number of lines) and the denominator (number of man-months) vary with a host of factors related to the environment and management practices in complex, ill-understood, nonlinear ways that cause it to behave unintuitively" (Putnam, 1991). The result is that the LOC metric is wrong approximately 90 percent of the time.

In the late 1980s and in the 1990s, emphasis on measurement has been renewed. MIS shops are now attempting to evaluate the reliability of software. In this chapter, a series of issues is raised in this area that the professional intent on installing a measurement program will want to review carefully.

PROCEDURES/ISSUES/POLICIES

1. Putnam defines a set of workable metrics as that which is simple, single valued, and which the boss understands. The following is the set that he recommends:
   - Quantity of function (such as source lines of code and function points)
   - Schedule (the elapsed calendar time)
   - People (the monthly head count)
   - Effort (the sum of the people applied over time)
   - Defects (the number of valid problem trouble reports over some time interval. This can easily be converted to mean time to defect.)
2. Making total quality realistic in a software engineering environment:
   - Take quality seriously.
   - Take productivity improvement seriously.
   - Measure progress with the right metrics.
   - Set realistic goals.
   - Focus MIS investment and education on the weaker spots.
   - Aim for a small gain every day.
3. Use statistical process control on projects. This technique couples statistical techniques with the metrics outlined above. The basics of software control:
   - Milestone accomplishments (schedule)
   - Effort expenditure (in man-months)
   - Code production
   - Defect identification (trouble reports)
4. These statistics should be captured each month and compared with the plan.
5. Unfavorable variations indicate slippage and overrun.
6. Statistical software packages should be used because a simple extrapolation to predict the future is not useful. Statistical curve-fitting techniques, readily available in this type of software, are a desirable tool for control.
7. Putnam's outlook for the future:
   - Control offices will be established to measure, plan, and control projects. This will be called the software-data repository and will be responsible for measuring process–productivity improvement as well as for generating realistic and consistent work plans for the individual project teams.
8. Executive managers will begin to take a more active interest in development because they realize that it is strategically important to the organization.

Reference

Putnam, L.H. (1991). Trends in measurement, estimation, and control, *IEEE Software*, March, 105–107.

Chapter 30
Sprague's Technique for Software Configuration Management in a Measurement-Based Software Engineering Program

ABSTRACT

The role of software configuration management (SCM) has increased in significance over the last few years. Sprague enumerates several reasons for SCM's expanded role:

The size of software projects has grown meaning that there are more components to manage.

The introduction of CASE tools has increased the number and types of machine-readable objects that must be maintained.

New computing topologies and application structures have come on the scene.

These reasons, coupled with an increasing awareness of the competitive and strategic organizational issues vis-a-vis technology, have placed an emphasis on being able to control the technology environment.

Sprague's definition of SCM expands on the traditional meaning, which is control over the source code. Sprague emphasizes that SCM should consider all of the work products associated with a project including:

- Contracts
- Memorandums
- Letters
- Project plans
- Schedules
- System and software requirements
- Design documentation
- Source, object, and executable code
- Data
- Build and installation files
- Test descriptions, results, and reports
- Systems and network options
- Metrics
- Technical reports
- Education and training documents
- Presentation slides
- Videos
- Business models and plans

SCM is a formal engineering discipline, as described in the 1983 IEEE standard 828–1983. "Standard for Software Configuration Management Plans" is the means through which the integrity of the software product is recorded, communicated, and controlled. Derived from hardware-oriented configuration management (CM), SCM's objective is the cost-effective management of a software system's life cycle and the resultant configuration. As Sprague (1991) suggests, "it is the process of ensuring the software and associated products are visible, traceable, and formally controlled throughout their evolution."

Perhaps the most important concept behind SCM is baseline management. A baseline is a specification or product, formally reviewed and agreed upon, which thereafter serves as the basis for further development — one that can be changed only through formal change control procedures.

Four functions are employed to manage the baseline and its products: configuration identification, configuration control, configuration status accounting, and configuration auditing. This chapter presents an overview of SCM as well as a process for implementing it.

PROCEDURES/ISSUES/POLICIES

1. Configuration identification is the process of designating the configuration items in a system and recording their characteristics. This process entails determination of the constituent parts of the software and of the relationship of those parts, assignment of a label and a name to each part, and graphical depiction of the identified software.

2. Configuration control provides the administrative mechanism for precipitating, preparing, evaluating, approving or disapproving, and implementing every change to all the products in a baseline. The purpose of configuration control is to assure:
   - Comprehensive system impact analysis
   - Cost and schedule impact analysis
   - Optimum and coordinated implementation
   - Accurate configuration records
   - Supportability

3. Configuration status accounting is the process of collecting, recording, and reporting on configuration control information. The following information is typically maintained as well as archived:
   - The time at which each baseline was established
   - The time at which each item and change was included in the baseline
   - A description of each software configuration item
   - The status of each software-related engineering change
   - The description of each software change
   - The documentation status for each baseline
   - The changes planned for each identified future baseline.

4. Configuration auditing is the process of verifying that all required configuration items have been produced, that the current version agrees with the specified requirements, that the technical documentation describes the configuration items, and that all change requests have been resolved.

PROCEDURES FOR DEVELOPING AN SCM PROCESS

1. Develop an SCMP.
   - The first step is to develop a plan tailored to the needs of the project and organization. The plan addresses the four components of SCM described above. The SCMP should address the following:
   - The characteristics of the work products controlled
   - The work products to be controlled
   - The different interfaces to be managed

- The expected duration of the project
- The available resources
- The organizational responsibilities of project members
- The identification procedures that will be used on each project
- The procedures for checking items into and out of the software libraries
- The procedures for managing the change process
- The authority, membership, and decision-making process of the group charged with this information's control
- The procedures to create and approve the promotion of a baseline
- The membership data that will be collected, stored, and reported
- The procedures to collect, store, and report the measurement data
- The mechanism to transfer objects between repositories
- The procedures for releasing versions
- The automated tools that will be used to support the SCM process
- The procedure for recovering work products in the event of a disaster

2. Implement the SCMP:
    - This step requires that those charged with the SCM take actions to ensure that it is implemented. This implies that the SCMP be periodically reviewed — and revised, if necessary.
3. Identify and control the work products.
    - This task is accomplished by identifying each object checked into the repository, securing an electronic or paper copy of the object, placing the object in a location where it cannot be modified, and, finally, making a log entry describing the events that took place during the transaction.
4. Collect, store, and report preliminary measurements.
    - This should be done at each phase of the development project. The benefits derived from collecting and analyzing the measurements at each stage provide the manager with insight into how the project is doing in terms of cost, schedule, and size.
5. Transfer the work products to the work group responsible for SCM, who will secure and control it.
6. Deliver the work products to the customer.
7. Collect, store, and report the final measurements to project members and users, as well as to senior management.

Reference

Sprague, K.G. (1991). The role of software configuration management in a measurement-based software engineering program, *ACM SIGSOFT Software Eng. Notes*, 16, 1–10.

Selected Bibliography

Bryan, W.L. and Siegel, S. (1988). *Software Product Assurance: Techniques for Reducing Software Risk*, Elsevier Science Publishing, New York.

Forte, G. (1990). Configuration management survey, *CASE Outlook*, 90, 24–51.

Humphrey, W.S. (1989). *Managing the Software Process*, Addison-Wesley Publishing Co., Reading, MA.

Tichy, W.F. (1989). Tools for software configuration management, 11th International Conference on Software Engineering, May 15–18, 1989.

Chapter 31
Corbin's Methodology for Establishing a Software Development Environment

ABSTRACT

The software development environment (SDE) is actually the integration of a number of processes, tools, standards, methodologies, and related elements whose purpose is to provide a framework for building quality software (Corbin, 1991). This chapter discusses the elements of SDE and shows how to develop one.

PROCEDURES/ISSUES/POLICIES

1. The elements of SDE:
   - Project management
   - Business plan
   - Architecture
   - Methodologies
   - Techniques
   - Tools
   - Metrics
   - Policies and procedures
   - Technology platform
   - Support
   - Standards
   - Education and training

2. The benefits of SDE:
   - Improved problem definition
   - Selection of the "right" problem according to the customer
   - Joint customer and IS responsibility and accountability
   - Acknowledgment of customer ownership of system
   - Reduced costs of systems development and maintenance
   - Reusability of software, models, and data definitions
   - Acceptance of the disciplined approach to software engineering using a consistent methodology
   - Productivity improvements through team efforts and tools such as CASE
3. Sample goals of SDE:
   - Reduce systems development costs
   - Reduce maintenance costs
   - Reduce MIS turnover rate

   These goals should be quantifiable wherever possible. For example, the first goal could be stated as "reduce systems development costs by 50 percent over the next five years."
4. Architecture: many organizations do not have a formal, documented architecture. There are three types:
   - Business architecture is a model of the business and identifies such things as processes and entities in the form of models.
   - Computing architecture, at a minimum, identifies hardware, software, and data communications. This breaks out into components such as operating systems, data resource management, network protocols, and user interface.
   - Enterprise architecture is a combination of business and computing architectures.
5. Business plan:
   - Create a steering committee that provides direction to the MIS function
   - Translate the organization's business plan into an actionable MIS plan that supports the company's goals and objectives
   - The steering committee should be responsible for funding projects, setting priorities, resolving business issues, and reviewing MIS policies and procedures.
6. Education and training: make sure that analysts, programmers, and users are trained and ready to start the development project. Training might include the following:
   - Software engineering concepts
   - Prototyping
   - System development life cycle
   - Joint application development
   - Software quality assurance and testing
   - Project management

- Data and process modeling
- CASE

7. Methodologies: whether the methodology chosen by the MIS department is a standard one, supplied from a vendor, or developed internally, the MIS group must follow one to ensure consistency from project to project. This will enable staff to be able to move from project to project without retraining while, at the same time, ensuring consistent deliverables. Questions to ask when selecting a methodology are:
   - Does your methodology support the entire systems development life cycle?
   - Does it include maintenance?
   - Is it clearly documented?
   - Does it focus on deliverables instead of activities?
   - Is it CASE tool-independent?
   - Can you use your metrics and techniques with it?

8. Project Management: questions to ask include:
   - Do you have a formal project management discipline in place?
   - Do you have a training program to support this?
   - Is a software tool used?
   - Do you have program planning and control to help manage the project?
   - Do you get routine reports showing the project work breakdown structure, status reports, resource loading, and cost projections?
   - Is there a formal reporting mechanism done on a timely basis to resolve problems?

9. Standards: some of the areas in which standards are required are:
   - Systems analysis and design
   - Data administration
   - Database administration
   - Systems testing
   - Prototyping
   - Documentation
   - Data entry
   - Systems production

   Change/configuration management questions to ask:
   - Have you identified all of the standards required to support your SDE?
   - Do you have someone responsible for developing and maintaining standards?

10. Support options:
    - External consulting
    - A sharing arrangement where you can provide services in exchange for those needed
    - User groups
    - Special-interest groups

11. Automated tool questions:
    - Have you identified the tools you need in the SDE?
    - Have they been approved, acquired, and installed?
    - Do they support the methodologies?
    - Do they support the technology platform?
    - Do they support the standards?
    - Is technical support available to support the tools?
    - Do you have templates for use in systems development?
    - Do you have a data dictionary or repository for your data?
    - Do you have tools to support each phase of the life cycle?

References

Corbin, D.S. (1991). Establishing the software development environment, *J. Syst. Manage.*, September, 28–31.

Chapter 32
Couger's Bottom-Up Approach to Creativity Improvement in IS Development

ABSTRACT

The majority of IS organizations use a top–down approach to generating productivity improvements. In this chapter, a process for generating productivity via a series of bottom–up creativity techniques is addressed. The authors are all staff members of the United Technologies Microelectronic Center who, upon a six-month review of all available IS literature, found that very little research had been published in the area of creativity generation techniques in information systems organization. Couger and co-workers (1991) decided to cull creativity-generating techniques that had been proven successful in other disciplines. As a result, a two-pronged approach was selected for the UTMC creativity program:

- Improvement of the environment for creativity and innovation
- Training in specific techniques for creativity generation and evaluation

The results of the institution of this approach were exciting. According to the authors, the creativity program more than paid for itself in efficiency improvements alone — in savings of computer processing time and computer programming time. In addition, the UTMC group saw great improvements in the effectiveness of their systems.

PROCEDURES/ISSUES/POLICIES

1. Survey participants were to obtain perceptions on the environment for creativity and innovation. This same instrument should be used to obtain new perceptions as a measurement of the results.

2. Participants were asked to keep a "creativity log" in which they keep track of their creativity improvements.
3. A training workshop was instituted to teach a variety of creativity generation and evaluation techniques.
4. One third of the workshop was spent in discussing how to improve the climate for creativity in the IS organization. The methodology used for this assessment was to ask the employees to identify positive and negative contributors to the creativity environment.
5. Creativity generation and evaluation techniques were used:
   - *Analogy/metaphor.* An analogy is a statement about how objects, people, situations, or actions are similar in process or relationship. Metaphors, on the other hand, are merely figures of speech. Both of these techniques can be used to create fictional situations for gaining new perspectives on problem definition and resolution.
   - *Brainstorming.* This technique is perhaps the most familiar of all the techniques discussed here. It is used to generate a large quantity of ideas in a short period of time.
   - *Blue slip.* Ideas are individually generated and recorded on a 3×5 in. sheet of blue paper. Because this is done anonymously to make people feel more at ease, people readily share ideas. Each idea is on a separate piece of blue paper, so the sorting and grouping of like ideas is facilitated.
   - *Extrapolation.* A technique or approach, already used by the organization, is stretched to apply to a new problem.
   - *Progressive abstraction technique.* By moving through progressively higher levels of abstraction, it is possible to generate alternative problem definitions from an original problem. When a problem is enlarged in a systematic way, it is possible to generate many new definitions that can then be evaluated for their usefulness and feasibility. Once an appropriate level of abstraction is reached, possible solutions are more easily identified.
   - *5Ws and H technique.* This is the traditional journalistic approach of "who–what–where–when–why–how." Use of this technique serves to expand a person's view of the problem and to assist in making sure that all related aspects of the problem have been addressed and considered.
   - *Force field analysis technique.* The name of this technique comes from its ability to identify forces contributing to or hindering a solution to a problem. This technique stimulates creative thinking in three ways:
     — It defines direction.
     — It identifies strengths that can be maximized.
     — It identifies weaknesses that can be minimized.

- *Peaceful setting.* This is not so much a technique as it is an environment. Taking people away from their hectic surroundings enables "a less cluttered open mental process."
- *Problem reversal.* Reversing a problem statement often provides a different framework for analysis. For example, in attempting to come up with ways to improve productivity, try considering the opposite: how to decrease productivity.
- *Associations/image technique.* Most of us have played the game, at one time or another, where a person names a person, place, or thing and asks for the first thing that pops into the second person's mind. The linking of combining processes is another way of expanding the solution space.
- *Wishful thinking.* This technique enables people to loosen analytical parameters to consider a larger set of alternatives than they might ordinarily consider. By permitting a degree of fantasy in the process, the result just might be a new and unique approach.
6. Follow-up sessions were scheduled for reinforcement. At these meetings, primarily staff meetings, employees were invited to identify results of creative activity.

Reference

Couger, J.D., McIntyre, S.C., Higgins, L.F., and Snow, T.A. (1991). Using a bottom–up approach to creativity improvement in IS development, *J. Syst. Manage.*, September, 23–36.

Chapter 33
Shetty's Seven Principles of Quality Leaders

ABSTRACT

Y. K. Shetty, a professor of management at Utah State University's College of Business and the co-editor of *The Quest for Competitiveness* (Quorum Books, 1991), suggests that even though most corporate executives believe that quality and productivity are the most critical issues facing American business, many do not know how to achieve it. Shetty lists 16 organizations that have vigorously attacked this challenge: Hewlett-Packard, IBM, Procter and Gamble, Johnson & Johnson, Maytag, Dana Corporation, Intel, Texas Instruments, 3M, Caterpillar, Delta, Marriott, McDonald's, Dow Chemical, Xerox, and General Electric. Shetty's chapter discusses the common principles shared by this elite group.

PROCEDURES/ISSUES/POLICIES

Principle 1: Quality improvement requires the firm commitment of top management. All top management, including the CEO, must be personally committed to quality. The keyword here is "personally." Many CEOs pay only lip service to this particular edit. Therefore, top management must be consistent and reflect its commitment through the company's philosophy, goals, policies, priorities, and executive behavior. Steps that management can take to accomplish this end include:

- Establish and communicate a clear vision of corporate philosophy, principles, and objectives relevant to product and service quality.
  - Channel resources toward these objectives and define roles and responsibilities in this endeavor.
  - Invest time to learn about quality issues and monitor the progress of any initiatives.
  - Encourage communication between management and employees, among departments, and among various units of the firm and customers.
  - Be a good role model in communication and action.

Principle 2: Quality is a strategic issue.

- It must be a part of a company's goals and strategies.
- Must be consistent with and reinforce a company's other strategic objectives.
- It must be integrated into budgets and plans — the way the company does business.
- It must be a corporate mission with planned goals and strategies.
- Quality should be at the heart of every action.

Principle 3: Employees are the key to consistent quality.

- The organization must have a people-oriented philosophy.
- Poorly managed people convey their disdain for quality and service when they work.
- Pay special attention to employee recruitment, selection, and socialization.
- Reinforce socialization and quality process with continuous training and education. This should include training in:
  - Awareness of quality
  - Each employee's role in the process
  - Statistical process control
  - Problem-solving techniques
- Incorporate quality into performance appraisal and reward systems.
- Encourage employee participation and involvement.
- Effective communication throughout the department, between departments, and throughout the organization is required to reinforce the deep commitment of management and create an awareness and understanding of the role of quality and customer service.

Principle 4: Quality standards and measurements must be customer-driven. They can be measured by:

- Formal customer surveys
- Focus groups
- Customer complaints
- Quality audits
- Testing panels
- Statistical quality controls
- Interaction with customers

Principle 5: Many programs and techniques can be used to improve quality, such as:

- Statistical quality control
- Quality circles
- Suggestion systems
- Quality-of-work-life projects
- Competitive benchmarking

Principle 6: All company activities have potential for improving product quality; therefore, teamwork is vital.

- Quality improvement requires close cooperation between managers and employees and among departments.
- Total quality management involves preventing errors at the point where work is performed.
- Every employee and department is responsible for quality.

Principle 7: Quality is a never-ending process.

- Quality must be planned.
- Quality must be organized.
- Quality must be monitored.
- Quality must be continuously revitalized.

Reference

Shetty, Y.K. (1991–1992). A point of view: seven principles of quality leaders, *Natl. Productivity Rev.*, Winter, 3–7.

Chapter 34
Simmons' Statistics Concerning Communications' Effect on Group Productivity

ABSTRACT

In this chapter Simmons (1991) details the many factors that dominate software group productivity. He defines dominator as a single factor that causes productivity to decline tenfold. The two dominators discussed are communications and design partition. What follows is a set of rules and statistics that the reader can use as a comparison in his or her own efforts to increase productivity.

PROCEDURES/ISSUES/POLICIES

1. Factors that developers must cope with in developing large systems:
   - Personnel turnover
   - Hardware/software turnover
   - Major ideas incorporated late
   - Latent bugs
2. A Delphi survey performed by Scott and Simmons (1974) to uncover factors that affect productivity found that the main factors are:
   - External documentation
   - Programming language
   - Programming tools
   - Programmer experience
   - Communications
   - Independent modules for task assignment (design partition)
   - Well-defined programming practices

3. Improvement statistics:
   - Any step toward the use of structured techniques, interactive development, inspections, etc. can improve productivity by up to 25 percent.
   - Use of these techniques in combination could yield improvements of between 25 and 50 percent.
   - Change in programming language can, by itself, yield a productivity improvement of more than 50 percent.
   - Gains of between 50 and 75 percent can be achieved by single high achievers or teams of high achievers.
   - Gains of 100 percent can be achieved by database user languages, application generators, and software reuse.
4. Dominators are factors that can suppress the effects of other factors and can reduce software group productivity by an order of magnitude.
5. Poor design partition can dominate group productivity. To obtain high productivity in the development of large software systems, the designer must break down the system in chunks that can be developed in parallel. The difference between great and average designers is an order of magnitude.
6. Communications can dominate productivity. Most project problems arise as the result of poor communications between workers. If n workers are on the team, then there are n(n — 1)/2 interfaces across which communications problems may occur.
7. Productivity of individual programmers varies as much as 26 to 1.
8. An individual working alone has no interruptions from fellow group members and, therefore, the productivity can be quite high for a motivated individual. It is estimated that one programmer working 60 hours a week can complete a project in the same calendar time as two others working normal hours, but at three-quarters of the cost.
9. Small groups of experienced and productive software developers can create large systems. An example is given of a company, Pyburn Systems, which scours the country for the best analytical thinkers. Its senior programmers typically earn $125,000 a year and can be paid bonuses of two to three times that amount. They work in small teams, never more than five, to produce large, complex systems. In comparison, most MIS departments produce large systems using normal development teams with developers of average ability.
10. In general, the difference between the cost to produce an individual program to be run by the program author and the cost to produce a programming system product developed by a software group is at least nine times more expensive.
11. At some point coordination overheads outweigh any benefits that can be obtained by the addition of further staff. Statistics that support this were pioneered during the 19th century in work on a military

organization. It was noted that as the number of workers who had to communicate increased arithmetically, from two to three to four to five..., the number of communication channels among them increased geometrically, from one to three to six to ten.... From this study, it was concluded that the upper limit of effective staff size for cooperative projects is about eight.

12. It has been shown in studies that when the number of staff increased to 12 or more, the efficiency of the group decreased to less than 30 percent.

13. The productive time of a typical software developer during a working day can vary from 51 to 79 percent. It was found that the average duration of work interruption was five minutes for a typical programmer. The average time to regain a train of thought after an interruption was two minutes. Thus, the average total time spent on an interruption was seven minutes. If we assume five productive hours each day, then each interruption takes 2.33 percent of the working day; ten interruptions would take up 23 percent of the day and 20 interruptions would take approximately 50 percent.

14. The optimum group size for a software development team is between five to eight members. The overall design should be partitioned into successively smaller chunks, until the development group has a chunk of software to develop that minimizes intragroup and intergroup communications.

References

Scott, R.F. and Simmons, D.B. (1974). Programmer productivity and the Delphi technique, *Datamation*, 72–73.

Simmons, D.B. (1991). Communications: a software group productivity dominator, *Software Eng. J.*, November, 454–462.

Selected Bibliography

Factor, R.M. and Smith, W.B. (1988). A discipline for improving software productivity, *AT&T Tech. J.*, July/August 1988, 2–9.

Grady, R.B. and Caswell, D.L. (1987). *Software Metrics: Establishing a Company-Wide Program*, Prentice-Hall, Englewood Cliffs, NJ.

Jones, C. (1977). Program quality and programmer productivity, IBM Technical Report TR 02.764, January 1977, 42–78.

Simmons, D.B. (1972). The art of writing large programs, *Computer*, March/April, 43–49.

Software Productivity Metrics Working Group. (1989). Standard for software productivity metrics, IEEE, Standard P1045/32.0, November 20, 1989.

Chapter 35
Gould's Points on Usability

ABSTRACT

Few in the industry have added usability design to their rostrum of design issues. However, Gould, Boies, and Lewis (1991) note that this process leads to usable, useful, likable computer systems and applications. The authors present Strong evidence that readers can use to support their own efforts in this, perhaps, new terrain. This chapter also details a process that can be used to design effective and usable systems. In effect, this chapter proposes:

- Greater reliance on existing methodologies for establishing testable usability and productivity-enhancing goals
- A new method for identifying and focusing attention on long-term trends about the effects that computer applications have on end-user productivity
- A new approach to application development, particularly the development of user interfaces

The authors conclude that a three-way split among style of the user interface, content of the user interface, and the functional code allows changes to be made in the user interface that still preserve the integrity of the functional code. Iterative design, a necessity when looking toward usability, proceeds rapidly. On the style side, a particular style can be prototyped and iteratively engineered. From the set of styles developed over time, a subset of workable, usable styles will emerge that have attained the favor of organizations or end users. Ultimately, the best work of the style side and the functional side of development will be better leveraged.

PROCEDURES/ISSUES/POLICIES:

1. The usability process consists of four activities:
   - Early focus on users should be via interviews, surveys, observations, and participatory design with an aim toward understanding users' cognitive, behavioral, and attitudinal characteristics.

- All facets of usability, for example, user interface, help system, training plan, and documentation, should evolve in parallel, rather than be defined sequentially and be under one management.
- User testing should be early and continual. This should include observation and measurement of user behavior and careful evaluation of feedback. Ultimately, a strong motivation to make design changes should exist.
- Iterative design must be used. Because the system under design must be continually modified due to results of behavioral tests of function, the system must have the ability to be changed continually.

2. This type of development effort has been used with great success:
   - Xerox's Star system
   - Apple's Lisa system
   - IBM Audio Distribution Systems (ADS)
   - IBM's Rexx
   - Tektronix's Graphic Input Workstation
   - Boeing's banking terminal
   - Digital Equipment Corporation's VAX text processing utility
   - IBM's QMF
   - Lotus Development Corporation's Lotus 1–2–3

3. Six interacting, organizational reasons why usability design is not used:
   - Usability is seldom a goal in development.
   - There is a belief that usability cannot be measured — even though there is much evidence to the contrary.
   - An apparent conflict between meeting deadlines and achieving usability exists. Project managers often lack confidence in managing something that does not have clear goals or the tools to address problems efficiently as they arise.
   - Designers report that software development is not organized to carry out the process of usability. Iterative design is thought to be too risky, time consuming, and too difficult.
   - Designers need better tools to do iterative design.
   - Nearly every new application creates its own user interface, which creates an enormous amount of work. Also, these interfaces are not usually developed by people skilled in user-interface design.

4. Usability metrics can be created. They must be clearly stated, easily communicated, and verifiable. The results must be made public. Experience has shown that these results are then taken seriously by management. This has always been the case in logging system performance data. This operation-room metric is a viable usability metric. Measures here include percent system available, downtime per

Exhibit 35-1. Usability Engineering Approach

Attribute	Measuring Concept	Measuring Method	Worst Case	Planned Level	Best Case	Now Level
Installability	Install task	Time to install	1 day with media	1 hour without media	10 minutes with media	Many cannot install
Learning rate						
Fear of seeming foolish						

day, and average user satisfaction rating. Digital Equipment Corporation has developed an analogous usability engineering approach, as shown in Exhibit 1.

5. Creation of goals is a group process. The group must decide what the relevant usability attributes are, how to measure them, and what the target goals should be. The goals are clearly stated and communicated, just as they are for other components of the system.

6. End-user activity involves four operations: filling in forms, selecting among prescribed choices, manipulating lists, and reading information.

7. The four end-user operations can be tied to four corresponding building blocks that are sufficient to describe user interfaces abstractly:
   - Form blocks
   - Choice blocks
   - List blocks
   - Info blocks

8. It is possible to separate the design of these blocks, i.e., the user interface, from functional code. In the process described here, experts structure their applications in terms of the form, choice, list, and info blocks. Style designers write rules about how these blocks will be rendered on an end user's screen under various circumstances. The benefits of this approach are that groups can work in parallel and independently, and it promotes code reuse and iterative design.

9. Content or application experts know the jobs of the end users. They can structure this knowledge into a computer-executable form. Application experts create the user-interface content specifications.

10. Application (content) programmers write the programs.

11. Style designers have skills in human factors and graphic design. Their role is mainly of advocacy; they identify problems and describe solutions. They specify style rules.

12. Style programmers write programs necessary for making an interaction work.

13. Content (application) specifications are created by the application expert and include the messages to end users, flow of control, connections to function, and guidance to style.

14. Content (application) actions are created by application programmers. These are atomic programs with general utility. For example, a module might transfer the contents of one list to another.

15. Style specifications are created by the style designers. These are the rules regulating the set of human–computer interaction techniques used to render content, including interaction methods (e.g., entry vs. selection), appearance of the end user's screen, and the interaction devices.

16. The team works with a series of tools. Over time, they build up a library of well-tested approaches to human interface, which can then be mapped onto an application's content blocks.

Reference

Gould, J.D., Boies, S.J., and Lewis, C. (1991). Making usable, useful, productivity-enhancing computer applications, *Commn. ACM*, 34,.

Selected Bibliography

Attewell, P. (1990). The productivity paradox, unpublished manuscript.

Good, M., Spine, T.M., Whiteside, J., and George, P. (1986). User-derived impact analysis as a tool for usabiliuty engineering, Human factors in computing systems, CHI'86 Proceedings, ACM, New York, 241–246.

Gould, J.D. (1988). How to design usable systems, in *Handbook of Human–Computer Interaction*, Helander, M., Ed., Elsevier Science North-Holland Publishers, 757–789.

Hartson, R. (1989). User interface management control and communication, *IEEE Software*, January, 62–70.

Wiecha, C., Bennett, W., Boies, S., and Gould, J. (1989). Generating highly interactive user interfaces, Proceedings of CHI'88 (Austin, Texas, April 30-May 4, 1989), ACM, New York, 277–282.

Chapter 36
Prescott's Guidelines for Using Structured Methodology

ABSTRACT

The science of software engineering is composed of many methodologies and each has its own variations. In this chapter, Prescott (1991) offers an itemized set of guidelines for those interested in using structured methodology to ensure their project's success.

Structured methodology is an approach to defining a particular task and in defining a solution to that task. It provides a methodology for partitioning a complex task into a manageable series of "black boxes." The underlying organization of this network of black boxes progresses from abstraction at the top level to details at the lower levels. Not only are the specifics of each black box charted out, but the interfaces between each of these black boxes are also specified.

One of the main reasons for using structured methodology is the sheer complexity and cost of a problem. The discipline associated with this technique is reflected in the need to document each particular phase of development to ensure compliance with demanding requirements for quality, performance, and reliability.

PROCEDURES/ISSUES/POLICIES

1. Structured methodology will only be successful if:
   - The company's management is willing to make a firm commitment to the substantial time investment required to build a quality project.
   - A software development plan for the development of software is used. It provides management with the means to coordinate schedules, control resources, initiate actions, and monitor progress of the development effort. It also provides detailed knowledge of the schedule, organization, and resource allocation

planned by the contractor. In addition, it contains definitions and discussions of software quality and configuration management, as well as design and programming standards and conventions.

- Walkthroughs of at least five people for up to one and three quarters hours at the most are held in the requirements, design, coding, and testing phases.

2. A software requirement must be expressed in very clear English.
3. Decompose each function into related subfunctions. For example, initialization may be decomposed into initialize local variables and initialize global variables subfunctions.
4. For each function or task and subfunction, a narrative is written that clearly describes the function in terms of what the function does. The source of the required data and its destination as output from the function must also be defined and documented. The narrative should include the following:
- Module name
- Module called by
- Module purpose
- Inputs
- Outputs
- Unit description
5. Define a local database that will house the data items pertinent to the data requirements.
6. For each function, a detailed design document must be created that will, ultimately, be used to create the code. This document contains the following information:
- Name of function
- Function's purpose
- Description
- Calling sequence — if this submodule is called by another module or calls another module
- Calling parameters — if called or calling, then what are the parameters passed
- Updates — the files that it updates
- Variables — the variables that it uses
- Algorithm — pseudocoded processing logic such as:
  — Clear error flag
  — If code entered is equal to code in table
  — Update table.
7. Module is then coded using programming standards that enforce readability and understanding.
8. A test plan is created that takes into consideration schedule, environment, and available resources.
9. Test procedures that test each requirement must be documented. This translates into a series of test cases or scenarios. The test, the

input, and the expected output are documented. This document is known as a requirements traceability matrix, which establishes the correspondence between a software product specification and the successful testing of each such specification.

10. Systems integration and maintenance must be considered.
11. Tools and techniques that assist in the process of structured methodology:
    - Use of formal walkthroughs
    - A structured approach to software design, coding, and testing
    - Use of structured programming
    - The use of standardized coding conventions
    - The use of graphics devices such as a functional block diagram for module specification

Reference

Prescott, J.R. (1991). Using structured methodology for software project success, *J. Syst. Manage.*, July, 28–31.

Chapter 37
Kemayel's Controllable Factors in Programmer Productivity

ABSTRACT

Based on extensive research performed in Tunisia by Kemayel et al., this chapter seeks to identify the characteristics of the programmer's work potential. The impact of certain controllable factors in the productivity of programmers is investigated. These factors are divided into three categories: factors pertaining to personnel, factors pertaining to the process, and factors pertaining to the user community.

PROCEDURES/ISSUES/POLICIES

1. Programmer productivity paradoxes:
   - *There is an enormous variance in the productivity of programmers.* This variance can be as wide as a factor of one to ten. (Other researchers report an even wider variance.) There is a large opportunity to improve programmer productivity within this wide range.
   - *Productivity invariance with respect to experience.* According to statistical measures by Boehm (1981), when the experience of a programmer increases from one month to three years (36-fold increase), productivity is improved by only 34 percent. This appears to show that experience has no effect on software project costs.
   - *Productivity invariance with respect to tools.* According to Boehm, the difference in productivity between a programmer who uses no tools at all and one who uses the most up-to-date, powerful tools available, on the most powerful machines, is no larger than 50 percent.

349

- *Suitability of motivation factors.* Studies have shown that programmers have a motivation pattern different from that of their managers and those of workers in other industries. This difference might well explain why some well-intentioned software managers fail to motivate their programmers.

2. The 33 productivity factors that are proposed can be divided into three categories:
   - Factors related to personnel
   - Factors related to the software process
   - Factors related to the user community

3. Personnel factors. Two sets of controllable factors are likely to affect the productivity of data processing personnel: motivation factors and experience factors.

4. Personnel motivation consists of many factors; 16 derived from research appear below:
   - *Recognition.* This is the reaction of the organization to the programmer's performance. Indifference leads to a drop in motivation, which leads to a decline in productivity.
   - *Achievement.* This represents the satisfaction that the programmer gets from doing a challenging task. This implies that the organization must keep supplying the programmer with challenging tasks to maintain motivation.
   - *The work.* The nature of the tasks that must be executed is a powerful tool to motivate a programmer.
   - *Responsibility.* This is derived from basic management theory. That is, if you want something to happen, make someone specifically responsible for it.
   - *Advancement.* A programmer who feels that he or she has the possibility of career advancement in the organization is more motivated than one who does not.
   - *Salary.* A programmer who feels that he or she is paid adequately, and who anticipates that salary increases will continue on par with performance, will be more motivated than one who does not.
   - *Possibility for growth.* This factor measures the possibilities for professional growth within a programmer's company.
   - *Interpersonal relations with subordinates.*
   - *Status.* This measures the importance of the worker in his or her company, e.g., participation at meetings, participation in decision making, ceremonial functions, usage of restricted services, and privileges of the corporation.
   - *Interpersonal relations, superiors.* This is controllable to the extent that the manager has latitude in assigning group leaders.

- *Interpersonal relations, peers.* Because teamwork is a key ingredient for the success of any group effort, the manager should take care in dividing staff into working groups.
- *Technical supervision.* This measures the willingness of the programmer's supervisor to help the programmer solve technical problems, orient efforts, and make choices.
- *Company policy and administration.* This factor measures how clearly the command structure of the company is defined, how rational it is, and how easy it is to determine to whom each worker reports.
- *Working conditions.* This factor represents working conditions in the traditional sense, such as office space, light.
- *Factors in personal life.* Given that the programmer's personal life influences motivation and job performance, the manager can assign key positions or tasks to those that have the best conditions.
- *Job security.* This factor is very important.

5. Personnel experience is equally important. Four factors are discussed:
   - Applications domain experience
   - Virtual machine experience — the aggregate of hardware, operating system, utilities, and software packages
   - Programming language experience
   - Experience with the user community — to what extent the programmer is familiar with the user community as a working partner

6. Two classes of controllable factors pertaining to the software process have been identified by the authors: project management and programming environments.

7. Project management consists of four controllable factors:
   - *Using a goal structure* — to what extent the programming team uses a goal structure, and to what extent the team depends on it for its day-to-day decision making.
   - *Adherence to a software life cycle* — to what extent a team uses and depends on a software life cycle.
   - *Adherence to an activity distribution* — to what extent the programming team uses a precise definition of life cycle activities, and to what extent they depend on it for decision making.
   - *Usage of cost estimation procedures* — to what extent the programming team uses a software cost-estimation model and to what extent they depend on it for decision making.

8. Programming environment is composed of four controllable factors:
   - *Programming tools.* To what extent the programmer uses software tools and how powerful these tools are (i.e., debuggers, editors).

- *Modern programming practices.* To what extent does the programmer use modern programming practices and how powerful are they? This includes modular programming, program libraries, and reuse.
- *Programming standards.* To what extent are standards used, how stringent are they, and how strictly are they adhered to? Examples include test standards, verification standards, validation standards, and standards of unit size.
- *Power of equipment used.* Barry Boehm introduced two factors pertaining to the power of equipment used: a factor that measures memory space limitations and a factor that measures time limitations.

9. The participation of users has been found to have an important impact on programmer productivity. Well prepared users reduce the cost of software maintenance.
    - *Previous education in computing.* What is the duration level of the users' previous education in computing.
    - *Experience in computing.* To what extent has the user used computers in the past? Previous experience gives users a better sense of what computers can do for them and enables them to express their desires more effectively.
    - *Experience with the type of application.* Experience in building computer systems in the same application domain is valuable. The major incentive for rapid prototyping is to have a high rating for this factor.
    - Experience with the group of programmers and analysts.

10. Survey results on Tunisian subjects:
    - Of the 16 motivation factors, 5 were statistically significant and account for 18.89 percent of programmer productivity: technical supervision, working conditions, achievement, responsibilities, and recognition.
    - Of the four personnel experience factors, only two were found to be statistically significant and account for 7.49 percent of programmer productivity: experience with the virtual machine and user community.
    - Of the factors used to assess project management, two were proved significant and explain 5.57 percent of programmer productivity: the definition and use of a software life cycle and software cost estimation.
    - In the programming environment area two factors explained 9.62 percent of programmer productivity: the use of modern programming practices and the power of equipment used for development.

- Two user factors were found to be significant and explained a 5.33 percent of programmer productivity: experience of the user community with computers and the experience of the user community with the group of programmers and analysts.

References

Boehm, B.W. (1981). *Software Engineering Economics*. Prentice-Hall, Englewood Cliffs, NJ.

Kemayel, L., Mili, A., and Ouederni, I. (1991). Controllable factors for programmer productivity: a statistical study, *J. Syst. Software*, 16, 151–163.

Selected Bibliography

Basili, V.R. and Weiss, D.M. (1984). A methdology for collecting valid software engineering data, *IEEE Trans. Software Eng.*, SE-10, 728–737.

Mills, H.D. (1983). *Programmer Productivity*, Little, Brown and Co., Boston, MA.

Chapter 38
AT&T's "Estimeeting" Process for Developing Estimates

ABSTRACT

This chapter presents a method for estimating a software development effort in the early phases of a large software-intensive project. For each feature of the project to be estimated, a "feature team" generates a detailed feature definition that is used in what the Taff, Borchering, and Hudgins (1991) term an "estimeeting." Using this process it is possible to build in software quality, by design, in the early stages of development and not added on later in a series of fixes to problems uncovered in testing. Building in quality requires "front loading" the development process, yielding better designs and fewer errors that are more easily and cleanly isolated and repaired.

More complete work in the early stages can serve to identify tools or special testing needs earlier. If the estimates for a project are too low, then project staffing will also be too low. As needs become apparent, staff are "back-end loaded," which is the reverse of what is desirable for a high-quality product. The "estimeeting" process described in this chapter can be used to estimate a software project accurately. The benefits of this process, as identified by the authors, are as follows:

- *Better estimates.* There is an ability to predict resources more accurately.
- *Earlier and closer subsystem involvement.* Subsystem owners attend meetings earlier, see what new features may be down the pike, and as a result, can make allowances.
- *Early direct relationships.* The meetings foster teamwork.
- *Early expert high-level designs.* Byproducts of these meetings are ideas that are useful for the next level of design.

- *Problem detection.* There is a better understanding of potential problems of resources and performance.
- *General acceptance of estimates.* Results are readily accepted as official.
- *Clearly defined milestones.* The process has clearly defined outputs and events.
- *Better transitions to development.* Smoother transitions occur between stages.
- *Better quality.* Multiexpertise team leads to better definition, requirements, and design.
- *Features interactions and synergy.* This leads to a better understanding of how all features interact.
- *Project knowledge base.* This improves the expertise and knowledge base for estimators, helping to produce more system experts.
- *Confidence.* The product management organization has increased confidence in the estimates.

PROCEDURES/ISSUES/POLICIES

1. An estimeeting is a standardized working meeting with regularly attending estimators. The meeting capitalizes on the synergy of having the key people together. The preparation for and agenda of these meetings are described. Success requires good feature requirements and a high-level design proposal in advance and attendance by a specific group of experienced people.
2. The front-end process constitutes the selection process through which feature candidates are picked for development. It begins with a list of feature candidates and ends when a subset has been approved for development. This process attempts to balance the conflicting needs of business. One of these needs is to respond quickly to changes in market conditions; a conflicting need is to reduce "throw-away" effort by deciding early what will be developed. Another need is to reduce risks. These conflicting needs can be resolved by reviewing the list of features three times, during which the set of potential features in a release is refined and distilled. Each of the three iterations generates a list of features for which further work will proceed but work is stopped on features that do not make the cuts. These "cut" features may be reconsidered for a later release. The needs of the market are considered as well as technical feasibility. Estimates of development cost will play a critical role.
3. Project-planning. Estimates are used for project management once the project begins. In addition to project planning, long-range planning is also based on development estimates. Multirelease planning tries to account for: 1) experienced staff, 2) test facilities, and 3) interactions with other products such as billing, etc.

4. Software is grouped into subsystems. The subsystems are organized functionally for the various tasks that the ultimate product must perform. Each subsystem is the responsibility of people knowledgeable in the details of existing hardware and software and standard industry practice for the subsystem function.

5. The large size of a project has implications. Project planning and management have large economic impacts; errors in estimation can have serious consequences.

6. Estimation can be broken down into two major parts. The first is job size, which is the size and complexity of the code. The second part of estimation is the effort required once the size is known. This effort depends on the productivity of the development organization.

7. In this model, people compare the job they are estimating with their own experience. Estimates are made on a highly componentized system. This breaking down of the problem into components is a key element of this methodology. The model has these advantages:
   - The components will better match the past jobs done by the estimators.
   - Statistical errors in estimating the components often cancel, giving a higher probability that the resultant number is correct.
   - Potentially overlooked parts of the job have a better chance of being exposed.

8. The estimeeting methodology evolved from three principles:
   - Estimates are important numbers because they help determine product content. Underestimating can cause failure to meet commitments with dire consequences for business. Estimates impact quality because they control the distribution of effort over the development cycle
   - Experienced people give the best values. Estimators compare the job to be estimated with one from their own experience. Therefore, the more extensive the experience, the more likely it is that the estimate will be accurate.
   - Cooperative meetings give excellent results. It has been proven that team consensus improves on the best individual solution.

9. The concept behind the estimeeting is to get into one room people highly experienced in all the major aspects of feature and subsystem development and with the authority to represent the technical viewpoint of their organizations. In this meeting, they come to a common understanding of a new feature, agree on an informal, nonbinding, high-level design proposal, and estimate development effort in their own areas of expertise.

10. With a preliminary recommendations feature list, a schedule is set down and for each feature on the list a feature team is formed. Over a chosen time period, each team produces two outputs — the

SOFTWARE ENGINEERING HANDBOOK

external feature requirements (FSPs) and the internal feature design (FAP).

11. These documents are distributed to estimators, the engineers with in-depth knowledge of the subsystems. The estimators are not on feature teams; they represent the development interests of their subsystems and receive these requirements and design documents for every feature that impacts their subsystems.

12. Team members are drawn from the concerned organizations (systems engineering, development). Some individuals join more than one feature team. Each feature team is responsible for estimeeting preparation, presentation, and follow-up for its feature. Although composition of the team may evolve, it is initially composed of:

- *Systems engineer* — owns and ensures the completeness and timely delivery of the FSP with the feature's mandatory and optional requirements. The engineer presents the requirements at the estimeeting.
- *The feature engineer* — owns the technical aspects of the feature's operation. Even when the feature is in production, the feature engineer will serve as a point of contact with a vested interest in design and resolution of issues. Along with the system architect, the feature engineer owns and generates the high-level design proposal (FAP) and identifies impacted subsystems. This person gives the high-level design and subsystem impact portions of the estimeeting presentation.
- *The system architect* — works with the feature engineer on the FAP and ensures its completeness and timely delivery. The system architect describes the FAP's architectural impact during the estimeeting. In nonestimeeting work, the system architect develops broad architectural guidelines.
- *The planner* — is a technical person who participates in the front-end process early in the release cycle. He or she is knowledgeable about proposed features when feature teams are formed. Planners are coordinators of the feature teams and may co-author the FAP. After the estimeeting, the responsibility for the feature moves from the planner to the feature engineer. Planners share their expertise about the features.
- *The product manager* — is responsible for ensuring that the scope and design of the feature remains consistent with the strategic intent and cost goals throughout the estimeeting process.

13. The FAP (feature architecture proposal) can be thought of as an existence proof for the feature. It is an informal document that does not require signoff signatures. The intent is to produce this document quickly with a minimum cost. It contains:

- Description of new internal architectures where applicable

- High-level functional description of how the feature works from hardware and software design viewpoints
- Itemization of all impacted areas internal and external to the feature
- Expected feature performance
- Dependencies and interactions with other new or existing features
- Open issues of design and architecture and proposed solutions

14. The FSP (feature selection proposal) consists of:
    - Feature operation (typical user scenarios)
    - Feature interaction with other features
    - Feature impact
    - Constraints
    - Restrictions

15. Contents of subsystem estimation form:
    - Feature name and number
    - Date estimate made
    - Estimator's name
    - Area (subsystem) represented
    - Estimator's experience in this area in years
    - Estimator's preparation time
    - Consultation time with FAP authors in hours
    - Estimator's quality assessment (1 to 5 scale) of FSP and FAP
    - Estimate for mandatory part of feature
    - Estimate for optional part of feature
    - Assumptions made to arrive at estimate
    - Concerns and uncertainties that could affect the estimate
    - Itemized work areas that make up estimate

16. Prior to the first estimeeting, the following package is assembled:
    - Cover sheet with meeting specifics and feature team membership
    - People expected to attend
    - FSP (external requirements)
    - FAP (design and system-impact checklist)
    - Subsystem estimation form

17. The estimeeting takes about two hours for a single feature. A moderator begins by introducing the feature team members and may briefly discuss the agenda and ground rules.

18. The system engineer presents feature description and requirements and delineates what is optional and mandatory.

19. The system architect and feature engineer jointly present the feature design. The architect gives the architectural impact perspective and the feature engineer covers the impact on subsystems.

20. A secretary, often the planner, takes notes and records assumptions and issues. A question and answer period typically follows the presentations.
21. Estimators are asked to complete their individual subsystem estimation forms in an "estimate collection" interval. Estimators and engineers consult with each other over finer points.
22. Following the estimeeting, the feature engineer is responsible for resolving any open issues resulting from the estimeeting and collecting any outstanding subsystem estimates. The feature engineer then completes a feature estimate summary form, audits the estimeeting outputs for completeness, and reports the estimeeting results. The estimate, FSP, and FAP now become the formal output of the front-end-process and form the project baseline.

Reference

Taff, L.M., Borchering, J.W., and Hudgins, Jr., W.R. (1991). Estimeetings: development estimates and a front-end process for a large project, *IEEE Trans. Software Eng.*, 17, 839–849.

Selected Bibliography

Lehder, Jr., W.D., Smith, D.P., and Yu, W.D. (1988). Software estimation technology, *AT&T Technol. J.*, 67, 10–18.

Londeix, B. (1987). *Cost Estimation for Software Development*. Addison-Wesley, Reading, MA.

Myers. W. (1989). Allow plenty of time for large-scale software, *IEEE Software*, 6, 92.

Chapter 39
Burns' Framework for Building Dependable Systems

ABSTRACT

The role and importance of nonfunctional requirements in the development of complex critical applications have, up until now, been inadequately appreciated. It has been shown, through experience, that this approach fails to produce dependable systems.

Nonfunctional requirements include dependability (e.g., reliability, availability, safety, and security), timeliness (e.g., responsiveness, orderliness, freshness, temporal predictability, and temporal controllability) and dynamic change management (i.e., incorporating evolutionary changes into a nonstop system).

The purpose of the framework described in this chapter (Burns and Lister, (1991) is to:

- Impose a design discipline that ensures that appropriate abstractions are used at each level of the design
- Allow assertions to be developed that the nonfunctional requirements can be met by the design if implemented in a particular environment
- Allow interactions between these nonfunctional requirements to be analyzed so that dependencies can be identified
- Allow the nonfunctional and functional requirements to be traded off against each other

PROCEDURES/ISSUES/POLICIES

1. A constructive way of describing the process of system design is a progression of increasingly specific commitments that define properties of the system design which designers operating at a more detailed level are not at liberty to change. For example, early in the design there may already be commitments to the structure of a system, in terms of module definitions and relationships.

2. Those aspects of a design to which no commitment is made at some particular level in the design hierarchy are the subject of obligations that lower levels of design must address. For example, the behavior of the defined "committed to modules" is the subject of obligations that must be met during further design and implementation.

3. The process of refining a design — transforming obligations into commitments — is often subject to constraints imposed primarily by the execution environment.

4. The execution environment is the set of hardware and software components on top of which a system is built. It may impose resource constraints (e.g., processor speed) and constraints of mechanism (e.g., data locking).

5. The framework controls the introduction of necessary implementation details into the design process by distinguishing two phases in the construction of an architectural design of any application:

   - *Logical architecture* — embodies commitments that can be made independently of the constraints imposed by the execution environment and is aimed at satisfying the functional requirements.
   - *Physical architecture* — takes constraints into account and embraces nonfunctional requirements.

6. The nonfunctional requirements of an application can be considered as projections onto the physical architecture. Distinct projects apply to timeliness, safety, etc. The physical architecture makes it explicit where projections interact and enables criteria to be developed that cater for these interactions.

7. The framework is grounded in the object-oriented approach to system design. This approach is widely regarded as offering a conceptual framework for mastering the complexities of the design process:

   - Objects are an adequate modeling tool for the functional requirements of the system.
   - They can be used to provide traceability through all stages of the design process.
   - They are an adequate basis for expressing nonfunctional requirements.
   - They provide an appropriate granularity for replication, checkpointing, dynamic change management, configuration, and dynamic reconfiguration.
   - They assist error containment through encapsulation.
   - They can support dynamic security by access right mechanisms on operations.
   - They can represent schedulable entities.
   - Commonly encountered standard architectures can be implemented by means of redefined classes and methods.

8. The logical architecture is concerned with defining a set of object classes, their interfaces, and relationships, which together meet all the functional requirements. In the logical architecture, communication between the classes is represented by invocation of methods.

9. The physical architecture is concerned with objects, that is, instances of the classes defined in the logical architecture. It refines the logical architecture in two ways:
   - It instantiates objects from the classes defined in the logical architecture and maps them onto the target execution environment.
   - It annotates the objects and their methods with attributes (such as deadlines) derived from the nonfunctional requirements.

Reference

Burns, A. and Lister, A.M. (1991). A framework for building dependable systems, *Computer J.*, 34, 173–181.

Selected Bibliography

Burns, A. and Wellings, A.J, (1989). *Real-Time Systems and Their Programming Languages*, Addison Wesley, Reading, MA.

Burns, A. and Lister, A.M. (1990). An architectural framework for timely and reliable distributed information systems (TARDIS): description and case study,. YCS. 140, Department of Computer Science, University of York, U.K..

Meyer, B. (1987). Reusability: the case study for object-oriented design, *IEEE Software*, 4, 50–64.

Meyer, B. (1988). *Object-Oriented Software Construction*, Prentice-Hall, Inc., Englewood Cliffs, NJ.

Chapter 40
Avison's Multiview Meta-Methodology

ABSTRACT

The proliferation of systems development methodologies has resulted in much confusion. In fact, it has been estimated that hundreds of more or less similar methodologies exist. In practice, most organizations have developed their own methodology. There have been many attempts to compare methodologies; past research by Avison managed to categorize methodologies into six broad themes. This chapter describes a contingency framework, called Multiview (Avison and Wood-Harper,1991), which includes descriptions of relevant techniques and tools. Analysts and users select those aspects of the approach appropriate to the application, in effect, creating a unique methodology for each application.

PROCEDURES/ISSUES/POLICIES

1. Problems with methodologies in practice:
   - Failure to meet needs of management
   - Unambitious systems design
   - Inflexibility due to the output-driven design
   - User dissatisfaction
   - Problems with documentation
   - Maintenance workload
   - Application backlog
2. Categories:
   - *Category 1:* Systems approach highlights the importance of the relationship between an organization and its environment, and of multidisciplinary teams to understand organizations.
   - *Category 2:* Planning approaches involve strategic management in information systems work so that their needs are analyzed and information systems are implemented that do more than computerize the operations level applications. This approach attempts to identify the needs of management and plans the ways of meeting these needs.

- *Category 3:* In a participative approach all users are expected to contribute to and gain from any information system; this should increase the potential for success.
- *Category 4:* Prototyping enables users to comment on the proposed information system and its inputs, processing, and outputs before the system has been designed in its final form.
- *Category 5:* Structured approaches aid the understanding of a complex problem through functional decomposition and the associated documentation techniques. This approach tends to emphasize decision trees, decision tables, data-flow diagrams, etc.
- *Category 6:* Data analysis is a useful modeling tool in which the data model produced is likely to be relevant for a longer period than models of processes, which can be unstable.

3. It has been suggested that one approach cannot be the answer:
   - The tools and techniques appropriate for one set of circumstances may not be appropriate for others.
   - The fuzziness of some applications requires attack on a number of fronts.
   - As an information system develops, it takes on very different perspectives and any methodology adopted should be able to incorporate these views.

4. It has been argued that the contingency approach to information systems development, an approach where the methodology chosen will depend on the particular circumstances where it will be applied, might be the solution. The methodology selected will be contingent on the particular situation according its level of uncertainty.

5. The choice of tools and techniques used in an application following a contingency framework will depend on:
   - The comprehensiveness and depth of the information systems design process required
   - Whether the designers choose a goal-oriented strategy or an alternative-oriented strategy. The goal-oriented strategy negotiates on what is to be achieved, and then finds ways to accomplish the tasks. The alternative-oriented strategy does not assume that consensus can be reached on the goals, but rather that negotiation must occur on how to do things.
   - The choice of an appropriate adaptation strategy reflecting the perception about future events. One choice is to ignore future requirements, the second is to presume they are predictable, and the third is to presume that they are unpredictable, but can be dealt with.
   - The choice of an appropriate implementation strategy

6. Multiview is a contingency approach that provides a flexible framework as an alternative to choosing between different methodologies

or standardizing on one particular methodology. Multiview is a blended methodology drawing on aspects from each of the six categories of methodologies as summarized above. It is an explorative structure which can be called a meta-methodology.

7. The multiview meta-methodology:

- *Step 1: Analysis of human activity.* This stage concerns the search for view of the organization, representing a subjective as well as objective perception of the problem situation in diagrammatic and pictorial form. It is used to identify problem themes. Through debate within the organization, it is possible to identify relevant systems that may relieve problem themes. The root definition describes the system on which to focus attention. The root definition is analyzed to make sure that all necessary elements have been identified including the owner of the system, the client, the transformation that takes place, and the environment in which it takes place.

- *Step 2: Analysis of information.* At this stage, the entities and functions of the system described are analyzed. By using functional decomposition, it is possible to break down the main function (clear in a well-formed root definition) into subfunctions. Using data-flow diagrams, it is possible to analyze the sequence of events. In developing an entity model, the problem solver extracts and names entities, relationships between entities, and attributes that describe the entities.

- *Step 3: Analysis and design of sociotechnical aspects.* At this stage, the problem solver produces a design from an analysis of people and their needs and the working environment along with consideration for the organizational structure, computers, and the necessary work tasks. The social and technical objectives are set and alternatives specified and compared so that the best solution can be selected. Once selected, computer tasks, role tasks, and people tasks can be defined. The emphasis at this stage is not on development, but on a statement of alternatives, according to important social and technical considerations.

- *Step 4: Design of the human computer interface.* Decisions are made as to batch versus online versus command, etc. Specific conversations and interactions are then designed; users are expected to be the major contributors of this stage. Technical requirements to fulfill these human–computer interfaces can then be designed.

- *Step 5: Design of technical aspects.* Using the entity model created in Step 2 and the technical requirements from Step 4, a more technical view can be taken by the analyst because human considerations are already integrated with the forthcoming technical considerations. The technical design will include the application subsystems and the nonapplication subsystems. These include the information retrieval subsystem, database, database maintenance subsystem, control subsystem, etc.

8. These five stages incorporate five different views that are appropriate to the progressive development of an analysis and design project. Because it is a multiview approach, it covers computer-related questions and also matters relating to people and business functions Each step addresses one of the following five questions:

- How is the information system supposed to further the aims of the organization using it?
- How can it be fit into the working lives of the people in the organization who will use it?
- How can individuals concerned best relate to the computer in terms of operating it and using the output from it?
- What information processing function is the system to perform?
- What is the technical specification of a system that will come close enough to doing the things written down in the answers to the other four questions?

Reference

Avison, D.E. and Wood-Harper, A.T. (1991). Information systems development research: an exploration of ideas in practice, *Computer J.*, 34(2).

Selected Bibliography

Avison, D.E. and Wood-Harper, A.T. (1986). Multiview — an exploration in informal system development, *Aust. Computer J.*, 18 ,.

Avison, D.E. and Fitzgerald, G. (1988). *Information Systems Development — Methodologies, Techniques and Tools*, Blackwell Scientific Publications, Oxford.

Avison, D.E. and Wood-Harper, A.T. (1990). *Multiview: an Exploration in Information Systems Development*, Blackwell Scientific Publications, Oxford.

Davies, L.J. and Wood-Harper, A.T. (1989). Information systems development: theoretical frameworks, *J. Appl. Syst. Anal.*, 16.

Hirschheim, R. and Klein, H.R. (1989). Four paradigms for information systems development, *Commn. ACM*, 32.

Iivari, J.A. (1989). Methodology for IS development as an organizational change: a pragmatic contingency approach, in Klein & Kumar (1989).

Chapter 41
Byrne's Reverse Engineering Technique

ABSTRACT

The problem of reimplementing an existing system in a different programming language is a problem around which there are three general approaches:

- Manually rewrite the existing system.
- Use an automatic language translator.
- Redesign and reimplement the system.

There are problems with each of these approaches. Manually translated source code often retains the style and flavor of the original implementation. This approach is labor intensive and error prone. Automatic translation, a better technique, has problems as well.

The source language may not yield itself to simple translation into the target language. Most automated translator tools perform the easier parts of the translation process, leaving the more complex details for a human. Perhaps the biggest problem with this technique is, as Byrne (1991) suggests, its tendency to replicate the same problems plaguing the original version — in other words, "garbage in, garbage out."

Of the three approaches, redesign and reimplementation has the best chance of producing a successful system; however, this technique has its disadvantages too. This approach has the highest cost because it is the equivalent of building a new system. Perhaps the most serious disadvantage is that, for many systems, it may not be possible to redesign from system requirements because the requirements may not exist.

Reverse engineering provides a new approach by producing a reconstructed design that captures the functionality of the system. This chapter describes a reverse engineering technique that successfully translated a FORTRAN program into the Ada language.

PROCEDURES/ISSUES/POLICIES

1. Collect information. The reverse engineering process begins by extracting detailed design information and from that extracting a high-level design abstraction. Detailed design information is extracted from the source code and existing design documents. This information includes structure charts as well as data descriptions to describe processing details. In the collect information step, all possible information about the program is collected. Sources of information include source code, design documents, and documentation for system calls and external routines. Personnel experienced with the software should also be identified. This last requirement is not to be underestimated; lack of "domain knowledge" can make design recovery extremely difficult, if not impossible.

2. Examine information. In this step the information collected in step one is examined to allow the person doing the recovery work to become familiar with the system and its parts. Staff responsible for reverse engineering formulate a plan for dissecting and recording the recovered information. It should be noted that becoming familiar with the language implementation of the module can bias the reverse engineering effort by influencing the perspective of what should be recovered and how it should be expressed.

3. Extract the structure. The information is reviewed in an attempt to identify the structure of the program. This is used to create a set of structure charts where each node in the chart corresponds to a routine called in the program. Therefore, the chart created actually records the calling hierarchy of the program. For each edge in the chart, the data passed to a node and returned by that node must be recorded. It should be noted that software tools are generally available to assist in the development of structure charts. Associating structure chart nodes with source code routines raises the issue of traceability. In reverse engineering, it is desirable to record the links between the recovered design and the original source code or documentation. In this case, it would be desirable to give a node a meaningful name and record the name of the implemented function to which it corresponds. As the structure chart is recorded, the data items passed between nodes should also be recorded.

4. Record functionality. For each node, the processing done by that node is recorded. At this step, the program routines' functionality as well as the functionality of system and library routines is described in English or using a more formal notation. If debugging statements are used within the program, then they should be recorded as well. Conditional compilation code, that is, the procedural code that directs the software to a particular hardware platform, needs to be reviewed carefully.

5. Record data-flow. The recovered program structure and processing logic can be analyzed to identify the data transformations in the software that show the actual data processing done in the program. This information can be used to develop a set of hierarchical data-flow diagrams that model the software.

6. Record control flow. At this stage the high-level control of the program is identified. This refers to the level of control that affects the overall operation of the software. A problem in this step might be in distinguishing between low-level control structures that involve the implementation of a routine and high-level control structures that serve to control the software operation. The former should be included as part of the processing described in the detailed design; the latter needs to be recorded in a control-flow diagram and its control specification. Byrne found that there is a temptation to recover too much of the control structure.

7. Review the recovered design for consistency. At this stage, missing items are identified and an attempt is made to locate them. The design is now checked to see if it accurately represents the program.

8. Generate documentation. This last step's purpose is to generate design documentation. Information explaining the purpose of the program, program overview, history, etc. will be recorded.

Reference

Byrne, E.J. (1991). Software reverse engineering: a case study, *Software — Pract. Exp.*, 21, 1349–1364.

Selected Bibliography

Biggerstaff, T.J. (1989). Design recovery for maintenance and reuse, *Computer*, 22, 36–49.

Chikofsky, E.J. and Cross II, J.H. (1990). Reverse engineering and design recovery: a taxonomy, *IEEE Software*, 7, 13–17.

Choi, S.C and Scacchi, W. (1990). Extracting and restructuring the design of large systems, *IEEE Software*, 7, 66–71.

Ricketts, J.A., DelMonaco, J.C., and Weeks, M.W. (1989). Data re-engineering for application systems, Conference on Software Maintenance, Miami Florida, October 16–19, 174–179.

Chapter 42
Prieto-Diaz' Reusability Model

ABSTRACT

Software reuse is still far from a standard practice in the software engineering community even though it was first conceived of over 20 years ago. The problem, according to Prieto-Diaz (1991), is not one of technology but of unwillingness to address the most important issues influencing software reuse.

A model for implementing software reuse programs is discussed in this chapter. This model is based on an incremental strategy and addresses many issues that were thought to be external to the software process. This includes managerial, economic, performance, cultural, and technology transfer issues. The approach addressed here is practical and effective, and has potential to make reuse a regular practice in the software development process.

PROCEDURES/ISSUES/POLICIES

1. Factors that influence reuse include:
   - *Managerial factors* — organizational, motivational, and financial
   - *Economic factors* — integrating reuse in cost/benefit analysis, system costing and estimation, pricing criteria, contracting strategies, and support costs
   - *Legal factors* — software copyright, liabilities, proprietary issues, contractual requirements
2. Justifications for an incremental approach:
   - Provides an immediate return on investment
   - Builds confidence within the organization
   - Easier to manage
   - Allows for tuning and refining the reuse process
   - Facilitates monitoring and evaluating reuse
3. A key ingredient is management support, which is a common factor in all successful reuse programs (Raytheon, Toshiba, Hartford). This commitment is necessary because reuse programs demand changes in the way software is developed.

4. Inputs to the reuse program include software from existing systems and requirements for future systems.
5. The products of a reuse program include a series of software catalogs, an automated library system, generic architectures, and a collection of reusable components.
6. The assessment report includes: feasibility analysis, domain stability assessment, cost/benefit analysis, and an implementation plan.
7. Questions for a feasibility analysis:
   - Does the organization have enough financial and human resources to implement a reuse program?
   - Can the organization afford it?
   - Is reuse necessary in the organization?
   - Does the organization want to do it?
   - Is management committed to implementing a reuse program?
   - How many systems of the same kind will be produced?
   - Are variations from implementation to implementation large or small?
   - Is existing software already available for reuse? What would be the estimated cost for each alternative?
   - Does a critical mass of software engineers exist?
   - Is software production large enough to justify a reuse program?
8. Questions for an analysis of domain suitability:
   - Is the domain, line of business, broad or narrow?
   - Is the domain mature and well understood or is it new and not well understood?
   - Is the domain complex or simple?
   - Is the domain stable or rapidly changing?
   - Is the domain very technology dependent?
   - Is it in a state of developing concepts or does it rely on well-established principles, methods, and formalisms?
9. Questions for cost/benefit analysis:
   - How much does it cost?
   - Is a reuse program economically feasible?
   - What alternatives exist for implementing a reuse program?
   - What is the scope?
   - How big a program is contemplated?
   - What are the expectations?
   - What is the desired level of reuse (partial, opportunistic, formal, total)?
10. The following organizational structure is recommended to establish a successful reuse program:
   - *Asset management group* — provides initiatives, funding, and policies for reuse.

- *Identification and qualification group* — identifies potential reusability areas and collects and certifies new additions to the collection.
- *Maintenance group* — maintains and updates reusable software components.
- *Development group* — creates new reusable components.
- *Reuser support group* — assists and trains users and runs tests and evaluations of reusable components.
- *Librarian* — updates and distributes catalogs, classifies new assets, maintains library system, and manages asset orders. Several roles may be assigned to one person. However, staff size for a large corporate endeavor might exceed ten.

11. A reuse program can be implemented in four basic stages: initiation, expansion, contraction, and steady state.

12. *Stage 1: Initiation.* Existing software is analyzed to select potentially reusable components. Descriptors of these components are extracted manually or automatically and a preliminary index is produced. A stage 1 catalog is produced. This catalog informs software engineers in the organization about potentially reusable software.

13. *Stage 2: Expansion.* The size of the catalogs increases as more of the existing software is identified for reuse. At this point, a classification scheme is necessary. An initial faceted classification scheme is produced and included with the stage 2 catalog. Based on the feasibility study, a case can be made to support an automated library system. The faceted classification scheme requires the resources of a librarian and a domain expert. A faceted scheme provides basic domain models in the form of taxonomies and standard descriptions or lexicons, which in turn support bootstrapping the domain analysis process.

14. *Stage 3: Contraction.* In this stage, domain analysis is the key activity. Early domain models from stage 2 coupled with more detailed information from existing systems and from requirements for future systems are used for domain analysis. Standard architectures and functional models are derived and common components are grouped to support basic generic functions. Redundant and ineffective components are identified and retired from the collection. This results in contraction in the size of the collection. The collection and classification are updated and a stage 3 catalog is made available. In this stage, a domain analyst, one or more domain experts, a software engineer, and a librarian are required.

15. *Stage 4: Steady State.* Now that the essential components have been identified for a specific domain, these components are progressively replaced by components supporting domain-specific functions. These components are reusable because they are designed to plug directly into the architecture.

Reference

Prieto-Diaz, R. (1991). Making software reuse work: an implmentation model, *ACM SIGSOFT, Software Eng. Notes*, 16, 61–68.

Selected Bibliography

Barnes, B.H. and Bollinger, T.B. (1991). Making reuse cost-effective, *IEEE Software*, 8, 13–24.

Basili, V.R. and Rombach, H.D. (1988). Towards a comprehensive framework for reuse: a reuse-enabling software evolution environment, Tech. Report CS-TR-2158, Dept of Computer Science, University of Maryland, College Park, MD,.

Frakes, W.B. (1991). A survey of software reuse, position paper for the 1st International Workshop on Software Reuse, Dortmund, Germany, July 1991.

Freeman, P. (1983). *Reusable Software Engineering: Concepts and Research Directions, in Workshop on Reusability in Programming*, Alan Perlis, ed., 3–26. ITT Programming, Newport, RI.

Prieto-Diaz, R. (1991). Implementing faceted classification for software reuse, *Commn. ACM*, 34, 88–97.

Chapter 43

Farbey's Considerations on Software Quality Metrics during the Requirements Phase

ABSTRACT

In this chapter Farbey (1990) expands on the general view of quality as the difference between what is expected and what is experienced:

quality = expectations – experience

Four questions are addressed:

- *Effectiveness.* Does the specification, considered as a solution, solve the right problem?
- *Serviceability.* Does the specification, considered as a starting point, provide a firm basis on which to proceed?
- *Prediction.* Does the requirement specification (together with the system test specification) provide useful measures for predicting the final quality outcome?
- *Process.* Does the process by which the specification is produced encourage effectiveness, serviceability, and quality prediction?

PROCEDURES/ISSUES/POLICIES

1. *Effectiveness.* The first question concerns the quality of the specification as a solution — how well does the specification capture the problem? The ultimate effectiveness of a system depends not on the quality of software or specification, but on the degree to which the problem is correctly perceived. Focus on the specification as a product by asking questions like the ones that follow:

- Is the process by which it has been produced conducive to bringing out and clarifying objectives?
- Is it complete in that it exhausts the objectives and needs that are known?
- Is the specification maintainable?
- Is it readable?

Quality attributes covered here include:

- *Functionality.* Does the specification capture all of the required functions?
- *Performance.* Does the specification meet the users' demands?
- *Usability.* Does the specification offer ease of use, learning, and relearning?

2. *Serviceability.* The second question concerns the quality of its content and implications for later system development. The following is a list of questions of efficiency, in this context meaning "doing things right:"
   - Are the requirements consistent?
   - Are the requirements unambiguous?
   - Are the requirements compatible with the methods of later development stages?
   - Are the requirements readable?
   - Are the requirements modifiable?
   - Are the requirements traceable?
   - Are the requirements usable after implementation?
   - Are the requirements maintainable?
   - Are the requirements in compliance with documentation standards?

3. *Prediction.* The third question concerns the value of measures of quality that will act as predictor measurements for the eventual quality of the finished software. A predictor metric is used to predict the value of a property of a system that will become directly observable only during a later stage of system development.

4. *Process.* Three processes of development are worth considering:
   - A life-cycle process such as SSADM (structured systems analysis and design) is based on a waterfall model. In this model requirements specification occurs at an early stage and is then fixed as any associated metrics would be.
   - A prototyping approach offers an early normalization, but also offers a more flexible model of system development that recognizes the problem of changing requirements.

- Approaches recognize specifically the social setting in which requirements specifications takes place. Control of quality during any process will probably be one of instituting checklists together with a program for completing them and acting on the results. Questions to ask at this point include:
  — Is the system easy to learn?
  — Is the system easy to relearn?
  — Is there stability and maturity in the system?

Reference

Farbey, B. (1990). Software quality metrics: considerations about requirements and requirement specifications, *Inf. Software Technol.*, 32, 60–64.

Selected Bibliography

Schafer, G. (1988). *Functional Analysis of Office Requirements — a Multi-Perspective Approach*, John Wiley & Sons, Chichester, U.K.

Stamper, R. (1984). Information: mystical fluid or a subject for scientific inquiry? *Computer J. Symp.*, November.

Watts, R. (1988). Measuring software quality NCC, Manchester, U.K.

Chapter 44

Redmill's Quality Considerations in the Management of Software-Based Development Projects

ABSTRACT

It comes as no surprise that the majority of software development projects are late, over budget, and out of specification. Project managers point to a number of technical problems, most of which are related to technical tasks specific to software development. This chapter shows that inadequate management and a lack of attention to quality are the main causes of the problem (Redmill, 1990).

PROCEDURES/ISSUES/POLICIES

1. Most common reasons given by project managers for failure to meet budget, time scale, and specification are as follows:
   - Incomplete and ambiguous requirements
   - Incomplete and imprecise specifications
   - Difficulties in modeling systems
   - Uncertainties in cost and resource estimation
   - General lack of visibility
   - Difficulties with progress monitoring
   - Complicated error and change control
   - Lack of agreed-upon metrics
   - Difficulties in controlling maintenance
   - Lack of common terminology

- Uncertainties in software or hardware apportionment
- Rapid changes in technology
- Determining suitability of languages
- Measuring and predicting reliability
- Problems with interfacing
- Problems with integration

2. Audits of systems development efforts reveal shortcomings in projects:
   - Lack of standards
   - Failure to comply with existing standards
   - Nonadherence to model in use
   - No sign-off at end of stages
   - Lack of project plans
   - No project control statistics recorded or stored
   - No quality assurance (QA) procedures
   - No change-control procedures
   - No configuration control procedures
   - No records of test data and results

3. The three causes for the lack of control of projects:
   - Attitude to quality
   - Attitude to management
   - Attitude to project

4. In finding solutions, the principal reasons for project management shortcomings should be reviewed, e.g., the project manager:
   - Has no experience working where a quality culture predominates
   - Has not been trained in TQM (total quality management)
   - Has not received adequate management training
   - Has not been managed in accordance with TQM principles by supervisors
   - Has not overcome an inclination toward technical matters and finds that they offer a more friendly environment than the less familiar affairs of management

5. Solutions:
   - *Training:* project manager and team must be trained in TQM.
   - *Management commitment:* must always be seen to be 100 percent.
   - *Standards:* a comprehensive set of standards for all aspects of work should be instituted and used. The project life cycle must be covered as well as other pertinent issues.
   - *Guidelines, procedures, and checklists:* assist workers to meet the standards and QA agents to check the products.
   - *Quality assurance:* should be carried out at all stages of the life cycle and for all end-products.
   - *QA team:* should be independent of the development team.

- *Audits:* should be carried out during the project to ensure that management and QA procedures are adhered to. The project manager should always initiate a review of the auditors' recommendations and of all resulting correction action.
- *Planning:* the project manager should be fastidious in drawing up plans and ensuring their use for control. Plans should include the project plan, stage plans, and a quality plan, which details the quality requirements of the project.
- *Reporting:* a reporting system should be instituted to ensure that problems are quickly escalated to the management level appropriate to the action needed.
- *Feedback:* statistics that assist in project control and the improvement of quality should be collected, analyzed, and used.
- *Continuous review:* the whole quality system (components, mode of operation, and quality of results) should be reviewed and improved continuously.
- *Project manager:* must not be too technically involved. Technical duties should be delegated to a development team manager who reports to the project manager.
- *Nontechnical support team:* should be appointed to assist in nondevelopmental matters including coordination and interpretation of resource and time statistics, recording all expenditures and tracking against budget, and tracking milestones. This team should report to project manager.

Reference

Redmill, F.J. (1990). Considering quality in the management of software-based development projects, *Inf. Software Technol.*, 32, 18–22.

Selected Bibliography

Rathbone, M. (1988). Software quality system, *Computer Tech.*, February.

Redmill, F.J. (1987). Difficulties of specifying users' requirements for computer systems and methods of mitigating them, *Br. Telecommn. Eng.*, 6, Part 1, April.

Wingrove, A. (1987). Software failures are management failures, in *Software Reliability: Achievement and Assessment*, Littlewood, B., Ed., Blackwell, Oxford, U.K.

Chapter 45
Contel's Software Metrics in the Process Maturity Framework

ABSTRACT

The Contel Technology Center's software engineering lab has as one of its prime goals the improvement of software engineering productivity. As a result of work in this area, Pfleeger and McGowan (1990) have suggested a set of metrics for which data is to be collected and analyzed. This set of metrics is based on a process maturity framework developed at the Software Engineering Institute at Carnegie Mellon University. The SEI framework divides organizations into five levels based on how mature (i.e., organized, professional, aligned to software tenets) the organization is. The five levels range from initial, or ad hoc, to an optimizing environment. Contel recommends that metrics be divided into five levels as well. Each level is based on the amount of information made available to the development process. As the development process matures and improves, additional metrics can be collected and analyzed.

PROCEDURES/ISSUES/POLICIES

1. *Level 1: Initial Process.* This level is characterized by an ad hoc approach to software development. Inputs to the process are not well defined but the outputs are as expected. Preliminary baseline project metrics should be gathered at this level to form a basis for comparison as improvements are made and maturity increases. This can be accomplished by comparing new project measurements with the baseline ones.
2. *Level 2: Repeatable Process.* At this level the process is repeatable in much the same way that a subroutine is repeatable. The requirements act as input and the code as output; constraints are such things as budget and schedule. Even though proper inputs produce

385

proper outputs, there is no means to discern easily how the outputs are actually produced. Only project-related metrics make sense at this level because the activities within the transitions from input to output are not available to be measured. Measures at this level can include:

- Amount of effort needed to develop the system
- Overall project cost
- Software size: noncommented lines of code, function points, object and method count
- Personnel effort: actual person-months of effort, reported person-months of effort
- Requirements volatility: requirements changes

3. *Level 3: Defined Process.* At this level the activities of the process are clearly defined. This additional structured means that the input to and output from each well-defined functional activity can be examined, which permits a measurement of the intermediate products. Measures include:

- *Requirements complexity:* number of distinct objects and actions addressed in requirements
- *Design complexity:* number of design modules, Cyclomatic complexity, McCabe design complexity
- *Code complexity:* number of code modules, Cyclomatic complexity
- *Test complexity:* Number of paths to test, of object-oriented development, then number of object interfaces to test
- *Quality metrics:* defects discovered, defects discovered per unit size (defect density), requirements faults discovered, design faults discovered, fault density for each product
- Pages of documentation

4. *Level 4: Managed Process.* At this level, feedback from early project activities is used to set priorities for later project activities. Activities are readily compared and contrasted, and the effects of changes in one activity can be tracked in the others. At this level measurements can be made across activities and are used to control and stabilize the process so that productivity and quality can match expectation. The following types of data are recommended to be collected. Metrics at this stage, although derived from the following data, are tailored to the individual organization.

- *Process type.* What process model is used and how is it correlated to positive or negative consequences?
- *Amount of producer reuse.* How much of the system is designed for reuse? This includes reuse of requirements, design modules, test plans, and code.

- *Amount of consumer reuse.* How much does the project reuse components from other projects? This includes reuse of requirements, design modules, test plans, and code. (By reusing tested, proven components, effort can be minimized and quality can be improved.)
- *Defect identification.* How and when are defects discovered? Knowing this will indicate whether those process activities are effective.
- *Use of defect density model for testing.* To what extent does the number of defects determine when testing is complete? This controls and focuses testing as well as increases the quality of the final product.
- *Use of configuration management.* Is a configuration management scheme imposed on the development process? This permits traceability, which can be used to assess the impact of alterations.
- *Module completion over time.* At what rates are modules completed? This reflects the degree to which the process and development environment facilitate implementation and testing.

5. *Level 5: Optimizing Process.* At this level measures from activities are used to change and improve the process; this change can affect the organization and the project as well. Studies by SEI report that 85 percent of organizations are at level 1, 14 percent at level 2, and 1 percent at level 3. None of the firms surveyed had reached levels 4 or 5; therefore, the authors have not recommended a set of metrics for level 5.

6. Steps to take in using metrics:
   - Assess the process: determine the level of process maturity
   - Determine the appropriate metrics to collect
   - Recommend metrics, tools, and techniques
   - Estimate project cost and schedule
   - Collect appropriate level of metrics
   - Construct project database of metrics data that can be used for analysis and to track value of metrics over time
   - Cost and schedule evaluation: when the project is complete, evaluate the initial estimates of cost and schedule for accuracy and determine which of the factors may account for discrepancies between predicted and actual values
   - Form a basis for future estimates

Reference

Pfleeger, S.L. and McGowan, C. (1990). Software metrics in the process maturity framework, *J. Syst. Software*, 12, 255–261.

Selected Bibliography

Boehm, B.W. (1988). A spiral model of software development and enhancement, *IEEE Computer*, May.

Conte, S.D., Dunsmore, H.E., and Shen, V.Y. (1986). *Software Engineering Metrics and Models*, Benjamin-Cummings Publishing Co., Menlo Park, CA.

Humphrey, W. (1989). *Managing the Software Process*, Addison-Wesley, Reading, MA.

Pfleeger, S.L. (1989). Recommendations for an initial set of metrics, Contel Technology Center Technical Report CTC-TR-89–017, Chantilly, VA.

Chapter 46
Kydd's Technique to Induce Productivity through Shared Information Technology

ABSTRACT

Organizations have made large investments in shared information technology (SIT) over the years under the guise of electronic mail systems, distributed databases, and group decision support systems. Kydd and Jones (1989) contend that SIT may not be appropriate for every organization — that, in order for SIT to be successful, the corporate culture must be one that supports sharing of information across boundaries. In this chapter, the authors give general guidelines that can be used concerning conditions under which high-return SIT can be implemented.

PROCEDURES/ISSUES/POLICIES

1. There are two organizational prerequisites for successful investment in SIT:
   * The organizational culture must be "right," that is, appropriate for and supportive of the sharing of information.
   * Successful execution of a significant number of jobs must require timely access to shared information.
2. In "excellent" companies, a great deal of communication takes place among people in different functional areas. There may also be cross-functional management of cost, quality, and scheduling. This implies that communication occurs across traditional organizational boundaries and that information is shared.
3. In traditional American businesses, the organization is through a hierarchical structure in which corporate norms have dictated that

389

communications paths follow the hierarchy — allowing certain managers to monopolize information. SIT, in contrast, allows workers to work in a cooperative manner across traditional organizational boundaries.

4. Rich communications media foster productivity:
   - Group meetings
   - One-on-one meetings
   - Telephone contact
5. Guidelines for implementing high-return SIT:
   - Assess the environment within the organization to determine whether shared information will further the strategic objectives of the organization. In addition, determine whether or not the culture of the organization fosters information sharing.
   - If SIT is not strategically important, defer SIT until it is.
   - If it is strategically important but the culture does not encourage information sharing, then plan and implement an improvement program that focuses on a single, measurable objective of strategic importance (such as a quality improvement program) and requires involvement by everyone in the organization. The objective is to develop a culture in which everyone is concerned with continuous improvement, measurable results, and shared information. Ensure that management behavior is consistent with the objectives of the program and that the organization's reward system encourages information sharing.
   - If the improvement program is successful, develop a plan for implementing SIT. This plan should include plans for developing an information infrastructure with standardized definitions of key data elements, an information technology infrastructure that provides access to corporate and external data bases, and a uniform set of user-friendly tools. This set should include tools that establish communication protocols between individuals and reinforce the new collaborative norms.

Reference

Kydd, C.T. and Jones, L.H. (1989). Corporate productivity and shared information technology, *Inf. Manage.*, 17, 277–281.

Selected Bibliography

Draft, R.L. and Lengel, R.H. (1986). Organizational information requriements, media richness and structural design, *Manage. Sci.*, 5, 554–571.

Chapter 47
Bellcore's Software Quality Metrics

ABSTRACT

The Bellcore quality assurance engineering software (QAES) group for Bellcore client companies (BCCs) has developed and implemented a comprehensive quality assurance program that focuses on resolving the underlying problems associated with developing quality software (Hon, 1990). The objective of QAES' surveillance program is to develop "cooperative" relationships that cause vendors to focus on (1) implementing methods and techniques to improve control of software development, (2) improving the effectiveness of the underlying process used to develop and support software, thus improving the quality, and (3) understanding the needs and requirements of the BCCs. This chapter discusses this approach and explores measurements utilized whose objectives are to assure adequate vendor quality control, minimize defects, and optimize buyer satisfaction.

PROCEDURES/ISSUES/POLICIES

1. Assure adequate vendor quality control. Measures have been implemented in the surveillance program to track the accomplishment of milestone criteria. These include:
   - Requirements, design, coding, and unit test-phase measurements:
     — Phase deliverable completion
     — Number of open correction actions requests
     — Review coverage
   - Test-phase measurements:
     — Test coverage as measured by structure, functions, or paths
     — Number of test cases executed and passed
     — Number of trouble reports
     — Number of open trouble reports by severity
     — Trouble report initiation rates
     — Product-specific quality, reliability, and stability
2. Minimize defects and improve the effectiveness of the software development process:

- Review of software development artifacts (e.g., requirements, specifications, and code) and testing results provide measurable evidence about the effectiveness of the implemented software development process, that is, specific information about the type and quantity of defects produced.
- Specific measurements used in "real time" to minimize defects include:
  — Average number of defects detected in modules and subsystems by type
  — Historical system, subsystem, and module fault densities
  — Number of defects detected during reviews
3. A long-term approach is to collect comprehensive defect data. Information about defect type, its origin, the mechanism used for detection, and defect severity are required to isolate ineffective processes and detection mechanisms. Defects found during reviews and testing are classified according to the phase detected (x axis) and originated (y axis). After defect data is accumulated, simple calculations will determine the percentage of total defects attributable to certain phases of the life cycle and the effectiveness of phase defect detection efforts. For example, the percentage of total defects attributable to "requirements" is calculated as the total number of requirements defects divided by the total number of defects multiplied by 100.
4. Quality and reliability measures include:
   - Number and duration of system outages due to software failure
   - Number of customer trouble reports
   - Customer trouble report cause analysis
   - Patch statistics where a patch is defined as an interim fix
5. Buyer support measures include:
   - Customer service response time
   - Number of open trouble reports
   - Site distribution of open fault reports
   - Aging of open customer trouble reports by severity
   - Time-to-correct customer trouble reports

Reference

Hon, S.E. (1990). Assuring software quality through measurements: a buyer's perspective, *J. Syst. Software*, 13, 117–130.

Selected Bibliography

Grady, R.B. (1987). Measuring and managing software maintenance, *IEEE Software*, September, 35–45.

Jones, T.C. (1986). *Programmer Productivity*, McGraw-Hill, New York.

Chapter 48
Keyes' Value of Information

ABSTRACT

If it will be difficult to make the point that the corporate information resource is a worthy vehicle to protect with a dictionary workbench, then calculating the value of information (VOI) will be a useful exercise (Keyes, 1992). It will assist the organization in determining the true worth of its investment in information. The ultimate goal of this exercise is to assign a monetary value to each unitary piece of information. In this way an organization accustomed to assessing relative worth based on bottom-line statistics can instantly recognize the value of information in terms that it understands.

PROCEDURES/ISSUES/POLICIES

The following steps should be taken for this assessment:

1. Assign each system (i.e., payroll) a weighting relative to its importance to the organization. Permissible weights for the entirety of this exercise are one for a low relative value, two for a middle relative value, and three for a high relative value.
2. For each data element within a system, assign a weighting that shows that data element's importance relative to that system. Again, use weightings one through three.
3. Multiply these two numbers to get the total weighting of a data element relative to all data in the organization.
4. Each data element should have an annotation next to it indicating the number of systems in which this data element is cross referenced. For example, it is possible that "customer name" is used in the sales, inventory, and marketing systems. This would give a total of three systems. The product calculated in instruction three is now multiplied by the number determined in this instruction.
5. Convert this number to a percentage.
6. Using the last audited net income amount for the organization (for a quarter or for an entire year), calculate the VOI by multiplying the percentage calculated in instruction five by the net income amount.

Reference

Keyes, J. (1992). *INFOTRENDS: the Competitive Use of Information*, McGraw-Hill, New York.

Chapter 49
Pfleeger's Method for CASE Tool Selection Based on Process Maturity

ABSTRACT

A wide variety of computer-assisted software engineering (CASE) tools are available in the software market for various types of applications in the software development process. It is not a trivial issue for an organization to make the appropriate selections and incorporate the CASE tools at the right stages for its own environment. The five process maturity levels defined by the Software Engineering Institute can be used as guidelines for an organization to determine the proper types of CASE tools to use based on its own process maturity (Pfleeger and Fitzgerald, Jr., 1991).

It is obvious that the CASE tools chosen for a particular project have direct impacts on its success in terms of productivity, schedule, quality, etc. Without any clearly defined procedures or guidelines, it is rather difficult for an organization to make intelligent decisions on selecting proper CASE tools to use for a particular process and for a particular project. The method presented here clearly defines the most suitable types of tools to use based on the software development process maturity of an organization. It is valuable for organizations that have already introduced CASE tools with emphasis on continuous process improvement or organizations that plan on migrating from no previous CASE tools involvement to a process with fully integrated CASE tools support.

PROCEDURES/ISSUES/POLICIES

The table in Exhibit 49-1 describes the characteristics for each process maturity level defined by the Software Engineering Institute.

Exhibit 49-1. Software Engineering Institute's Process Maturity Levels

Level	Characteristics
5. Optimizing	Improvement fed back to process
4. Managed	Measured process (quantitative)
3. Defined	Process defined, institutionalized
2. Repeatable	Process dependent on individuals
1. Initial	Ad hoc

Level 1: Initial Process

For this level of process maturity, the inputs to the process are not well defined; however, the outputs are usually defined. The software process neither defines nor controls the transition from inputs to outputs. The CASE tools selection for this level should focus on adding structure and definition to the inputs and outputs of the process. A tool that structures and controls the requirements is useful for process at this level of maturity.

Level 2: Repeatable Process

For this level of process maturity, the inputs, outputs, and constraints are identified for the process. This process is repeatable. Proper inputs will always produce proper outputs even though there is no mechanism to keep track of how the outputs are produced. The process at this level is completely dependent on individuals working on the project. The CASE tools selection for this level should focus on documenting and retaining the information produced in the software development process and making it available to other members in the project team. Tools for requirements modeling, specification, and analysis are useful and project management tools will help track the project constraints at this level of process maturity.

Level 3: Defined Process

For this level of process maturity, the process is now refined into activities according to various phases in the development cycle. The entry and exit criteria for all activities in the process are clearly defined. The inputs for any particular activity should be ready and evaluated before the actual activity takes place. The inputs and outputs associated with each activity are considered intermediate products. The CASE tools selection for this level should focus on measuring the characteristics of the intermediate products to ensure the goals are met and to monitor the process deviations. CASE tools should be selected to produce, analyze, and organize those intermediate products at this level of process maturity.

Level 4: Managed Process

For this level of process maturity, the software development process tends to be dynamic in the sense that feedback and experience learned from early project activities can be used to determine and modify the priority of later project activities. The effectiveness of process factors such as reuse, testing, and reviews can be evaluated. The causal analysis can be done throughout the development process to prevent future mistakes and to analyze defects injected in the early activities. The software development process is now carefully controlled rather than just monitored. The CASE tools selection for this level should focus on collecting and analyzing process-wide metrics for confidence measurement and course correction to allow management and control of the development process.

Level 5: Optimizing Process

This is the ultimate level of process maturity. Projects in this level are fully dynamic in terms of real-time intra- and interprocess improvements and modifications. The software process evolves and corrects itself. The CASE tools selection for this level should focus on dynamic evaluation, configuration, and reconfiguration of an environment based on the current status of the process to ensure product confidence level is met. Process programming and process simulation tools should be considered for process at this level of maturity.

Reference

Pfleeger, S.L. and Fitzgerald, Jr., J.C. (1991). Software metrics tool kit: support for selection, collection and analysis, *Inf. Software Technol.*, September, 33(7).

Selected Bibliography

Boehm, B.W. (1988). A spiral model of software development and enhancement, *Computer,* May.

Guidelines: a framework for the evaluation and comparison of software development tools (FIPS Publication 99), National Bureau of Standards, Gaitherburg, MD, March, 1983.

Humphrey, W. (1989). *Managing the Software Process*, Addison-Wesley, Reading, MA.

Pfleeger, S.L. and McGowan, C.L. (1990). Software metrics in a process maturity framework, *J. Syst. Software*, July.

Chapter 50
McCabe's Complexity Metric

ABSTRACT

McCabe's (1976) metric to assess the complexity of software is perhaps one of the most well-known and well-used metrics. It is presented here in a simplified format.

PROCEDURES/ISSUES/POLICIES

McCabe's proposal for a cyclomatic complexity number was the first attempt to quantify the "flow of control" complexity of software objectively. The metric is computed by decomposing the program into a directed graph that represents its flow of control. The cyclomatic complexity number is then calculated using this formula:

$$V(g) = \text{edges} - \text{nodes} + 2$$

In its shortened form, the cyclomatic complexity number is a count of decision points within a program with a single entry and a single exit plus one.

Reference

McCabe, T.A. (1976). Complexity measure, *IEEE Trans. Software Eng.*, December, 308–320.

Chapter 51
Halstead's Effort Measure

ABSTRACT

In the 1970s, Maurice Halstead (1977) developed a theory regarding the behavior of software. Some of his findings evolved into software metrics. One of these is referred to as "effort" or just "E," and is a well-known complexity metric.

PROCEDURES/ISSUES/POLICIES

The effort measure is calculated as:

$$E = \text{Volume/Level}$$

where Volume is a measure of the size of a piece of code and Level is a measure of how "abstract" the program is. The level of abstracting varies from almost zero for programs with low abstraction to almost one for programs that are highly abstract.

Reference

Halstead, M. (1977). *Elements of Software Science*, Elsevier, New York.

Chapter 52
DEC's Overview of Software Metrics

ABSTRACT

Nowhere are productivity and quality more important than in a hardware/software vendor. Digital Equipment Corporation's view of productivity and quality is presented in this chapter and provides a fine overview of the principles of this book (DEC, 1990). DEC was later acquired by Compaq, which itself has been acquired by HP.

PROCEDURES/ISSUES/POLICIES

1. *Software productivity*: why do we care?
   - Expectations of customers and users
   - Increasing complexity
   - Effective use of technology
   - Missed opportunities
   - Shortage of skilled software developers
   - Increasing need for higher-quality software
2. *Productivity:* what do we really want?
   - Better products
   - Better focus
   - Better resource utilization
   - Better control
3. *Productivity:* why measure?
   - Quantify the project's progress
   - Quantify attributes of the software system
4. Why use metrics?
   - Understand and manage the process
   - Measure the impact of change to the process: new methods, training
   - Know when a goal has been met: usability, performance, test coverage
5. Software system metrics:
   - Characterization of the parts of the system
     - Requirements
     - Specifications

- — Code
- — Documentation
- — Tests
- — Training
- Attributes include
  - — Usability
  - — Maintainability
  - — Extendibility
  - — Size
  - — Defect level
  - — Performance
  - — Completeness

6. Software development process metrics:
   - Characterizations of the process of developing the system
   - Attributes include cost of development, predictability of schedule, rate of defect discovery, and repair

7. Characteristics of metrics
   - Collectable
   - Reproducible
   - Pertinent
   - System independent

8. Questions to ask:
   - How is time spent on a project?
   - Has the defect rate gone down?
   - What tools are being used?
   - What are the reasons for rework?
   - Are problem reports under control?
   - Is this a reasonable schedule?

9. Caveats:
   - Behavior modifies toward what is being measured
   - Measure the attributes that are important
   - Measure multiple attributes
     - — Size versus quality
     - — Source code versus source + comments
     - — Executable lines of code versus data declarations

10. Product metrics:
    - *Size:* lines of code, pages of documentation, number and size of test, token count, function count
    - *Complexity:* decision count, variable count, number of modules, size/volume, depth of nesting
    - *Reliability:* count of changes required by phase, count of discovered defects, defect density = number of defects/size, count of changed lines of code

11. Process metrics:
    - *Complexity:* time to design, code, and test, defect discovery rate by phase, cost to develop, number of external interfaces, defect fix rate
    - *Methods and tool use:* number of tools used and why, project infrastructure tools, tools not used and why
    - *Resource metrics:* years experience with team, years experience with language, years experience with type of software, MIPS per person, support personnel to engineering personnel ratio, non-project time to project time ratio
    - *Productivity:* percent time to redesign, percent time to redo, variance of schedule, variance of effort
12. What is productivity?
    - How do you define it?
    - In what context?
    - What about quality and predictability?
    - Productivity itself is not the goal
13. Classes of productivity:
    - *Product:* quality, reliability, bug rate, maintainability, complexity level
    - *People:* how much is done in a unit of time, effects of training, type of problem, morale, creativity versus discipline
    - *Process:* what can be automated and at what cost, predictability of what and when delivered, getting problems out of the system and getting control in
14. Operational definitions:
    - Identify the attributes
    - Determine the metric and measuring technique
    - Measure to understand where you are
    - Establish worst, best, planned cases
    - Modify process
    - Remeasure to see what has changed
    - Reiterate
    - Work with data that is already available
    - Determine additional data to collect and method of collection
15. Software quality dimensions:
    - Software capabilities
    - Publications
    - Packaging
    - Installability
    - Ease of use
    - Performance
    - Reliability
    - Maintainability
    - Compatibility

- Evolvability
- Cost
- Timeliness

16. The relative cost of fixing problems:

• Just before code	1
• During code	1.5
• Just before test	10
• During test	60
• In the field	100

Reference

Digital Equipment Corporation. (1990). Software metrics: an overview — tools for managing software development, company presentation.

Chapter 53

Hewlett Packard's TQC (Total Quality Control) Guidelines for Software Engineering Productivity

ABSTRACT

Engineering productivity is extremely important to HP because the company relies on new product development to maintain its competitive strength. On average, HP introduces one new product every business day; 70 percent of HP's engineers are involved in software development and half of all R&D projects are exclusively devoted to software development.

It was this significant investment in software development that prompted HP's president to issue a challenge to achieve a tenfold improvement in software quality within five years. He also asked that new product development time be reduced by 50 percent.

This chapter points out the techniques Hewlett Packard (1989) utilized to meet this vast quality and productivity challenge.

PROCEDURES/ISSUES/POLICIES

1. HP's productivity equation:

    Productivity = function of doing the right things * function of doing things right
2. Cultural and organizational issues are addressed to be able to motivate and support positive changes. Productivity managers are used in each division:

- Understand productivity and quality issues
- Evaluate, select, and install CASE tools
- Communicate best software engineering practices
- Training
- Establish productivity and quality metrics
- A group productivity council created to share the best R&D practices across divisions
- Metrics definition
- Metrics tracking
- Productivity councils
- Software quality and productivity assessment
- Communication of best practices

3. A software metrics council was created composed of R&D and QA managers and engineers whose objective was to identify key software metrics and promote their use.

4. Project/product quality metrics:
   - Break-even time measures return on investment. It is defined as time until development costs are offset by profits. The three numbers plotted are: R&D investment in dollars, operating profit in dollars and time, and sales revenue in dollars and time.
   - Time-to-market measures responsiveness and competitiveness. It is defined as time from project go-ahead until release to market.
   - Kiviat diagram measures variables that affect software quality and productivity. It is a bull's eye chart that graphs results of quality and productivity assessment.

5. Process quality metrics:
   - Progress rate measures accuracy of the schedule. It is defined as the ratio of planned to actual development time.
   - Open, critical, and serious KPR measures effectiveness of support processes. It is defined as the number of service requests classified as known problems (of critical or serious severity level) that are not signed off.
   - Post-release defect density measures effectiveness of design and test processes. It is defined as the total number of defects reported during the first 12 months after product shipment.

6. People quality metrics:
   - Turnover rate measures morale; it measures the percent of engineers leaving company.
   - Training measures investment in career development. It is defined as the number of hours per engineer per year.

7. Basic software quality metrics:
   - Code size (KNCSS, which is thousands of lines of noncomment source statements)
   - Number of prerelease defects requiring fix
   - Prerelease defect density (defects/KNCSS)

- Calendar months for prerelease QA
- Total prerelease QA test hours
- Number of post-release defects reported after one year
- Post-release defect density (defects/KNCSS)
- Calendar months from investigation checkpoint to release
8. Strategy for code reuse:
   - Share code (use exactly as is) whenever possible.
   - If sharing is not possible, try to leverage (minimal modifications).
   - If neither sharing nor leveraging is possible, look for similar algorithms (design reuse).
   - As a last resort, invent something new.
9. The systems software certifications program was established to ensure measurable, consistent, high-quality software. The four metrics chosen were:
   - *Breadth* — measures the testing coverage of user-accessible and internal functionality of the product.
   - *Depth* — measures the proportion of instructions or blocks of instructions executed during the testing process.
   - *Reliability* — measures the stability and robustness of a product and its ability to recover gracefully from error conditions.
   - *Defect density* — measures the quantity and severity of reported defects found and a product's readiness for use.

Reference

Hewlett Packard. (1989). Software Engineering Productivity, company report.

Chapter 54
Motorola's Six Sigma Defect Reduction Effort

ABSTRACT

In 1987 Motorola set in motion a five-year quality improvement program called Six Sigma. The term "six sigma" is one used by statisticians and engineers to describe a state of zero defects. This program has resulted in productivity gains of 40 percent, as well as winning the Malcolm Baldrige National Quality Award in 1988 (Rifkin, 1991). Benefits include:

- Increased productivity by 40 percent
- Reduced backlog from years to months
- Increased customer service levels
- Shifted IS time from correcting mistakes to value-added work
- More motivated staff
- Saved $1.5 billion in reduced cost

PROCEDURES/ISSUES/POLICIES

1. Identify your product. Determine what service or product you are producing. IS must align what they do with what the customers want.
2. Identify customer requirements. IS must determine what the customer perceives as a defect-free product or service. The unit of work that the user is dealing with must be considered, for example, a general ledger system in which the user worries about defects per journal voucher and not defects per thousand lines of code.
3. Diagnose the frequency and source of errors. Four categories of metrics were established to target defect reduction:
   - New software development
   - Service delivery
   - Cycle time
   - Customer satisfaction, which is composed of a detailed service with the intent of validating the first three metrics

4. Define a process for doing the task. Motorola refers to this process as mapping, but closely aligned to the re-engineering process. The process involves using personal computer-based tools to determine flow-through of processes and answering the following questions:
   • Which processes can be eliminated?
   • Which processes can be simplified?
5. Make the process mistake proof. By streamlining a process and eliminating any unnecessary steps, it is possible to make the process mistake proof. By using metrics, a process control mechanism is put into place so that problems can be addressed before they affect output.
6. Put permanent control measures in place. Once Six Sigma is reached, this level must be maintained. At this step, the Six Sigma metrics are set up to be used to monitor the process continuously:
   • Monthly quality review meetings are held where each person discusses his or her metric, its trend, diagnosis of source cause of errors, and action plan to correct them.

Reference

Rifkin, G. (1991). No more defects, *Computerworld*, July, 59–62.

Chapter 55
Lederer's Management Guidelines for Better Cost Estimating

ABSTRACT

Inaccurately estimating software project costs wastes limited resources, fails to make expected contributions, and ultimately destroys the credibility of estimators and developers. This chapter results from a study by Lederer and Prasad (1992) of the cost-estimating practices reported by 115 computing managers and professionals.

PROCEDURES/ISSUES/POLICIES

1. Causes of inaccurate estimates: (listed in order of descending value)
   - Frequent requests for changes
   - Overlooked tasks
   - Users lack understanding of their own requirements
   - Insufficient communication between user and analyst
   - Poor or imprecise problem definition
   - Insufficient analysis when developing estimate
   - Lack of coordination between systems development, technical services, operations, etc.
   - Lack of an adequate methodology or guidelines for estimating
   - Changes in information systems department personnel
   - Insufficient time for testing
   - Lack of historical data regarding past estimates and actuals
   - Lack of setting and review of standard duration for use in estimating
   - Pressure from managers, users, or others to increase or reduce estimate
   - Inability to anticipate skills of project team members
   - "Red tape"

- Lack of project control comparing estimates and actuals
- Users lack data processing understanding
- Inability to tell where past estimates failed
- Reduction of project scope or quality to stay within estimate, resulting in extra work later
- Lack of careful examination of estimate by management
- Lack of participation in estimating by systems analysts and programmers who develop system
- Performance reviews do not consider whether estimates were met
- Lack of diligence by systems analysts and programmers
- Removal of padding from the estimate by management

2. Influences on the estimate: (listed in order of descending value)
   - Complexity of proposed system
   - Required integration with other systems
   - Complexity of programs in system
   - Size of the system in number of functions
   - Capabilities of the project team members
   - Size of the system in number of programs
   - Project team's experience with the application
   - Anticipated frequency or extent of potential changes in user requirements
   - Project team's experience with the programming language
   - Data management system
   - Number of project team members
   - Extent of programming or documentation standards
   - Availability of software productivity tools
   - Development mode (batch or online)
   - Particular programming language used
   - Project team's experience with the hardware
   - Availability of testing aids
   - Availability of test time on the hardware
   - Computer memory and secondary storage constraints
   - Size of the system in number of lines of code

3. The uses of cost estimates: (listed in order of descending value)
   - Staff projects
   - Control or monitor project implementation
   - Select proposed projects for implementation
   - Schedule projects
   - Quote charges to users for projects
   - Audit project success
   - Evaluate project developers
   - Evaluate project estimators

4. Software packages in use: (listed in order of descending value)
   - Estimacs
   - Spectrum/Estimator
   - In-house package
   - Project Workbench
   - Nolan/Prompt
   - AGS PAC III
   - DEC/VAX Software Project Manager
   - Microsoft Project
5. *Guideline one:* Assign the initial estimating task to the final developers. There are two schools of thought concerning the estimation process. One is that a separate group of people should be given the responsibility of estimating all software projects — much in the same way as a professional estimator estimates construction projects. This study found that this was not valid; the best estimates come from the ultimate developers of the product.
6. *Guideline two:* Delay finalizing the initial estimate until the end of a thorough study. If the estimators cannot come up with an accurate estimate, then they should delay announcing it until it can be as accurate as possible. Project overruns are a direct result of improvising an estimate. The researchers found that coming up with an estimate under pressure serves no purpose because revising an estimate may not correct it.
7. *Guideline three:* Anticipate and control user changes. Estimators should thoroughly understand the user requirements that motivated the proposed system before they estimate the costs. By doing so, they can probably reduce and therefore control the frequent requests for changes.
8. *Guideline four:* Monitor the progress of the proposed project. The study found that the percentage of large projects that overrun their estimates and the percentage of those for which formal monitoring of project progress compares it to its project plan were negative. Thus, formal monitoring is important.
9. *Guideline five:* Evaluate proposed project progress by using independent auditors. The monitoring of a project is usually done by those involved with it. The survey shows, however, that more accurate estimates occur when independent auditors are present. Apparently, an independent evaluation is an advance warning to estimators and developers that computing management is concerned about creating an accurate estimate and meeting it. It also makes it harder to cheat. Within systems analysts and programmers, 25 percent refrain from accurately reporting their actual hours in order to meet the estimates; 36 percent of computing departments postpone the delivery of part of a project and then claim on-time delivery for the rest of the project, and 68 percent of the

projects in this study had programmers work disproportionately harder in the final days of the project to meet the targeted completion date.

10. *Guideline six:* Use the estimate to evaluate project personnel. Greater accuracy is found in estimating when such evaluation is done. The authors recommend informing personnel in advance of the intended use of the estimate and giving favorable recognition to personnel whose projects meet their estimates.

11. *Guideline seven:* Computing management should carefully study and approve the cost estimate. For 58 percent of an organization's large projects, a cost/benefit analysis is used to justify systems development. Computing management approval, rather than user management approval, increases estimating accuracy.

12. *Guideline eight:* Rely on documented facts, standards, and simple arithmetic formulas rather than on guessing, intuition, personal memory, and complex formulas.

13. *Guideline nine:* Do not rely on cost estimating software for an accurate estimate. The study found that the use of software estimating packages had no significant effect on reducing overruns.

Reference

Lederer, A.L. and Prasad, J. (1992). Nine management guidelines for better cost estimating, *Commn. ACM*, 35, 51–59.

Selected Bibliography

Albrecht, A.J. (1979). Measuring application development productivity, *GUIDE/SHARE Appl. Dev. Symp. Proc.*, February, 83–92.

Conte, S.D., Dunsmore, H.E., and Shen, V.Y. (1986). *Software Engineering Metrics and Models*, Benjamin/Cummings Publishing Company, Inc., Menlo Park, CA.

Lederer, A.L., Mirani, R., Neo, B.S., Pollard, C., Prasad, J., and Ramamurthy, K. (1990). Information system cost estimating: a management perspective, *MIS Q.*, 14, 159–178.

Chapter 56
Kanter's Methodology for Justifying Investment in Information Technology

ABSTRACT

A survey of over 100 corporate CEOs found that 64 percent felt that their organizations were not getting the most for their information systems investments (Kanter, 1990). This short chapter focuses on how to justify the IS function.

PROCEDURES/ISSUES/POLICIES

1. Decide whether or not you need to justify the past or whether you want to work only on new expenditures. A strong argument can be made for comprehensive budgeting of past activities as a base point for future planning.
2. Once a scoping is made, budgets can be sorted by many categories such as specific department and activity or by qualitative breakouts such as architecture, skills mix, and systems development.
3. Many IS executives measure information technology expenditures against industry averages. To assure balance, analyze by major application areas such as marketing, manufacturing, or finance. Use one or more third-party yardsticks to measure strategic or competitive advantage applications such as:
   - *Computerworld Premier 100* — based on a six-part formula that includes:

- — Annual IS budget as percent of revenue (30 percent)
- — Market value of equipment as percent of revenue (15 percent)
- — Company profitability over five years (15 percent)
- — Percent of IS budget for people (10 percent)
- — Percent of IS budget on education (15 percent)
- — Number of PCs/Terminals as percent of total headcount (15 percent) (percent = weighting value)
- *CIO Magazine Top 100* —MIS operations evaluated by experts on four factors that foster a competitive edge:
  - — Demonstrated importance of customer service
  - — Not who you know, but how you connect to them
  - — Value of information as equal to money as an asset
  - — Illuminate shifts in IS usage
- *Nolan, Norton* — IT expenditure by industry compared to total revenue, then application portfolio by function, compared to business strategy and broken out by spending for:
  - — Institutional systems
  - — Professional support
  - — Physical automation
  - — External support
- *SoCal Gas Company* — based on a University of St. Louis method, company evolved a four-point plan:
- Economic impact (65 pts)
- Strategic alignment (22)
- MIS support (13)
- Definitional uncertainty (plus/minus pts)
- *Rivard & Kaiser* — value placed on intangible and probabilistic returns including:
  - — Incremental analysis
  - — Value analysis
  - — Expected value
  - — Worst/most likely/best case analysis
- *Index Group PRISM* — broad use of questionnaires to measure user satisfaction and performance within corporate culture and strategy guidelines
4. Conduct a qualitative survey, application by application, of all major systems. Have two groups respond. For each application, IS staff should rate cost/value in terms of maintainability, adequacy of hardware/software, staffing requirements, etc. Each user department should rate effectiveness of each application in terms of mission, fulfillment, timeliness, adequacy, method of reporting, productivity benefit, etc. This survey permits:

- Gain alignment and consensus for action
- Make cuts
- Clearly identify high-ROI applications

5. The next step is to assess future costs. Best approach builds on basic value analysis as represented by return-on-investment measurement. In this instance, it is important to place value on intangible benefits and strategic uses of information technology.

Example: Placing terminals in customers' offices has an intangible value unless you ask: how much more will that customer buy? How many customers do we normally lose in a year, and how many will we keep now? The answers can be found by extrapolation, projection, or survey.

The expected-value method can be used to assess the probabilities of certain outcomes. This allows you to draw and adjust quantified value conclusions of the type that senior management will respect.

Example: Assume average annual downtime for a paper mill is two weeks with each down week costing $2 million. A new information system has a goal of reducing downtime by improving maintenance decisions. If the assumption is made that a 50 percent chance downtime can be reduce 10 percent, then these are tangible figures that can be brought to management.

Reference

Kanter, J. (1990). It's time to justify your organization's investment in information technology, *Cambex STOR/age*, 1, from a paper prepared for MIS sponsors of Babson College's Center for Information Management.

Chapter 57
The "Make–Buy" Decision

ABSTRACT

Many projects can make use of package software to satisfy part or all of a functional requirement. In making this decision, the purchase cost of the package must be weighed against the development costs estimated as part of the planning step. As part of this process the questions in this chapter should be answered.

PROCEDURES/ISSUES/POLICIES

1. Does the vendor-supplied software meet all functional requirements defined in the scope of the plan? If not, what percentage of the function will need to be enhanced or added locally? What costs are associated with these enhancements?
2. Has the vendor-supplied software been developed using software engineering methods? Is it maintainable? Does a good documentation base exist? What documentation is supplied with the package?
3. Does the vendor-supplied software meet human interface requirements for the system to be developed?
4. Does the vendor-supplied software already have a user base? How many users are working in an environment identical to (hardware, operating system, database)? Are current users happy with the package and with vendor's support of the package? Is there a user group?
5. What is the vendor's policy on software maintenance and on error correction and reporting? What are the vendor's rates for future adaptation or enhancement of the software? Does a maintenance contract exist? Is the vendor the original developer of the package?
6. Will the vendor supply source code or will the source code be placed in escrow?
7. Have adequate benchmark and validation tests been conducted on the vendor's software?
8. Is there more than one candidate vendor package? Have all the candidates been evaluated? Have benchmark tests been conducted?

9. How are new releases of the package handled? How long are the older releases supported? What is the frequency (based on past performance) of new releases?
10. Is special training required to use the package? To operate the package? Is training conducted at the local site? Is any cost associated with training?

Reference

General Electric Company. (1986). *Software Engineering Handbook*, McGraw-Hill, New York.

Chapter 58
Software Selection from Multiple Packages

ABSTRACT

Many projects can make use of package software to satisfy part or all of a functional requirement. In making this decision, the purchase cost of the package must be weighed against the development costs estimated as part of the planning step. The decision is further complicated when more than one software package is evaluated. This chapter provides a recommended evaluation procedure.

PROCEDURES/ISSUES/POLICIES

1. *Cost* — the real cost of vendor-supplied software (purchase price + cost to modify + cost to add + maintenance fee)
2. *Service and support* — based on other users with identical environments
3. *Documentation* — for users and local maintenance
4. *Expandability and flexibility* — to address future applications or changes in environment
5. *Reputation* — of the vendor and the vendor-supplied software
6. *Stability* — based on the age of the package and the number of releases over the past two years
7. *Machine or operating system dependency* — based on programming languages used, special features tied to special hardware
8. *Completeness* — of function and performance based on software scope

A *software evaluation matrix* should be developed to evaluate software packages against each other. First, establish a weight factor, based on importance, for each characteristic. Grade each candidate package on a scale of one to ten for each characteristic listed above. The final grade for each package is:

$$\Sigma\,[(\text{characteristic})_k(\text{weighting factor})_k]$$

where k = 1 to 8.

Reference

General Electric Company. (1986). *Software Engineering Handbook*, McGraw-Hill, New York.

Chapter 59
The Boehm COCOMO Model

ABSTRACT

COCOMO (constructive cost model) describes factors that affect the ultimate cost of computer software. The factors fall into four broad categories: product, computer, personnel, and project. Each of these factors is assigned quantitative values.

The software development effort is modeled as a nonlinear function of the number of estimated lines of code to be developed. COCOMO equations take the form of:

$$m = c_1 * KLOC^a * PROD[f_i]$$

where:

    m = number of person-months for development effort
    c_1 = model coefficient
    a = model exponent
    f_i = cost factors (i = 1 to 16)

Each model cost factor is assigned values based on the degree of its importance and impact.

PROCEDURES/ISSUES/POLICIES

1. Product cost factors
   - *Required software reliability:* degree to which effort will be expended to assure software reliability (number of reviews, quality assurance effort)
   - *Data base size:* size and complexity of the database to be developed or integrated (number of information elements, access methods)
   - *Software product complexity:* logical and structural complexity of the software to be developed
2. Computer cost factors
   - *Execution time constraints:* degree to which program execution time is tied to successful accomplishment of software requirements
   - *Memory constraint:* memory limitations

- *Environmental volatility:* frequency and extent to which the environment external to the software (i.e., operating system, hardware, etc.) will change during development
- *Computer turnaround time:* responsiveness of the programming environment

3. Personnel cost factors
   - *Analyst capability:* experience and expertise
   - *Application experience:* experience of development personnel with user application domain
   - *Programmer capability:* experience and expertise
   - *Environment expertise:* experience and expertise with software environment
   - *Language experience:* experience and expertise in programming language

4. Project cost factors
   - *Programming practices:* use of modern programming practices during project
   - *Software tools:* availability of software tools for each of the software engineering steps
   - *Schedule constraints:* the degree to which scheduling constraints will affect the application of software engineering techniques

5. Other cost considerations
   - *Language:* Cost per source instruction in assembly language is about twice the cost per source instruction in a higher level language.
   - *Real-time applications:* Cost per instruction is about five times that of conventional applications.
   - *Point on learning curve:* An experienced programming group requires 50 to 100 percent more effort to develop an unfamiliar program than some variant of a familiar program.
   - *Amount of documentation:* Documentation costs run about 10 percent of the total software development cost.
   - *Amount of previous software used:* The cost of adapting existing software into a new project may be determined by estimating the modification and interface costs for the new application.
   - *Representations of development environment:* The added cost required to adapt software to actual operational conditions can be quite significant — up to 95 pecent — but can only be estimated subjectively.

Further Readings

Boehm, B. (1981). *Software Engineering Economics*, Prentice-Hall, New York.

Boehm, B. (1975). The high cost of software, in *Practical Strategies for Developing Large Software Systems*, Horowitz, E., Ed., Addison-Wesley, Reading, MA, 4–14.

Chapter 60
IEEE Standard Dictionary of Measures to Produce Reliable Software

ABSTRACT

The IEEE standards were written with the objective of providing the software community with defined measures currently used as indicators of reliability. By emphasizing early reliability assessment, this standard supports methods through measurement to improve product reliability. This chapter presents a subset of the IEEE standard easily adaptable by the general IS community.

PROCEDURES/ISSUES/POLICIES

1. *Fault density.* This measure can be used to predict remaining faults by comparison with expected fault density, determine if sufficient testing has been completed, and establish standard fault densities for comparison and prediction.

$$F_d = F/KSLOC$$

where:

F = total number of unique faults found in a given interval resulting in failures of a specified severity level

$KSLOC$ = number of source lines of executable code and nonexecutable data declarations in thousands

2. *Defect density.* This measure can be used after design and code inspections of new development or large block modifications. If the defect density is outside the norm after several inspections, it is an indication of a problem.

$$DD = \frac{\sum_{i=1}^{I} D_i}{KSLOD}$$

where:

D_i = total number of unique defects detected during the ith design or code inspection process

I = total number of inspections

KSLOD = in the design phase, the number of source lines of executable code and nonexecutable data declarations in thousands

3. *Cumulative failure profile.* This is a graphical method used to predict reliability, estimate additional testing time to reach an acceptably reliable system, and identify modules and subsystems that require additional testing. A plot is drawn of cumulative failures versus a suitable time base.

4. *Fault-days number.* This measure represents the number of days that faults spend in the system from their creation to their removal. For each fault detected and removed during any phase, the number of days from its creation to its removal is determined (fault-days). The fault-days are then summed for all faults detected and removed, to get the fault-days number at system level, including all faults detected and removed up to the delivery date. In cases where the creation date of the fault is not known, the fault is assumed to have been created at the middle of the phase in which it was introduced.

5. *Functional or modular test coverage.* This measure is used to quantify a software test coverage index for a software delivery. From the system's functional requirements, a cross reference listing of associated modules must first be created.

$$\text{Functional (Modular) Test Coverage Index} = \frac{FE}{FT}$$

where:

FE = number of the software functional (modular) requirements for which all test cases have been satisfactorily completed

FT = total number of software functional (modular) requirements

6. *Requirements traceability.* This measure aids in identifying requirements that are missing from or in addition to the original requirements.

$$TM = \frac{R1}{R2} * 100\%$$

where:

R1 = number of requirements met by the architecture
R2 = number of original requirements

7. *Software maturity index.* This measure is used to quantify the readiness of a software product. Changes from previous baselines to current baselines are an indication of current product stability.

$$SMI = \frac{M_T - (F_a + F_c + F_{del})}{M_T}$$

where:

SMI = maturity index
M_T = number of software functions (modules) in the current delivery
F_a = number of software functions (modules) in the current delivery that are additions to the previous delivery
F_c = number of software functions (modules) in the current delivery that include internal changes from a previous delivery
F_{del} = number of software functions (modules) in the previous delivery that are deleted in the current delivery

The software maturity index may be **estimated** as:

$$SMI = \frac{M_T - F_c}{M_T}$$

8. *Number of conflicting requirements.* This measure is used to determine the reliability of a software system resulting from the software architecture under consideration, as represented by a specification based on the entity–relationship-attributed model. A list of the system's inputs and outputs and a list of the functions performed by each program are reqiured. The mappings from the software architecture to the requirements are identified. Mappings from the same specification item to more than one differing requirement are examined for requirements inconsistency. Additionally, mappings from more than one spec item to a single requirement are examined for spec inconsistency.

9. *Cyclomatic complexity.* This measure is used to determine the structured complexity of a coded module. The use of this measure is designed to limit the complexity of the module, thereby promoting understanding of the module.

$$C = E - N + 1$$

where:

C = complexity
N = number of nodes (sequential groups of program statements)
E = number of edges (program flows between nodes)

10. *Design structure.* This measure is used to determine the simplicity of the detailed design of a software program. The values determined can be used to identify problem areas within the software design.

$$DSM = \sum_{i=1}^{6} W_i D_i$$

where:

DSM = design structure measure
P1 = total number of modules in program
P2 = number of modules dependent on input or output
P3 = number of modules dependent on prior processing (state)
P4 = number of database elements
P5 = number of nonunique database elements
P6 = number of database segments
P7 = number of modules not single entrance/single exit

The design structure is the weighted sum of six derivatives determined by using the primitives given above.

D1 = designed organized top down
D2 = module dependence (P2/P1)
D3 = module dependent on prior processing (P3/P1)
D4 = database size (P5/P4)
D5 = database compartmentalization (P6/P4)
D6 = module single entrance/exit (P7/P1)

The weights (Wi) are assigned by the user based on the priority of each associated derivative. Each Wi has a value between 0 and 1.

11. *Test coverage.* This is a measure of the completeness of the testing process from developer and user perspectives. The measure relates directly to the development, integration, and operational test stages of product development.

$$TC(\%) = \frac{(\text{implemented capabilities})}{(\text{required capabilities})}$$

$$* \frac{(\text{program primitives tested})}{(\text{total program primitives})} * 100\%$$

where:

program functional primitives are either modules, segments, statements, branches, or paths
data functional primitives are classes of data
requirement primitives are test cases or functional capabilities

12. *Data or information flow complexity.* This is a structural complexity or procedural complexity measure that can be used to evaluate: the information flow structure of large scale systems, the procedure and module information flow structure, and the complexity of the interconnections between modules and the degree of simplicity of relationships between subsystems, as well as to correlate total observed failures and software reliability with data complexity.

$$\text{weighted IFC} = \text{length} * (\text{fanin} * \text{fanout})^2$$

where:

IFC = information flow complexity

fanin = local flows into a procedure + number of data structures from which the procedure retrieves data

fanout = local flows from a procedure + number of data structures that the procedure updates

length = number of source statements in a procedure (excluding comments)

The flow of information between modules and subsystems needs to be determined through the use of automated techniques or charting mechanisms. A local flow from module A to B exists if one of the following occurs:

a. A calls B

b. B calls A and A returns a value to B that is passed by B

c. A and B are called by another module that passes a value from A to B

13. *Mean time to failure.* This measure is the basic parameter required by most software reliability models. Detailed record keeping of failure occurrences that accurately track time (calendar or execution) at which the faults manifest themselves is essential.

14. *Software documentation and source listings.* The objective of this measure is to collect information to identify the parts of the software maintenance products that may be inadequate for use in a software maintenance environment. Questionnaires are used to examine the format and content of the documentation and source code attributes from a maintainability perspective. The questionnaires examine the following product characteristics:

a. Modularity

b. Descriptiveness

c. Consistency

d. Simplicity

e. Expandability

f. Testability

Two questionnaires, the software documentation questionnaire and the software source listing questionnaire, are used to evaluate the software products in a desk audit.

For the software documentation evaluation, the resource documents should include those that contain the program design specifications, program testing information and procedures, program maintenance information, and guidelines used in preparation of the documentation. Typical questions from the questionnaire include:

1. The documentation indicates that data storage locations are not used for more than one type of data structure.
2. Parameter inputs and outputs for each module are explained in the documentation.
3. Programming conventions for I/O processing have been established and followed.
4. The documentation indicates the resource (storage, timing, tape drives, disks, etc.) allocation is fixed throughout program execution.
5. The documentation indicates that there is a reasonable time margin for each major time-critical program function.
6. The documentation indicates that the program has been designed to accommodate software test probes to aid in identifying processing performance.

The software source listings evaluation reviews high-order language or assembler source code. Multiple evaluations using the questionnaire are conducted for the unit level of the program (module). The modules selected should represent a sample size of at least 10 percent of the total source code. Typical areas include:

1. Each function of this module is an easily recognizable block of code.
2. The quantity of comments does not detract from the legibility of the source listings.
3. Mathematical models as described or derived in the documentation correspond to the mathematical equations used in the source listing.
4. Esoteric (clever) programming is avoided in this module.
5. The size of any data structure that affects the processing logic of this module is parameterized.
6. Intermediate results within this module can be selectively collected for display without code modification.

Reference

IEEE Standard of Measures to Produce Reliable Software. Standard 982.1–1988. IEEE Standards Department. Piscataway, NJ.

Note:

Chapter 61
IEEE Framework for Measures

ABSTRACT

Software reliability measurements take place in an environment that includes user needs and requirements, a process for developing products meeting those needs, and a user environment within which the deliver software satisfies those needs. This measurement environment establishes a framework for determining and interpreting indicators of software reliability. This chapter provides IEEE's recommended process for measurement. This process formalizes the data collection practices in development and support and provides for product evaluation at major milestones in the life cycle. It also relates measures from one life cycle phase to another. It is the basis for reliability measurement of a product.

PROCEDURES/ISSUES/POLICIES

The process can be described in nine stages, which may overlap or occur in different sequences depending on organization needs. Each of these stages in the measurement process influences the production of a delivered product with the potential for high reliability. Other factors influencing the measurement process include the following: a firm management commitment to continually assess product and process maturity, or stability, or both during the project; use of trained personnel in applying measures to the project in a useful way; software support tools; and a clear understanding of the distinctions among errors, faults, and failures.

1. Product measures:
   - *Errors, faults,* and *failures* is the count of defects with respect to human cause, program bugs, and observed system malfunctions.
   - *Mean time to failure* and *failure rate* is a derivative measure of defect occurrence and time.
   - *Reliability growth* and *projection* is the assessment of change in failure-freeness of the product under testing or operation.
   - *Remaining product faults* is the assessment of how fault-free the product is in development, test, or maintenance.

- *Completeness* and *consistency* is the assessment of the presence and agreement of all necessary software system parts.
- *Complexity* is the assessment of complicating factors in a system.
2. Process measures
   - *Management control* measures address the quantity and distribution of error and faults and the trend of cost necessary for defect removal.
   - *Coverage* measures allow one to monitor the ability of developers and managers to guarantee the required completeness in all the activities of the life cycle and support the definition of corrective actions.
   - *Risk, benefit,* and *cost evaluation* measures support delivery decisions based on technical and cost criteria. Risk can be assessed based on residual faults present in the product at delivery and the cost with the resulting support activity.
3. Errors, faults, and failures:
   - *Errors* — human action that results in software containing a fault.
   - *Faults* — accidental condition that causes a functional unit to fail to perform its required function. It is also a manifestation of an error in software that, if encountered, may cause a failure.
   - *Failure* — termination of the ability of a function unit to perform its required function. It is also an event in which a system or system component does not perform a required function within specified limits. A failure may be produced when a fault is encountered.
4. *Stage 1: Plan organizational strategy.* Initiate a planning process. Form a planning group and review reliability constraints and objectives, giving consideration to user needs and requirements. Identify the reliability characteristics of a software product necessary to achieve these objectives. Establish a strategy for measuring and managing software reliability. Document practices for conducting measurements.
5. *Stage 2: Determine software reliability goals.* Define the reliability goals for the software being developed in order to optimize reliability in light of realistic assessments of project constraints, including size scope, cost, and schedule.
   - Review the requirements for the specific development effort, in order to determine the desired characteristics of the delivered software. For each characteristic, identify specific reliability goals that can be demonstrated by the software or measured against a particular value or condition. Establish an acceptable range of values. Consideration should be given to user needs and requirements.
   - Establish intermediate reliability goals at various points in the development effort.

6. *Stage 3: Implement measurement process.* Establish a software reliability measurement process that best fits an organization's needs. Review the rest of the process and select stages that best lead to optimum reliability. Add to or enhance these stages as needed. Consider the following suggestions:
   - Select appropriate data collection and measurement practices designed to optimize software reliability.
   - Document the measures required, the intermediate and final milestones when measurements are taken, the data collection requirements, and the acceptable values for each measure.
   - Assign responsibilities for performing and monitoring measurements and provide necessary support for these activities from across the internal organization.
   - Initiate a measure selection and evaluation process.
   - Prepare educational material for training personnel in concepts, principles, and practices of software reliability and reliability measures.
7. *Stage 4: Select potential measures.* Identify potential measures that would be helpful in achieving the reliability goals established in stage 2.
8. *Stage 5: Prepare data collection and measurement plan.* Prepare a data collection and measurement plan for the development and support effort. For each potential measure, determine the primitives needed to perform the measurement. Data should be organized so that information related to events during the development effort can be properly recorded in a database and retained for historical purposes.
   - For each intermediate reliability goal identified in stage 2, identify the measures needed to achieve this goal. Identify the points during development when the measurements are to be taken. Establish acceptable values or a range of values to assess whether the intermediate reliability goals are achieved.
   - Include in the plan an approach for monitoring the measurement effort. The responsibility for collecting and reporting data, verifying its accuracy, computing measures, and interpreting the results should be described.
9. *Stage 6: Monitor the measurements.* Once the data collection and reporting begins, monitor the measurements and the progress made during development, so as to manage the reliability and thereby achieve the goals for the delivered product. The measurements assist in determining whether the intermediate reliability goals are achieved and whether the final goal is achievable. Analyze the measure and determine if the results are sufficient to satisfy the reliability goals. Decide whether a measure result assists in affirming the reliability of the product or process being measured. Take corrective action.

10. *Stage 7: Assess reliability.* Analyze measurements to ensure that reliability of the delivered software satisfies the reliability objectives and that the reliability as measured, is acceptable.

    • Identify assessment steps that are consistent with the reliability objectives documented in the data collection and measurement plan. Check the consistency of acceptance criteria and the sufficiency of tests to demonstrate satisfactorily that the reliability objectives have been achieved. Identify the organization responsible for determining final acceptance of the reliability of the software. Document the steps in assessing the reliability of the software.

11. *Stage 8: Use software.* Assess the effectiveness of the measurement effort and perform necessary corrective action. Conduct a follow-up analysis of the measurement effort to evaluate reliability assessment and development practices, record lessons learned, and evaluate user satisfaction with the software's reliability.

12. *Stage 9: Retain software measurement data.* Retain measurement data on the software throughout the development and operation phases for use by future projects. This data provides a baseline for reliability improvement and an opportunity to compare the same measures across completed projects. This information can assist in developing future guidelines and standards.

Reference

IEEE Guide for the Use of IEEE Standard Dictionary of Measures to Produce Reliable Software. Standard 982.2–1988. June 12, 1989. IEEE Standards Department, Piscatawy, NJ.

Chapter 62

Gillies' Method for Humanization of the Software Factory

ABSTRACT

In order to introduce computer-assisted software engineering technology successfully to an organization, human issues such as goals, objectives, fears, job impacts, etc. must be taken into consideration first. A method is presented here to address those human issues and at the same time to develop a quality definition that is agreed upon by the entire software development community of an organization (Gillies, 1991). The method takes the following approach:

- Educate people about quality.
- Resolve different viewpoints of quality.
- Reach a realistic consensus view of quality that is achievable by all parties.

The CASE technology has been widely used in the computer software industry for many years. As more CASE tools become available and CASE technology becomes mature, it is more noticeable that CASE education is beyond technology; the human issues must also be focused on such that when those issues are addressed, the CASE users such as software development staff will be more likely to perceive that the new technology will serve as an aid to the staff instead of a threat to jobs. The method described here should be considered part of CASE education for the introduction of any new CASE technology to an organization to ensure that the cooperation of staff will help in realization of the potential of new technology.

PROCEDURE

1. Educate People about Quality.

The following definitions of quality from various sources can serve as a starting point for education on quality:

Quality is the degree of excellence.

— *The Oxford English Dictionary*

The totality of features and characteristics of a product or services that bear on its ability to satisfy specified or implied needs

— *The International Organization for Standardization*

The transcendent view: relates quality to innate excellence.

The product-based view: the economist's view — the higher the quality, the higher the cost.

The user-based view can be summarized as fitness for purpose.

The manufacturing view: quality measured in terms of conformance to requirements.

The value-based view: the ability to provide what the user wants at an affordable cost.

— *Garvin*

Quality means the degree of user satisfaction. Previously, good quality meant that a national or an in-house standard was satisfied, This is necessary, but it is not sufficient alone for producing high-quality products. Quality depends upon user satisfaction,

- Software match to specification
- Specification match to user needs

— *Yasuda*

It is important to realize that the purpose of a starting point for a discussion of quality is to understand that the definition of quality varies dramatically from different viewpoints. Any one of these quality definitions is not sufficient by itself but is necessary to be considered for reaching a corporate consensus on quality.

2. Resolve Different Viewpoints of Quality. Establish Relationship Characteristics.

This is done by a two-part exercise involving an enabler and a mix of personnel from developers and users. The first part of the exercise focuses on reaching a consensus on quality that reflects the beliefs of all parties. The second part focuses on understanding the interrelationship and conflicts that exist between different quality criteria. Relationships between characteristics are classified in terms of trade-offs (if A is enhanced, B is degraded), affinity (if A is enhanced, B is affected), and resonance (if A is enhanced, B is enhanced).

The purpose of establishing the relationship between quality characteristics is for people to have realistic expectations. All quality criteria are desirable, but perfection is almost impossible to achieve with all aspects of quality characteristics included. Previous experiences indicate that the success of quality improvement is based on critical criteria, not the entire set. The relationships help people to appreciate clearly the consequences of emphasizing only those characteristics.

3. Reach a Realistic Consensus View of Quality.

The purpose of this step is to ensure a higher probability for the acceptance of quality definition and improvement. It is noted that, if all parties involved feel that the quality consensus takes their special needs into consideration and understands the needs of others, then it is more likely that the quality consensus will be accepted. In an environment where quality consensus is reached and clearly defined, CASE technology can then be introduced as the means to achieve specific goals identified in the quality consensus model. This obviously increases the likelihood of CASE being viewed as an aid rather than a hindrance to the software developer.

Reference

Gillies, A.C. (1991). Humanization of the software factory, *Inf. Software Technol.*, 33, 641–646.

Selected Bibliography

Gavin, D. (1984). What does product quality mean? *Sloane Manage. Rev.*, 4.

Gilb, T. (1988). *Principles of Software Engineering Management*, Addison- Wesley, Reading, MA.

International Organization for Standardization (ISO), www.iso.ch, Switzerland (1986).

Yasuda, K. (1989). Software quality assurance activities in Japan, in *Japanese Perspectives in Software Engineering*, Matsumoto, Y., Ed., Addison-Wesley, Reading, MA.

Chapter 63
Pfleeger's Approach to Software Metrics Tool Evaluation

ABSTRACT

The process and environment for software development are constantly changing as technology advances. Different projects usually utilize different quantified data for their usage in terms of project management, control, and forecast. For an organization that employs software metrics tools in its software development environment, it is not uncommon to have a wide range of software metrics tools available for various projects. Often product managers make the selection of tools based on sources such as previous experience, vendor specifications, input from other groups, etc. As more software metrics tools are acquired, it becomes more important to identify the characteristics common to each tool and to store this information in a repository. The repository is desirable because the comparison can be easily made against various tools in order to select the best set of tools for a particular use.

Software metrics are widely used in understanding, managing, and controlling the software development process. Attempts have been made to quantify the characteristics of various aspects of the software development process in terms of metrics. Software metrics tools are often used to collect and analyze data specific to project process maturity, development environment, and management needs and preferences. The approach suggested here describes a comprehensive way to collect essential information for each software metrics tool, and a project metrics database that supports monitoring, decision making, trend analysis, predictions, and setting up standards for future projects.

PROCEDURES/ISSUES/POLICIES

Pfleeger and Fitzgerald, Jr. (1991) describe a two-stage approach to evaluation below.

1. First Stage: paper evaluation.

This stage includes activities involving reviewing the product literature and documentation from various sources such as vendors, third-party evaluations, etc. The first level of information is a set of basic tool data collected according to the following sample categories:

- Tool name
- Vendor name
- Vendor address
- Contact
- Evaluation date

The tool information is then further refined by following a scheme known as faceted classification, which defines orthogonal facets as independent indices used to group similar objects. Each facet uniquely describes an attribute of an object that cannot be described by any other facet. The repository storing the evaluation result will be organized according to the facets employed. The following set of facets is suggested:

- Purpose of the tool
- MS = list of 5-seep.2
- Platform
- Target application

2. Second Stage: extended evaluation.

This stage involves the use of a tool in a real-life setting with hands-in evaluation. The results of the evaluation are recorded as the third level of information according to the following sample categories:

- Version number
- Platform evaluated
- Operation system run on
- Cost
- Tool strength

The fourth level of information is collected by performing subjective evaluation of the tool's strengths and weaknesses. The sample categories are listed below:

- Performance and speed
- Data import and export
- User interface
- Documentation
- Tool accuracy
- Vendor support
- Cost

For each category, a raw score is obtained based on evaluation results; a weight based on project needs and goals is assigned. The final score for each category is computed by multiplying the raw score by the assigned weight. The overall rating of the tool is calculated by summing the final score of each category. The repository will hold all four levels of information for each tool evaluated. Project managers can then retrieve the level of information desired and build the software metrics tools kit based on interests and needs.

Reference

Pfleeger, S.L. and Fitzgerald, Jr., J.C. (1991). Software metrics tool kit: support for selection, collection and analysis, *Inf. Software Technol.*, 33, 477–482.

Selected Bibliography

Humphrey, W. (1989). *Managing the Software Process*, Addison-Wesley, Reading MA.

Pfleeger, S.L. (1989). Recommendations for an initial set of software metrics, Technical report CTC-TR-89–017 Contel Technology Center, Chantilly, VA.

Pfleeger, S.L. and McGowan, C.L. (1990). Software metrics in a process maturity framework, *J. Syst. Software*, July.

Prieto-Diaz, R. and Freeman, P. (1987). Classifying software for reusability, *IEEE Software*, January.

Chapter 64

Maiden's Method for Reuse of Analogous Specifications through Human Involvement in Reuse Process

ABSTRACT

The concept of software reuse has been applied in various software deliverables such as design, coding, test cases, etc., and has been realized with the advance of CASE tools revolution. An alternative paradigm is proposed by Maiden (1991) for reuse of specifications during requirement analysis through the concept of analogy. The analogy recognition process is knowledge intensive and requires involvement from a software analyst in a pragmatic approach to perform problem classification, reusable specification candidate selection, and customization of the selected reusable specification for the new problem domain.

Specification reuse is a concept that should be implemented at some level higher than reusable code or reusable design. Reusable code or reusable design addresses only an isolated piece-wise solution that usually is identified at the design or coding phase of the software life cycle. Reusable specification must be identified during the requirement analysis; thus, it provides a better picture of software productivity and quality during those early stages of software life cycle and avoids costly faults and omissions that could happen in its later phases.

PROCEDURES

A good definition or analogy can be found from Carbonell (1985):

> Analogical problem solving consists of transferring knowledge from past problem-solving episodes to new problems that share significant aspects with corresponding past experience — and using transferred knowledge to construct solutions to new problems.

Analogy is not a process that matches for syntactic similarities; it basically transfers a network of domain and method knowledge representing solution in its entirety. Analogy is concerned with finding the affinities between the problem domains rather than just the reusable specifications. This domain and method knowledge is best presented by a set of interconnected causal relations constrained by abstraction. Normally domain and method knowledge are separately stored in the existing systems, but expert software engineers usually memorize abstract and concrete specifications in a form integrated with domain and method knowledge. Method and problem domain knowledge is usually required by intelligent CASE tools to assist the analytic problem-solving process. This indicates that specifications reuse must be a human-supported task; the important role of the software analyst must be emphasized to achieve a successful analogy process.

The analogy process for specification reuse can never be achieved solely by software tools. It involves the following steps in which extensive analyst participation is essential:

1. Retrieve the correct specification from a repository. Considerable knowledge is obviously needed to understand different problem domains and the analogy between them. The analyst is required to bring knowledge of the target domain to the process, which requires that key features of the new problem be defined and applied as inputs to the reusable specifications retrieval mechanism. The key features are used to match critical features of those candidate software engineering problems in the repository. This is normally an iterative process of retrieval and understanding.
2. Selection of candidate specifications under the same problem category. The requirement analyst must use his knowledge of the target and the reusable domains to understand each candidate and compare it against the functional and nonfunctional requirements of the target problem. Supports such as diagnostics and explanation tools are needed for the analyst to identify possible misconceptions about the analogy and to guide him during specification reuse so that the most appropriate specification will be selected.
3. Customization of the selected specification to the new domain. This also requires an analyst with extensive knowledge of the target and reusable domains to make successful modifications of a reusable

specification. Functional requirements of the new problem should be tested against the analogous specifications. Prototyping is appropriate to provide confidence that the reused specification will most likely meet the target problem requirements.

References

Carbonell, J.G., (1985). Derivational analogy: a theory of reconstructive problem solving and expertise acquisition, Technical report CMU-CS-85–115 Computer Science Department, Carnegie-Mellon University, Pittsburgh, PA.

Maiden, N.A.M. (1991). Saving reuse from the noose: reuse of analogous specification through human involvement in reuse process, *Inf. Software Technol.*, 33, 780–790.

Selected Bibliography

Maiden, N.A.M. (1991). Analogy as a paradigm for specification reuse, *Software Eng. J.*, 6, 3–15.

Maiden, N.A.M. and Sutcliffe, A.G. (1991). Analogical matching for specification reuse, in *Proc. 6th Knowledge-Based Software Eng. Conf.*, IEEE Computer Society Press.

Chapter 65
Tate's Approaches to Measuring Size of Application Products with CASE Tools

ABSTRACT

Computer-assisted software engineering (CASE) tools have been widely used in the software development environment. CASE tools have evolved and are now equipped with the capability to generate end products in various forms, including programming language source codes, graphical user interface, data dictionary entries, etc. This implies that counting lines of code (LOC) in many cases is no longer adequate for measuring productivity as well as process performance. Methods such as dictionary token counts, vector metrics, and function metrics are considered as alternative approaches for productivity measurements.

Measuring the size of the CASE application product is basically an attempt to measure the technology productivity and the development productivity. Technology productivity indicates the performance of a specific type of CASE technology or CASE tool. Development productivity focuses on the performance of an individual developer or a development group. Because software deliverables may come in various forms, it is necessary to include all objects of the end products in order to make comprehensive measurements. These measurements can then be used to produce tangible productivity numbers such as development cost, development effort, or time-per-unit size of the job done, etc.

PROCEDURE

The overall size of any software product basically should consist of representations from all object types delivered for the end product, and can be determined by one of the following two ways (Tate and Verner, 1991).

1. Find a common measure, for example, lines of code counts, for all objects.
2. Construct a composite measure that is a function of different weighted objects. This is commonly known as function points or function weight.

Three different types of measurements are listed as possible approaches for measurement of CASE application products (CAPs).

1. *Dictionary token counts.* CASE tools are concerned with a wide array of object types, e.g., source codes, entities, relationships, data types, data flows, graphical interfaces, forms, etc. All objects should be entered in a dictionary as tokens or fields. Those tokens can then be weighted and added together to form a single measurement. The following advantages are noted: tokens are simple and easy to count; tokens provide a useful measure across many CASE tools; a token can be considered as an atomic decision instance that the developer makes, thus better representing the software development effort as a whole. It is noted that tokens are most suitable for general purposes and for objective target sizes.
2. *Size metric vectors.* This approach implies that a concept such as size has more than one dimension and should not be represented in a single value. Many objects, such as data-flow diagrams, data models, user interfaces, etc., can be sized separately. The size metric vectors should be tailored based on the objects involved in the end products. It is noted that size metric vectors should not replace common or composite size metrics. They are simply complementary to one another.
3. *Function metric vectors (composite units of size measure).* One common composite measure is function points. The composite measures provide early size measures based on a partial system model. The success of composite measures is based on the purpose for which they are constructed and their suitability for that purpose. Some possible purposes include the forecast of
   - Downstream effort and cost for particular stages and CAP parts, or for a completed CAP
   - Downstream development time for similar categories
   - Downstream size in tokens or lines of source or machine code

Composite metrics are most suitable for particular purposes because they assign weights to different component types and object counts can be tailored for special needs.

Reference

Tate, G. and Verner, J.M. (1991). Approaches to measuring size of application products with CASE tools, *Inf. Software Technol.*, 33, 622–628.

Selected Bibliography

Basili, V.R. and Rombach, H.D. (1988). The TAME project: towards improvements oriented software environments, *IEEE Trans. Software Eng.*, 14, 758–773.

Verner, J., Tate, G., Jackson, B., and Hayward, R. (1989). Technology dependence in function point analysis: a case study and critical review, in *Proc. llth Int. Conf. Software Eng.*, Pittsburgh, PA.

Verner, J. (1989). A generic model for software size estimation based on component partitioning, Ph.D. Thesis, Massey University, New Zealand.

Section III

Section III

Appendices

These 19 appendices are filled with guides, templates, forms, and filled-out examples for every facet of software engineering.

Appendix A
System Service Request Form

System Service Request

Requestor
_____

Requestor Department
_____

Secondary Contact
_____

Request Date   Needed Date

Urgency: ☐ Low   ☐ Medium   ☐ High

Request Type: ☐ Maintenance
              (Fix or Modify System)

              ☐ New Development
              (New Capability)

Description:

☐ Please attach documentation: Screen shots with annotations for required changes are required for any maintenance to screens. This can be done by hitting the "print screen" key and pasting into a Word document. Provide program or function name if known.

☐ Additional information or interaction with other systems if pertinent.

☐ Can you provide test data?

Questions? Need Assistance? Call ext. xxx
or e-mail xxx@xxxx.com

Appendix B
Project Statement of Work

TABLE OF CONTENTS

Project manager:	<name>
Created:	<date>
Last updated:	<date>
Created by:	<name>

PROJECT INFORMATION

Project Request

This project has been requested to provide various business lines new or improved functionality within the <application name> System. Some of the requested changes will be beneficial for the customer also.

Project Number and Title

This project will be referred to as the "?? Project." The project number is ??.

Executive Sponsor or Delegate

The business group head for this project is <group head name> of <company name> and the executive sponsor is <executive sponsor name>, group technology executive.

PROJECT DEFINITION

Background

There are several requirements requested for Release ??. These requirements will be funded by various business lines and will benefit several different areas as well as the customer in many cases.

Release ?? is one of two remaining releases scheduled for <year> by the enterprise. The planned implementation date for Release ?? is <date>. This release will be coordinated with the <project name> scheduled between <month> and <month> <year>.

Project Objectives

To provide more functionality and data accessibility in the ?? system to the business lines and the customer in the least amount of time for the most reasonable cost

Business Units Involved

Internal. Impacts to the following applications were determined in the initial data gathering phase of this project. Certain applications have been defaulted to testing only because no response was obtained during the data gathering phase. Formal sizing has been gathered from all impacted applications as a part of the requirements phase of this project. This list represents the internal interfaces.

Internal Applications/Areas:	Impacts:
1. Application name:	No development — setup and testing needed
2. Application name:	**Application name** — Development, testing needed
	Application name — Development
	Application name — Testing needed
3. Application name:	Development, testing needed
Subsystem name	Testing needed
Subsystem name	No development; setup and testing needed
Subsystem name	Testing needed

External. The external organizations impacted by this project include:

Third party package name	New process and procedures; development, testing needed

Business Impacts. This project will have the following business impacts:

1. Changes for all <application name> customers
2. Changes for wholesale sales and relationship managers
3. Changes for regional managers
4. Changes for operations
5. Changes for central implementation and regional implementation centers

Business Benefits. This project will have the following business benefits:

1. Improved presentation of customer statements and reports
2. Productivity gains on automating various processes.
3. Productivity gains on making specific data more readily available to analysts for problem resolution
4. Compliance with corporate branding standards

Risks

Risk Rating. The risk score for this project is 82. As a result of the risk rating, this project has been rated as a medium-risk project. There is additional risk due to some of the requested changes to be implemented in conjunction to the release implementation date. There is a conflict between the release date and the upgrade date. See Appendix B-2 Risk Assessment form.

Identified Risks. The risks identified for this project include the following:

- Late deliverables if resource constraints
- Resource constraints if work needed on other higher priorities such as production issues
- Retaining key project team resources
- Conflicting project priorities
- Communication, coordination, and task management of all affected applications is necessary for successful implementation
- Risk of impacted customers due to the complexity of some changes

Risk Mitigation. The following actions will be taken to address the identified risks.

- Hire contractors as necessary to assist the team in completing the assigned tasks.
- Work with business lines early in the requirements gathering phase to document detailed requirements.
- Produce more accurate estimates due to detailed business requirements.
- Hold regularly scheduled meetings to keep all affected applications up to date on tasks.
- Include adequate checkpoint reviews in the project process to ensure accurate and complete information.
- Coordinate testing with all impacted applications to ensure the changes are correct.

PROPOSED SOLUTION

Current

Not all functionality was built into the new <application name> system from the old <application name> system. This lack of functionality is causing many manual work-arounds and in some cases loss of revenue. Some of the requested changes also position <application name> in compliance with the <company name> strategic standards.

PROPOSED SOLUTION

The <application name> management team is working with the project manager to ensure that detailed business requirements are fully documented and to prioritize those requirements based on business need. Those requirements have been sized and presented to the various business lines. A resource plan will be updated to reflect the number of resources available during the Release ?? timeframe. The business lines will then obtain funding for the requirements that can be completed in that Release ?? timeframe. The project plan will be updated and an issues log and task plan will be maintained throughout the term of the project.

PROJECT SCOPE

Inclusions

The scope of this project includes the following:

- Defining and communicating the business requirements to all affected applications that are included in the Release ?? requirements.
- Assessing and managing the impacts to the various Operational/Support Groups/Business Lines.
- Participation in development of customer, department, and vendor communications.
- Participation in development of customer or internal training.
- Participation in development of user documentation and procedures.
- Participation in regression testing.
- Validation of requirements, design, development, and unit and system testing of application changes necessary to the applications listed in the Business Units Involved.
- Changes needed for other applications requirements.

A list of the requirements scheduled for Release ?? is attached as Appendix B-6.

Exclusions

The scope of this project does not include the following:

- Any non-<APPLICATION NAME> accounts
- <APPLICATION NAME> (??) application conversion (although it is a dependency).

Security Statement

The security plan is prepared to ensure that appropriate controls are designed to meet security policy and standards. The plan should identify risks and exposures to information, systems, and networks that may result from any exceptions to the standards. The system managers are responsible for ensuring that the security plans are updated or created for all systems.

PROJECT APPROACH

Project Management

<Project Manager name> has been assigned to manage the project. The responsibilities of the project manager will be:

- Establish and execute a project plan
- Ensure completion of project estimates, as required
- Track actual costs against budget/planned costs
- Assist in maintaining the overall project direction
- First point of escalation of project issues
- Obtain project resource commitments
- Define project milestones
- Create and maintain a project issues log
- Schedule and conduct project status meetings
- Complete project status meeting minutes
- Complete project status reports
- Contact lists for all project participants with defined roles and responsibilities
- Ensure detailed test plans are complete
- Participate in the post event review
- Communicate with the other end-to-end project managers
- Close the project

Methodology

This project will follow the <methodology name> methodology. One overall project manager will be assigned as the end-to-end project manager as well as the technical lead. This project manager will manage the details of the <APPLICATION NAME> system development efforts. The project manager will maintain a common format for issues, project plans, and technical requirements. The project manager will provide day-to-day management for the technical team and provide a roll up of all issues, plans, and requirements.

Deliverables

Key Project Deliverables. Key deliverables from this project include:

- Statement of work
- Risk assessment
- Project change requests
- Project requirements document
- Design documents
- Communication plan
- Data security plan
- Resource plan
- Critical success factors document
- Master test plan
- Training plan
- Implementation plan
- Post-implementation review

Approvals. Approval of key project deliverables must be received from the individuals listed in Exhibit B-1. See Appendix B-1 for a signature sheet.

Acceptance Criteria

This project will be considered completed when the following acceptance criteria have been met:

- Each system change has passed all levels of test successfully and is implemented into production successfully.
- Delivered system functionality meets agreed-upon functionality
- No undue fallout up to two weeks after implementation.

Assumptions

The following assumptions are made for this project:

1. Resources assumption — the key resource assumptions for labor, space, and equipment are:
   - Technical lead will be identified and assigned.
   - A test coordination leader is identified and assigned for <APPLICATION NAME>.
   - Testing assumptions in general:
     1. Test coordination with all affected applications will be managed by an assigned resource from testing. Other testing resources will be drawn from each of the applications.
     2. Testing by all affected applications will be conducted at the specified time established by release management for this release.
   - All business line resources are available to the overall project.
   - Project support resources are available to the overall project.

Exhibit B-1. Approval of Key Project Deliverables

Area					Deliverables								
	1	2	3	4	5	6	7	8	9	10	11	12	13
\<manager name\> Operations Manager	A	A	A	A	A	A	R	A	A	A	A	A	A
\<manager name\> Technical Manager	A	A	A	A	A	A	R	A	A	R	R	A	A
\<manager name\> TM Product Manager	A	A	A	A	A	A	A	A	A	A	A	R	A
\<manager name\> Operations Manager	A	A	A	A	A	A	R	A	A	A	A	A	A
\<manager name\> Project Manager	A	A	A	A	A	A	R	A	A	A	R	A	A
\<manager name\> Wholesale Services	A	A	A	A	A	A	R	A	A	R	A	R	A
\<manager name\> Wholesale Integration	A	A	A	R	R	A	R	A	A	A	A	R	A
Audit Representative	R	R	R	R	R	R	R	R	R	R	R	R	R

Note: A = Approval required; R = Review only

2. Production support has the highest priority for resources. Other resource issues will be addressed and prioritized at the steering committee meeting level.
3. The Release ?? key dates will not be changed and various phases of the project will start and end on time.

Key Facts

Key facts identified for this project include the following:

- If the ?? requirement is not implemented with this release, we will continue to lose revenue at the rate of approximately $?? a month.
- If the new statement paper and logo requirement are not implemented with this release, <APPLICATION NAME> will continue to be out of compliance with enterprise standards.
- If <requirement> is not implemented with this release, there will be staffing impacts to the operations group.
- All <APPLICATION NAME> and <application name> related changes must be implemented concurrently.
- If <requirement> is not implemented, there will be customer and operational impacts.
- If the file format changes are not made, there will be customer impacts.
- If the <requirement> changes are not made, there will be customer impact.

Issue Management

Project related issues will be tracked, prioritized, assigned, resolved, and communicated as follows:

- The project manager and participants will report issues that are identified throughout the life of the project.
- The project manager will maintain a log of all issues and report on the status of issues.
- The project manager will assign the priority to and ownership of the issue. If necessary, the executive sponsors will assist the project manager in assigning appropriate ownership for resolution.
- Individual team members assigned to resolve the issue will be responsible for communicating the issue status to the project manager.

See Appendix B-5 for the issue log template.

Change Management

A change management procedure will be used by this project to help ensure that changes impacting the project are assessed, understood, and agreed upon by stakeholders before the change is made or before initiating

469

Exhibit B-2. Project Schedule and Major Milestones

Milestone	Start Date	Completion Date
Requirements	<date>	<date>
Analysis	<date>	<date>
Design	<date>	<date>
Development	<date>	<date>
Testing	<date>	<date>
Implementation	<date>	<date>
Post-Implementation support	<date>	<date>
Project closure	<date>	<date>

specific actions to accommodate the change. The purpose of this procedure is to control change and impacts to the project and not to discourage change.

A project change request form (PCR) must be submitted to the project manager for any changes that impact the project's cost, schedule, or scope. The project manager will review the proposed change request with the project team members affected by the change to assess the impact of the change. The project manager will present the change request to the steering committee to approve or reject the request. The decision will be communicated to the requester and project team.

See Appendix B-4 for the project change request form and instructions.

Communication Plan

A project communication plan will be completed. This plan identifies the approach that will be used to share information with key internal and external parties throughout the project. The key elements of the communication plan include:

- Who must receive the information
- What length intervals the information will be shared
- Who will provide the information
- What medium will be used

Project Status

The status of this project will be communicated in multiple ways (see Exhibit B-2). These include:

- Weekly project team status meeting
- Weekly project management status meeting
- Monthly project status reporting to the business lines
- Monthly online project status reporting to the PMO
- Project plan updates

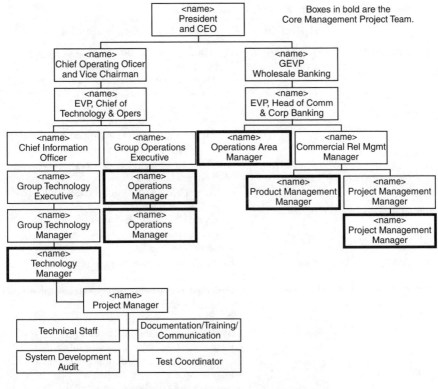

Exhibit B-3. Project organization.

A meeting agenda will be published prior to the meetings so that participants can be prepared for the meeting. Meeting minutes will be distributed after the meeting so that the team is aware of the discussion at the meeting.

Project Team

The Project Organization Chart is shown in Exhibit B-3.

Project Team Roles and Responsibilities

Roles and responsibilities of team members are listed in Exhibit B-4.

Project Estimates and Costs

Project estimates and costs are listed in Exhibit B-5.

Research and Experimentation Tax Credit Eligibility

An evaluation was completed for this project to determine if the project qualifies as an eligible R&E activity. The result of the evaluation indicates that it does not qualify as an eligible R&E activity. See Appendix B-3 for the completed R&E Tax Credit evaluation.

Exhibit B-4. Project Team Roles/Responsibilities

Area	Individuals	Roles/Responsibilities
Project manager	<name>	First point of escalation of project issues
		Obtain project resource commitments
		Complete project estimates, as required
		Establish and execute a project plan
		Define project milestones
		Create and maintain a project issues log
		Schedule and conduct project status meetings
		Complete project status meeting minutes
		Compete project status reports
		Monitor and manage financial status of project
		Participate in the post-implementation review meeting
		Communicate with the other end-to-end project managers
		Close the project
Technical lead	<name>	Review and approve change requests
		Create systems project plan
		Participate in weekly project status meetings
		Conduct system training, as needed
		Conduct system status meetings
		Assist in user acceptance testing
		Ensure system testing is completed
		Complete the technical design and review
		Review and approve the project plan
		Develop the systems support plan
		Develop system conversion programs, as needed
		Complete system development and unit testing
		Update system documentation
		Complete production support plan
		Ensure technical activities are included in the project timeline
		Ensure technical resources are available to complete technical activities
Technical systems manager	<name>	Review and approve business requirements
		Approve project plan
		Review and approve change requests
		Review and approve project plan
		Review and approve user design
		Review test plans
		Review and approve the project implementation plan
		Review and approve the support plan

(continued)

Exhibit B-4. (continued)   Project Team Roles/Responsibilities

Area	Individuals	Roles/Responsibilities
Product management project lead	\<name\>	Complete product research and analysis
		Review product implementation workflow
		Define business requirements
		Approve project plan
		Review and approve change requests
		Review and approve project plan
		Communicate product changes and delivery plan to project team and line staff
		Review and approve user design
		Perform gap analysis of old product vs. new product
		Review and approve customer transition workflow
		Complete product risk assessment
		Define product pricing structure
		Review test plans
		Resolve product issues
		Assist with development of customer communications
		Review the project implementation plan
		Review and approve the support plan
Operations project leader	\<name\>	Review and approve change requests
		Create operations project plan
		Participate in weekly project status meetings
		Conduct operations team status meetings, as necessary
		Participate in user acceptance testing
		Train operations staff, as needed
		Provide operations requirements
		Review and approve the technical design
		Review and approve user design
		Review and approve the project plan
		Update operations documentation
		Develop the operations support plan
		Review the project implementation plan
		Review and approve the support plan
		Ensure operations resources are available to complete operation activities
Customer services project leader	\<name\>	Review and approve change requests
		Participate in weekly project status meetings
		Participate in user acceptance testing
		Train customer services staff, as needed
		Provide customer service requirements
		Review and approve the technical design
		Review and approve user design

(continued)

Exhibit B-4. (continued) Project Team Roles/Responsibilities

Area	Individuals	Roles/Responsibilities
Customer services project leader	<name>	Review and approve the project plan Update customer service documentation Review the project implementation plan Review and approve the support plan Ensure customer services resources are available to complete customer service activities
Integration project leader	<name>	Review and approve change requests Participate in weekly project status meetings Participate in user acceptance testing Train implementation staff, as needed Provide implementation requirements Review and approve the technical design Review and approve user design Review and approve the project plan Update Implementation documentation Review the project implementation plan Review and approve the support plan Ensure implementation resources are available to complete Implementation activities
Documentation and training	<name>	Coordinate with various bank training groups to ensure proper updates are made to documentation and to assess the need for training
Test coordination	<name>	Identification of testing participants, organization of test team, and definition of responsibilities Coordinate cross-project testing dependencies with other testing project leads Identification of business and operations end users that may need to validate Confirm testing environment provided will meet needs Schedule testing with dependencies based on design, training, and conversion schedule Completion of test plan and approval Completion of test scripts and approval Establish and communicate testing schedule Communicate testing status with project team Monitoring of test cycles Ensure validation complete Track testing issues for fixes to be made and ensure appropriate resolution Obtain testing signoffs Types of testing to manage for CTG: IAT (integrated application testing) UAT (user acceptance testing)

Exhibit B-5. Project Estimates and Costs

	Description	Dollars
Capital (hardware/software)	(if applicable)	N/A
Labor costs		
Employee	# hours	$
Contract labor	# hours	$
Total labor	Hours	$
Test CPU	(if applicable)	N/A
Test dasd	(if applicable)	N/A
Other (list all)[a]	Travel/training	$
	Depreciation	N/A
	Software	N/A
	Teleconference	$ not budgeted
	Training	N/A
Total dollars		Total $[a]

[a] Ball Park Estimate

Appendices

APPENDIX B-1: STATEMENT OF WORK APPROVAL

Project Number ??

Project Name <APPLICATION NAME> Release ?? Project

Phase Name Design

Authorization

Name Signature Approval Date

<name>

Operations manager

<name>

Technology manager

<name>

Project manager

<name>

Treasury management product management

<name>

Operations manager

<name>

Client services

<name>

Wholesale integration

APPENDIX B-2: SUPPORT DOCUMENTATION RISK ASSESSMENT FORM

Project Number F1250   Application   <APPLICATION NAME>

Project Title   <application name> Release ??   Project Manager   <name>

Date   <date>

1.	**Type of Project:**	2	5.	**Number of years the project manager has been a project manager:**	0
	- Maintenance (correct problems)	1		- More than three	0
	- Enhancement (add new features)	2		- One to three	5
	New development: replace existing automated system	3		- Less than one	10
	New development: replace manual system	5			
	New development: develop system to support new business	6			
	- Implementation of software package in-house	6			
	- Outsourcing to external vendor	6			
	- Re-engineering of system's architecture	6			
2.	**Impact to Business Operations: (includes data/staffing/monetary)**	10	6.	**Number of years (on average) business group area has worked with specific application to be developed:**	0
	- Limited change to business operation	5		- More than three	0
	- Medium change to business operation	10		- One to three	5
	- Major change to business operation	20		- Less than one	10
3.	**Number of years business organization has been in business:**	0	7.	**Number of years (on average) technology project team has worked with specific application to be developed:**	2
	- More than three	0		- More than three	0
	- One to three	2		- One to three	2
	- Less than one	4		- Less than one	4
4.	**Number of years the business group and technology group have worked together:**	0	8.	**Number of years technology team has performed the duties they will be asked to perform on the project (i.e., analysis, design, coding, testing):**	0
	- More than three	0		- More than three	0
	- One to three	2		- One to three	4
	- Less than one	4		- Less than one	8

APPENDIX B-2: (CONTINUED)

9.	Number of years (average) technology team has worked with the technology to be used on the project (e.g., CICS, PACBASE, IMS):	0	14.	Number of years the project technology has been used in the organization:	4
	- More than three	0		- More than three	0
	- One to three	3		- One to three	4
	- Less than one	6		- Less than one	8
10.	Number of vendors involved:	4	15.	Amount and level of documentation currently available:	5
	- One	2		- Extensive, detailed documentation	1
				- Extensive documentation, but not detailed	2
	- Two	4		- Limited documentation, but detailed	4
	- Three or more	8		- Limited or no documentation, not detailed	5
11.	Number of project team members:	8	16.	Number of organizational entities (besides systems) that need to be involved:	18
	- One to five	2		- None to two	3
	- Six to ten	4		- Three to five	9
	- 11 to 15	8		- More than five	18
	- 16 or more	12			
12.	Approximate length of time to complete project:	10	17.	Availability of business partner to technology group:	4
	- Less than four months	5		- Assigned to desired level of involvement and available to DP immediately when needed	0
	- Four to seven months	10		- Assigned to desired level of involvement, but likely not available immediately when needed	4
	- Seven to twelve months	15		- Not assigned to the desired level of involvement	16
	- More than 12 months	25			
13.	Impact to Customer:	20	18.	Legal/regulatory impact:	0
	Limited product/portfolio customer base affected	5		- Limited legal/regulatory ramifications	0
	Partial product/portfolio customer base affected	10		- Moderate legal/regulatory ramifications	5
	Entire product/portfolio customer base affected	20		- Significant legal/regulatory ramifications	10

APPENDIX B-2: (CONTINUED)

19.	Estimated costs for hardware/software/conversion:	0	24.	Project requirements:	0
	- Less than $600,000	0		Requirements are clear, complete and stable	0
	- $600,000 to $3,000,000	5		Requirements are documented, but some unclear, incomplete, or unstable information	5
	- More than $3,000,000	10		Minimal or no requirements documented	10
20.	Number of interfaces:	5	25.	Service or functionality provided to customers or end-users by the technology:	18
	- Less than four	0		Maintenance	3
	- Four to twelve	5		Standard enhancement	6
	- Twelve or more	10		Extended functionality	9
				New functionality/service/ product/architecture	18
21.	Technology options explored/researched:	0	26.	Can sizing and capacity for technology be evaluated and incorporated into design?	10
	Three or more	0		Current and future sizing and capacity analysis is identified	2
	Two	2		Only current sizing and capacity analysis is identified	5
	One	5		No sizing and capacity analysis can be identified	10
	None	10			
22.	Was this technology option selected as a second choice based upon cost or schedule?	0	27.	Changes to existing systems, including infrastructure, necessary in order to implement the technology:	2
	No	0		Limited	2
	Yes	4		Moderate	5
				Significant	10
23.	Technology used in the project:	0	28.	Number of dependencies on other projects, changes, services, vendors, suppliers, or contractors:	15
	None of the technology used is new	0		None	0
	New to the business line	5		One	5
	New to the organization	10		Two or more	15
	New to the industry	20			

APPENDIX B-2: (CONTINUED)

29.	**Number of applications or systems impacted:**	**10**	**33.**	**Type of third-party connectivity (nonorganization connectivity) used in project or technology:**		**5**
	One or less	5		No third-party connectivity		0
	Two or three	10		Existing third-party connectivity involved		5
	Four to twelve	15		New third-party connectivity involved		10
	More than 12	25				
30.	**Incorporation of the corporate business continuity planning process into the design of the project:**	**4**	**34.**	**Outage during the implementation of the technology:**		**0**
	Extensive involvement in the systems design	0		No outage required		0
	Minimal involvement in the systems design	4		Outage after business hours		4
	No involvement in the systems design	8		Outage during business hours		8
	No contingency plan exists	12				
31.	**Impact to the customer or environment if the technology fails:**	**5**	**35.**	**Level of training necessary for customers and end users:**		**5**
	No impact	0		None		0
	Limited impact	5		Limited training necessary		5
	Moderate impact	10		Extensive training necessary		10
	Significant impact	20				
32.	**Impact to the customer or environment if the exit plan must be executed:**	**4**	**36.**	**Amount of training materials/documentation budgeted and necessary for customers and end users to use the new technology:**		**4**
	Limited impact	2		Limited or no documentation needed		2
	Moderate impact	4		Limited documentation, but detailed		4
	Significant impact	8		Extensive documentation, but not detailed		6
				Extensive and detailed documentation		8

APPENDIX B-2: (CONTINUED)

37.	Formal RFP process used during technology selection:	0	38.	Level of vendor support necessary for the technology after implementation:	5
	RFP process followed	0		No support necessary	0
	RFP process followed, but only one response	3		Minor support necessary, i.e., maintenance	5
	RFP process NOT followed	6		Major support necessary, i.e., programming, upgrades, etc.	10

Score Range Risk:

0 to 60   Low
61 to 110   Medium
111+   High

Total Score _____

Risk Level _____

APPENDIX B-3: POTENTIAL TAX CREDIT TESTS

The following analysis evaluates if this project qualifies as an eligible R&E activity.

Yes	No	Qualification Tests

☐ ☐ **First test**

Do the activities qualify as research in the laboratory or experimental sense by:

1. Relating to, or supporting, the development or improvement of a product

2. Intending to discover information that would eliminate uncertainty concerning the development or improvement of a product or process

☐ ☐ **Second test**

Is the research undertaken for the purpose of discovering information that is technological in nature?

☐ ☐ **Third test**

Do the activities undertaken include the elements of the process of experimentation (i.e., were alternative designs evaluated using the scientific method or did the development of the final design require experimentation)?

<u>Yes</u>   <u>No</u>   <u>**Qualification Tests (continued)**</u>

☐   ☐   **Fourth test**

Is the activity being conducted for a permitted purpose: new or improved function, performance, reliability, quality, or significant cost reduction?

If software is developed for *internal management function* it does not qualify for tax credit unless it meets the following three-part test:

<u>Yes</u>   <u>No</u>

☐   ☐   **First test**

Is the software innovative in that it results in a reduction of costs or improvement in speed that is substantial and economically significant?

☐   ☐   **Second test**

Does the development involve significant economic risk in that the company commits substantial resources to the development and there is substantial uncertainty, because of technical risk, that such resources would not be recovered in a reasonable period?

☐   ☐   **Third test**

Is the software in development commercially available (i.e., can the software be obtained elsewhere and used for the intended purpose without modifications that would satisfy the first and second tests above)?

APPENDIX B-4: CHANGE MANAGEMENT FORM AND INSTRUCTIONS

Procedure

At the conclusion of the requirement phase of the project, the requirements will be considered static and unchangeable because they will form the basis for subsequent project activities. In the event that a change is necessary, the following process must be followed in order to ensure that the change is implemented into the project plan and impacts are adequately assessed.

A change is identified as a result of an issue or of some change to the project environment (for example, regulatory or competitive changes). The person who is requesting the change completes a project change request form and sends it to the project manager. This form will require the following information from the requester:

- *Date of the request* —the date the request form is filled out
- *Requester* — the name of the individual requesting the change
- *Description of change* — a detailed description of the requested change
- *Business reason for change* — a detailed description of the business reason why the change must be implemented as part of this project
  1. The project manager will review the change request with all impacted team members to determine the project tasks that will be added or impacted by the change request and estimate the impacts of the change.
  2. After assessing the impact of the requested change on the project and completing an estimated cost and schedule impact, the request will be presented to the executive sponsors and either approved or denied.
  3. The project manager will contact the requester by sending a completed change request form to the requester with the final decision and informing the impacted areas of the decision. If the change request is denied, the project manager will include a reason in the "reason for denial" section.
  4. A copy of the project change request form will be included in the project file for permanent record and the project task plan will be updated accordingly.

Procedure

Complete the change control form.

Submit to <APPLICATION NAME> application systems manager or team leader.

Systems will estimate the effort.

Systems will respond within ten business days indicating if the change can be absorbed in the release requested.

If the request can be absorbed, work will be queued as appropriate.

If the request cannot be absorbed, the systems group will call a meeting to discuss reprioritizing requirements or moving the request to another release.

See bottom of form for approval instructions.

Project Change Request Form

<APPLICATION NAME> Release ??
Change Control Request Form

Instructions	Requester must complete this side of form.
Name of Change	
Date Requested	
Release Requested (cannot request change control on any release scheduled to move to ET in 60 days or less)	
Funding Source	
Estimated Hours to Complete	
Estimated Dollars to Complete (number of hours multiplied by the current development rate of $100.00)	
Cost Savings Realized by Implementing this Request (describe in dollars the savings realized on a monthly or yearly basis)	
State the Requirements	
Current Work-Around Being Employed	
Background or Other Important Facts	
Operations Approval Must have operations mgmt. approval before submission to systems for estimating	Insert approval e-mail in this section and copy operations mgmt. on the e-mail when sent to systems
Product approval Must have Product Mgmt. approval before being submitted to Systems for estimating	Insert approval e-mail in this section and copy product mgmt. on the e-mail when sent to systems
Systems Approval Approval will be granted after the estimate is completed	Insert approval e-mail in this section and copy systems mgmt. on the e-mail when the response is e-mailed to operations and product mgmt. within ten business days of the request

APPENDIX B-5: ISSUES LOG

<APPLICATION NAME> Release ?? Issues Log

Issue #	Open Date	Opened By	Issue Description	Assigned To	Due Date	Closed Date	Status	Priority	Comments/Resolution
					OPEN ISSUES				
						CLOSED ISSUES			

Priority Codes: High = Show Stopper — cannot continue without issue resolution; Medium = Caution — may continue without immediate resolution; Low = Not Critical — can continue without issue resolution.

Status Codes: (A)ctive; (R)esolved; (D)eferred; (P)ending

APPENDIX B-6: LIST OF REQUIREMENTS SCHEDULED FOR RELEASE ??

<APPLICATION NAME> New File Format

New File Format

New <APPLICATION NAME> Stmt Paper and Logo

Appendix C
Feasibility Study Template

PURPOSE

- To provide a structured method to focus on problems, identify objectives, evaluate alternatives, and aid in the selection of the best solution
- To improve confidence that the recommended action is the most viable solution to the problem
- To assure that projects requiring information systems resources can be done, should be done, and will be done

WHO SHOULD USE

- Individuals who must solve a problem, respond to an opportunity, or meet a mandate that involves the use of information systems should use the feasibility study, which is the initial justification needed to determine if a project is "doable."

RESPONSIBILITIES

This section describes each participant's role in the feasibility study process.

- Executive management ensures that the project is a priority, the proposed alternative represents a good business decision, and capital will be provided to support the project.
- Staff management assigns work, monitors progress, and verifies the work activities involved in preparing the feasibility study.
- Requester prepares the feasibility study including data gathering, analysis, preparation, and presentation functions.
- End user validates problem statement and recommended solution.
- Information systems staff provides technical advice and assistance to help define the current environment.
- Fiscal or budget officer assists in cost determination and validates financial data contained in the document.

DEFINITION

- A feasibility study is a controlled process for identifying problems, opportunities, or mandates, determining objectives, describing current situations and successful outcomes, and assessing the range of costs and benefits associated with several alternatives for solving a problem.

OUTLINE FOR PREPARING A FEASIBILITY STUDY

- Part 1: describe problem
- Part 2: identify success factors
- Part 3: describe current situation
- Part 4: consider approaches
- Part 5: prepare solution analysis
- Part 6: prepare implementation schedule
- Part 7: obtain management approval
- Part 8: prepare supporting documentation

The *amount* of detail will vary. Some feasibility studies *may be* one to two pages, others *may run considerably* longer. Length and detail of the study should be *commensurate* with the complexity and novelty of the effort.

PART 1: DESCRIBE PROBLEM

As answers depend upon the questions asked, so do solutions depend upon the problem statement. Otherwise, you will not know if the solution is an appropriate and adequate way to fix the problem. Your job here is to write a concise statement of the problem to be solved, opportunity available to you, or mandate to which you must respond.

Task 1: Describe the Problem, Opportunity, or Mandate

Step 1: Identify the Problem, Opportunity, or Mandate
- Problems adversely affect clients or members within your organization. Do you have a problem that *should be* resolved?
- Opportunities are potentially favorable — other departments with which you work or circumstances that may allow your department to operate more effectively or efficiently. Is an opportunity available to your department that *could be* realized?
- Mandates are statutory or managerial requirements of your department to do something new or different. Are you faced with a task that must be done?

Step 2: Describe the Problem
- Try to keep your description to one paragraph. It should discuss what you are unable to do now, not what you want to do (ends) or how you want to do it (means).

Task 2: Support Your Statement

Step 1: Explain who or what prompted your department into action on the subject. Try to keep your description to one paragraph.

Step 2: List affected parties. Explain briefly how the following are affected or what they are currently unable to do:
- Clients your department serves
- Other departments with which you work
- Groups or individuals inside your department

Task 3: Validate the Statement

Step 1: Test the statement — verify that your description is not a symptom, solution, or someone else's problem.

Step 2: Critique for accuracy — ask several affected parties to critique the problem statement for accuracy, completeness, and authenticity.

Step 3: Amend if necessary.

Step 4: Obtain concurrence — if you identified someone in task 2, step 1, as initiating the study, obtain concurrence that your statement is accurate

PART 2: IDENTIFY SUCCESS FACTORS

Your job in this part of the study is to determine what results must be achieved to satisfy the problem defined in part 1. Also, identify items that would contribute to the success of your project.

Task 1: Write a Scenario for Success

You cannot see the future, but visualizing the way things should be can be a step in making things come true. Some techniques you may find useful in determining desired outcomes are:

Step 1: Assemble a think tank —a small group of your staff who are knowledgeable of the project.

Step 2: Time travel — have the group pick a time in the future that would be appropriate to assess the project's positive performance in solving the problem. Probably six to twelve months would be appropriate in most cases.

Step 3: List players — include affected parties identified in part 1 along with the individuals and groups who will be responsible for this project.

Step 4: Describe success in functional terms — satisfaction from new products, services, or capabilities; limitations of time or money; resolved issues or mandates; existing policy or operations considerations; performance characteristics such as reliability or ease of use; or any other factors that would be important to the affected parties identified in part 1 or the individuals and groups responsible for the project.:

- Example: The group leader starts out with, "Imagine that it is one year from now — our boss is elated and congratulates everyone for fixing our problem." The group leader then asks everyone, 'What results caused the boss to say this?" Under the title "BOSS," list each item. Add a new category, "SELF." What should happen in the next year to make YOU feel that excitement from success?

Step 5: Consolidate the requirements and develop success factors. Review the requirements of each group for common themes. Develop a list of outcomes that must occur (success factors) to satisfy all the requirements.

Task 2: Rank and Evaluate The Key Success Factors

Step 1: Rank the success factors. List the factors from most to least important.

Step 2: Evaluate the factors. Underline the success factors that absolutely must get done to distinguish from those that could be done.

Task 3: Set Objectives

Ask yourself who needs to do what by when to accomplish the prioritized list of success factors.

Task 4: Validate the Objectives

Start with the first item on the list of success factors. Describe:

- What must be done?
- Who will be responsible?
- When must it be completed?

Repeat the process for each success factor.

Step 1: Achievable and doable? Are the objectives achievable and will you know when they have been accomplished?

Step 2: Acceptable? Will the affected parties concur that meeting these objectives will allow them to do what they were unable to do to in an acceptable time frame?

Step 3: Harmonious? Are the objectives logical? Do they work toward the same end or do they contradict each other?

Step 4: Capable? Is each individual capable of achieving the objectives assigned?

Step 5: Say yes! If you say yes to the preceding steps — good job!
* Examples of objective statements:
  — By May, 2003, DMV's project manager, Otto Mobile, will reduce the citizen's average waiting time at DMV offices to less than five minutes.
  — By December, 2004, without increasing personnel, Ida Fixit of the license section will use an online licensing system to certify 3000 automobile mechanics.

PART 3: DESCRIBE CURRENT SITUATION

Providing a "snapshot" of your organization allows others to understand your environment. Things that may appear obvious to you may not be obvious to others (even in your work group). Documenting the important features of your organization, work processes, products, and clients will bring the pieces together in an understandable format. Your job in this part of the study is to identify how things are done now and what resources are available.

Task 1: Describe How Things Are Done Currently

Step 1: Describe your organization. Briefly explain the structure and purpose. For example, 30 employees conduct environmental studies required for project approvals. They are organized in four work groups: the administration unit has five employees, including the section manager...

Step 2: Explain the purpose of each group. Support the description used in step 1.
* For example, the administration unit is responsible for personnel, budget, policy, and clerical support...

Step 3: Describe the information flow. Include the data's source, destination, method of filing (manual and automated), and frequency. (Often a flow diagram is useful for this step.)

Step 4: Develop your assessment. Identify strengths and weaknesses of the system. Give it an overall grade.

Task 2: List Existing Resources

Step 1: People: in task 1 you described the organizational structure, purpose, and business functions. In this step identify their skills and availability.

Step 2: Tools: list what types of mechanical and electronic tools are available (in terms of access and capacity) and how they are used. This step primarily will describe your existing automation and uses. Include what systems you need to access outside your organization.

Step 3: Funds: identify how much money is available and whether it is from general fund, department revenue, federal, grant, or other sources.

PART 4: CONSIDER APPROACHES

Chance dictates the future when you do not have information about your choices. During a feasibility study, chance and doubt are replaced with control and confidence. You will know what is in each box and can make an informed choice. Your job in this part is to list practical approaches, describe them in a consistent format, and select the best alternative. For comparison, always include retaining the current system for a baseline.

Task 1: Identify Approaches

Step 1: List the approaches that merit consideration. Approaches you will want to consider include:
- Retaining the current system
- Reorganizing
- Expanded manual operations
- Modifying the current system
- Adding new or expanding automation

Complete tasks 2 through 5 for each approach.

Task 2: Determine Life Cycle

Step 1: Determine life cycle. How many years do you expect to use the system that you select for solving the problem?

Task 3: Estimate Costs

Step 1: New costs: estimate the cost of new resources required to develop and operate the project for this approach. Quantify these values in categories of personal services, services and supplies, and capital investment through the project life cycle.
Step 2: Use of existing resources: estimate the amount of existing resources required to develop and operate the project with this approach. List the people and the hours required throughout the project life cycle.
Step 3: Describe adverse impacts: describe any adverse environmental, organizational, or procedural impacts from this approach.

Task 4: Estimate Benefits

Step 1: Tangible: identify anticipated benefits in three categories:
- Cost savings: estimate anticipated dollar savings in categories of cost reduction, new revenue, or reimbursements tied directly to this method throughout the life cycle.
- Staff time to be gained: list people or positions and estimate the staff time to be gained throughout the project life cycle.
- New products or services: describe what they are and list the recipients.

Step 2: Intangible: describe any new potential, increased control, or other advantages that would come from this approach (i.e., improved worker morale).

Task 5: Evaluation

Step 1: Assessment: rate each approach for its ability to solve your problem and meet your success factors.

Step 2: Special consideration: are any assumptions, conditions, factors, variables, or practices for or against one or more of the approaches?

Task 6: Select Approach

Step 1: Reduce your list of approaches to a manageable number. If you have more than three, eliminate any that are too costly or obviously unacceptable. Provide justification for deciding to eliminate them.

Step 2: Compare the costs and benefits. Use the project life cycle to calculate the net difference of new costs to develop and operate versus anticipated dollars to recover and staff time required versus anticipated hours to be gained. Compare these figures and your assessments of the adverse and beneficial aspects of each approach.

Step 3: Recommend approach: select the approach you believe is best for your department.

Step 4: Give reasons: discuss the significant reasons for your choice of this option.

PART 5: PROVIDE SOLUTION ANALYSIS

TASK 1: IMPACT ANALYSIS

Step 1: Describe impacts of recommended approach. Your review should include any changes or new requirements for the following:
- Training
- Modifications to space and facilities

- Staffing effects (+ or –)
- Changes in procedures
- Changes in forms
- Impacts to manual or automated systems
- Individual resistance to change
- Organizational changes
- Security
- Procurement requirements

PART 6: PROVIDE IMPLEMENTATION SCHEDULE

Your job in this part is to identify critical implementation elements and establish reporting milestones.

Task 1: Plan

Step 1: Identify activities. List the major tasks. Include checkpoints for review and approval. Consider tasks relating to procurement, installation, and commissioning.

Step 2: Add logic. Rank the tasks in the order they must be performed. A diagram is useful for more complex plans.

Step 3: Assign resources. Identify who is responsible for completing each task.

Task 2: Schedule

Step 1: Estimate the duration. Determine if hours, days, weeks, or months are the appropriate time unit. Estimate a duration for each activity. Milestones will not have duration.

Step 2: Schedule the activity. Review the logic and duration of each activity against your target completion and the availability of each resource. Assign forecasts for activity starts and compilation. (Computer-assisted project management tools may be useful for complex schedules.)

For further assistance see project management guideline.

PART 7: OBTAIN MANAGEMENT APPROVAL

Your job in this part is to obtain key players' endorsement and your management's approval.

Task 1: Endorsement

Review your findings with end users, the data processing manager, key program managers, department budget analyst, and the department administrator to verify they agree with your recommendation. An example of a formal authorization is shown below.

Task 2: Obtain Formal Authorization

We have read through this feasibility study and concur with its recommendations. We believe this project can be done, should be done, and will be done.

Appendix D
Sample Cost/Benefit Analysis Worksheets

Cost/Benefit Study

Form 1: Developmental Costs

Project Name:
Alternative:
Date:

Division:

Prepared by:

CATEGORIES	Fiscal Year 1	Fiscal Year 2	Fiscal Year 3	Fiscal Year 4	Fiscal Year 5	TOTAL (Years) 6
PERSONAL SERVICES						
New Personnel						$0
Benefits Package (O.P.E)						$0
Other (Specify)						$0
Subtotal	$0	$0	$0	$0	$0	$0
SERVICES & SUPPLIES						
Training and Education						$0
Travel and Lodging						$0
Outside Professional Services						$0
Supplies						$0
Maintenance						$0
Billable Computing Services						$0
Equipment and Software						$0
Telecommunications						$0
Facility						$0
Utilities						$0
Other (Specify)						$0
Subtotal	$0	$0	$0	$0	$0	$0

CAPITAL OUTLAY					
Equipment and Software					$0
Facility					$0
Other (Specify)					$0
					$0
					$0
Subtotal	$0	$0	$0	$0	$0
TOTAL DEVELOPMENT COSTS	$0	$0	$0	$0	$0
CURRENT PERSONNEL ALLOCATED TO PROJECT					
Project Staff					0.0
Administrative Staff					0.0
Support Staff					0.0
Other (Specify)					0.0
					0.0
TOTAL ALLOCATED HOURS	0.0	0.0	0.0	0.0	0.0
List assumptions in calculating these costs					

Cost/Benefit Study

Form 2: Operating Costs
Project Name:
Alternative:
Date:
(Do not fill in shaded areas)

Division:

Prepared by:

CATEGORIES	Fiscal Year 1	Fiscal Year 2	Fiscal Year 3	Fiscal Year 4	Fiscal Year 5	LIFE CYCLE (Years) 6
PERSONAL SERVICES						
New Personnel						$0
Benefits Package (O.P.E)						$0
Other (Specify)						$0
Subtotal	$0	$0	$0	$0	$0	$0
SERVICES & SUPPLIES						
Training and Education						$0
Travel and Lodging						$0
Outside Professional Services						$0
Supplies						$0
Maintenance						$0
Billable Computing Services						$0
Equipment and Software						$0
Telecommunications						$0
Facility						$0
Utilities						$0
Other (Specify)						$0
						$0

Subtotal	$0	$0	$0	$0	$0
REDUCED REVENUE					$0
					$0
Subtotal	$0	$0	$0	$0	$0
CAPITAL OUTLAY					
Equipment and Software					$0
Facility					$0
Other (Specify)					$0
					$0
Subtotal	$0	$0	$0	$0	$0
TOTAL OPERATING COSTS	$0	$0	$0	$0	$0
CURRENT PERSONNEL ALLOCATED TO PROJECT					
Project Staff					0.0
Administrative Staff					0.0
Support Staff					0.0
Other (Specify)					0.0
					0.0
TOTAL ALLOCATED HOURS	0.0	0.0	0.0	0.0	0.0
List assumptions in calculating these costs					

Cost/Benefit Study

Form 3: Tangible Benefits
Project Name: Division:
Alternative:
Date: Prepared by:
(Do not fill in shaded areas)

CATEGORIES	Fiscal Year 1	Fiscal Year 2	Fiscal Year 3	Fiscal Year 4	Fiscal Year 5	LIFE CYCLE (Years) 6
COST REDUCTION						
						$0
						$0
						$0
						$0
						$0
						$0
						$0
						$0
						$0
						$0
Subtotal	$0	$0	$0	$0	$0	$0
REVENUE/REIMBURSEMENT						
						$0
						$0
						$0
						$0
						$0
						$0

Subtotal	$0	$0	$0	$0	$0	$0
TOTAL BENEFITS			$0	$0	$0	$0
HOURS ACCRUED TO PROJECT						
LIST RECIPIENTS & ESTIMATED HOURS						0.00
						0.00
						0.00
						0.00
						0.00
						0.00
						0.00
						0.00
						0.00
						0.00
TOTAL ACCRUED HOURS	0.00	0.00	0.00	0.00	0.00	
List assumptions in calculating these costs						

505

Cost/Benefit Study

Form 4: Intangible Costs (–) and Benefits (+)

Project Name: Division:
Alternative:
Date: Prepared by:

+/–	DESCRIPTION	RECIPIENTS

Examples of Intangible Benefits
1. Reduced turnaround time
2. Improved customer satisfaction
3. Compliance with mandates
4. Enhanced interagency communication

Cost/Benefit Study

Form 5: Final Discounted Costs (–) and Benefits (+)

Project Name: Division:

Alternative:

Date: Prepared by:

(Do not fill in shaded areas)

(For sample discount rate, see table below)

FISCAL YEAR		BENEFITS	–	COSTS	=	NET BENEFITS	×	DISCOUNT RATE	=	PRESENT VALUE
FY	1	$0		$0		$0				$0
FY	2	$0		$0		$0				$0
FY	3	$0		$0		$0				$0
FY	4	$0		$0		$0				$0
FY	5	$0		$0		$0				$0
				NET BENEFITS		$0		DISCOUNTED NET BENEFITS		

Final Personnel Costs and Benefits (Hours)

Fiscal Year		Accrued Hours	Allocated Hours	–	Net Hours	=	
FY	1	0.00	0.00	–	0.00	=	0.00
FY	2	0.00	0.00	–	0.00	=	0.00
FY	3	0.00	0.00	–	0.00	=	0.00
FY	4	0.00	0.00	–	0.00	=	0.00
FY	5	0.00	0.00	–	0.00	=	0.00
	Totals:	0.00	0.00		0.00		

Cost/Benefit Study (continued)

Discount Rate Table

Years	3%	4%	5%	6%	7%	8%	9%	10%	11%	12%	13%
1	0.9709	0.9615	0.9524	0.9434	0.9346	0.9259	0.9174	0.9091	0.9009	0.8929	0.8850
2	0.9426	0.9246	0.9070	0.8900	0.8734	0.8573	0.8417	0.8264	0.8116	0.7972	0.7831
3	0.9151	0.8890	0.8638	0.8396	0.8163	0.7938	0.7722	0.7513	0.7312	0.7118	0.6931
4	0.8885	0.8548	0.8227	0.7921	0.7629	0.7350	0.7084	0.6830	0.6587	0.6355	0.6133
5	0.8626	0.8219	0.7835	0.7473	0.7130	0.6806	0.6499	0.6209	0.5935	0.5674	0.5428
6	0.8375	0.7903	0.7462	0.7050	0.6663	0.6302	0.5963	0.5645	0.5346	0.5066	0.4803
7	0.8131	0.7599	0.7107	0.6651	0.6227	0.5835	0.5470	0.5132	0.4817	0.4523	0.4251
8	0.7894	0.7307	0.6768	0.6274	0.5820	0.5403	0.5019	0.4665	0.4339	0.4039	0.3762
9	0.7664	0.7026	0.6446	0.5919	0.5439	0.5002	0.4604	0.4241	0.3909	0.3606	0.3329
10	0.7441	0.6756	0.6139	0.5584	0.5083	0.4632	0.4224	0.3855	0.3522	0.3220	0.2946

Appendix E
Sample Business Use Case

PROCUREMENT SYSTEM USE CASES

Team C's project is to develop and implement a procurement system for JCE. The company currently handles its purchase orders manually. A few external entities will interact with this procurement system. Different menus are displayed depending on the user's access. Orders are allowed for entry as long as the user is authorized for the order amount requested. If the order amount exceeds the user's authorized amount, a message is displayed on the screen. Due to limited knowledge of procurement systems, ideas were gathered from EventHelix.com Inc., which is dedicated to developing tools and techniques for real-time and embedded system development. Following are ten of the use cases for the procurement system.

Requestor

The requestor requests a product (see Exhibit E-1), requests a change in the product, or cancels an ordered product. The requestor can make requests by telephone, fax, or keying the information directly into the system, if authorized.

Requestor Logs into the System to Submit a New Request:

1. Requestor keys in his log-on ID and six- to eight-digit password, which are then verified against valid IDs and passwords in the procurement database. If the ID or password does not match, an error message is displayed on the screen. The requestor is prompted to re-key the ID or password. The requestor is allowed three attempts to log in. If unsuccessful, the password is flagged and a message is displayed to call data security for resolution. If successful, the procurement menu is displayed.
2. The requestor selects the menu option ENTER PURCHASE REQUEST by pressing the radio button next to that option.
3. The system displays the purchase request order form on the screen. The requestor keys the department name, number, and cost center in the appropriate fields. The requestor also keys the product

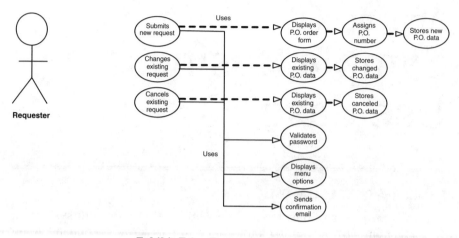

Exhibit E-1. Requestor Use Case

numbers, selections, and quantities and then presses the radio button for SUBMIT ORDER.

4. A purchase order number is automatically assigned by the system
   and is displayed on the screen as confirmation of the order taken.

5. An e-mail is also sent to the requestor confirming the order.

Requestor Logs into the System to Change an Existing Request:

1. Requestor keys in his log-on ID and six- to eight-digit password,
   which are then verified against valid IDs and passwords in the procurement database. If the ID or password does not match, an error
   message is displayed on the screen. The requestor is prompted to
   re-key the ID or password. The requestor is allowed three attempts
   to log in. If unsuccessful, the password is flagged and a message is
   displayed to call data security for resolution. If successful, the procurement menu is displayed.

2. The requestor selects the menu option CHANGE EXISTING PUR-
   CHASE ORDER REQUEST by pressing the radio button next to that
   option.

3. The system displays the change purchase order form on the screen.
   The requestor keys the purchase order number and presses the
   SUBMIT radio button.

4. The system finds the purchase order and displays the order request
   information on the screen. The fields that can be changed are open
   for change; all other fields are protected. The requestor keys the
   needed changes such as quantity, color, or type, as appropriate and
   then presses the radio button for SUBMIT CHANGE.

5. A message is displayed on the screen as confirmation of the order
   changes.

6. An e-mail is also sent to the requestor confirming the order changes.

Requestor Logs into the System to Cancel an Existing Request:

1. Requestor keys in his log-on ID and six- to eight-digit password, which are then verified against valid IDs and passwords in the procurement database. If the ID or password does not match, an error message is displayed on the screen. The requestor is prompted to re-key the ID or password. The requestor is allowed three attempts to log in. If unsuccessful, the password is flagged and a message is displayed to call data security for resolution. If successful, the procurement menu is displayed.
2. The requestor selects the menu option CANCEL EXISTING PURCHASE ORDER by pressing the radio button next to that option.
3. The system displays the cancel purchase order form on the screen. The requestor keys the purchase order number and presses the SUBMIT radio button.
4. The system finds the purchase order and displays the order request information on the screen. The requestor presses the radio button for CANCEL ORDER.
5. A message is displayed on the screen as confirmation of the canceled order.
6. An e-mail is also sent to the requestor confirming the order cancellation.

Purchasing Agent

The purchasing agent requests a product (see Exhibit E-2), requests a change in the product, or cancels an ordered product when the request is telephoned or faxed to the purchasing department.

Purchasing Agent Logs into the System to Submit a New Request:

1. Purchasing agent keys in his log-on ID and six- to eight-digit password, which are then verified against valid IDs and passwords in the procurement database. If the ID or password does not match, an error message is displayed on the screen. The purchasing agent is prompted to re-key the ID or password. The purchasing agent is allowed three attempts to log in. If unsuccessful, the password is flagged and a message is displayed to call data security for resolution. If successful, the procurement menu is displayed.
2. The purchasing agent selects the menu option ENTER PURCHASE REQUEST by pressing the radio button next to that option.
3. The system displays the purchase request order form on the screen. The purchasing agent keys the department name, number, and cost center in the appropriate fields. The purchasing agent also keys the product numbers, product selections, and quantities. If this order is

511

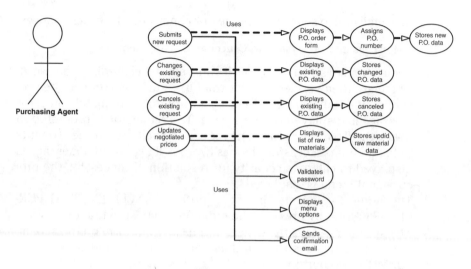

Exhibit E-2. Purchasing Agent Use Case

for a department other than the purchasing agent's department, he flags the order in a special field to indicate that this order is an authorized over-ride. The purchasing agent presses the radio button for SUBMIT ORDER.

4. A purchase order number is automatically assigned by the system and is displayed on the screen as confirmation of the order taken.

5. An e-mail is also sent to the original *requestor* confirming the order.

Purchasing Agent Logs into the System to Change an Existing Request:

1. Purchasing agent keys in his log-on ID and six- to eight-digit password, which are then verified against valid IDs and passwords in the procurement database. If the ID or password does not match, an error message is displayed on the screen. The purchasing agent is prompted to re-key the ID or password. The purchasing agent is allowed three attempts to log in. If unsuccessful, the password is flagged and a message is displayed to call data security for resolution. If successful, the procurement menu is displayed.

2. The purchasing agent selects the menu option CHANGE EXISTING PURCHASE ORDER REQUEST by pressing the radio button next to that option.

3. The system displays the change purchase order form on the screen. The purchasing agent keys the purchase order number and presses the SUBMIT radio button.

4. The system finds the purchase order and displays the order request information on the screen. The fields that can be changed are open

for change; all other fields are protected. The purchasing agent keys the needed changes such as quantity, color, or type, as appropriate. If this change is for a department other than the purchasing agent's department, he flags the order in a special field to indicate that this change is an authorized over-ride. The purchasing agent presses the radio button for SUBMIT CHANGE.

5. A message is displayed on the screen as confirmation of the order changes.
6. An e-mail is also sent to the original *requestor* confirming the order changes.

Purchasing Agent Logs into the System to Cancel an Existing Request:

1. Purchasing agent keys in his log-on ID and six- to eight-digit password, which are then verified against valid IDs and passwords in the procurement database. If the ID or password does not match, an error message is displayed on the screen. The purchasing agent is prompted to re-key the ID or password. The purchasing agent is allowed three attempts to log in. If unsuccessful, the password is flagged and a message is displayed to call data security for resolution. If successful, the procurement menu is displayed.
2. The purchasing agent selects the menu option CANCEL EXISTING PURCHASE ORDER by pressing the radio button next to that option.
3. The system displays the cancel purchase order form on the screen. The purchasing agent keys the purchase order number and presses the SUBMIT radio button.
4. The system finds the purchase order and displays the order request information on the screen. If this cancel is for a department other than the purchasing agent's department, he flags the order in a special field to indicate that this cancel is an authorized over-ride. The purchasing agent presses the radio button for CANCEL ORDER.
5. A message is displayed on the screen as confirmation of the canceled order.
6. An e-mail is also sent to the original *requestor* confirming the order cancellation.

Purchasing Agent Logs into the System to Update Negotiated Prices:

1. Purchasing agent keys in his log-on ID and six- to eight-digit password, which are then verified against valid IDs and passwords in the procurement database. If the ID or password does not match, an error message is displayed on the screen. The purchasing agent is prompted to re-key the ID or password. The purchasing agent is allowed three attempts to log in. If unsuccessful, the password is flagged and a message is displayed to call data security for resolution. If successful, the procurement menu is displayed.

2. The purchasing agent selects the menu option UPDATE PRICES by pressing the radio button next to that option.
3. The system displays another menu with various options for changing prices. The purchasing agent selects the RAW MATERIAL PRICES radio button.
4. The system displays on the screen a list of the raw materials listed in the database. The purchasing agent selects the appropriate raw material by paging through the list of raw materials and clicking the left side of the mouse button over the raw material name or by keying the name of the raw material in the SEARCH field and pressing the SUBMIT radio button.
5. The system finds the raw material in the database and displays the raw material's specifications on the screen. Some of the information displayed is price, suppliers, supplier codes, description, raw material ID, etc. Because the purchasing agent has authorization to update these fields, he changes the price of the raw material and presses the SUBMIT radio button.
6. The system returns to the raw material list and the new price is reflected.
7. The system records this status change in the historical database and reports the change on the monthly status report log.

Receiving Department

The receiving department (Exhibit E-3) receives the purchase order for the raw material, checks it for accuracy and good condition, and places the raw material into stock.

Receiving Department Receives the New Purchase Order:

1. Receiving department receives an e-mail notifying it of the new purchase order. Receiving agent logs into the procurement system to verify and accept the order. Receiving agent keys in his log-on ID and six- to eight-digit password, which are then verified against valid IDs and passwords in the procurement database. If the ID or password does not match, an error message is displayed on the screen. The receiving agent is prompted to re-key the ID or password. The receiving agent is allowed three attempts to log in. If unsuccessful, the password is flagged and a message is displayed to call data security for resolution. If successful, the procurement menu is displayed.
2. The receiving agent selects the menu option ACCEPT NEW PURCHASE ORDER by pressing the radio button next to that option.
3. The receiving agent keys the purchase order number and presses the SUBMIT radio button.

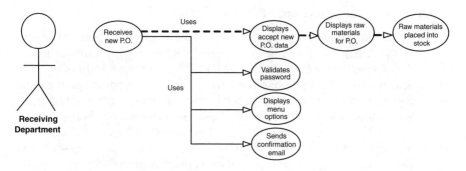

Exhibit E-3. Receiving Department Use Case

4. The system displays a list of the raw materials needed for the new purchase order on the screen. The receiving agent reviews the purchase order against the raw materials list and also examines the raw materials. If the order and raw materials meet required guidelines, the receiving agent presses the radio button for ORDER ACCEPTED.
5. The raw materials are then placed into stock/inventory, a bill is sent to accounts payable in accounting, and an e-mail is sent to the purchasing agent notifying him of the acceptance.
6. If the order and raw materials do not meet the required guidelines, the receiving agent flags the order in a special field to indicate that this order or raw materials are unacceptable. The receiving agent presses the radio button for ORDER DENIED.
7. An e-mail is sent to the purchasing agent notifying him of the denial.

Accounting Department

The accounting department (see Exhibit E-4) has a division called accounts payable, which verifies the unit cost on the purchase order against the unit cost on the invoice, and closes out purchase orders.

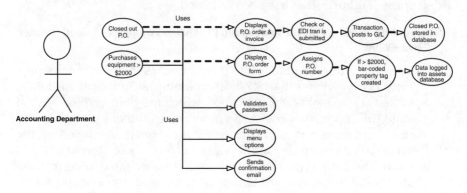

Exhibit E-4. Accounting Department Use Case

Accounts Payable Closes out a Purchase Order:

1. Accounts payable (A/P) receives an e-mail notifying them of the purchase order invoice. The A/P agent logs into the procurement system to verify and accept the order. A/P agent keys in his log-on ID and six- to eight-digit password, which are then verified against valid IDs and passwords in the procurement database. If the ID or password does not match, an error message is displayed on the screen. The A/P agent is prompted to re-key the ID or password. The A/P agent is allowed three attempts to log in. If unsuccessful, the password is flagged and a message is displayed to call data security for resolution. If successful, the procurement menu is displayed.

2. The A/P agent selects the menu option CLOSE OUT PURCHASE ORDER by pressing the radio button next to that option.

3. The A/P agent keys the purchase order number and presses the SUBMIT radio button.

4. The system displays the purchase order as well as its associated invoice. The A/P agent verifies the unit cost on the purchase order against the unit cost on the invoice. If the verification is approved, the A/P agent presses the radio button for SUBMIT PAYMENT.

5. A check or an EDI transaction is submitted, depending on the supplier's request, for payment of the invoice. An e-mail is sent to the purchasing agent notifying him of the payment approval. The transaction is then posted to the general ledger and the purchase order is closed.

6. If the verification is not approved, the A/P agent presses the radio button for PAYMENT DENIED.

7. An e-mail is sent to the purchasing agent notifying him of the payment denial.

The accounting department monitors equipment with a value over $2000. The equipment can be purchased through the procurement system provided proper authorization has been obtained.

Accounting Agent or Authorized Person Purchases Equipment Priced Greater Than $2000:

1. The accounting agent logs into procurement system to order equipment priced greater than $2000. Accounting agent keys in his log-on ID and six- to eight-digit password, which are then verified against valid IDs and passwords in the procurement database. If the ID or password does not match, an error message is displayed on the screen. The accounting agent is prompted to re-key the ID or password. The accounting agent is allowed three attempts to log in. If unsuccessful, the password is flagged and a message is displayed to call data security for resolution. If successful, the procurement menu is displayed.

2. The accounting agent selects the menu option ENTER PURCHASE REQUEST by pressing the radio button next to that option.
3. The system displays the purchase request order form on the screen. The accounting agent keys the department name, number, and cost center in the appropriate fields. The accounting agent also keys the product numbers, product selections, and quantities and then presses the radio button for SUBMIT ORDER.
4. A purchase order number is automatically assigned by the system and is displayed on the screen as confirmation of the order taken.
5. An e-mail is also sent to the accounting agent confirming the order.
6. If the equipment requested is priced greater than $2000, the system assigns a bar-coded equipment property tag. The property tag number is logged into the database.
7. Once the equipment purchase order is closed out, the information about the equipment is also logged into the company assets database along with the property tag number.

Appendix F
Sample Project Plan

TABLE OF CONTENTS

1. GOALS AND OBJECTIVES

The online resource scheduling system (ORSS) is a Web-based scheduling system designed for colleges, universities, and schools. The purpose of this system is to provide an online service for the faculty to reserve any type of resource such as computer systems, VCRs, projectors, and videotapes. This scheduling system can accept the requestors' orders, make a schedule for the orders, and perform some critical checks. It will enable the faculty to place their orders at any time and from any place. The system will be able to create new orders and update old orders.

1.1 System Statement of Scope

1.1.1 General Requirements

The following general requirements were specified for our project titled ORSS:

- A Web-based application allowing users easy access and use
- The ability to originate or update resource reservations
- The ability to link to the faculty database to verify "authorized users"
- A method to maintain and update a resource database
- The ability to limit simultaneous reservations against total resources available
- A way to search for resources available
- A method to disallow duplication of "special" classrooms
- The ability to disallow duplicate orders from the same user
- A method to print a confirmation from the Website
- The ability to send e-mail confirmations to the user
- The ability to print a daily list

1.1.2 Database Administration Interface

There will be a need for the resource center office to maintain the database of the resources and to link to the faculty database to verify "authorized users." If neither of these databases exists, Global Associates will need to create them and train personnel in their maintenance and administration.

1.1.3 Online Help

We will need to develop an online help program for this system, which will include a detailed help menu and "online" telephone assistance.

1.1.4 Training

We will need to conduct training for the resource center staff as well as for all full-time faculty. We may consider a training manual for the adjunct faculty or conduct training sessions at times that they are available

1.2 System Context

Multiple users will be using the product simultaneously from many different locations. The only requirement is access to the Internet.

1.3 Major Constraints

1.3.1 Security

This project will be uploaded to a server that will be exposed to the outside world, so we need to research and develop security protection. We will need to know how to configure a firewall and how to restrict access to "authorized users." We will need to know how to deal with load balance if the amount of visits to the site is very large at one time.

1.3.2 Database

We will need to know how to maintain the database in order to make it more efficient, and what type of database we should use. We will also have a link to the faculty database to verify the users.

2. PROJECT ESTIMATES

This portion of the document provides cost, effort, and time estimates for the project using two estimation techniques — process-based and lines of code (COCOMO II model).

2.1 Historical Data Used for Estimates

We obtained the following data according to "2001 Computer Industry Salary Survey" from EDP Staffing Service Inc. for the Northeast:

Job Function: Web Developer (Java/ASP)
Low	US$ 79,500
Median	US$ 92,500
High	US$ 105,500

Job Function: Sr. Database Analyst/Admin.
Low	US$ 78,100
Median	US$ 87,200
High	US$ 105,900

Low is the salary paid at the 25th percentile of all respondents in this data set; median is the 50th percentile and high is the 75th percentile (EDP Staffing Service Inc., 2001).

We estimate labor cost per month for two Web programmers and one database analyst using the low salary level. (The low salary level is used due to the slowdown in the U.S. economy.) Note that 15 percent overhead is added in the average labor cost per month

$$\$(((79{,}500/12)*2 + (78{,}100/12)*1)/3) * 1.15 \approx \$7{,}500$$

Note: Members' roles will be discussed in the section on project team organization.

2.2 Estimation Techniques Applied and Results

Two estimation techniques have been used to generate two independent results for higher accuracy.

- Process-based
- Lines of code (LOC) → COCOMO II Model

2.2.1 Process-Based Estimation

The process is divided into smaller tasks for process-based estimation purposes. We estimated, in person-months, the effort required to perform each task. We defined the following software functions as:

- User interface   UI
- Database management   DB
- Report generation   RG
- Bug fixing   BF
- Program integration   PI

Based on the historical data obtained, the estimated effort is approximately 7.5 person-months and the estimated project cost is $7500 × 7.5 ≈ $56,250 (see Exhibit F-1).

2.2.2 LOC-Based Estimation

The estimates in Exhibit F-2 are based on "best-effort" estimation from previous programming experiences and existing software size.

The estimates for LOC are plugged into the COCOMO II formula for effort and duration estimation. The basic COCOMO II model is used (See Exhibit F-3).

Results in Exhibit F-4 indicate that total effort is 8.8 person-months to finish the project. Because we have three team members, we will finish the project in approximately three months. Based on that calculation, the estimated project cost will be $7500 × 3 × 3 ≈ $67,500.

Exhibit F-1. Process-Based Estimation Table

Activity → Task → Function →	Cust. Comm.	Planning	Risk Analysis	Engineering		Construction Release		Cust. Eval.	Totals
				Analysis	Design	Code	Test		
UI	0.50	0.20	0.05	0.10	0.30	0.50	0.80	0.10	2.55
DB	—	0.30	0.10	0.20	0.30	0.20	0.20	—	1.30
RG	0.20	0.20	0.02	0.05	0.40	0.40	0.10	0.05	1.42
BF	0.20	0.10	0.02	0.10	0.10	0.30	0.10	0.05	0.97
PI	0.02	0.10	0.05	0.20	0.10	0.30	0.50	—	1.27
Total	0.92	0.90	0.24	0.65	1.20	1.70	1.70	0.20	7.51
% Effort	12.25	11.98	3.20	8.66	15.98	22.64	22.64	2.66	100.0

Exhibit F-2. LOC-Based Estimation

Functions	Estimated LOC
User interface UI	1000
Database management DB	500
Report generation RG	500
Bug fixing BF	500
Program integration PI	200
Total estimated lines of codes	2700

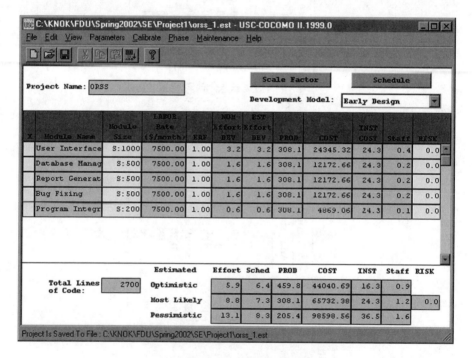

Exhibit F-3. COCOMO II

2.3   Project Resources

2.3.1   People

This project requires two Web developers and one database analyst in order to be finished in time. The developers must have adequate experiences in Web designing and have knowledge in HTML, JavaScript, Photoshop, ASP (VB Script), and Access. Experience on how to set up a Web server is preferred. The database analyst should be able to analyze, design, and maintain an efficient and secure database. The candidates must also have good personal communication skills.

Exhibit F-4.   Total Effort Estimate

Project Name ORSS
Total Size 2700
Total Effort 8.764317

Overall	Schedule (%)	Schedule (Months)	Effort (%)	Effort	Staff
Plans and requirements	16.23	1.187959	7.00	0.6135	0.516434
Product design	24.12	1.764864	17.00	1.4899	0.84422
Programming	55.53	4.063943	63.65	5.5785	1.372679
Integration and test	20.35	1.489218	19.35	1.6959	1.138782

2.3.2   Minimal Hardware Requirements

Development

Three IBM PC or compatibles with the following configurations:

- Intel Pentium III 700 MHz processor
- 512 MB SDRAM
- 40G hard disk space
- Internet connection

2.3.3   User Server Side

IBM PC or compatible with the following configurations:

- Intel Pentium IV 1.7GHz processor
- 512 MB SDRAM
- 80G hard disk space
- Internet connection

2.3.4   User Client Side

IBM PC or compatible with the following configurations:

- Intel Pentium III 450MHz processor
- 128 MB SDRAM
- 20 GMB Hard disk space
- Internet connection

2.3.5   Minimal Software Requirements

Development

- Windows 2000 Professional Version
- FrontPage 2000 or DreamWeaver 4.0
- Microsoft Access 2000

User Server Side

- Windows 2000 Server Version with Internet Information Server (IIS)
- Microsoft Access 2000

User Client Side

- Windows 98 or higher operating system
- Internet Explorer Browser 4.0 or Netscape Navigator 4.0

3. RISK MANAGEMENT

3.1 Scope and Intent of RMMM Activities

This project will be uploaded to a server that will be exposed to the out-side world, so we need to develop security protection. We will need to configure a firewall and restrict access to "authorized users" through the linked faculty database. We will need to know how to deal with load balance if the amount of visits to the site is very large at one time.

We will need to know how to maintain the database in order to make it more efficient, what type of database we should use, who should have the responsibility to maintain it, and who should be the administrator. Proper training of these personnel is very important so that the database and the system contain accurate information.

3.2 Risk Management Organizational Role

The software project manager must track the efforts and schedules of the team. They must anticipate any "unwelcome" events that may occur during the development or maintenance stages and establish plans to avoid these events or minimize their consequences.

It is the responsibility of everyone on the project team — with the regular input of the customer — to assess potential risks throughout the project. Communication among everyone involved is very important to the success of the project. In this way, it is possible to mitigate and eliminate possible risks before they occur. This is known as a proactive approach or strategy for risk management.

3.3 Risk Description

This section describes risks that may occur during this project.

3.3.1 Description of Risks

Business Impact Risk:

This risk would entail that the software produced does not meet the needs of the client who requested the product. It would also have a business impact if the product no longer fits into the overall business strategy for the company.

Customer Characteristics Risks:

This risk is the customer's lack of involvement in the project and non-availability to meet with the developers in a timely manner. Also, the customer's sophistication as to the product being developed and ability to use it are part of this risk.

Development Risks:

Pressman (2001) describes this as "risks associated with the availability and quality of the tools to be used to build the product." The client-provided equipment and software on which to run the product must be compatible to the software project being developed.

Process Definition Risks:

Does the software being developed meet the requirements as originally defined by the developer and client? Did the development team follow the correct design throughout the project? These are examples of process risks.

Product Size:

The product size risk involves the overall size of the software being built or modified. Risks involved would include the customer not providing the proper size of the product to be developed or if the software development team misjudges the size or scope of the project. The latter problem could create a product that is too small (rarely) or too large for the client and could result in a loss of money to the development team because the cost of developing a larger product cannot be recouped from the client.

Staff Size and Experience Risk:

This would include appropriate and knowledgeable programmers to code the product as well as the cooperation of the entire software project team. It would also mean that the team has enough team members who are competent and able to complete the project.

Technology Risk:

Technology risk could occur if the product being developed is obsolete by the time it is ready to be sold. The opposite effect could also be a factor: a product so "new" that the end users would have problems using the system and resisting the changes made. The "newness"of a technological product could also result in problems using it. This type of risk would also include the complexity of the design of the system being developed.

Exhibit F-5.   Risks Table (sorted)

Risks	Category	Probability (%)	Impact
Customer will change or modify requirements	PS	70	2
Lack of sophistication of end users	CU	60	3
Users will not attend training	CU	50	2
Delivery deadline will be tightened	BU	50	2
End users resist the system	BU	40	3
Server may not be able to handle larger number of users simultaneously	PS	30	1
Technology will not meet expectations	TE	30	1
Larger number of users than planned	PS	30	3
Lack of training of end users	CU	30	3
Inexperienced project team	ST	20	2
System (security and firewall) will be hacked	BU	15	2

Note: Impact values: 1 — catastrophic; 2 — critical; 3 — marginal; 4 — negligible.

Category abbreviations: BU — business impact risk; CU — customer characteristics risk; PS — process definition risk; ST — staff size and experience risk; TE — technology risk.

3.4   Risk Table

The risk table provides a simple technique to view and analyze the risks associated with the project. The risks were listed and then categorized using the description of risks listed in the previous section. The probability of each risk was estimated and then its impact on the development process was assessed. A key to the impact values and categories appears at the end of the table.

3.4.1   Probability and Impact for Risk

The table in Exhibit F-5 is the sorted version of the risk table by probability and impact. Exhibit F-5 was sorted first by probability and then by impact value.

4.   PROJECT SCHEDULE

Following are the master schedule and deliverables planned for each stage of the project development life cycle and their respective planned completion dates.

4.1   Deliverables and Milestones

See Exhibit F-6 for deliverables and milestones.

4.2   Work Breakdown Structure

See Exhibit F-7 for a work breakdown structure.

5.   PROJECT TEAM ORGANIZATION

The structure of the team and the roles of the team members are defined in this section. The project team organization is divided into four parts:

1. Conceptual planning
2. Software design and development
3. Editing, master testing, and maintenance
4. Training and user documentation

5.1   Team Structure

We separate part of the team project by following the responsibilities of the team members and dividing the functions of the system.

5.1.1   Conceptual Planning

- Interview and specify software scope
- Database re-engineering
- Overall process specifications
- Draft documentation

5.1.2   Software Design and Development

- Database design and development
- User interface and control facilities
- Function development
- Report generation
- Draft documentation

5.1.3   Editing, Master Testing, and Maintenance

- Maintenance system
- Integration testing
- Report software errors
- System documentation

5.1.4   Training and User Documentation

- Training sessions
- User documentation

This organization of the project team allows the project planner to know the area of responsibility for each team member and all of the functions of the team project.

Exhibit F-6. Deliverables and Milestones

Activities	Deliverable	From Date	To Date	Milestone
Meetings	Weekly meetings	02/04/02	05/07/02	05/07/02
	Assess functional requirements	02/18/02	02/22/02	
	Demonstrate system	02/19/02	02/27/02	
Requirements	Evaluation of testing needs	02/25/02	02/27/02	
	Assess nonfunctional requirements	02/18/02	02/27/02	
	Final requirements specification	02/27/02	03/01/02	03/01/02
	Quality assurance plan	02/04/02	02/06/02	
	Project plan	02/07/02	02/15/02	
	Requirements document	02/18/02	03/01/02	
	Design document	03/04/02	03/15/02	
Documentation	User guide	04/30/02	05/02/02	
	Final project notebook	04/29/02	05/03/02	
	Maintenance plan	04/29/02	05/03/02	05/03/02
Programmer Training	Web design training	03/01/02	03/07/02	
	Database design training	03/08/02	03/12/02	03/12/02

Phase	Task			
Preliminary Design	Brainstorming	03/13/02	03/14/02	
	Architectural layout	03/15/02	03/20/02	03/20/02
Detailed Design	Design user interface	03/21/02	04/01/02	
	Database design	03/21/02	04/01/02	04/01/02
	Build database	04/02/02	04/04/02	
Coding	User interface of campus version	04/05/02	04/19/02	
	User interface of in-house version	04/05/02	04/19/02	04/19/02
Integration Testing	In-house testing	04/22/02	04/26/02	
	Necessary modifications	04/23/02	04/26/02	04/26/02
Post-Test	On-campus testing	04/29/02	05/03/02	
	Necessary modifications	04/30/02	05/03/02	05/03/02
Modification	"Clean up" & finalized for delivery	05/06/02	05/07/02	05/07/02
Faculty Training	In-house training	05/08/02	05/08/02	
	Campus training	05/09/02	05/10/02	05/10/02

Exhibit F-7. Work Breakdown Structure

(a)

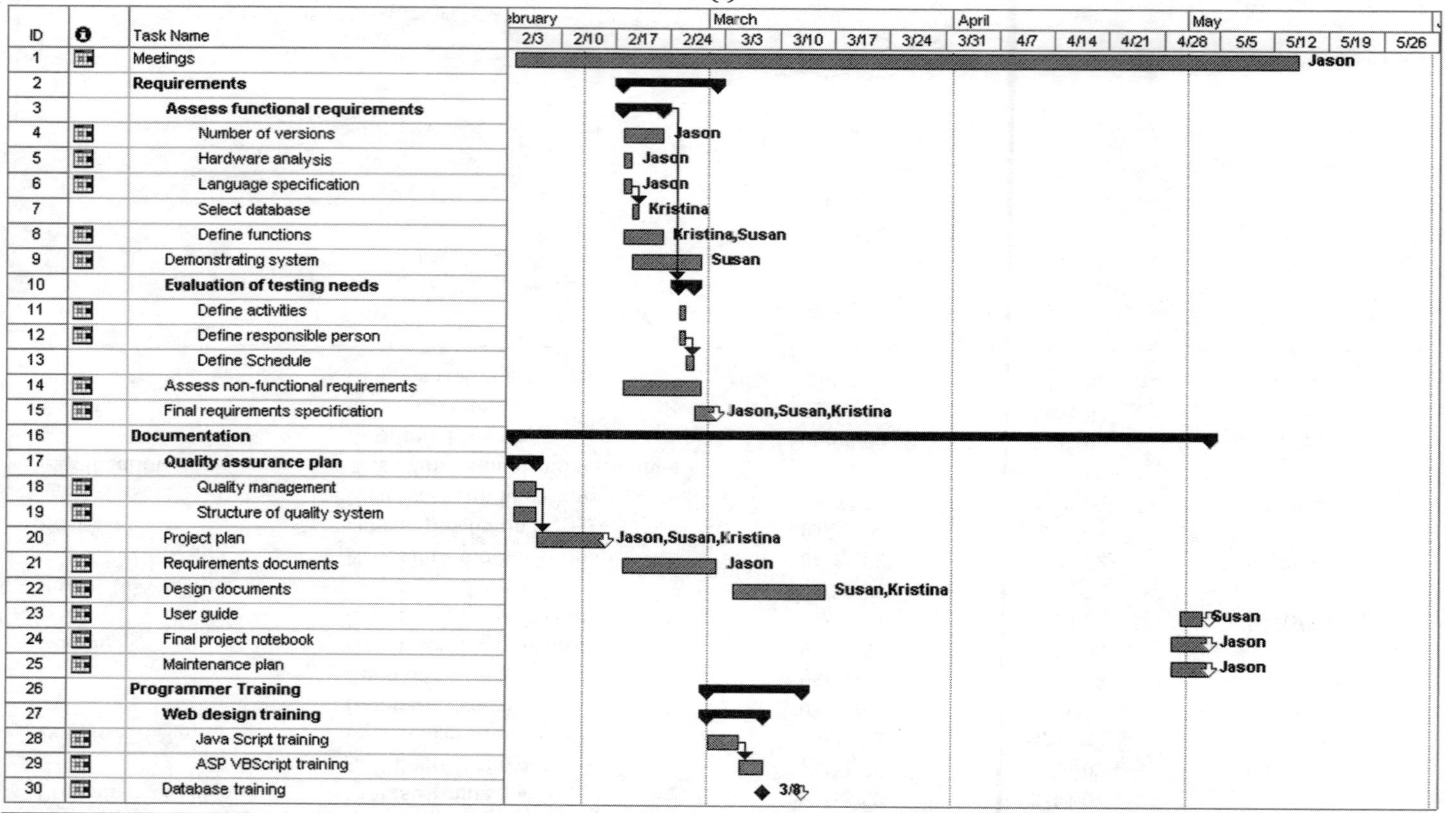

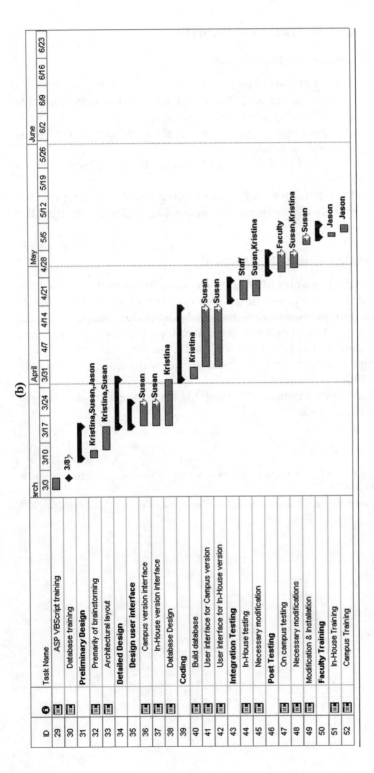

(b)

6. TRACKING AND CONTROL MECHANISMS

6.1 Quality Assurance Mechanisms

- Careful monitoring of the project
- Maintaining close contact with the client by using weekly meetings and regular e-mail contacts to communicate
- Periodic status meetings in which each team member reports on his or her progress and problems
- Careful monitoring of each phase as it relates to the milestone dates listed in Chapter 4
- Paying careful attention to all of the testing results, making needed changes as quickly and reasonably as possible, and then retesting the changes

6.2 Change Management and Control

- A change request is submitted and evaluated to assess technical merit, potential side effects, overall impact on other configuration objects and system functions, and the projected cost of the change.
- An engineering change order is generated for each approved change.
- Access control and synchronization control are implemented.
- The change is made, and appropriate software quality assurance (SQA) activities are applied.
- Appropriate version control mechanisms are used to create the next version of the software.

References

EDP Staffing Service Inc. (2001). Data: 2001 computer industry salary survey. http://www.edp-staffing.com/salary.html.

Pressman, R.S. (2001). *Software Engineering: a Practitioner's Approach*, 5th ed., McGraw Hill, New York, 117–118.

Appendix G
Sample SRS

TABLE OF CONTENTS

Revision Chart

Version	Primary Author(s)	Description of Version	Date Completed
Final	Project Team 2	Draft created for distribution and review comments.	03–11–02

1. INTRODUCTION

1.1 Purpose

The purpose of this software requirements specification is to capture requirements for developing a library management system for a small- to medium-sized library. The document is intended for use by all stakeholders involved in the development of such a system. Stakeholders include customer representatives (marketing personnel) and software representatives (analysts, developers, and testers). This document has been prepared to capture the requirements of all stakeholders so that those requirements are traceable to the end product. Capturing requirements in the early stages of the development cycle reduces the risk of schedule slippage or budget overspending and enables developers to develop the system in a more efficient manner.

1.2 Scope

The ACME Library Management System is intended for use in a small- to medium-sized library, such as a library in a small town or on a college campus. It is not intended to support very large libraries such as the New York Public Library. The system includes the hardware and software to support the day-to-day operation of the library. It provides services to members, librarians, and administrators. These services have been designed to help users get their jobs done faster and more efficiently. The system also provides services to remote users via the Internet.

The goal is to provide a system that is responsive, efficient, reliable, easy to use, and easy to maintain. The system must provide a good user experience for all users.

1.3 Definitions, Acronyms, and Abbreviations

Definitions for some of the common terms used throughout this document are:

- *Administrator* — a person responsible for administering the system
- *Asset database* — a database that contains information about all the assets in the library
- *Librarian* — a person responsible for serving the needs of the members
- *Member* — a person that has a membership number and password to gain access to the system from a member terminal on the library premises
- *Member database* — a database that contains information about all members of the library
- *Public* — a person that accesses the services of the library from a remote terminal via the Internet

The following acronyms and abbreviations are used in this document:

- *ADO* — active data object
- *DBMS* — database management system
- *GUI* — graphical user interface
- *IIS* — internet information server
- *LAN* — local area network
- *ODBC* — open database connectivity

1.4 References

- Roger Pressman, Software Engineering, "A Practitioner's Approach" — 5th edition, McGraw-Hill, January 2001
- Web site associated with the book immediately above at: http://www.mhhe.com/engcs/compsci/pressman/student_index.html
- Course web site at: http://www.newartech.com/se
- Thomas Connolly, "Database Systems" — 3rd edition, Addison-Wesley, 2002
- Ian Summerville, "Software Engineering," 5th edition, Addison-Wesley, 1995
- Edward Yourdon, "Modern Structured Analysis," Prentice Hall, 2000
- Suzanne Robertson, James Robertson, "Mastering the Requirement Process," Addison-Wesley, 1999
- Some useful background information on function points is located at: htpp://ourworld.compuserve.com/homepages/softcomp/fp-faq.htm#WhatAreFunctionPoints
- Product documentation for Microsoft Windows 2000 Server is located at: http://www.microsoft.com/windows2000/en/server/help
- Product documentation for Microsoft Internet Information Server (IIS) is located at: http://www.microsoft.com/windows2000/en/server/iis/
- Product documentation for Microsoft SQL Server is located at: http://www.microsoft.com/qul/techinfo/productdoc/2000/books.asp

1.5 Overview

The remainder of this document describes the system requirements for the ACME library management system. The next section contains a description of the overall system, assumptions, dependencies, constraints, and its intended users. The third section on specific requirements contains a detailed description of system requirements necessary for testing the ACME library management system. The fourth section on metrics contains information on the function points metric that was chosen to gauge the size of the system relative to other systems of this type developed by our company.

2. OVERALL DESCRIPTION

2.1 Product Perspective

The ACME library management system provides the hardware, software, and interfaces to support the various system users. For each user type, the system will operate in a different mode:

- *Public mode* — for library members and users accessing the system via the Web
- *Private mode* — for librarians
- *Administration mode* — for administrators

In each mode, a user has access to a different set of services helping to control access to the system and maintain the integrity of the data stored in the library databases.

PCs placed at strategic locations throughout the library provide the hardware interfaces through which members access the system. There are also PCs at the librarian and administrator desks. At the librarian's desk, a bar code reader provides an additional hardware interface. This reader enables the librarian to scan membership cards and asset bar codes, thus alleviating the need to enter the information manually.

Web browsers running on the various PCs provide the user interfaces to the system. A system access page is displayed on each PC type and each user must enter a username and password to gain access. Depending on the user type and the PC from which the system is accessed, different services are accessible:

- Members have access to services such as the ability to check the status of any checked-out assets with overdue fees (if applicable), search for an asset in the library, reserve, etc.
- Librarians have access to services such as the ability to check in or check out assets, the ability to accept payment of overdue fees, etc.
- Administrators have access to services such as the ability to add an asset, remove an asset, check the status of an asset, etc.

In addition, remote users can browse the library's Web page and access a subset of the member services with some additional services for remote users, such as the ability to enter a home location and get directions to the library from that location.

The system also has a number of software interfaces to other software products. These software products include the internet information server (IIS) and a database management system (DBMS). The IIS provides support for the Web pages that make up the user interface and the DBMS hosts databases for membership and asset information and processes all information queries generated by the system.

The communication interfaces include the library's previously installed Ethernet network, which is used to interconnect the various system components, its previously installed Internet gateway that provides access for remote users, and a firewall to restrict access to selected services.

2.1.1 System Interfaces

System interfaces for the ACME library management system include interfaces of the following types:

- *User interfaces* — describe how users (members, librarians, and administrator) access and interact with the system.

- *Hardware interfaces* — describe the hardware components in the system, such as PCs, bar code reader, etc. and how they connect to the system.
- *Software interfaces* — describe how the software being developed interfaces with other major software components in the system, such as the operating system, the IIS, and the DBMS.
- *Communication interfaces* — describe how the various components in the system communicate with each other.

2.1.2 User Interfaces

All user interfaces are implemented in HTML format and displayed inside an Internet web browser. Because the system is designed to support members of the public from a wide variety of backgrounds, the graphical user interface (GUI) will be designed to be both intuitive and easy-to-user. The same look-and-feel will be used for members, remote users, librarians, and administrators. (See Section 3.1.1.)

2.1.3 Hardware Interfaces

Hardware interface requirements for the ACME library management system include the following:

- Each PC will be equipped with a 10/100 BASE-T Ethernet network interface card that will enable the PC to connect to a hub or router on the LAN.
- The bar code reader will connect directly to the serial port on the librarian's PC and use serial transmission to communicate with the PC. (See Section 3.1.2 for specific requirements.)

2.1.4 Software Interfaces

The software developed for the ACME library management system must interoperate with several other software components in the system including:

- The operating system running on each PC
- The Internet information server running on the administrator's PC
- The DBMS running on the administrator's PC

See Section 3.1.3 for specific requirements.

2.1.5 Communications Interfaces

The communication interfaces in the system include:

- Remote users use their home telephone lines to access the remote services provided by the ACME library management system.
- The bar code reader connects to the librarian's PC via the PC's serial port.

See Section 3.1.4 for specific requirements.

2.1.6 Memory Constraints

To support reliable and efficient operation of the various PCs running the Microsoft Windows operating system, the following memory configurations are required for the PCs associated with each of the user types:

- Member's PC — 128 MB
- Librarian's PC — 128 MB
- Administrator's PC — 512 MB

The larger memory size on the administrator's PC reflects the fact that this PC is running the IIS and the DBMS. Also, the administrator's PC has a much higher disk space requirement: 1 GB, as opposed to the disk space requirement of 200 MB for member and librarian PCs.

2.1.7 Operations

The system will experience most use during normal opening hours of the library 9:30 a.m. to 9:30 p.m. During this time the system will be capable of sustaining service without undue delays in processing requests by members or the librarian. The system will be capable of handling multiple client requests without dropping a request.

Membership and asset data will be stored in databases managed by the DBMS system. The database information will be automatically backed up each night at 2:00 a.m. This will provide one level of protection against data loss should a failure occur.

A procedure will be developed to provide instructions for the administrator to perform a recovery operation in the event of a failure during daytime hours. The objective of such a procedure will be to bring the system back into normal operation within two hours.

2.1.8   Site Adaptation Requirements

The system will use the library's previously installed Ethernet network. The network is a 10BASE-T network and therefore the PCs will need to be equipped with network interface cards that support the 10BASE-T network type. The system will also use the library's existing Internet gateway. The gateway will connect to the library's network and provide firewall protection against remote users' accessing unauthorized services.

2.2   Product Functions

The ACME library management system will control user access and provide services to the various user types. The different users and the services provided for each user are:

- Members
  — Check the status of checked-out assets
  — Search for an asset
  — Reserve an asset
  — View list of coming events
  — View library floor map
  — View general library information
- Remote User
  — Search for an asset
  — Get library directions
  — View list of coming events
  — View library floor map
  — View general library information
- Librarian
  — Check out or check in an asset
  — Assess and collect fees
  — Print overdue notices
  — Reserve assets
  — Determine asset status
  — Determine member's records
  — Read membership card and asset numbers with bar code reader
- Administrator
  — Manage library assets
  — Maintain membership
  — Generate reports

2.3   User Characteristics

Because the ACME library management system is intended for small-to medium-sized libraries, people from many different educational backgrounds will want to take advantage of the services provided by the library.

Exhibit G-1. PC Requirements

PC	Memory	Disk Requirements
Member	128 MB	200 MB
Librarian	128 MB	200 MB
Administrator	512	1 GB

Remote users should not require any special skills to access and use the library services provided.

Similarly, user interfaces for librarians should be simple enough that only the most basic training will be required. Librarians should not need any special skills to use the system.

The administrator must be a qualified engineer knowledgeable about the Internet information server and database management systems in general. The administrator will need sufficient knowledge to be able to converse with customer support organizations should problems arise following the deployment of the system.

2.4 Constraints

2.4.1 Regulatory Policies

The system will comply with all local regulatory policies. The gateway providing access to remote users will comply with FCC regulations for the transmission of data via the Internet.

2.4.2 Hardware Limitations

The different user PCs must meet the requirements specified in Exhibit G-1. These requirements are critical to reliable and efficient use of the system.

2.4.3 Interfaces to Other Applications

The ACME library management system will be a Windows-based system and consequently all PCs must be running the Windows operating system. In addition, other system components must be interoperable with the Windows operating system. The system uses two other major applications, that is, an IIS and a DBMS. The servers for these products are hosted on the administrator's PC.

2.4.4 Parallel Applications

The ACME library management system will use the client/server architecture and therefore be capable of handling multiple service requests concurrently. For example, during busy periods many users may request a search for an asset when the librarian needs to perform an asset check-out operation for another member. In these circumstances, the system will process all requests without significant delays. (See Section 3.6 Performance Requirements for more information.)

2.4.5   Audit Requirements

No auditing functions are required in this system.

2.4.6   Control Functions

The only control functions provided in the system are those functions used to manipulate the data in the asset and membership databases.

2.4.7   High Order Language Functions

The ACME library management system uses a DBMS to manage the databases for membership and asset information. The system will use structured query language (SQL) to query for and update any information in the database.

2.4.8   Signal Handshaking Protocols

The ACME library management system will use cookies to help identify users attempting to access the system via the Internet. This will provide another level of security.

2.4.9   Reliability Requirements

The DBMS software will provide a backup capability to ensure protection of the data in the database. In addition, the DBMS software provides a transaction recording feature that can be used to keep track of all transactions during normal daytime operation. If a failure occurs, the transaction record can be used to roll back to the last successful transaction so that a minimum amount of information is lost.

2.4.10   Criticality of the Application

Although failure of the system will never be life threatening, providing a reliable and continuous service to users is one of the key requirements of the system. When a failure occurs, system downtime will be kept to a minimum. The target is to have the system operational within two hours following a serious failure.

2.4.11   Safety and Security of the System

Access to the ACME library management system by remote users will be controlled by the Internet gateway installed on the library premises. The gateway will provide a firewall that allows access to a subset of the services provided to library members. In addition, the IIS and the DBMS provide extensive security features to help protect data in the system. All system components must comply with regulations for equipment in a public location.

2.5 Assumptions and Dependencies

The ACME library management system uses equipment already installed at the library premises, including the existing network and the Internet gateway.

Over time, the technologies employed by the ACME library management system may change. New versions of the IIS and the DBMS will become available. New features will help the administrator maintain the databases, improve the response time for simultaneous transactions, and prompt the development of new features for librarians and members.

2.6 Apportioning of Requirements

The ACME library management system will be designed so that new features for member, librarian, or administrator can be added very easily. The combination of the IIS and the DBMS provide the mechanism through which the data stored in the membership and asset databases can be used in many different ways to provide new services.

3. SPECIFIC REQUIREMENTS

3.1 External Interface Requirements

3.1.1 User Interfaces

All user interfaces will be HTML-based and will be displayed in a web browser.

3.1.1.1. Process Member Access Screens

- Validate membership screen (see Exhibit G-2)
- Reserve asset screen (see Exhibit G-3)
- Request search screen (see Exhibit G-4)
- Request status screen (see Exhibit G-5)
- Coming event screen (see Exhibit G-6)
- Get library directions screen (see Exhibit G-7)
- View floor map screen (see Exhibit G-8)
- View general information screen (see Exhibit G-9)

3.1.1.2. Process Librarian Access Screens

- Check out asset screen (see Exhibit G-10)
- Check in asset screen (see Exhibit G-11)
- Generate reports screen (see Exhibit G-12)

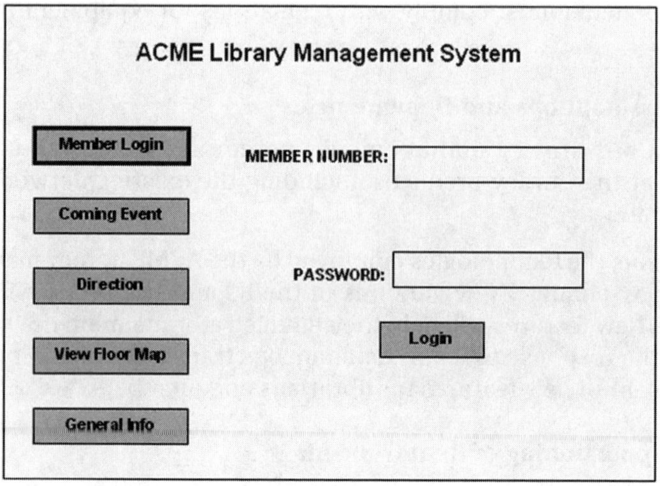

Exhibit G-2.   Member Screen: Validate Membership

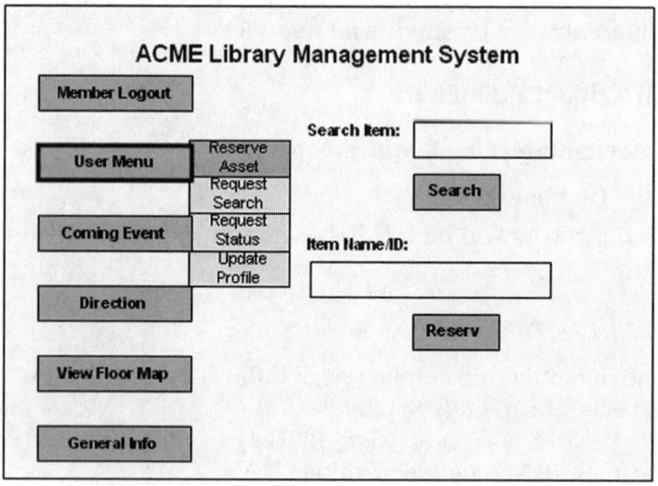

Exhibit G-3.   Member Screen: Reserve Asset

3.1.1.3.   Process Administrator Access Screens

- Manage library assets (see Exhibit G-13)
- Maintain membership (see Exhibit G-14)
- Generate reports (see Exhibit G-15)

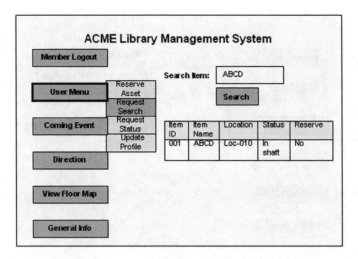

Exhibit G-4. Member Screen: Request Search

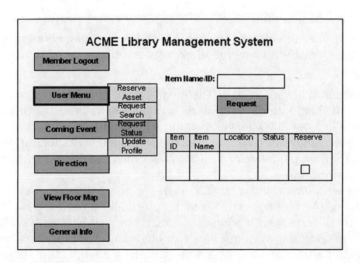

Exhibit G-5. Member Screen: Request Status

3.1.2 Hardware Interfaces

The hardware interfaces in the ACME library management system include:

- The connection of PCs to the LAN using 10/100BASE-T network interface cards
- The connection of the bar code reader to the librarian's PC using the serial port

ACME Library Management System

	Event Date	Event Description
Member Logout	Mar 30 2002	TAX Filing Event – TAX expert, Candy Wu, is going to give a one hour presentation on how to avoid taxes.
User Menu	April 01 2002	April Fool Event – Candy Wu, a well-known history teacher is going to give a presentation to our kids.
Coming Event	April 04 2002	Kids day– Everyone can borrow a book on this day and not return it.
Direction		
View Floor Map		
General Info		

Exhibit G-6. Member Screen: Coming Events

3.1.3 Software Interfaces

The software developed for the ACME library management system must interoperate with several other software components in the system including:

- *Microsoft Windows 2000* — The member and librarian PCs will run Microsoft Windows 2000 standard version. The administrator's PC will run Windows 2000 Server version to host the other servers in the system (see below). For detailed product documentation on Windows 2000 Server, please refer to http://www.microsoft.com/windows2000/en/server/help.
- *Internet Information Server (IIS)* — IIS is a group of Internet servers (including a Web or hypertext transfer protocol server and a file transfer protocol server) with additional capabilities for Microsoft's Windows Server operating systems. IIS also includes a set of programs for building and administering Web sites, a search engine, and support for writing Web-based applications that access databases. It is these capabilities that the ACME library management system will use to fulfill its requirements. The IIS is tightly integrated with Windows 2000 Servers, resulting in faster Web page serving. For detailed product documentation, please refer to http://www.micorosft.com/windows2000/en/server/iis/.
- *Database Management System (DBMS)* — The ACME library management system will use Microsoft SQL Server 2000 as the DBMS of choice. The interface between the system and DBMS will use an open database connectivity (ODBC) connection. Applications will use the active data object (ADO) library to access the database. For detailed

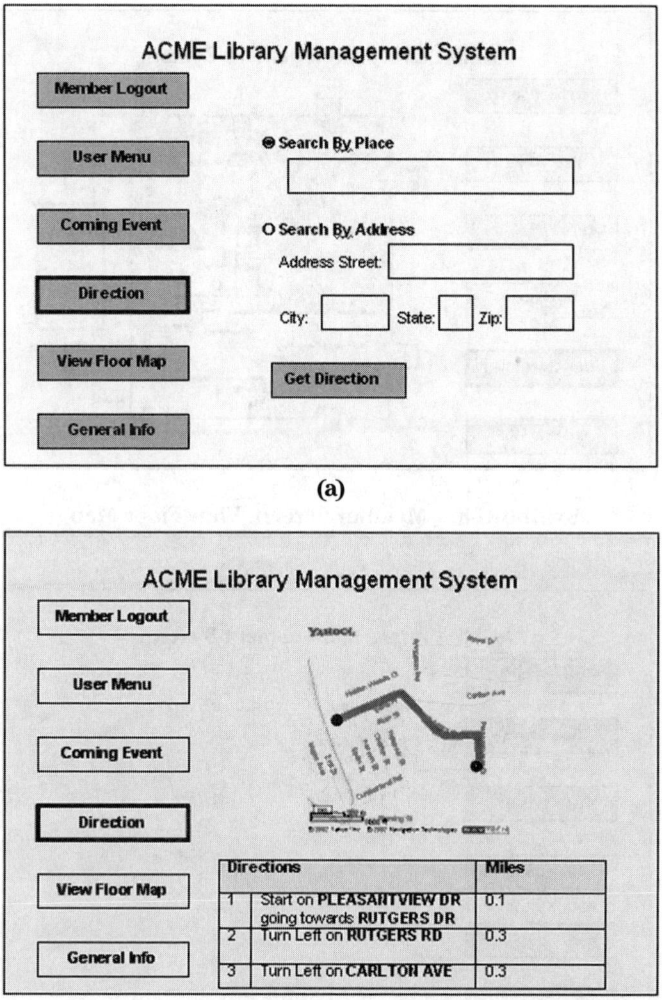

ACME Library Management System

| Member Logout |
User Menu	⊕ Search By Place
Coming Event	O Search By Address
	Address Street:
Direction	City: [ ] State: [ ] Zip: [ ]
View Floor Map	Get Direction
General Info

(a)

ACME Library Management System

| Member Logout |
| User Menu |
| Coming Event |
| Direction |

Directions		Miles
1	Start on **PLEASAHTVIEW DR** going towards **RUTGERS DR**	0.1
2	Turn Left on **RUTGERS RD**	0.3
3	Turn Left on **CARLTOH AVE**	0.3

| View Floor Map |
| General Info |

(b)

Exhibit G-7.   Member Screen: Get Library Directions

product documentation, please refer to http://www.mi-crosoft.com/qul/techinfo/productdoc/2000/books.asp.

3.1.4   Communications Interfaces

The ACME library management system requires communication interfaces to interconnect the various system components and to enable remote users to access the services allowed by the firewall in the Internet gateway. The communication interfaces are supported by the operating system and other subsystems:

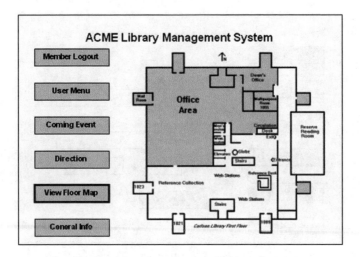

Exhibit G-8. Member Screen: View Floor Map

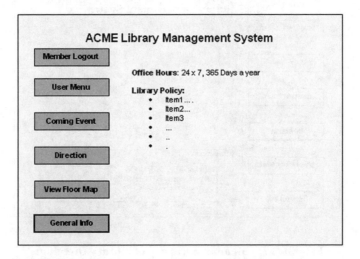

Exhibit G-9. Member Screen: General Information Display

- Windows supports most commercially available LAN interfaces for connection to communications servers or hosts. These include all normal communications APIs, and specific socket interfaces for all major TCP/IP vendors.
- Also, the Windows Sockets interface provides access to vendor-independent TCP/IP. Direct support is provided for synchronous cards for polled VIP connections; several commercial gateways for X.25 and TGX connections are also supported.

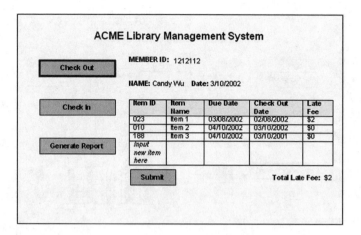

Exhibit G-10. Librarian Screen: Check Out Asset

ACME Library Management System

Check Out	**Item ID:**	*Item ID* **Item Name:** *Item Name*
	Status :	*On Hold/On Shelf/Returned*
Check In		
	Date Returned :	*MM/DD/YYYY*
Generate Report	**Check Out Date:**	*MM/DD/YYYY*
	Submit	

Exhibit G-11. Librarian Screen: Check In Asset

- For the firewall, a set of three layers of protocols standardizes the way in which the host system interfaces with users. Physical layer: defines the transmission media permissible under fire wire and the electrical and signaling characteristics of each. Link layer: describes the transmission of data in the packets. Transaction layer: defines a request–response protocol that hides the lower layer details of firewall from applications.

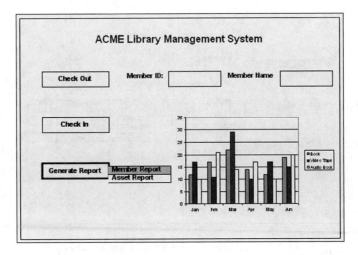

Exhibit G-12.   Librarian Screen: Generate Reports

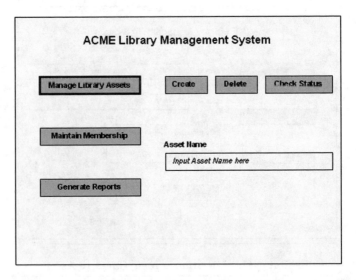

Exhibit G-13.   Administrator Screen: Manage Library Assets

3.2   Software Product Features

The Acme library management system comprises three major software subsystems: the inquiry subsystem, the database management system, and the administration subsystem. Their interactions are illustrated in the Exhibit G-16.

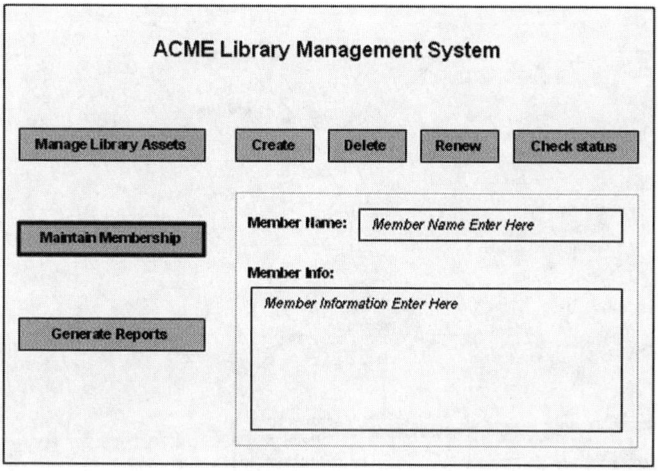

Exhibit G-14. Administrator Screen: Maintain Membership

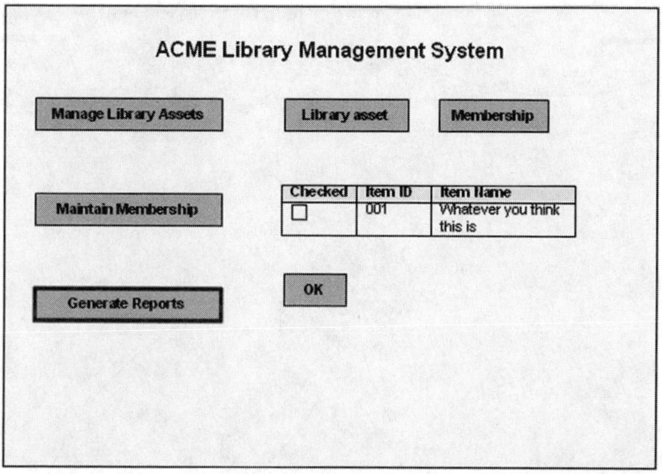

Exhibit G-15.   Administrator Screen: Generate Reports

3.3   Inquiry Subsystem (Process 1.0)

The inquiry subsystem is responsible for handling transactions and requests between the library and the user. Users fall into two categories: member and public. A member is allowed to view his membership status, perform searches, and reserve library assets. A public user is allowed to perform searches and request library information. The inquiry subsystem is decomposed into two major processes to handle these user actions. Exhibit G-17 illustrates their data flows.

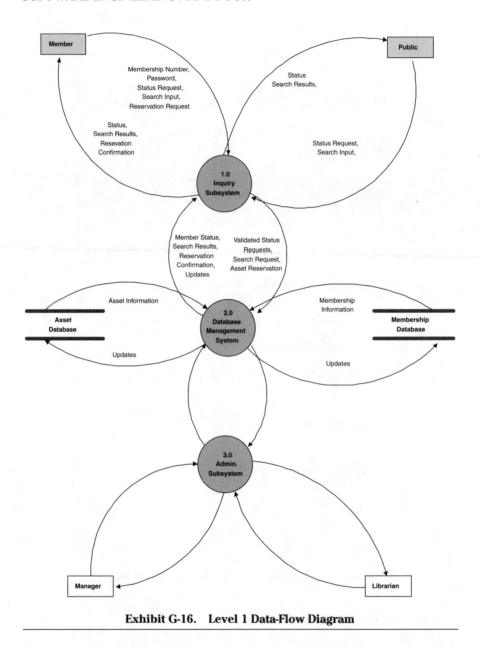

Exhibit G-16.   Level 1 Data-Flow Diagram

3.3.1   Member Access (Process 1.1)

3.3.1.1.   Purpose

The purpose of this function is to process member requests for status, process search requests, and allow members to reserve assets. Membership is validated with a comparison between the member-entered

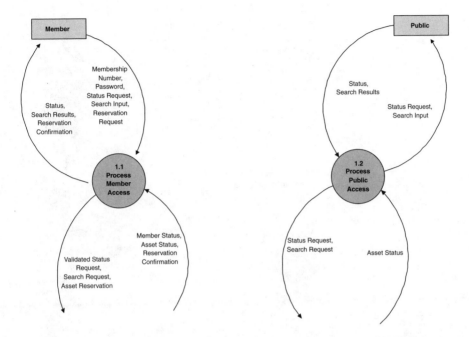

Exhibit G-17.   Inquiry Subsystem (Process 1.0) Data-Flow Diagram

password and the password stored in the membership info store. The store receives updates from the DBMS.

3.3.1.2.   Stimulus/Response Sequence

This functionality will be triggered whenever a member submits a request via a member terminal. (Refer to Exhibit G-18.) Stimulus is in the form of messages and member input. Responses are in the form of messages and member output.

3.3.1.3.   Associated Functional Requirements

- Validate membership (Process 1.1.1): This process validates a member's membership number and password. The member's membership number and password are compared to the information in the member data store for validity.
  - *Inputs:* The inputs to this process are membership number and password from the member and member info from the member data store. The member data store receives updates from the DBMS (Process 2.0).
  - *Processing:* This process accepts the membership number and password from the user and reads the corresponding member info from the member data store. If the password given by the member

555

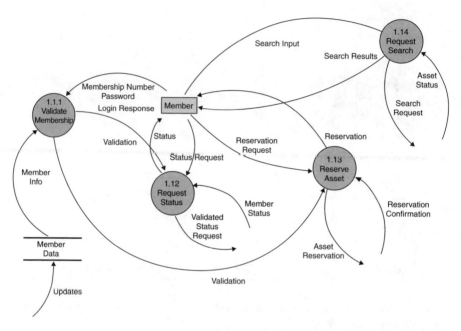

Exhibit G-18. Process 1.1 Data-Flow Diagram

matches the password in the member data store then the process passes a validation message to the request status and request asset processes. If the password does not match, then no message is sent. The process also sends a login response to the member based on the outcome of the password comparison.

— *Outputs:* The outputs of this process are a validation message and a log-in response. The validation message is sent to the request status and reserve asset processes and is used to validate requests and reservations. The login response is sent to the member's terminal and indicates whether or not the password was successful.

• *Request status (Process 1.1.2):* The purpose of this function is to generate validated status requests from members.

— *Inputs:* The inputs to this process are a status request message from the member's terminal and a member status message from the DBMS (Process 2.0).

— *Processing:* This process accepts a status request message from a member and a validation request from the validate membership process and generates a validated status request message. The validated status request message is sent to the DBMS process (Process 2.0). This process also accepts a member status message from the DBMS process and sends a status message to the member's terminal.

— *Outputs:* The outputs of this process are the status message that is sent to the member's terminal and the validated status request message sent to the DBMS (Process 2.0).

- *Reserve asset (Process 1.1.3):* The purpose of this function is to generate reserve library assets through member requests.

  — *Inputs:* The inputs to this process are a reservation request message from the member's terminal and reservation confirmation message from the DBMS (Process 2.0).

  — *Processing:* This process accepts reservation request messages from the member's terminal and a validation message from the validate member process. If the reservation request originates from a validated member, the reservation request message is translated into an asset reservation message and sent to the DBMS process (Process 2.0). This process also accepts reservation confirmation messages from the DBMS process and translates them into reservation messages destined for the member's terminal.

  — *Outputs:* The outputs from this process are an asset reservation message to the DBMS and a reservation message to the member's terminal.

- Request Search (Process 1.1.4)

  — *Inputs:* The inputs to this process are a search input message from the member's terminal and an asset status message from the DBMS process (Process 2.0).

  — *Processing:* This process accepts the search input message from the member terminal and generates a search request message destined for the database management process. The search input message must have at least one field (as defined in the data dictionary) that is not null. This field is used to create the search asset message. The asset status message from the DBMS process is accepted and translated into a search results message destined for the member terminal. Unsuccessful searches will have null values in the fields of the asset status message. The null values will be translated into a search result message indicating that the item was not found. If the search was successful, the asset status message will be translated into a search results message indicating the status of the asset.

    - *Outputs:* The outputs of this process include the search request message destined for the DBMS and the search results message destined for the member terminal.

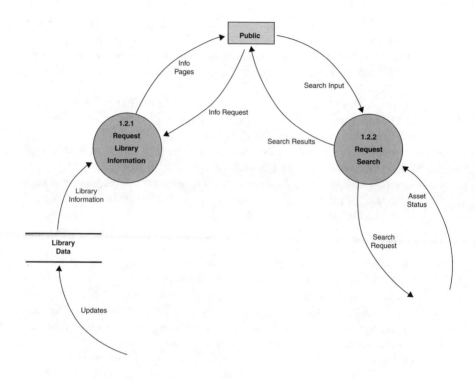

Exhibit G-19.   Process 1.2 Data-Flow Diagram

3.3.2   Process Remote Access (Process 1.2)

3.3.2.1.   Purpose

The purpose of this function is to process public requests for library information and to process search requests.

3.3.2.2   Stimulus/Response Sequence

This functionality will be triggered whenever the public user submits requests via the Internet. Stimulus is in the form of messages and public input; responses are in the form of messages and public output. Refer to Exhibit G-19 for their interaction.

3.3.2.3.   Associated Functional Requirements

- Request library information (Process 1.2.1): This process handles info request messages for library information from the public terminal. The public terminals are connected to the Acme library management system via the Internet.

—*Inputs:* The inputs to this process are the info request messages from the public terminal and library information messages from the library data store. The library data store receives updates from the DBMS (Process 2.0).

—*Processing:* This process accepts the info request message from the public terminal and selects the appropriate Web page to send to the public terminal.

—*Outputs:* The output of this process is a Web page for display on the public terminal.

- Request Search (Process 1.2.2)

—*Inputs:* The inputs to this process are a search input message from a public terminal and an asset status message from the DBMS process (Process 2.0).

—*Processing:* This process accepts the search input message from the public terminal and generates a search request message destined for the DBMS process. The search input message must have at least one field (as defined in the data dictionary) that is not null. This field is used to create the search asset message. The asset status message from the database management process is accepted and translated into a search results message destined for the public terminal. Unsuccessful searches will have null values in the fields of the asset status message. The null values will be translated into a search result message indicating that the item was not found. If the search was successful, the asset status message will be translated into a search results message indicating the status of the asset.

- *Outputs:* The outputs of this process include the search request message destined for the DBMS and the search results message destined for the public terminal.

3.4 Database Management System (Process 2.0)

The DBMS maintains the asset and membership databases. The asset database stores information about the library's books, magazines, videos, CD ROMS, and library equipment. The membership database stores information about the library's patrons and members. The DBMS provides the necessary interfaces between the physical storage units and the inquiry and administration subsystems. It handles the transactions and requests between the databases and the two subsystems: inquiry and administration. Exhibit G-20 illustrates their data flows.

3.4.1 Process Query (Process 2.1)

3.4.1.1. Purpose

The purpose of this function is to process queries from the various users. Queries include searches, status requests, and reservation requests.

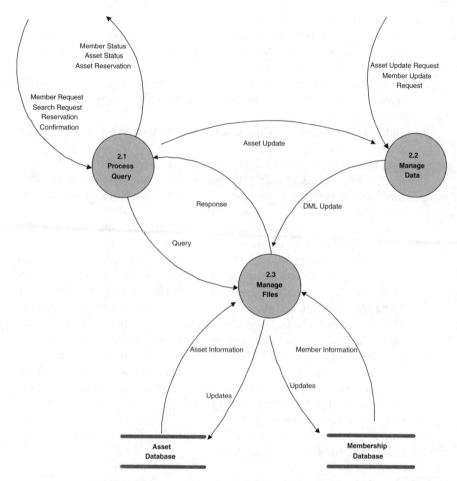

Member Status
Asset Status
Asset Reservation

Asset Update Request
Member Update
Request

Member Request
Search Request
Reservation
Confirmation

Asset Update

**2.1
Process
Query**

**2.2
Manage
Data**

Response

DML Update

Query

**2.3
Manage
Files**

Asset Information

Member Information

Updates

Updates

Updates

**Asset
Database**

**Membership
Database**

Exhibit G-20.   Database Management System (Process 2.0) Data-Flow Diagram

3.4.1.2.   Stimulus/Response Sequence

This functionality will be triggered whenever a request is sent by another process. No direct interaction with the user is available. The response is in the form of messages sent to the requesting process. Refer to the Exhibit G-21.

3.4.1.3.   Associated Functional Requirements

- Query Decomposition (Process 2.1.1)
  - *Inputs:* The inputs to this process are search member request messages and search request messages from other processes and responses from the manage file process.

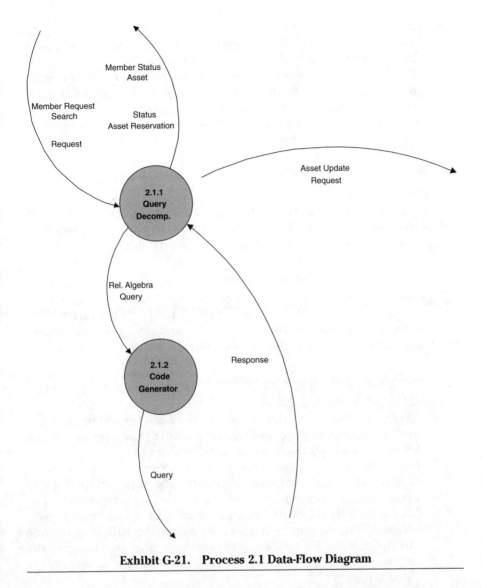

Exhibit G-21. Process 2.1 Data-Flow Diagram

— *Processing:* This process transforms the high-level queries (member request, search request) into a relational algebra query. It also checks that the query is syntactically and semantically correct.
— *Outputs:* The outputs from this process are member status, asset status, and asset reservation messages. It also generates relation algebra query messages for the code generator process, as well as asset update request messages destined for the request reservation process.

- Code Generator (Process 2.1.2)
  - *Inputs:* The inputs to this process are relation algebra query messages from the query decomposition process.
  - *Processing:* This process transforms the relational algebra query messages into runtime code for execution. It also checks that the query is syntactically and semantically correct.
    - *Outputs:* The outputs from this process query messages destined for the manage file process.

3.4.2 Manage Data (Process 2.2)

3.4.2.1. Purpose

The purpose of this function is to manage and maintain the meta-data for the database catalog. It also generates the data manipulation language for updating the membership database and asset database.

3.4.2.2. Stimulus/Response Sequence

The stimulus for this function is requests for update messages from other processes within the Acme library management system. The responses include member status, asset status, and asset reservation messages. See Exhibit G-22 for an illustration of the data flow.

3.4.2.3. Associated Functional Requirements

- DDL Compiler (Process 2.2.1)
  - *Inputs:* The inputs to this process are the asset update request and member update request messages from other processes and the table messages from the database catalog store.
  - *Processing:* This process accepts requests for updates to the member and asset databases and generates the appropriate code to update them. It maintains the database catalog and uses the information for generation of the appropriate DML update messages.
    - *Outputs:* The outputs from this process are the DML update code to the manage file process and member status and asset status messages to other processes. The Asset Reservation message is also generated.

3.4.3 Manage Files (Process 2.3)

3.4.3.1. Purpose

The purpose of this function is to manipulate the underlying storage files and manage the allocation of storage space on disk. It establishes and maintains the lists of structures defined in the internal schema for the membership and asset databases.

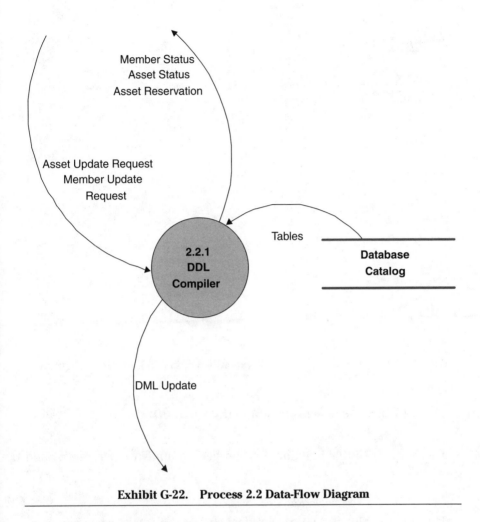

Exhibit G-22.   Process 2.2 Data-Flow Diagram

3.4.3.2.   Stimulus/Response Sequence

The stimuli for this function are queries and DML updates. The responses are member information and asset information messages.

3.5   Administration Subsystem (Process 3.0)

The administration subsystem (see Exhibit G-23) provides application software to handle transactions at the librarian's terminals and at the administrator's terminals. Transactions at the librarian's terminal include checking in and checking out books, searches, asset status, and bar code reading of books and membership cards. Transactions at the administrator's terminals include creation and deletion of library assets, creation and deletion of memberships, and report generation.

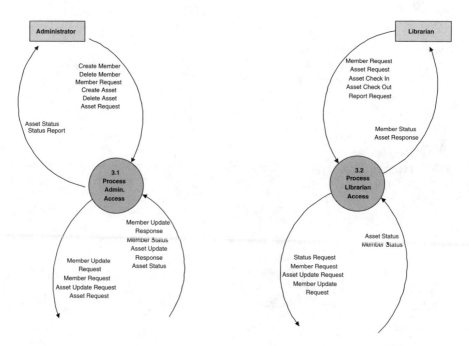

Exhibit G-23. Administration Subsystem (Process 3.0) Data-Flow Diagram

3.5.1   Process Administrator Access (Process 3.1)

3.5.1.1. Purpose

The purpose of this function is to process administrator requests and transactions.

3.5.1.2. Stimulus/Response Sequence

This functionality will be triggered whenever the administrator submits requests or transactions to the system. Stimulus is in the form of messages and other administrator generated input. Responses are in the form of messages and terminal output. Refer to Exhibit G-24 for their interaction.

3.5.1.3. Associated Functional Requirements

- *Manage assets (Process 3.1.1):* The purpose of this feature is to allow the administrator to control and manage the library assets by the ACME library management system. The administrator can choose the following actions: create asset, delete asset, or check asset status.
  - *Inputs:* The inputs to this process are create asset, delete asset, and asset request messages from the administrator terminal. It also accepts the asset status and asset update response messages from the DBMS process (Process 2.0).

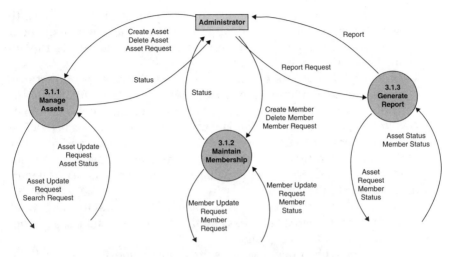

Exhibit G-24.   Process 3.1 Data-Flow Diagram

— *Processing:* This process accepts the create asset and delete asset messages from the administrator's terminal and generates asset update messages destined for the DBMS process. This process responds with an asset update message indicating success or failure of the update; this message is relayed to the administrator's terminal in the status message. Update requests messages are also accepted from the administrator's terminal and translated into search request messages destined for the DBMS process. The asset status response message is sent to the administrator's terminal.

— *Outputs:* The outputs of this process are the asset update request and search request messages destined for the DBMS process and the status messages destined for the administrator's terminal.

• *Maintain membership (Process 3.1.2):* The purpose of this process is to provide the library administrator with mechanisms to maintain and manage the member information of the ACME library management system. The administrator can choose the following actions: create member, delete member, or check member status.

— *Inputs:* The inputs to this process are create member, delete member, and member request messages from the administrator terminal. It also accepts the member status and member update response messages from the DBMS process (Process 2.0).

— *Processing:* This process accepts the create member and delete member messages from the administrator's terminal and generates member update messages destined for the DBMS process. This process responds with a member update message indicating success or failure of the update. This message is relayed to the administrator's terminal in the status message. Update requests messages are also accepted from the administrator's terminal and translated into search request messages destined for the database management process. The member status response message is sent to the administrator's terminal.

— *Outputs:* The outputs of this process are the member update request and search request messages destined for the DBMS process and the status messages destined for the administrator's terminal.

- *Generate report (Process 3.1.3):* The purpose of this process is to allow the administrator to generate reports of library assets and member status controlled by the ACME library management system. The administrator can choose the following: generate asset report or generate membership report.

  — *Inputs:* The inputs to this process are the member status and asset status from the DBMS process and the report request message from the administrator's terminal.

  — *Processing:* This process accepts the report request from the administrator's terminal and generates the appropriate member request and asset request messages destined for the DBMS process (process 2.0) based on a predefined set of reports. This process receives the member status and asset status messages from the DBMS process and formats them into the necessary fields of the report message. The report message is sent to the administrator's terminal.

    - *Outputs:* The outputs of this process are the member request and asset request messages destined for the DBMS process and the report message destined for the administrator's terminal.

3.5.2   Process Librarian Access (Process 3.2)

3.5.2.1.   Purpose

The purpose of this function is to process the librarian's requests and transactions.

3.5.2.2.   Stimulus/Response Sequence

This functionality will be triggered whenever the librarian submits requests or transactions to the system. Stimulus is in the form of messages and librarian input. Responses are in the form of messages and terminal output. Refer to Exhibit G-25 for their interaction.

3.5.2.3.   Associated Functional Requirements

- *Check-Out Process (Process 3.2.1):* This process handles check out of library assets.
  — *Inputs:* The inputs to this process are the member information from the card reader, the asset information from the bar code reader, and the check-in request from the librarian's terminal. Member update

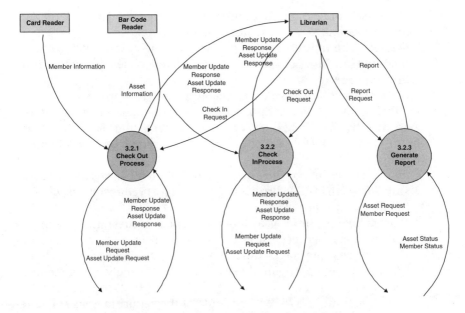

Exhibit G-25. Process 3.2 Data-Flow Diagram

responses and asset update responses are also accepted from the DBMS (Process 2.0).

— *Processing:* This process accepts the member information, asset information, and check-in request and generates a member update request and asset update request destined for the DBMS. The member update request and asset update request fields are modified to indicate a member is checking out an asset. Member update responses and asset update responses are received from the DBMS, formatted, and sent to the librarian's terminal.

— *Outputs:* The outputs of this process are the member update request and asset update request destined for the DBMS and member update responses and asset update responses destined for the librarian's terminal.

• *Check-In Process (Process 3.2.1):* This process handles check in of library Assets.

— *Inputs:* The inputs to this process are the asset information from the bar code reader and the check-in request from the librarian's terminal. Member update responses and asset update responses are also accepted from the DBMS (Process 2.0).

— *Processing:* This process accepts the asset information and check-in request and generates a member update request and asset update request destined for the DBMS. The asset update request fields are modified to indicate an asset has been returned. Member update

567

responses and asset update responses are received from the DBMS, formatted, and sent to the librarian's terminal.

— *Outputs:* The outputs of this process are the asset update request destined for the DBMS and asset update responses destined for the librarian's terminal.

- *Generate Report (Process 3.2.3):* The purpose of this process is to allow the librarian to generate reports of library assets and member status controlled by the ACME library management system. The administrator can choose the following: generate asset report or generate membership report.

    — *Inputs:* The inputs to this process are the member status and asset status from the DBMS process and the report request message from the librarian's terminal.

    — *Processing:* This process accepts the report request from the librarian's terminal and generates the appropriate member request and asset request messages destined for the DBMS process (Process 2.0) based on a predefined set of reports. It receives the member status and asset status messages from the DBMS process and formats them into the necessary fields of the report message. The report message is sent to the librarian's terminal.

    - *Outputs:* The outputs of this process are the member request and asset request messages destined for the DBMS process and the report message destined for the librarian's terminal.

3.6 Performance Requirements

The ACME library management system will support up to five member PCs, two librarian PCs, and one administrator PC. The bar code reader at the librarian's desk will be capable of reading membership cards and bar codes on assets with no noticeable delay. The response time should be no greater than 0.5 seconds.

Under normal operating conditions, a user (member, librarian, or administrator) can expect a response from the system within five seconds. Time-consuming operations such as search operations that require the retrieval of a large amount of data from the database will be designed with performance in mind. For example, part of the result set can be displayed while the query continues in parallel. More results are displayed if requested by the user.

The system will be capable of handling up to ten simultaneous transactions (including transactions to handle remote users) without any noticeable degradation of service to the supported users and without dropping any of the requested services.

The existing Internet gateway will not impose any degradation of performance on the system. Response to remote users is partly dependent on Internet traffic and therefore cannot be the sole responsibility of the ACME library management system.

The system will be tested to ensure conformance to the performance requirements mentioned in this section. A separate *functional test specification* will be developed containing details of on-site tests required to test the system under normal and load conditions. User interaction (including remote users) will be simulated to get a reading on how well the system performs and provide indications of how to improve performance if necessary. The response time for each service provided for each user type will be measured and evaluated.

Databases will need to be tuned to optimize queries against them. Such tuning can only be done effectively after the databases are populated and the system is up and running.

3.7 Design Constraints

The location of the PCs for members, librarians, and administrator must conform to the limitations imposed by the network topology. For example, if a PC connects to a hub or router, it must be located as close to the hub or router as deemed necessary by the specification.

3.8 Software System Attributes

3.8.1 Reliability

The system must be properly installed and tested by ACME engineers.

The software and hardware used by the system will be compatible to increase the reliability of the overall system. Where possible, software from a single vendor will be used to improve interoperability and reliability.

3.8.2 Availability

The system will remain operational even when the library is not open to the public. It is anticipated that the administrator will perform many tasks during periods of lower activity, such as when the library is closed. Also, the system needs to remain operational to provide service to remote users accessing the system via the Internet.

The system will not be available, even via the Internet, while the databases are backed up. This operation will be performed during the early hours of the morning when the system is not expected to be used.

3.8.3 Security

The system will provide a number of different security features. First, all members must log into the system at member PCs and must provide a username and password before gaining access to the system. Similarly, the librarian and administrator access the system via their respective PCs and are authenticated by username and password. Second, remote users access the system via a gateway that provides a firewall. The firewall allows access to services designated as remote access services, but blocks access to all other services, such as administrator services. Cookies will also be used to aid in identifying remote users.

The DBMS provides a high level of security. Security profiles for the different user types will be created so that specific users have only the permissions (create, update, delete) on selected data objects. For example, only the administrator will have create and delete permissions in the asset database. Stored procedures will be used to maintain referential integrity in the databases.

3.8.4 Maintainability

The system will be designed so that it will be easily extensible; that is, new services for each user type (member, librarian, and administrator) can be added using the same paradigm. While developers are required to extend the system, the code to develop new services is not expected to be complex. Software from a single vendor will be used to improve interoperability and reliability.

3.8.5 Portability

This section is not applicable. The system will integrate PCs running the Windows platform. There is no requirement to port the system to any other platform.

3.9 Logical Database Requirements

3.9.1 Types of Information

The types of data that will be stored in the database will be the standard numeric, string, date, and enumeration data types. Information members and assets will be stored in databases. Username and passwords for user access will be stored in a separate file

Exhibit G-26 shows the data dictionary that identifies by name each piece of data that will be stored by the ACME library management system and the general type of each piece of data.

3.10 Other Requirements

Not applicable.

Exhibit G-26. Data Dictionary Entries for the ACME Library Management System

Name:	Asset Database
Aliases:	None
Where Used/How Used:	Used by the DBMS to process requests and return results to the inquiry and administration subsystems
Content Description:	Attributes associated with each asset including:

- Asset Number = 16 Numeric Digits
- ISBN Number = 16 Alphanumeric Characters
- Library of Congress Classification Number = 16 Alphanumeric Digits
- Asset Title = 64 Alphanumeric Characters
- Author = 32 Alphanumeric Characters
- Dewey Decimal Classification Number = 16 Numeric Digits
- Media Type = Enumeration {BOOK I MAGAZINE I CDROM I REFERENCE}
- Status = Enumeration {IN I OUT I LOST I MISSING I DUE_DATE}
- Category = Enumeration {FICTION I NONFICTION}
- Published = 32 Alphanumeric Characters
- Keywords = 64 Alphanumeric Characters
- Date Acquired = Date
- Location = 16 Alphanumeric Characters

Name:	Membership Database
Aliases:	None
Where Used/How Used	Used by the DBMS to process requests and return results to the inquiry and administration subsystems
Content Description:	Attributes associated with each asset including:

- Membership Number = 10 Numeric Digits
- Member Since Date = Date
- Last Name = 16 Alphanumeric Characters
- First Name = 16 Alphanumeric Characters
- Address = 64 Alphanumeric Characters
- Phone Number = 11 Numeric Digits (1, area code, phone number)
- Assets on Loan = Array containing 10 strings each containing 64 Alphanumeric Characters
- Assets Overdue = Array containing 10 strings each containing 64 Alphanumeric Characters
- Late Fees Due = 10 Numeric Digits
- Maximum Allowed Loans = 2 Numeric Digits

Name:	Member Data
Aliases:	None
Where Used/How Used	A file used to validate username and passwords for members, librarians, and administrator when attempting to access the system. The username and password entered are compared with the username and password in this file. Access is granted only if a match is found.

(continued)

Exhibit G-26. (continued)

Content Description:	Attributes associated with each asset including: • Member Username = 16 Alphanumeric Digits • Member Password = 16 Alphanumeric Digits
Name:	**Library Data**
Aliases:	None
Where Used/How Used	Files maintained by the administrator and used to provide general information about the library
Content Description:	HTML files for: • General Library Information (Policy, etc.) • Coming Events • Library Floor Map • Library Directions Screen
Name:	**Database Catalog**
Aliases:	None
Where Used/How Used	Used by the DDL compiler process
Content Description:	Contains detailed information about the various objects in the databases including tables, indices, integrity constraints, security constraints, etc.

4. METRICS

As part of our company's metrics program, the project team used the function points metric to gauge the relative size of the ACME library management system. The function points metric is suitable for GUI-based, client/server systems and provides valuable information for the ongoing measurement of productivity within the organization. The FP value for the system can be compared with FP values of previous projects to gain an estimate of the relative size of the system. The function point value is calculated in the three steps:

1. Complete the function point table.
2. Calculate the value adjustment factor (VAF).
3. Compute the final function points (FP) value.

Each of these steps is described in the following sections and a conclusion is drawn in the final section.

More detailed information on the use of function points as a valuable metric is available at: http://ourworld.compuserve.com/homepages/softcomp/fpfaq.htm#WhatAreFunctionPoints.

Exhibit G-27.   ACME Library Management System Function Point Table

Measurement Parameter	Count	Weighting Factor			Total
		Simple	**Average**	**Complex**	
Number of user inputs	55	**3**	4	6	165
Number of user outputs	60	**4**	5	7	240
Number of user enquiries	55	3	**4**	6	220
Number of files	30	**7**	10	15	210
Number of external interfaces	80	**5**	7	10	400
Count Total					1235

4.1   Function Point Metric

4.1.1   Completing the Function Point Table

The completed function point table for the ACME library management system is shown in Exhibit G-27.

4.1.2   Calculating the VAF

The total degree of influence (TDI) factor, an interim factor necessary for the calculation of the VAF, is calculated by answering the questions in the table shown in Exhibit G-28. The options for the degree of influence range from not applicable (0) to absolutely essential (5). The total value is calculated by summing the values in the rows.

Using the TDI factor, the VAF can be calculated using the following formula:

VAF = (TDI * 0.01) + 0.65
VAF = (31 * 0.01) + 0.65 = **0.96**

4.1.3   Computing the Final FP Value

The final FP value can be calculated using the formula:

FP = Count Total ("FP metric" section) * VAF ("other metrics" section)
FP = 1235 * 0.96 = **1186**

4.1.4   Conclusion

An FP value of 1186, when compared with the historical data maintained for other projects, does not indicate a very large or complex system. The data for this project will be captured so that it can be used for comparison with other projects.

Exhibit G-28. Total Degree of Influence (TDI) Factor

General System Characteristic	Degree of Influence
1. Does the system require reliable backup and recovery?	4
2. Are data communications required?	1
3. Are there distributed processing functions?	3
4. Is performance critical?	2
5. Will the system run in an existing, heavily utilized operational environment?	1
6. Does the system require online data entry?	3
7. Does the online entry require the input transaction to be built over multiple screens or operations?	2
8. Are the master files updated online?	0
9. Are the inputs, outputs, files, or enquires complex?	2
10. Is the internal processing complex?	2
11. Is the code designed to be reusable?	3
12. Are conversion and installation included in the design?	2
13. Is the system designed for multiple installations in different organizations?	1
14. Is the application designed to facilitate change and ease of use by users?	5
Total Degree of Influence (TDI)	**31**

4.2 Other Metrics

Our company employs other metrics to assess the quality of the software product. Metrics are used to measure the quantity and quality of the source code by measuring various aspects of the code and the lines of codes (LOC). The metrics are described in the following categories:

- Source code size metrics
- Code understandability metrics
- Function metrics

4.2.1 Source Code Size Metrics

4.2.1.1. LOC Metric

A common basis on which to estimate a software project is the LOC metric. LOCs are used to determine time and cost estimates; the LOC estimate becomes the baseline to measure the degree of work performed on a project. Once a project is underway, the LOC becomes a tracking tool that can measure the degree of progress on a project. Experienced developers can gauge an LOC estimate using prior knowledge of previous projects.

4.2.1.2. *Effective Lines of Code*

An effective line of code is the measurement of all lines that are not comments, blank lines, or standalone braces or parentheses. This measurement more closely represents the quantity of work performed. It is common for programmers to use a single brace or parenthesis on a line to denote a specific block of code. A single character on a line should not really count as a line of code. This type of coding style can therefore increase the LOC metric by 20 to 40 percent.

4.2.2 Code Understandability Metrics

4.2.2.1. *Comment Line Metric*

The number of comments in a source program is a measure of the care taken by the programmer to make the source code and algorithms understandable. Code that is not well commented is very difficult to maintain. Comments can occur by themselves on a physical line or be co-mingled with source code. A line is considered a comment line if the physical line contains a comment.

4.2.2.2. *Blank Line and White Space Metric*

The number of blank lines within a program determines the readability. White space highlights the logical grouping of constructs and variables. Programs that use few blank lines are difficult to read and more expensive to maintain.

4.2.3 Function Metrics

4.2.3.1. *Function Count Metric*

The total number of functions within a program determines the degree of modularity. This metric is used to quantify the average number of LOC per function, maximum LOC per function, and the minimum LOC per function.

4.2.3.2. *Average LOC/Function Metric*

The average LOC/function indicates how the code meets the accepted standard. The accepted industry standard of 200 LOC/function is desired as the average. Functions that have a larger number of lines of code per function are difficult to understand and difficult to maintain. They provide a good indication that a function should be broken into smaller functions.

4.2.3.3. *Maximum LOC/Function Metric*

Although the average LOC per function gives an interesting source code trend, the maximum LOC per function gives an indication of the largest function in the system.

4.2.3.4. Minimum LOC/Function Metric

An LOC value of 2 may indicated that functions are just prototypes and will need to be completed later.

Selected Bibliography

Connolly, T. (2002). *Database Systems*, 3rd ed., Addison-Wesley, Reading, MA.

Pressman, R. (2001). *Software Engineering, a Practitioner's Approach,* 5th ed., McGraw-Hill, New York. (Web site associated with Pressman's book at: http://www.mhhe.com/engcs/comp-sci/pressman/stundent_index.html).

Robertson, S. and Robertson, J. (1999). *Mastering the Requirements Process*, Addison-Wesley, Reading, MA.

Summerville, I. (1995). *Software Engineering*, 5th ed., Addison-Wesley, Reading, MA.

Yourdon, E. (2000). *Modern Structured Analysis*, Prentice Hall, New York.

Course web site at: http://www.newartech.com/se.

Some useful background information on function points is located at: http://ourworld.compuserve.com/homepages/softcomp/fpfaq.htm#WhatAreFunctionPoints.

Product documentation for Microsoft Windows 2000 Server is located at: http://www.microsoft.com/windows2000/en/server/help.

Product documentation for Microsoft Internet Information Server (IIS) is located at: http://www.microsoft.com/windows2000/en/server/iis/.

Product documentation for Microsoft SQL Server is located at: http://www.microsoft.com/qul/techinfo/productdoc/2000/books.asp.

Appendix H
Sample Survey

Does your company recognize that Y2K certification is an ongoing effort and that modifying any program or file structure from now on will have Y2K ramifications? (i.e., a program has already been Y2K certificated and now needs changes made for some reason unrelated to Y2K. Scenario 1: the programmer creates new code that is not Y2K compliant. Scenario 2: the programmer inserts new code making existing Y2K-compliant code noncompliant some time in the future.) The established change management process will not detect new code that is not Y2K compliant. To depend solely on established change management processes or comprehensive Y2K types of testing as ongoing Y2K certification vehicles will delay production implementation and adversely affect the company's bottom line. In light of this problem, we are researching the feature set of a possibly automated Y2K certification and quality assurance tool that protects your company's Y2K investment and reduces your ongoing certification and quality-assurance labor cost. Your input is greatly appreciated.

If you were to search for a tool that prevents Y2K recontamination by automating an ongoing automated certification process, what would be the desired features of the tool? In the feature list below, please rate the importance of that feature using the scale of 1 to 5, with 1 being the most important.

MANAGEMENT ASPECTS (YOU MAY WANT TO COMPLETE THE TECHNICAL PART OF THE SURVEY FIRST):

1. The tool is used as part of program development cycle to improve quality   1 2 3 4 5
2. The tool is used as part of program development cycle to enforce standards   1 2 3 4 5
3. The tool has the flexibility of being used on an as-needed basis   1 2 3 4 5
4. The tool has the flexibility of being made a mandatory part of the process   1 2 3 4 5
5. The tool is also useful for non-Y2K-related certification   1 2 3 4 5
6. If this tool would not be useful beyond Y2K, why not? _____

7. Given the potential savings in labor and the protection of your investment, what price would you pay for a product such as this? (ballpark figure) _____
8. What features would interest you in a tool such as this? _____

TECHNICAL ASPECTS:

1. Is the tool enabled during compile time and does it generate diagnostics similar to those now familiar to programmers (e.g., Level E or Level W)?   1 2 3 4 5
2. The tool works under MVS   1 2 3 4 5
3. The tool works under VSE   1 2 3 4 5
4. The tool works under AS/400   1 2 3 4 5
5. The tool works under UNIX   1 2 3 4 5
6. The tool works under other platforms (name)   1 2 3 4 5
7. The tool can be run on a PC   1 2 3 4 5
8. The tool has the ability to link source with copybook and subroutines   1 2 3 4 5
9. The tool runs outside or front-end change management process   1 2 3 4 5
10. The tool interfaces with CA/Librarian or CA/Panvalet   1 2 3 4 5
11. The tool can support IBM Millennium Language Extensions   1 2 3 4 5
12. The tool permits user input of dates or other variables for verification and does this in an expert system rules-based format   1 2 3 4 5
13. The tool can uncover nonobvious date and year references (e.g., wy, which might mean work year)   1 2 3 4 5
14. The tool has the ability to detect source code changes from baseline   1 2 3 4 5
15. The tool has the ability to electronically store all compiler listings for automated retrieval, version control, audit, and reduction of storage space   1 2 3 4 5
16. The tool provides automated source code management   1 2 3 4 5
17. The tool has the ability to map all program relationships based on program calls and track compilation and linkage editor LIBRARY and INCLUDE statements to identify out of sync conditions   1 2 3 4 5

Thank you for your input. Your responses will be kept private.

Appendix I
Sample Architectural Design

1 INTRODUCTION

This section provides an introduction to the Dog E-DayCare system's architectural design.

1.1 Purpose

The purpose of this document is to provide a logical architectural view of the Dog E-DayCare system. This document will describe the system in terms of its conceptual organization, using the layers architectural pattern.

1.2 Scope

The Dog E-DayCare system will connect dog owners to dog care service providers by providing a Web-based forum to locate, purchase, and monitor dog care services. The Dog E-DayCare system will allow dog owners to search for dog care service providers within a location of their choice, based on their specific needs. Once a dog owner selects a service, the Dog E-DayCare system will permit the user to communicate with the selected dog care service provider, submit all required information, schedule, and pay for services. Depending upon the dog care service provider selected, dog owners will also be able to view their dogs online, receive an update of the dog's status, and participate in discussion forums and chat rooms dedicated to dog care.

The Dog E-DayCare system will support dog care service providers through two different forums: client software resident on the dog care service provider's workstations and through a Web-based forum. The system will notify dog care service providers of potential clients and permit them to communicate with dog owners and access information submitted by dog owners seeking a dog care service provider. In using the Dog E-DayCare system, dog care service providers will be able to coordinate scheduling of multiple clients, relay updates and messages, and bill their clients. In addition, in an effort to foster a greater sense of community, discussion forums and chat rooms will also be available for dog care service providers, to be used as a service for their clients.

The Dog E-DayCare system will maintain information about dog care service providers, dog owners, and their dogs. Information will be stored in a database accessible to dog care service providers and dog owners. This access will be through a Web-based forum for the dog owners and a combination of client software and a Web-based forum for the dog care service providers.

2 OVERALL SYSTEM ARCHITECTURE

This section provides an overview of the Dog E-DayCare system's architectural design.

2.1 Description

The Dog E-DayCare application is composed of six layers containing various subsystems that interact with each other in order to accomplish the many functions involved within the system. The six layers are: presentation, application, domain, business infrastructure, technical services, and foundation.

- The presentation layer is responsible for representing the range of user interfaces required for the Dog E-DayCare system. Each package contains the classes responsible for displaying information through a browser and through a client workstation.
- The application layer can be described as the mediator between the presentation and domain layers. Its responsibility is to provide the session façade for each request coming from a specific user interface. The application layer "directs traffic" between the presentation and domain layers.
- The domain layer contains the packages and classes that implement domain-level services. The domain layer handles application layer requests and implements domain-level business rules.
- The business infrastructure layer contains a package and classes that implement business infrastructure-level services. Services include those that pertain to establishing a sense of community for Dog E-DayCare clients.
- The technical services layer includes the subsystems that provide high-level technical services and frameworks; it consists of the persistence, logging, rule engine, and SOAP subsystems. The persistence framework is a general-purpose, reusable, and extendable set of types that provides functionality to support persistent objects. The persistence subsystem provides the service to domain layer subsystems. The logging and tracing functionalities can be organized as the logging subsystem in the technical services layer, which provides these functions for the upper layers such as domain, presentation, and application layers. The rule engine subsystem provides a full capability to "reason" based on a provided set of knowledge in the form of declarative rules. This will provide the system with the potential capability of adding complex schedule rules and work flow management. The SOAP subsystem is a lightweight protocol for exchange of information in a decentralized, distributed environment. SOAP allows remote method invocation from subsystems deployed to client-to-server subsystems.
- The foundation layer includes subsystems and packages that provide low-level technical services, including a relational database, and string and math utilities. The relational database is required to provide the application with storage location for all pertinent data; this subsystem supports the persistent subsystem in the technical services layer. The String and math utilities subsystem provides the packages and functions that will support many of the upper layer subsystems.

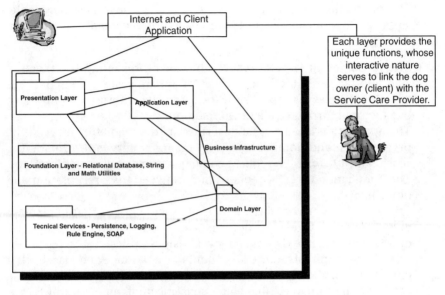

Exhibit I-1. Application

2.2 Major Subsystems

The diagram in Exhibit I-1 represents the layers and the subsystems involved in accomplishing the functions within the Dog E-DayCare application.

3 LAYERS

This section provides an in-depth understanding of the Dog E-DayCare system's architectural design from a layers perspective.

3.1 Presentation

The presentation layer will consist of several packages representing the range of user interfaces required for the Dog E-DayCare system. Each package would contain classes responsible for displaying information through a browser and through a client workstation. A brief description of each package in the presentation layer is provided below.

- *SearchUI* creates the screens that allow customers to search for service providers by type of service, location of service, cost of service, etc.
- *OrderUI* is responsible for the interfaces that allow users to select an order, place an order, revise an order, track an order, and cancel an order.

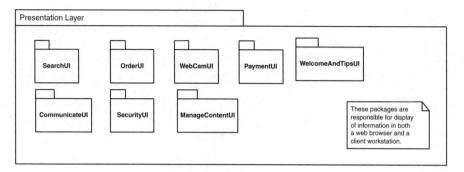

Exhibit I-2. Presentation Layer

- *WebCamUI* would create the interfaces necessary for selection and viewing of a customer's dog while in the care of a service provider.
- *PaymentUI* handles the interfaces necessary for service providers to request payment (i.e., bill), track payment, and confirm payment, as well as the interfaces necessary for customers to provide payment information, make a payment, and track status of payment.
- *WelcomeandTipsUI* handles display of text information to the user, e.g., welcome text, help screens, or tips of the day.
- *CommunicateUI* provides all the interfaces to receive feedback, hold a discussion, submit a rating, or participate in a chat.
- *SecurityUI* is responsible for the log-in, registration, and related administrator interfaces.
- *ManageContentUI* provides the interfaces for system administrators to manage text content.

The objects within the presentation layer would be developed based on the Javax Swing package using JFrame, JPanel, JLabel, and JButton, and will also employ HTML to display text (see Exhibit I-2).

3.2 Application

The application layer (Exhibit I-3) can be described as the mediator between the presentation and domain layers. The project team felt it was necessary to include an application layer because of the multiple user interfaces required for the Dog E-DayCare system. This layer contains packages that correspond to each of the presentation packages, providing the session façade for each request coming from a specific user interface. The application layer will be implemented using Enterprise Java Beans Object (see the section on application interactions for further details).

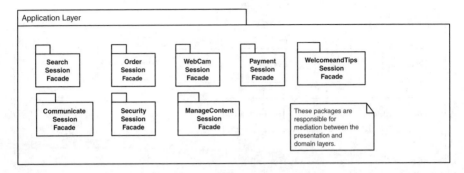

Exhibit I-3.   Application Layer

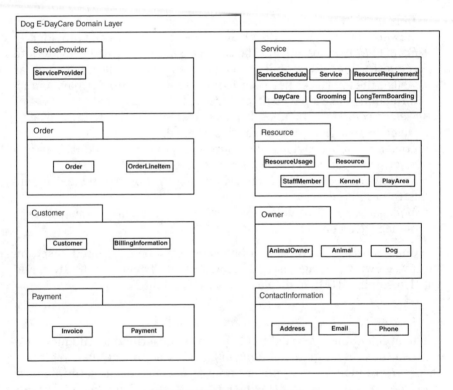

Exhibit I-4.   Domain Layer

3.3   Domain

The Dog E-DayCare domain layer diagram (Exhibit I-4) contains the packages and classes that implement domain-level services. Services include service provider, service, resource, order, customer, owner, payment, and contact information. Each of these subsystems was described in

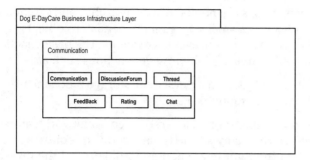

Exhibit I-5.   Infrastructure Layer

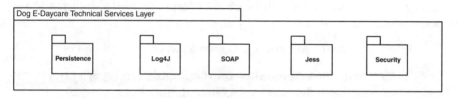

Exhibit I-6.   Technical Services Layer

detail in the software requirements specification. The domain layer handles application layer requests and implements domain-level business rules. Separating domain-level services from the other layers achieves a higher degree of cohesion, with a corresponding lower level of coupling.

3.4   Business Infrastructure

The Dog E-DayCare business infrastructure layer diagram (Exhibit I-5) contains a package and classes that implement business infrastructure level services. Services included are those that pertain to establishing a sense of community for Dog E-DayCare clients. Those community-oriented services are discussion forums, feedback, ratings, and chat. This subsystem was described in detail in the software requirements specification.

3.5   Technical Services

The technical services layer (Exhibit I-6) includes subsystems that provide high-level technical services and frameworks.

3.5.1   Persistence Subsystem

The Dog E-DayCare system requires string and retrieving information in a persistent storage mechanism such as a relational database. To lower coupling and promote high cohesion, the project team proposes a persistence framework in the technical services layer of architectural design.

585

The persistence framework is a general-purpose, reusable, and extendable set of types that provides functionality to support persistent objects. This subsystem provides service to domain layer subsystems. The basic functionality of the persistence subsystem should provide functions such as:

- Storing and retrieving objects in a persistent storage mechanism
- Commit and rollback transactions

Building an industrial-strength object persistence framework can consume man-years of effort; the many subtle issues involved require specialized expertise. Based on the tight implementation timeline of the project, the project team is in favor of using an open source or a commercial off-the-shelf package to achieve the functionality. Many of these packages are available. A final selection will be made later in the project timeline through an evaluation process. The following is a good resource for information on persistence frameworks:

http://www.ambysoft.com/persistenceLayer.html.

The persistence subsystem relies on the foundation layer subsystems, such as the relational database subsystem, to function.

3.5.2 Logging Subsystem

To improve the supportability of the Dog E-DayCare system, it is essential to develop logging and tracing functionality as a core component of the system. These functionalities can be organized as the logging subsystem in the technical services layer, which provides these functions for upper layers such as the domain, presentation, and application layers.

The project team has conducted a preliminary study and chosen to acquire the Log4J package from the Apache's Jakarta project to provide the functionality. The choice is based on the fact that the Log4j package is a Java open source system that can fully integrate with the system with the required functionality. Log4J also has a large user and developer community.

3.5.3 Rule Engine Subsystem

To provide enhanced supportability and extendibility for the scheduler subsystem, the project team is considering the inclusion of a rule engine subsystem to provide full capability to "reason" based on a provided set of knowledge in the form of declarative rules. This will provide the system with the potential capability of adding complex schedule rules and work flow management.

3.5.4 SOAP

To allow remote method invocation from subsystems deployed to client-to-server subsystems, the project team has chosen to use simple object access protocol (SOAP).

SOAP is a lightweight protocol for exchange of information in a decentralized, distributed environment. It is an XML-based protocol that consists of three parts: an envelope that defines a framework for describing what is in a message and how to process it, a set of encoding rules for expressing instances of application-defined data types, and a convention for representing remote procedure calls and responses. SOAP can be used in combination with a variety of protocols such as HTTP.

The advantage of SOAP is that it is based on industry standards like XML and HTTP. It is platform independent and can be used inside and across network boundaries such as a firewall.

3.5.5 Security

The security subsystem manages the users and roles of the system and controls access to the system by users.

3.6 Foundation

The Dog E-DayCare foundation layer (Exhibit I-7) includes subsystems and packages that provide low-level technical services. Those services include a relational database, and string and math utilities.

3.6.1 Relational Database

The project team has chosen to use a relational database as the persistent storage mechanism for storing the system information. The relational database subsystem supports the persistent subsystem in the technical services layer.

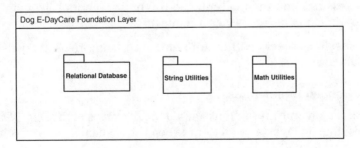

Exhibit I-7.   Foundation Layer

3.6.2 String and Math Utilities

String and math utilities will also be used in the system. They are packaged in string and math utilities subsystems that will support many of the upper layer subsystems.

4 INTERPACKAGE AND INTERLAYER COUPLING

This section provides an in-depth understanding of the Dog E-DayCare system's coupling among layers, packages, and classes.

4.1 Presentation Interactions

The packages in the presentation layer are highly coherent and have no explicit dependencies among them. (Within the packages, there would be dependencies among the various classes.) The most relevant interactions for the presentation layer are those with the application layer, with each presentation package having a counterpart session façade package in the application layer.

4.2 Application Interactions

The application layer has no significant interactions among its packages. Nevertheless, it has critical interactions with the presentation and the domain layers. As mentioned above, the application layer's primary function is to direct traffic between these layers.

The presentation layer may ask the domain layer for information. The request is received at the application layer and the corresponding session façade is invoked. This session, in turn, takes the request to the domain layer, where the information is processed and retrieved. The domain layer then sends the information back to the presentation layer via the application layer's session façade. Each session is an integral part of the overall system architecture. The session bean is accessed by a single client at a time (a session) and then is removed by the server. Its "life span" is the length of time it takes to service a request.

The session objects will be implemented using the Enterprise Java Beans Object.

4.3 Domain Interactions

There are several interactions among the packages of the Dog E-DayCare system's domain layer, as well as between the domain layer and other layers in the system.

Within the domain layer, the service provider package is coupled to the service package and the contact information package. The service package

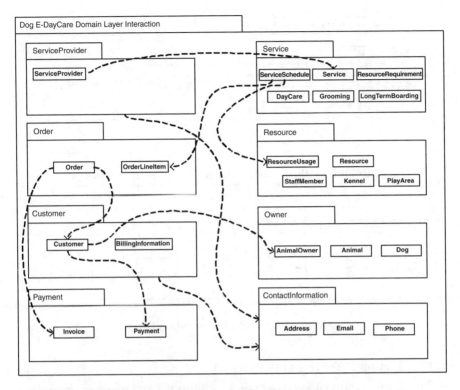

Exhibit I-8.   Domain Layer Interactions

is coupled to the order and resource packages. In turn, order is coupled to customer and payment classes. Finally, customer is coupled to the owner, payment, and contact information packages.

The domain layer also interacts across the Dog E-DayCare system architecture. The domain layer's service provider and customer packages are coupled to the business infrastructure layer's communication package. They are also coupled to the technical services layer's security package. These interlayer interactions are diagrammed in Exhibit I-8.

4.4   Business Infrastructure Interactions

Within the business infrastructure layer's communication package, the communication class interacts with the feedback, rating, chat, and discussion forum classes. The latter in turn depends on the thread class. With respect to the preceding description of the domain layer, the business infrastructure layer interacts with the domain layer. It also interacts with the foundation layer (see Exhibit I-9).

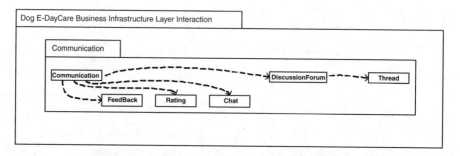

Exhibit I-9. Business Infrastructure Layer Interaction

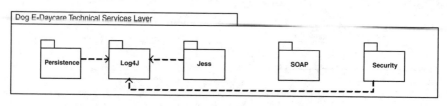

Exhibit I-10. Technical Services Layer

4.5 Technical Services Interactions

Within the technical services layer (Exhibit I-10), the persistence, Jess, and security subsystems depend on Log4J subsystem to log information.

4.6 Foundation Interactions

Subsystems inside the foundation layer no significant interactions. Nevertheless, there are interactions between the foundation layer and the technical services layer.

4.7 Summary

Many of the interlayer interactions have been described earlier; however, the following provides an overall summary along with a diagram that illustrates the interactions:

- The presentation layer is coupled with the application layer in that the application layer maintains session information. For each functional area, a session façade package in the application layer is coupled with the corresponding package in the presentation layer.
- The application layer packages are coupled with the corresponding packages in the domain layer as they use the operations in the domain layer to execute the system functions.

- In the domain layer, ServiceProvider and customer packages are coupled with the communication package in the business infrastructure layer. The ServiceProvider and customer packages are also coupled with the security subsystem in the technical services layer. The service package is also coupled with the Jess subsystem to obtain support for rule-based processing. In general, the packages in the domain layer are coupled with the persistence and logging subsystems. They also rely on the SOAP package to pass remote function invocations.
- The technical services layer's persistence subsystem is coupled with the relational database subsystem in the foundation layer. The string and math utilities packages are coupled with any package in the system that uses their functions.

Exhibit I-11 shows the interlayer coupling of the subsystems to different system layers.

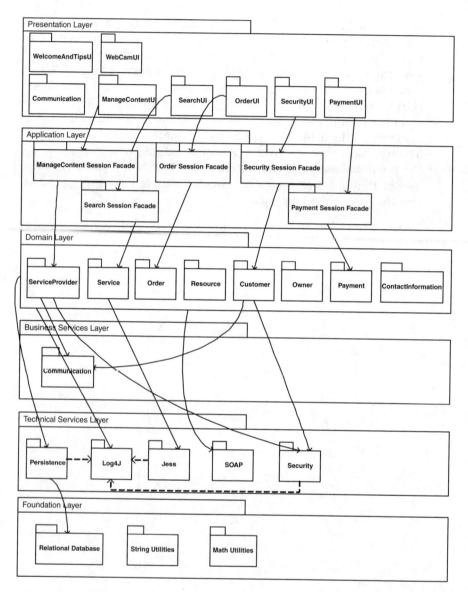

Exhibit I-11. Interlayer Coupling of the Subsystems to Different System Layers

Appendix J
Sample SDS

TABLE OF CONTENTS

REVISIONS

Version	Primary Author(s)	Description of Version	Date Completed
First Draft		Initial draft to be submitted and reviewed for comments.	4/14/2002

1   INTRODUCTION

1.1   System Overview

The Online Resource Scheduling System is a Web-based scheduling system designed for colleges, universities, and schools. The purpose of this system is to provide an online service for the faculty to reserve any type of resource such as computer systems, VCRs, projectors, and videotapes. This scheduling system can accept the requestors' orders, make a schedule for the orders, and do some critical checks. It will enable the faculty to be able to submit their orders at any time and from any place. The system will be able to create new orders and update old orders.

1.2   Purpose

The purpose of this software requirement specification is to produce a Web-based (online) scheduling system that will be used at colleges, universities, and schools. The faculty will be able to reserve equipment, classrooms, films, and other peripherals to be used during their classes. The staff of the resource center will be able to monitor these resources and to see what equipment is needed, by whom, at what time, and for what date. The resources will be maintained in a database created by ORSS that will be an easy method to keep track of the equipment. By testing these specifications as we progress through the design stage, we will be able to find errors and misjudgments as they occur instead of at the end of the project. This will save time in the long run; because mistakes are identified and corrected earlier, project development will not be delayed.

1.3 Document Overview

This document describes the proposed online registration system and the system requirements necessary to make the registration system effective. The second section describes design considerations, assumptions and dependencies, drivers and constraints, design methodology, and risks. The third section describes the different architecture styles and how they are incorporated into our design of the online resource scheduling system. The fourth section describes the high-level design, including DFD level 1 and 12 different processes. The fifth section describes the low-level design, including the procedures and details. We have included the structured English description of the different processes here, as well as the data dictionary. The last section is an appendix that describes use cases and includes the user interface screens.

1.4 Supporting Material

Roger Pressman, *Software Engineering, "A Practitioner's Approach"* — 5th edition, McGraw-Hill, January 2001.

"Handbook of Software Engineering Productivity," editor Jessica Keyes, McGraw-Hill, 1993

http://www.laynetworks.com/users/webs/cs10.htm

http://www.mhhe.com/engcs/compsci/pressman/student_index.mhtml

http://www.newarttech.com/se

http://www.uburst.com/uReserve

1.5 Definitions and Acronyms

- *Campus user interface* —the sign-on page allowing the faculty to connect to the system
- *IIS* — Internet information server
- *JSP* — Java server page
- *Materials* — a table in the resource database that is an in-house catalog of all available films and videos by type and format
- *ORSS* — online resource scheduling system, which is a Web-based scheduling system providing an online service for faculty to reserve any type of resource
- *SSL* — secure socket layer

2 DESIGN CONSIDERATIONS

2.1 Assumptions and Dependencies

2.1.0 Frequency of Use

ORSS is designed for continuous 24 hours a day, 7 days a week operation. This demands a high-availability architecture, which often requires a back-up server that needs to be in sync with the primary server. Clustering can also be used to supply high availability.

2.1.1 Database Requirement

- A faculty directory service is available now and will continue to be available to integrate directly with ORSS.
- A resource database is not available now and needs to be created and maintained by the database administrator of ORSS.

2.1.2 Track Resources

It is always assumed that the user will check out and return the reserved resource as scheduled. Currently no automatic mechanism traces the status of the resource. Either the administrator manually logs the activity or a future enhancement is added when a scanner and bar code system can automate this data entry effort.

2.1.3 User

The ORSS is designed for colleges, universities, and schools. Most of the users of this system are faculty. The user interface is designed so that the users can access the system more easily. For the basic education of users, they should have the knowledge to operate the computer, such as entering the system online, turning the system on, inputting data such as password, and information about the resource needed. This knowledge will require a minimum education level of middle school or higher. Moreover, faculty members should have the ability to use the Internet. Because most of the users of the system are the faculty of the school, they should have this knowledge (and a higher education level). The users do not need to have more than a basic technical knowledge. A help menu will include a detailed help list; this menu will help a user who does not understand when using and accessing the process.

2.2 Drivers and Constraints

2.2.0 Memory Constraints

Because we need to run I.E. or Netscape on the Windows operating system, the client's computer must have at least 64 MB of memory. The server must have at least 128 MB of memory because it will need to do a lot of data processing.

2.2.1 Regulatory Policies

The data will be transmitted over the Internet and needs to allow online processing.

2.2.2 Hardware Limitations

The memory for the client site computer will be limited to at least 64 MB of memory because the user needs to access our Website by using a Web browser that must run on a Windows platform. The memory for the server needs to be at least 128 MB. The bandwidth should be at least 512 Kbps because many users could possibly access the server at the same time. The hard drive for our server must have at least 8 GB of space in order to store a lot of data (i.e., the databases).

2.2.3 Interfaces to Other Applications

The online resource scheduling system will be Windows based so that all of the systems work with each other; therefore, the system must be Windows compliant. The ORSS will be a Web-based system. We use ADO as an interface with the MS Access databases.

2.2.4 High Order Language Requirements

ORSS uses a client/server architecture that makes use of the JavaScript, HTML, and ASP.

2.2.5 Reliability Requirements

ORSS will have a UPS installed so that, if the power is lost, the system will continue to operate as normal and no information will be lost.

2.2.6 Criticality of the Application

The server must run 24 hours a day, 7 days a week. The system will need to perform some checks so that the users do not make conflicting requests or complete the orders incorrectly. Moreover, a clustering technology is needed to make sure that the server is always running.

2.2.7 Security Constraints

Security is the most important issue in our system. To avoid hackers invading our system, we need to set up a firewall and apply a security patch. This product will be uploaded to a server exposed to the outside world, so we need to research and develop adequate security protection. We will need to know how to configure a firewall and how to restrict access to only "authorized users." We will need to know how to deal with load balance if the amount of visits to the site is very large at one time.

2.2.8 Databases

We will need to know how to maintain the different databases in order to make them more efficient, and the appropriate type of database that we should use. We will also have a link to the faculty database to verify the users.

2.3 System Environment

The ORSS has three interfaces: user, software, and communications interfaces.

- The user interface allows the user to interact with the system, providing Web pages that will display information. It also provides the different forms for users to use to input their requests.
- The software interface comprise ORSS and the operating system, the IIS, and the databases.
- The communications interface allows users to utilize campus networks or their ISP from home in order to use the system through the Internet.

2.3.0 User Interfaces

ORSS allows the user to make requests through a Website. The user interface will be composed of several Web pages that will be displayed on the user's Web browser. There should be two different versions of the user interface: one for the faculty and one for the resource center staff. Each of them will include many pages that have different purposes.

Campus version:

- Campus log-on
- Make request
- Update request
- Search resource
- Confirmation

The user gains access to the ORSS by entering user name and a unique numeric password. Once the user has correctly entered name and password into ORSS, he will be able to make requests, update old requests, and search all of the resources from the resource database. Clicking the items in the user menu can activate each of these functions.

The Request Form page allows the user to select the equipment and materials needed for reservations. Users can select equipment by clicking the dropdown list and checking the boxes that contain all of the equipment types. There is a total of five kinds of equipment (audio, video, digital, projection, and PCs) to use during presentations; each category consists of several pieces of equipment. The user should be able to select the equipment by checking the check box beside the type of equipment. Also, the user will be able to select the quantity needed.

In the Request Form, the user will be able to enter material numbers and titles for requests in one of two ways. One is to let the system automatically fill out the textboxes after the user selects specific items in the Search Material page. Another way is for the users to fill out the material numbers and titles (if they know them). Users need to fill out their general information before they submit requests. The general information includes name, department, phone number, etc.

The Search Material page helps users to find out the material numbers and titles that they want by using some keywords. The page must be able to pass the result to the Request Form after the user clicks the "select" button. The Confirmation page needs to display all of the information about that specific request, and needs to have a "print" button that will allow users to print out their confirmations. The Search Resource page will allow users to do two types of searching. One is to search the materials and the other one is to search for the equipment. Users who want to search the materials can enter the material number or the material title to make a query. When the users want to search the equipment, they can enter the equipment name or the equipment type to make a query.

Resource Center Version:

- Resource center staff log on
- Request form
- Search request
- Update request
- Search resource
- Add new resource
- Update resource
- Display daily list

The resource center system has the same functions as the campus version plus additional functions to be used only by the employees who work in resource center.

The Display Request page provides an interface for the user to make a daily report of requests for a specific date. The Search Request form will allow users to search a specific request by entering the confirmation number of that request or any information on the request, such as user name, extension number, date required, or room number. The system must allow users to update requests (modify or cancel requests). This function will be implemented by the Update Request form. The Search Resource form allows the users to search for a specific resource by entering the resource name, resource number or resource type. The resource center user will be able to add new resources or update the resources. This function will be implemented by the Update Resource form.

2.3.1 Software Interfaces

Client site:

- The ORSS will run on any Windows operating system with a browser on the client's computer.

Server site:

- The server side needs to run on the Windows NT operating system or Windows 2000 professional operating system that has the IIS. The Windows 2000 server can also be used to run this program.
- The operating system also needs Microsoft Access to use for the databases.
- The software will be designed and coded in ASP, JavaScript, and HTML.

2.3.2 Communications Interfaces

The users can access campus networks or their ISP from their homes in order to use the system through the Internet.

2.4 Processes, Policies, Conventions, and Tactics

Not applicable.

2.5 Design Methodology

Global Associates used a traditional structured approach in designing the ORSS. We used the linear sequential model, which begins at the system level and progresses through analysis, design, coding, testing, and support.

2.6 Risks and Volatile Areas

2.6.0 Performance Risks

The system needs to ensure that the following cross checks are in place in order to function adequately:

- The user cannot make a request for weekends.
- Notice of 24 hours is required for reservations.
- The system must not allow a user to reserve the same materials at the same time.
- The system must not allow a user to use the same equipment in the same room at the same time.

2.6.1 Technology Risks

The following enhancements need to be implemented to ensure that the product retains its competitive edge:

- Confirmation messages (e-mail) need to be sent to the user reserving the resource.
- Some type of alert needs to be sent to a user when a resource is overdue or a reserved resource becomes unavailable for some reason.
- Tracking of the equipment by order and faculty is very important.
- A bar code and scanner system needs to be implemented to log the check-out and check-in activities of the resources. This way the system will have real time information about the resource's availability.
- The user needs to be held accountable for violating certain rules, like reserving a certain item without actually using it, returning an item late, damaging the item, etc. The penalty may include a fine, or temporary or permanent suspension of certain privileges.
- We need to add equipment repair information and a possible database for these records.
- Automated monthly reports by equipment usage and room usage are necessary.

3 ARCHITECTURE

3.1 Overview

This section will analyze architectural styles and how they are incorporated into our design of the online resource scheduling system.

Data-centered architectures access a data store, which is a file or a database, as the center of their operation. This data store is also accessed by other components that may modify the data in the data store — adding, deleting, or updating any information contained in the data store. The ORSS design has the Material data store (D3), the Equipment data store (D4), and the Resource_Schedule data store (D5) that may be accessed by other components and updated. The Equipment and Material data stores may only be modified (adding or deleting inventory) by the resource center staff; the Resource_Schedule data store is actively modified as each reservation is made or updated. The latter database also sends out confirmations pertaining to the reservations made. This system also relies on the Faculty and the Resource_Staff data stores, which are passive. These are used to compare log-in names and passwords to authorize access. Each client can access the data and act independently of other clients.

Data-flow architecture style is used when input data is transformed into output data. A set of components ("filters") is connected by "pipes" that transmit data from one component to the next. Each filter works independently of the components before or after it. The ORSS DFD level 1 reflects how each filter (bubble in DFD) has several pipes remitting information from one filter to another. If the data flow collapses into a single line of pipes and filters, it is called a *batch sequential* pattern.

Call and return architectures incorporate *main program/subprogram architectures* or *remote procedure call architectures.* The former uses a "control hierarchy" in which a main program calls upon a number of program components (functions), which in turn may call upon other components. The latter style has the components of the former architectural style distributed across many computers on a network. This style makes it relatively easy for a software designer to modify, but it does not lend itself to the ORSS system design.

Object-oriented architectures use the techniques of object-oriented programming. The components of a system use the encapsulation principle in which the data about the object and the operations that must be used to manipulate the data are "packaged" together. Communication between components is by way of message passing. This architectural method is very good for reusability.

Layered architectures use a number of different layers, each of which is defined. At the outer layer, the components service user interface operations. At the inner layer, components perform operating system interfacing. Intermediate layer components include application software functions and provide utility services. This is not applicable to our system.

3.2   Subsystem, Component, or Module 1...n

Not applicable.

3.2.0   Sub Element 1...n.

Not applicable.

3.3   Strategies

Not applicable.

3.3.0   Strategy 1...n.

Not applicable.

4   HIGH-LEVEL DESIGN

4.1   ORSS: DFD Level 1: see Exhibit J-1.

List of procedures:

- Campus user interface
  — Campus_Login (Process # 1)
  — Campus_Menu (Process # 3)
- Resource center user interface

ORSS: DFD Level 1

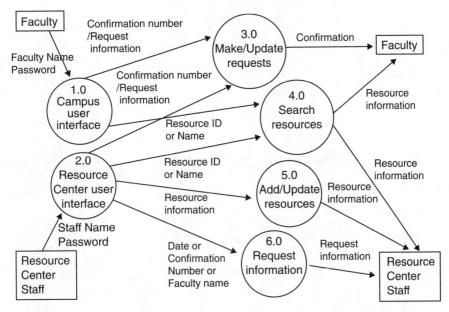

Exhibit J-1. ORSS: DFD Level 1

- — ResourceCenter_Login (Process # 2)
- — ResourceCenter_Menu (Process # 4)
- • Make/update requests
  - — Make_Request (Process # 5)
    - • Check_Request (Process # 6)
    - • Save_Request (Process # 7)
    - • Display_Confirmation (Process # 8)
  - — Update_Request (Process # 9)
    - • Check_Request (Process # 6)
    - • Save_Request (Process # 7)
    - • Display_Confirmation (Process # 8)
- • Request information
  - — Search_Request (Process # 10)
- • Search resource
  - — Search_Resource (Process # 11)
- • Add/update resource
  - — Add_Resource (Process # 12)
  - — Update_Resource (Process # 13)

4.2 Procedures

Process # 1
Campus_Login

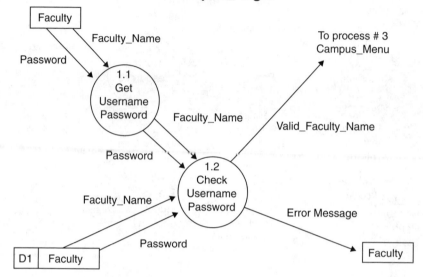

Exhibit J-2. Process 1: Campus Login

Process # 2
Resource Center_Login

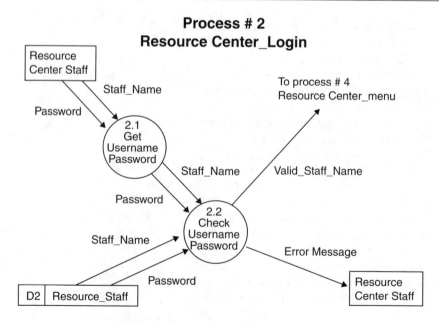

Exhibit J-3. Process 2: Resource Center Login

Process # 3
Campus_Menu

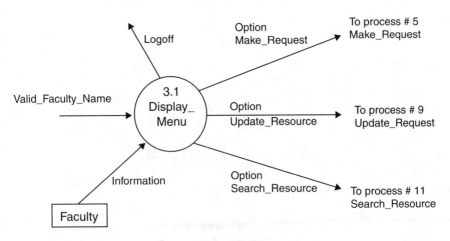

Exhibit J-4.   Process 3: Campus Menu

Process # 4
ResourceCenter_Menu

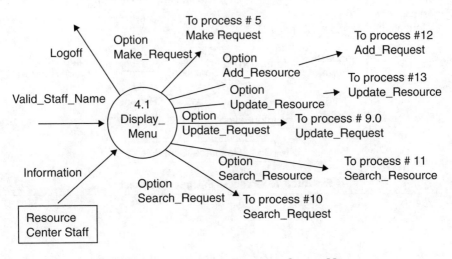

Exhibit J-5.   Process 4: Resource Center Menu

Process # 5
Make_Request

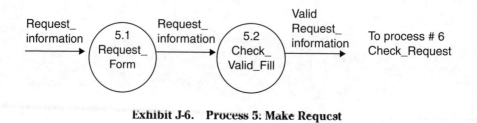

Exhibit J-6.   Process 5: Make Request

Process # 6
Check_Request

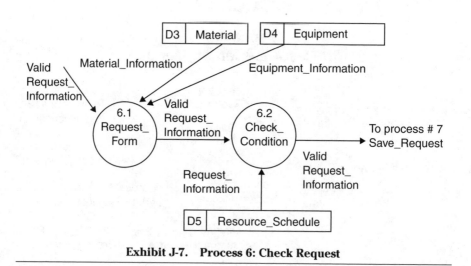

Exhibit J-7.   Process 6: Check Request

Process # 7
Save_Request

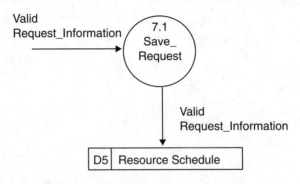

Exhibit J-8. Process 7: Save Request

Process # 8
Save_Confirmation

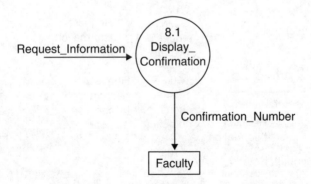

Exhibit J-9. Process 8: Display Confirmation

Process # 9
Update_Request

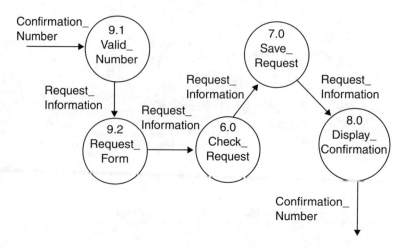

Exhibit J-10.   Process 9: Update Request

Process # 10
Search_Request

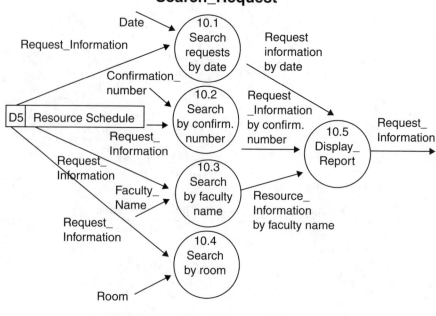

Exhibit J-11.   Process 10: Search Request

Process # 11
Search_Resource

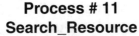
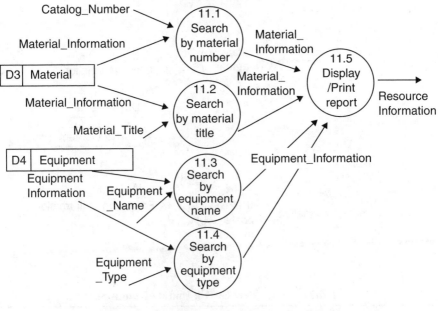

Exhibit J-12.   Process 11: Search Resource

Process # 12
Add_Resource

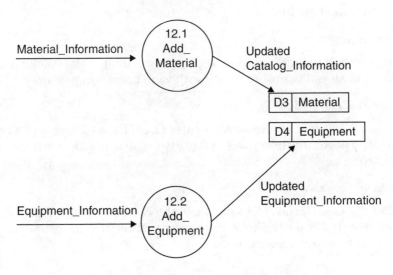

Exhibit J-13.   Process 12: Add Resource

Process # 13
Update_Resource

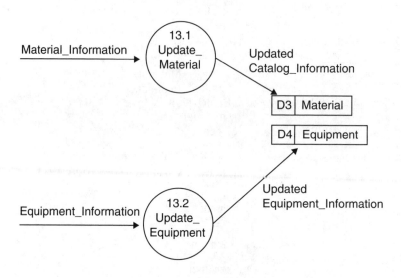

Exhibit J-14.   Process 13: Update Resource

5   LOW-LEVEL DESIGN

5.1   Procedures and Details

The following are the procedures and their details.

Campus_Login

Program will redirect Campus Login page to Campus Main Menu page if the user name and password match with valid name and password.

ResourceCenter_Login

Program will redirect Resource Center Login page to Resource Center Main Menu page if the user name and password match with valid name and password.

Campus_Menu

After the user (faculty) logs on ORSS, the campus menu will display on the screen. It allows the user to make decisions to make/update the request or to search resources.

Resource Center_Menu

After the user (staff) logs on ORSS, the resource center menu will display on the screen. It will open other Web pages when the user makes his selection.

Make_Request

This allows the user to make a new request. When he selects "make a new request," a blank request form will display on the screen. The procedure will check some information after the user submits the request.

Check_Request

The process will compare the new request with the requests in the database asking for equipment or materials at the same time. The purpose of this procedure is to make sure that no conflict between a new request and existing requests occurs.

Save_Request

Save request to database if the new request is acceptable.

Display_Confirmation

Display a confirmation page to the user. This page will include all of the information about the reservation that the user just requested.

Update_Request

Allow user to enter request number. Retrieve the requested information from the database. After the user modifies the reservation, the form is checked and if everything is ok, then it is saved.

Search_Requests

Procedure will search requests in the database and display all that match the conditions.

Search_Resources

Procedure will search the resources in the database and display all that match the conditions.

Add_Resource

This will allow resource center staff to add new resources to the database.

Update_Resource

This allows resource center staff to update resource information or delete resources from the database.

5.2 Processes and Details

Process #1

- Name: (Campus_Login)
- Number: 1
- **Name**: Campus_Login
- **Description**: The faculty member will log in to ORSS with the user-name and password through this process. Once he enters his name and password, the system will check whether or not the name and password are valid. If valid, the system will allow the user to make the reservation.
- **Input data**: Faculty member's name and password from log-in form
- **Output data**: Valid faculty member's name to the cookie; error messages
- **Type of process**: Manual check
- Process logic:

```
Begin
    Display S1: (Campus Login Screen)
    Accept user name and password from Campus Login Screen.
    Check if the user name or the password is empty.
    If Username or password is empty, display a
        message:"Sorry, please complete form." Give a link
        to go back to the CampusLogin.htm page.
    Else
        Execute SQL for checking whether username and password
            is in "Faculty" database.
        If Username exists, check if the password is correct.
        If password does not match the user, then display a
            message: "Sorry, Your password is incorrect." Give
            a link to go back to the CampusLogin.htm page.
        Else
            Create Cookie for this user.
            Display S2: (Campus Menu).
        End if
        Else
            Display a message:" No such user. Please try again."
                Give a link to go back to the Campus Login
                Screen.
        End if
    End if
End Procedure
```

Process #2

- Name: (ResourceCenter_Login)
- Number: 2
- **Name**: ResourceCenter_Login
- **Description**: Resource center staff member will log in to ORSS with the username and password through this process. Once name and password are entered, the system will check whether or not they are valid. If valid, then the system will allow the user to make the reservation.
- **Input data**: Resource center staff member's name and password from login form
- **Output data**: Resource center staff member's name to the cookie; error messages
- **Type of process**: Manual check
- Process logic:

```
Begin
    Display S3: (Resource Center Login Screen)
    Accept user name and password from login form
    Check if the user name or the password is empty.
    If Username or password is empty, display a
        message:"Sorry, please complete form," Give a link
        to go back to the ResourceCenterlogin.htm page.
    Else
        Execute SQL for checking whether username and password
            is in "ResourceCenter_Login" database.
        If Username exists, check if the password is correct.
            If password does not match, display a
                message:"Sorry, Your password is incorrect,"
                Give a link to go back to the
                ResourceCenterlogin.htm page.
            Else
                Create Cookie for this user.
                Display S4: (Resource Center Menu).
            End if
        Else
            Display a message:"No such user. Please try again."
                Give a link to go back to the Resource Center
                Login Screen.
        End if
    End if
End Procedure
```

Process #3

- Name: (Campus_Menu)
- Number: 3
- **Name**: Campus_Menu
- **Description**: Campus_Menu process will display a menu on the screen. It allows the user to be able to make a new request, update an existing request, and search for resources by clicking items in the menu.
- **Input data**: Faculty member's name as the cookie
- **Output data**: Option: make request, update request, search resources
- Type of process:
- Process logic:

```
Begin
    If Cookie is empty then
        Display S1: (Campus Login Screen)
    Else
        Display S2: (Campus Menu Screen)
        1. Make New Request
        2. Update Request
        3. Search Resources
        4. Log Off
        If user selected "Make New Request" Then
            Display S5: (New Request Screen)
        End if
        If user selected "Update Request" Then
            Display S6: (Update Request Screen)
        End if
        If user selected "Search Resources" then
            Display S7: (Search Resources Screen)
        End if
        If user selected "Log off" then
            Delete Cookie
            Display S1: (Campus Login Screen)
        End If
    End If
End Procedure
```

Process #4

- Name: (ResourceCenter_Menu)
- Number: 4
- **Name**: ResourceCenter_Menu
- **Description**: ResourceCenter_Menu process will display a menu on the screen. It allows the user to be able to make new requests, update

requests, search for requests, add resources, update resources, and search resources by clicking items in the menu.
- **Input data**: Staff's name as the cookie
- **Output data**: Option: make request, update request, display request, add new resource, update resource, search resource
- Type of process:
- Process logic:

```
Begin
    If Cookie is empty then
        Display S3: (Resource Center Login Screen)
    Else
        Display S4: (Resource Center Menu Screen)
        1. Make New Request
        2. Update Request
        3. Search Requests
        4. Add Resource
        5. Update Resource
        6. Search Resources
        7. Log Off
        If user selected "Make New Request" Then
            Display S5: (New Request Screen)
        End if
        If user selected "Update Request" Then
            Display S6: (Update Request Screen)
        End if
        If user selected "Display Request" Then
            Display S8: (Display Request Screen)
        End if
        If user selected "Add New Resource" Then
            Display S9: (New Resource Screen)
        End if
        If user selected "Update Resource" Then
            Display S10: (Update Resource Screen)
        End if
        If user selected "Search Resources" Then
            Display S7: (Search Resources Screen)
        End if
        If user selected "Log off" Then
            Delete Cookie
            Display S1: (Campus Login Screen)
        End If
    End If
End Procedure
```

Process #5

- Name: (Make_Request)
- Number: 5
- **Name**: Make_Request
- **Description**: Make_Request process will allow the user to make a new request. When the user selects "make a new request," a blank request form will display on the screen. The user will be asked to complete all of the required information on that form before he submits it. If he forgets to fill out any required information, an error message will be displayed on the screen until all of the required information has been filled out.
- **Input data**: Option to make a new request
- **Output data**: All of the information about the new request
- Type of process:
- Process logic:

```
Begin
    If Cookie is empty then
    Display S3: (Resource Center Login Screen)
    Else
       Display S5: (New Request Screen)
       If user submits request form then
          Check if user finished all of the required textboxes.
          If the user name is empty, then
            Display a message: "Please enter your name."
          End if
          If the required date is empty then
            Display a message: "Please enter the required
                 date."
          End if
          If the required time is empty then
            Display a message: "Please enter the required
                 time."
          End if
          If required room is empty then
            Display a message: "Please enter the required
                 room."
          End if
          Call Check_Request Procedure
       End if
    End if
End Procedure
```

Process #6

- Name: (Check_Request)
- Number: 6
- **Name:** Check_Request
- **Description**: Check_Request process will compare the new request with existing requests in the database that have asked for equipment or materials at the same time. If there is a conflict, then the procedure will display the error message on the screen. The user can cancel the order or go back to the previous page to change his request.
- **Input data**: All of the information about a request that has not been checked
- **Output data**: All of the information about the request that has been checked
- Type of process: Manual check
- Process logic:

```
Begin
    Redirect Check.asp page.
    Check if the required date and required time are valid or
        not.
    If required date < today then
      Display a message: "Please check your required date."
    End if
    If required day = Saturday or Sunday then
      Display a message: "Cannot deliver on Weekend."
    End if
    If required time > 5:00PM or < 8:00AM then
      Display a message: "Cannot deliver at non-office hour
        time."
    End if
    If request form does not reserve any resource then
      Display a message: "Please select at least one piece of
        equipment or material."
      Give a link to go back to the request form page.
    End if
    Do cross check in order to avoid conflict.
    Execute SQL that will read database "Request" Where
        date_required = Date_Required, and time_required =
        Time_Required.
    Do while not rs.eof
      If resource has been reserved then
        Display error message: "Resource has been reserved."
        Give a link to go back to the request form page.
      End if
      If the room has been reserved then
```

```
        Display error message: "Room has been reserved for
            another class."
        Give a link to go back to the request form page.
    End if
Loop
If everything is ok then call Save_Request Procedure
End Procedure
```

Process #7

- Name: (Save_Request)
- Number: 7
- **Name:** Save_Request
- **Description**: Save_Request process will save request into request database.
- **Input data**: All of the information about a request that has been checked
- **Output data**: All of the information about the request that has been checked (include a confirmation number)
- Type of process:
- Process logic:

```
Begin
    Redirect Save.asp page.
    Generate a confirmation Number.
    Execute SQL that will open "Request" database.
    Add new request to the database.
    Update Request Database
    Close Database
    Call Display_Confirmation Procedure.
End Procedure
```

Process #8

- Name: (Display_Confirmation)
- Number: 8
- **Name:** Display_Confirmation
- **Description**: Display_Confirmation process will display on the screen all of the information that the user just entered. This information should contain a confirmation_Number generated by our system after the check_request procedure accepts all of the information from the user. This page will provide a print button so that the user may print a hard copy of the confirmation page. Also, the procedure will automatically send a confirmation e-mail to the user.
- **Input data**: All of the information about a request that has not yet been checked

- **Output data**: All of the information about the request that has been checked
- Type of process:
- Process logic:

```
Begin
    Display S11: (Confirmation Screen)
    If user clicks print button, then
       Print out the confirmation page.
    End if
    Automatically send a confirmation email to the user.
End Procedure
```

Process #9

- Name: (Update_Request)
- Number: 9
- **Name:** Update_Request
- **Description**: Update_Request will allow the user to modify his/her request after he/she has submitted it. The procedure will ask the user to enter the request number (confirmation number) and retrieve this request from the database. The user can modify the request and resubmit it. After submitting the changed request, the procedure will check to verify that all of the required information has been completed.
- **Input data**: Option to update request; confirmation_Number of the request
- **Output data**: All of the information about the request from database
- Type of process:
- Process logic:

```
Begin
    Display S6: (Update Request Screen)
    Accept the confirmation number after submiting the
        request form.
    Execute SQL that will read database "Request" Where
        Confirmation_Number = ConfirmationNumber.
    If the Confirmation_Number does not exist, then
       Display an error message to the user.
    Else
       Read each field value of that specific request and fill
          out the corresponding textbox in update request
          form.
    End if
    After user modifies the request then
    Check if user completed all of the required textboxes.
    If the user name is empty, then
       Display a message: "Please enter your name."
```

```
      End if
      If the required date is empty then
         Display a message: "Please enter the required date."
      End if
      If the required time is empty then
         Display a message: "Please enter the time that is
               required."
      End if
      If required room is empty then
         Display a message: "Please enter the room that is
               required."
      End if
      Call Check_Request Procedure
      Call Save_Request Procedure
      Call Display_Confirmation Procedure
   End Procedure
```

Process #10

- Name: (Search_Request)
- Number: 10
- **Name:** Search_Request
- **Description**: The Search_Request procedure will retrieve all requests that match the conditions that the user entered. The user can search requests four different ways. If the user selects to search a single request by entering its confirmation_number, then the procedure will retrieve that request from the database and display all information about that request on the screen. If the user selects to search requests that match a specific room, specific name, or specific required date, then the procedure will retrieve all of the requests from the database that match the condition and display the list on the screen.
- **Input data**: Option to search request; Confirmation_Number, Date_Required, Faculty_Name, Room
- **Output data**: All of the information about the requests
- Type of process:
- Process logic:

```
   Begin
      Display S8: (Display Request Screen)
         List an Option List that allows users to make their
               decision if they want to search request by date,
               by faculty name or by confirmation number.
      Accept condition after user submits form.
      If Option = faculty_name then
         Execute SQL that will open "Request" database where
               User_Name = UserName.
         Do while not rs.eof
```

```
            Display each request one line by one line on the
                  Screen.
         Loop
         Close rs, Close database.
      End if
      If Option = Confirmation_Number then
      Execute SQL that will open "Request" database where
            Confirmation_Number = ConfirmationNumber.
      Display all of the information about that specific
            request on the screen.
         Close rs, Close database.
      End if
      If Option = Date_Required then
      Execute SQL that will open "Request" database where
            Date_Required = DateRequired.
         Do while not rs.eof
            Display each request one line by one line on the
                  Screen.
         Loop
         Close rs, Close database.
         If user clicks "print" button on the screen then
            Print all of the requests of that specific date.
         End if
      End if
      If Option = Room then
      Execute SQL that will open "Request" database where Room
            = Room.
         Do while not rs.eof
            Display each request one line by one line on the
                  Screen.
         Loop
         Close rs, Close database.
         If user clicks "print" button on the screen then
            Print all of the requests of that specific date.
         End if
      End if
   End Procedure
```

Process #11

- Name: (Search_Resource)
- Number: 11
- **Name:** Search_Resource
- **Description**: Search_Resource procedure will retrieve all of the resources that match the conditions that the user requested. The user can search two types of resources: Materials and Equipment. In order

to search the materials, he must obtain the Material_Number or the Title of the material. If the user wants to search the equipment, he must obtain the type of equipment or the name of the equipment. Our procedure will search the resources in the database and display the information on the screen.

- **Input data**: Option to search resource; Material_Number, Title, Equipment_Name, Equipment_Type
- **Output data**: All of the information about the resources
- Type of process:
- Process logic:

```
Begin
    Display S7: (Search Resource Screen)
    This page will allow user to enter the condition of the
        resources that he wants to search.
    Accept search condition.
    If search type = Material then
      If search method = equal_to then
        Execute SQL that will open "Material" database where
            Material_Number = MaterialNumber or
            Material_Title = MaterialTitle
        Display briefly information on each Material that
            matches the condition on the screen line by
            line.
    End if
    If search method = like then
        Execute SQL that will open "Material" database where
            Material_Number like MaterialNumber or
            Material_Title like MaterialTitle
        Display briefly information on each Material that
            matches the condition on the screen line by
            line.
      End if
    End if
    If search type = Equipment then
      If search method = equal_to then
        Execute SQL that will open "Equipment" database
            where Equipment Number = Equipment Number or
            Equipment_Type = EquipmentType
        Display briefly information on the equipment that
            matches the condition on the screen line by
            line.
    End if
    If search method = like then
```

```
            Execute SQL that will open "Equipment" database
                where Equipment_Number like EquipmentNumber or
                Equipment_Type like EquipmentType
            Display briefly information on each piece of
                equipment that matches the condition on the
                screen line by line.
        End if
      End if
   End Procedure
```

Process #12

- Name: (Add_Resource)
- Number: 12
- **Name:** Add_Resource
- **Description**: Add_Resource procedure will allow user to add new resources into the database. It will check what kind of resource the user wants to add and provide the user with different forms to fill out. Also, the procedure will check whether or not all of the required information that the user has filled out is complete. If everything is acceptable, then the procedure will save that resource in the equipment database or the material database.
- **Input data**: The option to add a new resource
- **Output data**: All of the information about a new resource
- Type of process:
- Process logic:

```
   Begin
        Display S11: (Add Resource Screen)
        This screen will display an option list that allows user
            to make his decision to add equipment or material.
        If option = Material then
           Display S12: (New Material Screen)
           Accept resource form after user submits it.
           Check if the user has completed all of the required
               information about the material.
           If some required information is missing then
           Display a message: "Please complete the information."
           Redirect New Material Screen.
           End if
           Execute SQL that will open "Material" database.
           Add new resource to the database.
           Close database.
        End if
        If option = Equipment then
           Display S13: (New Equipment Screen)
           Accept resource information after user submits it.
```

```
            Check if the user has finished all of the required
                information about the equipment.
            If some required information is missing then
                Display a message: "Please complete the
                    information."
                    Redirect New Equipment Screen
            End if
            Execute SQL that will open "Equipment"
            Add new resource to the database.
            Close database.
        End if
    End procedure
```

Process #13

- Name: (Update_Resource)
- Number: 13
- **Name:** Update_Resource
- **Description**: The Update_Resource procedure will allow the user to update resources from the database. The user must tell the procedure what kind of resource he is going to update. If he chooses to update a material, then he must tell the procedure the material's number. If the user chooses to update the equipment, then he must tell the procedure the equipment's number or the equipment's name. The procedure will retrieve the resource from database and display the information. The user can modify it and then resubmit it.
- **Input data**: Option to update resource; Material_Number, Title, Equipment_Type, Equipment_Name
- **Output data**: All of the information about the resource that has been modified
- Type of process:
- Process logic:

```
Begin
    Display S10: (Update Resource Screen)
    Display an Option List on the screen that allows the user
        to make a decision if he wants to update the
        equipment or material.
    If option = Material then
    Execute SQL that will open "Material" database where
        Material_Number = MaterialNumber
        Display all of the information about that material.
        If user selects delete that material then
            Remove that material from database.
            Close database
        Else
            Accept resource form after user submits it.
```

624

```
            Check if the user has completed all the required
                information about the material.
            If some required information is missing then
               Display a message: "Please complete the
                   information."
               Redirect material information form.
            End if
            Execute SQL that will open "Material" database where
                Material_Number = Material_Number and Title =
                Title.
            Update resource to the database.
            Close database.
         End if
      End if
      If option = Equipment then
         Execute SQL that will open "Equipment" database where
             Equipment_Type = EquipmentType and Equipment_Name
             = EquipmentName
         Display all the information about that equipment.
         If user selects to delete the equipment then
            Remove that equipment from database.
            Close database
         Else
            Accept resource form after user submits it.
            Check if the user has completed all of the required
                information about the material.
            If some required information is missing then
               Display a message: "Please complete the
                   information."
               Redirect material information form.
            End if
            Execute SQL that will open "Equipment" database
                where Equipment_Type = Equipment_Type and
                Equipment_Name = Equipment_Name.
            Update resource to the database.
            Close database.
         End if
      End if
   End procedure
```

5.3 Data Dictionary Entries for ORSS

D1: Faculty
    Where used and how used:
    It will do the password checking when the user logs into the
    scheduling system.

Content description:
Faculty_Name = 20 characters (primary key)
     Password = 10 characters

D2: Resource_Staff
     Where used and how used:
     It will do the password checking when a resource center staff
        member logs into the scheduling system.
     Content description:
     Staff_Name = 20 characters (primary key)
        Password = 10 characters

D3: Material
     Where used and how used:
          It contains all of the information about the materials such
             as which type of tape: 1/2 in. VHS, 16 mm files, etc. The
             user can locate materials from this database with the
             searching interface.
          Content description:
               Material_Number = 20 characters (primary key)
               Title1 = 100 characters
               Title2 = 100 characters
               Format = 20 characters
               Color = Boolean operator
               Sound = 10 characters
               Length = 5 digits
               ReleaseDate = 4 characters
               Components = 2 digits
               Distributor = 20 characters
               Series_Title = 50 characters
               Language = 20 characters
               OrderDate = 10 characters
               Description memo
     Supplementary description:
     Format Possible Values: "audiocassette," "CD-Rom," "1/2 in.
        video," "media KIT," "16-mm film"
     Color Possible Values: "0," "–1"
     Sound Possible Values: "stereo," "mono"

D4: Equipment
     Where used and how used
     It contains all of the information about the equipment. The staff
        of the resource center may add, delete, or update equipment
        from this database.
     Content Description:

EquipmentID = 10 characters (primary key)
RegisterNumber = 30 characters
Equipment_Name = 30 characters
Equipment_Model = 20 characters
Manufacturer = 50 characters
OrderDate = 10 characters
Equipment_Type = 10 characters
Supplementary description:
EquipmentType values: projection, audio, digital, video

D5: Resource_Schedule
Where used and how used:
It contains all of the information about the reserved orders. When a new order has been made, the detailed information about this order will be saved in this database. The staff of the resource center can retrieve data from this database and print their daily delivery list. The faculty in the university can update orders that are saved in this database.
Content description:
Confirmation_Number = 10 characters (primary key)
Date_Required = 10 characters
Day_Required = 5 characters
Date_Pickup = 10 characters
From_Time = 5 characters
To_Time = 5 characters
Time_Type = 10 characters
FirstName = 20 characters
LastName = 20 characters
Department = 30 characters
Building = 20 characters
Room = 10 characters
HomePhone = 10 characters
University_Ext = 4 characters
E-Mail = 30 characters
UserType = 10 characters
Projection = 255 characters
Audio = 255 characters
Video = 255 characters
Digital = 255 characters
Other equipment = 255 characters
Materials = 255 characters
Supplementary description:
The values for all of the equipment could be numeric digits from 1 to 10.

The domain of FromTime and ToTime is the time the class is scheduled or the time the user wants the order delivered or reserved.

The values of DayRequired are: "Mon," "Tue," "Wed," "Thu," "Fri," "Sat," "Sun."

TimeType values: "regular," "summer," "regularother," "summerother."

The domain of Department is the list of departments in the university.

The value of Building is a list of buildings that are part of the university.

UserType values: "faculty," "staff."

The values of Digital could be: zipdrive, LCD.

The values of Video could be: laser, DVD, VHS.

The values of Audio could be: CD, cassette, public address system.

The values of Projection could be: screen, slide, opaque, overhead.

6 APPENDIX

6.1 Use Cases

Faculty initially log in through the system:

1. Faculty member enters his/her name and password; the name and password are compared with the name and password stored in the faculty database. If either the name or password is incorrect, the system will send an error message and the user is prompted to re-enter the name and password.
2. If the user name and the password match the name and password stored in the database, the system shows the main menu that consists of these choices: request form, update form, and search resource form.
3. For the request form, the system prompts the user to enter the data to request information.
4. The update request form has the system prompt the user to enter information such as the confirmation number or the data to request information.
5. For the search resource form, the system prompts the user to enter the material number, title, equipment name, or equipment type.

Resource center staff initially log in through the system:

1. Resource center staff member enters his or her staff name and password. The staff name and password are compared with the name and password stored in the resource_staff database. If either is incorrect, the system will send an error message and the staff member is prompted to re-enter the name and the password.
2. If the user name and password match the name and password stored in the database, the system shows the main processing menu that offers these choices: add resource form, update resource form, and request information form.

Make the request:

1. After the faculty or resource center staff member logs in to the system, they may make a request for equipment or materials. The system prompts the user to enter specific information to complete the request form.
2. The request information details will be compared to one or more of these databases: equipment, materials, and resource schedule.
3. If the information of this request is correct and available, the system will process the request and create a confirmation number and send the confirmation to the faculty member.
4. This information will be updated in the resource schedule table.

Update the request:

1. After the faculty or resource center staff member logs in to the system, they may update existing requests. The system prompts the user to enter the confirmation number.
2. If the confirmation number is a valid number, the system will display the current reservation information.
3. The user can update any information. The update request information will be updated in the resource schedule table.
4. The system will send an updated confirmation to the faculty member and keep the original confirmation number on the updated request.

Search resources:

1. The system prompts the user (a faculty or resource center staff member) with a menu to search resources. These options include allowing the user to search by material number, material title, equipment name, or equipment type.

2. To search by material number, the system prompts the user to enter the catalog number of the material. The number will be compared with the material number in the material database and the information on that material will be displayed.

3. To search by material title, the system prompts the user to enter the material title. The title will be compared with the titles in the material database and the information on that material will be displayed on the screen.

4. For a search by equipment name, the system prompts the user to enter the equipment name. The name will be compared with the names in the equipment database and the information on that equipment will be displayed on the screen.

5. For a search by equipment type, the system prompts the user to enter the type of equipment. The type will be compared with the type in the equipment database and the details about that equipment will be displayed.

6. The faculty and staff will be able to display and print the report of the results of the search.

Resource center staff member adds resource:

1. The system prompts the staff member to enter the material information (details about the new material) in order to add the new material information into the material database.

2. The system prompts the staff member to enter the equipment information (details about the new equipment) in order to add the new equipment information into the equipment database.

Resource center staff member updates resource:

1. The system prompts the staff member to enter or change the material information in order to update the material database.

2. The system prompts the staff member to enter the equipment information in order to update the equipment database.

Search to request information:

1. The screen offers four options of a search to request information. The user can search the request information by date, by confirmation number, by faculty name, and by room number.

2. For search request information by date, the user enters the date the resources are requested for. This request date is compared to the data in the resource schedule table. The system will display all of the requests for that date. The user will need to select the correct request. The information for that request will be displayed on the screen and the user will be able to print this information.

3. For search request information by confirmation number, the user enters the confirmation number. This number is compared to the confirmation numbers in the resource schedule table. If the number that the user entered is a valid number, the system will display the information in the request on the screen. The user may then print the information.

4. For search request information by faculty name, the user enters the name of the faculty member that requested the resources. This request name is compared to the data in the resource schedule table. If more than one request is displayed for that faculty member, the user will need to select the appropriate request. The information for that request will be displayed on the screen and the user will be able to print the information.

5. To search request information by room number, the user enters the room number where the resources are requested. This room number is compared to the data in the resource schedule table. The system will display all of the requests for that room number. The user will need to select the correct request and the information for that request will be displayed on the screen. The user may print the information.

6.2 User Interface Screens

- Screen S1: Campus Login Screen (see Exhibit J-15)
- Screen S2: Campus Menu Screen (see Exhibit J-16)
- Screen S3: Resource Center Log-in Screen (see Exhibit J-17)
- Screen S4: Resource Center Menu Screen (see Exhibit J-18)
- Screen S5: New Request Screen (see Exhibit J-19)
- Screen S6: Update Request Screen (see Exhibit J-20)
- Screen S7: Search Resources Screen (see Exhibit J-21)
- Screen S8: Display Request Screen (see Exhibit J-22)
- Screen S9: New Resource Screen (see Exhibit J-23)
- Screen S10: Update Resource Screen (see Exhibit J-24)
- Screen S11: Confirmation Screen (see Exhibit J-25)
- Screen S12: New Material Screen (see Exhibit J-26)
- Screen S13: New Equipment Screen (see Exhibit J-27)

Supporting Material

Keyes, J., Ed., *Handbook of Software Engineering Productivity.* (1993). McGraw-Hill, New York.

Pressman, R. (2001). *Software Engineering, a Practitioner's Approach,* 5th ed., McGraw-Hill, New York.

http://www.laynetworks.com/users/webs/cs10.htm.

http://www.mhhe.com/engcs/compsci/pressman/student_index.mhtml.

http://www.newarttech.com/se.

http://www.uburst.com/uReserve.

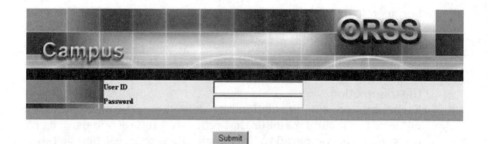

Exhibit J-15.   Screen S1: Campus Login Screen

Exhibit J-16.   Screen S2: Campus Menu Screen

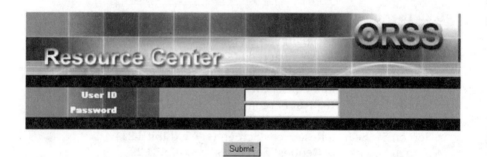

Exhibit J-17.   Screen S3: Resource Center Login Screen

Exhibit J-18.   Screen S4: Resource Center Menu Screen

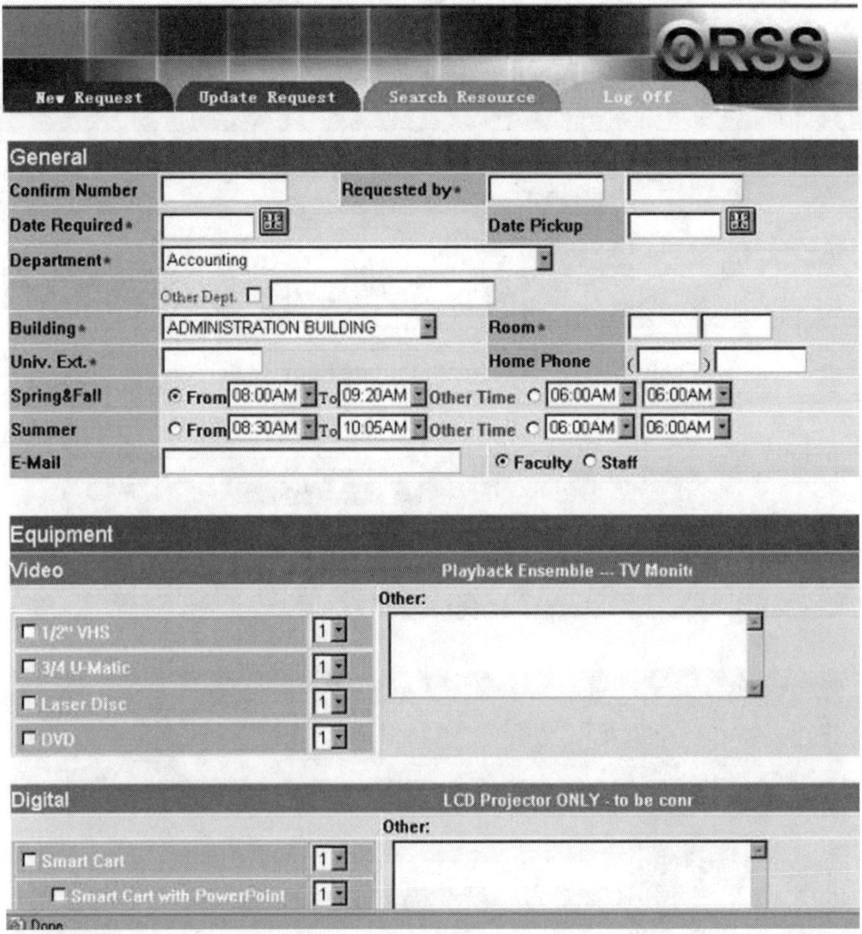

Exhibit J-19.   Screen S5: New Request Screen

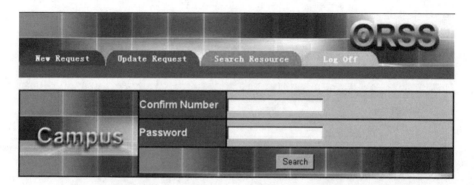

Exhibit J-20.   Screen S6: Update Request Screen

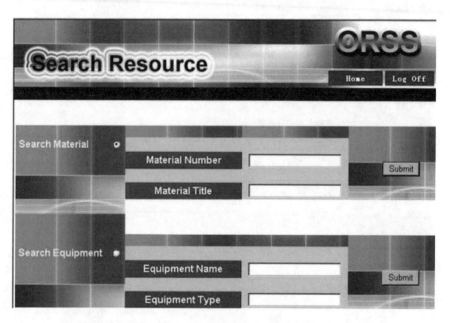

Exhibit J-21.   Screen S7: Search Resources Screen

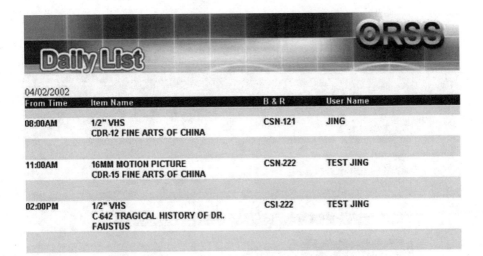

Exhibit J-22.   Screen S8: Display Request Screen

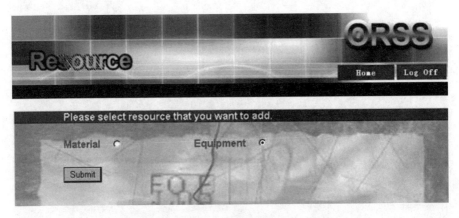

Exhibit J-23.   Screen S9: New Resource Screen

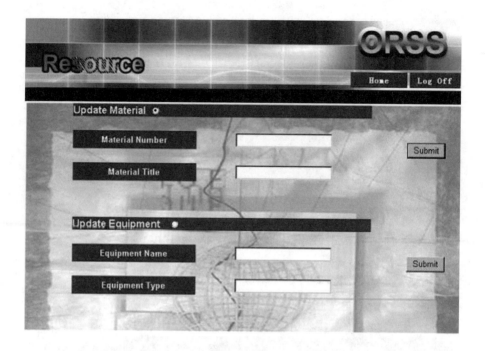

Exhibit J-24.   Screen S10: Update Resource Screen

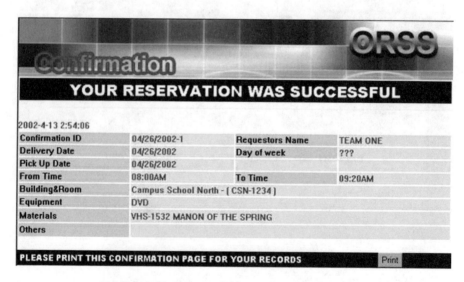

Exhibit J-25.   Screen S11: Confirmation Screen

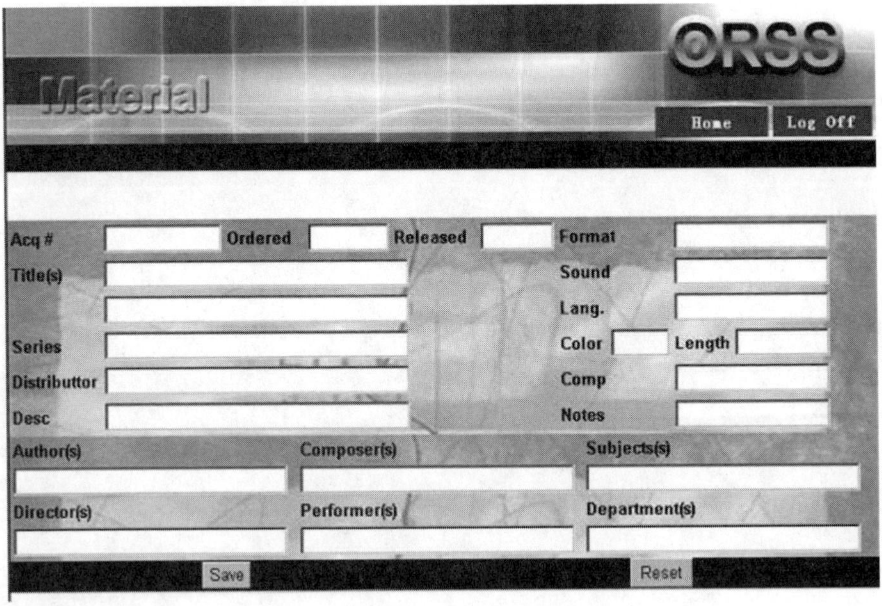

Exhibit J-26.   Screen S12: New Material Screen

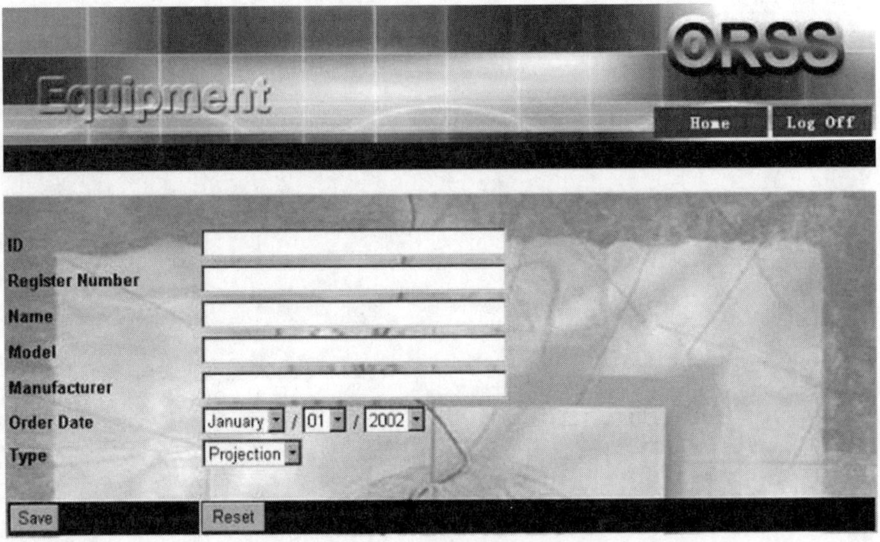

Exhibit J-27.   Screen S13: New Equipment Screen

Appendix K
Sample Data Dictionary

Data Dictionary Entries for the ACME Library Management System

Name:	Asset Database
Aliases:	None
Where Used/How Used:	Used by the database management system to process requests and return results to the inquiry and administration subsystems
Content Description:	Attributes associated with each asset including: • Asset number = 16 numeric Digits • ISBN number = 16 alphanumeric characters • Library of Congress classification number = 16 alphanumeric digits • Asset title = 64 alphanumeric characters • Author = 32 alphanumeric characters • Dewey decimal classification number = 16 numeric digits • Media type = Enumeration {BOOK I MAGAZINE I CDROM I REFERENCE} • Status = Enumeration {IN I OUT I LOST I MISSING I DUE_DATE} • Category = Enumeration {FICTION I NONFICTION} • Published = 32 alphanumeric characters • Keywords = 64 alphanumeric characters • Date acquired = Date • Location = 16 alphanumeric characters
Name:	Membership Database
Aliases:	None
Where Used/How Used	Used by the database management system to process requests and return results to the inquiry and administration subsystems
Content Description:	Attributes associated with each asset including: • Membership number = 10 numeric digits • Member since date = date • Last name = 16 alphanumeric characters • First name = 16 alphanumeric characters • Address = 64 alphanumeric characters • Phone number = 11 numeric digits (1, area code, phone number) • Assets on loan = array containing 10 strings each containing 64 alphanumeric characters • Assets overdue = array containing 10 strings each containing 64 alphanumeric characters • Late fees due = 10 numeric digits • Maximum allowed loans = 2 numeric digits
Name:	Member Data
Aliases:	None
Where Used/How Used	A file used to validate username and passwords for members, librarians, and administrator when they attempt to access the system. The username and password entered are compared with the username and password in this file. Access is granted only if a match is found.

Data Dictionary Entries (continued)

Content Description:	Attributes associated with each asset including: • Member username = 16 alphanumeric digits • Member password = 16 alphanumeric digits
Name:	**Library Data**
Aliases:	None
Where Used/How Used	Files maintained by the administrator and used to provide general information about the library
Content Description:	HTML files for: • General library information (policy, etc.) • Coming events • Library floor map • Library directions screen
Name:	**Database Catalog**
Aliases:	None
Where Used/How Used	Used by the DDL compiler process
Content Description:	Contains detailed information about the various objects in the databases including tables, indices, integrity constraints, security constraints, etc.

Appendix L
Sample OO SDS

1. INTRODUCTION

1.1 Goals and Objectives

The main purpose of Dog E-DayCare System (DEDS) is to provide a database-driven, Web-enabled application to manage and track services provided by a canine care facility. The goals of DEDS are:

- To maintain a database of customer and canine information
- To accept inquiries for and scheduling of canine services
- To track services and specific instructions on customer canines individually
- To process financial transactions and provide billing services to customers
- To utilize a simple, elegant Web interface for interaction with all users

1.2 Scope

Your dog is by nature a gregarious animal, needing socialization and attention that can be provided by the high-quality care and comfort of the Dog E-DayCare System (DEDS). The DEDS is a pet daycare service specializing in pampered pet lodging, dog training, and a variety of in-house care services. Our pet spa services feature the finest in pet grooming for all breeds of dogs. We take pride in accommodating most special requests. We are committed to providing the best care in a relaxing environment suitable for all pets.

Our services also consist of providing daycare for dogs in an open, cage-free environment. Special activities are included, such as playtime with staff and other dogs, nature walks, and obedience training. We also have a veterinarian on site for treatment of any medical problems. Certified dog trainers are available for help with behavioral problems. In addition we offer a full-service grooming salon and an on-site professional obedience trainer

The DEDS system will interact with clients through a Web interface for data entry and business transactions. The system will accept information from existing and future clients and will provide an interface for specific care instructions, present available dog services, accept inquiries for available services, provide a means for scheduling services and appointments, collect relevant dog information (from the client and care-giver), and track provided services and billing for services rendered.

A database will be maintained on a Web-connected personal computer for dog and client information to be entered, updated, and removed. This database will also be searchable and viewable based on various provided criteria.

1.3 Context

The DEDS system will service a perceived market opportunity to provide a complete, user-friendly application to canine care facilities enabling them to provide a wealth of increased and efficient services to their potential customers. Through the use of the Internet, the DEDS system will interact with trained employees as well as individual lay customers.

2. DEDS OVERALL SYSTEM ARCHITECTURE

2.1 Overall Architecture Description

The Web architectural design chosen for the Dog-E-DayCare System is a hierarchical design. Most functionality is funneled through a top-level component, which delegates functionality to additional subcomponents. These subcomponents in turn delegate functionality down to additional subcomponents. Most of the subcomponents utilize their own top-level component as a manager for the package. However, communication is not strictly vertical; several subcomponents communicate among themselves creating the hierarchical architecture.

Communication between components is accomplished using a request/response messaging scheme. Components communicate by requesting some functionality be performed by a component, which returns the response back to the requesting component. In this manner, components can encapsulate their functionality and provide a simple straightforward interface to other components.

Functionality is broken down into packages, each of which handles a particular aspect of functionality for the system (see Exhibit L-1). As with each component, each package is encapsulated and provides a relatively small interface for communication among other packages. As each package is encapsulated, the removal or corruption of most packages will have limited effect on the system as a whole. However, several key packages exist that are accessed by most other packages, and these must be strenuously tested and validated.

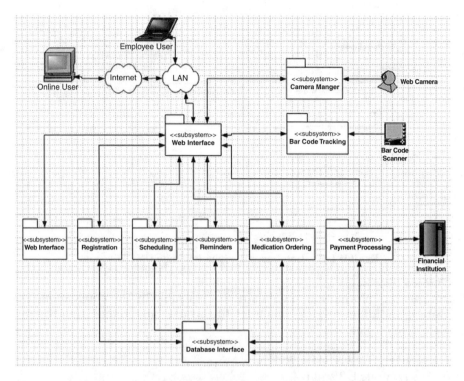

Exhibit L-1. Overall DEDS Application Package Architecture

3. ARCHITECTURAL PACKAGES

3.1 Database Interface Package

3.1.1 Conceptual Description

The database interface package handles interaction and formatting between the DEDS application and the database used to store all information. Serving as the conceptual foundation of the DEDS application, the database interface package provides many low-level core services, structures, and utilities. In addition, this package encapsulates all operations with the database providing the technical service of database management.

The database interface package (see Exhibit L-2) consists of a Database Manager component and a DatabaseMiddleware component. The Database Manager component serves as the interface between the DEDS application and services relevant to database storage. Other components within the DEDS application interact solely with the Database Manager component for communication with the database. This component honors requests by interfacing with the database to obtain the requested information and

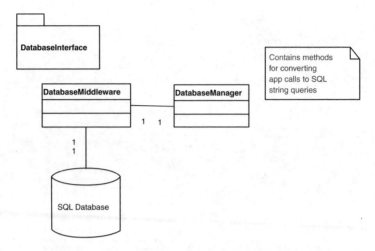

Exhibit L-2. DatabaseInterface Package UML Diagram

returns the information in data structures usable by the application. The DatabaseMiddleware layer handles the actual calls to and from the raw database format.

3.1.2   UML Object Models.

See Exhibits L-3 and L-4.

3.1.3   Collaboration Graph

See Exhibit L-5.

3.1.4   PSPEC

3.1.4.1. DatabaseManager Package

```
PACKAGE DatabaseManager IS
PROC addAppObject(appObject:IN, statusBoolean:OUT);
PROC modifyAppObject(appObject:IN, statusBoolean:OUT);
PROC deleteAppObject(appObject:IN, statusBoolean:OUT);
PROC queryAppObject(appObject:IN, resultObject:OUT);
PROC loadDatabase(databaseFileName:IN, statusBoolean:OUT);
PROC saveDatabase(databaseFileNameIN, statusBoolean:OUT);
PROC convertAppToSQL(appObject:IN, sqlObject:OUT);
PROC convertSQLToApp(sqlObject:IN, appObject:OUT);
PROC issueDBCommand(sqlCommand:IN, statusBoolean:OUT);
PROC getDatabaseResult(resultObject:OUT);

//////////////////////////////////////////////////////////////
// addAppObject - Adds an application object to the database
```

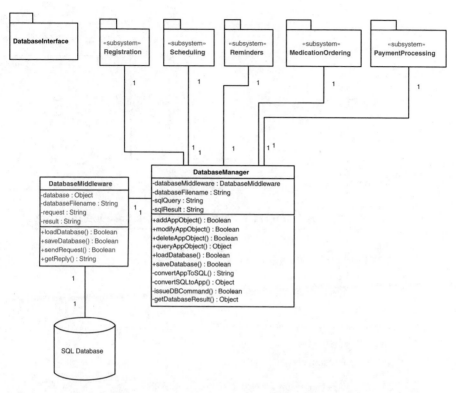

Exhibit L-3.   Database Interface UML Diagram

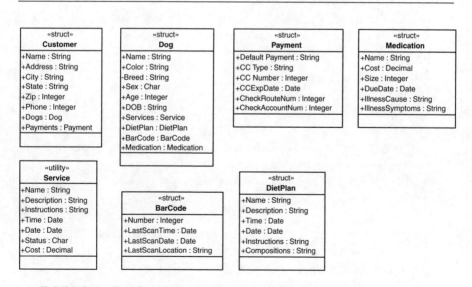

Exhibit L-4.   Database Interface Package Public Application Structures

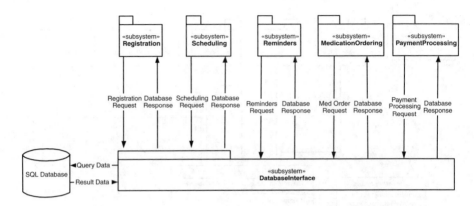

Exhibit L-5. Database Interface Package UML Collaboration Diagram

```
// returns BOOLEAN
//      TRUE — success
//      FALSE — error
//////////////////////////////////////////////////////////
PROC addAppObject(appObject:IN, statusBoolean:OUT)
   TYPE returnCode IS INTEGER;
   TYPE sqlCommand IS STRING;

   sqlCommand = converTAppToSQL(appObject)

   If sqlCommand ! = " "
      convert sqlCommand to ADD returned sqlCommand;
      returnCode = issueDBCommand(sqlCOmmand);
   else

      returnCode = FALSE;
   RETURN returnCode;
END PROC
//////////////////////////////////////////////////////////
// modifyAppObject — modifies an object in the database
// returns BOOLEAN
//      TRUE — success
//      FALSE — error
//////////////////////////////////////////////////////////
PROC modifyAppObject(appObject:IN, statusBoolean:OUT);
   TYPE returnCode IS INTEGER;
   TYPE sqlCommand IS STRING;

   sqlCommand = converTAppToSQL(appObject)
```

```
    If sqlCommand ! = ""
        convert sqlCommand to MODIFY returned sqlCommand;
        returnCode = issueDBCommand(sqlCommand);
    else
        returnCode = FALSE;

    RETURN returnCode;
END PROC

//////////////////////////////////////////////////////////
// modifyAppObject — deletes an object in the database
// returns BOOLEAN
//        TRUE — success
//        FALSE — error
//////////////////////////////////////////////////////////

PROC deleteAppObject(appObject:IN, statusBoolean:OUT);
    TYPE returnCode IS INTEGER;
    TYPE sqlCommand IS STRING;

    sqlCommand = convertAppToSQL(appObject)

    If sqlCommand ! = ""
        convert sqlCommand to REMOVE returned sqlCommand;
        returnCode = issueDBCommand(sqlCOmmand);
    else
        returnCode = FALSE;
    RETURN returnCode;
END PROC

//////////////////////////////////////////////////////////
// queryAppObject — queries and returns the current state
// of an object in the database
// returns OBJECT
//////////////////////////////////////////////////////////
PROC queryAppObject(appObject:IN, resultObject:OUT)
    TYPE returnObject IS OBJECT;
    TYPE sqlCommand IS STRING;

    sqlCommand = convertAppToSQL(appObject)

    If sqlCommand ! = ""
        convert sqlCommand to RETURN returned sqlCommand;
        returnCode = issueDBCommand(sqlCOmmand);
        if returnCode ! = FALSE
            getDatabaseResult(returnObject);
```

```
        else
           returnObject = null;

        RETURN returnObject;
    END PROC

///////////////////////////////////////////////////////////
// loadDatabase — loads the database from the sent fileName
// and sets the database variable
// returns BOOLEAN
//       TRUE — success
//       FALSE — error
///////////////////////////////////////////////////////////
PROC loadDatabase(databaseFileName:IN, statusBoolean:OUT)
    TYPE returnStatus IS BOOLEAN;
    TYPE sqlCommand IS STRING;

    returnStatus =
       databaseMiddleware.loadDatabase(databaseFileName,
       database);

    RETURN returnStatus;
END PROC

///////////////////////////////////////////////////////////
// saveDatabase — saves the database to the sent fileName
// returns BOOLEAN
//       TRUE — success
//       FALSE — error
///////////////////////////////////////////////////////////
PROC saveDatabase(databaseFileName:IN, statusBoolean:OUT)
    TYPE returnStatus IS BOOLEAN;
    TYPE sqlCommand IS STRING;

    returnStatus =
       databaseMiddleware.saveDatabase(databaseFileName,
       database);

    RETURN returnStatus;
END PROC

///////////////////////////////////////////////////////////
//convertAppToSQL — converts an application object into a SQL
//      command representing the object
//returns STRING
///////////////////////////////////////////////////////////
```

```
PROC convertAppToSQL(appObject:IN, sqlObject:OUT)
   TYPE sqlObject IS STRING;
   TYPE objectType IS STRING

   ObjectType = Reflect on appObject to determine class type;
   IF (objectType = = "Service")
      SqlObject = create blank Service SQL statement;
      WHILE (variables)
   Append sqlObject string with variable and values;
   Variables = variable.next;
   ELSE IF (objectType = = "Payment")
      SqlObject = create blank Payment SQL statement;
      WHILE (variables)
   Append sqlObject string with variable and values;
   Variables = variable.next;
   ELSE IF (objectType = = "Customer")
      SqlObject = create blank Customer SQL statement;
      WHILE (variables)
   Append sqlObject string with variable and values;
   Variables = variable.next;

   ELSE IF (objectType = = "Dog")
      SqlObject = create blank Dog SQL statement;
      WHILE (variables)
   Append sqlObject string with variable and values;
   Variables = variable.next;
   ELSE IF (objectType = = "DietPlan")
      SqlObject = create blank DietPlan SQL statement;
      WHILE (variables)
   Append sqlObject string with variable and values;
   Variables = variable.next;
   ELSE IF (objectType = = "BarCode")
      SqlObject = create blank BarCode SQL statement;
      WHILE (variables)
   Append sqlObject string with variable and values;
   Variables = variable.next;
   ELSE IF (objectType = "Reminder")
      SqlObject = create blank Reminder SQL statement;
      WHILE (variables)
   Append sqlObject string with variable and values;
   Variables = variable.next;
   //Continue on with possible object in database
```

651

```
        RETURN sqlObject;
    END PROC

    ///////////////////////////////////////////////////////
    //convertSQLTOApp — converts sql string results from the
                    database
    //              into objects within the application
    //returns OBJECT
    ///////////////////////////////////////////////////////
    PROC convertSQLToApp(sqlObject:IN, appObject:OUT)
        TYPE returnObject IS OBJECT;
        TYPE sqlType IS STRING;

        sqlType = sqlObject.getType;
        if (sqlType = = "Service")
            returnObject = new Service object;
            while (variables)
              returnObject.variable.setValue =
            service.variable.g.,etValue;
              variable = variable.next;
        ELSE IF (sqlType = = "Payment")
            returnObject = new Payment object;
            while (variables)
            returnObject.variable.setValue =
            payment.variable.g.,etValue;
            variable = variable.next;
        ELSE IF (sqlType = = "Customer")
            returnObject = new Customer object;
            while (variables)
        returnObject.variable.setValue =
            customer.variable.g.,etValue;
        variable = variable.next;
        ELSE IF (sqlType = = "Dog")
            returnObject = new Dog object;
            while (variables)
        returnObject.variable.setValue =
            og.variable.g.,etValue;
        variable = variable.next;
        ELSE IF (sqlType = = "DietPlan")
            returnObject = new DietPlan object;
            while (variables)
        returnObject.variable.setValue =
            dietPlan.variable.g.,etValue;
```

```
      variable = variable.next;
      ELSE IF (sqlType = = "BarCode")
         returnObject = new BarCode object;
         while (variables)
      returnObject.variable.setValue =
         barCode.variable.g.,etValue;
      variable = variable.next;
      ELSE IF (sqlType = = "Reminder")
         returnObject = new Reminder object;
         while (variables)
      returnObject.variable.setValue =
         reminder.variable.g.,etValue;
      variable = variable.next;
      RETURN returnObject;
   END PROC

//////////////////////////////////////////////////////////
//issueDBCommand — issues the actual SQL command to the
      database middleware
// RETURNS BOOLEAN
//      TRUE — success
//      FALSE — error
//////////////////////////////////////////////////////////
PROC issueDBCommand(sqlCommand:IN, statusBoolean:OUT)
   TYPE returnStatus IS BOOLEAN;

   returnStatus =
      databaseMiddleware.sendRequest(sqlCommand);
      RETURN returnStatus;
   END PROC

//////////////////////////////////////////////////////////
// getDatabaseResult — retrieves the result from the previous
         database command
// RETURNS OBJECT
//////////////////////////////////////////////////////////
PROC getDatabaseResult(resultObject:OUT)

   returnObject = databaseMiddleware.g.,etReply();

   RETURN returnObject;
   END PROC
END PACKAGE
```

3.1.4.2 DatabaseMiddleware Package

```
PACKAGE DataBaseMiddleware IS

   PROC loadDatabase(fileName:IN, returnStatus:OUT);
   PROC saveDatabase(fileName:IN, returnStatus:OUT);
   PROC sendRequest(sqlCommand:IN);
   PROC getReply(sqlReply:OUT);

   ///////////////////////////////////////////////////////////
   // loadDatabase — loads the actual physical database in the
   //       middleware layer using native database calls
   // returns BOOLEAN
   //       TRUE — success
   //       FALSE — error
   ///////////////////////////////////////////////////////////
   PROC loadDatabase(fileName:IN, returnStatus:OUT)
      TYPE returnStatus IS INTEGER;
      TYPE sqlCommand IS STRING;

      sqlCommand = load database command with fileName;
      database = database.load(sqlCommand);

      IF (database = = null)
         ReturnStatus = FALSE;
      ELSE
         ReturnStatus = TRUE;
      RETURN returnStatus;
   END PROC

   ///////////////////////////////////////////////////////////
   // saveDatabase — saves the actual physical database in the
   //    middleware layer using native database calls
   // returns BOOLEAN
   //       TRUE — success
   //       FALSE — error
   ///////////////////////////////////////////////////////////
   PROC saveDatabase(fileName:IN, returnStatus:OUT)
      TYPE returnStatus IS INTEGER;
      TYPE sqlCommand IS STRING;

      sqlCommand = save database command with fileName;

      returnStatus = database.save(sqlCommand);

      RETURN returnStatus;
```

```
END PROC
////////////////////////////////////////////////////////////
//sendRequest — sends the sql command to the database driver
//    for communication with the native SQL database
// returns BOOLEAN
//        TRUE — success
//        FALSE — error
////////////////////////////////////////////////////////////
PROC sendRequest(sqlCommand:IN);
    TYPE returnStatus IS INTEGER;

    returnStatus = database.request(sqlCommand);

    RETURN returnStatus;
END PROC

////////////////////////////////////////////////////////////
//getReply — returns the reply from the previous issued
//        request to the database
//returns STRING
////////////////////////////////////////////////////////////
PROC getReply(sqlReply:OUT)

    sqlReply = database.reply;

    RETURN sqlReply;
END PROC
END PACKAGE
```

3.2   Tutorial Package

3.2.1   Conceptual Description

The Tutorial package handles the browsing, searching, formatting, and display of the tutorial functionality of the DEDS application. This package provides many business infrastructure layer services such as templates used to provide the user with a common view and functionality associated with the tutorials. The package's ability to apply GUI templates and present this information to the user also represents a significant service in the presentation layer.

Four components comprise the Tutorial package (see Exhibit L-6): TutorialManager, TutorialTemplates, Tutorials, and Tutorial GUI. The TutorialManager component handles the browsing and display of tutorial information to the user. Through its interactions with the TutorialTemplates and TutorialSearch components, the TutorialManager provides the sole interface into the tutorial functionality. The TutorialTemplates com-

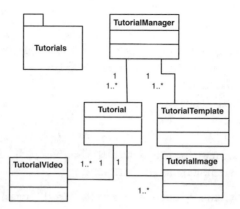

Exhibit L-6.   Tutorials Package UML Diagram

ponent is concerned with formatting tutorial information based on pre-configured templates. Tutorial data is applied to these templates and returned to the TutorialManager for display to the user in a common GUI format. The Tutorials contain information relevant to each tutorial such as images, text, description, title, and keywords. The TutorialGUI controls the display of information within the Tutorial Package; it deals with formatting the Tutorial portion of the GUI and displaying the preformatted Tutorial information. When a specific Tutorial is requested, the Tutorial-Manager picks the correct one from its vector of Tutorials, applies the applicable TutorialTemplate for formatting, and displays it on the TutorialManagerGUI. TutorialVideo handle videoClips within the Tutorial to present the user video images. TutorialImages handles high-quality image display within the tutorials.

3.2.2   UML Object Model.

See Exhibit L-7.

3.2.3   Collaboration Graph.

See Exhibit L-8.

3.2.4   PSPEC

3.2.4.1   TutorialManager

```
PACKAGE TutorialManager IS

    PROC addTutorial(tutorial:IN, returnStatus:OUT);
    PROC deleteTutorial(tutorialName:IN, returnStatus:OUT);
    PROC keywordSearchTutorial(string:IN, tutorialVector:OUT);
    PROC returnTutorial(tutorialName:IN, tutorial:OUT);
    PROC applyTemplate(tutorial:IN, template:IN, html:OUT);
```

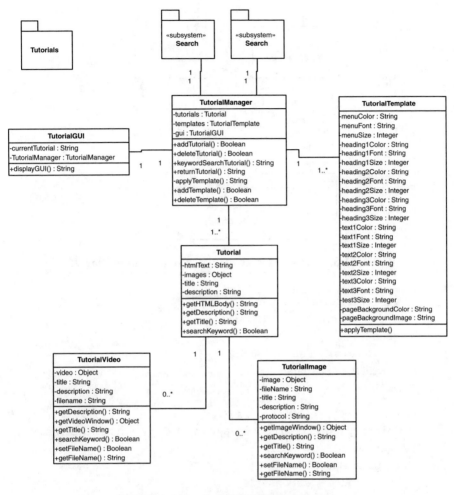

Exhibit L-7.   Tutorial UML Diagram

```
PROC addTemplate(template:IN, returnStatus:OUT);
PROC deleteTemplate(templateName:IN, returnStatus:OUT);
//////////////////////////////////////////////////////////
// addTutorial — adds a tutorial to the internal vector of
// tutorials returns BOOLEAN
//         TRUE — success
//         FALSE — failure
//////////////////////////////////////////////////////////
PROC addTutorial(tutorial:IN, returnStatus:OUT)
    TYPE returnStatus IS BOOLEAN;
```

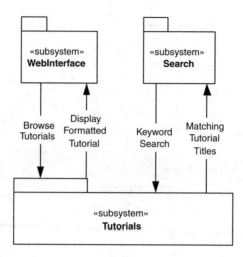

Exhibit L-8.   Tutorials Package UML Collaboration Diagram

```
IF tutorials.add(tutorial)
    ReturnStatus = TRUE;
ELSE
    ReturnStatus = FALSE;
RETURN returnStatus
END PROC

//////////////////////////////////////////////////////////////
//deleteTutorial — removes a tutorial from the internal
// vector of tutorials.
//returns BOOLEAN
//      TRUE — success
//      FALSE — failure
//////////////////////////////////////////////////////////////
PROC deleteTutorial(tutorial:IN, returnStatus:OUT)
    TYPE returnStatus IS BOOLEAN;

    IF tutorials.remove(tutorial)
        ReturnStatus = TRUE;
    ELSE
        ReturnStatus = FALSE;
    RETURN returnStatus
END PROC

//////////////////////////////////////////////////////////////
//keywordSearchTutorials — parses through all the tutorials
```

```
//      in the vector and checks if the tutorial contains
//      the keyword If it does then it is added to the return
//      vector
//returns VECTOR
//      contains name of tutorials
//////////////////////////////////////////////////////////
PROC keywordSearchTutorial(string:IN, tutorialVector:OUT)
    TYPE returnVector IS VECTOR;

    WHILE (tutorials)
        IF tutorial.searchKeyword =  = TRUE
    TutorialVector.add(tutorial.getName);
        Tutorial = tutorial.next;
    RETURN tutorialVector;
END PROC


//////////////////////////////////////////////////////////
//returnTutorial — returns the tutorial with the given
        tutorial name
//returns TUTORIAL
//  tutorial object containing tutorial information or null
//  if not existing in tutorialVector
//////////////////////////////////////////////////////////
PROC returnTutorial(tutorialName:IN, tutorial:OUT)
    TYPE returnTutorial IS TUTORIAL;

    If tutorials.contains(tutorialName)
        ReturnTutorial = tutorials.getTutorial(tutorialName);
    ELSE
        ReturnTutorial = null;
    RETURN returnTutorial;
END PROC


//////////////////////////////////////////////////////////
//applyTemplate — applies the given template to the given
//  tutorial and returns the resulting HTML code
//returns STRING
//      html of the tutorial with the template applied
//////////////////////////////////////////////////////////
PROC applyTemplate(tutorial:IN, template:IN, html:OUT)
    TYPE html IS STRING;

    Html = template.apply(tutorial);

    RETURN html;
```

659

```
END PROC

/////////////////////////////////////////////////////////
//addTemplate — adds a template to the internal vector of
//          templates
//returns BOOLEAN
//       TRUE — success
//       FALSE — failure
/////////////////////////////////////////////////////////
PROC addTemplate(template:IN, returnStatus:OUT)
   TYPE returnStatus IS BOOLEAN;

   IF templates.add(template)
      ReturnStatus = TRUE;
   ELSE
      ReturnStatus = FALSE;

   RETURN returnStatus
END PROC

/////////////////////////////////////////////////////////
//deleteTemplate — removes a template from the internal
//                   vector of tutorials.
//returns BOOLEAN
//       TRUE — success
//       FALSE — failure
/////////////////////////////////////////////////////////
PROC deleteTemplate(template:IN, returnStatus:OUT)
   TYPE returnStatus IS BOOLEAN;

   IF templates.remove(template)
      ReturnStatus = TRUE;

   ELSE
      ReturnStatus = FALSE;

   RETURN returnStatus
   END PROC

END PACKAGE
```

3.2.4.2   Tutorial Package

```
PACKAGE Tutorial IS

   PROC getHTMLBody(returnHTML:OUT);
   PROC getDescription(returnDescription:OUT);
```

```
PROC getTitle(returnTitle:OUT);

PROC searchKeyword(keyword:IN, found:OUT);

///////////////////////////////////////////////////////////////
//getHTMLBody — gets the html body of the tutorial
//returns STRING
//        html body
///////////////////////////////////////////////////////////////
PROC getHTMLBody(returnHTML:OUT)
    TYPE returnHTML IS STRING;
    ReturnHTML = description;

    RETURN returnHTML;
END PROC

///////////////////////////////////////////////////////////////
//getDescription — gets the description of the tutorial
//returns STRING
//        description
///////////////////////////////////////////////////////////////
PROC getDescription(returnDescription:OUT)
    TYPE returnDescription IS STRING;

    ReturnDescription = description;

    RETURN returnHTML;
END PROC

///////////////////////////////////////////////////////////////
//getTitle — gets the title of the tutorial
//returns STRING
//        title
///////////////////////////////////////////////////////////////
PROC getTitle(returnTitle:OUT)
    TYPE returnTitle IS STRING;

    returnTitle = description;

    RETURN returnTitle;
END PROC

///////////////////////////////////////////////////////////////
//searchKeyword — searches the tutorial description and html
//        for the sent keyword and returns whether
//        it was found
//returns BOOLEAN
```

661

```
//        TRUE — found keyword
//        FALSE — did not find keyword
////////////////////////////////////////////////////////
PROC searchKeyword(keyword:IN, found:OUT)
   TYPE found IS BOOLEAN;

   FOUND = FALSE;

   IF title.indexOf(keyword) ! = —1
      Found = TRUE;
   ELSE if htmlText.indexOf(keyword ! = —1)
      Found = TRUE;
   ELSE
      WHILE (images)
   Found = Image.keywordSearch(keyword)
   Image = images.next;
      WHILE (videos)
   Found = video.keywordSearch(keyword)
   Video = video.next;
   RETURN Found;
   END PROC
END PACKAGE
```

3.2.4.3   TutorialVideo

```
PACKAGE TutorialVideo IS
PROC getVideoWindow(videoPanel:OUT);
PROC getDescription(returnDescription:OUT);
PROC getTitle(returnTitle:OUT);
PROC searchKeyword(keyword:IN, found:OUT);
PROC setFileName(fileName:IN, returnResult:OUT);
PROC getFileName(fileName:OUT);

////////////////////////////////////////////////////////
//getVideoWindow — returns a panel containing the video
//      player to be displayed to the user
//returns PANEL
//        video window
////////////////////////////////////////////////////////
PROC getVideoWindow(videoPanel:OUT)
   TYPE videoPanel IS JPanel;

   JavaX Multimedia Extensions get codec
   Get codec player
   VideoPanel = Codec player.getPanel();
```

```
    RETURN videoPanel;
END PROC

/////////////////////////////////////////////////////////////
//getDescription — gets the description of the video
//returns STRING
//       description
/////////////////////////////////////////////////////////////
PROC getDescription(returnDescription:OUT)
    TYPE returnDescription IS STRING;

    ReturnDescription = description;

    RETURN returnHTML;
END PROC

/////////////////////////////////////////////////////////////
//getTitle — gets the title of the video
//returns STRING
//       title
/////////////////////////////////////////////////////////////
PROC getTitle(returnTitle:OUT)
    TYPE returnTitle IS STRING;

    returnTitle = description;

    RETURN returnTitle;
END PROC

/////////////////////////////////////////////////////////////
//searchKeyword — searches the tutorial descrpition and html
//       for the sent keyword and returns whether
//       was found
//returns BOOLEAN
//       TRUE — found keyword
//       FALSE — did not find keyword
/////////////////////////////////////////////////////////////
PROC searchKeyword(keyword:IN, found:OUT)
    TYPE found IS BOOLEAN;

    IF title.indexOf(keyword) ! = —1
        Found = TRUE;
    ELSE if description.indexOf(keyword ! = —1)
        Found = TRUE;
    ELSE
        Found = FALSE;
```

```
      RETURN Found;
   END PROC

   ////////////////////////////////////////////////////////////////
   //setFileName — sets the internal filename if the video was
   //      found
   //returns BOOLEAN
   //      TRUE — success
   //      FALSE — failure, file does not exist
   ////////////////////////////////////////////////////////////////
   PROC setFileName(fileName:IN, returnResult:OUT)
      TYPE returnResult IS BOOLEAN;

      IF fileName.exists()
         This.fileName = fileName
         ReturnResult = TRUE;
      ELSE
         ReturnResult = FALSE;

      RETURN returnResult
   END PROC

   ////////////////////////////////////////////////////////////////
   //getFileName — returns the fileName of the video
   //returns STRING
   //      Filename of the video or null if no fileName
   ////////////////////////////////////////////////////////////////
   PROC getFileName(fileName:OUT);
      TYPE fileName IS STRING;

      FileName = this.fileName;

      RETURN fileName;
   END PROC
END PACKAGE
```

3.2.4.4   TutorialImage Package

```
PACKAGE TutorialImage IS

   PROC getImageWindow(imagePanel:OUT);
   PROC getDescription(returnDescription:OUT);
   PROC getTitle(returnTitle:OUT);
   PROC searchKeyword(keyword:IN, found:OUT);
   PROC setFileName(fileName:IN, returnResult:OUT);
   PROC getFileName(fileName:OUT);
```

```
/////////////////////////////////////////////////////////////
//getImageWindow — returns a panel containing the image
//     to be displayed to the user
//returns PANEL
//     video window
/////////////////////////////////////////////////////////////
PROC getVImageWindow(imagePanel:OUT)
    TYPE videoPanel IS JPanel;

    JavaX Multimedia Extensions get codec
    Get codec player
    imagePanel = Codec player.getPanel();

    RETURN imagePanel;
END PROC

/////////////////////////////////////////////////////////////
//getDescription — gets the description of the image
//returns STRING
//       description
/////////////////////////////////////////////////////////////
PROC getDescription(returnDescription:OUT)
    TYPE returnDescription IS STRING;

    ReturnDescription = description;

    RETURN returnHTML;
END PROC

/////////////////////////////////////////////////////////////
//getTitle — gets the title of the image
//returns STRING
//       title
/////////////////////////////////////////////////////////////
PROC getTitle(returnTitle:OUT)
    TYPE returnTitle IS STRING;

    returnTitle = description;

    RETURN returnTitle;
END PROC

/////////////////////////////////////////////////////////////
//searchKeyword — searches the description and title for the
//sent keyword and returns whether was found
//returns BOOLEAN
```

665

```
//      TRUE — found keyword
//      FALSE — did not find keyword
////////////////////////////////////////////////////////////
PROC searchKeyword(keyword:IN, found:OUT)
   TYPE found IS BOOLEAN;

   IF title.indexOf(keyword) ! = —1
      Found = TRUE;
   ELSE if description.indexOf(keyword ! = —1)
      Found = TRUE;
   ELSE
      Found = FALSE;

   RETURN Found;
END PROC

////////////////////////////////////////////////////////////
//setFileName — sets the internal filename if the image was
      found
//returns BOOLEAN
//      TRUE — success
//      FALSE — failure, file does not exist
////////////////////////////////////////////////////////////
PROC setFileName(fileName:IN, returnResult:OUT)
   TYPE returnResult IS BOOLEAN;

   IF fileName.exists()
      This.fileName = fileName
      ReturnResult = TRUE;
   ELSE
      ReturnResult = FALSE;

   RETURN returnResult
END PROC

////////////////////////////////////////////////////////////
//getFileName — returns the fileName of the image
//returns STRING
//      Filename of the image or null if no fileName
////////////////////////////////////////////////////////////
PROC getFileName(fileName:OUT);
   TYPE fileName IS STRING;

   FileName = this.fileName;

   RETURN fileName;
```

```
  END PROC
END PACKAGE
```

3.2.4.5. *TutorialGUI Package*

```
PACKAGE TutorialGUI IS
   PROC displayGUI(guiHTML:OUT);

   /////////////////////////////////////////////////////////
   //displayGUI - returns the html for the entire tutorial GUI
   //    menu screen
   //returns STRING
   //       html of the tutorial screen
   /////////////////////////////////////////////////////////
   PROC displayGUI(guiHTML:OUT)
      TYPE guiHTML IS STRING;

      GuiHTML = tutorialManager.applyTemplate(tutorial,
         options.templates);
      Append GuiHTML with Menu HTML
      While (videos)
         Video.getVideoWindow();
         Append VideoWindow reference to guiHTML
         Video = videos.next;
      WHILE (images)
         Image.g.,etImageWindow();
         Append imageWindow reference to guiHTML
         Image = images.next

      RETURN guiHTML;
   END PROC
END PACKAGE
```

3.2.4.6. *TutorialTemplate Package*

```
PACKAGE TutorialTemplate IS
   PROC applyTemplate(tutorial:IN, html:OUT);
   /////////////////////////////////////////////////////////
   //applyTemplate - returns the html for the entire tutorial
   //    GUI menu screen
   //returns STRING
   //       html of the tutorial screen with template applied
   /////////////////////////////////////////////////////////
   PROC applyTemplate(tutorial:IN, html:OUT)
      TYPE html IS STRING;
```

```
html = tutorial.getHTMLBody();
html.replace(H1 color with template H1 color);
html.replace(H1 font with template H1 font);
html.replace(H1 size with template H1 size);
html.replace(H2 color with template H2 color);
html.replace(H2 font with template H2 font);
html.replace(H2 size with template H2 size);
html.replace(H3 color with template H3 color);
html.replace(H3 font with template H3 font);
html.replace(H3 size with template H3 size);
html.replace(text1 color with template text1 color);
html.replace(text1 font with template text1 font);
html.replace(text1 size with template text1 size);
html.replace(text2 color with template text2 color);
html.replace(text2 font with template text2 font);
html.replace(text2 size with template text2 size);
html.replace(text3 color with template text3 color);
html.replace(text3 font with template text3 font);
html.replace(text3 size with template text3 size);
html.replace(menuColor with template menuColor);
html.replace(menuFont with template menuFont);
html.replace(menuSize with template menuSize);
html.replace(backgroundColor with template
    backGroundColor);
html.replace(backgroundImage with template
    backgroundImage);
RETURN html;
END PROC
END PACKAGE
```

3.3   Payment Package

3.3.1   Conceptual Description

Payment subsystem is responsible for setting up different payment methods, processing payment requests, and billing information for a customer. It also conducts the verification operations with external financial institutions for automatic debit operations.

The Payment package provides many business infrastructure layer services such as security, currency conversion routines, automatic debit process, and credit card validation used to provide the user with a common view and functionality associated with the payment. This package provides the ability to apply GUI templates and present this information to the user;

it also represents a significant service in the presentation layer. The Payment subsystem provides the following features:

- *Security:* payment subsystem verifies the user authenticity to use the payment processing and billing information.
- *Credit card validation:* payment subsystem validates the user credit card for its correct information with the external systems.
- *Currency conversion:* payment subsystem provides utility to convert the local currency into different currencies.
- *Automatic debit process:* user can set up automatic debit from his or her checking account or charge to a credit card. The Payment subsystem processes these charges on a periodic basis.

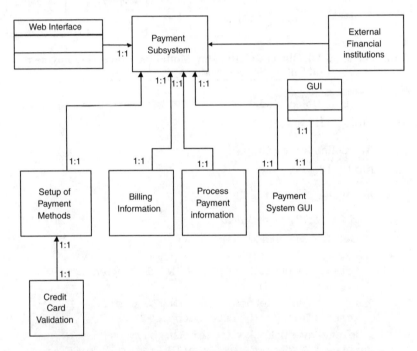

Exhibit L-9. Payment Package UML Object Relationship Model

Four major components comprise the Payment package (Exhibit L-9): Payment method setup, Billing Information, Payment Process information, and GUI presentation. The Payment package interacts with Payment method to set up processes, with payment method validation with external financial systems. The Payment package also interacts with the Billing Information package, with security and currency conversion routines. The Payment package interacts with the payment process information package, with security and currency conversion and automatic debit process from checking accounts or charge to credit accounts. The Payment package also presents a presentation layer to display the payment information on the screen for the user (see Exhibit L-10).

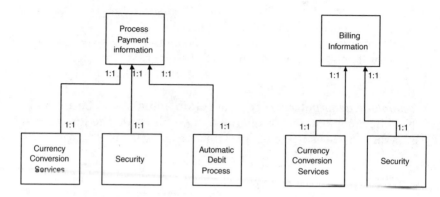

Exhibit L-10. UML Object Relationship Model for Processing Payment and Billing Sub-Subsystems

3.3.2   UML Object Model

See Exhibit L-11.

3.3.3   Collaboration Graph

See Exhibit L-12.

3.3.4   PSPEC

3.3.4.1   SetPaymentMethod

```
PACKAGE SetPaymentMethod IS
    PROC addPaymentMethod(owner:IN, paymentType:IN,
        creditCardNo:IN, expDate:IN, defPayment:IN
        returnCode:OUT);
    PROC setDefPaymentMethod(owner:IN, paymentType:IN,
        creditCardNo:IN, returnCode:OUT);
    PROC deletePaymentMethod(owner:IN, paymentType:IN,
        creditCardNo:IN, expDate:IN, returnCode:OUT);
    PROC validateCreditCard(ownerName:IN, creditCardNo:IN,
        expDate:IN, returnCode:OUT);
////////////////////////////////////////////////////////////
//addPaymentMethod — store paymentMethod against user in
        database
//returns INTEGER
//        0 — success
//        1 — error
////////////////////////////////////////////////////////////
```

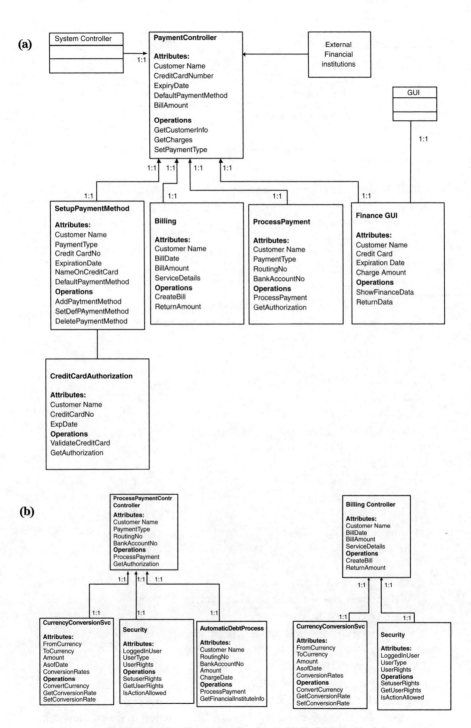

Exhibit L-11. Payment Package UML Object Model

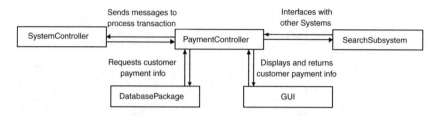

Exhibit L-12. Payment Package UML Collaboration Graph

```
PROC addPaymentMethod(owner:IN, paymentType:IN,
     creditCardNo:IN, expDate:IN, defPayment:IN
     returnCode:OUT)
   TYPE returnCode IS INTEGER;
   Get OwnerId from owner object for a given Owner.
   If owner does not exist in owner object
      returncode = error;
   Add a new payment record in database for the given Owner.
   If defPayment = 'Y', set this payment method as default
      payment method.
   returnCode = success;

   RETURN returnCode;
END PROC
///////////////////////////////////////////////////////////
//setDefPaymentMethod — setPaymentMethod as default
     paymentMethod.
//returns INTEGER
//      0 — success
//      1 — error
///////////////////////////////////////////////////////////
PROC setDefPaymentMethod(owner:IN, paymentType:IN,
     creditCardNo:IN, returnCode:OUT)
   TYPE returnCode IS INTEGER;
   Get OwnerId from owner object for a given Owner.
   If owner does not exist in owner object
      returncode = error;
   Get PaymentMethod of a given owner with specified
      PaymentType and creditCardNo.
   If paymentMethod does not exist for this owner
      returncode = error;
   Set defaultPayment = 'Y' for this paymentMethod.
   Set defaultPayment = 'N' for all other paymentMethods
      defined for this user, if any.
```

```
        returnCode = success;
     RETURN returnCode;
  END PROC
  ////////////////////////////////////////////////////////////
  //deletePaymentMethod — delete paymentMethod from the
        database for this owner.
  //returns INTEGER
  //      0 — success
  //      1 — error
  ////////////////////////////////////////////////////////////
  PROC deletePaymentMethod(owner:IN, paymentType:IN,
        creditCardNo:IN, returnCode:OUT)
     TYPE returnCode IS INTEGER;
     Get OwnerId from owner object for a given Owner.
     If owner does not exist in owner object
        returncode = error;
     Get PaymentMethod of a given owner with specified
        PaymentType and creditCardNo.
     If paymentMethod does not exist for this owner
        returncode = error;

     Delete selected paymentMethod for this owner.
     RETURN returnCode;
  END PROC
  ////////////////////////////////////////////////////////////
  //validateCreditCard — Validate creditCards using external
        interface.
  //returns INTEGER
  //      0 — success
  //      1 — error
  ////////////////////////////////////////////////////////////
  PROC validateCreditCard(ownerName:IN, creditCardNo:IN,
        expDate:IN, returnCode:OUT);
     TYPE returnCode IS INTEGER;
     Validate specified credit card using external interface.
     If creditCard is valid
        ReturnCode = success
     Else returnCode = error;

     RETURN returnCode;
  END PROC
END PACKAGE
```

3.3.4.2 *CurrencyConversionSvcClass*

```
PACKAGE CurrencyConversionSvc IS
  PROC convertCurrency(fromCurrency:IN, toCurrency:IN,
        asOfDate:IN, Amount:IN, outValue:OUT,
        returnCode:OUT);
  PROC getConversionRate(fromCurrency:IN, toCurrency:IN,
        asOfDate:IN, convRate:OUT, returnCode:OUT);
  PROC setConversionRate(fromCurrency:IN, toCurrency:IN,
        asOfDate:IN, convRate:IN, returnCode:OUT);

  ////////////////////////////////////////////////////////
  //convertCurrency — Convert the currency value from
        fromCurrency to toCurrency
  //returns INTEGER
  //        0 — success
  //        1 — error
  //returns outValue as a converted currency.
  ////////////////////////////////////////////////////////
  PROC convertCurrency(fromCurrency:IN, toCurrency:IN,
        asOfDate:IN, Amount:IN, outValue:OUT, returnCode:OUT)
    TYPE returnCode IS INTEGER;
    GetConversionRate for fromCurrency, toCurrency,asOfDate.
    If returnCode is not error then
        OutValue = ConvRate *amount;
    RETURN returnCode;
  END PROC

  ////////////////////////////////////////////////////////
  //getConversionRate — get the conversion rate asOfDate from
        fromCurrency to
  //toCurrency
  //returns INTEGER
  //        0 — success
  //        1 — error
  //returns convRate as a conversion Rate.
  ////////////////////////////////////////////////////////
  PROC getConversionRate(fromCurrency:IN, toCurrency:IN,
        asOfDate:IN, convRate:OUT, returnCode:OUT)
    TYPE returnCode IS INTEGER;
    Get conversion rate for fromCurrency, toCurrency,
        asOfDate from database into convRate.
    If conversion rate is not defined for fromCurrency,
        toCurrency, asOfDate, ReturnCode = error;
    RETURN returnCode;
```

```
END PROC
/////////////////////////////////////////////////////////////
//setConversionRate — set the conversion rate asOfDate from
      fromCurrency to
//toCurrency in database.
//returns INTEGER
//      0 — success
//      1 — error
/////////////////////////////////////////////////////////////
PROC getConversionRate(fromCurrency:IN, toCurrency:IN,
      asOfDate:IN, convRate:IN, returnCode:OUT)
   TYPE returnCode IS INTEGER;
   Check if Conversion rate is already defined for
      fromCurrency, toCurrency, asOfDate from database.
   If conversion rate is already defined, returnCode =
      error.
   Else {
      Set conversion rate into database for fromCurrency,
         toCurrency, asOfDate.
      ReturnCode : = error;
         }
      RETURN returnCode;
   END PROC
END PACKAGE
```

3.3.4.3 *PaymentSecurity*

```
PACKAGE PaymentSecurity IS
   PROC setUserRights(user:IN, rights:IN, returnCode:OUT);
   PROC getUserRights(user:IN, rights:OUT, returnCode:OUT);
   PROC isActionAllowed(user:IN, action:IN, allowed:OUT);
   /////////////////////////////////////////////////////////////
   //setUserRights — sets the user rights to database.
   //returns INTEGER
   //      0 — success
   //      1 — error
   /////////////////////////////////////////////////////////////
   PROC setUserRights(user:IN, rights:IN, returnCode:OUT)
      TYPE returnCode IS INTEGER;
      If User right is already specified in database,
         returnCode = error;
      Insert specified rights into database for specified user;
      ReturnCode = success;
```

```
        RETURN returnCode;
    END PROC

    ///////////////////////////////////////////////////////////
    //getUserRights — gets the user rights from database.
    //returns INTEGER
    //        0 — success
    //        1 — error
    ///////////////////////////////////////////////////////////
    PROC setUserRights(user:IN, rights:IN, returnCode:OUT)
        TYPE returnCode IS INTEGER;
        If User right is not defined in database, returnCode =
            error;
        Select rights feom database for specified user;
        Concatenate them in a string format.
        ReturnCode = success;
        RETURN returnCode;
    END PROC
    ///////////////////////////////////////////////////////////
    //getUserRights — gets the user rights from database.
    //returns Y if right exists, N if not.
    ///////////////////////////////////////////////////////////
    PROC isActionAllowed(user:IN, action:IN, allowed:OUT)
        TYPE returnCode IS INTEGER;
        If User right is defined in database,allowed = 'Y';
        Else allowed = 'N'
        RETURN allowed;
    END PROC
END PACKAGE
```

3.3.4.4   AutomaticDebitProcess

```
PACKAGE EventLog IS
    PROC ProcessPayments(owner:IN, routingNumber:IN,
        AccountNumber:IN, amount:IN, authorization:OUT,
        returnCode:OUT);
    PROC getFinancialInstituteInfo(routingNumber:IN,
        bankName:OUT);

    ///////////////////////////////////////////////////////////
    //ProcessPayments — Process Payments to be automatically
        debted from bank
    //accounts.
    //returns INTEGER
```

```
//      0 - success
//      1 - error
//returns authorization as INTEGER
///////////////////////////////////////////////////////
PROC ProcessPayments(owner:IN, routingNumber:IN,
        AccountNumber:IN, amount:IN, authorization:OUT,
        returnCode:OUT)
    TYPE returnCode IS INTEGER;
    Validate given routingNumber;
    Validate given accountNumber;
    Post 'amount' onto given routingNumber+accountNumber
        account.
    If Error during posting amount, returnCode = error.
    getAuthorization.
    RETURN returnCode;
END PROC
///////////////////////////////////////////////////////
//getFinancialInstituteInfo - Get bank name for a given
        routing Number
//returns INTEGER
//      0 - success
//      1 - error
///////////////////////////////////////////////////////
PROC getFinancialInstituteInfo(routingNumber:IN,
        bankName:OUT)
    TYPE returnCode IS INTEGER;
    From external system, get bank name for routingNumber.
    RETURN returnCode;
    END PROC
END PACKAGE
```

3.3.4.5   Billing

```
PACKAGE Billing IS
    PROC createBill(customer:IN, ServiceDetails:IN,
        BillDate:OUT, BillAmount:OUT, returnCode:OUT);
    PROC returnAmount(customer:IN, billDate:IN, billAmount:OUT,
        returnCode:OUT);
    ///////////////////////////////////////////////////////
    //createBill - create a bill for given service details for a
        customer.
    //returns INTEGER
    //      0 - success
    //      1 - error
```

677

```
//returns billDate as date
//returns billAmount as float
//////////////////////////////////////////////////////////
PROC createBill(customer:IN, ServiceDetails:IN,
        BillDate:OUT, BillAmount:OUT, returnCode:OUT)
    TYPE returnCode IS INTEGER;
    Get OwnerId for given customer.
    If Customer does not exist, returnCode = error;
    From the service details provided,
        Build a string of all services provided for all his
            dogs.
        Compute the total price of all services.
    Set the billDate as today.
    Set the paymentDateas Today + 20 days.
    returnCode = success
    RETURN returnCode;
END PROC
//////////////////////////////////////////////////////////
//returnAmount — retrieve the amount of bill for a customer
        and billdate
//returns INTEGER
//        0 — success
//        1 — error
//returns billAmount as float
//////////////////////////////////////////////////////////
PROC returnAmount(customer:IN, billDate:IN, billAmount:OUT,
        returnCode:OUT)
    Get OwnerId for given customer.
    If Customer does not exist, returnCode = error;
    TYPE returnCode IS INTEGER;
    Get billAmount from database for a specified customer and
        billDate.
    RETURN returnCode;
END PROC
END PACKAGE
```

3.4   Reminders Package

3.4.1   Conceptual Description

Reminders subsystem of DEDS is responsible for creating and sending out birthday, medication, and registration reminders to dog owners as and when required. The Reminders subsystem will accept system message, then connect to data objects, which interface with DB, to generate reminders to send to the user.

The Reminders package provides many business infrastructure layer services such as reminder templates used to provide the user with a common view and functionality associated with the reminders. This package's ability to apply GUI templates and present this information to the user also represents a significant service in the presentation layer.

Three components comprise the Reminders package (see Exhibit L-13): Birthday Reminders, Medication Reminders, and Registration Reminders.

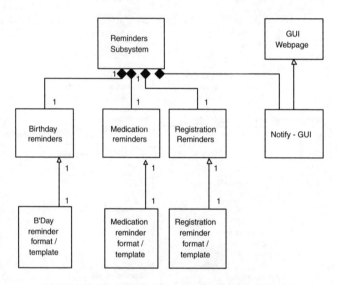

Exhibit L-13.   UML Object Relationship Model

Each of these reminders can have multiple sets of templates to be selected for use. The Reminders component handles the browsing and display of reminder information to the user. Through its interactions, the Reminder subsystem provides the sole interface into the tutorial functionality.

3.4.2   UML Object Model.

See Exhibit L-14.

3.4.3   Collaboration Graph

See Exhibit L-15.

3.4.4   PSPEC

3.4.4.1   *BirthDay Reminder*

```
PACKAGE BirthDayReminders IS
```

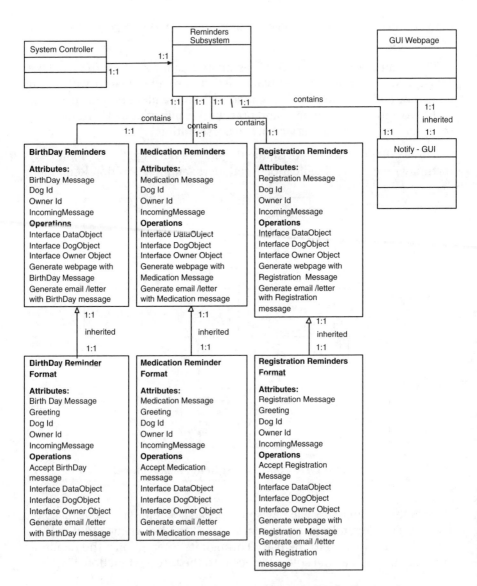

Exhibit L-14. Reminders Package UML Object Model

```
PROC selectBDayReminderFormat(aFormat:IN, returnCode:OUT);
PROC createBDayReminder(aDog:IN, birthDayMessage:IN,
      greeting:IN returnCode:OUT);
PROC sendOutReminders(aReminder:IN, returnCode:OUT);
/////////////////////////////////////////////////////////////
//selectBDayReminderFormat — Select the format to be used for
      birthday
```

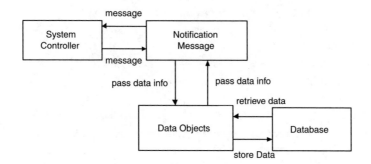

Exhibit L-15.   Camera Package UML Collaboration Graph

```
//reminders
//returns INTEGER
//       0 — success
//       1 — error
////////////////////////////////////////////////////////////
PROC selectBDayReminderFormat(aFormat:IN, returnCode:OUT)
   TYPE returnCode IS INTEGER;
   If aFormat exist
      set the format to be used to a format.
      Set returnCode = Success;
   Else
      Set returnCode = Error;
   RETURN returnCode;
END PROC
////////////////////////////////////////////////////////////
//createBDayReminder — Create the Birthday reminders
//returns INTEGER
//       0 — success
//       1 — error
////////////////////////////////////////////////////////////
PROC createBDayReminder(aDog:IN, birthDayMessage:IN,
      greeting:IN returnCode:OUT);
   TYPE returnCode IS INTEGER;
   Get DogName, BirthDate information from dog Object.
   Get Owner name, address, communicationMethod and greeting
      from owner object.

   Get BdayFormat selected.
   In selected BdayFormat, insert dogName, birthDate,
      OwnerGreeting, ownerName, address to create
      birthdayLetter.
```

```
        If birthDayLetter created successfully
            returnCode = Success
        else
            returnCode = error
        RETURN (returnCode);
    END PROC
    ///////////////////////////////////////////////////////////
    //sendOutReminders — Sends the reminders out
    //returns INTEGER
    //        0 — success
    //        1 — error
    ///////////////////////////////////////////////////////////
    PROC sendOutReminders(aReminder:IN, returnCode:OUT);
        TYPE returnCode IS INTEGER;
        If communication type is email then
            send email to address specified.
            ReturnCode = Success;
        elseif communication type is usps then
            print the reminder letter.
            ReturnCode = Success;
        else return code — error;

        RETURN returnCode;
    END PROC
END PACKAGE
```

3.4.4.2   *Medication Reminder*

```
PACKAGE MedicationReminders IS
    PROC selectMedicationReminderFormat(aFormat:IN,
            returnCode:OUT);
    PROC createMedicationReminder(aDog:IN,
            MedicationMessage:IN, greeting:IN
    returnCode:OUT);
    PROC sendOutReminders(aReminder:IN, returnCode:OUT);

    ///////////////////////////////////////////////////////////
    //selectMedicationReminderFormat — Select the format to be
            used for medication
    //reminders
    //returns INTEGER
    //        0 — success
    //        1 — error
    ///////////////////////////////////////////////////////////
```

```
PROC selectMedicationReminderFormat(aFormat:IN,
      returnCode:OUT)
   TYPE returnCode IS INTEGER;
   If aFormat exist
      set the format to be used to a format.
      Set returnCode = Success;
   Else
      Set returnCode = Error;
   RETURN returnCode;
END PROC

///////////////////////////////////////////////////////////////
//createMedicationReminder — Create the Medication reminders
//returns INTEGER
//      0 — success
//      1 — error
///////////////////////////////////////////////////////////////
PROC createMedicationReminder(aDog:IN,
      medicationMessage:IN, greeting:IN returnCode:OUT);
   TYPE returnCode IS INTEGER;
   Get DogName, BirthDate information from dog Object.
   Get Owner name, address, communicationMethod and greeting
      from owner object.

   Get MedicationFormat selected.
   In selected MedicationFormat, insert dogName, birthDate,
      OwnerGreeting, ownerName, address to create
      MedicationLetter.
   If medicationLetter created successfully
      returnCode = Success
   else
      returnCode = error

   RETURN (returnCode);

END PROC
///////////////////////////////////////////////////////////////
//sendOutReminders — Sends the reminders out
//returns INTEGER
//      0 — success
//      1 — error
///////////////////////////////////////////////////////////////
PROC sendOutReminders(aReminder:IN, returnCode:OUT);
   TYPE returnCode IS INTEGER;
```

```
        If communication type is email then
            send email to address specified.
            ReturnCode = Success;
        elseif communication type is usps then
            print the reminder letter.
            ReturnCode = Success;
        else return code = error;
        RETURN returnCode;
    END PROC
END PACKAGE
```

3.4.4.3   Registration Reminders

```
PACKAGE RegistrationReminders IS
    PROC selectRegistrationReminderFormat(aFormat:IN,
            returnCode:OUT);
    PROC createRegistrationReminder(aDog:IN,
            registrationMessage:IN, greeting:IN returnCode:OUT);
    PROC sendOutReminders(aReminder:IN, returnCode:OUT);

    /////////////////////////////////////////////////////////////
    //selectRegistrationReminderFormat — Select the format to be
        used for
    //registration reminders
    //returns INTEGER
    //      0 — success
    //      1 — error
    /////////////////////////////////////////////////////////////
    PROC selectRegistrationReminderFormat(aFormat:IN,
            returnCode:OUT)
        TYPE returnCode IS INTEGER;
        If aFormat exist
            set the format to be used to a format.
            Set returnCode = Success;
        Else
            Set returnCode = Error;
        RETURN returnCode;
    END PROC
    /////////////////////////////////////////////////////////////
    //createRegistrationReminder — Create the Registration
        reminders
    //returns INTEGER
    //      0 — success
    //      1 — error
```

```
//////////////////////////////////////////////////////////
PROC createRegistrationReminder(aDog:IN,
      registrationMessage:IN, greeting:IN returnCode:OUT);
   TYPE returnCode IS INTEGER;
   Get DogName, BirthDate information from dog Object.
   Get Owner name, address, communicationMethod and greeting
      from owner object.

   Get RegistrationFormat selected.
   In selected RegistrationFormat, insert dogName,
      birthDate, OwnerGreeting, ownerName, address to create
      registrationLetter.

   If registrationLetter created successfully
      returnCode = Success
   else
      returnCode = error

   RETURN (returnCode);

END PROC
//////////////////////////////////////////////////////////
//sendOutReminders — Sends the reminders out
//returns INTEGER
//       0 — success
//       1 — error
//////////////////////////////////////////////////////////
PROC sendOutReminders(aReminder:IN, returnCode:OUT);
   TYPE returnCode IS INTEGER;
   If communication type is email then
      send email to address specified.
      ReturnCode = Success;
   elseif communication type is USPS then
      print the reminder letter.
      ReturnCode = Success;
   else return code = error;

   RETURN returnCode;
END PROC
```

3.5 Search Package

3.5.1 Conceptual Description

The Search Package (Exhibit L-16) is used to provide facility for the user to search the DEDS based on the dog's information or dog owner's

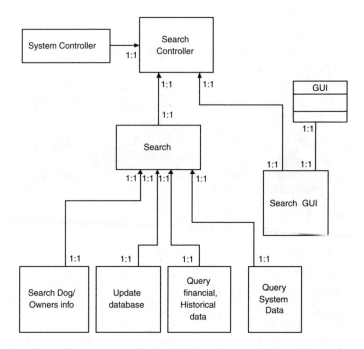

Exhibit L-16.   Search Package UML Object Relationship Model

information and get complete dog and dog owner information for all possible search matches. Search package also provides interface with tutorial, payment, reminders, scheduling, medication, ordering, registration, camera, and barcode subsystems. Moreover, the system manager can benefit from this module for searching statistical data about customers, revenue, and number of potential matches provided to users. System environment settings, network speed, database performance, and other relevant technical information required by the system administrator are also obtained by using this module of the system.

3.5.2   UML Object Model.

See Exhibit L-17.

3.5.3   Collaboration Graph.

See Exhibit L-18.

3.5.4   PSPEC

3.5.4.1   SeachDogOwnerInfo

```
PACKAGE SearchDogOwnerInfo IS
    PROC setDogOwnerSearchCriteria(anSearchCriteria:IN,
        returnCode:OUT);
```

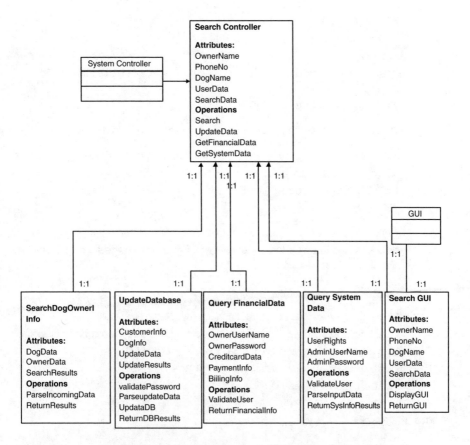

Exhibit L-17.   Search Package UML Object Model

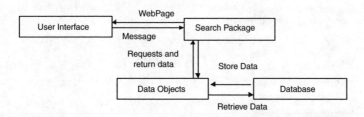

Exhibit L-18.   Search Package UML Collaboration Graph

```
PROC getDogOwnerSearchResults(SearchResults:OUT);

////////////////////////////////////////////////////////
//setDogOwnerSearchCriteria — set search criteria from user
      input.
//returns INTEGER
```

```
//      0 - success
//      1 — error
//////////////////////////////////////////////////////////
PROC setDogOwnerSearchCriteria(anSearchCriteria:IN,
        returnCode:OUT);

    TYPE returnCode IS INTEGER;

    Parse the search criteria for required columns.

    If required columns are identified, returnCode = success
    Else returnCode = error
    RETURN returnCode;
END PROC

//////////////////////////////////////////////////////////
//getDogOwnerSearchResults — retrieve dog/owner information
        from the database
//based on search criteria
//////////////////////////////////////////////////////////
PROC getDogOwnerSearchResults(SearchResults:OUT);
    Get Dog and Owner information for the set search criteria.
    Retrieve columns using database package.
    Cast the results into a searchResults object
    Return SearchResults;
    END PROC
END PACKAGE
```

3.5.4.2 SearchFinancialInfo

```
PACKAGE SearchFinancialInfo IS
    PROC setFinancialSearchCriteria(anSearchCriteria:IN,
            returnCode:OUT);
    PROC getFinancialSearchResults(SearchResults:OUT);

//////////////////////////////////////////////////////////
//setFinancialSearchCriteria — set search criteria from
        user input.
//returns INTEGER
//      0 — success
//      1 — error
//////////////////////////////////////////////////////////
PROC setFinancialSearchCriteria(anSearchCriteria:IN,
        returnCode:OUT);

    TYPE returnCode IS INTEGER;

    Parse the search criteria for required columns.
```

```
          If required columns are identified, returnCode = success
          Else returnCode = error

          RETURN returnCode;
     END PROC
//////////////////////////////////////////////////////////////
//getFinancialSearchResults — retrieve Financial
     information from the database
//based on search criteria
//////////////////////////////////////////////////////////////
     PROC getFinancialSearchResults(SearchResults:OUT);
        .Get Financial information of dog owners for the set search
           criteria.
        Retrieve columns using database package.
        Cast the results into a searchResults object
        Return SearchResults;
     END PROC
END PACKAGE
```

3.5.4.3 *SearchSystemInfo*

```
PACKAGE SearchSystemInfo IS
   PROC setSystemSearchCriteria(anSearchCriteria:IN,
        returnCode:OUT);
   PROC getSystemSearchResults(SearchResults:OUT);
//////////////////////////////////////////////////////////////
//setSystemSearchCriteria — set search criteria from user
     input.
//returns INTEGER
//       0 — success
//       1 — error
//////////////////////////////////////////////////////////////
   PROC setSystemSearchCriteria(anSearchCriteria:IN,
        returnCode:OUT);
      TYPE returnCode IS INTEGER;

      Parse the search criteria for required columns.

      If required columns are identified, returnCode = success
      Else returnCode = error

      RETURN returnCode;
   END PROC
//////////////////////////////////////////////////////////////
```

```
//getSystemSearchResults — retrieve System information from
      the database
//based on search criteria
///////////////////////////////////////////////////////////////
PROC getSystemSearchResults(SearchResults:OUT);
    Get System information for the set search criteria.
    Retrieve columns using database package.
    Cast the results into a searchResults object
    Return SearchResults;
  END PROC
END PACKAGE
```

3.6 Registration Package

3.6.1 Conceptual Description

The Registration package is responsible for allowing new customers to register with the DEDS. This package will take the customer's name, address, and emergency phone number, establish a user ID and password, as well as take information on the pet. Verification of customer and dog registration information for the DEDS application is performed and then this vital information is stored to the database.

Four components make up the Registration package (see Exhibit L-19): Registration Manager, Customer Registration, Dog Registration, and Registration GUI. As mentioned earlier, the Registration Manager could be considered one of the key components in the business work flow process and therefore serve as a component in the application layer. It will handle the collection and display of the relevant information and send it to the respective components.

The format of information is then checked in the Customer Registration and Dog Registration components and sent to the Registration GUI component. The Customer Registration and Dog Registration components interface with the database subsystem to check for duplication of information. If appropriate, the information is written to the database. This subsystem should be included in the technical services layer as an information exchange service.

3.6.2 Registration Object Model.

See Exhibit L-20.

3.6.3 Registration Collaboration Graph.

See Exhibit L-21.

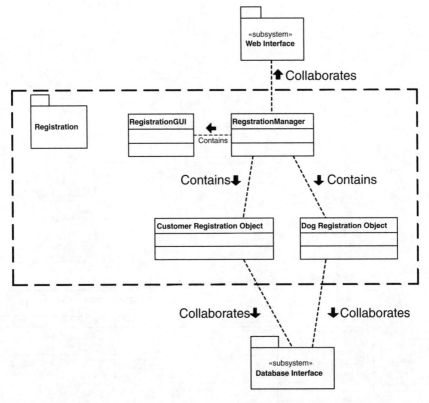

Exhibit L-19.   Registration Package UML Object Relationship Model

3.6.4   PSPEC

3.6.4.1   *Customer Registration Package*

```
PACKAGE customerRegistrationRecord IS
   TYPE customerRegistrationRecord data
   PROC setFirstName, setLastName, setStreetaddress,
   PROC setState, setZipCode, setCustphone, setCustEmail,
   PROC setID, setPassword

   PRIVATE
      PACKAGE BODY customerRegistrationRecord IS
      PRIVATE
      OwnerFirstName, OwnerLastName, streetAddress,
      state, phoneNumber, eMailAddress, OwnerId,
      password IS STRING LENGTH (20);
///////////////////////////////////////////////////
//setFirstName — set the customer's first name.
```

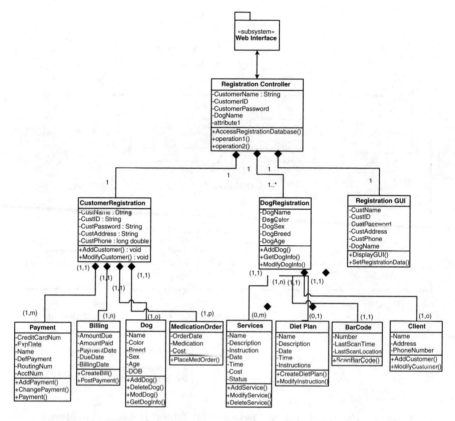

Exhibit L-20.   Registration Package UML Object Model

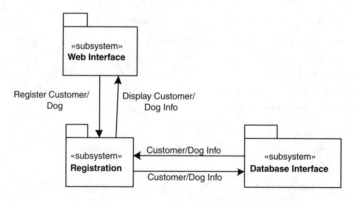

Exhibit L-21.   Registration Package UML Collaboration Graph

```
PROC setFirstName(String first)
   OwnerFirstName = first;

END PROC

//////////////////////////////////////////////////
//getFirstName — return the customer's first name.
//
//returns — STRING
//////////////////////////////////////////////////

PROC getFirstName
   return OwnerFirstName;

END PROC

//////////////////////////////////////////////////
//setLastName — set the customer's last name.
//
//////////////////////////////////////////////////
PROC setLastName (String last)
   OwnerLastName = last;

END PROC

//////////////////////////////////////////////////
//getLastName — return the customer's last name.
//
//returns — STRING
//////////////////////////////////////////////////

PROC getlastName
   return OwnerLastName;

END PROC

//////////////////////////////////////////////////
//setStreetaddress — set the customer's street
//address.
//
//////////////////////////////////////////////////

PROC setStreetaddress(stAddress)
   streetAddress = stAddress;

END PROC
//////////////////////////////////////////////////
//getStreetAddress — return the customer's street
```

```
//address.
//
//returns - STRING
//////////////////////////////////////////////////

PROC getStreetAddress
   return streetAddress;

END PROC

//////////////////////////////////////////////////
//setState - set the customer's state.
//
//////////////////////////////////////////////////

PROC setState(st)
   state = st;

END PROC

//////////////////////////////////////////////////
//getState - return the customer's state.
//
//returns - STRING
//////////////////////////////////////////////////

PROC getState
   return state;

END PROC

//////////////////////////////////////////////////
//setZipCode - set the customer's postal code.
//
//////////////////////////////////////////////////
PROC setZipCode(zip)
   zipCode = zip;

END PROC

//////////////////////////////////////////////////
//getzipCode - return the customer's postal code.
//
//returns - STRING
//////////////////////////////////////////////////

PROC getZipCode
   return zipCode;
```

```
END PROC

///////////////////////////////////////////////////
//setCustPhone — set the customer's phone number.
//
///////////////////////////////////////////////////

PROC setCustPhone(phNum)
    phoneNumber = phNum;

END PROC

///////////////////////////////////////////////////
//getzipCode — return the customer's phone number.//
//returns — STRING
///////////////////////////////////////////////////

PROC getCustPhone
    return phoneNumber;

END PROC

///////////////////////////////////////////////////
//setCustEmail — set the customer's email address.
//
///////////////////////////////////////////////////

PROC setCustEmail (eMail)
    eMailAddress = eMail;

END PROC

///////////////////////////////////////////////////
//getCustEmail — return the customer's email address.//
//returns — STRING
///////////////////////////////////////////////////

PROC getCustEmail
    return eMailAddress;

END PROC

///////////////////////////////////////////////////
//setID — set the customer's identification.
//
///////////////////////////////////////////////////

PROC setID (id)
    OwnerId = id;
```

```
END PROC

///////////////////////////////////////////////////
//getID — return the customer's identification.
//
//returns — STRING
///////////////////////////////////////////////////

PROC getID
    return OwnerId;

END PROC

///////////////////////////////////////////////////
//setPassword — set the customer's password.
//
///////////////////////////////////////////////////

PROC setPassword (pwd)
    password = pwd;

END PROC

///////////////////////////////////////////////////
//getPassword — return the customer's password.
//
//returns — STRING
///////////////////////////////////////////////////

PROC getPassword
    return password;

  END PROC
END PACKAGE customerRegistrationRecord
```

3.6.4.2   *DogRegistrationRecord*

```
PACKAGE dogRegistrationRecord IS
  TYPE dogRegistrationRecord data
  PROC setDogName, setColor, setBreed, setSex, setAge,
    setBirthDate

  PRIVATE
    PACKAGE BODY dogRegistrationRecord IS
    PRIVATE

        dogName, dogColor, dogBreed
        IS STRING LENGTH (20);
```

```
        sex IS STRING LENGTH (7);,
        dogAge, birtDate IS INTEGER;
////////////////////////////////////////////////////
//setDogName - set the dog's name.
//
////////////////////////////////////////////////////

PROC setDogName(String name)
    dogName = name;

END PROC
////////////////////////////////////////////////////
//getDogName - return the dog's name.
//
//returns - STRING
////////////////////////////////////////////////////

PROC getDogName
    return dogName;

END PROC

////////////////////////////////////////////////////
//setColor - set the dog's color.
//
////////////////////////////////////////////////////

PROC setColor (String color)
    dogColor = color;

END PROC

////////////////////////////////////////////////////
//getColor - return the dog's color.
//
//returns - STRING
////////////////////////////////////////////////////

PROC getColor
    return dogColor;

END PROC

////////////////////////////////////////////////////
//setBreed - set the dog's breed.
//
////////////////////////////////////////////////////
```

```
PROC setBreed (String breed)
   dogBreed = breed;

END PROC

//////////////////////////////////////////////////////
//getBreed — return the dog's breed.
//
//returns — STRING
//////////////////////////////////////////////////////

PROC getBreed
   return dogBreed;

END PROC

//////////////////////////////////////////////////////
//setSex — set the dog's sex.
//
//////////////////////////////////////////////////////

PROC setSex (String sex)
   dogSex = sex;

END PROC

//////////////////////////////////////////////////////
//getSex — return the dog's sex.
//
//returns — STRING
//////////////////////////////////////////////////////

PROC getSex
   return dogSex;

END PROC

//////////////////////////////////////////////////////
//setAge — set the dog's age.
//
//////////////////////////////////////////////////////

PROC setAge (int age)
   dogAge = age;

END PROC

//////////////////////////////////////////////////////
//setAge — return the dog's age.
```

```
//
//returns — INTEGER
/////////////////////////////////////////////////////

PROC getAge
    return dogAge;

END PROC

/////////////////////////////////////////////////////
//setBirthDate — set the dog's date of birth.
//
/////////////////////////////////////////////////////

PROC setBirthDate (int DOB)
    birthDate = DOB;

END PROC

/////////////////////////////////////////////////////
//getBirthDate — return the dog's date of birth.
//
//returns — INTEGER
/////////////////////////////////////////////////////

PROC getBirthDate
    return birthDate;

END PROC
END PACKAGE dogRegistrationRecord
```

3.6.4.3 *RegistrationController*

```
PACKAGE RegistrationController IS
   TYPE RegistrationController data
   PROC addCustomer, modifyCustomer, deleteCustomer
   PROC addDog, modifyDog, deleteDog

   PRIVATE
       PACKAGE BODY RegistrationController IS
       PRIVATE

          dogName, dogColor, dogBreed
          IS STRING LENGTH (20);
          sex IS STRING LENGTH (7);,
          dogAge, birtDate IS INTEGER;

   /////////////////////////////////////////////////////
```

```
//addCustomer — uses previously defined processes to
//add a new customer. Parameters are obtained using
//getText operation for text boxes.
//
///////////////////////////////////////////////////

PROC setFirstName(first)
PROC setLastName(last)
PROC setStreetaddress(stAddress)
PROC setState(st)
PROC setZipCode(zip)
PROC setCustphone(phNum)
PROC setCustEmail(eMail)
PROC setID(id)
PROC setPassword(pwd)
END PROC

///////////////////////////////////////////////////
//modify Customer — uses previously defined processes
//to modify existing customer.
//
///////////////////////////////////////////////////

PROC getFirstName()
PROC getLastName()
PROC getStreetaddress()
PROC getState()
PROC getZipCode()
PROC getCustphone()
PROC getCustEmail()
PROC getID()
PROC getPassword()

PROC setFirstName(first)
PROC setLastName(last)
PROC setStreetaddress(stAddress)
PROC setState(st)
PROC setZipCode(zip)
PROC setCustphone(phNum)
PROC setCustEmail(eMail)
PROC setID(id)
PROC setPassword(pwd)

END PROC
```

```
/////////////////////////////////////////////////////
//delete Customer — uses previously defined processes
//to remove an existing customer.
//
/////////////////////////////////////////////////////

PROC getFirstName()
PROC getLastName()
PROC getStreetaddress()
PROC getState()
PROC getZipCode()
PROC getCustphone()
PROC getCustEmail()
PROC getID(OwnerId)
PROC getPassword()

database.remove(OwnerFirstName);
database.remove(OwnerLastName);
database.remove(streetAddress);
database.remove(state);
database.remove(zipCode);
database.remove(phoneNumber);
database.remove(eMailAddress);
database.remove(OwnerId);
database.remove(password);

END PROC

/////////////////////////////////////////////////////
//addDog — uses previously defined processes to
//add a new dog(s). Parameters are obtained using
//getText operation for text boxes.
//
/////////////////////////////////////////////////////

PROC setDogName(name)
PROC setColor(color)
PROC setBreed(breed)
PROC setSex(sex)
PROC setAge(age)
PROC setBirthDate(dob)

END PROC

/////////////////////////////////////////////////////
```

```
//modifyDog — uses previously defined processes to
//modify a dog(s) record. Parameters are obtained
//using getText operation for text boxes.
//
/////////////////////////////////////////////////////

PROC setDogName(name)
PROC setColor(color)
PROC setBreed(breed)
PROC setSex(sex)
PROC setAge(age)
PROC setBirthDate(dob)

END PROC

/////////////////////////////////////////////////////
//removeDog — uses previously defined processes to
//delete a dog(s) record from the database.
//Parameters are obtained using getText operation
//for text boxes.
//
/////////////////////////////////////////////////////

database.remove(name)
database.remove(color)
database.remove(breed)
database.remove(sex)
database.remove(age)
database.remove(dob)

END PROC

END PACKAGE RegistrationController
```

3.7 Camera Subsystem Architecture

3.7.1 Conceptual Description

The Camera package of DEDS will allow the customer to select a camera and view images using streaming video technology via the Internet. Two components comprise the Camera Package (see Exhibit L-22): Camera Manager and Camera GUI. The Camera Manager is responsible for sending the formatted information to the user. This component could be considered part of the technical services layer due to the information exchange characteristics. The Camera GUI component will provide information regarding the size of the screen and positioning. Video information is applied to the Camera GUI component and then sent on to the Camera

Manager. The Camera GUI component could be considered in the presentation layer of the architecture.

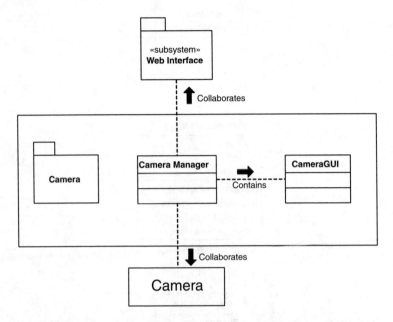

Exhibit L-22.   Camera Package UML Object Relationship Model

3.7.2   Registration Object Model.
See Exhibit L-23.

3.7.3   Registration Collaboration Graph.
See Exhibit L-24.

3.7.4   PSPEC

3.7.4.1   Camera Object

```
PACKAGE Camera IS
   TYPE camera data
   PROC zoomIn, zoomOut

PRIVATE
     PACKAGE BODY camera IS
     PRIVATE
     cameraID IS STRING LENGTH (8);

//////////////////////////////////////////////////////////
//setCamera — set the camera to be used for
//displaying the video
```

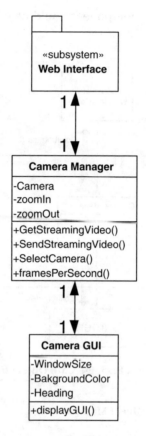

Exhibit L-23.   Camera Package UML Object Model

```
//
//////////////////////////////////////////////////

PROC setCamera(String cameraID)
   camera = cameraID;

END PROC

//////////////////////////////////////////////////
//getCamera — return the camera to be used for
//displaying the video
//
//returns — STRING
//////////////////////////////////////////////////

PROC getCamera
   return camera;
```

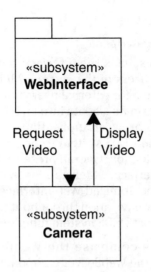

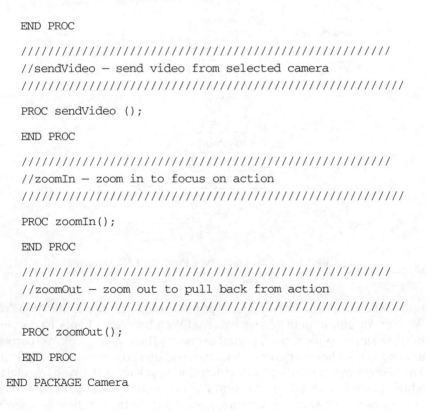

Exhibit L-24. Camera Package UML Collaboration Graph

```
END PROC

//////////////////////////////////////////////////////
//sendVideo — send video from selected camera
//////////////////////////////////////////////////////

PROC sendVideo ();

END PROC

//////////////////////////////////////////////////////
//zoomIn — zoom in to focus on action
//////////////////////////////////////////////////////

PROC zoomIn();

END PROC

//////////////////////////////////////////////////////
//zoomOut — zoom out to pull back from action
//////////////////////////////////////////////////////

PROC zoomOut();

END PROC

END PACKAGE Camera
```

3.8 WebInterface Package

3.8.1 Conceptual Description

The WebInterface package is the interface between the DEDS system and the external human users of the system. All information coming into and out of the DEDS system for external users flows through the WebInterface. The WebInterface formats all data into an HTML protocol allowing for display on common Web browser applications on a variety of platforms. Utilizing HTML allows the DEDS system to be accessed by nearly anyone with a Web browser application. Overall presentation of the information is controlled by the WebInterface, which applies templates to the overall site presentation creating a customized Web interface. The WebInterface provides a GUI that allows for navigation throughout the DEDS application providing the interface to most DEDS system functionality.

Several components comprise the WebInterface package (see Exhibit L-25). The first is the WebServer component that controls distribu-

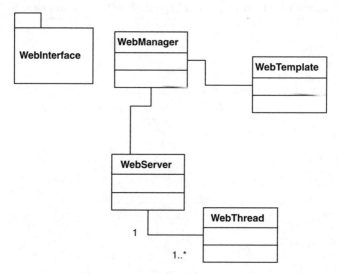

Exhibit L-25.   WebInterface Package UML Diagram

tion of HTML information and navigation through the site application. The WebServer component allows external Web browser clients to connect into the DEDS application. External users can then utilize their Web browsers and the WebServer component to navigate throughout the DEDS site. The second component of the WebInterface package is the WebTemplates, which provide overall site presentation in a customizable fashion. New templates can be added or existing ones modified to give the site a new or changed look and feel. Finally, the WebManager is the overall controlling component of the WebInterface package. Requests from the WebServer are funneled through the WebManager, which then interacts with other packages within the DEDS system. The returned information is then formatted by applying a WebTemplate and finally returned to the WebServer for transmission to the external user's Web browser. WebThreads handle the individual connection for each client because the transport protocol utilized is a connection-based protocol.

3.8.2   Object Model.

See Exhibit L-26.

3.8.3   Collaboration Graph.

See Exhibit L-27.

3.8.4   PSPEC

```
PACKAGE WebManager IS
    PROC startServer();
    PROC stopServer(stopStatus:OUT);
    PROC applyTemplate(template:IN, html:IN, returnHTML:OUT);

    /////////////////////////////////////////////////////////////
    //startServer - Starts the WebServer on the port and creates
    //        one
    //WebThread that is waiting for a connection
    //RETURNS void
    /////////////////////////////////////////////////////////////

    PROC startServer()
        Server.start();

    END PROC

    /////////////////////////////////////////////////////////////
    //stopServer - Stops the WebServer
    //RETURNS BOOLEAN
    //       TRUE - success
    //       FALSE - failure
    /////////////////////////////////////////////////////////////

    PROC stopServer(stopStatus:OUT)
        TYPE stopStatus IS STRING;

        StopStatus = server.StopServer();

        Return stopStatus;
    END PROC
    /////////////////////////////////////////////////////////////
```

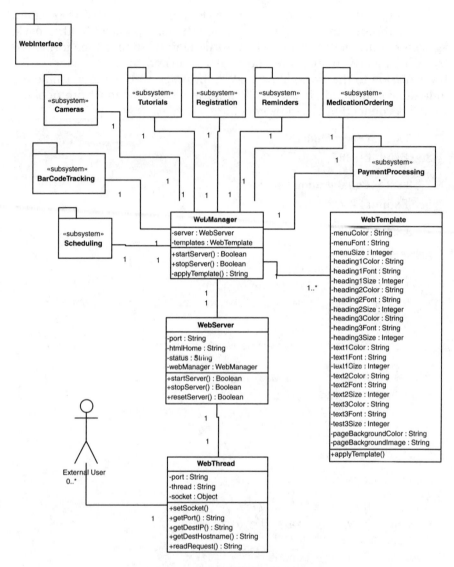

Exhibit L-26.   WebInterface UML Diagram

```
//applyTemplate — Applies the given template to the given
      html and
//returns the resulting html
//RETURNS STRING
//     html with site wide template applied
///////////////////////////////////////////////////////
PROC applyTemplate(template:IN, html:IN, returnHTML:OUT);
```

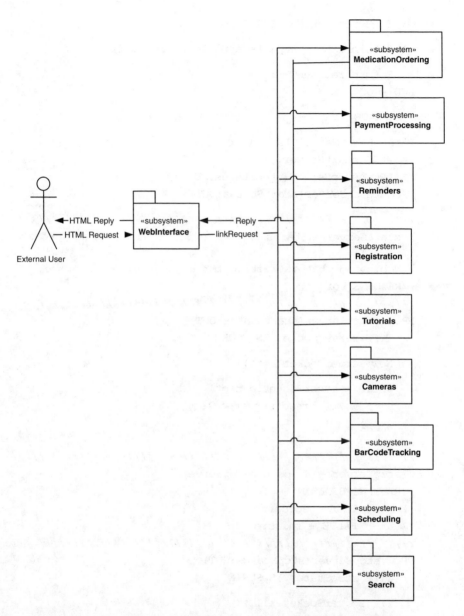

Exhibit L-27. Web Interface Package UML Collaboration Diagram

```
                  TYPE returnHTML IS STRING;

                  ReturnHTML = Template.applyTemplate(html);

                  Return returnHTML;
               END PROC

          END PACKAGE

             PACKAGE WebServer IS
                PROC startServer();
                PROC stopServer(stopStatus:OUT);
             PROC resetServer(startStatus:OUT);

          ////////////////////////////////////////////////////////
          //startServer - Starts the WebServer on the port and creates
                  one
          //WebThread that is waiting for a connection
          //RETURNS void
          ////////////////////////////////////////////////////////
          PROC startServer(startStatus:OUT)
             TYPE serverSocket IS SOCKET;

             New serverSocket(port)

             While (serverSocket.accept)
                New Webthread(serverSocket);

          END PROC

          ////////////////////////////////////////////////////////
          //stopServer - Stops the WebServer
          //RETURNS BOOLEAN
          //       TRUE - success
          //       FALSE - failure
          ////////////////////////////////////////////////////////
          PROC stopServer(stopStatus:OUT)
             TYPE stopStatus IS STRING;

             IF (serverSocket.kill)
                StopStatus = TRUE;
             Else
                StopStatus = FALSE;

             Return stopStatus;
          END PROC

          ////////////////////////////////////////////////////////
```

```
//resetServer — Stops the WebServer and then restarts it
//RETURNS BOOLEAN
//       TRUE — success
//       FALSE — failure
/////////////////////////////////////////////////////////
PROC resetServer(resetStatus:OUT)
   TYPE resetStatus IS STRING;

   ResetStatus = stopServer();
   StartServer();

   Return resetStatus;
END PROC

END PACKAGE
PACKAGE WebThread IS
   PROC setSocket(socket:IN);
   PROC getPort(portString:OUT);
   PROC getDestIP(destIPString:OUT);
   PROC getDestHostname(destHostname:OUT);
   PROC readRequest(request:OUT);
   PROC returnReply(reply:OUT);
   /////////////////////////////////////////////////////////
   //setSocket — sets the socket to the given socket
   //RETURNS void
   /////////////////////////////////////////////////////////
   PROC setSocket(socket:IN)
      This.socket = socket;
   END PROC

   /////////////////////////////////////////////////////////
   //getPort — gets the port the socket is connected to
   //RETURNS STRING
   //port number
   /////////////////////////////////////////////////////////
   PROC getPort(portString:OUT)
      TYPE portString IS STRING;

      PortString = socket.getPort();

      RETURN portString;
   END PROC
   /////////////////////////////////////////////////////////
   //getDestIP — gets the IP the socket is connected to
   //RETURNS STRING
```

```
        //IP
        ////////////////////////////////////////////////////////
        PROC getDestIP(destIPString:OUT)
            TYPE ipString IS STRING;

            ipString = socket.getDestIP();

            RETURN ipString;
        END PROC

        ////////////////////////////////////////////////////////
        //getDestHostname - gets the hostname the socket is connected
                to
        //RETURNS STRING
        //hostname
        ////////////////////////////////////////////////////////
        PROC getDestHostname(destHostname:OUT)
            TYPE hostname IS STRING;

            Hostname = resolve getDestIP();

            RETURN hostname;
        END PROC

        ////////////////////////////////////////////////////////
        //readRequest - reads the HTML request from the socket
        //RETURNS void
        ////////////////////////////////////////////////////////
        PROC readRequest(request:OUT)
            TYPE InputBuffer IS BUFFEREDINPUTSTREAM;
            TYPE request IS STRING;

            InputBuffer = Socket.getInputStream();
            Request = InputBuffer.getString();

            RETURN request;
        END PROC

    END PACKAGE

    PACKAGE WebTemplate IS
        PROC applyTemplate(tutorial:IN, html:OUT);

        ////////////////////////////////////////////////////////
        //applyTemplate - returns the html for the entire Web GUI
        //      menu screen
        //returns STRING
```

```
//        html of the Web screen with template applied
///////////////////////////////////////////////////////////////
PROC applyTemplate(html:IN, html:OUT)
    TYPE html IS STRING;

    html.replace(H1 color with template H1 color);
    html.replace(H1 font with template H1 font);
    html.replace(H1 size with template H1 size);
    html.replace(H2 color with template H2 color);
    html.replace(H2 font with template H2 font);
    html.replace(H2 size with template H2 size);
    html.replace(H3 color with template H3 color);
    html.replace(H3 font with template H3 font);
    html.replace(H3 size with template H3 size);
    html.replace(text1 color with template text1 color);
    html.replace(text1 font with template text1 font);
    html.replace(text1 size with template text1 size);
    html.replace(text2 color with template text2 color);
    html.replace(text2 font with template text2 font);
    html.replace(text2 size with template text2 size);
    html.replace(text3 color with template text3 color);
    html.replace(text3 font with template text3 font);
    html.replace(text3 size with template text3 size);
    html.replace(menuColor with template menuColor);
    html.replace(menuFont with template menuFont);
    html.replace(menuSize with template menuSize);
    html.replace(backgroundColor with template
        backGroundColor);
    html.replace(backgroundImage with template
        backgroundImage);

  RETURN html;
  END PROC
END PACKAGE
```

3.9 Scheduling Package

3.9.1 Conceptual Description

The Scheduling subsystem (see Exhibit L-28) is responsible for linking available services to customers. In doing so, it also manages the operating calendar schedule by adding and removing appointments with customers. The scheduler is available to the customer and to in-house staff, thereby allowing both parties to create and remove appointments. The scheduling subsystem is linked to the database because all the services and customer information are inherently stored in the database subsystem.

The interface of the package is extremely significant to its structure. All of the information is shown through various GUI displays; the ability to select services and select them on certain dates for the customer is run through a GUI view of a calendar. The major portions of the scheduling subsystem are the Scheduling Manager, Service Manager, and Verify Appointment Addition/Deletion. Their purposes are as follow:

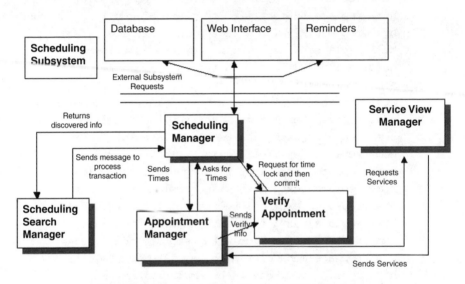

Exhibit L-28. Scheduling Package UML Diagram

- *Scheduling Manager:* allows the user to view the current schedule for any day on any upcoming or past week. This view can be for appointments, for vacant time slots, or for both. The staff user has full functional use, which means he or she can view information relating to the various appointments; the customer can only see that time slots are vacant or filled. Time slots also have a various amount of resources available to them because more than one service can be provided at a given time for different customers, depending on the scheduled services.
- *Scheduling Service Manager:* allows customer user to search for his upcoming appointments. Staff user has an additional option of searching for a certain service's upcoming date and times.
- *Service View Manager:* shows the available services for the customer and indicates the scheduling constraints uniquely innate to each.
- *Appointment Manager:* allows customer or staff user to select a service from the Service View Manager and a large enough time slot from the

scheduling, thereby creating an appointment. Appointments for a customer can also be cancelled by the same customer or employee with this portion of the subsystem. The added or removed appointment is recorded and the Scheduling Manager information is now included.

- *Verify Appointment Addition/Deletion:* once the appointment has been selected for addition or removal, a verification process is undertaken and ultimately the appointment time is updated. When the verification appointment process goes into effect, the Scheduling Manager, if invoked by another user, will display the given time slot as temporally taken so that other clients cannot attempt to fill the time slot's resources.

3.9.2 Schedule Service Object Model.

See Exhibit L-29.

3.9.3 Schedule Service Collaboration Graph.

See Exhibit L-30.

3.9.4 PSPEC

3.9.4.1 *SearchSchedulingManager*

```
PACKAGE SearchSchedulingManager IS
    PROC setSchedulingSearchCriteria(anSearchCriteria:IN,
        returnCode:OUT);
    PROC getSchedulingSearchResults(SearchResults:OUT);

//////////////////////////////////////////////////////////////
//setSchedulingSearchCriteria — set search criteria from
        user input.
//returns INTEGER
//        0 — success
//        1 — error
//////////////////////////////////////////////////////////////
PROC setSchedulingSearchCriteria(anSearchCriteria:IN,
        returnCode:OUT);
    TYPE returnCode IS INTEGER;

    Parse the search criteria for required columns.

    If required columns are identified, returnCode = success
    Else returnCode = error

    RETURN returnCode;
END PROC
```

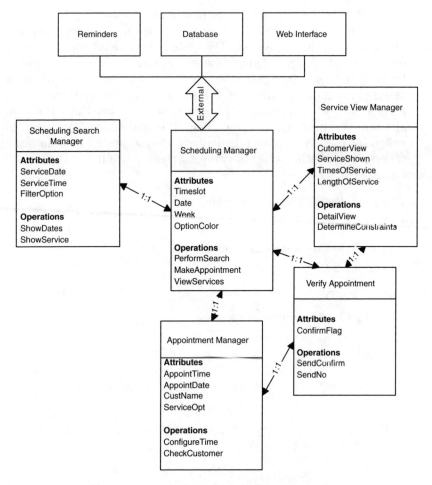

Exhibit L-29.   Schedule Service UML Diagram

```
//////////////////////////////////////////////////////////
//getSchedulingSearchResults — retrieve Schedule information
    from the database
//based on search criteria
//////////////////////////////////////////////////////////
PROC getSchedulingSearchResults(SearchResults:OUT);
    Get Scheduling information of dog owners for the set
        search criteria.
    Retrieve columns using database package.
    Cast the results into a searchResults object
    Return SearchResults;
END PROC
```

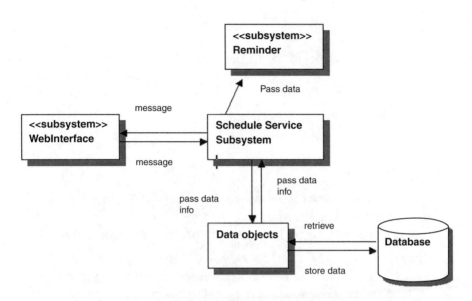

Exhibit L-30. Schedule Service Package UML Collaboration Diagram

```
END PACKAGE
```

  3.9.4.2   Verify Appointment

```
PACKAGE VerfiyAppointment IS
  PROC verifySelectedTime(timeslot:IN, returnCode:OUT);

///////////////////////////////////////////////////////////
//verifySelectedTime — takes the proposed Time Slot for
     Service
//and verifies appointment creation
//returns INTEGER
//      0 — Validated
//      1 — Cancelled
//      2 — Eror
///////////////////////////////////////////////////////////
PROC verifySelectedTime(aFormat:IN, returnCode:OUT)
    TYPE returnCode IS INTEGER;
    Get CurrentSelectedService information from Service View
        Manager
    Get Owner name, address, communicationMethod and greeting
        from owner object.
    Prompt User with action box with service, time slot
        information
    If Prompt is Yes
```

```
            returnCode = 0
        If Prompt is No
            ReturnCode = 1
        else
            returnCode = 2

        RETURN (returnCode);

    END PROC

END PACKAGE
```

3.9.4.3   Scheduling Manager

```
PACKAGE SchedulingManager IS
    PROC CreateAppointment(timeslot:IN, returnCode:OUT);

    ////////////////////////////////////////////////////////////
    //CreateAppointment — takes the proposed Time Slot for Service
    //and calls the verify process then adds it if validated
    //returns INTEGER
    //      0 — Validated
    //      1 — Canceled
    ////////////////////////////////////////////////////////////
    PROC CreateAppointment(timeslot:IN, returnCode:OUT)
        TYPE returnCode IS INTEGER;
        Get CurrentSelectedService information from Service View
            Manager
        Get Owner name, address, communicationMethod and greeting
            from owner object.
        Call verifySelectedTime
        If verifySelectedTime is validated
            Send Appointment to Database
            Return(0)
        Else
            RETURN (1)
        End proc

    END PROC

END PACKAGE
```

3.9.4.4   Service View Manager

```
PACKAGE ServiceViewManager IS
    PROC DetailView(custID:IN,services:OUT);
    PROC DetermineConstraints(custID:IN,constraintcode:OUT);
```

```
/////////////////////////////////////////////////////////////
//DetailView — Shows the services available to Given
//Customer
//returns ComboBox consisting of services
/////////////////////////////////////////////////////////////
    PROC DetailView(custID:IN,services:OUT)
    TYPE services IS ComboBox;
    Get Owner name, address, communicationMethod and greeting
        from owner object.
    Get Service, Service Description, ServiceLevel from
        Service object
    Call DetermineConstraints
    Show all Services allowed by DetermineConstraints return
        as combobox
    Return services
END PROC

/////////////////////////////////////////////////////////////
//DetermineConstraints — limits shown services available to
        Given
//Customer
//returns list of allowed service codes
/////////////////////////////////////////////////////////////
    PROC DetermineConstraints(custID:IN,constraintcode:OUT)
    TYPE constraintcode IS list;
    Use sql to create list of allowed for customer
    Get Service, Service Description, ServiceLevel from
        Service object
    Return constraintcode
    END PROC
END PACKAGE
```

3.10 Medication Ordering Package

3.10.1 Conceptual Description

The Medication ordering subsystem (see Exhibit L-31) is responsible for allowing the customer to order medication as well as ensuring the company has a reasonable supply of all prescribed medications in stock. It manages the company side and the customer side of the medicine spectrum. In doing so, it accesses the database for the various medicines' information. In regard to the customer, it accesses the customer information, knows when the medicine was given to the customer and when it should run out, and then communicates with the notification system for the customer's benefit. For the company, the medication ordering keeps a track of inventory and orders new medicine when needed. The subsystem also has a GUI system built in so that orders can be entered when initially assigned to a customer — also so that a stock can be increased if needed for some reason. (i.e., an outbreak of kennel cough) Customers are also able to order certain medications such as tick repellant via the GUI without visiting the physical site.

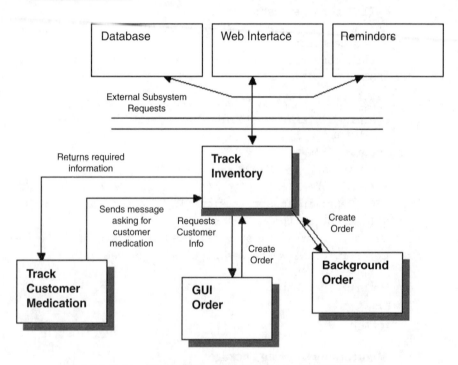

Exhibit L-31. Medication Ordering Package UML Diagram

The major portion of the medication ordering subsystem is the ability to track customer medication, track inventory, and order medication. Their purposes is as follows:

- *Track Customer Medication:* this works in congruence with the reminder subsystem. By retrieving when a reminder would be generated, a medication order can also be created.

- *Track Inventory:* whenever medication is given or sold to a customer, a record of its depletion is updated, thereby allowing for constant knowledge of a given medicine's stock.
- *GUI Order Medication:* through GUI screens orders can be generated for the customer and the staff users. The GUI screens are esthetically laid out and allowed medications can be browsed and added to a buy list. The GUI for the staff side allows a greater spectrum of options (in regard to what is available).
- *Background Order Medication:* background processing of medication orders creates order lists for the staff employees to fulfill. This function works in congruence with the track inventory function and orders medicine when asked.

3.10.2 Ordering Medication Object Model.
See Exhibit L-32.

3.10.3 Collaboration Graph.
See Exhibit L-33.

3.10.4 PSPEC

3.10.4.1 Track Inventory

```
PACKAGE TrackInventory IS
  PROC IncreaseQuant, DecreaseQuant,NewItem,RemoveItem,
      MedicationReport;

//////////////////////////////////////////////////////////
//IncreaseQuant — Increases certain Medication Quantity
//////////////////////////////////////////////////////////
  PROC IncreaseQuant(MedicationID:IN, Quantity:IN,
      Amount:IN,returncode:OUT)
    If exist
      Increase Quantity by amount
      Set returnCode = Success;
    Else
      Set returnCode = Error;
    RETURN returnCode;
  END PROC

//////////////////////////////////////////////////////////
//IncreaseQuant — increases certain Medication Quantity
//////////////////////////////////////////////////////////
  PROC IncreaseQuant(MedicationID:IN, Quantity:IN,
      Amount:IN,returncode:OUT)
    If exist
```

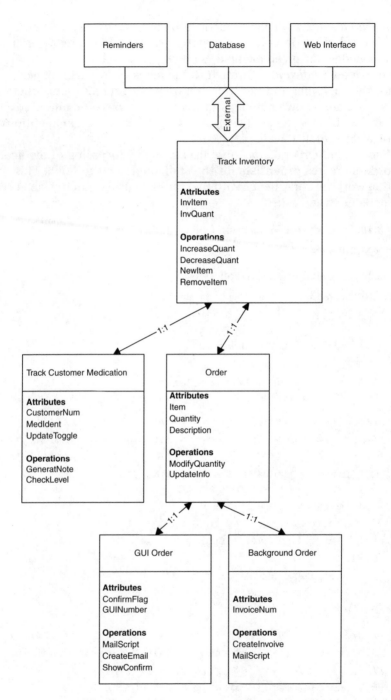

Exhibit L-32. Medication Ordering UML Diagram

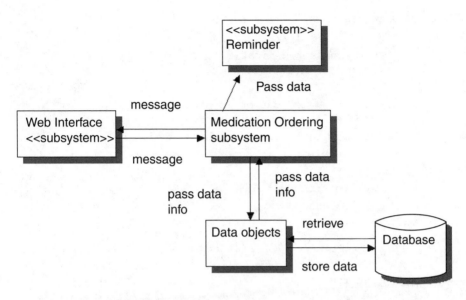

Exhibit L-33.   Medication Ordering Package UML Collaboration Diagram

```
        Decrease Quantity by amount
        Set returnCode = Success;
    Else
        Set returnCode = Error;
    RETURN returnCode;
END PROC

////////////////////////////////////////////////////////////
//AddItem — add new Item if carried
////////////////////////////////////////////////////////////
PROC AddItem(MedicationID:IN, Quantity:IN,returncode:OUT)
    If Unique MedicationID
        Set MedicationID in Database
        Prompt for Medication Information and add to Database
        Set Quantity by amount
        Set returnCode = Success;
    Else
        Set returnCode = Error;
    RETURN returnCode;
END PROC

////////////////////////////////////////////////////////////
//RemoveItem — remove Item if no longer carried, call report
        for
```

```
//excess leftover
//////////////////////////////////////////////////////////
PROC IncreaseQuant(MedicationID:IN, Quantity:IN,
        Amount:IN,returncode:OUT)
    If exist
    If Currently medication in stock Call
        medicationreport(MedicationID)
    Delete Medication from Database
        Set returnCode = Success;
    Else
        Set returnCode = Error;
    RETURN returnCode;
END PROC

//////////////////////////////////////////////////////////
//MedicationReport — print report of leftover medication for
        records
//////////////////////////////////////////////////////////
PROC MedicationReport(MedicationID:IN, Quantity:IN)
    Print document with medication id and info called from
        database
END PROC

END PACKAGE
```

3.10.4.2 Track Customer Medication

```
PACKAGE TrackCustomerMedication IS
    PROC GeneratNote, CheckLevel
    //////////////////////////////////////////////////////////
    //GenerateNote — creates note of Customer Medications
    //////////////////////////////////////////////////////////
    PROC GenerateNote(MedicationID:IN,
            CustomerID:IN,returncode:OUT)
        If exist
            Increase Quantity by amount
            Set returnCode = Success;
        Else
            Set returnCode = Error;
        RETURN returnCode;
    END PROC

    //////////////////////////////////////////////////////////
    //CheckLevel — checks level of Customer Medication quantity
    //////////////////////////////////////////////////////////
```

```
PROC CheckLevel(MedicationID:IN, Quantity:IN,
      Amount:IN,returncode:OUT)
   If exist
      Decrease Quantity by amount
      Set returnCode = Success;
   Else
      Set returnCode = Error;
   RETURN returnCode;
END PROC
```

END PACKAGE

3.10.4.3 Order Medication

```
PACKAGE OrderMedication IS
   PROC MakeOrder,UpdateInfo,PrintOrder
   ///////////////////////////////////////////////////////
   //MakeOrder - creates Order for Medication
   ///////////////////////////////////////////////////////
   PROC MakeOrder(MedicationID:IN, Quantity:IN)
      If exist
         Increase Quantity by amount
         Set returnCode = Success;
      Else
         Set returnCode = Error;
      RETURN returnCode;
   END PROC

   ///////////////////////////////////////////////////////
   //UpdateInfo - used to indicate pending order and arrival
   ///////////////////////////////////////////////////////
   PROC UpdateInfo(MedicationID:IN, Quantity:IN, Date:IN)
      If arrived
         Increase Quantity
         Remove Pending
      Else
      Increase Quantity
      Set Pending for Quantity with Date
   END PROC

   ///////////////////////////////////////////////////////
   //PrintOrder - createReadout
   ///////////////////////////////////////////////////////
   PROC PrintOrder(MedicationID:IN, Quantity:IN,DatE:IN)
```

```
        Call Database for Medication Details
        Create Printout for Medication Order
    END PROC

  END PACKAGE
```

4. GUI DESCRIPTION

The GUI for DEDS allows the user to perform all the necessary and imperative functions required to provide optimum dog care. The screens available to the user are all esthetically pleasing, while conforming to a standard powerful screen layout that allows fast and efficient use of DEDS. The system is available to users via the Internet as well as to employees located in house. Both will be shown identical screens, although the employees have access to a wider range of options. Regardless of the user type, the initial entrance into the system involves a welcome screen to the Dog-E-DayCare Website (see Exhibit L-34). From there the log-on process is invoked (see Exhibit L-35); ultimately the user will log-off and be bid adieu by the goodbye view. In between these two screens is a range of similarly designed screens allowing access to the various system features. The key screens involved in the GUI are as follows:

1. Welcome and Access Screen
2. New User Signup Page
3. Modify User Screen
4. Adding Service
5. Modifying/Deleting Service
6. Adding Reminder
7. Modifying/Deleting Reminder
8. Web Camera View
9. Submitting Payment
10. Tutorial Pages
11. Exit Screen

Users of the system are greeted with the greeting screen and have the ability to log in as an existing user or create a new account. Employees have specially assigned log-in names, while customers can log in using their user number or first and last name (middle initial requested upon multiple users with the same first and last name cases). New users can also view the daycare introduction before committing themselves to the new user process. Once logged in, a registered user can select any of the other available options.

If a user labels himself as a new user, then he goes through the signup page, where he provides pertinent information concerning living location, contact information, payment details, etc. New users also enter information concerning their dogs. For the dogs, they input all the information

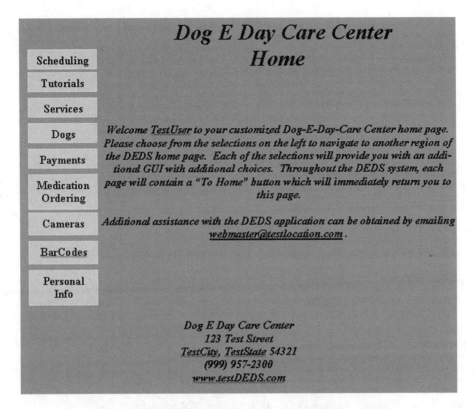

Exhibit L-34.   DEDS Personal Home Page GUI Screen Shot

they know including breed, weight, age, vaccinations, etc. The new account procedure double checks to ensure the customer is already registered and informs the user that he might be and suggests calling the clinic to find out.

Users can modify their information at any time after log-in. Any field pertaining to a user is updateable, although the information regarding canines is primarily brought up to date by employees in order to ensure accuracy. However, a user's address, payment, password, etc. are all modifiable fields.

Services can be added by picking a service and date. The calendar is displayed and available days will be shown in green. Those days can be selected and a display of the work hours appears and the user can pick open time slots. Also, a search can be done for a specific date or time slot so that the first available slot (such as 10:30 a.m.) will be displayed. Services can be selected prior to or after picking a time slot, providing the two fit together in terms of time required.

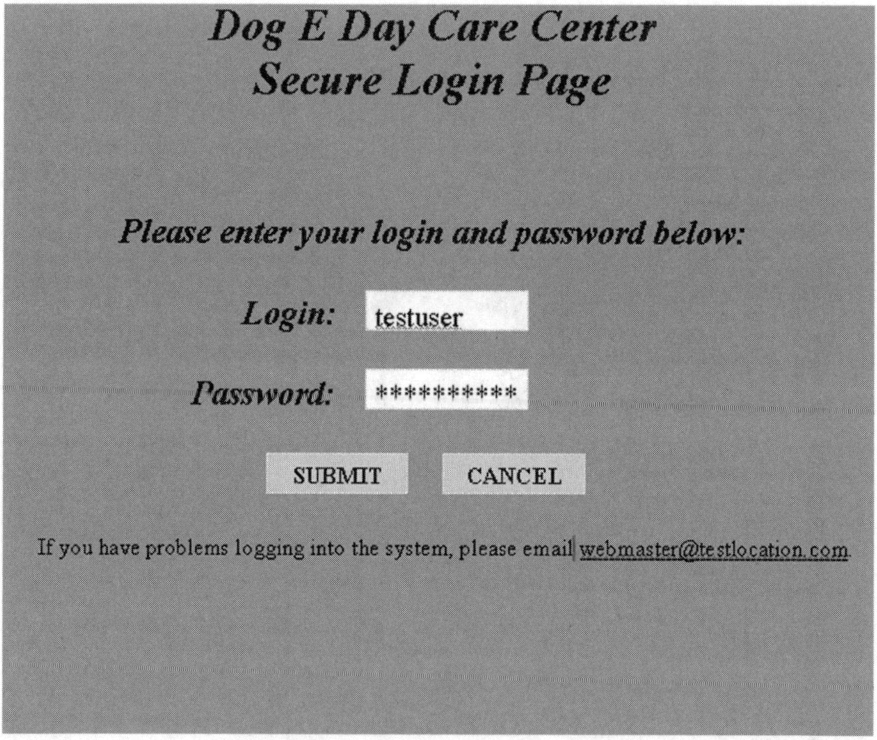

Dog E Day Care Center
Secure Login Page

Please enter your login and password below:

Login: testuser

Password: **********

SUBMIT   CANCEL

If you have problems logging into the system, please email webmaster@testlocation.com

Exhibit L-35. DEDS Login GUI Snapshot

Scheduled services can be modified or deleted upon logging on. If none are available, then a message box informs the user. Also, if the selected appointment is too close to the current day, the user is informed that he will be subject to a late notification fee. Otherwise, the user can delete the appointment or select a new date and time via the method described earlier.

Reminders can be created for users. They can involve almost anything, even for subjects unrelated to the daycare, although such nondaycare reminders can only take e-mail form. Otherwise, the user can select whether he wants a phone, e-mail, or mail reminder and for what. The background automatically creates some reminders as well. Reminders can be modified or deleted later by accessing them.

An existing user can select any of the various Web cameras located across the daycare. Each Web camera page can be selected to update automatically or simply upon a user refreshing the page. The views can be shown as real video or as an embedded java view video view.

Existing customers who owe the daycare money can submit payments. They are shown their current balance and can view an itemized account of their past performed services. An option to submit payments automatically is available if the customer has provided a credit card. Otherwise, the user can enter payment information and submit it electronically. All the pages are encrypted and further verification of customer and payment information is performed. A receipt page is displayed and sent to the user via mail and e-mail and also displayed to the screen for printing. Once payment has been accepted, the balance and itemization are updated and shown to the user.

The tutorial pages are available for user viewing. They go over all the various services, medications, doctors, breeds, and more. The information is available in downloadable form for future browsing, as well as online. A search engine is available to churn through the expansive tutorial quickly. A walkthrough is also available for users not particularly computer savvy to aid them in navigating the system and utilizing all of its options. Finally, the user can log out; a thank you and goodbye page is displayed.

5. DATA DICTIONARY

5.1. Database Interface Package

Name:	Database
Aliases:	None
Where used/how used:	As a reference to the actual database driver in middleware
Description:	Reference to the database driver that communicates with the SQL database server

Name:	DatabaseFilename
Aliases:	None
Where used/how used:	Used to store filename for database
Description:	String filename of the database

Name:	Request
Aliases:	None
Where used/how used:	Used to store the current request in middleware temporarily
Description:	String SQL request last issued by the databaseManager

Name:	Reply
Aliases:	None
Where used/how used:	Used to store the last reply in middleware temporarily
Description:	String SQL reply last returned from previous request

Name:	DatabaseMiddleware
Aliases:	None
Where used/how used:	As a reference to the middleware layer in manager
Description:	Middleware layer object controlling access to the database

Name:	sqlQuery
Aliases:	None
Where used/how used:	Used to store the current query to be sent to middleware
Description:	String SQL query to be sent to middleware layer

Name:	sqlResult
Aliases:	None
Where used/how used:	Used to store the last result obtained from middleware
Description:	String SQL reply last obtained from middleware layer

5.2   TutorialPackage

Name:	Tutorials
Aliases:	None
Where used/how used:	Contains list of tutorials in tutorial manager
Description:	Vector of tutorials so they can be accessed by the tutorial manager for searching, displaying, etc.

Name:	Templates
Aliases:	None
Where used/how used:	Contains list of templates in tutorial manager
Description:	Vector of templates so they can be accessed by the tutorial manager for applying template formatting

Name:	Gui
Aliases:	None
Where used/how used:	Used as reference in the tutorial manager to display the GUI
Description:	Reference to TutorialGUI which controls actual displaying of the tutorial information to the client

Name: HtmlText
Aliases: htmlBody
Where used/how used: HTML text for the tutorial
Description: HTML protocol text of the tutorial

Name: Images
Aliases: None
Where used/how used: Contains list of images in tutorial
Description: Vector of images so they can be accessed by the tutorial

Name: Title
Aliases: None
Where used/how used: Title of the image, tutorial, or video for display and searching
Description: String title of different objects

Name: Description
Aliases: None
Where used/how used: Description of the image, tutorial, or video for display and searching
Description: String description of different objects

Name: FileName
Aliases: None
Where used/how used: FileName of the image or video for display and searching
Description: String filename of actual file of image or video

Name: Protocol
Aliases: None
Where used/how used: Protocol of the tutorialImage to determine how to display
Description: String protocol type of the image

Name: TutorialManager
Aliases: None
Where used/how used: Reference to the TutorialManager in the TutorialGUI for displaying back to the WebInterface
Description: Reference to the TutorialManager

Name: CurrentTutorial
Aliases: None
Where used/how used: Used in GUI to know which tutorial is currently displayed

Description: String name of the current tutorial

Name: menuColor
Aliases: None
Where used/how used: Used in template to know which color to make the menu
Description: String name of the color

Name: menuFont
Aliases: None
Where used/how used: Used in template to know which font to make the menu
Description: String name of the font

Name: menuSize
Aliases: None
Where used/how used: Used in template to know which size to make the menu
Description: Integer size number

Name: heading1Color
Aliases: None
Where used/how used: Used in template to know which color to make heading1
Description: String name of the color

Name: heading1Font
Aliases: None
Where used/how used: Used in template to know which font to make heading1
Description: String name of the font

Name: heading1Size
Aliases: None
Where used/how used: Used in template to know which size to make heading 1
Description: Integer size number

Name: heading2Color
Aliases: None
Where used/how used: Used in template to know which color to make heading2
Description: String name of the color

Name: heading2Font
Aliases: None
Where used/how used: Used in template to know which font to make heading2

Description: String name of the font

Name: heading2Size
Aliases: None
Where used/how used: Used in template to know which size to make heading2
Description: Integer size number

Name: heading3Color
Aliases: None
Where used/how used: Used in template to know which color to make heading3
Description: String name of the color

Name: heading3Font
Aliases: None
Where used/how used: Used in template to know which font to make heading3
Description: String name of the font

Name: heading3Size
Aliases: None
Where used/how used: Used in template to know which size to make heading3
Description: Integer size number

Name: text1Color
Aliases: None
Where used/how used: Used in template to know which color to make text1
Description: String name of the color

Name: text1Font
Aliases: None
Where used/how used: Used in template to know which font to make text1
Description: String name of the font

Name: text1Size
Aliases: None
Where used/how used: Used in template to know which size to make text1
Description: Integer size number

Name: text2Color
Aliases: None
Where used/how used: Used in template to know which color to make text2

Description:	String name of the color

Name:	text2Font
Aliases:	None
Where used/how used:	Used in template to know which font to make text2
Description:	String name of the font

Name:	text2Size
Aliases:	None
Where used/how used:	Used in template to know which size to make text2
Description:	Integer size number

Name:	text3Color
Aliases:	None
Where used/how used:	Used in template to know which color to make text3
Description:	String name of the color

Name:	text3Font
Aliases:	None
Where used/how used:	Used in template to know which font to make text3
Description:	String name of the font

Name:	text3Size
Aliases:	None
Where used/how used:	Used in template to know which size to make text3
Description:	Integer size number

Name:	pageBackgroundColor
Aliases:	None
Where used/how used:	Used in template to know which color to make the background
Description:	String name of the background color

Name:	pageBackgroundImage
Aliases:	None
Where used/how used:	Used in template to know which image to set the background
Description:	String name of the background image file

5.3 WebInterfacePackage

Name:	Server
Aliases:	None

Where used/how used: Contains a reference to the WebServer object in manager

Description: WebServer object

Name: Templates

Aliases: None

Where used/how used: Contains list of templates in Web manager

Description: Vector of templates so they can be accessed by the Web manager for applying template formatting

Name: Port

Aliases: None

Where used/how used: Used as port number for server in the server and thread to know which port to bind to

Description: Integer port number for the server

Name: HTMLHome

Aliases: None

Where used/how used: Used in server to locate the home directory for Web pages

Description: Directory containing the HTML

Name: webManager

Aliases: None

Where used/how used: Reference to WebManager in the server to allow access to it

Description: WebManager object

Name: Thread

Aliases: None

Where used/how used: Used in Web thread to allow the class to be run by this thread of the operating system

Description: Native thread in the operating system

Name: Socket

Aliases: None

Where used/how used: Used in thread to allow access to the streams and connection status of that particular client

Description: Connection to the client

Name: menuColor

Aliases: None

Where used/how used: Used in template to know which color to make the menu

Description: String name of the color

Name: menuFont
Aliases: None
Where used/how used: Used in template to know which font to make the menu
Description: String name of the font

Name: menuSize
Aliases: None
Where used/how used: Used in template to know which size to make the menu
Description: Integer size number

Name: heading1Color
Aliases: None
Where used/how used: Used in template to know which color to make heading1
Description: String name of the color

Name: heading1Font
Aliases: None
Where used/how used: Used in template to know which font to make heading1
Description: String name of the font

Name: heading1Size
Aliases: None
Where used/how used: Used in template to know which size to make heading 1
Description: Integer size number

Name: heading2Color
Aliases: None
Where used/how used: Used in template to know which color to make heading2
Description: String name of the color

Name: heading2Font
Aliases: None
Where used/how used: Used in template to know which font to make heading2
Description: String name of the font

Name: heading2Size
Aliases: None
Where used/how used: Used in template to know which size to make heading2

Description: Integer size number

Name: heading3Color
Aliases: None
Where used/how used: Used in template to know which color to make heading3
Description: String name of the color

Name: heading3Font
Aliases: None
Where used/how used: Used in template to know which font to make heading3
Description: String name of the font

Name: heading3Size
Aliases: None
Where used/how used: Used in template to know which size to make heading3
Description: Integer size number

Name: text1Color
Aliases: None
Where used/how used: Used in template to know which color to make text1
Description: String name of the color

Name: text1Font
Aliases: None
Where used/how used: Used in template to know which font to make ext1
Description: String name of the font

Name: text1Size
Aliases: None
Where used/how used: Used in template to know which size to make text1
Description: Integer size number

Name: text2Color
Aliases: None
Where used/how used: Used in template to know which color to make text2
Description: String name of the color

Name: text2Font
Aliases: None
Where used/how used: Used in template to know which font to make text2

Description:	String name of the font
Name:	text2Size
Aliases:	None
Where used/how used:	Used in template to know which size to make text2
Description:	Integer size number
Name:	text3Color
Aliases:	None
Where used/how used:	Used in template to know which color to make text3
Description:	String name of the color
Name:	text3Font
Aliases:	None
Where used/how used:	Used in template to know which font to make text3
Description:	String name of the font
Name:	text3Size
Aliases:	None
Where used/how used:	Used in template to know which size to make text3
Description:	Integer size number
Name:	pageBackgroundColor
Aliases:	None
Where used/how used:	Used in template to know which color to make the background
Description:	String name of the background color
Name:	pageBackgroundImage
Aliases:	None
Where used/how used:	Used in template to know which image to set the background
Description:	String name of the background image file

5.4 Scheduling Package

Name:	DogId
Aliases:	None
Where used/how used:	To generate reminder and to look up dog information
Description:	Unique Identifier of a Dog — used from database

Name:	OwnerId
Aliases:	None
Where used/how used:	To generate reminder and to look up dog owner information
Description:	Unique Identifier of a Dog — used from database

Name:	TimeSlot
Aliases:	None
Where used/how used:	To indicate a given time period
Description:	Used to reserve a time on a certain day, used to create appointments

Name:	ScheduleDate
Aliases:	AppointDate
Where used/how used:	Date of a scheduled service, used to create appointment
Description:	Appointment date

Name:	ScheduleTime
Aliases:	AppointTime
Where used/how used:	Time of a scheduled service, used to create appointment
Description:	Appointment Time

Name:	FilterOption
Aliases:	None
Where used/how used:	Option used to show only certain appointments
Description:	Can view services based on criteria such as date, service, or customer

Name:	SendConfirm
Aliases:	None
Where used/how used:	Confirm selected service for making appointment
Description:	Used when selecting service to add

Name:	LengthOfService
Aliases:	None
Where used/how used:	Used in creating time slot size
Description:	Varies by service

Name:	ConfirmFlag
Aliases:	None
Where used/how used:	Used to confirm a scheduled service
Description:	Last step before creating appointment

5.5 Medication Ordering Package

Name:	OwnerId
Aliases:	None
Where used/how used:	To generate reminder and to look up dog owner information
Description:	Unique identifier of a dog — used from database

Name:	MedicineId
Aliases:	None
Where used/how used:	The ID linked to a given medicine
Description:	Unique identifier of a medicine — used from database

Name:	MedicineName
Aliases:	None
Where used/how used:	To generate forms and printouts in package
Description:	Name of a medicine — used from database

Name:	MedicationDescription
Aliases:	None
Where used/how used:	Used for print outs and forms
Description:	A detail description of related medicine

Name:	OrderDate
Aliases:	None
Where used/how used:	Date of a medication order, used for printouts and inventory
Description:	The order's date

Name:	InvoiceNum
Aliases:	None
Where used/how used:	Unique identifier for an invoice order
Description:	Invoice number

Name:	ConfirmFlag
Aliases:	None
Where used/how used:	Used to confirm an order
Description:	Last step before creating order

5.6 customerRegistrationRecord PACKAGE

Name:	OwnerFirstName
Aliases:	None
Where used/how used:	Used to register new customer and search on DEDS for existing account information
Description:	First name of the user

Name:	OwnerLastName
Aliases:	None
Where used/how used:	Used to register new customer and search on DEDS for existing account information
Description:	Last name of the user

Name:	streetAddress
Aliases:	None
Where used/how used:	Used to register new customer and search on DEDS for existing account information
Description:	Street address of user

Name:	state
Aliases:	None
Where used/how used:	Used to register new customer
Description:	Geographic state of user

Name:	phoneNumber
Aliases:	None
Where used/how used:	Used to register new customer and to search on DEDS for existing account information
Description:	Phone number of the user

Name:	eMailAddress
Aliases:	None
Where used/how used:	Used to register new customer
Description:	Internet e-mail address of user

Name:	OwnerId
Aliases:	None
Where used/how used:	To register new customer, generate reminder, and look up dog owner information
Description:	Unique identifier of a dog — used from database

Name:	password
Aliases:	None
Where used/how used:	Used to register new customer and permit access to account
Description:	Password of user

5.7 dogRegistrationRecord PACKAGE

Name:	DogName
Aliases:	None
Where used/how used:	Used to register new dog and to search on DEDS for existing account information

Description:	Name of the dog
Name:	dogColor
Aliases:	None
Where used/how used:	Used to register new dog and to search on DEDS for existing account information
Description:	Color of the dog
Name:	dogBreed
Aliases:	None
Where used/how used:	Used to register new dog
Description:	Type of the dog (breed)
Name:	dogSex
Aliases:	None
Where used/how used:	Used to register new dog and to search on DEDS for existing account information
Description:	Sex of dog (male/female)
Name:	dogAge
Aliases:	None
Where used/how used:	Used to register new dog
Description:	Age of dog
Name:	birthDate
Aliases:	None
Where used/how used:	Used to register new dog
Description:	Date of birth of dog

5.8 Camera PACKAGE

Name:	cameraID
Aliases:	None
Where used/how used:	Used to select proper camera for video transmission
Description:	Camera number

5.9 Reminder Package

Name:	DogId
Aliases:	None
Where used/how used:	To generate reminder and to look up dog information
Description:	Unique identifier of a dog — used from database
Name:	OwnerId
Aliases:	None

Where used/how used:	To generate reminder and to look up dog owner information
Description:	Unique identifier of a dog — used from database

Name:	IncomingMessage
Aliases:	None
Where used/how used:	To access any special instructions for reminders
Description:	Input value to reminders package

Name:	BirthDayMessage
Aliases:	None
Where used/how used:	System generates birth day message for dog
Description:	Birth day message for dog will be sent out to owner's address via e-mail and postal service

Name:	MedicationMessage
Aliases:	None
Where used/how used:	System generates medication message for dog
Description:	Medication message for dog will be sent out to owner's address via e-mail and postal service

Name:	RegistrationMessage
Aliases:	None
Where used/how used:	System generates medication message for dog
Description:	Medication message for dog will be sent out to owner's address via email/postal service

Name:	Greeting
Aliases:	None
Where used/how used:	Used while addressing the dog owner in letters and e-mails
Description:	Provides information about how dog owner needs to be addressed in letters and e-mails

5.10 Payment Package

Name:	CustomerName
Aliases:	None

Where used/how used: Linking payment information to customer
Description: Name of the customer

Name: PaymentType
Aliases: None
Where used/how used: Used to define payment method
Description: Type of credit card

Name: CreditCardNumber
Aliases: None
Where used/how used: Used to define payment method
Description: Credit card number

Name: Expdate
Aliases: None
Where used/how used: Used to define payment method
Description: Expiry date of credit card

Name: DefaultPaymentMethod
Aliases: None
Where used/how used: Used to identify default among multiple payment methods
Description: Indicator to show that this is the default payment method

Name: BillAmount
Aliases: None
Where used/how used: Used while generating bill
Description: Bill amount

Name: DefCurencyBilled
Aliases: None
Where used/how used: Used while generating bill
Description: Currency for the bill

Name: NameOnCreditCard
Aliases: None
Where used/how used: Used while accepting credit cards
Description: User name on the credit card

Name: BillDate
Aliases: None
Where used/how used: Used while generating bill
Description: Date on which bill is generated

Name: ServiceDetails
Aliases: None
Where used/how used: Displayed on bill

Description:	Details of various services charged

Name:	RoutingNo
Aliases:	None
Where used/how used:	Used for automatic debt process
Description:	Routing number of financial institution

Name:	BankAccountNo
Aliases:	None
Where used/how used:	Used for automatic debt process
Description:	User bank account number

Name:	ChargeAmount
Aliases:	None
Where used/how used:	Used for automatic debt process
Description:	Amount to be charged to user account

Name:	ChargeDate
Aliases:	None
Where used/how used:	Used for automatic debt process
Description:	Date on which amount to be charged to user account

Name:	FromCurrency
Aliases:	None
Where used/how used:	Used in currency conversion
Description:	From currency — conversion needs to be done

Name:	ToCurrency
Aliases:	None
Where used/how used:	Used in currency conversion
Description:	To currency — conversion needs to be done

Name:	Amount
Aliases:	None
Where used/how used:	Used in currency conversion
Description:	Amount needed to be converted

Name:	AsOfDate
Aliases:	None
Where used/how used:	Used in currency conversion
Description:	Conversion to be done as of what date

Name:	ConversionRate
Aliases:	None
Where used/how used:	Used in currency conversion

Description:	Rate of the conversion

Name:	LoggedUser
Aliases:	None
Where used/how used:	Used in security for payment package
Description:	Logged-in user

Name:	UserType
Aliases:	None
Where used/how used:	Used in security for payment package
Description:	Type of the user — clerk, admin, manager

Name:	UserRights
Aliases:	None
Where used/how used:	Used in security for payment package
Description:	Read/write permissions

5.11 Search Package

Name:	OwnerFirstName
Aliases:	None
Where used/how used:	Used to search on DEDS for existing account information
Description:	First name of the user

Name:	OwnerLastName
Aliases:	None
Where used/how used:	Used to search on DEDS for existing account information
Description:	Last name of the user

Name:	DogName
Aliases:	None
Where used/how used:	Used to search on DEDS for existing account information
Description:	Name of the dog

Name:	DogType
Aliases:	None
Where used/how used:	Used to search on DEDS for existing account information
Description:	Type of the dog (breed)

Name:	DogSex
Aliases:	None
Where used/how used:	Used to search on DEDS for existing account information
Description:	Sex of dog (male/female)

Name: PhoneNumber
Aliases: None
Where used/how used: Used to search on DEDS for existing account information
Description: Phone number of the user

Name: PaymentMethod
Aliases: None
Where used/how used: Used to display as part of search results
Description: Payment method of user

Name: ServiceDtls
Aliases: None
Where used/how used: Used to display as part of search results
Description: Details of the pet services scheduled for dog

Name: ServiceTime
Aliases: None
Where used/how used: Used to display as part of search results
Description: Timings of the pet services scheduled for dog

Appendix M
Sample Class Dictionary

Name:				Class_Header	
Aliases:				None	
Where used / How used:				Stores header information for document class types. The system allows for an unlimited number of document classes.	
Content Description:					
FIELD	DATATYPE	PK	FK	NULLS?	NOTES
chID	Int	Y		N	Identity
chName	Varchar				
ChDesc	Varchar				
ModifyBy	Varchar				
ModifyDate	Varchar				

Name:				Attrib_Header	
Aliases:				None	
Where used/How used:				Stores attribute information for each class type. For example, the tool kit part class has multiple dimensions and each dimension is defined as an attribute with a corresponding label. This allows the user to define new part/document class types dynamically.	
Content Description:					
FIELD	DATATYPE	PK	FK	NULLS?	NOTES
ahID	Int	Y		N	Identity
ahcID	Int		Y	N	Stores class ID
ahLabel	Varchar				Label that displays on the screen
ModifyBy	Varchar				
ModifyDate	Varchar				

Name:	Atrib_Detail				
Aliases:	None				
Where used/How used:	Stores the values for attributes defined in the attrib_header table. If a row in this table contains values for the part number, version, and revision fields, then that row stores attribute values for a specific part number or document. If a row in this table contains a value for AttribHeaderID table, then that row is used to define the structure of a class.				
Content Description:					
FIELD	DATATYPE	PK	FK	NULLS?	NOTES
AdID	Int	Y		N	Identity
adhID	Varchar		Y		Only present for class definition; stores attribute header ID
AdPN	Varchar				
AdRev	Varchar				
AdVer	Varchar				
adValue	Varchar				
adUnits	Varchar				
ModifyBy	Varchar				
ModifyDate	Varchar				

Name:	Attrib_Constraint				
Aliases:	None				
Where used / How used:	Stores validation rules for the attribute_details table. When attribute values are entered through the user interface, the application performs validation using this table.				
Content Description:					
FIELD	DATATYPE	PK	FK	NULLS?	NOTES
AcID	Int	Y		N	Identity
AchID	Int		Y	N	Stores attribute header ID
AcJoinType	Varchar				And—Or
acCondition	Varchar				Must be "=,<,>,Like, Not Like"
acValue	Varchar				Specified value
ModifyBy	Varchar				
ModifyDate	Varchar				

Name:				Workflow_State	
Aliases:				None	
Where used/How used:				Defines available workflow states	
Content Description:					
FIELD	DATATYPE	PK	FK	NULLS?	NOTES
WsID	Int	Y		N	Identity
WsName	Varchar				
WsDesc	Varchar				
ModifyBy	Varchar				
ModifyDate	Varchar				

Name:				Workflow_Template	
Aliases:				None	
Where used/How used:				Stores workflow template header information	
Content Description:					
FIELD	DATATYPE	PK	FK	NULLS?	NOTES
WtID	Int	Y		N	Identity
WtName	Varchar				
WtDesc	Varchar				
ModifyBy	Varchar				
ModifyDate	Varchar				

Appendix N
Control Sheet

DATE ORIGINAL PROGRAM:

1/18/02

DATE OF MODIFIED PROGRAM (THIS WILL BE THE SAME AS DATE ORIGINAL PROGRAM IF THIS IS A NEW PROGRAM):

1/25/02

PROGRAM NAME:

Currency Converter Utility

PROGRAMMER NAME:

Jerry V.

VERSION NUMBER (START AT V1.0):

V1.0
V1.1

DESCRIPTION OF PROGRAM:

Program converts one currency to another currency and displays in a table format.

CONFIGURATION:

Microsoft Visual C++

DESCRIPTION OF CHANGES:

Changes have been made to pull currencies from a text file. Also added option to print data.
No changes have been made for this release. Print option was added to version 1.1

Appendix O
Test Plan

1   REVISION HISTORY

The following is a revision history table for the Dog E-DayCare system's software test cases document:

Date	Version	Description	Author(s)

2   INTRODUCTION

Software testing is a critical quality assurance step in the software development process. Testing of the Dog E-DayCare system is undertaken to identify errors in the product before delivery to the client. Thorough testing ensures the product will meet user requirements, thus minimizing costs in the long run, bolstering client satisfaction, and promoting repeat business.

The purpose of this document is to provide the test plan for the Dog E-DayCare system, detailing the testing strategy, metrics, artifacts, schedule, procedures, and test cases. Two sets of sample test cases have been developed: class test cases and integration test cases. Class test cases focus on classes and their operations within a specific subsystem. Integration test cases take a larger view of the product, uncovering errors that could occur as subsystems interact.

2.1 Goals and Objectives

Dog E-DayCare connects dog owners to dog care service providers, providing a Web-based national forum to locate, purchase, and monitor pet care services. The mission of the Dog E-DayCare project team is to fill a gap in the current market for online pet care resources. For dog owners, finding a service that meets their immediate needs can be challenging; for dog care service providers, a vibrant market can be reached. Dog E-DayCare envisions bringing together dog owners and service providers nationally to support this challenge.

2.2 Statement of Scope

Although several online directories of pet care services are available, few e-businesses offer a service locator as well as the ability to purchase and monitor pet care services online.

The Dog E-DayCare system will be released in two phases. In the first phase, it will allow dog owners to search for services within a radius of their choice and based on their specific needs, whether they are looking for on-going in-home daycare, daycare outside the home, or an afternoon walk and grooming. Once a dog owner selects a service, the Dog E-DayCare system will allow him to submit all required information, and schedule, and pay for service.

Dog care service providers who have registered with Dog E-DayCare will have access to the system through two different forums: client software on their workstations and the Web. The system will notify service providers of potential clients, allowing them to communicate with dog owners and access submitted information. Service providers will be able to coordinate scheduling of multiple clients, and to e-mail and bill clients.

Phase II of the Dog E-DayCare system will introduce a range of additional tools to facilitate communication between the customer and service provider. Discussion forums, chat rooms, and instant messaging will greatly enhance customer-service provider relations. In addition, with selected service providers, customers will be able to view their dogs online and receive an update of the dog's status. Dog E-DayCare users will also be able to access dog care "tips of the day."

Dog E-DayCare also envisions partnering with community service organizations — for example, matching puppy raisers to puppies for Guiding Eyes for the Blind, or potential dog owners to rescued dogs on behalf of Lab Rescue. Community service is the foundation on which Dog E-DayCare is built.

2.3 Major Constraints

As identified in the Software Requirements Specification, the most obvious limitation in this project is the experience of the project team. This is our first attempt to go through the entire software development life cycle and present a product that satisfies requirements in a timely and efficient manner. Thorough testing is particularly imperative in this context.

3 TEST PLAN

The test plan provides an incremental and iterative process of testing from small to large. The Dog E-DayCare system has been designed using an object-oriented approach. Its smallest components are the classes that encapsulate the responsibilities and attributes associated with the system's various functions. Sets of related classes have been organized into subsystems. The testing process first examines the classes within subsystems through class testing, and then examines the interactions among subsystems through integration testing. Integration testing is followed by validation testing and system testing, which are not addressed in this plan.

The overall system description, test strategy, testing resources and output, and test schedule are detailed below.

3.1 System Description

The Dog E-DayCare system is composed of seven subsystems; each has an associated interface and represents a set of related responsibilities. The subsystems comprise the following:

- Application controller
- User management
- Resource management
- Order
- Accounting
- Customer relationship management (available in Phase II)
- Persistence

The application controller subsystem provides a "core" for the entire application, acting as "Grand Central Station" for every process that takes place within the scope of the application. The user management subsystem provides a central location for handling each piece of user data. The resource management subsystem provides the application with its overall scheduling capabilities and the order subsystem has responsibility for supporting the ordering of products and services from service providers by Dog E-DayCare clients. The accounting subsystem is responsible for processing financial transactions. The customer relationship management subsystem enables the application to provide an opportunity for interaction between customers and service care providers. (This feature set will be available in Phase II.) Finally, the persistence subsystem is responsible for storage, retrieval, and update of data.

The system collaboration diagram demonstrates the collaboration or "hand-shaking" that takes place throughout the major subsystems within the application. The application controller is the core of the system — each subsystem generates a request and a corresponding response. The application controller must handle the request and the response; it receives the request, processes a response, and returns the response to the calling function. This can also cross over into other layers of the system. For example, if the accounting subsystem request requires information from the ordering subsystem in order to accomplish its tasks, the application controller mediates between these subsystems to formulate a response and provide it to the requestor.

3.1.1   System Collaboration Diagram

Exhibit O-1 depicts the collaborations that exist between the major Dog E-DayCare subsystems.

3.2   Testing Strategy

In the object-oriented context, no operation can be tested in isolation; this poses a challenge to testers. The overall objective of testing is to uncover errors. The strategy for testing the Dog E-DayCare system entails first thoroughly testing the classes within subsystems through class testing, and then testing interactions among subsystems through scenario-based integration testing.

A set of test cases is developed for each testing method. Test cases for both methods must exercise the requirements of the system. For the purpose of this test plan, a sample of tests have been developed and are provided in Appendices 1 and 2. Further details on class and integration testing in general are provided in the section on testing procedures below.

3.3   Testing Resources

3.3.1   Staffing

The project team developing the Dog E-DayCare system consists of four members as detailed in the table below. Testing is a joint activity in which all team members participate. This activity is led by the documentation specialist.

Team Members:

- Senior Web software developer
- Senior Web designer
- Senior documentation specialist
- Project lead — software engineer

3.3.2   Tools

The hardware used for testing the Dog E-DayCare system will include:

- SQL server 2000 to host the system
- Desktop (Pentium III processor) with a standard 56 K modem to access the system
- Laptop to record test results

Software required for testing will include the stubs and drivers developed to support class testing.

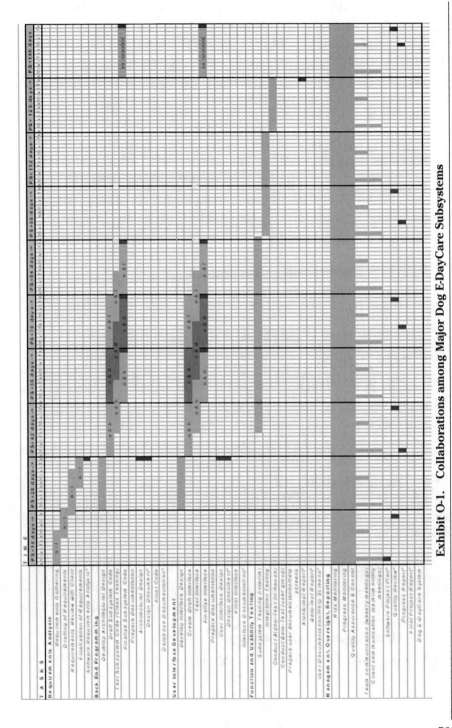

Exhibit O-1. Collaborations among Major Dog E-DayCare Subsystems

3.4 Testing Metrics

It is envisioned that class and integration testing will be carried out through several iterations until all errors are corrected. For each iteration, class testing will involve recording the following metrics:

- For each class, indicators of test failure (as identified in the test cases)
- Number of failure indicators per class
- Number of failure indicators per subsystem
- A categorization of failure indicators by severity
- Number of repeat failures (not resolved in the previous iteration)
- Hours spent by test team in test process
- Hours spent by development team in correcting failures

Integration testing will involve recording a similar set of metrics for each iteration; however, the level of analysis will be the scenario. In other words:

- For each scenario, indicators of test failure (as identified in the test cases)
- Number of failure indicators per scenario
- A categorization of failure indicators by severity
- Number of repeat failures (not resolved in the previous iteration)
- Hours spent by test team in test process
- Hours spent by development team in correcting failures

3.5 Testing Artifacts

The artifacts of testing provided to the client include:

- Test plan
- Test cases
- Test results
- Test report

3.6 Testing Schedule

Class testing will be undertaken as each set of subsystems is completed. The following provides general information on how testing will be scheduled:

- PS + 35 days: class testing of application controller and persistence subsystems
- PS + 49 days: class testing of user management and order subsystems
- PS + 64 days: class testing of resource management and accounting subsystems
- PS + 86 days: scenario-based integration testing

A detailed project schedule is provided in Appendix 3.

4 TEST PROCEDURES

4.1 Class Testing

Based on the project schedule, class testing will take place as pairs of subsystems have been completed. Test cases for class testing must be explicitly associated with the class to be tested; effective class testing depends on well-articulated test cases. The test cases detail the:

- *Description.* The description includes the test purpose, i.e., which class will be tested and the particular responsibilities to be tested.
- *Required stubs and drivers.* As stated previously, components of an object-oriented system cannot be tested in isolation. Because of the collaborations that must take place within and across subsystems, class testing will likely require the use of stubs and drivers. In object-oriented testing, a stub is a stand-in for a subclass and a driver is a type of tester class that accepts test case data, passes data back to the class, and prints relevant results.
- *Test steps.* The test steps detail the events and states the system will move through from the beginning through the end of the test.
- *Expected results.* The expected results provide indicators of test success and test failure.

4.2 Integration Testing

Based on the project schedule, integration testing will take place once all subsystems have been developed and tested. Test cases are scenario based, reflecting what users need to do with the Dog E-DayCare system. Similar to the preceding test cases, the integration test cases detail the:

- *Description.* The description includes the test purpose, i.e., which scenario or use case will be tested, and the particular subsystems that must interact in order for the scenario to be completed.
- *Required stubs andr drivers.* In object-oriented testing, stubs and drivers are critical for class testing. However, if class testing is thorough, stubs and drivers would not be necessary for completion of integration testing.
- *Test steps.* The test steps detail the events and states the system will move through from the beginning through the end of the test.
- *Expected results.* The expected results provide indicators of test success and test failure.

Sample class and integration test cases are provided in Appendices 1 and 2, respectively.

5   APPENDIX 1: CLASS TESTING TEST CASES

Class tests are developed for each subsystem of the Dog E-DayCare system. A sample of class test cases follows.

5.1   Application Controller Subsystem

The application controller subsystem provides a "core" for the entire application. The controller acts as "Grand Central Station" for every process that takes place within the scope of the application.

5.1.1   Test Case: ApplicationController:ApplicationController

5.1.1.1   Description

This test case tests to see if the user functions invoked by the application user interface are handled correctly. This interface is invoked by the other subsystems when actions are performed and requests are made from their respective user interfaces. This particular test focuses on the user who is attempting to search for a service care provider within his area.

5.1.1.2   Required Stubs/Drivers

- The SearchUI that is part of the presentation layer will be invoked.

5.1.1.3   Test Steps

1. The user will press the search button within the order subsystem, which is part of the presentation layer.
2. The user will be presented with a form to fill in the search criteria.
3. The search criteria will be concatenated to form a full select query against the database. ("Select * from ServiceSchedule where location = inputlocation and date/time = inputdatetime and servicetype = inputservicetype order by location")
4. The user's search criteria will be evaluated and the results displayed.
5. The user may then select the desired result and schedule the service.

5.1.1.4   Expected Results

Test success

1. The application controller subsystem successfully handles the routing of the information so that the query data goes from the presentation layer to the application controller layer, to the persistence layer and, ultimately, is used to query the database. Success will be measured by the accuracy of the information (results) returned as a result of the query string.

Test failure

1. The concatenation that must take place to form the query could be invalid, which would result in an error message when the query is executed against the database.
2. The route that the application controller must take may not be followed because of a flaw in the logic.
3. The query string concatenation may not be sufficient and the wrong data could be returned.

5.1.2   Test Case: ApplicationController:ApplicationController

5.1.2.1   Description

This test case tests to see if the user functions invoked by the application user interface are handled correctly. This interface is invoked by the other subsystems when actions are performed and requests are made from their respective user interfaces. This particular test will verify that the user is able to view the tip of the day when the tip-of-the-day button is pressed.

5.1.2.2   Required Stubs and Drivers

The CommunicationUI from the customer relationship management module will be used heavily in conjunction with the communication class within that same subsystem.

5.1.2.3   Test Steps

- The user will successfully log into the system.
- The user will press the tip-of-the-day button.
- The tip of the day will be displayed within the user interface.

5.1.2.4   Expected Results

Test successs

1. The success of the test must be measured based on the application controller subsystem's ability to use the system data to determine the date and then use that date as the query string to invoke the persistence subsystem, which will use the query string against the database. The test passes if the tip of the day is returned with the correct tip of the day for today's date.

Test failure

1. An exception may occur if the incorrect date is retrieved from the system time; therefore, the wrong tip of the day is returned.
2. An exception may also occur if the correct tip is displayed, but in an incorrect format.

5.1.3 Test Case: ApplicationController:ApplicationController

5.1.3.1 Description

This test case tests to see if the user functions invoked by the application user interface are handled correctly. This interface is invoked by the other subsystems when actions are performed and requests are made from their respective user interfaces. This specific test will determine if the user's account balance is updated after a payment is made.

5.1.3.2 Required Stubs/Drivers

1. The PaymentUI, which is part of the presentation layer, must have been invoked and a payment must be attempted.
2. The accounting subsystem and its interfaces will be invoked.

5.1.3.3 Test Steps

1. The user will successfully log into the system.
2. The user will navigate to his account information.
3. The user will select the option to make a payment on their balance.
4. The user will be presented a form with which to indicate the amount of the payment and to provide or change credit card information.
5. The user will enter an amount and use the preregistered credit card information.
6. The user will press the pay button.

5.1.3.4 Expected Results

Test success

1. The success of this test can be measured by the user's new balance reflecting the recent payment on the account balance. Performing a query against the database to determine if the account balance is correct will test this. The ApplicationController is tested because it is responsible for ensuring that the correct route is followed to ultimately commit the transaction and return a successful message.

Test failure

1. An exception may occur if the query string is malformed. This could be caused by invalid data entry or faulty logic.
2. An exception may also occur if the update is unsuccessful and the query returns an invalid balance.

5.1.4 Test Case: ApplicationController:ApplicationController

5.1.4.1 Description

This test case tests to see if the user functions invoked by the application user interface are handled correctly. This interface is invoked by the other subsystems when actions are performed and requests are made from their respective user interfaces. This particular test will ensure that the service care provider can successfully update scheduling information.

5.1.4.2   *Required Stubs/Drivers*

The resource management subsystem will be invoked with particular attention to the resource class, which is used for scheduling.

5.1.4.3   *Test Steps*

1. The service care provider will successfully log into the system.
2. The service care provider will press the resource button.
3. A form will be presented that will allow the service care provider to specify that he wants to edit the resource schedule.
4. The service care provider will modify the employee schedule to exclude the dog shearer on a particular day.

5.1.4.4   *Expected Results*

Test success

1. The success of this test can be determined by a query performed against the database, which is invoked when the user attempts to search for that particular service. The application controller will be tested because its responsibility is to accept the query string and commit the transaction to the database via the persistence subsystem.

Test failure

1. An exception may occur if the concatenation of the query string is faulty, which will result in a database SQL error.
2. An exception may also occur if the user cannot see the changes updated via the user interface, which indicates that the test was unsuccessful.

5.2   User Management Subsystem

The user management subsystem provides a central location for handling every piece of user data. This is very important in the parsing of the system.

5.2.1   Test Case: Security Manager :: addUser(in user : User)

5.2.1.1   *Description*

The purpose of the test is to determine whether the security manager class is carrying out its responsibilities as expected. Security manager is a critical class of the user management subsystem, adding and removing users and their roles, and authenticating users. This test will focus specifically on adding a user to the system.

5.2.1.2   Required Stubs/Drivers

Driver: IUserInterfaceDriver (smaller version of IUserInterface class)
RegisterUIDriver (smaller version of RegisterUI class)
Stubs: UserStub (smaller version of user class)
NextStub (captures next button clicks)

5.2.1.3   Test Steps

1. Open register user interface.
2. Input information "about you."
3. Click next.
4. Input information "about your dog."
5. Click next.
6. Input user name and password.
7. Click finish.
8. View results.

5.2.1.4   Expected Results

Test success

1. Driver displays information entered for user.

Test failure

1. Driver does not display information entered for user.

5.2.2   Test Case: Security Manager :: removeUser(in user : User)

5.2.2.1   Description

The purpose of the test is to determine whether the security manager class is carrying out its responsibilities as expected. Security manager is a critical class of the user management subsystem, adding and removing users and their roles, and authenticating users. This test will focus specifically on removing a user.

5.2.2.2   Required Stubs/Drivers

Driver: IUserInterfaceDriver (smaller version of IUserInterface class)
RegisterUIDriver (smaller version of RegisterUI class)
Stubs: UserStub (smaller version of user class)
NextStub (captures next button clicks)

5.2.2.3   Test Steps

1. Open register user interface.
2. Select option to "cancel registration."
3. Input user ID in appropriate field.
4. Click "remove."
5. View results.

5.2.2.4   Expected Results

Test success

1. User ID removed no longer appears in user ID table.

Test failure

1. User ID removed persists in user ID table.

5.2.3   Test Case: Security Manager :: authenticateUser(in user : User) : Boolean

5.2.3.1   Description

The purpose of the test is to determine whether the security manager class is carrying out its responsibilities as expected. Security manager is a critical class of the user management subsystem, adding and removing users and their roles, and authenticating users. This test will focus specifically on user authentication.

5.2.3.2   Required Stubs/Drivers

Driver: IUserInterfaceDriver (smaller version of IUserInterface class)
        LoginUIDriver (smaller version of LoginUI class)
Stubs: UserStub (smaller version of User class)
        NextStub (captures next button clicks)
        RoleStub (captures role assigned to user)

5.2.3.3   Test Steps

1. Open login user interface.
2. Input user name and password.
3. Click login.
4. View results.

5.2.3.4   Expected Results

Test success

1. User enters a correct user name and password, the welcome page appears and the name of the user is displayed in the upper right corner.
2. User enters an incorrect name and password. A login failure message is displayed asking the user to try again.

Test failure

1. User enters a correct user name and password. A login failure message is displayed.

2. User enters an incorrect user name and password, the welcome page appears and the name of the user is displayed in the upper right corner.

5.2.4 Test Case: Customer :: getDogs() : Collection

5.2.4.1 Description

The purpose of the test is to determine whether the customer class is carrying out its responsibilities as expected. The customer's role in the user management subsystem is to receive, store, and return a range of information associated with a particular customer. This test will focus specifically on retrieving a list of all dogs belonging to a specific customer.

5.2.4.2 Required Stubs/Drivers

Driver: IUserInterfaceDriver (smaller version of IUserInterface class)
SearchUIDriver (smaller version of SearchUI class)
Stubs: UserStub (smaller version of user class)
NextStub (captures next button clicks)
DogStub (small version of animal owner, animal, and dog classes)

5.2.4.3 Test Steps

1. Open search user interface (for service providers).
2. Input customer ID.
3. Click search.
4. View results.

5.2.4.4 Expected Results

Test success

1. The names of all dogs owned by the customer are listed in the results page.

Test failure

1. The names of dogs owned by other customers are listed in the results.
2. No dog names are listed in the results.

5.2.5 Test Case: Customer :: getInvoices() : Collection

5.2.5.1 Description

The purpose of the test is to determine whether the customer class is carrying out its responsibilities as expected. The customer's role in the user management subsystem is to receive, store, and return a range of information associated with a particular customer. This test will focus specifically on retrieving a correct list of all invoices associated with a customer.

5.2.5.2   Required Stubs/Drivers

Driver: IUserInterfaceDriver (smaller version of IUserInterface class)
SearchUIDriver (smaller version of SearchUI class)
Stubs: UserStub (smaller version of user class)
NextStub (captures next button clicks)
InvoiceStub (smaller version of invoice class)

5.2.5.3   Test Steps

1. Open Dog E-DayCare search interface (for service providers).
2. Enter customer ID.
3. Click on search.
4. View results.

5.2.5.4   Expected Results

Test success

1. All invoices associated with the customer are listed.

Test failure

1. Invoices associated with another customer are listed.
2. None of the invoices associated with the customer is listed.

5.2.6   Test Case: Service Provider :: addServiceOffering()

5.2.6.1   Description

The purpose of the test is to determine whether the service provider class is carrying out its responsibilities as expected. The service provider's role in the user management subsystem is to receive, store, and return a range of information associated with a particular service provider. This test will focus specifically on adding a service offering for a specific service provider.

5.2.6.2   Required Stubs/Drivers

Driver: IUserInterfaceDriver (smaller version of IUserInterface class)
RegisterUIDriver (smaller version of RegisterUI class)
Stubs: ServiceProviderStub (smaller version of service provider class)
ServiceStub(smaller version of service class)
NextStub (captures next button clicks)

5.2.6.3   Test Steps

1. Open service details page of company registration.
2. Input service information requested.
3. Click "add another service."
4. Input service information requested.

5. Click "next."
6. View results.

5.2.6.4 Expected Results

Test success

1. Services information for particular company is present in service table.

Test failure

1. Service information for particular company is not present in service table.

5.2.7 Test Case: Service Provider:: getAddress()

5.2.7.1 Description

The purpose of the test is to determine whether the service provider class is carrying out its responsibilities as expected. The service provider's role in the user management subsystem is to receive, store, and return a range of information associated with a particular service provider. This test will focus specifically on retrieving address information for a service provider.

5.2.7.2 Required Stubs/Drivers

Driver: IUserInterfaceDriver (smaller version of IUserInterface class)
SearchUIDriver (smaller version of SearchUI class)
Stubs: ServiceProviderStub (smaller version of ServiceProvider class)
NextStub (captures next button clicks)

5.2.7.3 Test Steps

1. Open Dog E-DayCare search interface (for customers).
2. Enter name of service provider.
3. Click on "search."
4. View results.

5.2.7.4 Expected Results

Test success

1. If address information is available, correct address information is displayed in search results.
2. If address information is not available, no address information is displayed in search results.

Test failure

1. If address information is available, incorrect address information is displayed in search results.
2. If address information is not available, someone else's address information is displayed in search results.

5.3 Resource Management Subsystem

This resource management subsystem provides the application with its overall scheduling capabilities. It uses various respective classes and subsystems to ensure that the user has up-to-date information regarding the services he is interested in.

5.3.1 Test Case: ResourceUI :: showCreate()

5.3.1.1 Description

The purpose of this test case is to test the resource management user interface class's (ResourceUI) showCreate() method to determine if it can display the "register company — resource details" screen as an add screen.

5.3.1.2 Required Stubs/Drivers

Driver: IUserInterfaceDriver (smaller version of IUserInterface class)
Stubs: ResourceStub (smaller version of resource class)
NextStub (captures next button clicks)
OtherButtonsStub (captures other buttons clicked)

5.3.1.3 Test Steps

1. Execute the IUserInterfaceDriver in a Web browser.
2. Select "staff" from the resource type drop down list.
3. Enter a staff member's first name (if resource type = staff).
4. Enter a staff member's last name (if resource type = staff).
5. Select an item in the position drop down list.
6. Determine that the height, width, and length fields are protected.
7. Press the next button.

5.3.1.4 Expected Results

Test success

1. The IUserInterfaceDriver should display the "Register company — resource details" screen in the Web browser.
2. The resource type drop down list should contain an entry for staff and permit its selection.
3. The staff member first name can be entered.
4. The staff member last name can be entered.

5. The position drop down list can be entered and should permit the selection of one of its items.
6. The height, width, and length fields should be protected.
7. The next stub should return a basic Web page.

Test failure

1. Report all failures.

5.3.2 Test Case: ResourceUI :: showEdit()

5.3.2.1 Description

The purpose of this test case is to test the resource management user interface class's (ResourceUI) showEdit() method to determine if it can display the "register company — resource details" screen as an edit screen.

5.3.2.2 Required Stubs/Drivers

Driver: IUserInterfaceDriver (smaller version of IUserInterface class)
Stubs: ResourceStub (smaller version of resource class)
NextStub (captures next button clicks)
OtherButtonsStub (captures other buttons clicked)

5.3.2.3 Test Steps

1. Execute the IUserInterfaceDriver in a Web browser.
2. Determine that "staff" is displayed from the resource type drop down list.
3. Update the staff member's first name (if resource type = staff).
4. Update the staff member's last name (if resource type = staff).
5. Select another item in the position drop down list.
6. Determine that the height, width, and length fields are protected.
7. Press the next button.

5.3.2.4 Expected Results

Test success

1. The IUserInterfaceDriver should display the "register company — resource details" screen in the Web browser.
2. The resource type drop down list should display an entry for staff.
3. The staff member first name should be updated.
4. The staff member last name should be updated.
5. The position drop down list should be enterable and permit the selection of one of its items.
6. The height, width, and length fields should be protected.
7. The next stub should return a basic Web page.

Test failure

1. Report all failures.

5.3.3 Test Case: ResourceUI :: showSearch()

5.3.3.1 Description

The purpose of this test case is to test the resource management user interface class's (ResourceUI) showSearch() method to determine if it can display resource search screen (example not present in SDS).

5.3.3.2 Required Stubs/Drivers

Driver: IUserInterfaceDriver (smaller version of IUserInterface class)
Stubs: ServiceProviderStub (smaller version of ServiceProvider class)
ResourceStub (smaller version of resource class)
SearchStub (captures search button clicks)
OtherButtonsStub (captures other buttons clicked)

5.3.3.3 Test Steps

1. Execute the IUserInterfaceDriver in a Web browser.
2. Determine that the service provider drop down list displayed.
3. Determine that the resource type drop down list displayed.
4. Select a service provider from the service provider drop down list.
5. Select a resource type from the resource type drop down list.
6. Press the search button.

5.3.3.4 Expected Results

Test success

1. The IUserInterfaceDriver should display the "register company — resource details" screen in the Web browser.
2. The service provider drop down list should display service providers.
3. The resource type drop down list should display the resource types that the selected service provider supports.
4. The service provider selected should be visible in the drop down list.
5. The resource type selected should be visible in the drop down list.
6. The search stub should return a basic Web page.

Test failure

1. Report all failures.

5.4   Order Subsystem

The Order Subsystem has responsibility for supporting the ordering of products and services from Service Providers by Dog E-DayCare™ clients.

5.4.1   Test Case: OrderUI :: showCreate()

5.4.1.1   Description

The purpose of this test case is to test the order user interface class's (OrderUI) showCreate() method to determine if it can display the "order — initiate order" screen (see SDS section 11.10) and if the drop down lists are populated.

5.4.1.2   Required Stubs/Drivers

Driver: IUserInterfaceDriver (smaller version of IUserInterface class)
Stubs: OrderStub (smaller version of order class)
         ServiceProviderStub (smaller version of ServiceProvider class)
         ServiceStub (smaller version of service class)
         AppointmentStub (smaller version of appointment class)
         OtherButtonsStub (captures other buttons clicked)

5.4.1.3   Test Steps

1. Execute the IUserInterfaceDriver in a Web browser.
2. Select an item in the service provider drop down list.
3. Select an item in the service drop down list.
4. Select an item in the service duration drop down list.
5. Select an item in the time frame drop down list.

5.4.1.4   Expected Results

Test success

1. The IUserInterfaceDriver should display the "order — initiate order" screen in the Web browser.
2. The service provider drop down list should contain a list of service providers.
3. The service drop down list should contain a list of services offered by the selected service provider.
4. The service duration drop down list should contain a list of service durations available for the selected service.
5. The time frame drop down list should contain a list of all opening for the selected service.

Test failure

1. Report all failures.

5.4.2 Test Case: OrderUI :: showEdit()

5.4.2.1 *Description*

The purpose of this test case is to test the order user interface class's (OrderUI) showEdit() method to determine if it can display the "order — order details" screen.

5.4.2.2 *Required Stubs/Drivers*

Driver: IUserInterfaceDriver (smaller version of IUserInterface class)
Stubs: OrderStub (smaller version of Order class)
        OtherButtonsStub (captures other buttons clicked)

5.4.2.3 *Test Steps*

1. Execute the IUserInterfaceDriver in a Web browser.
2. Determine if the correct service provider is displayed.
3. Determine if the correct service is displayed.
4. Determine if the correct location is displayed.
5. Determine if the correct phone number is displayed.
6. Determine if the correct e-mail address is displayed.
7. Determine if the correct appointment is displayed.

5.4.2.4 *Expected Results*

Test success

1. The IUserInterfaceDriver should display the "order — order details" screen in the Web browser.
2. The service provider name should display.
3. The service name should display.
4. The location should display.
5. The phone number should display.
6. The e-mail address should display.
7. The appointment should display.

Test failure

1. Report all failures.

5.4.3 Test Case: OrderUI :: showSearch()

5.4.3.1 *Description*

The purpose of this test case is to test the order user interface class's (OrderUI) showSearch() method to determine if it can display the "search" screen and conduct a search using a stub to display the "results."

5.4.3.2   Required Stubs/Drivers

Driver: IUserInterfaceDriver (smaller version of IUserInterface class)
Stubs: SearchStub (captures search button clicks)
         OtherButtonsStub (captures other buttons clicked)

5.4.3.3   Test Steps

1. Execute the IUserInterfaceDriver in a Web browser.
2. Enter a value in the customer ID field.
3. Press the search button.
4. Enter a value in the customer name field.
5. Press the search button.
6. Enter a value in the order ID field.
7. Press the search button.
8. Enter a value in the invoice ID field.
9. Press the search button.

5.4.3.4   Expected Results

Test success

1. The IUserInterfaceDriver should display the "search" screen in the Web browser.
2. The screen should permit entry of a customer ID.
3. The search stub should return a basic Web page.
4. The screen should permit entry of a customer name.
5. The search stub should return a basic Web page.
6. The screen should permit entry of an order ID.
7. The search stub should return a basic Web page.
8. The screen should permit entry of an invoice ID.
9. The search stub should return a basic Web page.

Test failure

1. Report all failures.

5.4.4   Test Case: OrderUI :: showList()

5.4.4.1   Description

The purpose of this test case is to test the order user interface class's (OrderUI) showList() method to determine if it can display the "search results — customer search results" screen.

5.4.4.2   Required Stubs/Drivers

Driver: IUserInterfaceDriver (smaller version of IUserInterface class)
Stubs: OrderStub (smaller version of order class)
         InvoiceStub (smaller version of the invoice class)

AddressStub(smaller version of the address class)
OtherButtonsStub (captures other buttons clicked)

5.4.4.3   Test Steps

1. Execute the IUserInterfaceDriver in a Web browser.
2. Determine if the correct customer name is displayed.
3. Determine if the correct address is displayed.
4. Determine if the correct e-mail address is displayed.
5. Determine if the correct phone number is displayed.
6. Determine if the correct order numbers are displayed.
7. Determine if the correct invoice numbers are displayed.

5.4.4.4   Expected Results

Test success

1. The IUserInterfaceDriver should display the "search results — customer search results" screen in the Web browser.
2. The customer name should display.
3. The address should display.
4. The e-mail address should display
5. The phone number should display.
6. The order numbers should display.
7. The invoice numbers should display.

Test failure

1. Report all failures.

5.4.5   Test Case: OrderLineItem

5.4.5.1   Description

The purpose of this test case is to test the OrderLineItem class to determine if it correctly handles order line item-related data.

5.4.5.2   Required Stubs/Drivers

Driver: OrderLineItem test driver: a small console application that assigns a value to the OrderLineItem and prints out the result in a console window

Stub: N/A

5.4.5.3   Test Steps

1. Execute the OrderLineItem test driver in a console window. The test driver application should execute the following methods of OrderLineItem class:
   a.   SetServiceName()
   b.   SetUnitPrice()

    c. SetQuantity()
    d. GetServiceName()
    e. GetUnitPrice()
    f. GetQuantity()
    g. GetTotalPrice()
    h. GetTax()
    i. GetTotalPriceWithTax()

2. Review the console printout to see if all property values are correctly assigned and returned.
3. Review the console printout to see if the getTotalPrice method return value is the result of quantity multiplied by UnitPrice and then add tax.

5.4.5.4 Expected Results

Test success

1. All property values assigned match property values returned.
2. The total price matches the calculation from quantity, unit price, and tax values.

Test failure

1. Property values assigned do not match property values returned.
2. Total price does not match the calculation from quantity, unit price, and tax values.

5.4.6 Test Case: ServiceResourceRequirement

5.4.6.1 Description

The purpose of this test case is to test the ServiceResourceRequirement class to determine if it correctly handles the service resource requirement-related data.

5.4.6.2 Required Stubs/Drivers

Driver: ServiceResourceRequirement test driver: a small console application that assigns a value to ServiceResourceRequirement and prints out the result in a console window.
Stubs: N/A

5.4.6.3 Test Steps

1. Execute the ServiceResourceRequirement test driver in a console window. The test driver application should execute the following methods of order class:
    a. SetQuantity()
    b. SetPercentage()

    c.   SetResourceType()
    d.   GetQuantity()
    e.   GetPercentage()
    f.   GetResourceType()

2. Review the console printout to see if all property values are correctly assigned and returned.

5.4.6.4 Expected Results

Test success

1. All property values assigned match property values returned.
2. If quantity value is less than 1, an exception is raised.
3. If percentage value is greater than 1, an exception is raised.

Test failure

1. Property values assigned do not match property values returned.
2. If quantity value is less than 1, no exception is raised.
3. If percentage value is greater than 1, no exception is raised.

5.4.7 Test Case: Service

5.4.7.1 Description

The purpose of this test case is to test the service class to determine if it correctly handles the service related data.

5.4.7.2 Required Stubs/Drivers

Driver: service test driver: a small console application that assigns a value to the order and prints out the result in a console window

Stubs: ServiceResourceRequirement class or stub

5.4.7.3 Test Steps

1. Execute the service test driver in a console window. The test driver application should execute the following methods of order class:
    a.   SetName()
    b.   SetDescription()
    c.   SetUnitCost()
    d.   GetResourceRequirement()
    e.   GetName()
    f.   GetDescription()
    g.   GetUnitCost()

2. Review the console printout to see if all property values are correctly assigned and returned.

Test success

1. All property values assigned match property values returned.

Test failure

1. Property values assigned do not match property values returned.

5.4.8   Test Case: Order

5.4.8.1   Description

The purpose of this test case is to test the order class to determine if it correctly handles the order-related data.

5.4.8.2   Required Stubs/Drivers

Driver: order test driver: a small console application that assigns a value to the order and prints out the result in a console window

Stubs: OrderLineItem class or stub
Invoice class or stub
Payment class or stub
Customer class or stub

5.4.8.3   Test Steps

1. Execute the order test driver in a console window. The test driver application should execute the following methods of order class:
    a. SetOrderDateTime
    b. SetCompletionDateTime
    c. SetOrderStatus
    d. GetOrderLineItems
    e. GetTotalPrice
    f. GetCustomer
    g. GetPayment
    h. GetInvoice
2. Review the console printout to see if all property values are correctly assigned and returned.
3. Review the console printout to see if the getTotalPrice method return value is the total of all OrderLineItem price.

5.4.8.4   Expected Results

Test success

1. All property values assigned match property values returned.
2. The total price matches the calculation from order line items.

Test failure

1. Property values assigned do not match property values returned.
2. Total price does not match the calculation from order line items.

5.5   Accounting Subsystem

The accounting subsystem is responsible for processing the financial transactions.

5.5.1   Test Case: Accounting:InvoicePrint

5.5.1.1   Description

The purpose of this test is to determine if the service care provider is able to print invoices for billing.

5.5.1.2   Required Stubs/Drivers

1. Orders must be placed against the service care provider in question via the order subsystem and the OrderService class.
2. The accounting subsystem will be invoked with the invoice class in particular.

5.5.1.3   Test Steps

1. A test customer order must be placed against a predetermined service care provider.
2. The service care provider must log into the system successfully.
3. The service care provider must select the invoices to be printed.

5.5.1.4   Expected Results

Test success

1. Invoices printing out successfully with the correct data will determine the success of the test.

Test failure

1. The test can be deemed unsuccessful if the invoice does not print.
2. The test will also be unsuccessful if the format is incorrect
3. The test will be unsuccessful if the wrong line items are printed.

5.5.2   Test Case: Accounting:Payment

5.5.2.1   Description

The purpose of this test is to determine if a representative of the service care provider can enter a payment receipt within the accounting subsystem.

5.5.2.2   Required Stubs/Drivers

The accounting subsystem will be invoked with particular attention to the payment class.

5.5.2.3   Test Steps

1. The service care provider must successfully log into the system.
2. The service care provider must invoke the accounting user interface to enter the payment receipt.
3. The service care provider must enter a payment receipt and press the button to commit the transaction.

5.5.2.4   Expected Results

Test success

1. A subsequent query indicates the customer's balance reflects the recent payment.
2. A successful message is displayed.

Test failure

1. The customer's balance does not reflect the payment receipt.
2. The customer's balance reflects an incorrect amount that is a result of faulty logic within the program.

5.5.3   Test Case: Accounting:InvoiceList

5.5.3.1   Description

The purpose of this test is to ensure that every time a service care provider requests to view invoices, the correct invoices will be displayed.

5.5.3.2   Required Stubs/Drivers

The application subsystem is required, with particular attention to the invoice class.

5.5.3.3   Test Steps

1. The service care provider will successfully log into the system
2. The service care provider will select the button to view invoices.
3. The system will determine who is logged on and display the appropriate invoices for that user.

5.5.3.4   Expected Results

Test success

1. All invoices for the particular service care provider are displayed with the correct information.

Test failure

1. The invoices displayed are for another service care provider.
2. The invoices indicate an incorrect balance or other incorrect information

5.6 Customer Relationship Management Subsystem

The customer relationship management subsystem provides the application with the ability to provide for interaction between the customers and service care providers. It also provides the system administrator with the ability to gain feedback from the customer in an effort to revamp the application continually.

5.6.1 Test Case: This Feature Set Will Be Available in Phase II.

5.7 Persistence Subsystem

The persistence subsystem has responsibility for supporting persistent data.

The purpose of this group of test cases is to determine whether the PersistenceManager class is carrying out its responsibilities as expected. PersistenceManager is a critical part of the system that handles the persistence activities of all objects. Based on the system architecture design, the persistence layer java code library from http://artyomr.narod.ru has been selected to execute the majority of the persistence functionality. The persistence layer code library uses an XML file to store the database map and class map information. So the correctness of the XML file in terms of correctly mapping the class structure design with the database design will essentially determine whether the objects can be correctly persisted to the database. This will be a major area of potential fault of the implementation and hence one of the major focuses of the testing of the persistence subsystem.

Due to limit of space, the document specifies in detail the example of customer object persistence. Note that tests in similar patterns will need to be executed for EVERY object that needs to be persisted.

5.7.1 Test Case: PersistenceManager :: loadXMLConfig()

5.7.1.1 Description/Purpose

This test case tests the persistence manager's functionality to load class map and database map from XML file. Potential errors are usually related to bad XML file entries that are not valid XML files or do not load correctly into the class map and database map.

5.7.1.2   Required Stubs/Drivers

1. DatabaseMap and ClassMap configuration XML file in format specified by http://artyomr.narod.ru/docs/pl/XMLConfigLoader.html

5.7.1.3   Test Steps

1. Edit Config.xml with all database map and class map information according to http://artyomr.narod.ru/docs/pl/XMLConfigLoader.html.
2. Start PersistenceManager application by running java PersistenceManager.class from command prompt, loading Config.xml as the configuration.
3. Exit PersistenceManager application.

5.7.1.4   Expected Results

Test success

1. The PersistenceManager application successfully starts without error messages.

Test failure

1. XML parser error when loading Config.xml
2. Error parsing class map and database map information

5.7.2   Test Case: PersistenceManager :: saveObject()

5.7.2.1   Description/Purpose

This test case tests the persistence manager's functionality to save the object to the database.

5.7.2.2   Required Stubs/Drivers

1. DatabaseMap and ClassMap configuration XML file in format specified by http://artyomr.narod.ru/docs/pl/XMLConfigLoader.html
2. Customer registration screens

5.7.2.3   Test Steps

1. Edit Config.xml with all database map and class map information according to http://artyomr.narod.ru/docs/pl/XMLConfigLoader.html.
2. Start PersistenceManager application by running java PersistenceManager.class from command prompt, loading Config.xml as the configuration.
3. Browse to Dog E-Day-Care home page from the Web site.
4. Click register button.
5. Input customer information.
6. Click register to create a new customer.
7. Use SQL tool to open the database.

8. Execute "SELECT * FROM CUSTOMER" SQL statement and review the result.
9. Execute "SELECT * FROM DOG" SQL statement and review the result.

5.7.2.4 Expected Results

Test success

1. The customer and dog information should exist in the database.

Test failure

1. RMI error when clicking register button
2. Error executing SQL statement
3. Customer and dog not get added to the database

5.7.3   Test Case: PersistenceManager :: retrieveObject()

5.7.3.1 Description/Purpose

This test case tests the persistence manager's functionality to retrieve an object from the database.

5.7.3.2 Required Stubs/Drivers

1. DatabaseMap and ClassMap configuration XML file in format specified by http://artyomr.narod.ru/docs/pl/XMLConfigLoader.html
2. Customer information screens

5.7.3.3 Test Steps

1. Edit Config.xml with all database map and class map information according to http://artyomr.narod.ru/docs/pl/XMLConfigLoader.html.
2. Start persistencemanager application by running java Persistence-Manager.class from command prompt, loading Config.xml as the configuration.
3. Browse to Dog E-Day-Care home page from the Web site.
4. Log in to Dog E-Day-Care system.
5. Click edit customer profile button
6. Review the information retrieved from persistence manager

5.7.3.4 Expected Results

Test success

1. The customer and dog information should be retrieved and match what was input.

Test failure

1. RMI error when clicking edit customer profile button
2. Cannot retrieve customer and dog information

3. Error executing SQL statement
4. Customer and dog information retrieved but does not match the data that was input

6 APPENDIX 2: INTEGRATION TESTING TESTS

Integration tests are scenario based, capturing key activities that the Dog E-DayCare System™ allows the user to perform.

6.1 Test Case: Customer Registration

6.1.1 Description

Registering with the Dog E-DayCare system is the key task that allows users to take advantage of the services Dog E-DayCare offers. Registration requires collaboration among three subsystems: user management, application controller, and persistence. The purpose of this test is to find errors in the interactions that must take place across these subsystems.

6.1.2 Required Stubs/Drivers

No stubs or drivers are required.

6.1.3 Test Steps

1. User opens Dog E-DayCare welcome page.
2. User selects "register."
3. Register customer/about you page displays.
4. User fills in fields and clicks next.
5. Register customer/about your dog page displays.
6. User fills in fields and clicks next.
7. Register customer/user ID, password page displays.
8. User fills in fields and clicks next.
9. Register customer/verify Information page displays with appropriate information.
10. User reviews information and clicks finish.
11. Register customer/thank you page displays.
12. User receives confirmation e-mail.

6.1.4 Expected Results

Test success

1. User is able to move through each step of the registration process successfully. User information displayed in the verify information page is correct. Thank you page appears and user receives e-mail confirmation.

Test failure

1. User cannot click from one step in the registration process to the next.
2. User information displayed in the verify information page is incorrect.
3. User does not receive a confirmation e-mail.

6.2 Test Case: Reallocate Resources

6.2.1 Description

One of the key services Dog E-DayCare provides to dog care companies is the ability to manage their resources (e.g., staff, kennels, and play areas), allocating and reallocating resources, for example, in response to staff illness, rainy weather, etc. Reallocating resources requires collaboration among several subsystems: user management, order, resource management, application controller, and persistence. The purpose of this test is to find errors in the interactions that must take place across these subsystems.

6.2.2 Required Stubs/Drivers

No stubs or drivers are required.

6.2.3 Test Steps

1. User opens schedule/this week page.
2. User selects appointment whose resources need to be reallocated.
3. Schedule/appointment details page displays.
4. User selects option to "reallocate" resources.
5. Schedule/resource details page displays.
6. User revises resource details as necessary and clicks next.
7. Schedule/confirm changes page displays.
8. User clicks finish.
9. Revised schedule/appointment details page displays.

6.2.4 Expected Results

Test success

1. User is able to move through each step of the reallocation process successfully. Reallocation information displayed in the confirm changes page is correct. Appointment details have been updated.

Test failure

1. User cannot click from one step in the reallocation process to the next.
2. User information displayed in the confirm changes page is incorrect.
3. Appointment details have not been updated.

6.3 Test Case: Search for Service Provider and Initiate Order

6.3.1 Description

The Dog E-DayCare system allows customers to search for service providers based on geographic location and service desired. From the search results, a user can initiate an order.

Searching for a service provider and initiating an order require collaboration among several subsystems: user management, order, application controller, and persistence. The purpose of this test is to find errors in the interactions that must take place across these subsystems.

6.3.2 Required Stubs/Drivers

No stubs or drivers are required.

6.3.3 Test Steps

1. User opens search for service provider page.
2. User enters required information and clicks "search."
3. Search results page displays all service providers that match criteria.
4. User selects "initiate order" button associated with the service provider of choice.
5. Order/initiate order page displays.

6.3.4 Expected Results

Test success

1. The search results page displays service providers matching the user's criteria. The order/initiate order page displays the name of the service provider selected and the services available from this provider in the appropriate fields.

Test failure

1. Search results page does not display.
2. Search results do not match criteria.
3. Order/initiate order page does not display correct service provider information.

6.4 Test Case: Place Order

6.4.1 Description

The Dog E-DayCare system allows customers to place an order for the service they need, from a service provider of their choice, within a desired timeframe. Placing an order requires collaboration among several subsystems: order, user management, resource management, application controller, and persistence. The purpose of this test is to find errors in the interactions that must take place across these subsystems.

6.4.2   Required Stubs/Drivers

No stubs or drivers required.

6.4.3   Test Steps

1. Order/initiate order page is displayed.
2. User fills in all fields.
3. User selects "view openings."
4. Order/openings page displays.
5. User selects an available appointment time.
6. Order/order details page displays.
7. User selects "place order."
8. Order/order confirmation page displays.
9. An e-mail is sent to user.

6.4.4   Expected Results

Test success

1. The user is able to move successfully through each step in the process of placing an order. The Order/openings page displays the correct information on available appointment times. The Order/order details page displays the correct information. An email is sent to the user.

Test failure

1. The order/openings page displays incorrect information
2. The order/order details page displays incorrect information.
3. An e-mail is not sent to the user.

6.5   Test Case: Pay for Service

6.5.1   Description

The Dog E-DayCare system allows customers to pay online for the dog care services they have received. Paying for service requires collaboration among several subsystems: accounting, order, user management, application controller, and persistence. The purpose of this test is to find errors in the interactions that must take place across these subsystems.

6.5.2   Required Stubs and Drivers

No stubs or drivers are required.

6.5.3   Test Steps

1. User opens the payment/initiate payment page.
2. User enters the order ID number and clicks "next."
3. The payment/payment details page displays.
4. User reviews payment details and selects "next."
5. The payment/billing address page displays.
6. User reviews information and clicks "next."
7. The payment/credit card details page displays.
8. User enters information and clicks "next."
9. The payment/make payment page displays.
10. User reviews information and clicks "pay now."
11. The payment/payment confirmation page displays.
12. An e-mail is sent to user.

6.5.4   Expected Results

Test success

1. The user is able to move successfully through each step in the process of making a payment for service. The payment/payment details page displays the correct information. The payment/billing address page displays the correct information. The payment/make payment page displays the correct information. An e-mail is sent to the user.

Test failure

1. The payment/payment details page displays incorrect information
2. The payment/billing address page displays incorrect information.
3. The payment/make payment page displays incorrect information.
4. An e-mail is not sent to the user.

7   APPENDIX 3: PROJECT SCHEDULE

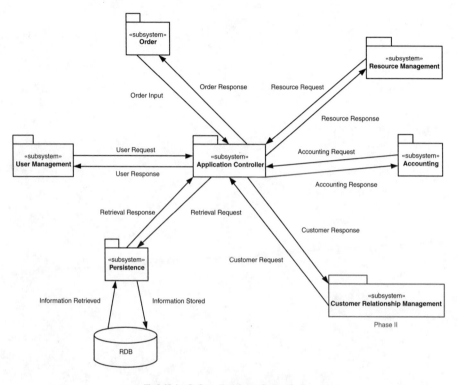

Exhibit O-2.   Project Schedule

Appendix P
QA Handover Document

QA Handover Document			

Submitted:	Dept.	Phone number	Submission date

Application/module	Product/form to test (required)		Implementation date

Handover item name/description	Version/built		New/modified

Brief but thorough description of the modification, along with any special testing requirements

_____

_____

_____

_____

_____

Testing done at the development stage (attach documentation [required])

_____

_____

_____

_____

_____

Known issues (documentation attached [required])

_____

_____

_____

_____

_____

Team member/developer _____

Project manager _____

QA analyst _____

QA manager _____

Systems manager _____

Appendix Q
Software Metrics Capability Evaluation Questionnaires

METRICS CUSTOMER PROFILE FORM

1. Point of contact information:

   a. Name: _____

   b. Position: _____

   c. Office symbol: _____

   d. Location: _____

   e. Phone #: _____   DSN: _____

   f. Fax number: _____

   g. E-mail address: _____

   h. Organization name: _____

   i. Products: _____

2. Environment information:

   a. Hardware platform: _____

   b. Languages used: _____

   c. Tools used for metrics: _____

3. Organization information:

   a. Copy of organization chart: _____
   _____

   b. Type(s) of software (real time, communication, command and control, MIS, other):_____
   _____

    c. Type(s) of activity (development, acquisition, maintenance, combination, other): _____

_____

    d. Do project teams comprise members from more than one organization? (If yes, please give examples) _____

_____

    e. Typical size of development organization for a particular program (or project) (less than 10, 10 to 40, more than 40 personnel): _____ _____

    f. Typical length of project (< 6 mo, 6 to 18 mo, 18 mo to 3 yr, > 3 yr):

_____

4. General background:

    a. What are the organization's strengths? _____

_____

    b. Can you demonstrate these strengths through measurements or other objective means? (If yes, please give examples): _____

_____

    c. What are the organization's biggest challenges? _____

_____

    d. Have measurements or other objective means been used to understand or to help manage these challenges? (If yes, please give examples): _____

_____

5. Metrics background:

    a. Does your organization require software development plans to be developed and used? _____

_____

    b. Are project management tools used? (If yes, please give examples): _____

_____

c. How is project status reported? (Please give examples): _____

_____

d. How is product quality reported? (Please give examples): ____

_____

e. What forces are driving the interest in metrics in your organization? _____

_____

ACQUISITION ORGANIZATION QUESTIONNAIRE

Questions for Metrics Capability Level 2

Theme 1: Formalization of Source Selection and Contract Monitoring Process

#	Question	Yes	No	NA	?
1a	Is a software capability evaluation (SCE) or software development capability evaluation (SDCE) for developers part of your source selection process? Comments:	☐	☐	☐	☐
1b	Is proof of a specific CMM level required from developers as part of your source selection process? Comments:	☐	☐	☐	☐
2	Does your organization require and evaluate developers' draft software development plans as part of the source selection process? Comments:	☐	☐	☐	☐
3	Are software metrics required as part of developers' software development plans (or other contractually binding metrics plans)? Comments:	☐	☐	☐	☐
4	Are software cost and schedule estimates required from the developer as part of the source selection process? Comments:	☐	☐	☐	☐

#	Question	Yes	No	NA	?
5	Is the developer's project performance monitored based on the cost and schedule estimates? Comments:	☐	☐	☐	☐
6	Are the acquirers' management plans developed, used, and maintained as part of managing a program? Comments:	☐	☐	☐	☐

Theme 2: Formalization of Metrics Process

#	Question	Yes	No	NA	?
1	Is there a written organizational policy for collecting and maintaining software metrics for this program? Comments:	☐	☐	☐	☐
2	Is each program required to identify and use metrics to show program performance? Comments:	☐	☐	☐	☐
3	Is the use of software metrics documented? Comments:	☐	☐	☐	☐
4	Are developers required to report a set of standard metrics? Comments:	☐	☐	☐	☐

Theme 3: Scope of Metrics

#	Question	Yes	No	NA	?
1	Are internal measurements used to determine the status of the activities performed for planning a new acquisition program? Comments:	☐	☐	☐	☐
2	Are measurements used to determine the status of software contract management activities? Comments:	☐	☐	☐	☐
3	Do your contracts require metrics on the developer's actual results (e.g., schedule, size, and effort) compared to the estimates? Comments:	☐	☐	☐	☐

#	Question	Yes	No	NA	?
4	Can you determine whether the program is performing according to plan based on measurement data provided by the developer? Comments:	☐	☐	☐	☐
5	Are measurements used to determine your organization's planned and actual effort applied to performing acquisition planning and program management? Comments:	☐	☐	☐	☐
6	Are measurements used to determine the status of your organization's software configuration management activities? Comments:	☐	☐	☐	☐

Theme 4: Implementation Support

#	Question	Yes	No	NA	?
1	Does the program (or project) have a database of metrics information? Comments:	☐	☐	☐	☐
2	Do you require access to the contractor's metrics data as well as completed metrics reports? Comments:	☐	☐	☐	☐
3	Does your database (or collected program data) include both developer's and acquirer's metrics data? Comments:	☐	☐	☐	☐

Theme 5: Metrics Evolution

#	Question	Yes	No	NA	?
1	Is someone from the acquisition organization assigned specific responsibilities for tracking the developer's activity status (e.g., schedule, size, and effort)? Comments:	☐	☐	☐	☐
2	Does the developer regularly report the metrics defined in the developer's software development plan (or other contractually binding metrics plan)? Comments:	☐	☐	☐	☐

#	Question	Yes	No	NA	?
3	Do your contracts have clauses that allow the acquirer to request changes to the developer's metrics based on program needs? Comments:	☐	☐	☐	☐

Theme 6: Metrics Support for Management Control

#	Question	Yes	No	NA	?
1	Do you track your developer's performance against the developer's commitments? Comments:	☐	☐	☐	☐
2	Are the developer's metrics results used as an indicator of when contract performance should be analyzed in detail? Comments:	☐	☐	☐	☐
3	Are metrics results used to support risk management, particularly with respect to cost and schedule risks? Comments:	☐	☐	☐	☐
4	Are program acquisition and program management metrics used to help determine when changes should be made to your plans (e.g., changes to schedules for completion of planning activities and milestones, etc.)? Comments:	☐	☐	☐	☐
5	Are measurements used to determine the status of verification and validation activities for software contracts? Comments:	☐	☐	☐	☐

Questions for Metrics Capability Level 3

Theme 1: Formalization of Source Selection and Contract Monitoring Process

#	Question	Yes	No	NA	?
1	Do you require developers to show proof of software development maturity at a minimum of CMM Level 3? Comments:	☐	☐	☐	☐

#	Question	Yes	No	NA	?
2	Is your software acquisition process reviewed for improvement periodically? Comments:	☐	☐	☐	☐
3	Does your organization have a standard software acquisition process? Comments:	☐	☐	☐	☐
4	Do one or more individuals have responsibility for maintaining the organization's standard software acquisition processes? Comments:	☐	☐	☐	☐
5	Does the organization follow a written policy for developing and maintaining the acquisition process and related information (e.g., descriptions of approved tailoring for standards based on program attributes)? Comments:	☐	☐	☐	☐

Theme 2: Formalization of Metrics Process

#	Question	Yes	No	NA	?
1	Do you have documented standards for metrics definitions and for reporting formats you require from developers? Comments:	☐	☐	☐	☐
2	Can these standards be tailored to the size, scope, and type of the software to be acquired? Comments:	☐	☐	☐	☐
3	Are specific metrics requested for each new acquisition based on your organization's metrics standards? Comments:	☐	☐	☐	☐
4	Is someone from your organization assigned specific responsibilities for maintaining and analyzing the contractor's metrics regarding the status of software work products and activities (e.g., effort, schedule, quality)? Comments:	☐	☐	☐	☐

Theme 3: Scope of Metrics

#	Question	Yes	No	NA	?
1	Do you collect, maintain, and report metrics data for all new (in the last three years) contracts? Comments:	☐	☐	☐	☐
2	Do you use automated tools that support metrics collection, maintenance, and reporting? Comments:	☐	☐	☐	☐
3	Do you and your developers use automated metrics tools that allow you to share contract metrics data? Comments:	☐	☐	☐	☐
4	During contract negotiations, do the program goals drive the metrics required for the contract? Comments:	☐	☐	☐	☐
5	Do the metrics collected include specific product metrics (e.g., quality, reliability, maintainability)? Comments:	☐	☐	☐	☐
6	Do you require metrics summary reports that show general program trends as well as detailed metrics information? Comments:	☐	☐	☐	☐

Theme 4: Implementation Support

#	Question	Yes	No	NA	?
1	Does your program metrics database include information on specific product metrics (e.g., quality, reliability, maintainability)? Comments:	☐	☐	☐	☐
2	Do you share metrics data across programs? Comments:	☐	☐	☐	☐
3	Is the metrics data shared through a common organizational database? Comments:	☐	☐	☐	☐

#	Question	Yes	No	NA	?
4	Does your organization have a standard length of time that you retain metrics data? Comments:	☐	☐	☐	☐
5	Does the organization verify the metrics data maintained in the metrics database? Comments:	☐	☐	☐	☐
6	Does your organization manage and maintain the metrics database? Comments:	☐	☐	☐	☐

Theme 5: Metrics Evolution

#	Question	Yes	No	NA	?
1	Do you use product metrics in making management decisions? (For example, a decision is made to delay the schedule because of known defects.) Comments:	☐	☐	☐	☐
2	Are product metrics reported during program management reviews (e.g., defects by severity or defects by cause)? Comments:	☐	☐	☐	☐
3	Are both project and product metrics used in making management decisions regarding contract performance? Comments:	☐	☐	☐	☐
4	Does your organization periodically review the current metrics set for ongoing usefulness? Comments:	☐	☐	☐	☐
5	Does your organization periodically review the current metrics set to determine if new metrics are needed? Comments:	☐	☐	☐	☐

Theme 6: Metrics Support for Management Control

#	Question	Yes	No	NA	?
1	Are measurements used to determine the status of the program office activities performed for managing the software requirements?	☐	☐	☐	☐

Comments:

2 Are product metrics used as an indicator for renegotiating the terms of contracts when necessary?   ☐ ☐ ☐ ☐
Comments:

3 Are product metrics used in reports forwarded to higher level management concerning contract performance?   ☐ ☐ ☐ ☐
Comments:

4 Are measurements used to forecast the status of products during their development?   ☐ ☐ ☐ ☐
Comments:

5 Are product metrics used as inputs to award fee calculations for cost-plus-award-fee contracts?   ☐ ☐ ☐ ☐
Comments:

6 Do metrics serve as inputs for determining when activities need to be initiated (or modified) to mitigate technical program risks?   ☐ ☐ ☐ ☐
Comments:

SOFTWARE DEVELOPMENT/MAINTENANCE ORGANIZATION QUESTIONNAIRE

Questions for Metrics Capability Level 2

Theme 1: Formalization of the Development Process

#	Question	Yes	No	NA	?
1a	Has your organization been assessed via the SEI CMM?[a] (This could be an independent assessment or an internal assessment supported by an SEI-authorized source.) Comments:	☐	☐	☐	☐
1b	Has your organization been assessed via some vehicle other than the SEI CMM? Comments:	☐	☐	☐	☐

#	Question	Yes	No	NA	?
2	Are software development plans developed, used, and maintained as part of managing software projects? Comments:	☐	☐	☐	☐
3	Are software metrics included in your software development plans or other contractual binding documents? Comments:	☐	☐	☐	☐
4	Does your organization have an ongoing software process improvement program? Comments:	☐	☐	☐	☐

Theme 2: Formalization of Metrics Process

#	Question	Yes	No	NA	?
1	Is there a written policy for collecting and maintaining project management metrics (e.g. cost, effort, and schedule)? Comments:	☐	☐	☐	☐
2	Do standards exist for defining, collecting, and reporting metrics? Comments:	☐	☐	☐	☐
3	Is each project required to identify and use metrics to show project performance? Comments:	☐	☐	☐	☐

Theme 3: Scope of Metrics

#	Question	Yes	No	NA	?
1	Are measurements used to determine the status of activities performed during software planning? Comments:	☐	☐	☐	☐
2	Are measurements used to determine and track the status of activities performed during project performance? Comments:	☐	☐	☐	☐
3	Does the project manager establish cost and schedule estimates based on prior experience? Comments:	☐	☐	☐	☐

Theme 4: Implementation Support

#	Question	Yes	No	NA	?
1	Is there a project database of metrics information? Comments:	☐	☐	☐	☐
2	Is the project manager responsible for implementing metrics for the project? Comments:	☐	☐	☐	☐
3	Do you keep metrics from project to project (historical data)? Comments:	☐	☐	☐	☐

Theme 5: Metrics Evolution

#	Question	Yes	No	NA	?
1	Do you report the project's actual results (e.g., schedule and cost) compared to estimates? Comments:	☐	☐	☐	☐
2	Is someone on the staff assigned specific responsibilities for tracking software project activity status (e.g., schedule, size, cost)? Comments:	☐	☐	☐	☐
3	Do you regularly report the metrics defined in the software development plan or other contractually required documents? Comments:	☐	☐	☐	☐

Theme 6: Metrics Support for Management Control

#	Question	Yes	No	NA	?
1	Do metrics results help the project manager manage deviations in cost and schedule? Comments:	☐	☐	☐	☐
2	Are measurements used to determine the status of software configuration management activities on the project? Comments:	☐	☐	☐	☐
3	Are measurements used to determine the status of software quality assurance activities on the project? Comments:	☐	☐	☐	☐

#	Question	Yes	No	NA	?
4	Are measurements used to determine the status of activities performed for managing the allocated requirements (e.g., total number of requirements changes that are proposed, open, approved, and incorporated into the baseline)? Comments:	☐	☐	☐	☐
5	Are cost and schedule estimates documented and used to refine the estimation process? Comments:	☐	☐	☐	☐
6	Do you report metrics data to the customer based on customer requirements? Comments:	☐	☐	☐	☐

Questions for Metrics Capability Level 3

Theme 1: Formalization of the Development Process

#	Question	Yes	No	NA	?
1	Is your software development process periodically reviewed for improvement? Comments:	☐	☐	☐	☐
2	Does your organization's standard software process include processes that support software management and software engineering? Comments:	☐	☐	☐	☐
3	Can your processes be tailored to the size and scope of the project? Comments:	☐	☐	☐	☐

Theme 2: Formalization of Metrics Process

#	Question	Yes	No	NA	?
1	Do you have documented organizational standards for metrics (e.g., metrics definitions, analyses, reports, and procedures)? Comments:	☐	☐	☐	☐
2	Can these standards be tailored to the size and scope of the software project? Comments:	☐	☐	☐	☐

#	Question	Yes	No	NA	?
3	Are standards established for the retention of metrics? Comments:	☐	☐	☐	☐
4	Are specific project and product metrics proposed for each software project based on the organization's metrics standards? Comments:	☐	☐	☐	☐
5	Is someone assigned specific responsibilities for maintaining and analyzing metrics regarding the status of software work products and activities (e.g., size, effort, schedule, quality)? Comments:	☐	☐	☐	☐
6	Does the organization collect, review, and make available information related to the use of the organization's standard software process (e.g., estimates and actual data on software size, effort, and cost; productivity data; and quality measurements)? Comments:	☐	☐	☐	☐

Theme 3: Scope of Metrics

#	Question	Yes	No	NA	?
1	Do project and organization management and technical goals drive the metrics required? Comments:	☐	☐	☐	☐
2	Do you collect, maintain, and report project and product metrics data for all projects? Comments:	☐	☐	☐	☐
3	Do you use automated tools that support metrics collection, maintenance, and reporting? Comments:	☐	☐	☐	☐
4	Do the metrics collected include specific product metrics (e.g., quality, reliability, maintainability)? Comments:	☐	☐	☐	☐

#	Question	Yes	No	NA	?
5	Do you report product metrics (e.g., problem/defect density by product, amount of rework, or status of allocated requirements) throughout the development life cycle? Comments:	☐	☐	☐	☐

Theme 4: Implementation Support

#	Question	Yes	No	NA	?
1	Does your metrics database include information on specific product metrics (e.g., quality, reliability, maintainability)? Comments:	☐	☐	☐	☐
2	Do you share metrics data across software projects? Comments:	☐	☐	☐	☐
3	Is the metrics data shared through a common organizational database? Comments:	☐	☐	☐	☐
4	Does your organization have a standard length of time that you retain metrics data? Comments:	☐	☐	☐	☐
5	Does your organization verify the metrics data maintained in the metrics database? Comments:	☐	☐	☐	☐
6	Does your organization manage and maintain the metrics database? Comments:	☐	☐	☐	☐
7	Have normal ranges been established for project metrics reported (e.g., the difference between planned and actual schedule commitments)? Comments:	☐	☐	☐	☐

Theme 5: Metrics Evolution

#	Question	Yes	No	NA	?
1	Do you use product metrics as well as project metrics in making management decisions? Comments:	☐	☐	☐	☐

#	Question	Yes	No	NA	?
2	Are product metrics as well as project metrics reported during program management reviews (e.g., the number of defects per SLOC)? Comments:	☐	☐	☐	☐
3	Do you report metrics to your internal manager? Comments:	☐	☐	☐	☐
4	Do you report metrics to your customer? Comments:	☐	☐	☐	☐

Theme 6: Metrics Support for Management Control

#	Question	Yes	No	NA	?
1	Are product metrics as well as project metrics used as indicators for renegotiating the terms of contracts when necessary (e.g., you decide to extend a schedule based on the known number of defects in the product)? Comments:	☐	☐	☐	☐
2	Do metric results help isolate technical problems? Comments:	☐	☐	☐	☐
3	Are improvements to the metrics process (including metrics standards, procedures, definitions, etc.) based on analysis and lessons learned? Comments:	☐	☐	☐	☐
4	Are measurements used to determine the quality of software products (i.e., numbers, types, and severity of defects identified)? Comments:	☐	☐	☐	☐
5	Do you maintain metrics specifically to help manage your project? Comments:	☐	☐	☐	☐

#	Question	Yes	No	NA	?
6	Are management decisions made as a result of metrics reported? (For example, is corrective action taken when actual results deviate significantly from the project's software plans?) Comments:	□	□	□	□
7	Are metrics reported to the customer consistent with internally reported metrics? Comments:	□	□	□	□

[a] Score only one correct for a yes response to either 1a or 1b. If neither is a yes answer, score only one no.

SOFTWARE METRICS CAPABILITY EVALUATION REPORT: ANNOTATED OUTLINE

The goals of the software metrics capability evaluation report are as follows:

1. Report the results of the evaluation. The results have two components:
    a. General results (i.e., metrics capability level and an overview of the organization's metrics-related strengths and weaknesses)
    b. Discussion of the organization's strengths and weaknesses based on each of the six measurement themes identified
2. Discuss recommendations for improvement. These recommendations will be based on the results of the evaluation and may include one or more of several elements, such as:
    a. A recommended set of high-payback activities that the organization could use to implement metrics capability improvements
    b. Recommendations to implement a metrics improvement program that would be tailored to meet the specific organization's goals based on follow-up consulting and plan preparation. These recommendations would include a brief description of the areas to be covered in the metrics improvement program to help open communication with the organization.
3. Recommendations to implement other management or engineering improvement activities that would be tailored to meet the specific organization's objective based on follow-up consulting and plan preparation. These recommendations would include a brief description of the areas to be covered in the program to help open communication with the organization.

ORGANIZATION INFORMATION FORM

Credibility:

1. How would you characterize the organization's customer satisfaction?

   ☐ Excellent ☐ Good ☐ Fair ☐ Poor

   Please explain: _____

2. How would you characterize the organization's ability to meet schedule commitments?

   ☐ Excellent ☐ Good ☐ Fair ☐ Poor

   Please explain: _____

3. How would you characterize the organization's ability to meet budget commitments?

   ☐ Excellent ☐ Good ☐ Fair ☐ Poor

   Please explain: _____

4. How would you characterize the organization's product quality?

   ☐ Excellent ☐ Good ☐ Fair ☐ Poor

   Please explain: _____

5. How would you characterize the organization's staff productivity?

   ☐ Excellent ☐ Good ☐ Fair ☐ Poor

   Please explain: _____

6. How would you characterize the organization's staff morale and job satisfaction?

   ☐ Excellent ☐ Good ☐ Fair ☐ Poor

   Please explain: _____

7. How frequently do the development projects have to deal with changes in customer requirements?

   ☐ Weekly or daily ☐ Monthly ☐ Less often ☐ Rarely if ever

   Please explain: _____

Motivation:

1. To what extent are there tangible incentives or rewards for successful metrics use?

   ☐ Substantial ☐ Moderate ☐ Some ☐ Little if any ☐ Don't know

   Please explain: _____

2. To what extent do technical staff members feel that metrics get in the way of their "real" work?

☐ Substantial ☐ Moderate ☐ Some ☐ Little if any ☐ Don't know

Please explain: _____

3. To what extent have managers demonstrated their support for rather than compliance to organizational initiatives or programs?

☐ Substantial ☐ Moderate ☐ Some ☐ Little if any ☐ Don't know

Please explain: _____

4. To what extent do personnel feel genuinely involved in decision making?

☐ Substantial ☐ Moderate ☐ Some ☐ Little if any ☐ Don't know

Please explain: _____

5. What does management expect from implementing metrics?

Please explain: _____

Culture/Change History:

1. To what extent has the organization used task forces, committees, and special teams to implement projects?

☐ Substantial ☐ Moderate ☐ Some ☐ Little if any ☐ Don't know

Please explain: _____

2. To what extent does "turf guarding" inhibit the operation of the organization?

☐ Substantial ☐ Moderate ☐ Some ☐ Little if any ☐ Don't know

Please explain: _____

3. To what extent has the organization been effective in implementing organization initiatives (or improvement programs)?

☐ Substantial ☐ Moderate ☐ Some ☐ Little if any ☐ Don't know

Please explain: _____

4. To what extent has previous experience led to much discouragement or cynicism about metrics?

☐ Substantial ☐ Moderate ☐ Some ☐ Little if any ☐ Don't know

Please explain: _____

5. To what extent are lines of authority and responsibility clearly defined?

☐ Substantial ☐ Moderate ☐ Some ☐ Little if any ☐ Don't know

Please explain: _____

Organization Stability

1. To what extent has there been turnover in key senior management?

☐ Substantial ☐ Moderate ☐ Some ☐ Little if any ☐ Don't know

Please explain: _____

2. To what extent has there been a major reorganization or staff downsizing?

☐ Substantial ☐ Moderate ☐ Some ☐ Little if any ☐ Don't know

Please explain: _____

3. To what extent has there been growth in staff size?

☐ Substantial ☐ Moderate ☐ Some ☐ Little if any ☐ Don't know

Please explain: _____

4. How much turnover has there been among middle management?

☐ Substantial ☐ Moderate ☐ Some ☐ Little if any ☐ Don't know

Please explain: _____

5. How much turnover has there been among the technical staff?

☐ Substantial ☐ Moderate ☐ Some ☐ Little if any ☐ Don't know

Please explain: _____

Organizational Buy-In

1. To what extent are organizational goals clearly stated and well understood?

☐ Substantial ☐ Moderate ☐ Some ☐ Little if any ☐ Don't know

Please explain: _____

2. What level of management participated in the goal setting?

☐ Substantial ☐ Moderate ☐ Some ☐ Little if any ☐ Don't know

Please explain: _____

3. What is the level of buy-in to the goals within the organization?

☐ Substantial ☐ Moderate ☐ Some ☐ Little if any ☐ Don't know

Please explain: _____

4. To what extent does management understand the issues faced by the practitioners?

☐ Substantial ☐ Moderate ☐ Some ☐ Little if any ☐ Don't know

Please explain: _____

5. To what extent have metrics been used for improving processes?

☐ Substantial ☐ Moderate ☐ Some ☐ Little if any ☐ Don't know

Please explain: _____

6. To what extent has there been involvement of the technical staff in metrics?

☐ Substantial ☐ Moderate ☐ Some ☐ Little if any ☐ Don't know

Please explain: _____

7. To what extent do individuals whose work is being measured understand how the metrics are or will be used in the management process?

☐ Substantial ☐ Moderate ☐ Some ☐ Little if any ☐ Don't know

Please explain: _____

Measurement Knowledge/Skills

1. How widespread is metrics knowledge and training?

☐ Substantial ☐ Moderate ☐ Some ☐ Little if any ☐ Don't know

Please explain: _____

2. What type of metrics training have members of the organization participated in?

☐ Statistical Process Control ☐ Data Analysis

☐ Metrics Application ☐ Basics ☐ Don't know

Other: _____

Appendix R
IT Staff Competency Survey

Directions: Please rate your perception of your abilities on a scale of 1 to 5, with 1 the lowest score and 5 the highest. In addition, please use the same scale to rate the importance of this trait in your current work environment.

COMMUNICATIONS

1. IT professionals must communicate in a variety of settings using oral, written, and multimedia techniques.

> **Your self rating:**
> Low   High
> 1   2   3   4   5

> **Importance of this trait to your organization:**
> Low   High
> 1   2   3   4   5

PROBLEM SOLVING

2. IT professionals must be able to choose from a variety of different problem-solving methodologies to formulate a solution analytically.

> **Your self rating:**
> Low   High
> 1   2   3   4   5

> **Importance of this trait to your organization:**
> Low   High
> 1   2   3   4   5

3. IT professionals must think creatively in solving problems.

> **Your self rating:**
> Low   High
> 1   2   3   4   5

> **Importance of this trait to your organization:**
> Low   High
> 1   2   3   4   5

4. IT professionals must be able to work on project teams and use group methods to define and solve problems.

Your self rating:
Low   High
1 2 3 4 5

Importance of this trait to your organization:
Low   High
1 2 3 4 5

ORGANIZATION AND SYSTEMS THEORY

5. IT professionals must be grounded in the principles of systems theory.

Your self rating:
Low   High
1 2 3 4 5

Importance of this trait to your organization:
Low   High
1 2 3 4 5

6. IT professionals must have sufficient background to understand the functioning of organizations because the information system must be congruent with and supportive of the strategy, principles, goals, and objectives of the organization.

Your self rating:
Low   High
1 2 3 4 5

Importance of this trait to your organization:
Low   High
1 2 3 4 5

7. IT professionals must understand and be able to function in the multinational and global context of today's information-dependent organizations.

Your self rating:
Low   High
1 2 3 4 5

Importance of this trait to your organization:
Low   High
1 2 3 4 5

QUALITY

8. IT professionals must understand quality, planning, steps in the continuous improvement process as it relates to the enterprise, and tools to facilitate quality development.

Your self rating:
Low   High
1 2 3 4 5

Importance of this trait to your organization:
Low   High
1 2 3 4 5

9. As the IT field matures, increasing attention is directed to problem avoidance and process simplification through re-engineering. Error control, risk management, process measurement, and auditing are areas that IT professionals must understand and apply.

Your self rating:
Low   High
1 2 3 4 5

Importance of this trait to your organization:
Low   High
1 2 3 4 5

10. IT professionals must possess a tolerance for change and skills for managing the process of change.

Your self rating:
Low   High
1 2 3 4 5

Importance of this trait to your organization:
Low   High
1 2 3 4 5

11. Given the advancing technology of the IT field, education must be continuous.

Your self rating:
Low   High
1 2 3 4 5

Importance of this trait to your organization:
Low   High
1 2 3 4 5

12. IT professionals must understand mission-directed, principle-centered mechanisms to facilitate aligning group as well as individual missions with organizational missions.

Your self rating:
Low   High
1 2 3 4 5

Importance of this trait to your organization:
Low   High
1 2 3 4 5

GROUPS

13. IT professionals must interact with diverse user groups in team and project activities.

Your self rating:
Low   High
1 2 3 4 5

Importance of this trait to your organization:
Low   High
1 2 3 4 5

14. IT professionals must possess communication and facilitation skills with team meetings and other related activities.

Your self rating:
Low   High
1 2 3 4 5

Importance of this trait to your organization:
Low   High
1 2 3 4 5

15. IT professionals must understand the concept of empathetic listening and utilize it proactively to solicit synergistic solutions in which all parties to an agreement can benefit.

Your self rating:
Low   High
1 2 3 4 5

Importance of this trait to your organization:
Low   High
1 2 3 4 5

16. IT professionals must be able to communicate effectively with a changing work force.

Your self rating:

Low   High

1   2   3   4   5

Importance of this trait to your organization:

Low   High

1   2   3   4   5

Reference

McGuire, E.G. and Randall, K.A. (1998). Process improvement competencies for IS professionals: a survey of perceived needs, ACM Special Interest Group on Computer Personnel Research, ACM Press.

Appendix S
Function Point Counting Guide

In the late 1970s IBM asked one of its employees, Allan Albrecht, to develop a language-independent approach to estimating software development effort. The result was the function point technique. Several years later a function point counting manual was produced by IBM's GUIDE organization. By the late 1980s, the International Function Point Users Group (IFPUG) had been founded and duly published its own counting practices manual. In 1994, IFPUG produced Release 4.0 of its counting practices manual. IFPUG is now up to Release 4.1.1 of the manual.

Function points are a measure of the size of computer applications and the projects that build them. The size is measured from a functional point of view. The counting methodology is independent of computer language, development methodology, technology, or capability of the project team used to develop the application. Function points are not a perfect measure of effort to develop an application or of its business value, although the size in function points is typically an important factor in measuring each.

Function points measure software by quantifying the functionality provided external to itself, based primarily on logical design. With this in mind, the objectives of function point counting are to:

- Measure what the user requested and received
- Measure independently of technology used for implementation
- Provide a sizing metric to support quality and productivity analysis
- Provide a vehicle for software estimation
- Provide a normalization factor for software comparison

In addition to meeting these objectives, the process of counting function points should be:

- Simple enough to minimize the overhead of the measurement process
- Simple yet concise, to allow for consistency over time, projects, and practitioners

The function point metric measures an application based on two areas of evaluation. The first results in the unadjusted function point count and reflects the specific countable functionality provided to the user by the application. The second area of evaluation, which produces the value adjustment factor (VAF), evaluates the general functionality provided to the user of the application.

UNADJUSTED FUNCTION POINT COUNT

An application's specific user functionality is evaluated in terms of *what* is delivered by the application, not *how* it is delivered; only user-requested and visible components are counted. These components are categorized into function types, which in turn are categorized as data or transactional.

Data:

- Internal logical files (ILFs) — internally maintained logical group of data
- External interface files (EIFs) — externally maintained logical group of data

Transactional:

- External inputs (EIs) — maintain internally stored data
- External outputs (EOs) — data output
- External inquiries (EQs) — combination of input (request) and output (retrieval)

Each function type is further categorized based on its relative functional complexity as:

- Low
- Average
- High

Function point values ranging from 3 to 15, depending on the function type and functional complexity rating, are assigned and totaled, producing the unadjusted function point count. The unadjusted function point count is then weighted by the VAF to produce the final function point count.

VALUE ADJUSTMENT FACTOR

The VAF comprises 14 general system characteristic (GSC) questions that assess the general functionality of the application:

1. Data communication
2. Distributed function
3. Performance
4. Heavily used configuration
5. Transaction rates
6. Online data entry
7. Design for end-user efficiency
8. Online update
9. Complex processing

10. Usable in other applications
11. Installation ease
12. Operational ease
13. Multiple sites
14. Facilitate change

The questions are answered using degrees of influence (DI) on a scale of zero to five:

- 0 Not present, or no influence
- 1 Incidental influence
- 2 Moderate influence
- 3 Average influence
- 4 Significant influence
- 5 Strong influence throughout

TYPES OF FUNCTION POINT COUNTS

Function point counts can be associated to projects or to applications. The three types of function point counts are:

- *Development (project) function point count* —function point count associated with the initial installation of new software. This count measures the function provided to the end users by the project. It includes the functionality provided by data conversion and associated conversion reporting requirements. The development function point count, minus those function points associated with conversion activities, becomes the application function point count once the project is installed.
- *Enhancement (project) function point count* — function point count associated with the enhancement of existing software. This count measures the modifications to the existing application that add, change, or delete user function within the scope of a project. It includes the functionality provided by data conversion and associated conversion reporting requirements. When an enhancement project is installed, the application function point count must be updated to reflect changes in the application's functionality.
- *Application function point count* — function point count associated with an installed application. It is also referred to as the baseline or installed function point count. This count provides a measure of the current function that the application provides to the end user. This number is initialized at the time the development function point count is completed. This count does *not* include the functionality provided by data conversion and associated conversion reporting requirements. It can therefore differ from the development function point count. It is altered every time an enhancement alters the application's function.

BOUNDARIES

Boundaries identify the border between the application or project measured and either external applications or the user domain. Boundaries are used to establish the scope of the work product measured. Additionally, they are used to establish data ownership and processing relationships that are required when conducting a function point count. Associated measurement data (e.g., effort, cost, defects) should be collected at the same level as the application or project boundaries.

Application Boundary

Look at the application from the *user's point of view* — what the user can understand and describe. The boundary between related applications should be based on separate business functions as seen by the user, not on technological concerns. Use the system external specifications or get a system flow chart and draw a boundary around it to highlight what is internal and what is external to the application. The boundary should be stable and correspond to how the application is maintained.

Development (Project) Boundary

Again, look at the application from the *user's point of view* — what the user can understand and describe. Use the system external specifications or get a system flow chart and draw a boundary around it to highlight what is internal and what is external to the application.

Enhancement (Project) Boundary

An enhancement project's boundary must conform to the boundaries already established for the application being modified. For ease of development, separate or small phases should not be considered separate project boundaries.

COUNTING RULES

The function point metric measures the application based on two areas of evaluation. The first produces the unadjusted function point count that is a measure of the specific, countable functionality provided to the user by the application. The second area of evaluation, which produces the VAF, evaluates the general functionality of the application. This is done based on the 14 general system characteristics discussed in detail in a later section. The five function types discussed briefly next are discussed in detail in following sections.

Unadjusted Function Point Count

Unadjusted function points are calculated based on those components of an application that are requested and visible to the user; these components are categorized into function types, which in turn can be categorized as data or transactional.

Data function types represent the functionality provided to the user to meet internal and external data requirements.

- Internal logical files (ILFs) reside internal to an application's boundary and reflect data storage functionality provided to the user. ILFs must be maintained and utilized by the application.
- External interface files (EIFs) reside external to an application's boundary and reflect the functionality provided by the application through the use of data maintained by other applications.

Although ILFs and EIFs contain the word "file" in their titles, they are not files in the traditional data processing sense. In this case, file refers to a logically related group of data and not the physical implementation.

Transactional function types represent the functionality provided to the user for processing data by an application.

- External inputs (EIs) reflect the functionality provided to the user for the receipt and maintenance (add, change, and delete) of data on internal logical files.
- External outputs (EOs) reflect the functionality provided to the user for output generated by the application from internal logical files or external interface files.
- External inquiries (EQs) reflect the functionality provided to the user for queries of internal logical files or external interface files.

INTERNAL LOGICAL FILES

Internal logical files represent an application's maintainable data storage requirements. These files are evaluated and contribute to the function point count based on their number and relative functional complexity.

Definitions

- An ILF is a *user-identifiable group of logically related data or control information maintained* and utilized within the boundary of the application.
- *User identifiable group of logically related data* refers to data related at such a level that an experienced user would identify the data as fulfilling a specific user requirement of the application. The data analysis equivalent to such high-level logical groupings is singularly named data stores on a data-flow diagram.
- *Control information* is data used by the application to ensure compliance with business function requirements specified by the user.
- *Maintained* is the ability to add, change, or delete data through a standardized process of application.

Methodology

Identification

- Identify all data that is:
  - Stored internal to the application's boundary
  - Maintained through a standardized process of the application
  - Identified as a requirement of the application by the users
- Group the data logically based on the user's view:
  - Group data at the level of detail at which the user can first categorize the data as satisfying unique requirements of the application.
  - View the data logically. Some storage technologies, such as tables in a relational DBMS or a sequential flat file, relate closely to internal logical files; however, do not assume that one physical file equals one logical file.

Examples

To identify potential ILFs, look at the type of data stored and how a user would view or group the data, rather than storage technology such as tables, flat files, indices, and paths. Each type of data on the following list can relate to one or more ELFs, depending on the user's view.

- Application data (master files such as those for tax information and personnel information)
- Application security data
- Audit data
- Help messages
- Error messages
- Edit data

The following are ILFs:

- *Back-up data* is counted ONLY if specifically requested by the user due to legal or similar requirements.
- ILFs maintained by more than one application are credited to both applications at the time each is counted.

The following are not ILFs:

- Temporary files
- Work files
- Sort files
- Suspense files (These are files containing incomplete transactions from an external Input. Do not count unless data on the suspense file can be accessed or maintained by the user through unique EIs, EOs, or EQs.)
- Back-up data required for corporate back-up and recovery procedures

- Files introduced only because of technology used; for example, a file containing JCL required for job submission
- Alternate indices (These are an alternative physical access method.)

Issues and Resolutions

The following are not discussed in Albrecht's 1984 document but are decisions of the IFPUG Counting Practices Committee (CPC):

1. *Back-up files* are counted *only* if specifically requested by the user to meet legal or similar requirements. Back-up files required for normal back-up and recovery procedures are not counted.
2. ILFs maintainable by more than one application are credited to both applications at the time each is counted.
3. *Suspense/carry around files* are counted as an ILF *only if* the suspense file can be accessed or maintained by the user through unique EIs, EOs, or EQs.

EXTERNAL INTERFACE FILES

External interface files represent an application's externally maintained data storage requirements. EIFs are evaluated and contribute to the function point count based on their number and relative functional complexity.

Definitions

- An EIF is a *user identifiable group of logically related data or control information* utilized by the application, but maintained by another application.
- *User identifiable group of logically related data* is defined as data related at such a level that an experienced user would identify the data as fulfilling a specific user requirement of the application.
- *Control information* is data used by the application to assure compliance with business function requirements specified by the user.

Methodology

Identification

- Identify all data that is:
  — Stored external to the application's boundary
  — Not maintained by this application
  — Identified as a requirement of the application by the users
- Group the data logically based on the user's view:
  — View data at the level of detail at which the user can first categorize the data as satisfying unique requirements of the application

— View the data logically. Some storage technologies, such as tables in a relational DBMS or a sequential flat file, relate closely to EIFs; however, do *not* assume that one physical file equals one logical file.

Examples

When identifying potential EIFs, look at the type of data and how a user would view it rather than storage technologies such as tables, flat files, indexes, and paths. Each type of data on the following list can relate to one or more EIFs, depending on the user's view:

- Reference data (external data utilized by the application, but not maintained on internal logical files)
- Help messages
- Error messages
- Edit data (criteria)

The following are not EIFs:

- Data received from another application that adds, changes, or deletes data on an ILF (This is considered transaction data and therefore the process of maintaining the data is counted as external input.)
- Data maintained by the application being counted, but accessed and utilized by another application
- Data formatted and processed for use by another application (counted as an external output)

Issues and Resolutions

The following decision of the IFPUG CPC differs from Albrecht's 1984 document:

> *EIF is not credited to the "sending application":* Albrecht's methodology credits EIFs to the application maintaining the data and to the application using the data by differentiating EIFs from EIs and EOs based on the directional flow and use of the data by the application.
>
> Function type determination is based on how the application that *receives* the data utilizes it. If the data is used to update an ILF, it is either an EI or EO, depending on data flow. If the data is not maintained on an ILF, it is an EIF, regardless of the data flow.

Two issues have been raised with Albrecht's 1984 method of identifying EIFs:

- Function point counts must be updated if, subsequent to the count, access to an ILF is given to another application.
- Because it cannot always be determined how the other application is using the data, various methods have evolved to handle this situation, resulting in inconsistent counting rules.

To resolve these problems, only the application receiving the data can have EIFs. As a result, an application's function point count is dependent only on the application as it currently exists and not on future events or another application's use of data.

EXTERNAL INPUTS

EIs represent an application's data maintenance and control processing requirements. They are evaluated and contribute to the function point count based on their number and relative functional complexity.

Definitions

- An EI processes data or processes *control information* that enters the application's external boundary. Through a unique logical process, the processed data *maintains* an ILF. Control information is data used by a process within an application boundary to assure compliance with business function requirements specified by the user. Control information may or may not directly maintain an ILF. An EI should be considered unique if it has a different format or if the logical design requires *processing logic* different from that of other EIs of the same format. An *external input* is considered unique if
  — Data is maintained on an ILF *and*
  — The input format is unique *or*
  — The processing logic is unique
- *Control information* is data used by the application to assure compliance with business function requirements specified by the user. Do not include the input side of an EI.
- *Maintain* is the ability to add, change, or delete data through a standardized process of the application.
- *Format* is defined as unique data elements or a unique arrangement or order of data elements.
- *Processing logic* is defined as unique edits, calculations or algorithms, and sorts specifically requested by the user.

Methodology

Identification

- Identify all processes that update an ILF.
- For each process identified:
  — Consider each format a separate process if the data used by the process can be received in more than one format.
  — Credit an EI for each data maintenance activity (add, change, and delete) performed.

Examples

Assuming the preceding conditions are met, the following are EIs:

- *Transactional data:* external data that is used to maintain ILFs.
- *Screen input:* count one EI for each function that maintains ILFs. If add, change, and delete capabilities are present, the screen would count as three EIs.
- *Batch input:* for each unique process that maintains an ELF, count one EI for each add, change, and delete.

Batch inputs should be identified based on the processing required to apply the data. One physical input file can, when viewed logically, correspond to a number of EIs. Conversely, two or more physical input files can correspond to one EI, if the processing logic and format are identical for each physical file.

One way to identify multiple EIs when processing one physical file is to look at the record types on the file. Exclude header and trailer records as well as those record types required due to physical space limitations. Look at the remaining record types for unique processing requirements and associate an EI for each unique process. Do not assume a one-to-one correspondence between the remaining record types and EIs.

- *Duplicate EIs:* see the section
- *Suspense file updates:* see the section on issues and resolution

The following are not EIs:

- *Reference data:* external data utilized by the application, but not maintained on ILFs
- *Input side of an EI:* data input used to drive selection for data retrieval
- *Menu screens:* see section on issues and resolution
- *Logon screens:* see the section on issues and resolution
- *Multiple methods of invoking the same input logic,* for example, entering "A" or "add" on a command line or using a PF key should be counted only once

Issues and Resolutions

The following are not discussed in Albrecht's 1984 document but are decisions of the IFPUG CPC:

- *Duplicate EIs:* input processes that, if specifically requested by the user, duplicate a previously counted EI, are each counted. An example is a banking system that accepts identical deposit transactions, one through an automated teller machine (ATM) transaction and a second through a manual teller deposit transaction.

- *Suspense file updates:* Input processes that maintain an ILF or a suspense/carry around file (depending on edit evaluation) should be counted based on the following:
  — If the suspense/carry around file is accessed or maintained by the user, it is counted as an ILF. Thus, count EIs for each data maintenance activity performed on *both* ILFs.
  — If the suspense/carry around file cannot be maintained or accessed by the user, count EIs for each data maintenance activity performed on the original ILF.

  In either instance, the process of reapplying data from the suspense/carry around file to the ILF is not counted.

- *Logon screen:* screens that facilitate entry into an application and do *not* maintain an ILF are not EIs.

The following decision of the IFPUG CPC is in agreement with Albrecht's 1984 document:

- Menu screens that provide only selection or navigational functionality and do NOT maintain an ILF are not counted.

EXTERNAL OUTPUT

EOs represent an application's output processing requirements; they are evaluated and contribute to the function point count based on their number and relative functional complexity.

Definitions

- An EO processes data or *control information that exits the* application's external boundary. An EO should be considered unique if it has a different format, or if the logical design requires *processing logic* different from other EOs of the same format. An external output is considered unique if:
  — The output format is unique *or*
  — The processing logic is unique
- *Control information* is data used by the application to assure compliance with business function requirements specified by the user.
- *Format* is defined as unique data elements or a unique arrangement or order of data elements.
- *Processing logic* is defined as unique edits, calculations or algorithms, and sorts specifically requested by the user.

Methodology

Identification

- Identify all processes that:
  — Send data external to the applications's boundary *or*
  — Control data external to the application's boundary
- For each process identified:
  — Consider each format a separate process if the data used by the process is sent in more than one format.
    - Credit an EO for each process

Examples

Assuming the preceding conditions are met, the following are EOs:

- *Data transfer to other applications:* data residing on an ILF that is formatted and processed for use by an external application. Outputs are identified based on the processing required to manipulate the data. One physical output file can, when viewed logically, correspond to a number of EOs. Conversely, two or more physical output files can correspond to one EO, if the processing logic and format are identical for each physical file.
- A method for identifying multiple EOs from the processing of one physical file is to look at the record types on the file. Exclude header and trailer records as well as those record types required due to physical space limitations. Review the remaining record types for unique processing requirements and associate an EO for each unique process. Do not assume a one-to-one correspondence between the remaining record types and EOs.
- *Reports:* each report produced by the application is counted as an EO. Two identically formatted reports at the detail and summary levels are counted as two EOs because each report requires unique processing logic and unique calculations.
- *Duplicate reports:* see the section on issues and resolutions
- *Online reports:* online output of data that is *not* the output side of an EQ
- *Error/confirmation messages:* see the section on issues and resolutions
- *Derived data:* derived data that does not necessarily update a file
- *Graphics:* see the section on issues and resolutions
- *Report Generators:* see the section on issues and resolutions

The following are not EOs:

- *Help:* see external inquiry
- *Multiple methods of invoking the same output logic:* for example, entering "R" or "report" on a command line or using a PF key should be counted only once

- *Error/confirmation messages associated with function types other than EIs:* for example, an EO would *not* be counted for the error/confirmation messages associated to an EQ.
- *Multiple reports/unique data values:* identical reports that have the same format and processing logic, but exist due to unique data values, are *not* counted as separate EOs. For example, two reports identical in format and processing logic where the first contains customer names beginning with "A" through "L" and the second has customer names beginning with "M" through "Z" are counted as only one EO.
- *Summary fields* (column totals): summary fields on a detail report do not constitute a unique EO.
- *Ad-hoc reporting:* when the user directs and is responsible for the creation (through the use of a language such as FOCUS or SQL) of an undefined number of reports, no EOs are counted.
- *Query language:* a tool used in the ad-hoc environment.

Issues and Resolutions

The following decisions of the IFPUG CPC are not discussed in Albrecht's 1984 document:

- *Duplicate reports:* identical reports, produced on different media due to specific user requirements, are counted as separate EOs. The processing required to produce different output media is considered to be unique processing logic. Identical reports, one on paper and one on microfiche, if specifically requested by the user, are counted as two EOs.
- *Graphical format:* graphical outputs should be counted as if they had been presented in textual format. Each different graphical display requested by the user should be counted as an EO. Statistical data presented in a table, bar chart, pie chart, and exploded pie chart should be counted as four EOs.
- *Report generator:* output developed for the user with a report generator should be counted as an EO for each specified unique report. If a report generator facility is requested by the user as part of an application for do-it-yourself report generation, one EI should be counted for each report definition parameter or unique command (e.g., select, compare, sort, merge, extract, calculate, summarize, format, etc.) requested by the user to control the report generation, and one EO should be counted for the total report program; and one ILF should be counted if a new file is created and saved.

The following decision of the IFPUG CPC is in agreement with Albrecht's 1984 document:

- *Error/confirmation messages:* an EO should be credited for each *external input* having error or confirmation messages.

External Inquiries

External inquiries represent an application's inquiry processing requirements; they are evaluated and contribute to the function point count based on their number and relative functional complexity.

Definitions

- An EQ is a unique *input/output combination* that results in the retrieval of data required for immediate output, does not contain derived data, and does not update an ILF. An EQ is considered unique if it has *a format* different from other those EQs in its input or output parts or if the logical design requires *edits and sorts* different from those of other EQs. An input/output combination is considered unique if:
  — The input format is unique *or*
  — The edits and sorts are different *or*
  — The output format is unique
- *Format* is defined as unique data elements or a unique arrangement or order of data elements.
- *Derived data* is defined as data that requires processing other than direct retrieval, editing, and sorting of information from ILFs or EIFs.

Methodology

Identification

- Identify all processes where an input triggers an immediate retrieval of data.
- For each process identified:
  — Verify that each input/output combination is unique and consider each unique input/output combination a separate process
  — Credit an EQ for each process

Examples

Assuming the preceding conditions are met, the following are EQs:

- *Immediate retrieval of data:* selection of data retrieval is based on data input.
- *Implied inquiries:* Change/delete screens that provide data retrieval capabilities prior to change/delete functionality are credited with an EQ, provided the inquiry capability can be and is used as a stand-alone function.
- If the input and output sides of the EQ are identical for change and delete functions, count only one EQ. If identical inquiry functions are available from the change/delete screens and a separate inquiry screen, count only one EQ.
- Menus having implied inquiries: see the section on issues and resolutions.

- *Log-on screens:* see the section on issues and resolutions.
- *Help:* see the section on issues and resolutions.

Two categories of help are considered EQs:

- *Full-screen help:* a help facility that is dependent on the application screen displays help text relating to the calling screen. Credit one low complexity EQ per calling screen regardless of the number of help panels or screens returned.
- *Field-sensitive help:* a help facility, dependent on the location of the cursor or some other method of identification, displays help documentation specific to that field. Credit one EQ per screen. Each field that is sensitive to help should be considered one DET on the input side.

The following are not EQs:

- Error/confirmation messages: see EOs.
- *Multiple methods of invoking the same inquiry logic:* multiple methods, such as entering "I" or "inq" on a command line, or using a PF key are counted only once.
- *Help text:* help that can be accessed from multiple areas or screens of an application, or accessed and browsed independently of the associated application, is counted only once.
- *Menu screens:* see the section on issues and resolutions.
- *Derived data:* derived data would be treated as an input/output versus retrieval of data.
- *Online documentation:* system documentation available online, in lieu of or in addition to that available in hard copy, is not counted. Online documentation by itself should not be considered software function delivered.
- *Test systems:* test systems are included in system development and should not be counted.

Issues and Resolutions

The following decisions of the IFPUG CPC differ from Albrecht's 1984 document:

- *Menu screens:* screens that provide only selection functionality are not counted.
- *Menus having implied inquiries:* menu screens that provide screen selection *and* data retrieval selection input for the called screen are counted as EQs because the menu is the input side of the EQ and the called screen is the output side.

The following are not discussed in Albrecht's 1984 document but are decisions of the IFPUG CPC:

- *Log-on screens:* log-on screens that provide security functionality are counted as EQs.
- *Help:* help is an inquiry pair where the input and the output (explanatory text) are each unique. Credit help text that can be accessed or displayed through different request techniques or from different areas of an application only once.
- *Duplicate output side:* identical queries, produced on different media due to specific user requirements, are counted as separate EQs.
- *Graphical formats:* each different graphical display requested by the user should be counted as an additional EQ.
- *User-maintained help facility:* a user-maintained help facility should be counted separately.
- *Independent teaching (tutorial) systems:* computer-assisted instruction (CAI), computer-based training (CBT) systems, or other independent software teaching systems that are different from the production system and maintained separately should be counted as separate applications. Training systems identical to the production system should be considered additional sites; do not count them as separate functions, but consider the sites when calculating general system characteristic 13 (multiple sites).

GENERAL SYSTEMS CHARACTERISTICS

Each general system characteristic (GSC) must be evaluated in terms of its degree of influence (DI) on a scale of zero to five. The descriptions listed under "score as" are meant to be guides in determining the DI. If none of the guideline descriptions fits the application exactly, a judgment must be made about which DI most closely applies to the application. The general system characteristics are:

1. Data communication
2. Distributed function
3. Performance
4. Heavily used configuration
5. Transaction rates
6. Online data entry
7. Design for end-user efficiency
8. Online update
9. Complex processing
10. Usable in other applications
11. Installation ease
12. Operational ease
13. Multiple sites
14. Facilitate change

The questions are answered using DI on a scale of zero to five.

- 0 Not present or no influence
- 1 Incidental influence
- 2 Moderate influence
- 3 Average influence
- 4 Significant influence
- 5 Strong influence throughout

Data Communications

The *data and control* information used in the application are sent or received over communication facilities. Terminals connected locally to the control unit are considered to be using communication facilities. Protocol is a set of conventions that permit the transfer or exchange of information between two systems or devices. All data communication links require some type of protocol.

Score as:

- 0 — Application is pure batch processing or a stand alone PC.
- 1 — Application is batch but has remote data entry or remote printing.
- 2 — Application is batch but has remote data entry and remote printing.
- 3 — Online data collection or TP (teleprocessing) is front end to a batch process or query system.
- 4 — More than a front end, but the application supports only one type of TP communications protocol.
- 5 — More than a front-end, but the application supports more than one type of TP communications protocol.

Distributed Data Processing

Distributed data or processing functions are a characteristic of the application within the application boundary.

Score as:

- 0 — Application does not aid the transfer of data or processing function between components of the system.
- 1 — Application prepares data for end-user processing on another component of the system such as PC spreadsheets and PC DBMS.
- 2 — Data is prepared for transfer, transferred, and processed on another component of the system (not for end-user processing).
- 3 — Distributed processing and data transfer are online and in one direction only.

- 4 — Distributed processing and data transfer are online and in both directions.
- 5 — Processing functions are dynamically performed on the most appropriate component of the system.

Performance

Application performance objectives, stated or approved by the user in response or throughput, influenced (or will influence) the design, development, installation, and support of the application.

Score as:

- 0 — No special performance requirements were stated by the user.
- 1 — Performance and design requirements were stated and reviewed but no special actions required.
- 2 — Response time or throughput is critical during peak hours. No special design for CPU utilization was required. Processing deadline is for the next business day.
- 3 — Response time or throughput is critical during all business hours. No special design for CPU utilization was required. Processing deadline requirements with interfacing systems are constraining.
- 4 — Stated user performance requirements are stringent enough to require performance analysis tasks in the design phase.
- 5 — In addition, performance analysis tools were used in the design, development, or implementation phases to meet the stated user performance requirements.

Heavily Used Configuration

A heavily used operational configuration, requiring special design considerations, is a characteristic of the application. (For example, the user wants to run the application on existing or committed equipment that will be heavily used.)

Score as:

- 0 — There are no explicit or implicit operational restrictions.
- 1 — Operational restrictions do exist, but are less restrictive than a typical application. No special effort is needed to meet the restrictions.
- 2 — Some security or timing considerations exist.
- 3 — There are specific processor requirements for a specific piece of the application.
- 4 — Stated operation restrictions require special constraints on the application in the central processor or a dedicated processor.
- 5 — In addition, there are special constraints on the application in the distributed components of the system.

Transaction Rate

The transaction rate is high and it influenced the design, development, installation, and support of the application.

Score as:

- 0 — No peak transaction period is anticipated.
- 1 — Peak transaction period (e.g., monthly, quarterly, seasonally, annually) is anticipated.
- 2 — Weekly peak transaction period is anticipated.
- 3 — Daily peak transaction period is anticipated.
- 4 — High transaction rates stated by the user in the application requirements or service level agreements are high enough to require performance analysis tasks in the design phase.
- 5 — High transaction rates stated by the user in the application requirements or service level agreements are high enough to require performance analysis tasks and, in addition, require the use of performance analysis tools in the design, development, or installation phases.

Online Data Entry

Online data entry and control functions are provided in the application.

Score as:

- 0 — All transactions are processed in batch mode.
- 1 — 1 to 7 percent of transactions are interactive data entry.
- 2 — 8 to 15 percent of transactions are interactive data entry.
- 3 — 16 to 23 percent of transactions are interactive data entry.
- 4 — 24 to 30 percent of transactions are interactive data entry.
- 5 — Over 30 percent of transactions are interactive data entry.

End-User Efficiency

The online functions provided emphasize a design for end-user efficiency. They include:

- Navigational aids (e.g., function keys, jumps, dynamically generated menus)
- Menus
- Online help/documents
- Automated cursor movement
- Scrolling
- Remote printing (via online transactions)
- Preassigned function keys
- Submission of batch jobs from online transactions
- Cursor selection of screen data

- Heavy use of reverse video, highlighting, colors, underlining, and other indicators
- Hard-copy user documentation of online transactions
- Mouse interface
- Pop-up windows
- As few screens as possible to accomplish a business function
- Bilingual support (supports two languages; count as four items)
- Multilingual support (supports more than two languages; count as six items)

Score as:

- 0 — None of the above
- 1 — One to three of the above
- 2 — Four to five of the above
- 3 — Six or more of the above but no specific user requirements related to efficiency
- 4 — Six or more of the above and stated requirements for end-user efficiency strong enough to require design tasks for human factors to be included (for example, minimize key strokes, maximize defaults, use of templates, etc.).
- 5 — Six or more of the above and stated requirements for end-user efficiency strong enough to require use of special tools and processes in order to demonstrate that objectives have been achieved

OnLine Update

The application provides online update for the ILFs.

Score as:

- 0 — None
- 1 — Online update of one to three control files; low volume of updating and easy recovery
- 2 — Online update of four or more control files; low volume of updating and easy recovery
- 3 — Online update of major ILFs
- 4 — In addition, protection against data loss essential and specially designed and programmed in the system
- 5 — In addition, high volumes bring cost considerations into the recovery process; highly automated recovery procedures with minimum of operator intervention

Complex Processing

Complex processing is a characteristic of the application. Categories are:

- Sensitive control (for example, special audit processing) or application-specific security processing
- Extensive logical processing
- Extensive mathematical processing
- Much exception processing resulting in incomplete transactions that must be processed again; for example, incomplete ATM transactions caused by TP interruption, missing data values, or failed edits
- Complex processing to handle multiple input/output possibilities; for example, multimedia, device independence

Score as:

- 0 — None of the above
- 1 — Any one of the above
- 2 — Any two of the above
- 3 — Any three of the above
- 4 — Any four of the above
- 5 — Any five of the above

Reusability

The application and the code in the application have been specifically designed, developed, and supported to be usable in other applications.

Score as:

- 0 — No reusable code
- 1 — Reusable code is used within the application
- 2 — Less than 10 percent of the application considered more than one user's needs
- 3 — 10 percent or more of the application considered more than one user's needs
- 4 — Application specifically packaged or documented to ease reuse and customized by user at source code level
- 5 — Application specifically packaged or documented to ease reuse and customized for use by means of user parameter maintenance

Installation Ease

Conversion and installation ease are characteristics of the application. A conversion and installation plan or conversion tools were provided and tested during the system test phase.

Score as:

- 0 — No special considerations were stated by user and no special set-up required for installation
- 1 — No special considerations were stated by user but special set-up required for installation

- 2 — Conversion and installation requirements stated by user and conversion and installation guides provided and tested impact of conversion on the project not considered to be important
- 3 — Conversion and installation requirements stated by the user and conversion and installation guides provided and tested; impact of conversion on the project considered to be important
- 4 — In addition to (2), automated conversion and installation tools provided and tested
- 5 — In addition to (3), automated conversion and installation tools provided and tested

Operational Ease

Operational ease is characteristic of the application. Effective start-up, back-up, and recovery procedures were provided and tested during the system test phase. The application minimizes the need for manual activities such as tape mounts, paper handling, and direct on-location manual intervention.

Score as:

- 0 — No special operational considerations, other than normal back-up procedures, were stated by the user.
- 1–4 — Select the following items that apply to the application. Each item has a point value of one, except as noted otherwise.
  — Effective start-up, back-up, and recovery processes were provided but operator intervention is required.
  — Effective start-up, back-up, and recovery processes were provided but no operator intervention is required (count as two items).
  — The application minimizes the need for tape mounts.
  — The application minimizes the need for paper handling.
- 5 — Application is designed for unattended operation. Unattended operation means *no operator intervention* is required to operate the system other than to start up or shut down the application. Automatic error recovery is a feature of the application.

Multiple Sites

The application has been specifically designed, developed, and supported to be installed at multiple sites for multiple organizations.

Score as:

- 0 — There is no user requirement to consider the needs of more than one user installation site.
- 1 — Needs of multiple sites were considered in the design and the application is designed to operate only under identical hardware and software environments.

- 2 — Needs of multiple sites were considered in the design and the application is designed to operate only *under similar* hardware and software environments.
- 3 — Needs of multiple sites were considered in the design and the application is designed to operate *under different* hardware and software environments.
- 4 — Documentation and support plans are provided and tested to support the application at multiple sites and application is as described by (1) or (2).
- 5 — Documentation and support plans are provided and tested to support the application at multiple sites and application is as described by (3).

Facilitate Change

The application has been specifically designed, developed, and supported to facilitate change. Examples are:

- Flexible query/report capability is provided.
- Business control data is grouped in tables maintainable by the user.

Score as:

- 0 — No special user requirement to design the application to minimize or facilitate change.
- 1–5 — Select which of the following items apply to the application:
  — Flexible query/report facility is provided that can handle simple requests; for example, *and/or* logic can be applied to only one ILF (count as one item).
  — Flexible query/report facility is provided that can handle requests of average complexity; for example, *and/or* logic can be applied to more than one ILF (count as two items).
  — Flexible query/report facility is provided that can handle complex requests; for example, *and/or* logic combinations on one or more ILFs (count as three items).
  — Control data is kept in tables maintained by the user with online interactive processes but changes take effect only on the next business day.
  — Control data is kept in tables maintained by the user with online interactive processes and the changes take effect immediately (count as two items.)

FUNCTION POINT CALCULATION

The function point calculation is a three-step process. Step 1 produces the unadjusted function point count. Step 2 produces the value adjustment factor (VAF). Step 3 adjusts the unadjusted function point count by the VAF to produce the final function point count.

Exhibit S-1. Calculation of Unadjusted Function Point Count

Function Type		Functional Complexity		Complexity Totals	Function Type Totals
ILF	Low	*	7	= _____	
	Average	*	10	= _____	
	High	*	15	= _____	_____
EIF	Low	*	5	= _____	
	Average	*	7	= _____	
	High	*	10	= _____	_____
EI	Low	*	3	= _____	_____
	Average	*	4	–	_____	_____
	High	*	6	= _____	_____
EO	Low	*	4	= _____	
	Average	*	5	= _____	
	High	*	7	= _____	_____
EQ	Low	*	3	= _____	
	Average	*	4	= _____	
	High	*	6	= _____	_____
Unadjusted function point count					_____

The formula used by Step 3 varies depending on the type of count — application (system baseline), development (project), or enhancement (project). The three last sections in this appendix discuss the final function point calculation for each type of count.

Unadjusted Function Point Calculation

The way you determine functional complexity depends on the function type. There are two types of function types:

- Data function types are ILFs and EIFs. The functional complexity of each identified data function type is based on the number of record types (RET) and data element types (DET).
- Transactional function types are EIs, EOs, and EQs. The functional complexity of each identified transaction function type is based on the number of file type referenced (FTR) and data element types (DET).

Once an application's components (specific data and processing requirement) have been categorized into the various function types, each component is assigned an unadjusted function point value based on its functional complexity. The unadjusted function point count value for each component is then summarized at the function type level and again at the application level. The resulting total at the application level is the

Exhibit S-2.   Internal Logical File (ILF) Complexity Matrix

	1 to 19 DET	20 to 50 DET	51 or more DET
1 RET	L	L	A
2–5 RET	L	A	H
6 or more RET	A	H	H

Note: Legend: RET = Record Element Type; DET = Data Element Type.
Functional Complexity: L = Low; A = Average; H = High.

application's unadjusted function point count and is used in the final calculation. The form in Exhibit S-1 can be used to facilitate the calculation of the unadjusted function point count.

Internal Logical Files

Each identified ILF is assigned a functional complexity based on the number of associated RETs and DETs.

- *Record element type identification:* RETs are subgroupings of ILFs based on the logical/user view of the data. The data analysis equivalent to such logical groupings is data entities. ILFs, which cannot be subcategorized, are considered to have one RET.
- *Data element type identification:* an ILF's DETs are user-recognizable, nonrecursive fields residing on the ILF.

Each field on the ILF is a DET with the following exceptions:

- Fields should be viewed at the user recognizable level; for example, an account number or date physically stored in multiple fields is counted as one DET.
- Fields that appear more than once in an ILF because of technology or implementation techniques should be counted only once. For example, if an ILF comprises more than one table in a relational DBMS, the keys used to relate the tables are counted only once.
- Repeating fields that are identical in format and exist to allow for multiple occurrences of a data value are counted only once. For example, an ILF containing 12 monthly budget amount fields and an annual budget amount field would be credited with two DETs, a DET for the monthly budget amount fields and a DET for the annual budget amount field.
- Each unique command or parameter is counted as a DET if an ILF is created and saved in a report generator facility requested by the user for do-it-yourself report generation. Use the matrix in Exhibit S-3 to translate an ILF's functional complexity to Unadjusted function points.

Functional complexity assignment for ILFs is based on the matrix shown in Exhibit S-2. Use the matrix in Exhibit S-3 to translate an ILF's functional complexity to unadjusted function points.

SOFTWARE ENGINEERING HANDBOOK

External Interface File

Each identified EIF is assigned a functional complexity based on the number of associated RETs and DETs.

- *Record element type identification:* RETs are subgroupings of EIFs based on the logical/user view of the data. The data analysis equivalent to such logical groupings is data entities. EIFs that cannot be subcategorized are considered to have one RET.
  - One physical interface file can, when viewed logically, correspond to a number of EIFs. Additionally, multiple RETs can be associated to each EIF identified.
  - One way to identify different EIF RETs from one physical file is to look at the record types on the file. Exclude header and trailer records, unless specifically requested for audit purposes, as well as those record types required by physical space limitations. Each unique record type corresponds to a RET.
- *Data element type identification:* an EIF's DETs are user-recognizable, nonrecursive fields residing on the EIF. Each field on the EIF is a DET with the following exceptions:
- *Fields should be viewed at the user recognizable level;* for example, an account number or date physically stored in multiple fields should be counted as one DET.
  - Fields that appear more than once in an EIF because of the technology or implementation techniques should be counted only once. For example, if an EIF comprises more than one record type in a file, the record ID field used to identify the records would be counted only once.

Exhibit S-3. Internal Logical File (ILF) Unadjusted Function Point Table

Functional Complexity Rating	Unadjusted Function Points
L(ow)	7
A(verage)	10
H(igh)	15

Exhibit S-4. External Interface File (EIF) Complexity Matrix

	1 to 19 DET	20 to 50 DET	51 or more DET
1 RET	L	L	A
2–5 RET	L	A	H
6 or more RET	A	H	H

Note: Legend: RET = Record Element Type; DET = Data Element Type.
Functional Complexity: L = Low; A = Average; H = High.

— Repeating fields that are identical in format and exist so that multiple occurrences of a data value can occur are counted only once. For example, an EIF containing 12 monthly budget amount fields and an annual budget amount field would be credited with two DETs, a DET for the monthly budget amount fields and a DET for the annual budget amount field.

Functional complexity assignment for EIFs is based on the matrix shown in Exhibit S-4. Use the matrix in Exhibit S-5 to translate an EIF's functional complexity to unadjusted function points.

External Inputs

Each identified EI is assigned a functional complexity based on the number of file type referenced (FTR) andDETs.

Exhibit S-5.   External Interface File (EIF) Unadjusted Function Point Table

Functional Complexity Rating	Unadjusted Function Points
L(ow)	5
A(verage)	7
H(igh)	10

Exhibit S-6.   External Input (EI) Complexity Matrix

	1 to 4 DET	5 to 15 DET	16 or more DET
0 - 1 FTR	L	L	A
2 FTR	L	A	H
3 or more FTR	A	H	H

Note: Legend: FTR = File Type Referenced; DET = Data Element Type.
Functional Complexity: L = Low; A = Average; H = High.

Exhibit S-7.   External Input (EI) Unadjusted Function Point Table

Functional Complexity Rating	Unadjusted Function Points
L(ow)	3
A(verage)	4
H(igh)	6

File Type Referenced Identification

An FTR is counted for each ILF maintained or referenced and each EIF referenced during the processing of the external input.

Data Element Type Identification:

The DET count is the maximum number of user-recognizable, nonrecursive fields that are maintained on an ILF by the EI.

Each field maintainable on an ILF by the EI is a DET with the following exceptions:

- *Fields should be viewed at the user-recognizable level*; for example, an account number or date physically stored in multiple fields should be counted as one DET.
- Fields that appear more than once in an ILF because of technology or implementation techniques should be counted only once. For example, if an ILF comprises more than one table in a relational DBMS, the keys used to relate the tables would be counted only once.

Additional DETs are credited to the EI for the following capabilities:

- Command lines or PF/Action keys that provide the capability to specify the action to be taken by the EI — one additional DET per external input, *not* per command PF/action key.
- Fields that are not entered by the user, but through an EI, are maintained on an ILF, should be counted. For example, a system generated sequenced key, maintained on an ILF, but not entered by the user, would be counted as a DET.

Functional complexity assignment for EIs is based on the matrix shown in Exhibit S-6. Use the matrix in Exhibit S-7 to translate an EI's functional complexity to unadjusted function points.

External Outputs

Each identified EO is assigned a functional complexity based on the number of FTR and DETs.

- *File type referenced identification:* an FTR should be counted for each ILF and EIF referenced during the processing of the EO.
- *Data element type identification:* a DET should be counted for each user-recognizable, nonrecursive field that appears on the EO.

Each field on the EO is a DET with the following exceptions:

- *Fields are viewed at the user-recognizable level*; for example, an account number or date physically stored in multiple fields is counted as one DET.

- Count a DET in the EO for each unique command or parameter in a report generator facility requested by the user for do-it-yourself report generation.
- Count a DET for each type of label and each type of numerical equivalent in a graphical output. For example, a pie chart might have two DETs: one for designating the category and one for the applicable percentage.
- Do not count literals as DETs.
- Do not count paging variables or system generated time/date stamps.

Additional DETs are credited to the EO for the following:

- Count additional DETs for each summary or total field appearing on the EO.
- Error/confirmation messages: Count a DET for each distinct error or confirmation message available for display by the External Input. Implementation techniques, whether Batch Error Reports or an Error Message Area, Box, or Window appearing on the EI or a separate physical screen, such as a Message Frame, do not affect the functional complexity or number of EOs associated to a particular External Input.

Functional complexity assignment for EOs is based on the matrix shown in Exhibit S-8. Use the matrix in Exhibit S-9 to translate an EO's functional complexity to unadjusted function points.

Exhibit S-8. External Output (EO) Complexity Matrix

	1 to 5 DET	6 to 19 DET	20 or more DET
0 - 1 FTR	L	L	A
2–3 FTR	L	A	H
4 or more FTR	A	H	H

Note: Legend: FTR = File Type Referenced; DET = Data Element Type.
Functional Complexity: L = Low; A = Average; H = High.

Exhibit 9. External Output (EO) Unadjusted Function Point Table

Functional Complexity Rating	Unadjusted Function Points
L(ow) 4	
A(verage) 5	
H(igh) 7	

External Inquiries

Use the following steps to assign an unadjusted function point value to each EQ:

1. Calculate the functional complexity for the input side of the EQ.
2. Calculate the functional complexity for the output side of the EQ.
3. Select the higher of the two functional complexities. Using the EQ unadjusted function point table, transcribe the complexity rating to unadjusted function points.

- *File type referenced identification — input and output sides:* an FTR is counted for each ILF and EIF referenced during the processing of the EQ.
- *Data element type identification — input side.* a DET is counted for those fields entered that specify the external inquiry to be executed or specify data selection criteria.
- *Data element type identification — output side:* a DET is counted for each user-recognizable, nonrecursive field that appears on the output side of the EQ.

Each field appearing on the EO is a DET with the following exceptions:

- *Fields are viewed at the user recognizable level;* for example, an account number or date physically stored in multiple fields is counted as one DET.
- Fields that, because of technology or implementation techniques, appear more than once in an ILF should be counted only once. Do not count literals as DETs.
- Do not count paging variables or system generated time/date stamps.

Additional DETs are credited to the EQ for the following:

- Count additional DETs for each summary or total field appearing on the EQ.

Help Messages

The three categories of help are full screen help, field sensitive help, and help subsystems. DET determination varies between each and is discussed below:

- Full-screen help: credit a low-complexity EQ per calling screen regardless of the number of FTRs or DETs involved.
- Field-sensitive help: credit an EQ having a complexity, using the input side, based on the number of fields that are field sensitive and the number of FTRs. Each field-sensitive field corresponds to a DET.
- Help subsystems: specific counting rules are not available at this time.

Exhibit S-10. External Inquiry (EQ) Input Complexity Matrix

	1 to 4 DET	5 to 15 DET	16 or more DET
0–1 FTR	L	L	A
2 FTR	L	A	H
3 or more FTR	A	H	H

Note: Legend: FTR = File Type Referenced; DET = Data Element Type.
Functional Complexity: L = Low; A = Average; H = High.

Exhibit S-11. External Inquiry (EQ) Output Complexity Matrix

	1 to 5 DET	6 to 19 DET	20 or more DET
0–1 FTR	L	L	A
2–3 FTR	L	A	H
4 or more FTR	A	H	H

Note: Legend: FTR = File Type Referenced; DET = Data Element Type.
Functional Complexity: L = Low; A = Average; H = High.

Exhibit 12. External Inquiry (EQ) Output Complexity Matrix

Functional Complexity Rating	Unadjusted Function Points
L(ow)	3
A(verage)	4
H(igh)	6

Functional complexity assignments for EQs are based on the matrices shown in Exhibits S-10 and S-11. Use the matrix in Exhibit S-12 to translate an EQ's functional complexity to unadjusted function points.

VALUE ADJUSTMENT FACTOR CALCULATION

The VAF is based on 14 general system characteristics (GSCs) that rate the general functionality of the application. These 14 are summarized into the VAF. When applied, the VAF adjusts the unadjusted function point count ±35 percent, producing the final function point count.

1. Evaluate the 14 GSCs on a scale from zero to five producing a DI for each of the GSC questions.
2. Sum the 14 DIs to produce the total degree of influence (TDI).
3. Insert the TDI into the following equation to produce the VAF:

$$(TDI * 0.01) + 0.65 = VAF$$

Exhibit S-13. Calculation of the VAF

General System Characteristics (GSC)	Degree of Influence (DI) 0 - 5
1. Data communication	_____
2. Distributed processing	_____
3. Performance	_____
4. Heavily used configuration	_____
5. Transaction rates	_____
6. Online data entry	_____
7. Design for end-user efficiency	_____
8. Online update	_____
9. Complex processing	_____
10. Usable in other applications	_____
11. Installation ease	_____
12. Operational ease	_____
13. Multiple sites	_____
14. Facilitate change	_____

Total Degree of Influence (TDI)

Value Adjustment Factor (VAF) _____ = (_____ * 0.01) + 0.65

$$VAF = (TDI * 0.01) + 0.65$$

where:

> TDI is the sum of the 14 DIs
>
> VAF is the value adjustment factor

The table in Exhibit S-13 facilitates the calculation of the VAF.

APPLICATION FUNCTION POINT CALCULATION

To produce the application function point count, complete the following formula:

$$[(UFPB + ADD + CHGA) — (CHGB + DEL)] * VAFA = AFP$$

where:

> UFPB is the application's unadjusted function point count *before* the enhancement project.
>
> ADD is the unadjusted function point count of those functions added by the enhancement project.
>
> CHGA is the unadjusted function point count of those functions modified by the enhancement project. This number reflects the functions *after* the modifications.

CHGB is the unadjusted function point count of those functions modified by the enhancement *before* the modification.

DEL is the unadjusted function point count of those functions deleted by the enhancement project.

VAFA is the VAF of the application *after* the enhancement project.

AFP is the application's adjusted function point count.

This formula can be used to establish an application's initial application function point count or re-establish an application function point count after an enhancement project has modified the application's functionality. (Do not include conversion requirements in an application function point count. If unavailable, the application's prior unadjusted function point count can be calculated using the following formula:

$$AFPB/VAFB = UFPB$$

where:

AFPB is the adjusted application function point count *before* the enhancement project. VAFB is the VAF of the application *before* the enhancement project.

UFPB is the application's unadjusted function point *before* the enhancement project.)

When establishing an application function point count in which functionality is only being added, not changed or deleted, the formula in effect becomes:

$$ADD * VAFA = AFP$$

where:

ADD is the unadjusted function point count of those functions that were installed by the development project.

VAFA is the VAF of the application.

AFP is the initial application function point count.

DEVELOPMENT (PROJECT) FUNCTION POINT CALCULATION

To produce the development (project) function point count, complete the following formula:

$$UFP * VAF = DFP$$

where:

UFP is the unadjusted function point count.

VAF is the value adjustment factor.

DFP is the development (project) function point count.

ENHANCEMENT (PROJECT) FUNCTION POINT CALCULATION

To produce the enhancement (project) function point count, complete the following formula:

$$((ADD + CHGA) * VAFA) + (DEL * VAFB) = EFP$$

where:

> ADD is the unadjusted function point count of those functions that were added by the enhancement project.

> CHGA is the unadjusted function point count of those functions that were modified by the enhancement project. This number reflects the functions *after* the modifications.

> DEL is the unadjusted function point count of those functions that were deleted by the enhancement project.

> VAFA is the VAF of the application *after* the enhancement project.

> VAFB is the VAF of the application *before* the enhancement project.

> EFP is the enhancement (project) function point count.

Reference

Deveaux, P. (1993). Counting function points, in *Software Engineering Productivity Handbook*, Keyes, J., ed., McGraw-Hill, New York.

Index